RETIREMENT AS
A RISKY PROJECT

RETIREMENT AS A RISKY PROJECT

Monitoring, Evaluating, and Managing a Retirement Income Portfolio

■ ■ ■

PATRICK J. COLLINS, PHD, CFA, CLU AND JOSH STAMPFLI, MS EESOR

Investments & Wealth Institute

Greenwood Village, Colorado

INVESTMENTS & WEALTH INSTITUTE®

Patrick Collins, PhD, CFA®, CLU, is a founder and principal emeritus of Schultz Collins Investment Counsel. He has taught extensively, including portfolio theory in the CFA program and CFA Level Three courses in investment policy and asset allocation. He has published widely in academic and trade journals and is co-author, with Huy D. Lam and Josh Stampfli, of *Longevity Risk and Retirement Income Planning* (2015). He earned a PhD in English and a professional designation in financial planning from the University of California, Berkeley.

Josh Stampfli, MS EESOR, is founder and chief executive officer of Wealthscry, a financial software firm focused on retirement planning analytics. Previously Stampfli worked for two decades on Wall Street where he built two electronic equity trading groups and managed trading, technology, research, and analytics. He earned an MS in engineering and economic systems operations research from Stanford University and a BS in aerospace engineering from Princeton University.

ABOUT INVESTMENTS & WEALTH INSTITUTE

The Investments & Wealth Institute® is a professional association, advanced education provider, and certification board for financial advisors, investment consultants, and wealth managers who continuously strive for excellence and hold themselves to the highest ethical standards.

INVESTMENTS & WEALTH INSTITUTE*

5619 DTC Parkway, Suite 600
Greenwood Village, CO 80111
+1 303-770-3377 • www.investmentsandwealth.org

Book Cover Artist: Florence G. Raker (1922–2005) • Title: *Boat in a Storm* (oil painting on canvas)
Designed by Tillie Creative
Printed in the United States of America

ISBN: 978-0-578-34601-4
This paper meets the requirements of ANSI/NISO Z39.48-1992 (Permanence of Paper).

CONTENTS

• • •

INTRODUCTION

...

Investors, investment advisors, and trustees of irrevocable family trusts face the challenge of providing sustainable periodic cash flows from financial asset portfolios. As the title suggests, this study gives primary emphasis to retirement-income planning for private investors.[1] Initially, the retirement-planning process focuses on designing a portfolio (usually in terms of strategic or tactical asset allocation approaches), deciding on spending (withdrawal) elections, memorializing decisions in a written investment policy statement, and implementing the portfolio through the acquisition of investments. Following the first-stage activities, retirement planning becomes a measuring and managing problem. Although this book does not ignore first-stage activities, it focuses primarily on retirement-income portfolio management where the term "management" encompasses an assessment of investment resources and goals, elucidation of options, and implementation of a process to decide which options are appropriate and prudent.

Retirement is a risky project. We use the term "project" in a real-options sense where the investor has the option to accept the project (start retirement immediately), delay the project (postpone the retirement start date), or, health permitting, reject the project (work for the remainder of life). This book demonstrates that real options are rarely binary. Rather, they exist along a decision path where the advisor invites the investor to consider which asset management options are available currently. Real options, evaluated intelligently, offer the investor both risk and opportunity.

This book examines retirement risk and opportunity by considering three metrics:

Feasibility: Is my retirement economically feasible or is it merely a pipe dream? Do I have sufficient resources to undertake the retirement project?

Sustainability: What resources do I need to support a retirement standard of living and is my standard of living sustainable for more than just a few years?

Flexibility: Will I have a financial cushion sufficient to survive economic setbacks from contingent or unanticipated expenses?

For all but the very wealthy, retirement is a risky project in the sense that questions abound and, for many investors, clear answers may be in short supply. What is the risk of deciding to reduce or terminate labor income upon retirement? Under what conditions is such a decision prudent? Is it feasible to retire now? Is retirement likely to be financially successful? These uncertainties confront investors on the threshold of retirement. How does the investor decide if his first-stage decisions will place him in a good position to sustain a desired standard of living? How dependent is his standard of living on the outcome of future events? What is the investor's attitude toward risk? These questions underlie investment decision-making at the time of initial retirement.

How do investors currently in retirement assess their financial situation? Has their health improved or deteriorated? For a given amount of financial resources, how much can a 75-year-old spend safely compared to a 65-year-old? After a multi-year sequence of investment and inflation realizations, compared to the economic position at the initial retirement date, is an investor more or less likely to be able to sustain target cash flows throughout the remainder of life? Has the initial risk to a successful outcome changed for better or worse?

This book focuses on monitoring, evaluating, and managing, and devotes less attention to strategic asset allocation (portfolio design), strategic investment approach (buy-and-hold, fixed-mix, etc.), and strategies for portfolio implementation (security selection, active-passive investing, tactical allocation, etc.). The best investment strategies cannot cure a large imbalance between wealth and consumption. The practical litmus test for any strategy is a successful outcome, where success is defined in terms of investor aims.

---

1.   The retirement-planning challenges faced by individual investors are, in many respects, similar to those faced by trustees. This is especially the case when a settlor defines an irrevocable trust's purposes and goals in terms of providing a lifetime income to one or more surviving beneficiaries. Trust documents may define the type of trust (net income, total return, etc.), the degree of trustee discretion regarding trust distributions (mandatory, ascertainable standard, etc.), and the income and terminal wealth interests of each beneficiary class (spouses, children, grandchildren).

A retirement portfolio's primary objective is to produce cash sufficient to meet the investor's retirement-income goals. Some economic needs can be identified and estimated, e.g., certain expenses associated with maintaining a desired lifestyle while others remain ambiguous, contingent, or unknowable, e.g., unanticipated financial emergencies. Retirement security is enhanced by having the flexibility or financial wherewithal to spend money when, and in the amount, needed.

Investors do not have a homogeneous definition of "security." Security can encompass the concept of stability of principal for investors wishing to provide multigenerational financial security for family members. The financial security of children or grandchildren, for example, is sometimes an important objective. Security, however, does not always equal stability of principal. In many cases it means the assurance of income when, and in the amount, required. Often, retired investors think of security in terms of securing the periodic lifetime income needed to fund a projected budget.

When does an investor have sufficient resources to provide security? When does keeping the nest egg secure jeopardize the goal of producing sufficient income? How much, and when, is it safe to spend? Should an investor front-load retirement income with the knowledge that continued survival is less and less likely with the passage of time, or should an investor back-load retirement income with the knowledge that end-of-life medical bills may quickly dissipate remaining family wealth?

For most investors, financial decision-making during retirement involves risk. Multiple goals and financial objectives may not be compatible. Progress in one direction may undermine efforts in another and the investor struggles with risk-reward trade-offs. He seeks to grasp more clearly the likely consequences of his decisions.

Even though key decisions often are financial in nature, some retirees consider the time series of inflation, stock, and bond returns as phenomena akin to weather patterns. The weather is sometimes benign and sometimes nasty, but because you can't do anything about it, hope for the best.[2] Other retirees (and perhaps their advisors) build retirement portfolios according to the label on the investment wrapper: "Critical" objectives are matched to "safe" investments. Investment-by-labels, despite an intuitive appeal, is a dubious method for securing a financial future. A principal guarantee is not a guarantee of adequate income and an income guarantee is not a guarantee of adequate funds, e.g., adequate purchasing power or financial flexibility.

The economic risks of retirement are complex and varied. The economic landscape is, for many, unfamiliar and uncertainties abound. Although risks intertwine with the vicissitudes of capital markets in complex patterns, at the end of the day retirees need to consider two basic questions:

1. Do I have enough money to retire?

2. Will I have sufficient financial resources to withstand personal or family changes, or unfavorable economic conditions?

The two questions can be parsed, decomposed, construed, interpreted, and restated in a million ways. The first question concerns feasibility—no matter how intense an investor's motivation, it is not possible to take 15 pounds out of a 10-pound sack. The second is about sustainability and flexibility—this involves understanding how vulnerable ("close-to-the-bone") an investor is during retirement. Information about retirement risk is the central rationale for monitoring a portfolio in terms of its ability to meet the economic requirements that the investor places on it. Portfolio management requires portfolio monitoring lest investment strategy devolve into mere wishful thinking. Portfolio monitoring is the measurement of financial flexibility. Flexibility provides security.

That's it—if long-term spending plans are economically infeasible under any reasonable allocation or portfolio investment strategy, the investor needs either to change them, or to begin an aggressive program of alcohol and cigarette consumption. If you lack financial flexibility, your retirement may be feasible, but your retirement security is at risk.

But feasibility implies solvency. If liabilities (defined as the money a retiree wishes to spend) are greater than assets (defined as the current value of financial resources), then an individual investor is technically insolvent. This is merely an extension of the idea of the solvency tests that regulators apply to banks, insurance companies, and other regulated institutions. Even if, at a given moment, a financial firm owns millions of dollars in money, securities, and other assets, regulators shut them down if assets do not cover projected liabilities. The firms are not economically viable and it is dangerous for them to continue operations. Likewise, the investor is not economically viable. Investors should consider carefully the risks of over-stressing economic resources by demanding unsupportable cash targets.

---

2.   Perhaps the man on TV, or the woman who sent the invitation to a free retirement seminar, is offering a chance to buy an umbrella?

Flexibility implies sustainability. Even a viable retirement may be a risky undertaking if financial resources are excessively vulnerable either to economic shocks (a bear market in stocks or bonds), or to unexpected large expenses. Flexibility is not measured solely by the market value of assets, but, rather, by the amount of the investor's economic surplus, where surplus is defined as the value of assets minus the value of liabilities. The greater the surplus, the greater the investor's financial flexibility, all else being equal. A financial surplus, if reasonably liquid, enhances an investor's ability to sustain retirement at an acceptable living standard. A surplus is a difference (between assets and liabilities), and maintaining a surplus makes all the difference with respect to retirement security.

Whereas both feasibility and sustainability encompass the concept of asset-liability management, it is worthwhile to begin by reviewing this topic.

CHAPTER ONE

ASSET-LIABILITY MANAGEMENT

■ ■ ■

Initially, asset-liability management (ALM) approaches to portfolio management were confined primarily to institutional investors such as banks, insurance companies, or defined benefit (DB) pension funds. Corporations sponsoring DB plans strive to maintain plan surplus lest they incur penalties from regulatory agencies or adverse effects on their financial statements.[1] Banks and insurance companies operate in regulatory and accounting environments that mandate strict adherence to solvency/reserve requirements. In many respects, within a retirement-income planning context, the concept of monitoring and managing economic surplus also applies to protecting a privately held portfolio against shortfall risk.

A series of articles authored by Martin Leibowitz and Roy Henriksson explicitly extends the concept of "surplus management" (an institutional ALM approach) to private investors. Leibowitz and Henriksson (1989) define "shortfall constraint" in terms of a minimum return that an investor must equal or exceed with a given probability. The analysis assumes a normal distribution of investment returns characterized completely by its mean and standard deviation—the square root of variance. Given this assumption, the authors remind investors that a portfolio with an expected return of 'R_p' and a standard deviation of 'σ_p' has only a 10-percent probability of producing a return less than 1.282 standard deviations below expected mean return.[2]

Leibowitz and Henriksson (1989) make the analysis more concrete through a close examination of a portfolio offering an 8-percent expected return with a 10-percent standard deviation. The mathematics of the symmetric normal distribution suggests that the portfolio has a 78.81-percent probability of exceeding a return of zero, a 95-percent probability of exceeding a return of -8.45, and a 90-percent probability of exceeding a return of -4.82 [$R_p - 1.282\sigma_p = -4.82\%$].

The authors argue that the mathematics of confidence limits gives investors the opportunity to secure a portfolio's floor value without resorting to a dynamic hedging strategy.[3] Dynamic hedging can fully guarantee success only in a market environment of frictionless and continuous trading.[4] A confidence-level approach provides a probabilistic assessment regarding the limits on downside risk. However, given the shape and level of the efficient frontier in the expected return/standard deviation plane, the set of feasible downside limits is itself limited by the geometry of line slopes and intercepts.

---

1. For example, an adequately funded plan avoids increased insurance premiums from the Pension Benefit and Guarantee Corporation. Other stakeholders, such as shareholders concerned with the market value of corporate securities, unions concerned with the security of member benefits, and retirees and their families concerned with the safe and timely arrival of pension checks, also have an interest in protecting and enhancing the plan's surplus.

2. Readers familiar with statistics will recognize the number 1.282 as a Z-score value that measures distance from the mean of the probability density function for a standard normal distribution.

3. Peter Albrecht discusses the mathematics of confidence limits for lognormal distributions in two presentations given in the early 1990s. Compounding returns over time brings the investor to mean expected wealth; adding the logarithms of return relatives brings the investor to median expected return—where the median outcome is the most likely to occur. See, for example, the initial presentation (Albrecht 1993) and the more developed presentation (Albrecht 1994). Although his audience is insurance actuaries charged with controlling investment shortfall risk over long planning horizons, the presentations contribute to the "surplus" management literature on the topic of liability-driven investing for individuals. It is possible to connect, at least intellectually, Albrecht's conference presentations to essays by authors such as Jarrod Wilcox. For example, Wilcox (2003) argues that discretionary wealth (consumer surplus) is the upper-bound amount that is prudent to risk. The proportion of risky assets held in a portfolio equals the ratio between the investor's surplus and the investor's wealth [D] times the ratio of Real Expected Median Return to Variance [Optimal Risky Asset Allocation = D(E/V)].

4. It is instructive to compare Leibowitz and Henriksson (1989), which offers a short course on risk-return trade-offs associated with a normal distribution (evaluated in discrete time), to Karagiannis (2014), which discusses the normal distribution in the context of continuous time mathematics originally developed by Robert Merton and others in the 1970s.

The Leibowitz and Henriksson articles prompted others to explore the general topic of portfolio optimization with downside risk control for both institutional investors (banks, insurance companies, pension funds) and, somewhat later, for individual investors. By 1990, William Sharpe turned his attention to these topics.[5] Following Sharpe, surplus management strategies (ALM approaches) begin to enter the private wealth management literature.

Surplus optimization using downside risk (semi-variance), shortfall constraints, and benchmark-relative targets are important concepts for understanding efficient use of portfolio resources for retired investors. The issue of liability-relative portfolio allocation is of great interest to retirees (and trustees) faced with managing portfolios designed to meet cash flow, gifting, and bequest "liabilities." The extensive literature on fixed income cash matching and immunization theory and techniques for institutional investors is beyond the scope this literature review. However, by the late 1990s, Moshe Milevsky discussed portfolio immunization, retirement cash-flow liabilities, and shortfall risk in the context of annuitization of privately held wealth—specifically, he asks when, if ever, is it optimal to trade financial wealth for an insurance company guaranteed lifetime annuity income stream (Milevsky 1998).

ALM approaches emerged within the practitioner community by the turn of the twenty-first century. For example, building upon consulting work done by William Ziemba at the Frank Russell Company,[6] a number of Russell associates advocated for using an ALM approach with private wealth clients. For example, Pittman and Greenshields (2012) advanced the proposition that advisors should focus on "funded ratio management"—the ratio of assets to liabilities—to promote better management of retirement-income portfolios. The "funded ratio" determines (1) if the client's wealth can support his desired lifestyle, and (2) if the benefits of exercising an option to purchase an immediate life annuity are worthwhile. By definition, tracking the funded ratio is a form of asset-liability monitoring: "… assets need to be managed considering the liabilities they will fund." The authors define assets as the value of liquid financial assets plus the present value of guaranteed income streams such as Social Security and guaranteed pension benefits. Liabilities are defined as the "… present value of future spending needs."[7]

Accounting-based methodologies using investor balance sheets also inform ALM studies for private investors. A balance-sheet approach underlies, for example, research by Wilcox (2004), Wilcox and Fabozzi (2009), and DiBartolomeo (2011). The Investments & Wealth Institute incorporates a "balance sheet" approach to retirement planning directly into the academic curriculum underlying the Retirement Management Analyst® (RMA®) program.[8] In the past decade, dozens of articles employing an ALM approach to private wealth management appeared in both academic and practitioner-oriented journals. The 500+ page annotated bibliography, found at the Schultz Collins, Inc. website, summarizes and comments on many important books and papers.[9] Interested readers may peruse this chronological survey of academic literature spanning the period 1965 through 2014.

This book discusses the linkage between investment wealth and funds required to support a retirement standard-of-living target. Grounding the discussion in the personal balance sheet context assures the investor that investment performance assessment includes reports on progress toward or retreat away from personal goals as well as reports on more quantitative-oriented topics. Its primary subject is monitoring, evaluating, and managing a retirement-income portfolio. Following a brief discussion of risk in retirement, the book presents a series of case studies illustrating how investors at the early, middle, and later stages of retirement learn about the risks that confront them, the opportunities that present themselves, and the investment management solutions that are both prudent and suitable to implement.

---

5.   Sharpe and Tint 1990) motivated further research in the area of asset-liability management. See, for example, Ezra (1991), Elton and Gruber (1992), Ho et al. (1994), Zhao et al. (2003), Medova et al. (2008), Berkelaar and Kouwenberg (2010), Ashton (2011), Ang et al. (2013).

     Berkelaar and Kouwenberg (2010) considers "surplus optimal portfolios," "maximum drawdown optimal portfolios," "optimal 90% conditional drawdown at risk portfolios," the "minimum risk portfolio," the "minimum surplus-risk portfolio," the "minimum drawdown portfolio," and the "traditional mean-variance portfolio." They assert: "Liabilities should be at the center of designing investment policies and serve as the ultimate reference point for evaluating and allocating risks and measuring performance. The goal of the investment policy should be to maximize expected excess returns over liabilities subject to an acceptable level of risk relative to liabilities."

6.   Described in Ziemba (2003).

7.   See Pittman and Greenshields, (2012), Fan et al. (2013), and Pittman (2013)

8.   The Investments & Wealth Institute® (formerly IMCA®) acquired the Retirement Management Analyst (RMA) program in September 2017.

9.   See "Introduction to My Annotated Bibliography on the Topic of 'Longevity Risk and Portfolio Sustainability," https://www.schultzcollins.com/resources/Annotated_Bibliography.pdf.

CHAPTER TWO

WHAT IS RISK?

■ ■ ■

Risk, at least so far as it is defined by many retired investors, is not having sufficient money to pay for necessities. Beyond spending risk (the inability to maintain an acceptable standard of living), there are other monetary risks. These are often multigenerational risks when they pertain to the financial security of the investor's family or risks to philanthropic goals when they pertain to supporting religious, cultural, or educational institutions. Irrespective of the context, and of the risk pecking order, risk is not having the cash that you need. Indeed, a primary objective of a financial asset portfolio is to meet the demand for cash at the time it arises. At the extreme, risk is portfolio depletion during one's lifetime.

Whenever an investor characterizes an investment goal primarily in terms of a target, risk metrics sort themselves into (1) an evaluation of the target's current feasibility, (2) the risk, in the future, of falling short of the target because financial outcomes fail to meet expectations, and (3) the vulnerability of the target to unexpected events and personal economic setbacks. This chapter discusses these topics in greater detail.

RETIREMENT RISK MODELS, RISK METRICS, AND PORTFOLIO MONITORING

Upon retiring completely or partially from the labor market, an investor, perhaps with the assistance of an advisor, designs and implements a portfolio to produce retirement cash flows sufficient to support a standard of living and, possibly, gift and bequest objectives.[1] The magnitude and timing of cash-flow requirements are uncertain with respect to their future purchasing power. Additionally, the investor may confront unexpected medical costs, non-medical financial emergencies, and a host of other unanticipated events. Initial decisions reflect the investor's views about expected returns, inflation, longevity, and other variables.

Investors can make informed estimates regarding some liabilities, e.g., deterministic liabilities such as the need to meet mortgage payments, or lifestyle liabilities defined either conservatively (food, clothing, shelter, and transportation) or liberally (travel, entertainment, and gifting). Non-deterministic liabilities are, by definition, stochastic in nature. Even deterministic liabilities have an uncertain present value by virtue of changes, over time, in applicable discount rates. When liabilities have a payment period measured in terms of an investor's life span, a credible and defensible valuation method uses the annuity pricing principle: The cost of providing lifelong cash flows is the sum of the periodic payments, adjusted for the probability of remaining alive to receive each payment, and discounted by a factor based on the applicable term structure of interest rates.

Likewise, at retirement, the investor knows the market value of publicly traded financial assets and, given a reasonable appraisal methodology, can estimate the value of illiquid projects such as real estate properties or a closely held business enterprise. Assuming a complete departure from the work force, the value of human capital at retirement is zero. Absent borrowing or intra-family support, retirement liabilities exceeding the value of pension and Social Security entitlements must be funded with available assets. Therefore, retirement is a risky economic proposition for many investors.

1.　We acknowledge the academic distinction between "risky" and "risk." The asset allocation decision focuses on the issue of how risky the investor wishes the portfolio to be. A risky portfolio has a distribution, usually asymmetrical, of potential results evidencing a large spread away from the mean. Asset allocation is the process of designing and implementing a specific distribution well suited to the investor's goals, e.g., spending objectives, and preferences. Primary issues are the investor's risk tolerance and risk capacity. Risk, on the other hand, usually refers to the location of actual investment or inflation outcomes within the investor's preferred investment distribution. Is the outcome a product of a bull or a bear market? Risk is the possibility that investment results will fail to achieve returns sufficient to meet critical investor targets. It is a measuring and evaluation issue rather than an asset allocation issue. Measuring provides insight into distance toward or away from goals; evaluation is fundamental to prudent portfolio management. Roy (1952) is a helpful article for understanding asset allocation risk. Academic studies of the nature of "risky" investments include Rothschild and Stiglitz (1970, 1971). An early article discussing downside risk and its implications for precautionary savings and investment choice is Menezes et al. (1980). Finally, an interested reader may wish to examine Brockett and Kahane (1992), which discusses the often-complex relationships between the nth-order derivatives of utility functions and the moments of a distribution of investment results. Time and tenure demands have brought forth a vast theoretical literature on the nature of decision-making and the economics of risk. This book touches on these subjects only tangentially and, most often, when discussing behavioral finance topics.

Some sophisticated investors and advisors quantify risk through a formal and comprehensive modeling process. Outputs are projections flowing from a retirement risk model that incorporates complex interactions among multiple data inputs. Outputs reflect distributional assumptions for variables such as longevity, investment returns, and inflation realizations. Future projections are informed guesses and the projections depend on the credibility of the underlying risk model's structure and assumptions. As such, the output manifests "model risk"—a risk that should be added to the list of risks faced by retirees working with advisors, internet calculators, robo-advice firms, and other technology-based information sources.[2] An initial retirement-income model is a set of *a priori* probabilities projected into the future.

The inputs to the decision-making process, whether they reflect an uninformed investor's subjective beliefs or are well-considered inputs into a sophisticated risk model, produce an output—the retirement portfolio model. The output may be optimized in the sense of maximizing the value of a utility function (aggregate utility, habit or Epstein-Zin[3] utility, state-preference utility, prospect-theory utility, and so forth) where the utility function can be continuous or discontinuous; where a relative or absolute risk-aversion function can be increasing, decreasing, or constant; where a bequest motive can compete with a consumption motive; and where consumption itself may by subject to an "impatience factor."

Solutions based on utility theory are, however, a source of controversy. Economists from the Behavioral Finance School point out:

1. Utility functions often are difficult to assess.

2. Decision-makers (investors and advisors) are unlikely to know how to generate mathematical expressions that accurately reflect personal risk tolerance at either a spot on the wealth domain or across the entire domain.

3. Many decision-makers do not define their objectives in terms of maximizing a portfolio's expected utility (state-preference or aggregate) as derived from consumption, lifetime gifting, and bequests.

Alternately, the retirement portfolio model's output can reflect the investor's sense of "satisficing," where the optimal solution path involves meeting individual goals within a "chanced constrained" framework (goal A should be met at a probability of 95 percent or better, goal B should be met at a probability of 80 percent or better, and so on).[4] The utility-based approach has been characterized, improperly, as the exclusive domain of the rationalist school of financial economics and the goals-based approach has been characterized, improperly, as the exclusive domain of the Behavioral Finance School.[5]

Retirement as a Risky Project largely sidesteps disputes between the Behavioral and Rational schools for at least two reasons: (1) Many disputes, at least in practitioner-level publications, are merely a thicket of silly back-and-forths. The fact is that both schools provide insights valuable for developing and communicating investment concepts and strategies. And, (2) we prefer an approach based on informed judgment rather than dogmatic adherence to academic or psychological doctrine.

---

2.   For a more complete discussion of model risk, see Collins et al. (2015a) and Pfleiderer (2014).

3.   For a discussion about Epstein-Zin utility, see Epstein and Zin (1989).

4.   For example, Yaari (1965) notes that the feasibility problem can be solved either through a "chance-constrained programming" methodology or through a "penalty function" procedure. "The chance-constrained programming approach requires that the constraint (in this case the wealth constraint) be met with probability λ or more, where λ is some number fixed in advance, say 0.95. ... This approach is, of course very common in statistics where many of the standard tests are based on the idea of maximizing some criterion subject to the constraint that the probability of type I error be less than, say .05." However, Yaari points out that the choice of λ is itself a decision problem: "... one might want to choose λ optimally rather than arbitrarily."

5.   Simplistically, the Rational School uses mathematical definitions of risk while the Behavioral Finance School employs psychological definitions of risk. Although the points of departure differ greatly, nevertheless, the literature is replete with examples of rational-school approaches that generate portfolio management recommendations that conform well to behaviorist principles, and vice versa. An early example is Fishburn (1977). A growing body of research focuses on synthesizing the tenets and viewpoints of the two schools, see Bordley and LiCalzi (2000), Ziemba (2003), Medova et al. (2008), and Das et al. (2010).

     Sharpe (2017) provides a good review of "utility" functions, investor preferences, and the interrelationships between behavioral and rational schools of finance. Sharpe's analysis, not surprisingly, builds from insights developed from a single-period equilibrium model. The model of choice is not the capital asset pricing model (CAPM), however, but the Arrow-Debreu state-preference model first developed in the 1950s. Sharpe's "criticism" of CAPM echoes, in many respects, both the tone and substance of commentaries written by behavioralists such as Ashvin Chhabra, Meir Statman, and others.

     By substituting the concept of the "felicity function" and by incorporating psychological parameters that carry specific discount rates, the concept of a "utility function" moves behavioral finance concepts toward Rational School commentary. A more complete discussion of these topics is found in Collins and Gadenne (2017), which provides links to extensive notes and appendixes that detail the history of academic research and provide commentaries thereon.

Getting an investor to the point at which informed judgment is possible is not an easy task. At the beginning of the analysis and advice process, the investor often lacks sufficient information to articulate personal preferences or, in the language of financial economics, personal utility/risk preference functions.[6] We argue that it is the advisor's job to help the investor discover the nature of his "risk appraisal function," i.e., his willingness and ability to accept retirement risk.[7] The advisor can facilitate the discovery process, without doubt, through probabilistic risk modeling—for example, by employing Monte Carlo risk models. More to the point, as previously discussed, an initial assessment of retirement risk is more credible when based on current observables rather than on projections of possible outcomes many years into the future.[8]

Often, retirement risks are categorized neatly into areas such as inflation or purchasing power risk, investment risk (most commonly, sequence of returns risk and portfolio depletion risk), health risks (the paradoxical risk of a long life), unexpected liability shocks, and variability in periodic consumption needs. It is easy to see that the investor must confront a number of complex issues. How does the investor gather information about important variables? How do uncertainties become more tractable probabilities in the face of incomplete information or lack of statistical data?[9]

Advisors traditionally address risk in one of three ways:

1. Ignoring it by pointing out that more money is always better than less and that the best portfolio is the expected return-maximizing portfolio.

2. Succumbing to the methodological flaw of basing decisions on point estimates rather than on the distribution of possible results. This flaw can take the form of a what's-my-retirement-number approach to retirement planning under the assumption that a safe lifetime spending amount is a function of initial portfolio value or a what's-a-safe-spending-rate number based on some combination of initial portfolio value and pre-set spending rules.

3. Projecting distributions of results (inflation and investment return realizations, changes in health and longevity expectations, changes in liability values). Most often, this approach uses Monte Carlo simulations to consider a variety of risk metrics including shortfall probability (risk of shortfall in either budget or wealth targets), shortfall magnitude, and shortfall duration.

Investment spreadsheet tools sometimes calculate shortfall-risk metrics using point estimates. Such an approach assumes a deterministic world where calculating success and failure is easy—historical returns average 8 percent, inflation averages 3 percent, life expectancy (an average) is 20 years, and the average of all the averages—a calculation methodology destined to generate a completely spurious output—is the investor's odds for success. Unfortunately, "Plans based on average assumptions are wrong on average. An apocryphal

---

6. We acknowledge the difference between "preferences" and "utility." Preferences are ordinal utility where the investor decides which choice is preferable, e.g., A is better than B, B is better than C, and so on. In this context, the expression "maximizing utility" indicates that the investor's choice is prudent and suitable. "Prudent" because it is a feasible solution path and "suitable" because it comports well with the investor's personal financial objectives. The term "utility" is also appropriate, however, because it usually refers to a mathematical function the output of which is a cardinal measure of preferences over outcomes within a given probability space. Unlike many academic papers, however, we do not attempt to discover (or impose) a specific function across the entire probability space or across the population of investors. Our goal is to help investors articulate their preferences for distributions of prospective outcomes. For additional insight into these issues, see Montesano (2009), Diecidue and Van De Ven (2008), Levy and Levy (2009), and Abbas and Matheson (2005).

7. Davies (2017) provides a helpful discussion of risk tolerance versus risk capacity: "For most investors, risk capacity is overwhelmingly more important than risk tolerance; the right level of risk for their investments is far more likely to be constrained by their lack of capacity to cope with capital losses than by the psychological aversion to long-term risk. … Investors with small flows in and out of their balance sheet relative to the size of the balance sheet (typically very wealthy people with large net asset values) will be likely to have high risk capacity since they have significant wealth with which to fund future liabilities as they arise. For them, risk tolerance is far more likely to be the binding constraint." (Davies 2017, 6).

8. Unfortunately, a vocabulary descriptive of a prudent decision-making process has been co-opted by those interested primarily in increasing product sales. A recent conference for insurance salespeople, for example, highlighted a speaker that specialized in boosting sales by showing an attendee how to become a "facilitator of decision making."

9. The reader might recall the joke about the ill statistician who asked his surgeon to perform an operation on him 30 times so that he could quantify the procedure's success rate with greater accuracy.

example concerns the statistician who drowned while fording a river that was, on average, only three feet deep ..." (Savage 2012, 11). Sometimes investment tools quantify shortfall risk by simulating economic outcomes. Outputs usually are more credible than those derived from point-estimate models if for no other reason than that simulation-based models allow for the possibility of more than one future outcome.[10]

Shortfall-risk metrics often focus on the portfolio's dollar value. They include:

Shortfall probability: The chance of falling below a threshold value or target rate of return given the model's distribution of economic outcomes.

Time to shortfall: The number of months until the onset of portfolio depletion or below-target value (distribution of the initial date of shortfall onset given a shortfall occurrence).

Magnitude of shortfall: The distribution of the dollar amount of the shortfall conditional on shortfall occurrence.

Duration of shortfall: The length of time of the shortfall conditional on its occurrence.

For example, if the investor is interested in the likelihood that the investment portfolio becomes depleted during the investor's lifetime, the metric of interest is shortfall probability. If the investor is interested in the distribution of time during which he is alive-but-broke, the metric of interest is duration of shortfall.

Advisors and investors also use shortfall-risk metrics with respect to periodic income as well as portfolio dollar values. Income-oriented metrics include:

Shortfall probability: The likelihood that income will ever be less than $x per period.

Shortfall duration: The likelihood that aggregate income will ever be less than $y over a deterministic or stochastic planning horizon.

Shortfall snapshots: The distribution of income at particular times (five-year, 10-year, period just before end of life) under given asset allocation and asset management elections.

Monitoring income-shortfall metrics is especially important when a retired investor's spending is proportional to the portfolio's current value. In a trust context, such an approach characterizes a unitrust distribution policy. For example, a trust beneficiary may be entitled to receive a yearly distribution equal to 4 percent of the average value of the trust over the previous 36 months. Spending is not fixed because portfolio value fluctuates depending, primarily, on capital market conditions.[11]

---

10. Although fixing unique values to parameters, whenever parameter values are uncertain, may give the model user the illusion of accuracy, this approach simply pushes the problem of predetermined outcomes back one level. Most Monte Carlo simulations, for example, rely on pre-parameterized distributions thereby ignoring the facts that (1) parameter values may be random or regime dependent (i.e., state dependent), and (2) the outcome is only a rough approximation of the true probability distribution. Variations in a model's mathematical structure and input assumptions can lead to outputs suggesting drastically different conclusions regarding the suitability of current asset management policies to a client's financial objectives. For example, even within the simplistic rolling-period-analysis approach, using historical returns spanning different time periods or varying the size of the rolling window can generate strikingly different success or failure probabilities. Understanding such sensitivities is essential to discerning the trustworthiness of outputs from a retirement-income risk model.

Although no investment risk model can predict the future, one hallmark of a credible model is that it enables investors to make good decisions within a wide range of possible futures. Thomas J. Sargent's Nobel Prize-winning research deals with how investors make decisions when they doubt the accuracy of their model. When confronted with ambiguity, they tend to use a family of models and to overweight bad outcomes as a mechanism for exercising caution. See, for example, Hansen and Sargent (2008).

Outputs based on financial modeling are best considered fictional in the sense that they are provisional, e.g., Bayesian Priors. This includes model outputs presented in this book. Language itself is a model in that it is a system of verbal and written elements designed to communicate information about reality. Although language is the most imprecise model in existence, most users find that it is both a necessary and a beneficial tool. Silver (2012, 230–231) quotes the statistician George E. P. Box: "All models are wrong, but some models are useful." Silver concludes "The key is in remembering that a model is a tool to help us understand the complexities of the universe, and never a substitute for the universe itself." In this book we do not delve into deeper philosophical questions of Pyrronism and Skepticism other than to reiterate the adage: "Take everything with a grain of salt."

11. When the claims of various beneficiary classes are likely to spark litigation alleging trustee breach of the duty of impartiality, the trustee's prior analysis—including documentation of income/dollar value shortfall metrics—takes center stage. For example, a trustee may demonstrate the "fairness" of trust administration by comparing the distribution of probable aggregate constant-dollar income benefit to the distribution of probable constant-dollar terminal wealth benefit. The Kolmogorov-Smirnov test is one of several statistical tools at the disposal of trustees seeking to substantiate the "closeness" of the income distribution to the terminal wealth distribution and, therefore, the impartiality of trust administration.

It is useful to rethink the nature and scope of retirement risk and to communicate to investors how the risks to their retirement objectives change through time. To this end, we present case studies to provide an enhanced perspective on retirement risk by focusing on three metrics:

- Feasibility
- Sustainability
- Flexibility

Although each of the first three case studies isolates and emphasizes one risk metric, it is the interaction of all three that determines success or failure in the context of investor-specific goals.[12] Briefly, a mapping of the risk metrics to quantitative performance measures produces:

Feasibility: The actuarial coverage ratio. This is a test for retirement solvency (does the current market value of financial assets exceed the actuarially determined present value of current liabilities?).[13]

Sustainability: Shortfall-risk metrics (at what confidence level does the retirement-income model peg the likelihood of success?).

Flexibility: This is a test for security. After funding target lifetime cash flows, how much, if any, surplus is available—both currently and in future years—to cover the cost of other financial needs or emergencies? In the context of retirement-income planning, a solvency risk metric estimates how far portfolio value would have to fall so that it can no longer produce required cash flows absent a market recovery or a change in withdrawal policy.

The case studies provide further details on both the quantitative and qualitative aspects of these risk metrics.[14]

---

12. It is cold comfort to the investor that her retirement portfolio beat an index or landed in the top peer-group quartile if the investment plan leaves her unable to pay the bills.

13. "[T]he aggregate consumption in states cannot exceed what is available in that state. ... This condition is, in fact, the feasibility condition" (Eeckhoudt et al. 2005, 170).

14. Bajtelsmit et al. (2013) provides a helpful review of risk metrics.

CHAPTER THREE

CASE STUDY 1—EMPHASIS ON FEASIBILITY

■ ■ ■

PART ONE: FEASIBILITY

Money management encompasses ongoing monitoring; effective monitoring helps the investor assess the continued feasibility of retirement objectives relative to financial resources at hand. A critical distinction must be drawn between sustainability—the probability calculated by the risk model that future financial market returns might be sufficient to fund cash-flow targets, and feasibility—the assessment that the current portfolio has the ability to produce the required cash flows. The feasibility condition requires that the current market value of assets equal or exceed the stochastic value of the lifetime target income plus, if relevant, any bequests, gifts, or other liabilities.

Conceptually, it is useful to consider portfolio monitoring as an activity within the set of "free boundary" problems. One class of free boundary problems involves estimating the demarcation between two regions where the line of demarcation is not fixed (Friedman 2000, 854).[1] A classic example is estimating the location of the boundary between solid ice and liquid water when the temperature drops below freezing. In winter, the depth of a Minnesota lake's boundary between ice and water fluctuates according to the random variable of water temperature. In cold weather, the ice pack is thick, in warmer weather it thins. Analogizing to retirement-income-portfolio monitoring in an asset-liability management (ALM) context, the investor faces the problem of determining the line of demarcation between two regions—a region of wealth surplus, in which the portfolio's current value is able to support financial objectives, and a region of wealth deficit, in which the portfolio's current value is not able to support financial objectives. We call the first region the "feasible region" and the second region the "infeasible region." A bull market tends to move a portfolio farther into the feasible region—the region of wealth surplus. A bear market, however, tends to move it toward the line of demarcation—the free boundary—that separates the regions. As wealth depletion pushes farther and farther toward the region of infeasibility, the consequences of investor actions or inactions are magnified in the sense that an ill-considered asset management election may not only generate losses, but losses from which the portfolio can never recover.

The investor has to know, in effect, the thickness of the ice pack, lest undue optimism induces the fatal mistake of conducting financial affairs on thin ice. Once the ice cracks, one falls through and is unable to climb out. No matter what the temperature is the next day, the disaster is irreversible. If a portfolio becomes too depleted, even spectacular subsequent market performance is of no use.

PART TWO: FACT PATTERN

A currently employed, 66-year-old, single, male investor in good health seeks retirement-planning information. The investor wants his investment portfolio to provide inflation-adjusted lifetime monthly income to supplement periodic benefits payable from government entitlements, employer-sponsored pensions, or privately held annuity contracts.

He calculates that his portfolio must generate a threshold $5,000 of inflation-adjusted lifetime monthly income to support a minimal acceptable lifestyle. We designate the $5,000 constant-dollar lifetime monthly income as the "threshold target." His desired lifestyle, however, requires a $7,000 constant-dollar lifetime monthly income. We designate the $7,000 constant-dollar lifetime monthly income as the "aspirational target." The financial asset portfolio consists of liquid, publicly traded securities with a $1.5 million current market value. Appendix A provides additional details regarding portfolio composition. This case study ignores possible gifting or bequest objectives to focus on the investor's primary objective—securing a target standard of living throughout retirement. It assumes that

---

1. An interesting extension of free boundary problems involves the mathematics of black holes, where the boundary location between normal space and the event horizon—the event horizon is the boundary at which light is no longer able to escape, so anything that penetrates the horizon is forever trapped—is both constantly shifting and unobservable. Passing through the event horizon is catastrophic. An interesting aspect of the event horizon is that you can pass through it without realizing it. Likewise, you could place yourself into what you believe to be a stable orbit only to spiral quickly into a black hole due to the smallest of perturbations. These nonlinear physical phenomena provide interesting perspectives into the portfolio risks discussed in this book. Without an effective monitoring program, an investor can pass into the region of danger without realizing it, or the investor can believe that his/her retirement is on a stable economic footing just before a nerve-wrenching downward trajectory. For further insight into what happens when you encounter a black hole, see the University of Colorado website: http://jila.colorado.edu/~ajsh/insidebh/schw.html.

the investor's budget calculations and withdrawal targets incorporate anticipated tax liabilities. Cash flows to meet future liability payments for financial emergencies including medical expenses are absent from Case Study 1. Case Study 1 acquaints the reader with a substantial amount of baseline information within a simplified fact pattern. Familiarity with this material will pay dividends when discussing subsequent case studies.

The investor wishes to understand the probable economic consequences of retiring now. Whenever a limited amount of capital must fund future cash-flow targets, the investment problem takes on aspects of an asset-liability approach to portfolio management. Can asset allocation create a portfolio capable of sustaining lifetime-income targets assuming prudent future asset management? Given an asset allocation decision, if retirement begins immediately, what is the likelihood that either the aspirational or the threshold lifestyle-income target is sustainable throughout the planning horizon?

Initially, the case analysis is based on two current observables: (1) cost of an inflation-adjusted annuity promising the lifetime target income and (2) current market value of assets. If the ratio of assets to annuity cost is greater than 1.00 (allowing for a reasonable loading factor for commercial single-premium, immediate annuity contracts), retirement is "feasible" in the sense that the present value of assets exceeds the present value of cash-flow liabilities as actuarially determined. The investor can lock in the cash flow today and avoid the future vicissitudes of inflation and market performance. Although an early resolution of uncertainty through annuitization may not be an optimal solution, nevertheless it is not without significant utility.[2]

Case Study 1 initially presents risk model output for a retirement-income portfolio maintaining a fixed allocation to 50-percent stocks and 50-percent bonds. The investor wishes to spend $7,000 per month adjusted for inflation. Figure 3.1 shows inflation-adjusted wealth, which is quantified on the left-side vertical axis, and feasibility, which is quantified on the right-side vertical axis. The horizontal axis measures time in years. An investor achieving a feasibility ratio (defined below) greater than 100 percent passes the feasibility test.

FIGURE 3.1: FEASIBILITY TEST—50–50 PORTFOLIO, $7,000 PER MONTH DISTRIBUTION

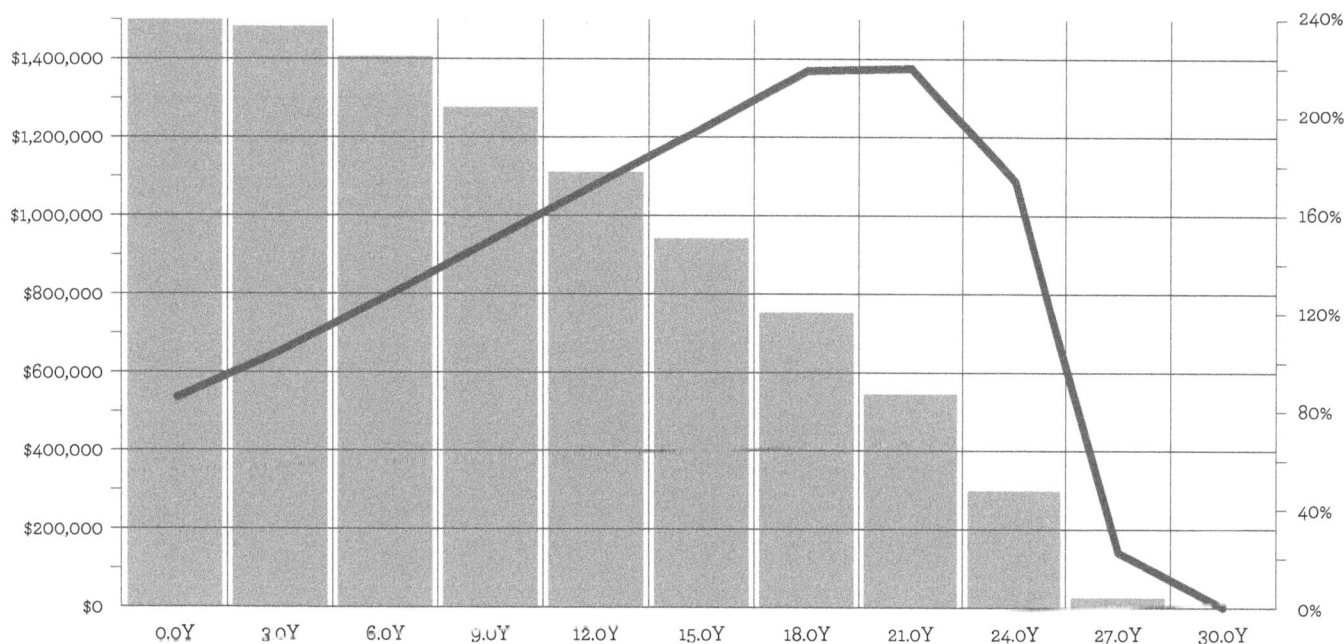

2.   We note that other fixed income benchmarks exist for quantifying the cost of retirement income. For example, when considering only nominal cash flows, the investor can
     calculate the present-value cost of a 30-year sequence of annually maturing zero-coupon bonds (Treasury STRIPS). A weakness of this benchmark lies in its inability to account
     for inflation—purchasing power risk. Alternately, the investor can build a 30-year Treasury Inflation-Protected Securities (TIPS) ladder. The present-value cost of the ladder is a
     measure of feasibility with respect to inflation-adjusted income. A weakness of this benchmark lies in its inability to account for longevity risk.

The columns record the portfolio's projected inflation-adjusted dollar value, at the median (50th percentile) of the joint distribution of investment, inflation, and spending outcomes, net of fees and withdrawals. The projection suggests that the portfolio can sustain a monthly, constant-dollar $7,000 withdrawal throughout most of a 30-year planning horizon. The left-side axis measures a range of portfolio value from the current $1.5 million through portfolio depletion at approximately year 28 under the assumption that the investor's retirement strategy (50–50 allocation with constant-dollar monthly spending of $7,000) continues on autopilot throughout the planning horizon. The financial model indicates that, assuming retirement does not continue beyond year 27 (age 93), the investor, on average, should have funds sufficient to support his aspirational consumption objective.

The line on figure 3.1 records the value of the actuarial coverage ratio (ACR). The ACR is the ratio of the portfolio's current market value to the current estimated cost of an actuarially fair annuity—decremented by an assumed 15-percent load factor—paying the target amount of inflation-adjusted lifetime income.[3] In this case, the investor's financial wealth falls short of the estimated annuity cost[4] by 14.4 percent, or the investor's current ACR value is 85.6 percent. The actuarial model indicates that current resources are insufficient to guarantee the investor's aspirational income target throughout his life span. It is not comforting to hear that his retirement plans have flunked the initial feasibility test. To the investor, this seems perplexing. One indicator is signaling a retirement green light (at least up to age 93), the other is flashing red.[5] Where does this leave the investor?

Both portfolio market value and annuity cost (fair price + estimated load) are current observables.[6] Figure 3.1, however, projects dynamically changing values over the planning horizon. The data table for figure 3.1 provides data chronologically over the 30-year period:

DATA TABLE FOR FIGURE 3.1: 50–50 PORTFOLIO, $7,000 PER MONTH DISTRIBUTION

	Percentile	Current Value	3.0Y	6.0Y	9.0Y	12.0Y	15.0Y	18.0Y	21.0Y	24.0Y	27.0Y	30.0Y
Portfolio Value	50th	$1,500,000	$1,482,814	$1,405,993	$1,276,351	$1,110,732	$942,133	$753,045	$545,575	$298,234	$25,721	$0
Actuarial Coverage Ratio	50th	85.60%	104.80%	126.90%	150.00%	173.00%	195.80%	219.30%	220.20%	174.00%	22.40%	0.00%

---

3.   Our findings are in line with previous studies. For example, Pang and Warshawsky, (2010) set the annuity expense load to 15 percent in their simulation model. Subjects in an experiment designed to ascertain the premium an individual may be willing to pay to avoid ambiguity usually paid 10 to 20 percent of expected value. Ahn et al. (2014) suggests that some investors may not find a 10-percent to 20-percent load to be onerous. However, Charness and Gneezy (2010) provide a counterpoint: "With ambiguity aversion, we do find a difference in behavior. ... However; this difference goes in the opposite direction from the prediction! [The result] certainly does not provide support for the hypotheses that people invest less when there is a higher degree of ambiguity."

4.   The annuity pricing factor is the sum of periodic cash flows, where each cash flow is adjusted for the probability of remaining alive to receive it and is discounted by the applicable rate on the yield curve. The cost of a lifetime unit of income (nominal or inflation-adjusted) changes with age, systematic (i.e., population) longevity risk factors, and discount rates. Actuarially fair annuities do not exist in the marketplace. Depending on (1) the investor's age and gender, and (2) the insurance company's sales and administrative expenses, reserving requirements, and profit objectives, investors should expect to multiply the actuarially fair cost by a substantial load factor. Stated otherwise, should an investor wish to exercise the option to trade financial wealth for an equivalent-value lifetime income stream, he must expect to pay a substantial cost. An ACR of 100 percent indicates that current wealth exactly equals the estimated current cost of a commercial annuity contract.

5.   Simulation is an investment test; ACR is an actuarial test.

6.   The investor can visit a number of websites to determine the exact cost of a particular carrier's single-premium, immediate annuity contract. The quoted price will include loads as well as applicable state taxes and policy fees. Quoted prices also reflect the investment opportunity set available to a particular insurance company (private placement bonds), the company's proprietary yield curve discounting methods and actuarial assumptions, the carrier's credit and financial strength ratings, as well as a host of other factors.

The investor notes that by year 3 he appears to be on the sunny side of the feasibility (ACR) ratio despite the fact that the inflation-adjusted value of the portfolio has decreased slightly.[7] Furthermore, despite monotonically decreasing wealth, the investor maintains an ACR value greater than 1.0 until the latter part of the planning horizon. The apparent anomaly is explained easily by noting that annuity contracts become cheaper as the investor's age increases. Although the insurance company will have less time to earn investment income, the expected payout period decreases. In the race between investment earnings and mortality credits, chronological age becomes the dominant factor—older individuals pay less for equivalent periodic life-time income streams.[8]

In the instant case, the investor lacks sufficient wealth to retire today and secure an annuity contract that, assuming continued insurance company solvency,[9] provides the desired lifetime monthly income. However, the data table for figure 3.1 suggests that sometime before year 3 he is likely to have the financial resources to exercise the annuity option should he choose to do so. Here are some issues:

- The data suggest that retirement success may be uncomfortably reliant on favorable financial conditions (market returns and realized inflation).
- If interest rates rise, future annuity costs may decrease, thus pushing attainment of the feasibility boundary closer in time. If interest rates fall, future annuity costs may increase, thus pushing the feasibility boundary further into the future, e.g., to years 4, 5, or 6.
- At whatever time the investor opts to annuitize, he loses the financial flexibility to confront other financial needs and objectives (unscheduled liabilities, gifts, bequests).
- If he fails to annuitize, he may confront purchasing-power risk and poor investment returns that will cause a further deterioration in his retirement security.

At this point, we cannot intuit the investor's reaction to this information. Does the investor take great discomfort in the fact that retirement is currently economically infeasible according to actuarial standards? Is the fact that he is operating close-to-the-bone likely to keep him up at night? What type of risk-reward trade-off is the investor able and willing to make? What additional information does the investor wish to examine? What additional issues might affect his decision making? These questions inform the Case Study 1 analysis.

PART THREE: ANALYSIS

The investor notes that the portfolio, running on autopilot, seems to have a life expectancy of approximately 27 years. This seems like a long time—a fact in which the investor takes comfort. Thus, a logical question is how well this time horizon matches the investor's life span.[10] In order to consider the possibility that the investor will outlive the unannuitized portfolio, the advisor adds a new data element: survival probability (see figure 3.2 and the data table for figure 3.2). There is 100-percent certainty that the investor is alive today—after all, he is currently meeting with the advisor; however, as time passes, the force of mortality increases:

7. Chapters Five and Eight provide further discussion on the evolution of ACR values and the dangers of assuming that a positive trend will continue throughout retirement. Like a black-hole's physics, ACR paths can be highly unstable.
8. See appendix E for details on future annuity cost projections and ACR calculations in a context where the future value of the income stream itself is linked to the Consumer Price Index.
9. A "second order" issue of great importance to an investor's financial security.
10. Life expectancy is not the same as life span. Life expectancy is a point estimate—in this case, 18 years. Life span is the investor's actual longevity. In other words, how likely is it that a 66-year-old, male, white-collar, high-income retiree, in good health, lives beyond 18 years? In particular, how likely is it that the investor lives beyond the projected 27-year life of the portfolio?

FIGURE 3.2: FEASIBILITY TEST—50–50 PORTFOLIO, $7,000 PER MONTH DISTRIBUTION

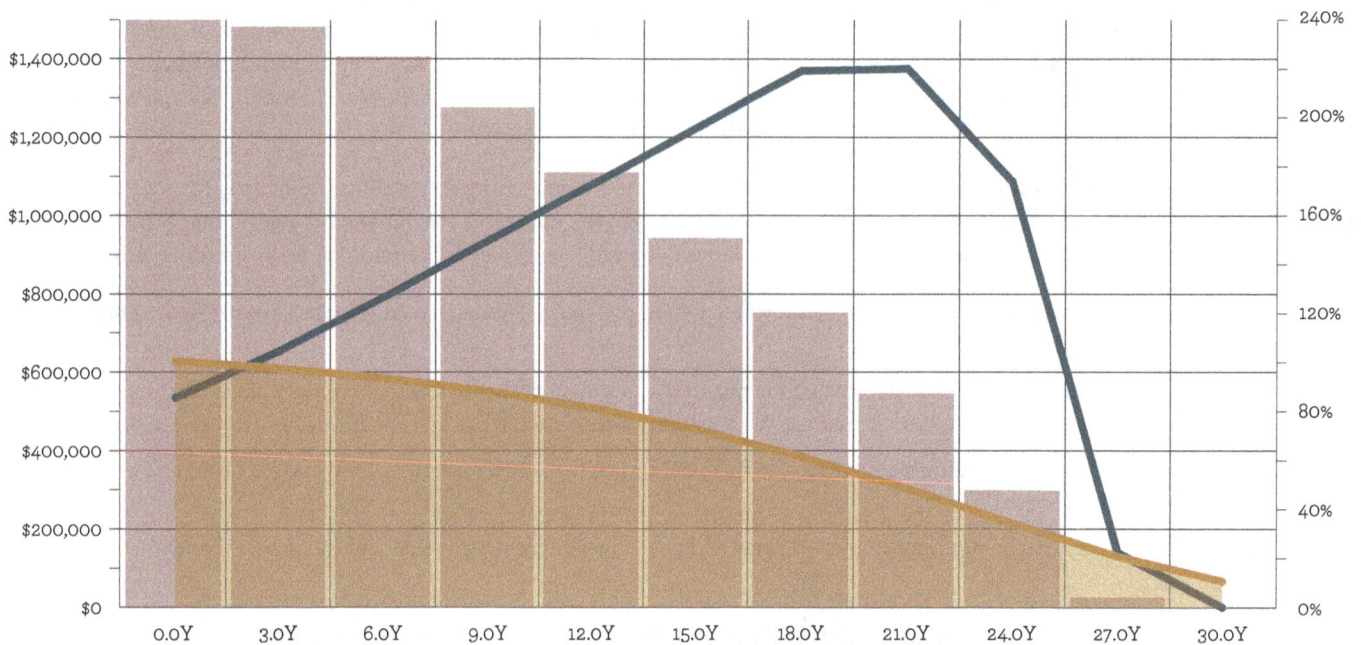

DATA TABLE FOR FIGURE 3.2: FEASIBILITY TEST—50–50 PORTFOLIO, $7,000 PER MONTH DISTRIBUTION

	Percentile	Current Value	3.0Y	6.0Y	9.0Y	12.0Y	15.0Y	18.0Y	21.0Y	24.0Y	27.0Y	30.0Y
Portfolio Value	50th	$1,500,000	$1,482,814	$1,405,993	$1,276,351	$1,110,732	$942,133	$753,045	$545,575	$298,234	$25,721	$0
Actuarial Coverage Ratio	50th	85.60%	104.80%	126.90%	150.00%	173.00%	195.80%	219.30%	220.20%	174.00%	22.40%	0.00%
Survival Probability		100.00%	97.00%	92.90%	87.70%	80.80%	72.30%	61.10%	48.20%	34.10%	20.50%	10.50%

The survival probability data suggests that the investor has an approximately 20-percent chance of outliving the portfolio. How does the investor react to the new information? On the one hand, the annuitization option, exercised at the right time, provides the promise of a lifetime income stream relatively free from investment monitoring and management tasks. Such a low-maintenance solution may be particularly attractive to investors fearing future cognitive impairment or other perils. On the other hand, considered from today's perspective, if the annuity option is exercised at year 3, there is a 20-percent probability that even a healthy investor will not remain alive by year 12. Should a change in health shortly after year 3 (age 69) increase the force of mortality, exercising the annuity option at the earliest feasible time may be catastrophic in terms of lost consumption opportunities, or lost flexibility to meet healthcare expenses. Annuitization carries the risk of brevity.

Longevity risk is the flip side of brevity risk. Given a 50–50 stock-to-bond allocation of his current financial resources, what is the interrelationship between longevity and the risk of portfolio depletion for the investor electing to spend an inflation-adjusted $7,000 per month? A definition of longevity risk is: time-alive-and-broke. Figure 3.3 depicts longevity risk graphically in the blue-shaded area; data table 3.3 quantifies it analytically.

FIGURE 3.3: FEASIBILITY TEST—50–50 PORTFOLIO, $7,000 PER MONTH DISTRIBUTION

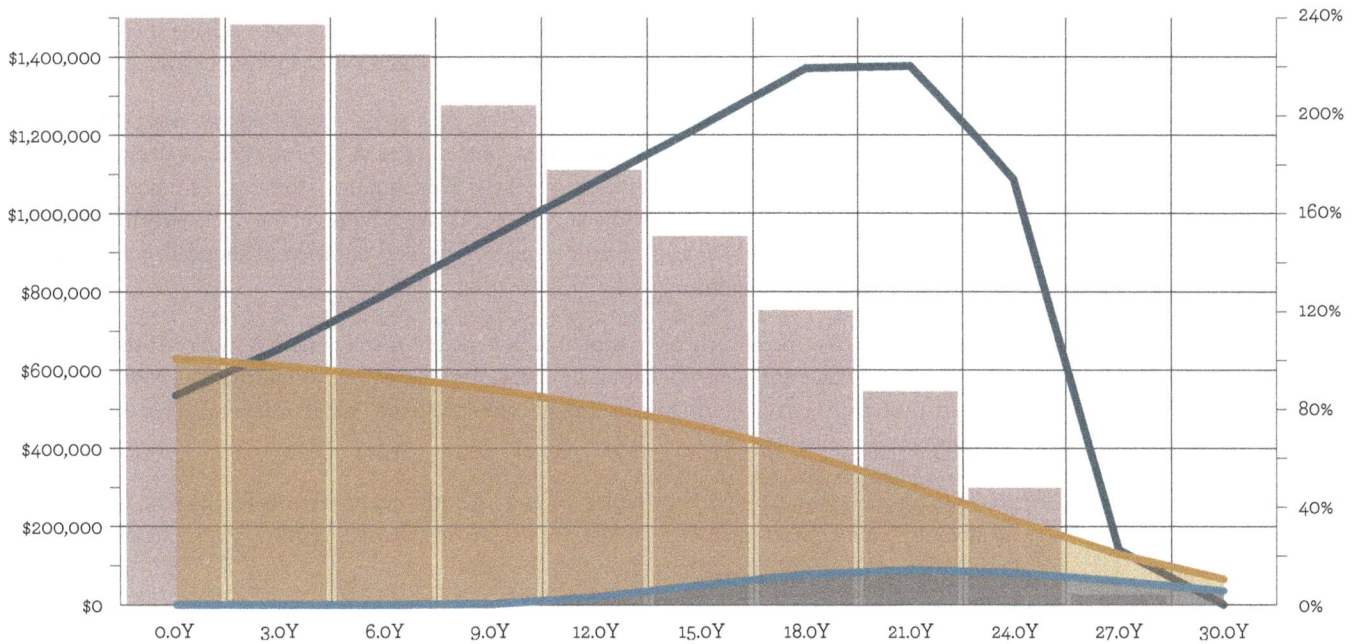

DATA TABLE FOR FIGURE 3.3: FEASIBILITY TEST—50–50 PORTFOLIO, $7,000 PER MONTH DISTRIBUTION

	Percentile	Current Value	3.0Y	6.0Y	9.0Y	12.0Y	15.0Y	18.0Y	21.0Y	24.0Y	27.0Y	30.0Y
Portfolio Value	50th	$1,500,000	$1,482,814	$1,405,993	$1,276,351	$1,110,732	$942,133	$753,045	$545,575	$298,234	$25,721	0
Actuarial Coverage Ratio	50th	85.60%	104.80%	126.90%	150.00%	173.00%	195.80%	219.30%	220.20%	174.00%	22.40%	0.00%
Survival Probability			100.00%	97.00%	92.90%	87.70%	80.80%	72.30%	61.10%	48.20%	34.10%	20.50%	10.50%
Probability of Depletion			0.00%	0.00%	0.00%	0.30%	3.20%	8.40%	12.90%	14.70%	13.70%	10.20%	5.90%

Longevity risk is a conditional probability. Mathematically it can be expressed as [(the percentage of surviving investors who lack funds) divided by (the total percentage of surviving investors)]. The blue-shaded area represents the number of surviving-and-broke investor trials. At the current time, all trials evidence a living investor who owns a $1.5-million portfolio. The distance between the top of the blue-shaded region and the top of the orange-shaded region is at a maximum. Currently, the conditional probability of portfolio "bankruptcy" is zero. By year 12, however, only 80.80 percent of trials evidence a living investor, and 3.20 percent of living investors have exhausted their financial portfolios. Thus, conditional depletion risk equals 3.20 percent divided by 80.80 percent, or approximately 4 percent. The distance between the top of the two shaded regions is decreasing. By year 21, longevity risk (the conditional probability of portfolio depletion while alive) equals 14.70 percent divided by 48.20 percent, or approximately 31 percent. Stated otherwise, there is an approximately one-in-three chance that if the investor lives for 21 years (and continues to fund a $7,000-per-month standard-of-living withdrawal) he will fully deplete his portfolio. The two regions approach each other asymptotically, figure 3.3 provides an intuitive understanding of the convergence rate.

A brief recap may be in order. The investor is trying to decide if he should retire now or postpone retirement until a future date. He owns a $1.5-million financial asset portfolio from which he wishes to spend $7,000 per month in inflation-adjusted dollars (his aspirational target). Under all economic circumstances, however, he must be able to spend a minimum of $5,000 (his threshold target).

To assist in the decision-making process, the investor enlists the services of an advisor. The advisor's initial test aims to determine if retirement is feasible. This is a solvency test—assets must exceed liabilities. Is the current value of financial assets equal to or greater than the actuarially determined cost of the investor's desired lifetime cash flow? If the answer is no, the insurance marketplace is signaling that the investor cannot expect to generate adequate income throughout retirement. It is unwise for an investor to ignore such a signal.

In Case Study 1, the investor considers a series of outputs from a retirement risk model. At a 50–50 stock-to-bond asset allocation, it appears as if retirement at his aspirational level is fraught with embedded risks that may emerge in the future. If he decides to retire today, the evolution of portfolio values and risk metrics will have to be monitored closely. This requires attention, as time unfolds, to a variety of risk metrics indicative of both (1) the distance between current assets and the boundary location in the dollar-wealth space that separates regions of feasibility and infeasibility and (2) shortfall risks—probability, magnitude, and duration of shortfall, conditional on its occurrence, in both the consumption space and the dollar-wealth space.

For now, however, the investor remains curious about the consequences of available investment management options. At the top of the list, he wishes to know the probable consequences of changing the allocation by increasing the equity weighting. Over long planning horizons, according to what he has previously read, stocks outperform bonds. Can he ameliorate the risk of unfavorable future results by increasing the portfolio's allocation to stocks?

To address this question, the advisor presents figures 3.4 and 3.5 and data tables 3.4 and 3.5 outlining the results (at the 50th percentile of outcomes) for both a 60–40 and a 70–30 stock-to-bond allocation:

FIGURE 3.4: FEASIBILITY TEST—60–40 PORTFOLIO, $7,000 PER MONTH DISTRIBUTION

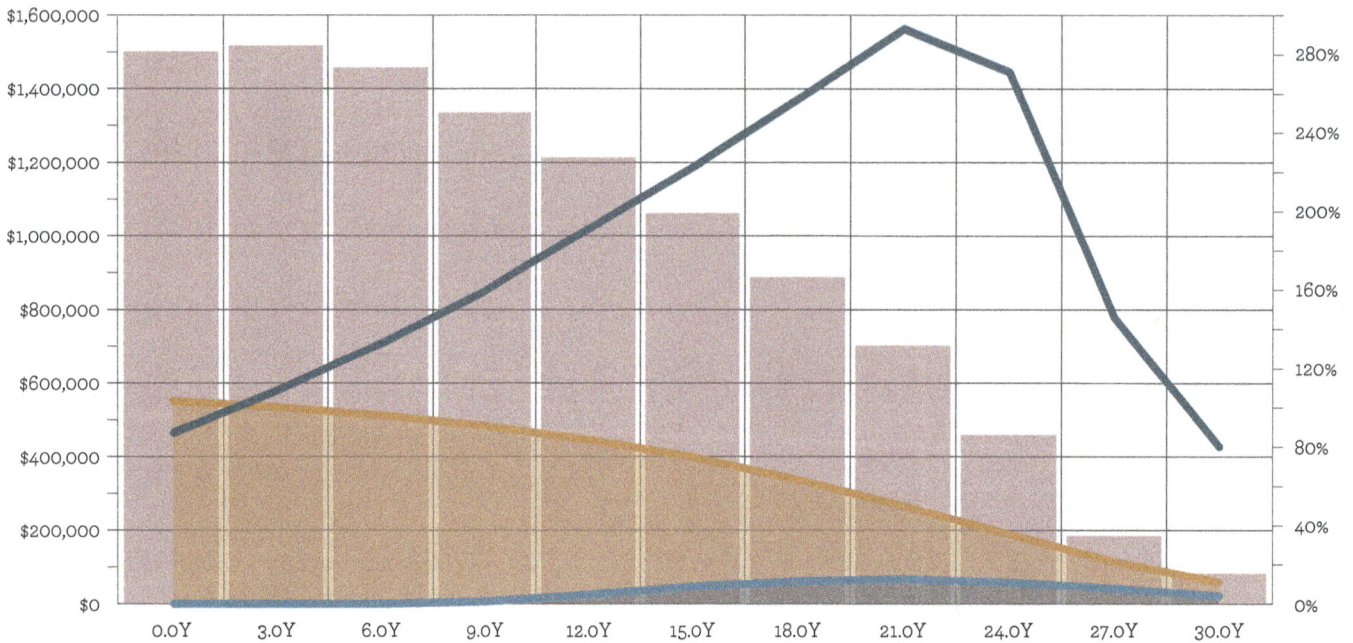

DATA TABLE FOR FIGURE 3.4: FEASIBILITY TEST—60–40 PORTFOLIO, $7,000 PER MONTH DISTRIBUTION

	Percentile	Current Value	3.0Y	6.0Y	9.0Y	12.0Y	15.0Y	18.0Y	21.0Y	24.0Y	27.0Y	30.0Y
Portfolio Value	50th	$1,500,000	$1,515,731	$1,456,487	$1,334,359	$1,212,265	$1,061,314	$887,302	$701,500	$458,780	$184,880	$82,303
Actuarial Coverage Ratio	50th	85.60%	107.10%	131.00%	157.50%	188.70%	219.80%	254.00%	289.20%	267.50%	143.60%	78.60%
Survival Probability		100.00%	97.00%	92.90%	87.70%	80.80%	72.30%	61.10%	48.20%	34.10%	20.50%	10.50%
Probability of Depletion		0.00%	0.00%	0.00%	1.40%	5.60%	10.50%	13.90%	15.00%	13.10%	9.50%	5.00%

FIGURE 3.5: FEASIBILTY TEST—70–30 PORTFOLIO, $7,000 PER MONTH DISTRIBUTION

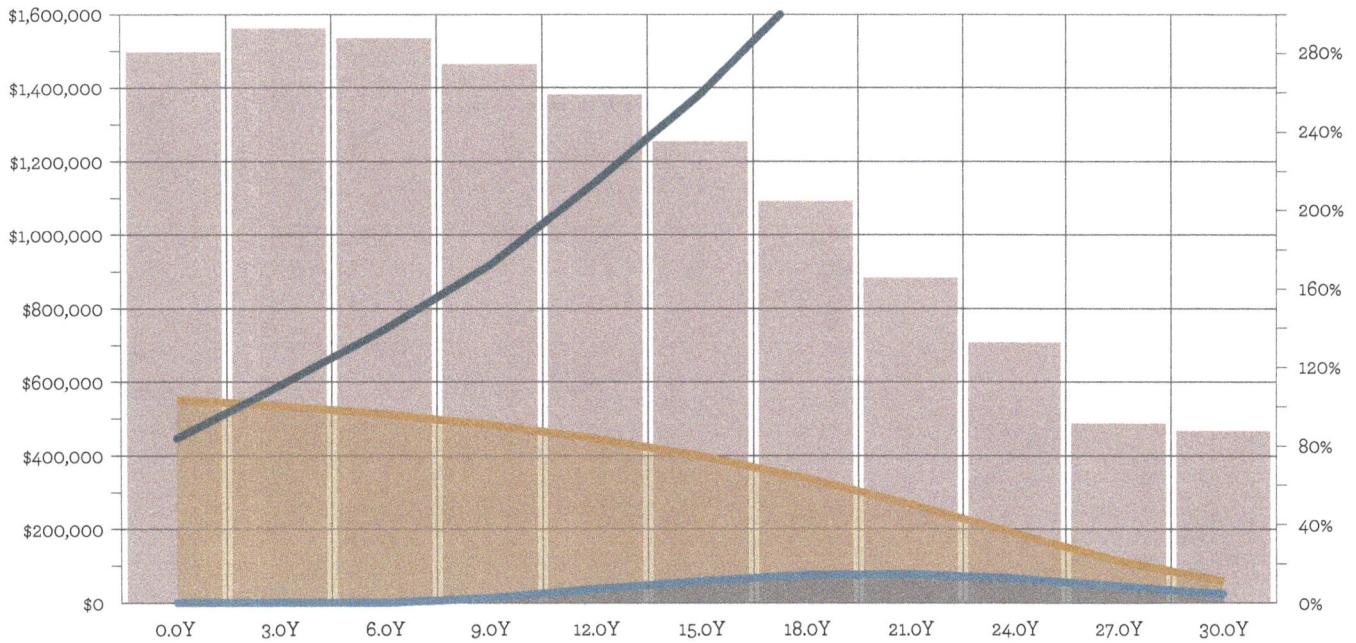

DATA TABLE FOR FIGURE 3.5: FEASIBILITY TEST—70–30 PORTFOLIO, $7,000 PER MONTH DISTRIBUTION

	Percentile	Current Value	3.0Y	6.0Y	9.0Y	12.0Y	15.0Y	18.0Y	21.0Y	24.0Y	27.0Y	30.0Y
Portfolio Value	50th	$1,500,000	$1,564,746	$1,538,683	$1,467,950	$1,384,054	$1,256,934	$1,093,822	$885,812	$708,105	$487,963	$468,159
Actuarial Coverage Ratio	50th	85.60%	110.40%	139.70%	171.60%	214.60%	259.20%	313.80%	360.60%	394.10%	386.70%	451.70%
Survival Probability		100.00%	97.00%	92.90%	87.70%	80.80%	72.30%	61.10%	48.20%	34.10%	20.50%	10.50%
Probability of Depletion		0.00%	0.00%	0.00%	2.30%	6.80%	11.00%	14.10%	14.40%	12.30%	8.40%	4.50%

What are the implications of this new information? An increase in equity exposure from 50 percent to 60 percent or 70 percent improves the expected safety-range of the ACR. Indeed, after year 3, the 70-30 allocation exhibits an increasingly favorable ACR value. However, the data reveal interesting trade-offs. The greater the exposure to equity, the greater is the likelihood of experiencing an early depletion. For example, the 50-50 allocation indicates that the year 9 portfolio depletion rate is 0.30 percent. This compares to year 9 depletion rates of 1.40 percent and 2.30 percent for the 60-40 and 70-30 allocations, respectively. However, the 50-50 allocation does not uniformly dominate the probability of depletion risk metric. In this case study, the 50-50 allocation dominates the 60-40 allocation through year 21 and the 70-30 allocation through approximately year 18. A lower-risk portfolio today may prove to be a higher-risk portfolio in the future. What is the long-term cost of safety?

The investor and advisor—as well as the reader—have digested a lot of information. During a short coffee break, the investor, heartened by the seemingly beneficial effects of increasing exposure to stocks, begins to ponder a troublesome notion. He knows that the stock market is notorious for its volatility and he wonders whether he is planning for the best while ignoring the worst. Following the break, he asks the advisor why they are discussing only the median (50th percentile) outcome. If the trajectory of the portfolio's future inflation-adjusted values tracks either above or below the median over time, do not these additional possibilities also merit consideration? The advisor concurs and, in response, offers the following information based on a 60-40 allocation model (see figure 3.6 and data table 3.6):

FIGURE 3.6: DISTRIBUTION OF WEALTH—$7,000 PER MONTH, 60-40 ALLOCATION

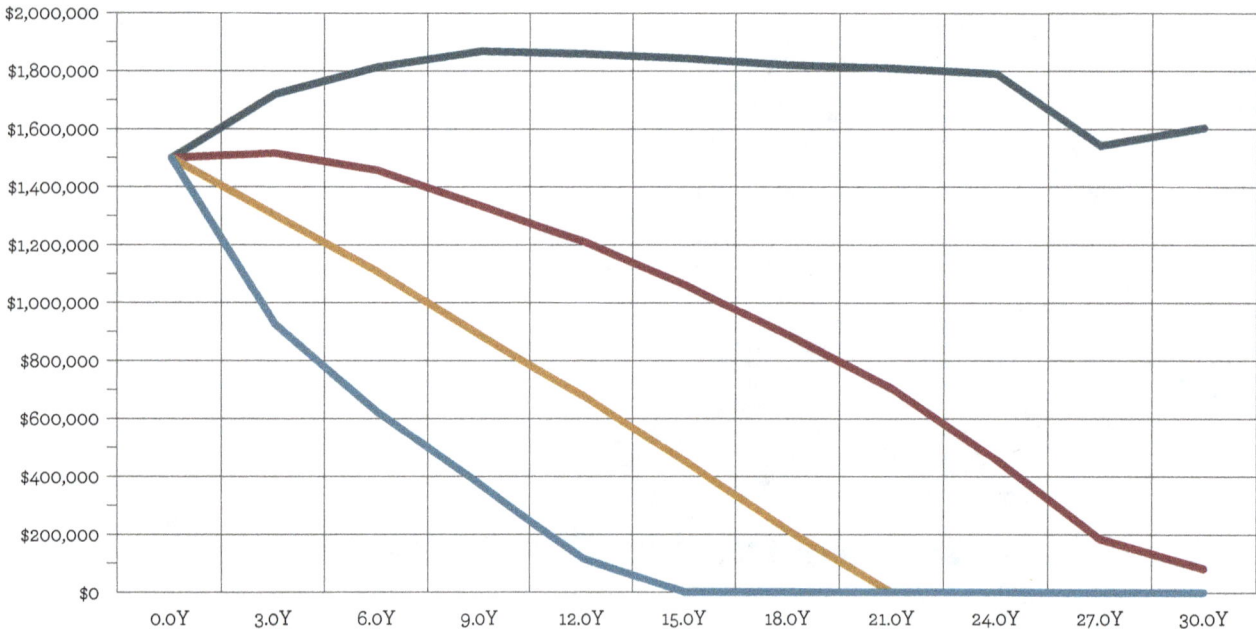

DATA TABLE FOR FIGURE 3.6: DISTRIBUTION OF WEALTH—$7,000 PER MONTH, 60–40 ALLOCATION

	Percentile	Current Value	3.0Y	6.0Y	9.0Y	12.0Y	15.0Y	18.0Y	21.0Y	24.0Y	27.0Y	30.0Y
Portfolio Value	70th	$1,500,000	$1,719,378	$1,813,094	$1,867,404	$1,859,075	$1,843,677	$1,820,289	$1,809,433	$1,790,569	$1,543,045	$1,602,994
Actuarial Coverage Ratio	50th	$1,500,000	$1,515,731	$1,456,487	$1,334,359	$1,212,265	$1,061,314	$887,302	$701,500	$458,780	$184,880	$82,303
Survival Probability	30th	$1,500,000	$1,301,363	$1,107,767	$885,135	$679,666	$451,715	$214,797	$0	$0	$0	$0
Probability of Depletion	10th	$1,500,000	$926,588	$621,431	$369,218	$117,870	$0	$0	$0	$0	$0	$0

The advisor explains that the left-side vertical axis measures portfolio value, the horizontal axis tracks time. Each line traces out, over time, the 60–40 portfolio's value at different percentiles of the distribution of wealth. The median value (red line) corresponds to the illustrated portfolio value on the previous 60–40 allocation's "feasibility test" graph. The portfolio, at the median percentile, provides the aspirational-target income throughout the 30-year period under consideration. At year 30, survival odds are approximately 10 percent and, conditional on survival, there is a 50-percent chance of being alive-and-broke. The median value indicates that 50 percent of trials recorded better outcomes and 50 percent of trials recorded worse outcomes (where an "outcome" represents complex interactions among spending, inflation, and investment return variables over time). For example, to preserve the inflation-adjusted value of the portfolio's original principal, investment results must fall into the 70th percentile—substantially better than the median. Stated differently, the model indicates, absent any mid-course corrections, there is only a 30-percent chance of generating the aspirational level of income and preserving the inflation-adjusted value of the initial principal. The far-left side (blue) line indicates, in 10 percent of the trials, the portfolio has zero value within approximately 15 years. There is a 10-percent chance of financial ruin—no income and no principal—by age 81 absent future changes in asset management elections. The accompanying table provides more precise information at various percentiles of the distribution. As a general rule, if future results are below the median, it is better to be in the 50–50 allocation; if future results are above the median, it is better to weight the allocation toward stocks.

The investor, not accustomed to thinking probabilistically, exhibits a blank stare and begins to form the opinion that his coffee was not sufficiently strong. After a deep breath, he requests the advisor take one more stab at an explanation. The advisor tells him that the only thing known with certainty is today's portfolio value: $1.5 million. As the future unfolds, a range of outcomes is possible: some good, some bad. The middle of the range is the 50th percentile—half the projected outcomes will have better results, half worse. The percentiles calibrate the odds of attaining either a better or worse result. For example, 30 percent of outcomes will be better than the 70th percentile value. However, at the 10th percentile, 90 percent of outcomes will be better and 10 percent will be worse. A percentile is like a marker to point out where an outcome falls on the worse/better scale of outcomes.

Evaluating the risk of retirement requires evaluation of the range rather than the average. If the investor had 10,000 separate and independent life spans, then the average outcome of all possible results would be close to the median. However, the investor does not have 10,000 chances at a successful retirement, he has only one chance. He cannot count on a statistical average, he can count only on the actual outcome, which can range from very bad (far below the median at a low probability) to very good (far above the median at a low probability).

Realizing that he is holding on by his mental fingertips, the investor asks two questions:

- Can you show me a quick glimpse of my situation if I'm willing to reduce my aspirational standard of living to my threshold budget requirements ($5,000 per month)?
- What happens to my retirement plans if, starting tomorrow, we head into a bear market?

After a brief discussion during which the investor says that he would like to split the difference between the 50–50 and 70–30 allocations when evaluating the financial consequences of taking a threshold distribution, the advisor displays a graphical sequence of portfolio values at the 50th, 30th, and 10th percentiles, assuming an inflation-adjusted monthly budget of $5,000 and a 60–40 constant-mix allocation. Figures 3.7, 3.8, and 3.9 also present the actuarial coverage ratio.

FIGURE 3.7: 50TH PERCENTILE FEASIBILITY TEST—$5,000 PER MONTH, 60-40 ALLOCATION

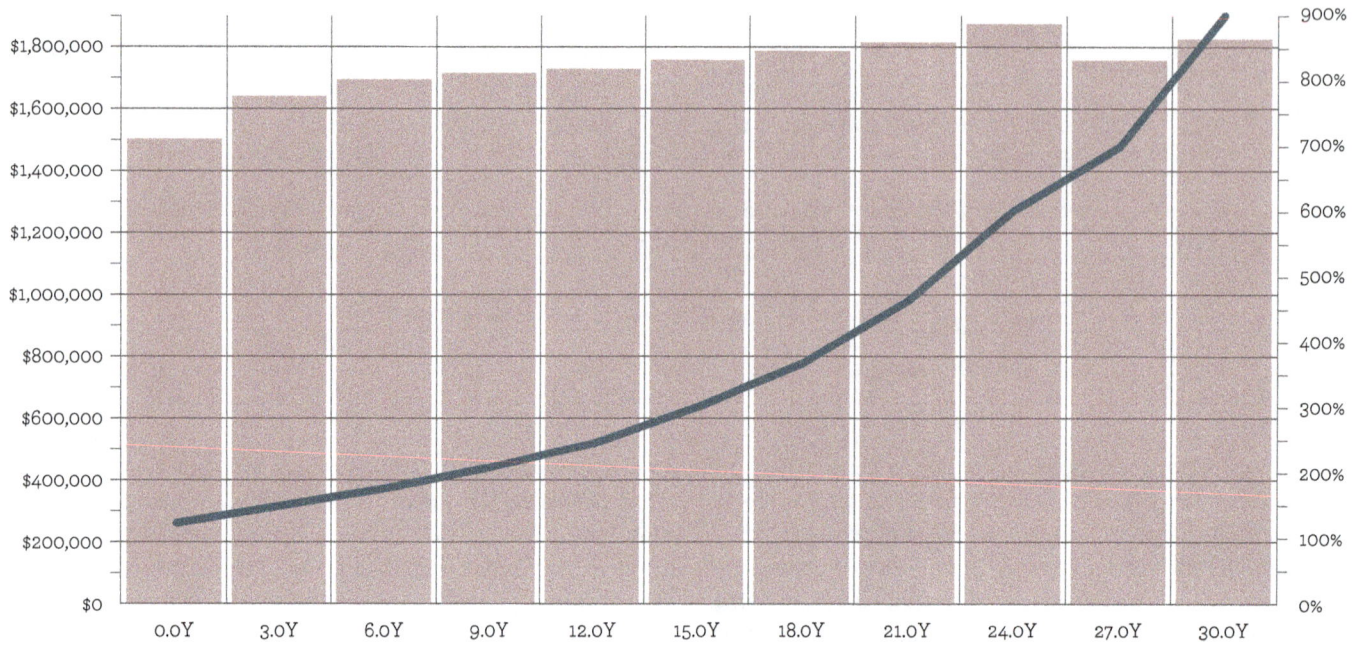

Note right side scale differences.

FIGURE 3.8: 30TH PERCENTILE FEASIBILITY TEST—$5,000 PER MONTH, 60-40 ALLOCATION

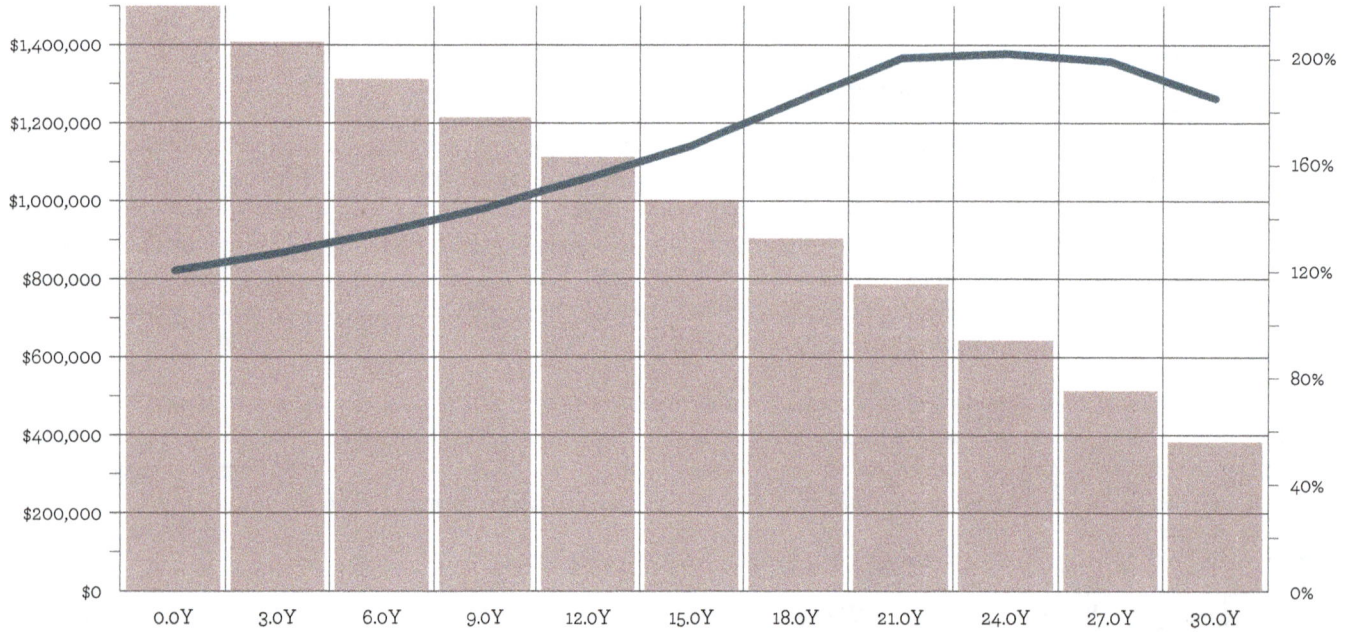

Note right side scale differences.

FIGURE 3.9: 10TH PERCENTILE FEASIBILITY TEST—$5,000 PER MONTH, 60–40 ALLOCATION

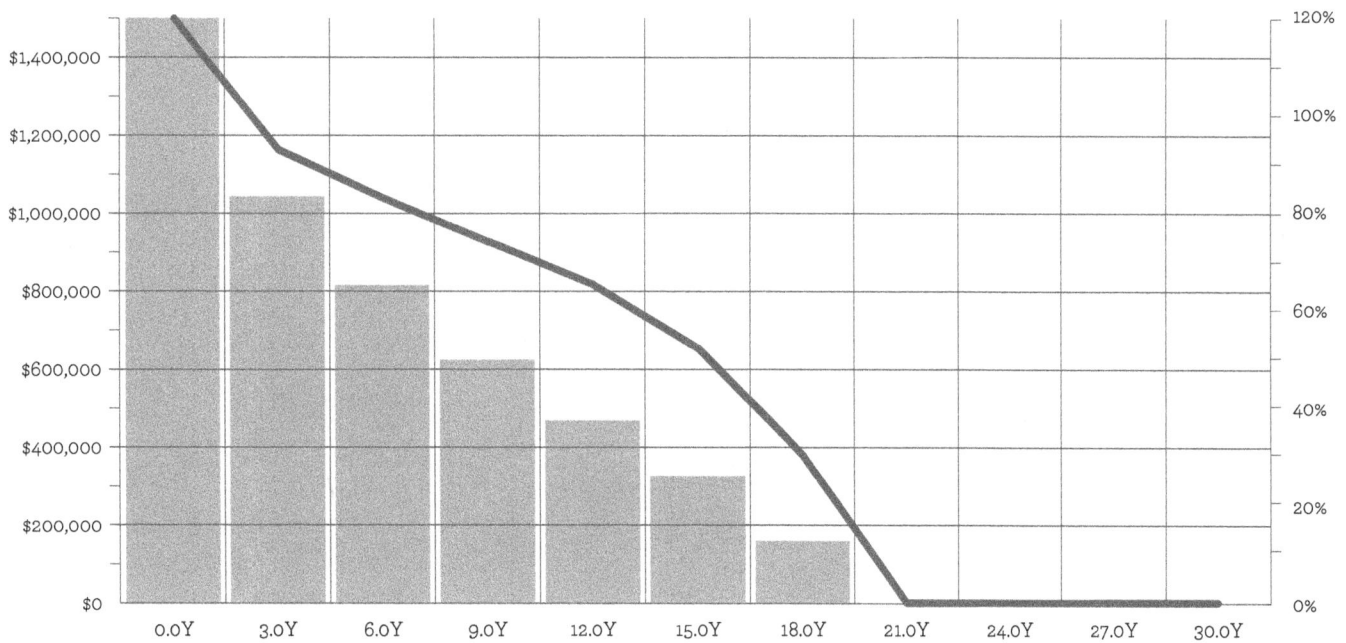

Note right side scale differences.

The sequence of graphs makes two things clear:

1. At the threshold budget level, the investor's initial cushion (ACR) is positive [120 percent]—immediate retirement is feasible, and

2. Although the investor can maintain a positive cushion (coverage ratio > 100 percent) for most of his planning horizon at the 50th and 30th percentile of results, things become somewhat dicey at the 10th percentile. Within three years the investor will face a 10-percent probability of having to make some quick, and potentially painful, asset management decisions.

Finally, the advisor presents information on the investor's single greatest fear: What if he retires today only to face a bear market in stocks beginning tomorrow? The advisor focuses on the 60-percent stock/40-percent fixed income allocation for both the aspirational-level income target and the threshold income target:

FIGURE 3.10: ASPIRATIONAL INCOME TARGET—$7,000 PER MONTH, INITIAL BEAR MARKET

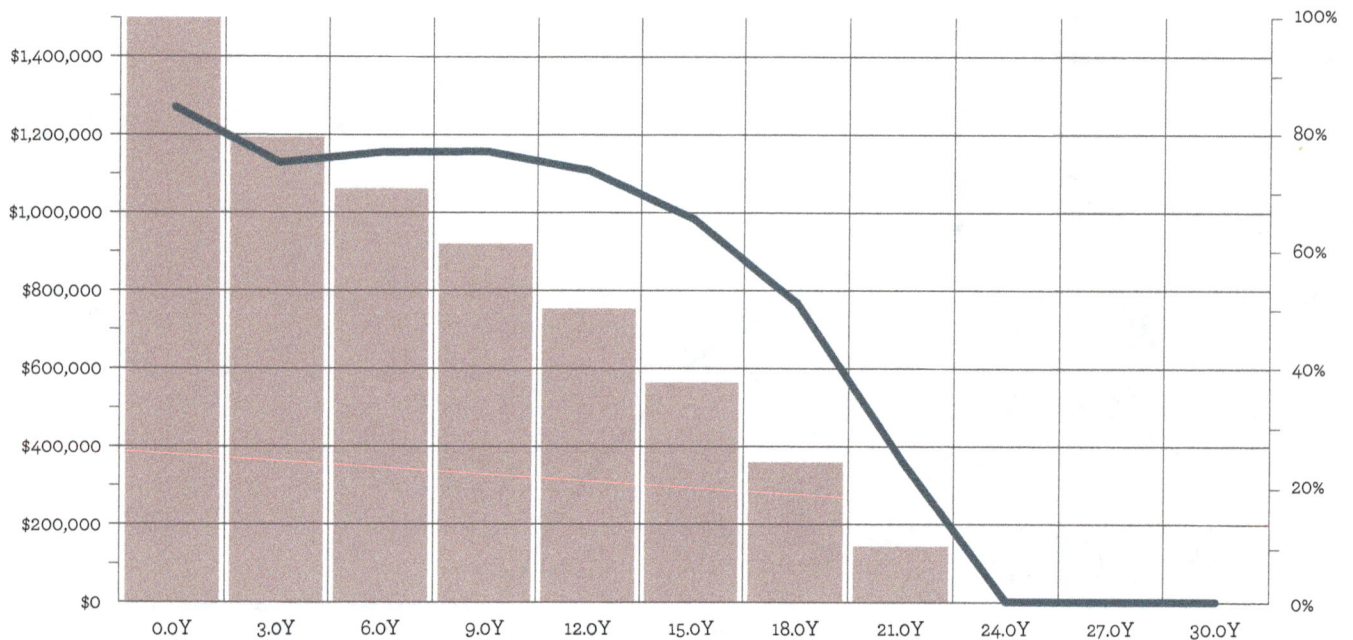

DATA TABLE FOR FIGURE 3.10: ASPIRATIONAL INCOME TARGET—$7,000 PER MONTH, INITIAL BEAR MARKET

	Percentile	Current Value	3.0Y	6.0Y	9.0Y	12.0Y	15.0Y	18.0Y	21.0Y	24.0Y	27.0Y	30.0Y
Portfolio Value	50th	$1,500,000	$1,187,146	$1,060,155	$916,859	$748,362	$558,373	$354,885	$134,792	$0	$0	$0
Actuarial Coverage Ratio	50th	85.60%	76.30%	77.80%	78.00%	74.90%	67.00%	52.00%	24.60%	0.00%	0.00%	0.00%

Figure 3.10 and its companion table illustrate the concept of retirement-as-a-risky-project. Should the investor accept this project by forcing a distributional stress on a financial asset portfolio that fails its initial feasibility test? Unlike a project that a corporation might undertake, the investor's project lacks any option for early abandonment should initial results prove disappointing. That is not to say that the investor lacks any asset management options—part-time employment, reverse mortgages, or other remedies may exist.

The investor opines that he is beginning to have a better liking for his job.

Figure 3.11 and its accompanying table explore the economic consequences of starting retirement at the threshold income level at the onset of a bear market:

FIGURE 3.11: THRESHOLD INCOME TARGET—$5,000 PER MONTH, INITIAL BEAR MARKET

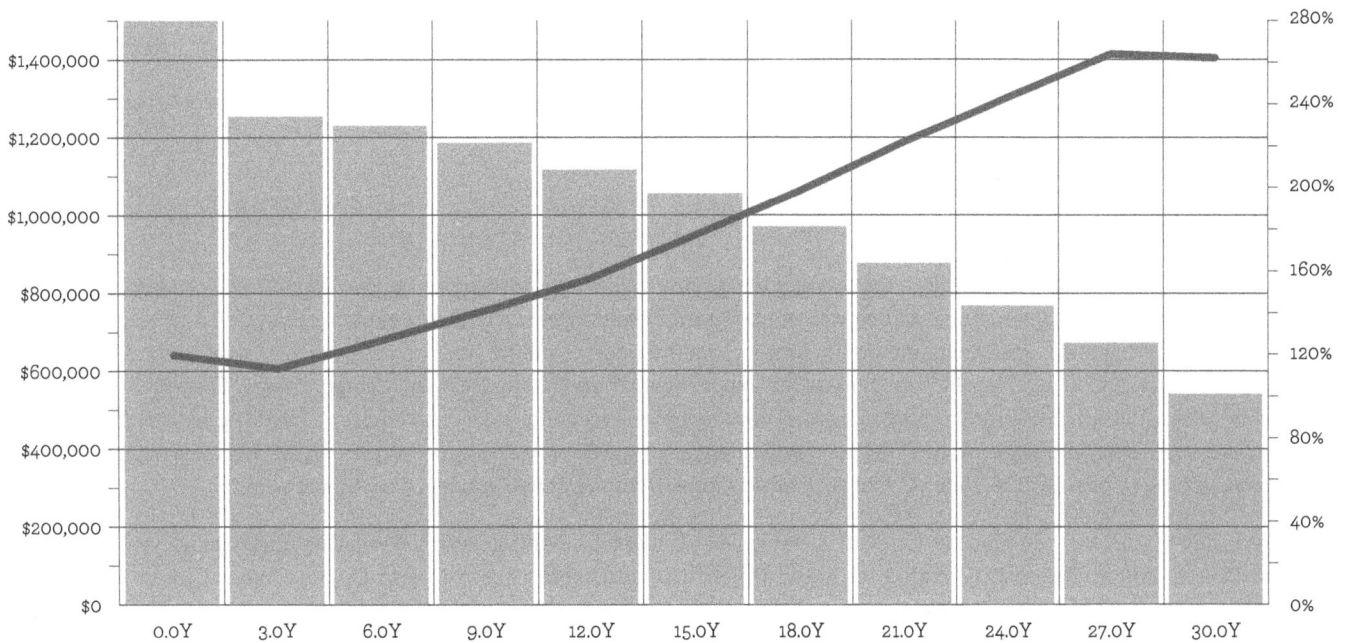

DATA TABLE FOR FIGURE 3.11: THRESHOLD INCOME TARGET—$5,000 PER MONTH, INITIAL BEAR MARKET

	Percentile	Current Value	3.0Y	6.0Y	9.0Y	12.0Y	15.0Y	18.0Y	21.0Y	24.0Y	27.0Y	30.0Y
Portfolio Value	50th	$1,500,000	$1,252,040	$1,229,712	$1,184,118	$1,117,284	$1,054,298	$968,647	$873,665	$762,076	$667,315	$535,477
Actuarial Coverage Ratio	50th	119.80%	112.60%	126.20%	140.70%	156.30%	176.80%	198.40%	222.20%	242.60%	262.80%	262.30%

At the threshold income level, the model suggests that the investor can negotiate the average bear market successfully should such a market emerge at the start of retirement. The advisor reminds the investor that the charts depict the median bear-market results and that there is also a distribution of results above and below the median that might be worth considering.

The investor, however, has seen enough for today. There is a lot of material to digest and he tells the advisor he would like to mull things over before making decisions. He suspects that additional questions will occur and asks to schedule a second meeting next week. Before leaving, the investor expresses his subjective assessment of the risk-reward trade-offs that he currently faces. Articulating his understanding of the situation serves as a check that he has not missed anything critical. Here is the investor's thinking process:

- I may have enough money to retire now and meet both my lifetime threshold and aspirational targets.

- My cushion, however, is not sufficiently large that I can easily withstand unfavorable future economic environments while maintaining a portfolio of liquid financial assets.

- There is a strong possibility that I may be forced to consider the option to annuitize wealth despite the large load demanded by the marketplace, despite several other unfavorable aspects of annuitization including loss of financial flexibility, and a permanent constraint on my budget.

- If I retire just before the onset of a bear market, I'm particularly vulnerable economically. Getting off to a bad start forces me to make quick decisions regarding extraordinarily consequential matters.

- If I retire just before the onset of a bull market, I'm likely to enjoy a prosperous economic future.

- If I seek an early resolution to my uncertainties by annuitizing in the near future, I lose the ability to annuitize later, if things go well, at a potentially much higher lifetime income level.

- If I annuitize in the future, however, I may lose the opportunity to make future gifts or a bequest should I so desire.

The advisor provides hardcopy printouts of all tables and figures. After thanking the advisor for helping him clarify important retirement-planning issues, the investor leaves the advisor's office. Back to work.

PART FOUR: A SECOND ADVISOR/CLIENT MEETING

During the week-long interval between meetings, the investor does some follow-up investigation concerning retirement-planning options. Specifically, he notices that several internet sites strongly recommend annuitization and he wishes to explore this option further. Additionally, he reads an article suggesting that retirement planning should not consist of tracking only the sufficiency of current assets to fund anticipated future spending, but also should consider ways to mitigate the exposures that drive both asset and liability values. The article named this process "liability-driven investing." He sends an email several days before the meeting to give the advisor a heads up on topics of interest. Finally, he has been wondering about the merits of delaying retirement until age 68 or 70 and is looking for guidance on this planning option. Specifically, he is looking to quantify the trade-offs between leisure time (retirement) and enhanced economic security.

The advisor is familiar with the planning options the investor wishes to explore and, before the meeting, prepares several charts and tables. The advisor recognizes the annuity strategy as one in which an investor locks in a contractually guaranteed income sufficient to support a threshold standard of living and invests excess funds in a performance-seeking portfolio. Such an approach has a number of theoretical advantages including:

- Lifetime assurance, subject to counterparty performance,[11] of an income sufficient to support a threshold standard of living,

- Freedom to improve the budget constraint imposed by the annuity by implementing an aggressive, performance-seeking portfolio to capture the expected higher returns on stocks (the equity-risk premium), and

- Preserving some non-annuitized wealth so that the option to annuitize further amounts at a future age remains in play should the portfolio become unable to sustain the cash flows it is asked to produce.

Annuitization of a floor income is a variation on bucketing approaches to designing a retirement-income portfolio. Bucketing involves setting aside sufficient funds to secure lifestyle flooring either for a limited number of time periods through cash-matching bond ladders or immunized fixed income portfolios, or for the long term through a sequence of zero-coupon bonds extending out to long-dated maturities, or through acquisition of single-premium immediate annuities. Funds used for either short-term or long-term flooring are deemed to have been put in a bucket. While enjoying life in the bucket, the funds are relatively free from many risks associated with financial asset portfolios invested primarily for capital appreciation.

Income, over time, is segregated by degree of importance (it is more critical to secure threshold income than excess amounts targeted for lifestyle aspirations) and the income streams (two-fold, in this case) are funded with financial instruments best suited to the investor's objectives: threshold with flooring; aspirational with a risky-asset portfolio. The short-term income/long-term income chronology gives rise to the term "time-segmentation," which is a variation on the theme of securing a floor income as quickly as resources allow. Time segmentation considers income needs at particular moments in time and "buckets" resources according to a time-priority criterion.

Bucketing approaches often use the geometric shape of a pyramid as a guide to portfolio construction. The base of the pyramid represents critical needs that are fully funded by safe (usually low-variance or principal-guaranteed) investments. Different goals occupy different pyramid layers with less-critical objectives located toward the top. Only when funding for the important goals (defined by time priority and/or need priority) is secured does an investor consider allocating excess resources, if any, to growth-oriented portfolios. Under a bucketing approach, equity allocation reflects investment of residual funds. This approach gives rise to the term "goal-segmentation." The advisor recognizes that both types of segmentation are operative in this case: Time-segmentation reflects the period over which investor goals are sustainable and goal-segmentation reflects the cost of funding the layers on the pyramid. After securing flooring, what will remain to invest for growth?

---

11. Munnell (2008) points out that annuity contracts are not risk free: "Two relatively large insurance companies ended up paying only 70 cents on the dollar after they got into trouble as a result of bad investments." For an example of a retirement risk model that explicitly incorporates a factor for insurance company failure see Warshawsky and Pang (2012).

The advisor recognizes that the article advocating for a liability-driven investing approach develops insights originally derived from Robert Merton's investigations into the mathematics of continuous time finance.[12] Merton, although focused on the analysis of wealth accumulation rather than retirement spending, argues that investors confront several types of economic risks: The risks of low returns during depressed economies, the risk to the safety of their wealth, and the risk of earning less than the return required to achieve financial success. He advocates a "three-fund solution" for investment portfolio optimization.

One part of the portfolio is devoted to the "hedge" portfolio with which the investor expects to attain adequate returns during a period of general economic decline. In such a period, attractive investment opportunities may be scarce and aggregate borrowing for capital investment decreases significantly. Interest rates generally mirror the general decline in economic activity and, in order to capture returns in a period of decreasing rates, the hedge portfolio consists of long-term bonds. As interest rates decline, bond values increase.

The second piece of the portfolio is devoted to performance assets. Merton made significant contributions to the literature on optimizing risky-asset portfolios and recommended, under certain assumptions and within certain mathematical contexts, that investors rebalance their performance-oriented portfolios to the "Merton optimum" {[expected risk premium – risk free rate] ÷ [portfolio variance × risk aversion coefficient]}.

Finally, to reflect the investor's risk tolerance preferences, Merton recommends a third fund consisting of the safe asset. Whereas the investor is interested primarily in inflation-adjusted income over time, the advisor decides to use U.S. Treasury Inflation-Protected Securities (TIPS) as the safe asset. The three-fund solution's allocation requires a portion of the portfolio invested in long-term government bonds, a portion in TIPS, and the remainder in a diversified portfolio of domestic and international equities. The three-fund solution is, in some respects, an extension of two-fund solutions flowing from: (1) academic literature, e.g., Sharpe's incorporation of the risk-free asset into the Markowitz portfolio optimization solution or Tobin's development of the two-fund portfolio separation theorem, and (2) the practitioner-oriented flooring + performance approaches discussed above.

In terms of a quasi "optimal control" perspective on analyzing retirement feasibility and sustainability, the investor seeks insight to the sensitivity of results to changes in the asset allocation control (a floor + performance allocation, or a three-fund solution allocation) and into the sensitivity of results to changes in the retirement date control. The investor's questions are both on-point and important—the advisor's challenge is to help the investor negotiate some intellectually deep waters in a manner that facilitates good decision-making.[13]

When the investor arrives, the advisor first offers him insights into the consequences of incorporating an annuity into the asset allocation. Given that the advisor laid a solid groundwork during the investor's previous visit, the graphical presentation is limited to 50th percentile (median) results.

The advisor explains that the cost of an annuity, if purchased in a low-interest-rate environment, is relatively high. Using the traditional principles of annuity pricing, the advisor estimates that the actuarially fair value of an immediate, single-premium annuity paying a lifetime monthly inflation-adjusted lifetime income of $5,000 is approximately $1.25 million based on the Freddie Mac yield curve—3.28 percent at year 5 and 3.50 percent at year 15.[14] The annuity's cost also reflects a load of 15 percent for a commercially available contract.[15] When the investor expresses surprise at the cost, the advisor reminds him that the insurance company bears the risk of providing income in investment markets and inflationary environments that reflect below median, i.e., unfavorable, results. In a low-interest-rate environment guarantees are expensive. A bank's guarantee of certificate of deposit principal results in an anemic rate of interest income; an insurer's annuity income guarantee requires a large and irrevocable transfer of principal. An increase in interest rates throughout the general economy, all else being equal, lowers the cost of acquiring annuity income; however, a carrier's reach for yield within its bond portfolio must be balanced against increased default risk. Annuities are akin to structured financial instruments, and the reserving portfolios are not immune from the economic forces that affect the underlying portfolio securities.

12. Robert C. Merton is Distinguished Professor of Finance at the MIT Sloan School of Management and recipient of the 1997 Nobel Memorial Prize in Economic Sciences (shared with Myron S. Scholes).

13. Advisors may be held to a fiduciary status. This entails both a standard of conduct (act in the best interest of the client) and a standard of competence.

14. Academic evidence indicates that insurance companies often seek yields higher than those available from U.S. Treasuries on their reserving portfolios (either through the private-placement bond market or through more-aggressive investing via duration mismatching). The "best-fit" discounting rate may be a term structure of interest rates derived from intermediate-term government obligations such as the curve for government-agency mortgage rates. Calculations based on summer 2017 yield curve.

15. The term "load" encompasses all fees, charges, expenses, commissions, profit targets, reserves against adverse selection, etc., more than the actuarially fair value. For further discussion of annuity costs, see Collins (2016a). Donnelly et al. (2014) state: "Consumers have no idea if annuity prices are fair, or if insurance companies are either making excessive profits or are grossly inefficient."

Assuming that the investor elects to lock in lifetime annuity flooring equal to his threshold $5,000 monthly budget requirement, the advisor presents figure 3.12 and its companion table. The portfolio under consideration is now a pure "performance portfolio" allocated 100 percent to stocks. Figure 3.12 depicts the dynamic evolution of variables with respect to the financial asset portfolio's ability to provide a $2,000 monthly lifetime inflation-adjusted excess income to sustain the investor's aspirational budget target. The actuarial coverage ratio is now calculated with respect to the $250,000 residual portfolio's ability to sustain the $2,000 monthly constant-dollar target.

FIGURE 3.12: PERFORMANCE PORTFOLIO—$5,000 PER MONTH, ANNUITY FLOOR IN LOW-INTEREST-RATE ENVIRONMENT

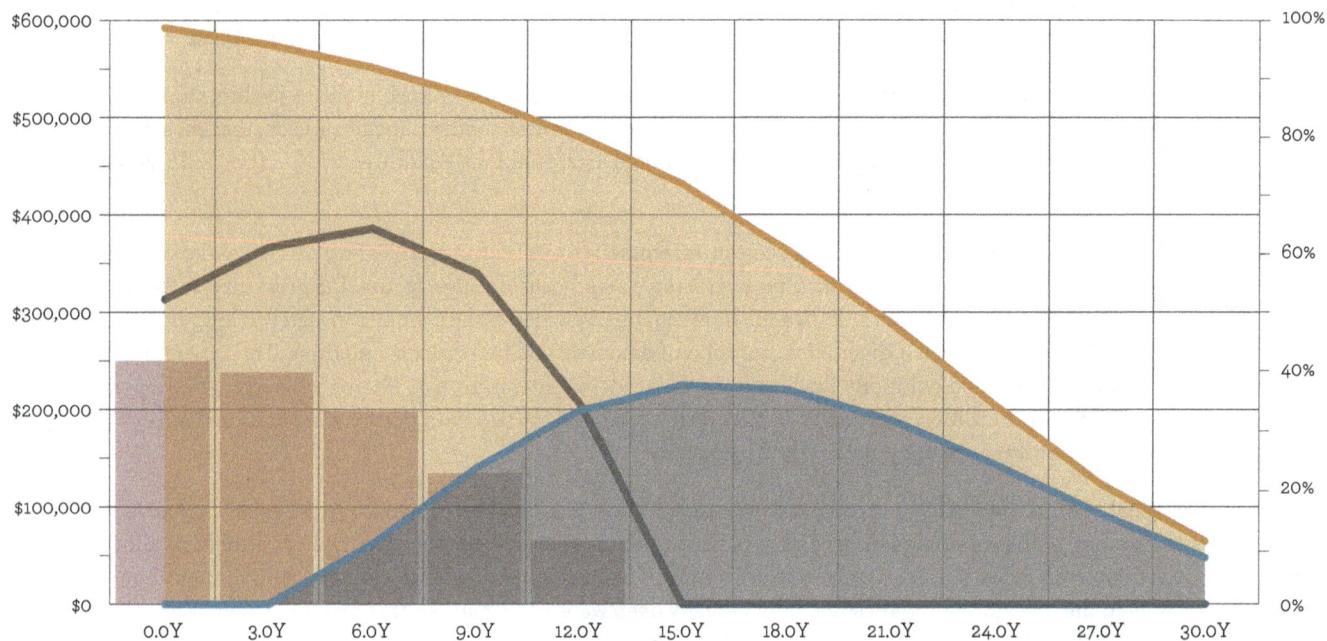

DATA TABLE FOR FIGURE 3.12: PERFORMANCE PORTFOLIO—$5,000 PER MONTH, ANNUITY FLOOR IN LOW-INTEREST-RATE ENVIRONMENT

	Percentile	Current Value	3.0Y	6.0Y	9.0Y	12.0Y	15.0Y	18.0Y	21.0Y	24.0Y	27.0Y	30.0Y
Portfolio Value	50th	$250,000	$237,173	$195,907	$134,082	$62,660	$0	$0	$0	$0	$0	$0
Actuarial Coverage Ratio	50th	49.90%	58.70%	62.20%	55.40%	33.60%	0.00%	0.00%	0.00%	0.00%	0.00%	0.00%
Survival Probability		100.00%	97.00%	92.90%	87.70%	80.80%	72.30%	61.10%	48.20%	34.10%	20.50%	10.50%
Probability of Depletion		0.00%	0.00%	9.80%	23.40%	33.10%	37.80%	36.90%	31.80%	23.90%	15.00%	7.80%

At no point does the portfolio attain a feasibility ratio equal to or greater than one. The trade-off for locking in a floor equal to the minimum budget demand is an expectation to sustain the aspirational budget only through age 78. Portfolio performance must achieve approximately the 75th percentile of the distribution to sustain the aspirational target throughout the planning horizon (data not shown). The median (50th percentile) results show the portfolio depleted by year 15; the 30th percentile of results by year 9. Of course, should the investment regime begin in a bear market state, the model's outputs would be worse.

Given the current low-interest-rate environment, there exists the possibility that rates may rise in the near future. The advisor calculates that the potential impact of an upward 50-basis-point parallel shift in the yield curve decreases the annuity's cost from approximately $1.25 million to $1.12 million. This increases the size of the residual performance portfolio to $380,000. Figure 3.13 and the accompanying data table illustrate results at the 50th percentile:

FIGURE 3.13: PERFORMANCE PORTFOLIO—$5,000 PER MONTH, ANNUITY FLOOR IN 50-BASIS-POINT-PLUS ENVIRONMENT

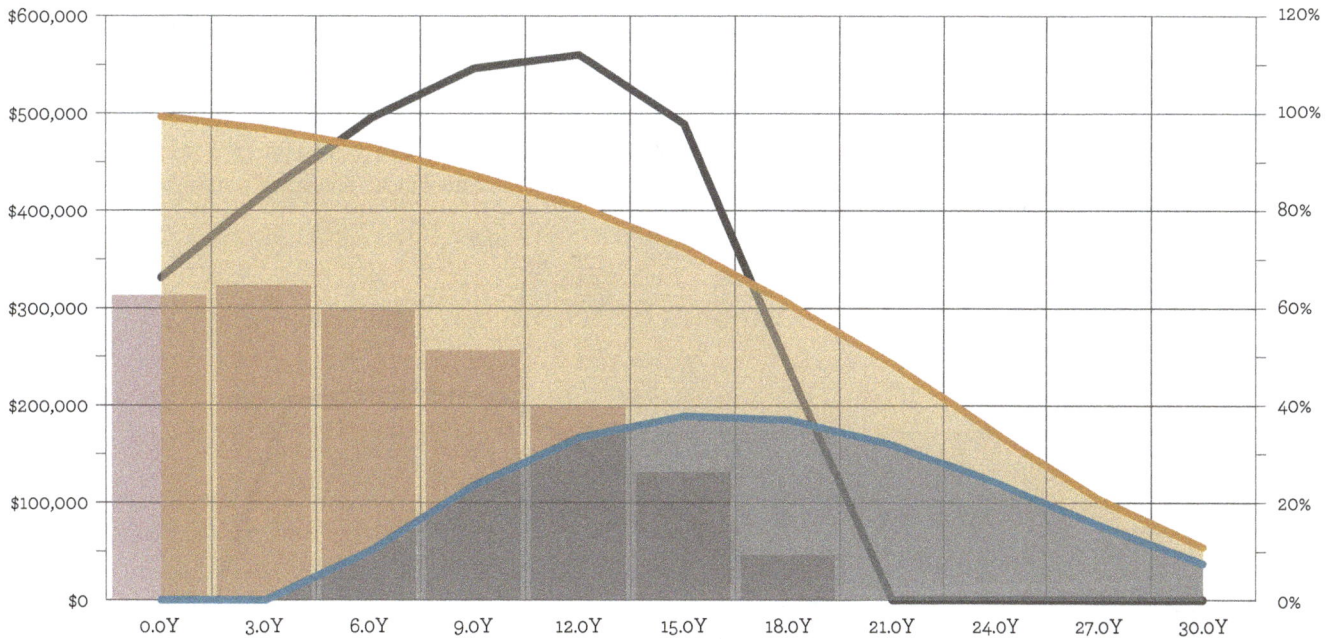

DATA TABLE FOR FIGURE 3.13: PERFORMANCE PORTFOLIO— $5,000 PER MONTH, ANNUITY FLOOR IN 50-BASIS-POINT-PLUS ENVIRONMENT

	Percentile	Current Value	3.0Y	6.0Y	9.0Y	12.0Y	15.0Y	18.0Y	21.0Y	24.0Y	27.0Y	30.0Y
Portfolio Value	50th	$380,000	$322,197	$298,548	$255,704	$195,534	$129,878	$45,209	$0	$0	$0	$0
Actuarial Coverage Ratio	50th	65.70%	83.30%	98.80%	109.20%	112.20%	98.00%	47.10%	0.00%	0.00%	0.00%	0.00%
Survival Probability		100.00%	97.00%	92.90%	87.70%	80.80%	72.30%	61.10%	48.20%	34.10%	20.50%	10.50%
Probability of Depletion		0.00%	0.00%	9.80%	23.40%	33.10%	37.80%	36.90%	31.80%	23.90%	15.00%	7.80%

There is a marginal improvement in results under a hypothetical 50-basis-point increase in the applicable term-structure of annuity pricing discount rates. At the 50th percentile, the performance portfolio's sustainability increases from approximately 15 to 18 years (age 84). The retirement-income-model output suggests that it requires an approximately 110-basis-point parallel shift upward in the yield curve to attain lifetime sustainability, at the distribution's 50th percentile of the aspirational income target (data not shown).

The risk-return trade-off of flooring is of great interest to the investor. Under some conditions, the cost of flooring is prohibitively expensive leaving almost no funds for the performance-seeking investment portfolio. In this case, in a low-interest-rate environment, the cost of flooring reduces the ACR for the aspirational $7,000 per month constant-dollar target from 85.6 to 65.7 (where a ratio value of 100 indicates feasibility under an actuarial benchmark criterion). The investor, by immediately electing the flooring option, never reaches an ACR value of 100 with respect to the aspirational income target. Only with a hypothetical 50-basis-point increase in interest rates can the investor expect to achieve sufficient wealth to elect the annuitization option to secure a constant-dollar, future value of $2,000 per month income, but this does not occur until six to nine years into the future. Furthermore, by electing the flooring option, the investor curtails financial flexibility, where flexibility is defined as a financial cushion sufficient to survive economic setbacks from contingent or unanticipated expenses.

The paradox of flooring in a low-interest-rate economy is: If you need it, you can't afford it; if you can afford it, you don't need it. In these circumstances, the old adage "more money is better than less" is truly operative. This observation raises the issue of the probable consequences of delaying retirement for one or more years. Before looking at the delay strategy, however, the advisor explores the liability-relative asset allocation strategy in terms of Merton's three-fund solution.[16]

The allocation of the $1.5-million, three-fund portfolio is 60-percent stocks and 40-percent fixed income with the economic-state "hedge portfolio" allocated 20 percent to long-term U.S. government bonds and the purchasing-power "safety-preserving" portfolio allocated 20 percent to TIPS. The stock portion of the portfolio resembles the proportional allocation of previously presented portfolios.[17] The investor considers figure 3.14 and its companion table:

FIGURE 3.14: THREE-FUND SOLUTION, LIABILITY-RELATIVE ALLOCATION

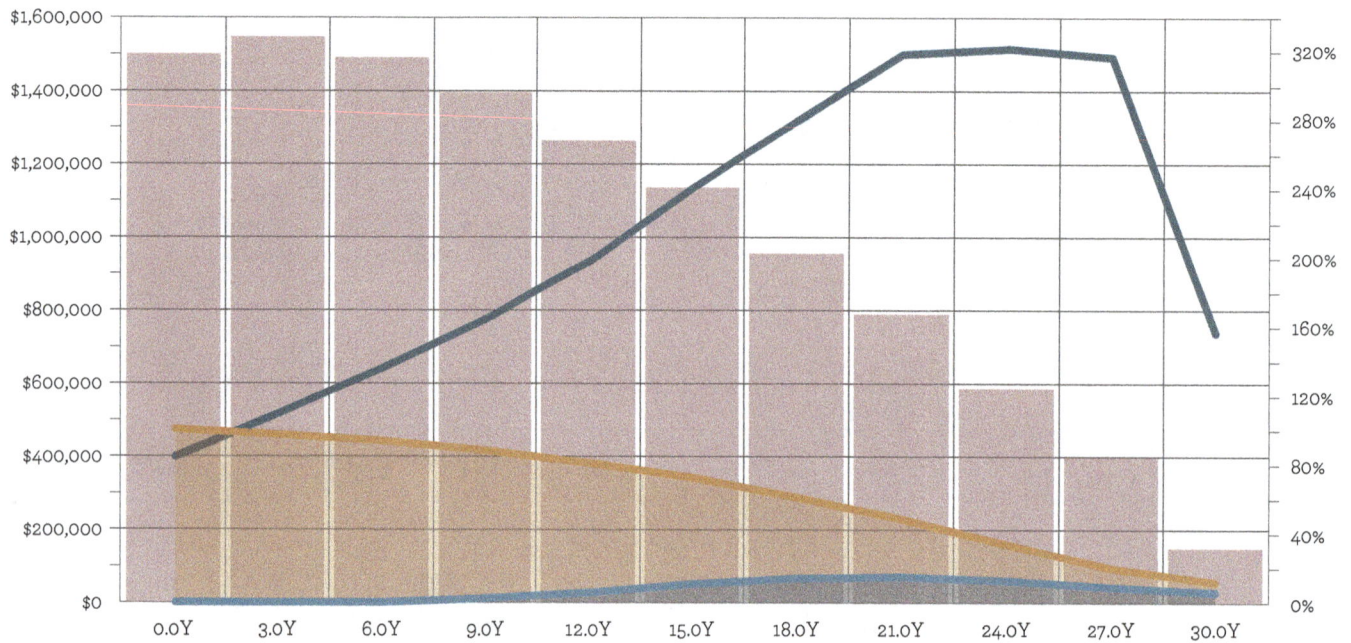

---

16. Merton recommended periodic recalculation of the "Merton optimum" within a dynamic asset allocation program. In the interest of keeping Case Study 1 relatively simple, we present model output in terms of a constant-mix portfolio allocation at this point in time. We present dynamic monitoring, evaluation, and asset management elections later in the book.

17. The allocation of the three-fund portfolio deliberately mimics the 60–40-macro allocation examples. Optimal allocation occurs at the point where the marginal benefit of adding or subtracting a dollar from the economic state hedge fund is exactly equal to the marginal benefit of adding or subtracting a dollar from the purchasing power safety fund and the performance portfolio. The return-to-risk profile of the resulting portfolio divided by (portfolio variance times the coefficient of investor risk aversion) is the metric for determining the "Merton optimum" portfolio composition. Menoncin and Scaillet (2003) review multiple fund solutions ranging from Tobin's two-fund solution and Merton's three-fund solution to their own model, which is a five-fund solution.

DATA TABLE FOR FIGURE 3.14: THREE-FUND SOLUTION, LIABILITY-RELATIVE ALLOCATION

	Percentile	Current Value	3.0Y	6.0Y	9.0Y	12.0Y	15.0Y	18.0Y	21.0Y	24.0Y	27.0Y	30.0Y
Portfolio Value	50th	$1,500,000	$1,549,974	$1,492,391	$1,392,676	$1,262,168	$1,135,471	$957,174	$783,732	$583,784	$397,329	$140,272
Actuarial Coverage Ratio	50th	85.60%	109.40%	135.80%	164.80%	198.10%	240.20%	279.90%	319.00%	321.70%	317.70%	156.40%
Survival Probability		100.00%	97.00%	92.90%	87.70%	80.80%	72.30%	61.10%	48.20%	34.10%	20.50%	10.50%
Probability of Depletion		0.00%	0.00%	0.00%	1.50%	5.30%	10.10%	13.40%	14.40%	12.70%	8.60%	5.00%

Although there is a marginal improvement in some metrics when the three-fund portfolio is compared to the 60–40 portfolio presented earlier, for all practical purposes the two portfolios replicate each other. This fact holds true at the 50th percentile of the distribution and at the other percentiles (70th, 30th, and 10th) illustrated previously (data not shown). It appears as if asset allocation has only limited ability to solve the problem of scarce resources relative to economic goals. The investor begins to realize that he cannot allocate himself out of a tight-money situation.

Curiously, multi-fund solutions are only a few steps away from segregated, or goal-relative, investment portfolios often recommended by behavioral finance (BHF) advocates. Although some commentators consider that a BHF approach radically differs from the modern portfolio theory-grounded approaches of Markowitz, Merton, Sharpe, and others, there may not be a great difference in the composition of recommended portfolios. Das et al. (2010) for example, demonstrate the close relationship between behavioral finance and modern portfolio theory portfolios.[18]

The investor now has sufficient insight to formulate some preliminary opinions:

- There is no asset allocation magic bullet.

- The risk-return trade-off operates over all portfolio elections. Investment is a prudent exchange of costs and risks. Lower risk entails higher costs both in terms of the amount of dollars required to secure safety and in terms of the opportunity costs entailed by maintaining safety.

- There is no objectively best portfolio. The interaction between the investor's personal appetite for risk and economic circumstances dictates the portfolio that he deems to be most appropriate.[19]

- If the risky retirement project is accepted immediately, there will be no opportunity to save more money in a retirement fund. With the absence of labor income, financial assets must bear the full burden of producing income in excess of entitlements. There is substantial risk that standard of living objectives will be unsustainable in the face of an early bear market economic regime.[20]

- It is the availability of the election to annuitize rather than the actual exercise itself that provides sufficient comfort to maintain a financial asset portfolio. However, retirement, when there is not enough money to purchase an annuity contract, is truly a risky proposition.

---

18. These topics are discussed in greater depth in Collins and Gadenne (2017).

19. Appetite for risk is best defined not in terms of a label (conservative, all-weather, growth-oriented, etc.) or in terms of statistical concepts (standard deviation, variance, etc.). Rather, risk is best presented in terms of retirement feasibility, retirement sustainability, and retirement security: How much? How long? How secure?

20. Case Study 5 discusses in further detail the financial consequences of a market decline at various points in the retirement-planning horizon.

PART FIVE: IMPACT OF DELAY

The investor states that he had hoped to see a better picture of his retirement possibilities. However, he tells the advisor that he has not yet decided against immediate retirement. He asks for guidance on the trade-off(s) between leisure time (created by immediate retirement from work) and financial feasibility, sustainability, and security (enhanced by delaying retirement to a future date). The investor ponders how much leisure he is willing to give up for additional assurances concerning his retirement standard of living. This is an important issue because leisure time seems particularly valuable while he remains in good health. Although postponement of retirement may better assure availability of future financial resources, a decision to delay may reduce utility if his health turns bad.

The advisor shows a series of figures and tables designed to show the economic effects of postponing retirement by one, two, or three years. Each figure/table begins at today's date (age 66) with a $1.5-million portfolio market value. The advisor decides to utilize the 60–40 portfolio allocation as a base case for comparison purposes. The advisor replicates the previously presented table of portfolio outputs over time for ease of reference (the companion table for figure 3.4):

FEASIBILITY TEST: 60–40 PORTFOLIO, $7,000 PER MONTH DISTRIBUTION

	Percentile	Current Value	3.0Y	6.0Y	9.0Y	12.0Y	15.0Y	18.0Y	21.0Y	24.0Y	27.0Y	30.0Y
Portfolio Value	50th	$1,500,000	$1,515,731	$1,456,487	$1,334,359	$1,212,265	$1,061.314	$887,302	$701,500	$458,780	$184,880	$82,303
Actuarial Coverage Ratio	50th	85.60%	107.10%	131.00%	157.50%	188.70%	219.80%	254.00%	289.20%	267.50%	143.60%	78.60%
Survival Probability		100.00%	97.00%	92.90%	87.70%	80.80%	72.30%	61.10%	48.20%	34.10%	20.50%	10.50%
Probability of Depletion		0.00%	0.00%	0.00%	1.40%	5.60%	10.50%	13.90%	15.00%	13.10%	9.50%	5.00%

The advisor reminds the investor that the above table lists model outputs for a portfolio model tasked with providing the aspirational ($7,000 per month) inflation-adjusted target income. The table values assume immediate retirement.

The challenge is to explain clearly to the investor the sensitivity of several critical reward and risk metrics to a delay-retirement strategy. Figure 3.15 shows the probable consequences of a one-year delay:

FIGURE 3.15: 60–40 PORTFOLIO, ONE-YEAR DELAY

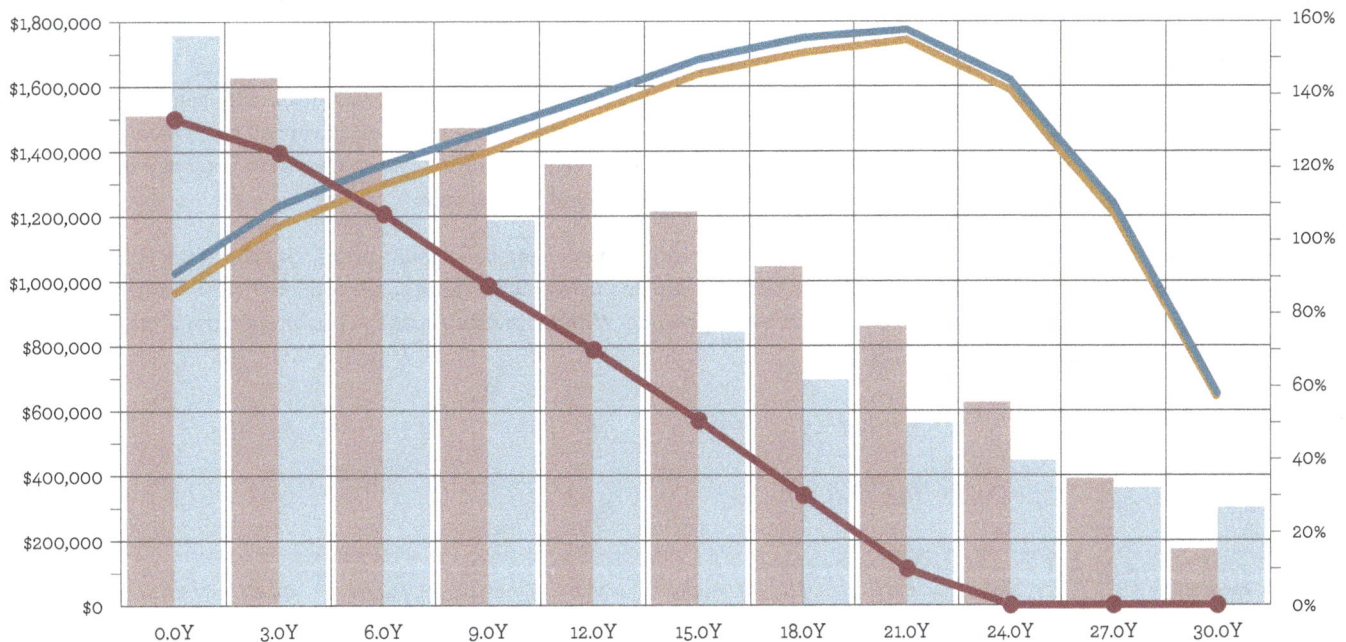

The advisor reiterates that the horizontal axis represents the 30-year planning horizon starting at the investor's current age 66. The left-hand axis provides a dollar-value scale that quantifies column outputs. The salmon-colored column replicates the portfolio's market value (inflation-adjusted) as it originally appears on figure 3.4. The blue-colored column quantifies the dollar-value needed to purchase a commercial annuity contract equal to an initial value of $7,000 per month adjusted for inflation.[21] As expected, the year-zero salmon bar shows a current value of $1.5 million, while the year-zero blue bar illustrates that a greater amount of money is required to meet the actuarial cost of retirement.

The investor interrupts to ask why more money is required under the actuarial-benchmark standard than under the investment-retirement-funding standard. After all, the investment value of the portfolio, although declining in later years, remains positive throughout the planning horizon. The advisor, realizing that this is a tough concept to grasp fully, reminds the investor:

1. The actuarial-cost benchmark builds in a guarantee that payments will continue even if the investor's life span extends to age 110.

2. The distribution of investment results depicted by the salmon bars is at the middle (median or 50th percentile) of the range of possible outcomes. The actual outcomes may be either better or worse than the median.

3. The stock and-bond indicator may signal that retirement is a go while the actuarial indicator may signal that retirement is a no go. Both viewpoints are valid and both should be considered carefully.[22]

The investor indicates that he "kind of gets it" and requests that the advisor continue explaining figure 3.15. The advisor wraps up his analysis of the column bars by noting that a one-year retirement date delay pushes the portfolio's expected (50th percentile) value above the annuity contract's cost by year 3. A positive surplus or cushion remains in place through year 27. Thereafter, the feasibility condition is again violated (blue bar higher than salmon bar) suggesting that the investor remains vulnerable to longevity risk—outliving his financial assets—absent a willingness to make midcourse spending adjustments.

---

21. There are two aspects to calculating inflation-adjusted annuity cost. The first aspect requires the initial contract value ($7,000 per month = $84,000 per year) to be increased by the stochastic inflation rate at the appropriate percentile of the distribution of Consumer Price Index results over the one-, two-, and three-year delay periods. This is a "growth-before-contract-payment-start" calculation. The second aspect is a "growth-after-payment-start" calculation. See appendix E for further details.

22. One might observe that if the expected equity risk premium is higher than the annuity return, the investor can fund retirement cash flows more cheaply by tilting the portfolio allocation toward risky assets. This is the case for investors with substantial surplus wealth who wish the opportunity to improve their budget constraint so that they can enjoy a higher future standard of living. More money is always better than less. However, as stated, the level of wealth relative to consumption requirements is critical in determining the lottery that an investor is willing to accept. Penetrating the free boundary [ACR < 1] established by the existence of a minimum periodic income need risks financial catastrophe, and is not a lottery that is easy to accept when acceptance is based on mere projections of future equity risk premiums. When investment returns are bad, asset management choices become difficult.

The advisor next calls attention to the orange and blue lines, the values of which are recorded on the right-side vertical axis. This axis quantifies the value of the ACR. Initially, the investor's portfolio covers only 85.6 percent of the cost of guaranteeing the aspirational income target via a commercial annuity. The orange line depicts the dynamically changing ACR value calculated under the applicable current yield curve used to determine the actuarially fair value of a lifetime income stream.[23] Initially, the orange line is below the 100-percent ACR value on the right-side axis; however, by year 3, it climbs above the ACR's lower-bound feasibility value. The blue line, which initially tracks above the orange line and which ultimately converges with the orange line at an advanced age, shows the effect of a 50-basis-point parallel increase in the yield curve. All else being equal, an increase in interest rates lowers the present value of future liabilities, i.e., monthly payments, and allows the investor to purchase an annuity at a lower cost.

Finally, the advisor explains that the red line marked with circles is the inflation-adjusted dollar value of the portfolio at the 30th percentile of the distribution of outcomes. If the interaction of inflation, withdrawals, and investment realizations produces below-median outcomes, the investor, if remaining in good health, should expect to cut back spending. Without revising spending downward, the portfolio runs out of money, at the 30th percentile, by year 24 (age 90).

The data table for figure 3.15 details chart values:

DATA TABLE FOR FIGURE 3.15: 60–40 PORTFOLIO, ONE-YEAR DELAY

	Percentile	Current Value	3.0Y	6.0Y	9.0Y	12.0Y	15.0Y	18.0Y	21.0Y	24.0Y	27.0Y	30.0Y
Portfolio Value	50th	$1,500,000	$1,621,105	$1,575,047	$1,465,807	$1,350,223	$1,212,496	$1,033,281	$850,175	$620,343	$378,368	$157,024
Target Annuity Cost	50th	$1,752,629	$1,556,247	$1,364,256	$1,178,451	$1,001,001	$834,526	$682,860	$549,969	$439,367	$352,716	$285,784
Actuarial Coverage Ratio	50th	85.60%	104.20%	115.50%	124.40%	134.90%	145.30%	151.30%	154.60%	141.20%	107.30%	54.90%
Actuarial Coverage Ratio + 50 bp shift	50th	90.20%	109.20%	120.50%	129.10%	139.40%	149.40%	155.00%	157.70%	143.60%	108.80%	55.60%
Portfolio Value	30th	$1,500,000	$1,403,926	$1,206,251	$984,730	$783,409	$568,836	$338,455	$100,973	$0	$0	$0

Although the purpose of reviewing model output is to gain an understanding of the economic consequences of delaying the retirement date, the model output also elucidates the rewards and risks of delaying the option to annuitize. Consider the dollar-value difference between the top row of the data table for figure 3.15 (constant-dollar value of the portfolio net of investment costs and withdrawals) and the row directly below it (inflation-adjusted cost of securing the aspirational income by purchasing an annuity contract). From year 3 through year 27 there is a positive surplus—the portfolio's market value is greater than the annuity's cost. A simple arithmetic calculation shows the expected evolution of the surplus (row one minus row two):

EVOLUTION OF SURPLUS

Year	3.0Y	6.0Y	9.0Y	12.0Y	15.0Y	18.0Y	21.0Y	24.0Y	27.0Y	30.0Y
Surplus	$64,858	$210,791	$287,356	$349,222	$377,970	$350,421	$300,206	$180,976	$25,652	−$128,760

---

23. The model, as stated, assumes a 15-percent load to cover commissions, expenses, and guarantee costs.

If it is prudent to delay annuitization, the investor can increase his retirement security significantly.[24] The option to annuitize has time value and, like many options, early exercise can be detrimental. Indeed, by year 15, the ability to delay option exercise increases expected wealth by $377,970 (inflation-adjusted)—or the present value equivalent of approximately 25-percent more financial wealth. Actuarial guarantees, cash-matched bond ladders, immunized portfolios, and other strategies promoting safety are expensive and often produce declining long-term portfolio value because asset allocation overweights fixed income instruments in the quest for short-term safety. This is the opportunity cost of safety.[25]

After some humorous back-and-forth about the best way to secure economic safety, e.g., "work till you die," the advisor presents the two- and three-year delay data (see figures 3.16 and 3.17):

FIGURE 3.16: 60–40 PORTFOLIO, TWO-YEAR DELAY

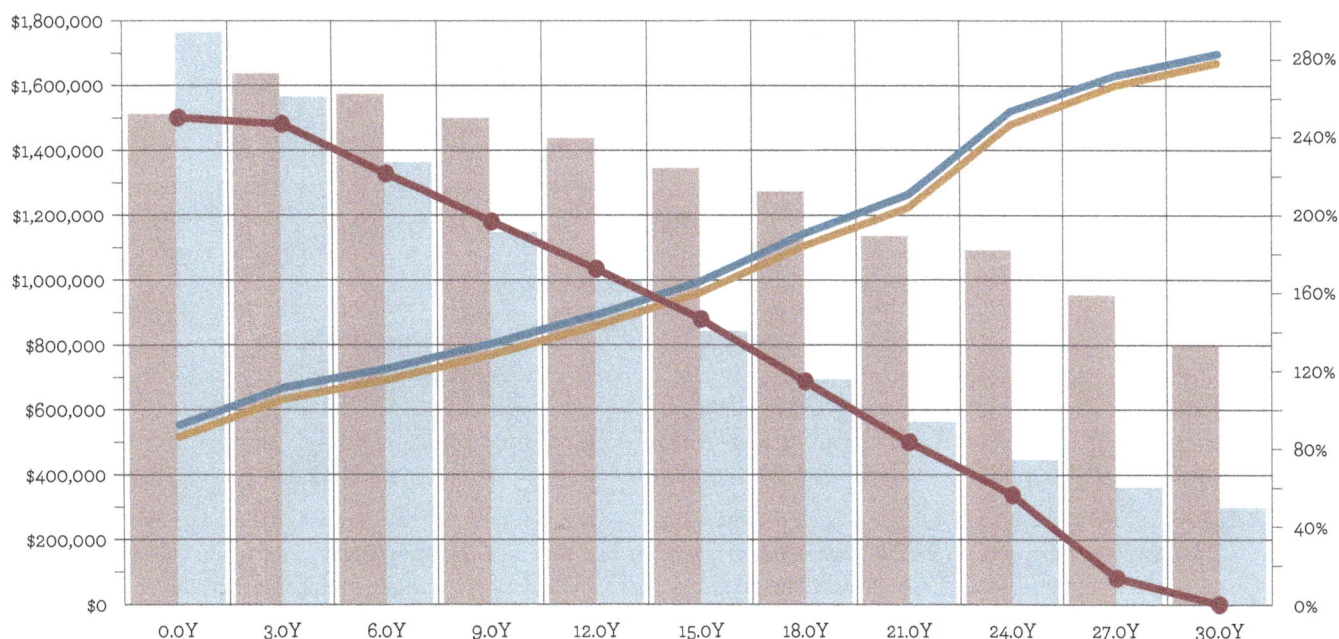

---

24. The investor's retirement security also may benefit if he elects to delay claiming Social Security benefits. Benefits are adjusted upward each year according to a "delayed retirement credits" formula.

25. See also, the Case Study 6 discussion regarding the cost of protecting against sequence of return risk during the initial years of retirement.

DATA TABLE FOR FIGURE 3.16: 60–40 PORTFOLIO, TWO-YEAR DELAY

	Percentile	Current Value	3.0Y	6.0Y	9.0Y	12.0Y	15.0Y	18.0Y	21.0Y	24.0Y	27.0Y	30.0Y
Portfolio Value	50th	$1,500,000	$1,629,068	$1,564,188	$1,495,699	$1,425,499	$1,333,863	$1,262,868	$1,129,779	$1,087,156	$942,403	$797,622
Target Annuity Cost	50th	$1,752,629	$1,556,247	$1,364,236	$1,178,451	$1,001,001	$834,526	$682,860	$549,969	$439,367	$352,716	$285,784
Actuarial Coverage Ratio	50th	85.60%	104.70%	114.70%	126.90%	142.30%	159.80%	184.90%	204.80%	247.40%	267.00%	279.10%
Actuarial Coverage Ratio + 50 bp shift	50th	90.20%	109.80%	119.60%	131.70%	147.10%	164.40%	189.40%	209.00%	251.70%	270.90%	282.50%
Portfolio Value	30th	$1,500,000	$1,479,578	$1,324,624	$1,175,895	$1,029,592	$870,989	$682,474	$494,911	$328,613	$78,777	$0

The above information is a bit of a revelation to the investor. He begins to balance two insights:

1. It appears as if a two-year delay enhances retirement security to the point where attaining the aspirational standard of living is possible at even below-median results (30th percentile). The actuarial coverage ratio is positive by the third year at the median, and within an eyelash of becoming positive by year 6 ($1.324-million portfolio value versus $1.364-million annuity cost) at the 30th percentile of the distribution. The projected long-term sustainability metrics also improve dramatically. The daunting prospect of being forced to exchange all financial wealth for a long-term income guarantee is, in the investor's mind, beginning to recede.

2. It appears as if a two-year delay puts the investor in a position where the sustainability of future cash flows and the magnitude of future security tend to increase, over time, even as the constant-dollar value of the nest egg decreases. Like many investors contemplating the decision to retire, the investor mentally links the portfolio's dollar value to its lifetime income-generating capacity. Older investors, especially, may become concerned about any portfolio value decrease because of a fear of running out of money. The missing element in their calculations, however, is the offsetting force of mortality. All else being equal, a 90-year-old can safely withdraw more funds from a portfolio than a 70-year-old owning a portfolio of comparable value and comparable allocation. Under the right circumstances, there is an inverse relationship between income potential and portfolio value.[26] Looking at the progression of model outputs, it is evident that the investor is better and better able to give himself a raise from a portfolio shrinking in value over time.

Figure 3.17 and the companion data table encapsulate the three-year delay information:

---

26. This topic is the subject of Case Study 5.

FIGURE 3.17: 60–40 PORTFOLIO, THREE-YEAR DELAY

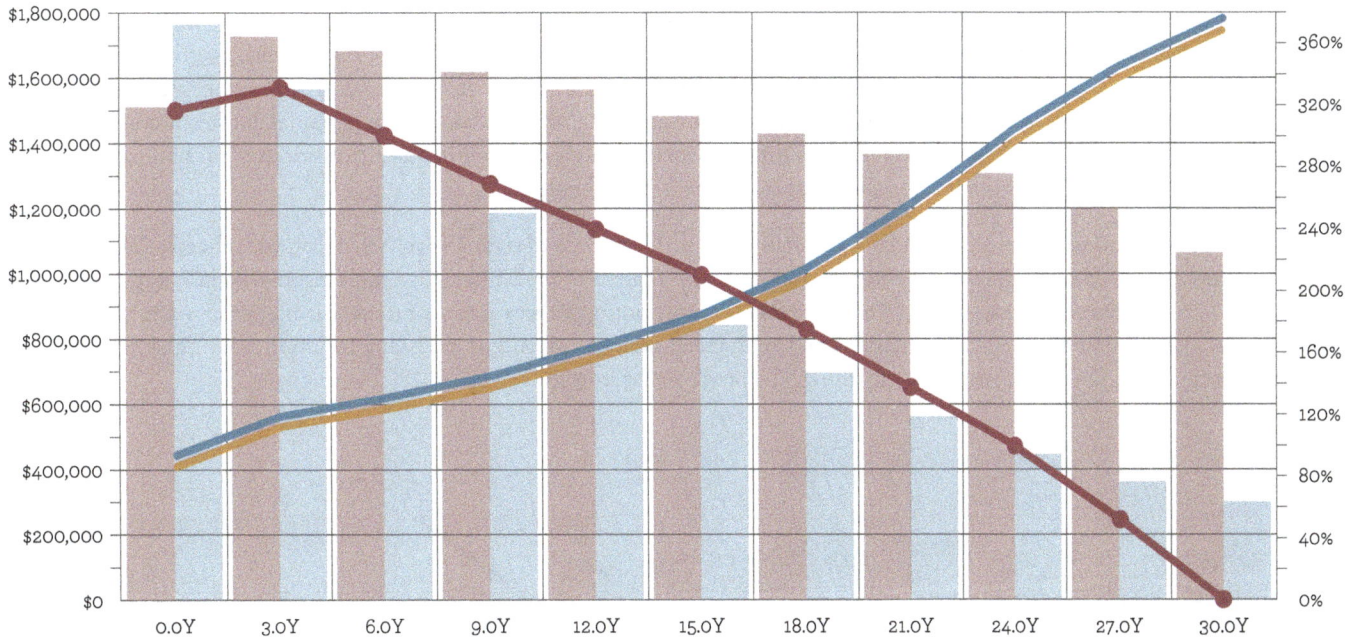

DATA TABLE FOR FIGURE 3.17: 60–40 PORTFOLIO: THREE-YEAR DELAY

	Percentile	Current Value	3.0Y	6.0Y	9.0Y	12.0Y	15.0Y	18.0Y	21.0Y	24.0Y	27.0Y	30.0Y
Portfolio Value	50th	$1,500,000	$1,722,938	$1,677,356	$1,611,903	$1,558,940	$1,472,774	$1,420,648	$1,364,095	$1,302,034	$1,196,274	$1,062,130
Target Annuity Cost	50th	$1,752,629	$1,556,247	$1,364,256	$1,178,451	$1,001,001	$834,526	$682,860	$549,969	$439,367	$352,716	$285,784
Actuarial Coverage Ratio	50th	85.60%	110.70%	122.90%	136.80%	155.70%	176.50%	208.00%	248.00%	296.30%	338.60%	369.20%
Actuarial Coverage Ratio + 50 bp shift	50th	90.20%	116.10%	128.30%	142.00%	160.90%	181.50%	213.00%	253.10%	301.40%	343.40%	373.60%
Portfolio Value	30th	$1,500,000	$1,564,865	$1,418,391	$1,271,742	$1,131,811	$987,573	$823,753	$645,520	$465,482	$240,885	$0

Although noticing a further improvement on the two-year delay reward-to-risk profile, the investor wonders if jettisoning an additional 12 months of leisure time is worth the improved economic projections.

By considering retirement as a risky project, the investor realizes that he can make prudent and well-timed decisions by matching portfolio outcomes to flooring costs (and to other variables such as health changes and unanticipated expenses) on a periodic basis. The set-flooring-in-place-as-soon-as-possible approach gives an early resolution to ambiguity and uncertainty that characterize acceptance of the retirement project. The implementation of flooring, however, destroys the value of optionality and flexibility in retirement-income planning. The annuity solution, for example, is the ultimate set-in-stone asset management approach.[27]

---

27. In a trust management context, acquisition of an annuity bears an uneasy relationship to trustee duties to take control of assets and make them productive. Analysis and documentation are critical components of prudent trust administration because few trust instruments explicitly grant the power to default asset management and distribution policy irrevocably to an insurance company.

PART SIX: CONTINGENT ASSETS/RETIRING INTO A BEAR MARKET

As the analysis of retirement-planning choices draws to a close, the investor asks if the expectation of an inheritance should be a factor in decision-making. In this case, the investor states that he has a long and close relationship with a spinster aunt who has given him reason to believe that he will receive a portion of her estate. The aunt recently nominated him as her estate executor/personal representative and he has agreed to serve in that capacity. A review of her current assets for estate-planning purposes and for potential durable-power-of-attorney use in the event of medical and end-of-life costs indicates that a conservatively estimated bequest, considering possible life-time care expenses, amounts to $350,000.[28] His aunt is age 93 and appears to be in good health.

The advisor agrees that the analysis should consider a possible bequest. The timing of such an event is, of course, unknown. Therefore, the advisor models the bequest date based on the Society of Actuaries 2014 table for the white-collar, high-income, female, and good-health population group's distribution of life expectancy. To isolate the effect of contingent assets (or contingent liabilities in other case studies), the advisor ignores opportunities to continue contributing retirement savings (or budget revisions resulting from delaying receipt of entitlements). Incorporating the contingent asset into the model produces figure 3.18:

FIGURE 3.18: 60–40 PORTFOLIO, THREE-YEAR DELAY, $5,000 INCOME, BEAR MARKET, BEQUEST

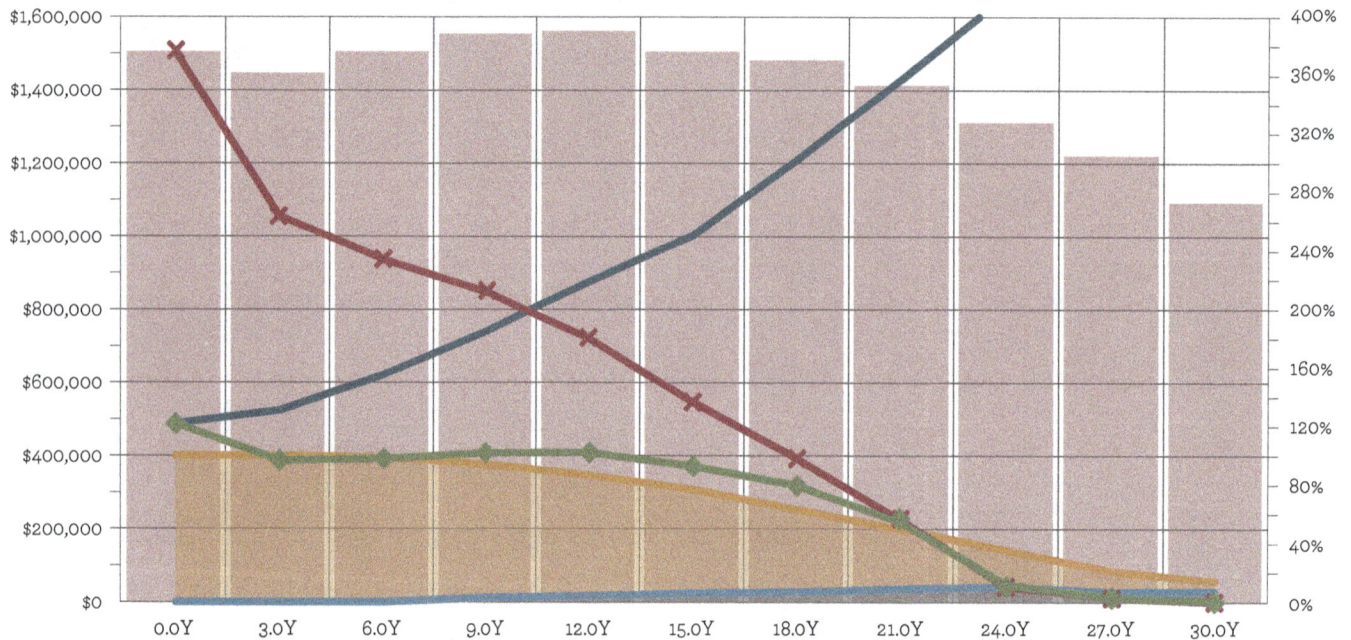

---

28. Life insurance contracts, if they remain in force, also provide a contingent expectation of future funds to named beneficiaries. For a detailed analysis on this topic, see Collins and Lam (2011). Life insurance is an important asset in Case Study 9. Contingent liabilities also may be of importance in developing and presenting retirement-income models.

DATA TABLE FOR FIGURE 3.18: 60–40 PORTFOLIO, THREE-YEAR DELAY, $5,000 INCOME, BEAR MARKET, BEQUEST

	Percentile	Current Value	3.0Y	6.0Y	9.0Y	12.0Y	15.0Y	18.0Y	21.0Y	24.0Y	27.0Y	30.0Y
Portfolio Value	50th	$1,500,000	$1,536,157	$1,648,681	$1,715,293	$1,731,466	$1,741,288	$1,754,161	$1,728,402	$1,671,181	$1,561,236	$1,450,166
Target Annuity Cost	50th	119.80%	138.20%	169.20%	203.70%	242.20%	292.10%	359.60%	440.00%	532.50%	619.70%	710.40%
Survival Probability		100.00%	98.80%	94.80%	89.40%	81.70%	72.40%	60.90%	48.10%	34.00%	20.20%	10.20%
Probability of Depletion		0.00%	0.00%	0.00%	0.00%	0.50%	2.10%	4.00%	5.00%	5.30%	4.00%	2.40%
Portfolio Value	20th	$1,500,000	$1,130,280	$1,040,002	$952,251	$823,232	$668,491	$511,101	$356,743	$173,245	$5,267	$0
Actuarial Coverage Ratio	20th	119.80%	101.70%	106.70%	113.10%	115.10%	112.10%	104.80%	90.20%	55.20%	2.10%	0.00%

The advisor informs the investor that the salmon-colored bar is the left-axis dollar value of the portfolio over time at the 50th percentile assuming a bear market starts immediately. The red line with the x pattern is the distribution of portfolio dollar value over time at the 20th percentile assuming a bear market starts immediately. The orange-shaded area is the probability of survival while the small blue-shaded area at the bottom is the conditional probability of portfolio depletion. The solid blue line with no marking is the 50th percentile ACR and finally, the green line with diamond markings is the 20th percentile ACR.

If he decides to delay retirement for three years, it would take a confluence of nasty events to knock the investor below the threshold standard of living that his portfolio must support. In an average initial bear-market return sequence, portfolio depletion first appears in year 12. Depletion, however, remains a low-probability event. The bottom two rows indicate that the portfolio would have to perform below the 20th percentile level of the "start bear" return sequence to present a significant danger to the investor's ability to support his threshold income target. A rough calibration indicates that even under this set of dire circumstances,[29] the investor has an 80-percent chance of a successful retirement outcome.

His spirits bolstered by this economic profile, the investor considers one final model output assuming (see figure 3.19):

- Aspirational inflation-adjusted monthly income ($7,000)
- Immediate retirement
- Immediate start of a bear market
- An inheritance ($350,000) at a stochastic future date

29. Analysis reflects the confluence of a low-probability bad event (immediate start of a bear market) and a second low-probability event (a bear market of greater-than-average severity). Cumulative probability is extremely low—although not zero.

FIGURE 3.19: 60–40 PORTFOLIO, NO DELAY, $7,000 INCOME, BEAR MARKET, BEQUEST

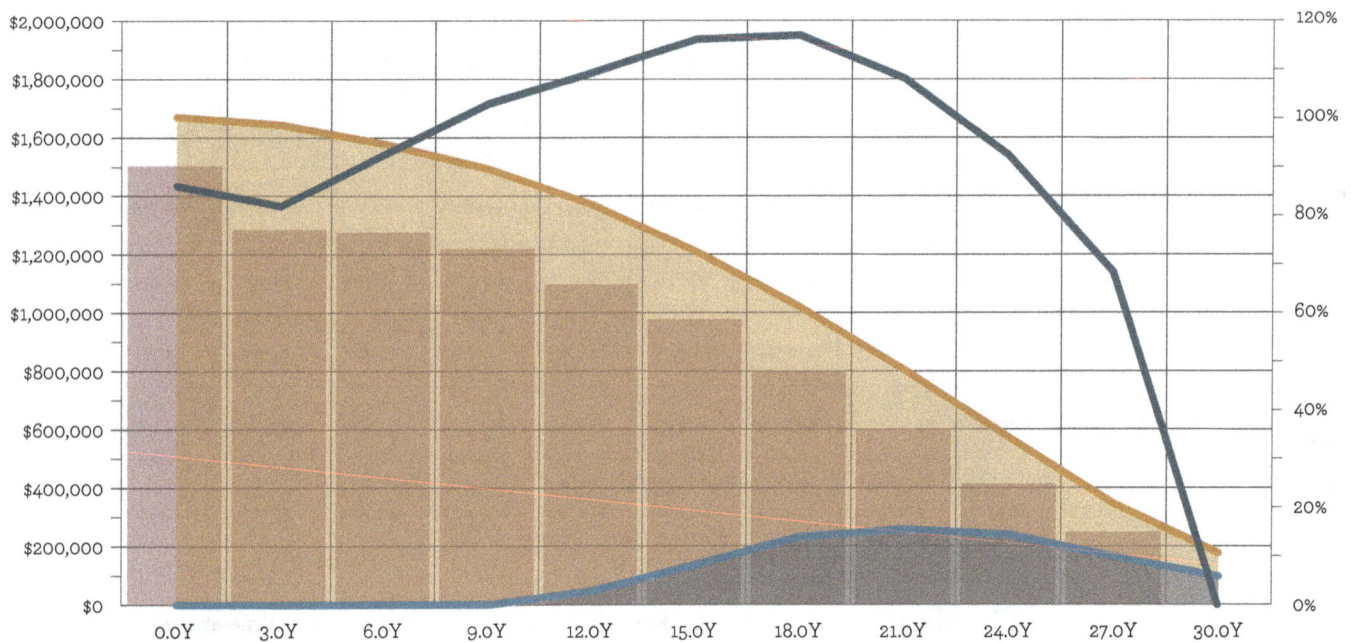

DATA TABLE FOR FIGURE 3.19: 60–40 PORTFOLIO, NO DELAY, $7,000 INCOME, BEAR MARKET, BEQUEST

	Percentile	Current Value	3.0Y	6.0Y	9.0Y	12.0Y	15.0Y	18.0Y	21.0Y	24.0Y	27.0Y	30.0Y
Portfolio Value	50th	$1,500.000	$1,266,270	$1,259,928	$1,212,559	$1,091,421	$967,240	$797,529	$594,985	$404,068	$238,750	$0
Actuarial Coverage Ratio	50th	85.60%	81.40%	92.30%	102.90%	109.00%	115.90%	$116.70%	108.20%	92.00%	67.70%	0.00%
Survival Probability		100.00%	98.80%	94.80%	89.40%	81.70%	72.40%	60.90%	48.10%	34.00%	20.20%	10.20%
Probability of Depletion		0.00%	0.00%	0.00%	0.20%	2.40%	7.90%	13.30%	15.40%	13.70%	9.20%	5.30%

For ease of comparison, the advisor reproduces the start-bear-market table from the first planning meeting (see table 3.1). The retirement-planning model indicates that the economic consequences of the contingent asset are twofold:

1. Long-term portfolio sustainability is, on average, significantly extended.

2. The bear market ACR achieves a positive value by year 9.

However, the prospects of an inheritance by no means eliminate the risks that accompany immediate acceptance of the retirement project. The current value of available resources remains insufficient in terms of the actuarial benchmark. Should the inheritance fail to occur, or fail to provide a sufficient amount of funds, the investor's standard of living may be in jeopardy. The test for retirement feasibility compares the current market value of assets to the present value of actuarially calculated liabilities. Failure to pass the feasibility test does not preclude a successful retirement, however, an ACR less than one makes finding a suitable retirement strategy difficult.

CHAPTER FOUR

CASE STUDY 2—EMPHASIS ON SUSTAINABILITY

• • •

PART ONE: FACT PATTERN

Case Study 2 examines feasible lifetime spending where an investor's consumption is a function of her preferences for specific spending patterns, e.g., money available for spending today is more valuable than money available for future spending.

The planning goal is to identify:

- Feasible lifetime spending levels
- Feasible lifetime spending patterns

Theoretically, optimal consumption is a feasible path that maximizes the investor's intertemporal utility function.

Much traditional financial planning analysis focuses, explicitly or implicitly, on the investor's degree of risk aversion regarding wealth fluctuation. For the population of retired investors, however, income security is an important—and often neglected—area for analysis. It is not obvious how wealth levels and income sustainability interact. Can you be more financially secure with less money?

Many retired investors define income security as having the amount of money they planned on having at the time they planned to have it.[1] Fixed wealth, however, often demands fluctuating income.[2] Fixed income often demands fluctuating wealth.[3]

If wealth is an asset that provides money to support financial goals, then the savvy investor is at least as concerned with the safety and sustainability of the goals as with transitory price levels of various global financial markets. As Nobel Prize-winner Robert Merton wrote: "[A]n investment that is risk-free from an asset value standpoint may be very risky in income terms" (Merton 2014, 1,403). However, many investors focus primarily on asset value. A disconnect in thinking occurs whenever an investor confuses stability in asset value with stability and sustainability in cash flows. The market watchers and prognosticators seldom speak in terms of a portfolio's ability to provide resources, over time, to pay the bills. Their vocabulary tends to trap listeners into a short-term dynamic based on fear and greed and their exhortations encourage buy-sell strategies that, more often than not, enrich only the brokers. If the goal is lifetime income, the primary risks are income insufficiency and the failure to achieve income sustainability (shortfall-risk metrics), not portfolio value fluctuations.

A low actuarial coverage ratio value [ACR < 1] is, within an asset-liability management (ALM) context, the economic equivalent of a negative surplus. As Case Study 1 demonstrates, planning, i.e., accepting the risky project of retirement, under these circumstances is problematic. Case Study 2 examines issues of income sustainability more closely. There are several aspects to this issue:

1. Whenever the portfolio's goal is to provide a lifetime income stream sufficient to support standard-of-living objectives, the sustainability issue translates into a concern to provide cash flows that align with consumption preferences.

2. Whenever the investor has a strong bequest motive, the sustainability issue translates into a concern to preserve portfolio value for the benefit of future generations.

---

1. A better definition is having the amount of money the investor needs at the time it's needed. This is the focus of Case Study 3 with its emphasis on retirement security.

2. An investor maintaining a fixed balance in a certificate of deposit finds that income fluctuates with each change in the interest rate offered at the certificate's renewal date. Over time, interest rates, i.e., retirement income, can vary enormously.

3. An extreme example is the transfer of all wealth to an insurance company for a fixed lifetime-income guarantee. Spendable wealth disappears when an investor buys a contract to provide specified periodic future income. Exchanging wealth for a guaranteed lifetime income provides an extreme example of a more-secure-with-less-wealth circumstance.

From the perspective of retirement as a risky project, the investor is better equipped to make spending decisions if she can quantify the trade-offs between sustainability (how long can the portfolio generate income?) and sufficiency (will the income be enough?). Elements of concern for the retirement project are the risk that:

- A bequest objective fails, or
- Periodic/aggregate spending goals are not met.

Of course, it is common for an investor to have both objectives. For example, if the investor is a trustee of an irrevocable family trust, there may be a duty to equilibrate the expected distribution of terminal wealth for the remaindermen and the expected distribution of lifetime income for the income beneficiary. Trust administration, in the presence of a duty of impartiality, often benefits from statistical analysis confirming that the distribution of expected results for one beneficiary class is not significantly better than for the other. However, if the investor acts in a nonfiduciary context, i.e., a private wealth investor, different preference weightings may exist between income and bequest objectives. For investors with modest amounts of financial resources, a dollar of spendable lifetime income often produces many times the satisfaction (utility) of a dollar available for bequest. Private wealth portfolio modeling may benefit from weighting outcomes—either in dollar wealth or utility-of-wealth—between consumption and bequests.

In Case Study 2, the advisor meets an investor who passes initial tests for feasibility. She is age 74, in good health, and has implemented a portfolio allocated 50 percent to stocks and 50 percent to fixed income securities. The portfolio's current value is $5 million and its lifetime periodic income target is $20,000 per month adjusted for inflation. The investor wishes the advisor to help her investigate several questions:

- If she withdraws the monthly target income, what are the chances that the full constant-dollar value of the portfolio will pass on to future generations?
- If she withdraws the monthly target income, what are the chances that the portfolio's future value will decrease to a level that will require substantial spending reductions or, worst case, will result in portfolio depletion?
- What are the consequences of increasing withdrawals in the near term while she is in good health and can fully enjoy travel and leisure activities? If such a strategy is possible, what is a good way to do it? By how much, if any, will her late-in-life income shrink?

The advisor recognizes that the interplay between consumption and bequest objectives is complex. Upon further inquiry, he discovers that the $20,000 per month is not a hard target. She has some financial flexibility both currently (near term) and intertemporally (long term). Based on further fact finding, the advisor conjectures[4] that the investor has the following economic preferences and constraints:

- An impatience factor (subjective discounting higher than the risk-free rate). This means that current spending is of greater value to her than future spending.[5]
- An elasticity of intertemporal substitution greater than one. This means that the investor is not extremely risk averse with respect to periodic fluctuations in monthly income over the planning horizon. She does not demand absolute budgetary certainty.
- A positive bequest motive, primarily for the benefit of grandchildren, due to the economic independence of her adult children.
- A Fisher utility-of-wealth function. Named after the economist Irving Fisher, this implies that money to pay for contingent expenses that may occur far into the future is not as important as money to support a high current standard of living.[6]

The advisor suspects that there is a possible tug-of-war between the bequest and consumption objectives—he looks forward to helping the investor make informed decisions.

---

4. At this stage of the retirement-income planning process, any statement regarding investor preferences is a conjecture. A primary purpose of advisor-investor discussions is to allow the investor an opportunity to reveal her preferences. This occurs as she considers the opportunity set and either embraces or rejects feasible outcomes and the solution paths leading thereto. Indeed, at this stage of the planning process many investors cannot clearly articulate their preferences. It is difficult to select a planning option if you are in the dark about which options are available to you, which are feasible, and which are prudent.

5. Although the interest rate is a financial factor and the preference rate is a subjective or psychological factor, the risk-free rate reflects the "average" impatience factor of all market participants. In Case Study 2, the investor demands a higher-than-average compensation (interest rate) for deferring spending until a future date. One consequence of the retirement-as-a-risky-project approach is that optimizing on a purely net present value criterion is not always appropriate. This is another point of tangency between rational and behavioral finance.

6. See Collins et al. (2015b), especially pp. 18–19, 43–49, and 62.

The advisor's first order of business is to explain how his portfolio modeling analysis will unfold. The risk model replicates the current $5-million portfolio value, as well as its current asset allocation (50-percent stocks/50-percent bonds), and its rebalance policy (constant mix).[7] Given the nature and scope of the investor's current assets and current asset-management elections, the advisor seeks to determine if they can support spending goals. The advisor presents four retirement-spending policies:

1. **A budget-certain spending policy:** A lifetime, fixed spending budget of $240,000 per year adjusted for inflation.

2. **A unitrust spending policy:** Consumption based on annually withdrawing 4.8 percent of the portfolio's end-of-previous-year value (with one-twelfth of the calculated annual amount withdrawn monthly). Such a spending policy eschews strict budgetary certainty in favor of linking consumption directly to the financial resources available to support it.[8]

3. **A hybrid spending policy:** This is a combination of fixed spending (budget certain) plus floating spending (percent of portfolio value).

4. **A front-loaded spending policy:** This withdrawal policy spends higher amounts in the current and immediately forthcoming years while tapering off later in retirement.[9]

The analysis employs the following terminology for graph headings:

- The model's output designates the budget-certain withdrawal strategy: "20K fixed spending" indicating that the strategy seeks to provide a certain, inflation-adjusted, $20,000 per month ($240,000 per year).

- The model's output designates the unitrust policy: "4.8% of Corpus" indicating that this is the annual percentage withdrawal amount.[10] The 4.8 percent of $5 million generates a $240,000 initial annual withdrawal. The 4.8-percent target provides an apples-to-apples comparison of spending policy options with respect to the initial amount.

- The model's output designates the hybrid spending policy: "10K Fixed/2.4% of Corpus" indicating that each month the investor will receive a fixed, inflation-adjusted, $10,000 amount plus a floating amount based on a monthly withdrawal of one-twelfth of the calculated amount.

- The model's output designates the front-loaded spending policy: "30K decreasing 12K per year to 180K" indicating that (1) the initial year's withdrawal amount is $360,000 and (2) each year thereafter spending decreases by $12,000 until it levels off in year 15 to a fixed $180,000, or $15,000 per month (with all values adjusted for inflation).

PART TWO: VERIFYING INITIAL INCOME FEASIBILITY

Feasibility is the first hurdle that any retirement-income project must overcome. In this case, however, a commercial annuity contract only replicates income strategy 1—a lifetime, fixed monthly inflation-adjusted income. Under spending strategies 2 and 3, if portfolio values fluctuate upward, spending increases. Conversely, if portfolio values fluctuate downward, spending decreases. However, fluctuations in feasible spending, i.e., spending levels that maintain a prudent ACR, do not change proportionately to changes in wealth. A 30-percent change in wealth does not necessarily call for a 30-percent change in spending. The fact that feasible retirement spending does not move in lockstep with changes in wealth is due to factors other than sensitivity to capital market fluctuations. These include:

- Age, which changes in only one direction—no Benjamin Buttons are included in our retiree population. All else being equal, a 90-year-old investor requires less wealth to produce a $20,000 monthly, inflation-adjusted lifetime income than does a 70-year-old investor.

- Changes in interest rates dynamically change the ACR value according to the interest-rate sensitivity of future liabilities and the interest-rate sensitivity of financial assets.

---

7.   See appendix A.

8.   In Case Study 2, the model does not incorporate a "smoothing function" rule, e.g., withdrawal amount is based on average portfolio value over the previous 'x' years. By incorporating such a function, the spending policy approaches the well-known "endowment spending policy" rules commonly employed by nonprofit institutions. A "unitrust" distribution rule is based on withdrawing a percent of corpus and is a commonly used alternative to net-income trust distribution rules. Trusts employing a unitrust distribution policy are "total return trusts." Some commentators characterize smoothing techniques as "accounting tricks." See, for example, Waring and Siegel (2015).

9.   The reverse strategy is "back-loaded" spending, which keeps initial spending low in the expectation of accumulating substantial wealth that can be used for end-of-life expenses or bequests. Unattended spending policies can, over time, unintentionally morph into front-loaded or back-loaded policies that may not be a good fit with investor spending preferences. Initial investment conservatism designed to protect wealth, for example, may produce back-loaded spending patterns that are misaligned with an investor's consumption preferences.

10. The unitrust withdrawal policy should not be confused with the ubiquitous 4-percent spending rule, which encourages investors to spend 4 percent (adjusted for inflation) of the portfolio's initial value. The unitrust spending policy reflects the portfolio's current value. Although the 4-percent rule continues to find adherents in the practitioner community, virtually every credible academic assessment yields a strongly negative critique.

We explore important relationships between wealth changes and feasible spending in greater detail in Case Study 3.

Spending strategy 4 requires a unique feasibility test. The ACR calculation, in this case, employs the annuity pricing principle using specified, but non-constant, cash flows.

The advisor explains that the ACR represents the division of "what you have by what you need." If the client has 100 percent of what she needs, she can, theoretically, guarantee a risk-free retirement through conversion into an annuity. At an ACR value equal to 1, the denominator is the actuarial equivalent to a guaranteed lifetime income. That is to say, the investor's retirement-spending plan is feasible. If she has more than 100 percent of what she needs, there is a financial cushion to mitigate poor investment results, unexpected expenses, higher than expected inflation, the costs associated with a long life span, and so forth.[11]

The advisor's solvency testing verifies the initial feasibility of each spending strategy, i.e., the ACR value exceeds a value of 100 percent for each spending election:

FIGURE 4.1: FEASIBILITY TEST—ACTUARIAL COVERAGE RATIO VALUES

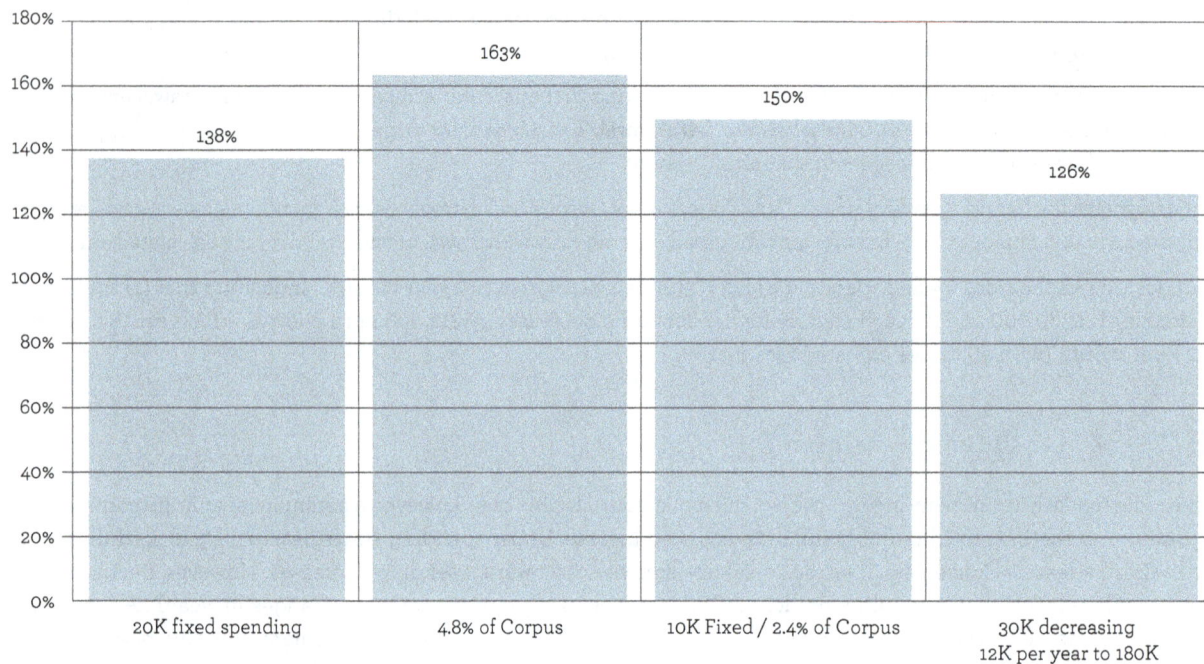

The lowest ACR is associated with the front-loaded spending strategy; the highest ACR is associated with the "floating" percentage of corpus strategy.[12]

---

11. A more complete characterization of ACR in terms of Case Study 1 is: A 100-percent ACR indicates the feasibility of funding an investor's threshold standard of living. ACR values in excess of 100 percent indicate the feasibility of funding aspirational standard-of-living levels. Case Study 2 tracks multiple ACR levels. The ACR metric is expressed sometimes as a wealth-to-consumption ratio. Ultimately, of course, no investor is inherently interested in the evolution of ACR values over time; rather, the investor wants to know if she will be able to pay the bills in retirement. This argues for a behavioral finance framework for reporting future progress toward or regression from personal financial objectives. However, such a behaviorist communications framework must have analytical credibility and, therefore, the need for a quantitative underpinning.

12. Even though the first three spending strategies begin with the same portfolio value ($5 million) and the same initial cash-flow demand ($20,000 per month), they manifest different ACRs. This is due primarily to two factors, each of which is associated with the future cash-flow demand. First, spending strategy number 1 grows spending at the rate of inflation, spending strategy number 2 grows spending as a function of portfolio value, and spending strategy number 3 grows spending by proportionally weighting strategies 1 and 2. Second, the ACR for the two strategies incorporating a floating-portfolio-withdrawal component assume that the floating withdrawal amount, recalculated annually, remains constant at that level throughout the remaining planning horizon. These factors explain, in part, why the ACR value for spending strategy 2 is the most favorable. During times of economic distress, the portfolio does not have to bear the stress of higher fixed inflation-adjusted distributions. However, these factors also explain, in part, why the ACR for spending strategies incorporating floating withdrawal elements are less-effective predictors of future solvency and sustainability probabilities.

PART THREE: PROJECTING FUTURE INCOME FEASIBILITY

The advisor congratulates the investor and remarks that the ACR values indicate that she can embark comfortably on a strategy that best reflects her cash-flow preferences. Under each election she has the expectation that the portfolio can adequately fund anticipated future spending.

In a static world, the investor can relax because values of key variables will not change. Under conditions of uncertainty, however, this may not be fully possible. The ACR reflects the interaction of critical variables (investment, inflation, health, interest rate, and liabilities) each of which may manifest changing parameter values as realizations emerge over time. Rather than average values (point estimates), the investor faces a multi-dimensional distribution of possible outcomes (range estimates). Granted that figure 4.1 provides information indicating the initial feasibility of investor goals, nevertheless, it is a point-in-time estimate (today) that bears close monitoring (tomorrow).

The investor says she understands that the future is not set in stone, but she is unsure about how ACR values can change from positive to unfavorable. If she has enough money to retire today, what is the possibility of waking up some morning to discover that this is no longer true? The advisor suspects that it is time to add a dynamic time dimension to the income feasibility analysis, but cautions the investor that (1) the dynamic analysis initially may seem to detour away from her main focus on the risk-reward trade-offs of various spending strategies, and (2) the detour may soak up a large portion of her attention span. On the positive side of the ledger, the advisor explains that tracking ACR value, i.e., portfolio sufficiency, is part of his firm's service set and that ACR monitoring is crucial lest the investor remain unaware of potential future dangers and opportunities.

The advisor states that he will present, in tabular and graphic form, a distribution (range) of future results from an asset-liability management perspective.[13] For each spending election under consideration, the distribution's range indicates the likelihood of a favorable ACR value continuing for the long term. He explains that an ACR value less than 100 percent suggests that reducing future spending may be prudent. An ACR value sufficiently greater than 100 percent suggests that the investor may have an option to increase consumption.[14] A low value (<100 percent) indicates that the investor has a "negative surplus" in an asset-liability management context and that she has entered a danger zone.

The following series of data presents, through time, dynamically projected ACR values for each spending strategy:

---

13. We reiterate that ACR value calculation can incorporate a number of deterministic or stochastic liabilities in addition to periodic spending objectives.

14. Managing a retirement-income portfolio is a process of identifying, over time, available options and evaluating the prudence of their implementation. It is only peripherally a process of buying five-star mutual funds or "strong-buy" stocks.

OPTION ONE

TABLE 4.1: OPTION ONE—RANGE OF ACTUARIAL COVERAGE RATIOS FOR CONSTANT-DOLLAR, $20,000 PER MONTH

	Years from Today										
	0.0Y	2.8Y	5.8Y	8.7Y	11.6Y	14.5Y	17.4Y	20.3Y	23.2Y	26.2Y	29.1Y
95%	138%	261%	327%	415%	557%	746%	1001%	1386%	1914%	2814%	3790%
90%	138%	228%	279%	350%	453%	596%	782%	1051%	1342%	1981%	2684%
80%	138%	190%	227%	275%	339%	431%	550%	713%	857%	1215%	1575%
70%	138%	167%	194%	231%	277%	343%	422%	528%	603%	742%	973%
60%	138%	147%	170%	197%	231%	274%	322%	384%	395%	473%	687%
50%	138%	131%	147%	168%	192%	216%	244%	268%	250%	253%	250%
40%	138%	116%	126%	140%	155%	169%	171%	169%	112%	60%	15%
30%	138%	100%	107%	114%	123%	122%	109%	82%	2%	0%	0%
20%	138%	83%	86%	87%	85%	75%	45%	0%	0%	0%	0%
10%	138%	62%	61%	57%	45%	22%	0%	0%	0%	0%	0%
5%	138%	47%	44%	38%	20%	0%	0%	0%	0%	0%	0%
Level 1	100%	100%	100%	100%	100%	100%	100%	100%	100%	100%	100%
Level 2	125%	125%	125%	125%	125%	125%	125%	125%	125%	125%	125%
Level 3	150%	150%	150%	150%	150%	150%	150%	150%	150%	150%	150%

The advisor explains that table 4.1 is a heat map. The green-shaded areas are regions of "surplus." The ACR value of 100 percent is the feasibility boundary. A value below 100 percent indicates that resources are inadequate with respect to the future monetary demands placed upon them. As the investor approaches the feasibility boundary from above, she enters into the yellow-shaded areas, which are regions of "awareness." If the ratio value moves closer to the lower bound, the color changes to orange, which signifies a region of "caution." Finally, if the portfolio penetrates the feasibility boundary, the maroon-shaded areas are regions of "danger." When the investor remarks that the table exhibits a heavy dose of "danger," the advisor cautions her not to jump to a hasty conclusion—things are not as perilous as they may first seem. He asks for permission to explain further the table's informational content.

The entire table represents a distribution of possible ACR values. After stating that the table shows a distribution of ratios, the advisor pauses for a moment. Failing to see any sign that the light bulb over the investor's head has clicked on, the advisor admits that the concept of a "distribution of ratio values" is tough to comprehend. The advisor takes a sheet of paper and writes some fractions:

$$\frac{Assets}{Liabilities} \quad = \quad \frac{Wealth}{Consumption} \quad = \quad \frac{Value\ of\ Portfolio}{Sum,\ in\ current\ dollars,\ of\ future\ spending\ assuming\ you're\ alive\ to\ buy\ things}$$

By definition, a fraction has a numerator and a denominator. This makes it a ratio—like miles per hour (distance ÷ time) or miles per gallon (distance ÷ number of gallons). The concept of ACR is complex because both the numerator and the denominator have multiple and continuously moving parts. The value of the portfolio in the numerator is an ever-changing number dependent on the random variables of inflation and investment returns.[15] The discounted sum of mortality-adjusted spending in the denominator constantly changes as a function of time (age) and liability values (changes in the discount rate used to value liabilities, or in the nature and scope of liabilities themselves).

---

15. A random variable is a variable the future value of which you cannot predict with certainty. The possible future value is from a distribution of probabilities for possible values—a range over the space of possible outcomes as opposed to a single point estimate.

In Case Study 2 the denominator is the actuarial cost, at a particular moment in time, for a guaranteed lifetime income.[16] Given so many moving parts (a person's financial situation never remains static because, all else being equal, it changes merely with the passage of time), it is no wonder that ratio values are variable. The simple answer is "things change" and this is why retirement is a risky project. There is uncertainty in the numerator (assets) and in the denominator (liabilities), and both elements contribute to retirement risk.

The far-left column divides the distribution into percentiles ranging from "worst case" (5th percentile) to "best case" (95th percentile). A brief discussion of probability, similar to the one from Case Study 1, ensues. Values in red, of course, indicate a negative surplus—an ACR less than 100 percent. The horizontal axis across the top records points in time for the evolution of ACR values over the applicable planning horizon (to approximately age 103). At time zero (0.0Y = today), the investor's ratio value (current portfolio value ÷ discounted value of future income targets calculated under the annuity pricing principle) equals 138 percent. Her retirement-spending strategy is feasible and, because today's ACR is based on current observables (market value of portfolio and actuarially determined cost of lifetime income), there is no guesswork—the ACR value is 138 percent at every percentile in the distribution of possible results. She is solvent; her retirement is feasible.

A key to understanding the table, according to the advisor, lies in the wording of the fraction:

Value of Portfolio

Sum, in current dollars, of future spending assuming you're alive to buy things.

"We know that the portfolio's value—the numerator—will change over time. However, the actual length of time for portfolio withdrawals is measured by an uncertain life span. Thus the key phrase is 'assuming you're alive to buy things.'" Or, "if you're alive in the future, what is the likelihood your portfolio will run out of money (hit an ACR value of 0 percent)?" The initial sample population of 74-year-old, healthy, female investors is 10,000. At time zero, the entire sample population is alive. The table does not record an ACR value of 0 percent until time 14.5 years. At that time, within the population of investors who remain alive to buy things, approximately 5 percent will have fully depleted their portfolio wealth assuming they made no mid-course spending adjustments. At time 20.3 years (investor age ≈ 94), of the remaining sample population, approximately 20 percent of those who remain alive will have run out of money assuming they made no mid-course spending adjustments. Finally, at time 29.1 years (investor age ≈ 103), of the remaining sample population, approximately 30 percent of those who remain alive, will have run out of money assuming they made no mid-course spending adjustments.

The state of "alive-and-broke" represented by an ACR value of zero occurs only at the intersection of three events: (1) the investor is fortunate enough to enjoy a long life span; (2) investment-inflation realizations are particularly unfavorable during the planning horizon and, perhaps most significant, (3) no one notices the unfolding economic danger and recommends corrective actions before wealth depletion. The heavy dose of red that alarmed the investor initially reflects conditional, rather than absolute, probabilities. To enter into the region of danger, the investor has to remain alive, suffer poor investment results, and remain unaware of her economic plight (or remain unwilling or unable to revise her spending policy).

The investor remarks: "When I looked at the table initially, I thought that it raised the specter of an approximately 30-percent chance of running out of money if I elect a $20,000 monthly, inflation-adjusted income. This is an unacceptable risk. However, if I understand the concept of conditional probability, I see that it suggests that approximately 30 percent of the very few sample investors who remain alive at age 103, and who continued the full monthly distribution from the investment portfolio, experience economic difficulty." The advisor sees the light bulb click on to 40 watts. The investor shakes her head and remarks that she feels she's swimming in intellectually deep water. At the advisor's suggestion, she readily agrees to take a break. When they resume, the advisor wants to show her a picture that, in his opinion, may make things clearer.

"So," the advisor remarks when the meeting resumes, "the ACR indicates when your portfolio's assets are worth more than your spending target. This is a good thing to know and is well quantified in the data we have been examining. Now, however, let's take a different look. In this view, the probability regions colored red, orange, yellow, and green require a somewhat different interpretation."

---

16. This is true for Case Study 2. Case Study 3 includes additional liability elements. In Case Study 3, both the nature and the scope of liabilities suddenly change.

The advisor directs the investor's attention to figure 4.2, which records:

1. Time on the bottom horizontal axis

2. The ACR value on the left vertical axis

3. The distribution of ACR values on the right vertical axis[17]

Locating the target ACR of 100 percent on the left vertical axis, the advisor notes the horizontal line extending, across time, to the chart's far side. Green represents regions that will occur in all but the low-probability (orange and maroon) strong bull-market outcomes. The deep shade of green, for example, indicates a region of investment outcomes that will be exceeded 95 percent of the time. Tracking an ACR value equal to 100 percent is an important monitoring objective because the 100-percent value is the boundary between retirement-income feasibility and infeasibility.

FIGURE 4.2: RANGE OF ACTUARIAL COVERAGE RATIOS, $20,000 FIXED

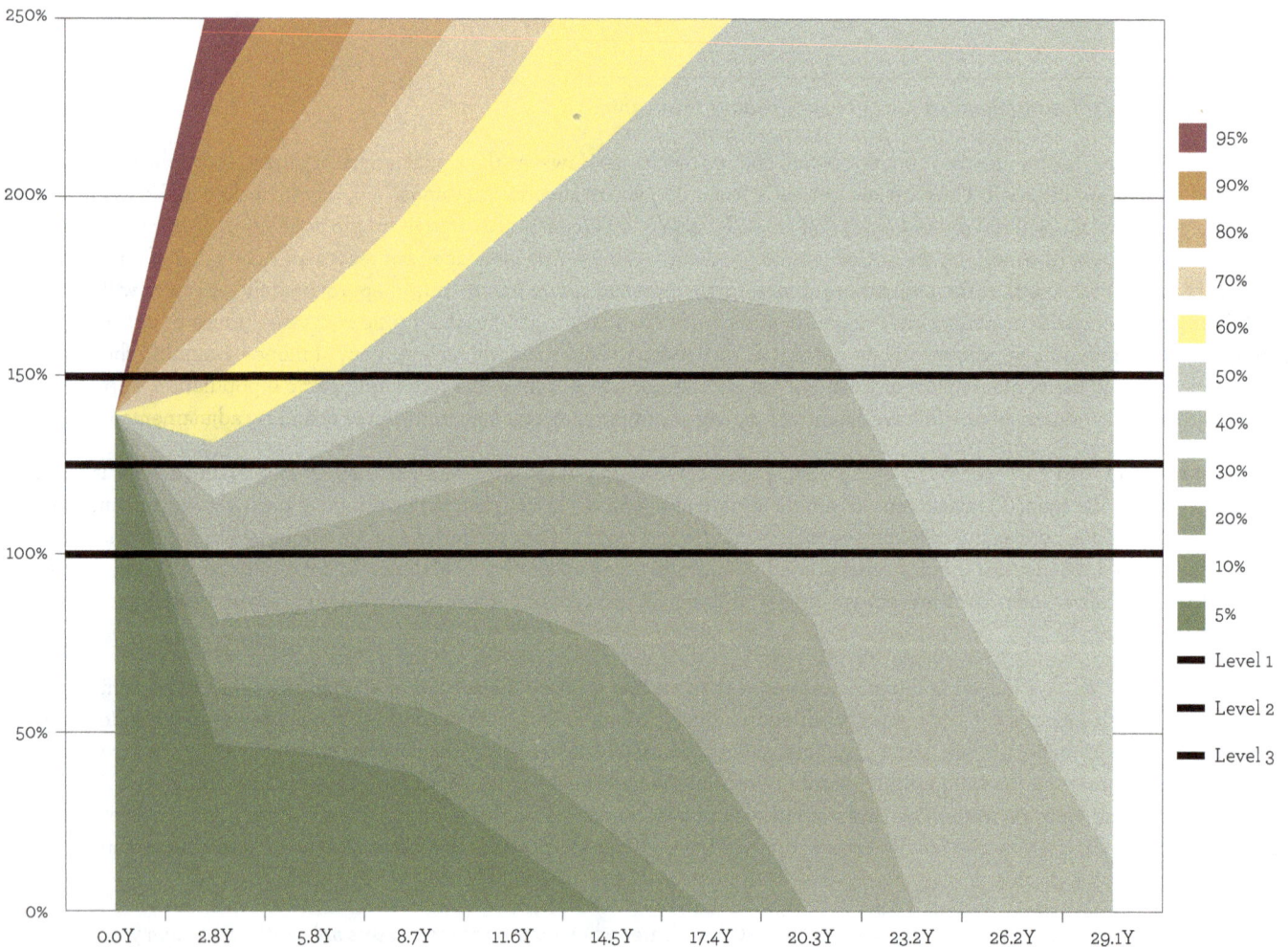

17. Note: The 95th percentile in maroon represents the low probability. The low probability outcome, in this case, is an extremely favorable investment performance—an outcome that would be dangerous to rely on when planning for sustainable retirement income. Maroon, for example, represents a 95-percent event level, or an event for which only 5 percent of outcomes are likely to be more favorable. The higher the target ACR level, the less likely an investor can achieve it, therefore, maroon is at the top of the chart. If orange or maroon represents a sizable portion of the graph or exists in a region of the graph in which the investor hopes to maintain ACR values, it is a danger signal that things have to go really well for the outcome to be realized.

ACR values greater than 100 percent represent margins of safety. At a 125-percent ACR (the horizontal line above the 100-percent level on figure 4.2), the investor again finds herself in the green throughout the applicable retirement planning horizon. And, although a target cushion of 150 percent is initially problematic, under most future trajectories, it returns to a feasible region.[18]

As the target ACR level increases, it becomes less likely to remain in the green throughout the planning horizon. Case Study 3 explores the trade-off between economic security and adequate sustainable income in greater detail. For now, the investor opines that figure 4.2 provides greater comfort because, if for no other reason, the maroon areas are not quite so prominent. It is time to evaluate the other spending strategies.

OPTION TWO

As the meeting continues, the advisor reminds the investor that their discussion about safety ratios, although important for understanding retirement risk, detours from her main topic of interest, i.e., what retirement-income strategies are safe, sustainable, and achievable, and what is the trade-off between income levels and bequest amounts. The advisor asks whether she wants to continue exploring the evolution of the ACR (feasibility) levels associated with each spending strategy. After pondering this question, she acknowledges the detour, but points out that the discussion has opened up dimensions of retirement risk that, although obviously important, have remained unknown to her for some reason. "You have my interest and attention. I've worked for many years to accumulate my nest egg and, at this point in my life, I don't want to trip over dangerous obstacles because I didn't take the time to look where I was walking. If we have to schedule a follow-on meeting, that's fine."

The advisor replies: "OK, here goes, but, fair warning, I'm going to play a trick on you." Figure 4.3 and its companion table are associated with spending strategy 2: withdrawing 4.8 percent of the portfolio's beginning of the year value.

DATA TABLE FOR FIGURE 4.3: OPTION TWO—RANGE OF ACTUARIAL COVERAGE RATIOS FOR 4.8 PERCENT OF PORTFOLIO VALUE ANNUAL WITHDRAWAL

	Years from Today										
	0.0Y	2.8Y	5.8Y	8.7Y	11.6Y	14.5Y	17.4Y	20.3Y	23.2Y	26.2Y	29.1Y
95%	163%	193%	220%	256%	305%	369%	453%	555%	677%	823%	990%
90%	163%	190%	217%	253%	300%	364%	446%	547%	669%	812%	964%
80%	163%	186%	213%	248%	295%	357%	437%	537%	658%	794%	949%
70%	163%	183%	210%	245%	291%	352%	432%	530%	648%	785%	937%
60%	163%	179%	205%	238%	283%	344%	421%	517%	633%	769%	914%
50%	163%	177%	202%	235%	280%	340%	416%	511%	626%	760%	901%
40%	163%	181%	207%	241%	287%	348%	426%	523%	641%	778%	925%
30%	163%	174%	199%	232%	276%	334%	410%	503%	616%	749%	888%
20%	163%	171%	196%	228%	271%	328%	401%	491%	604%	731%	872%
10%	163%	165%	189%	220%	262%	317%	388%	472%	578%	701%	836%
5%	163%	160%	184%	214%	254%	305%	372%	447%	535%	646%	779%
Level 1	100%	100%	100%	100%	100%	100%	100%	100%	100%	100%	100%
Level 2	125%	125%	125%	125%	125%	125%	125%	125%	125%	125%	125%
Level 3	150%	150%	150%	150%	150%	150%	150%	150%	150%	150%	150%

---

18. This parallels the situation in Case Study 1 where the about-to-retire investor favored a target income level that initially pushed the ACR value slightly below the feasibility threshold. In Case Study 1, however, the investor was playing roulette with his economic welfare because the target income level under evaluation was (1) close to his minimum standard of living consumption needs, and (2) at the feasibility-infeasibility boundary.

FIGURE 4.3: RANGE OF ACTUARIAL COVERAGE RATIOS, 4.8%

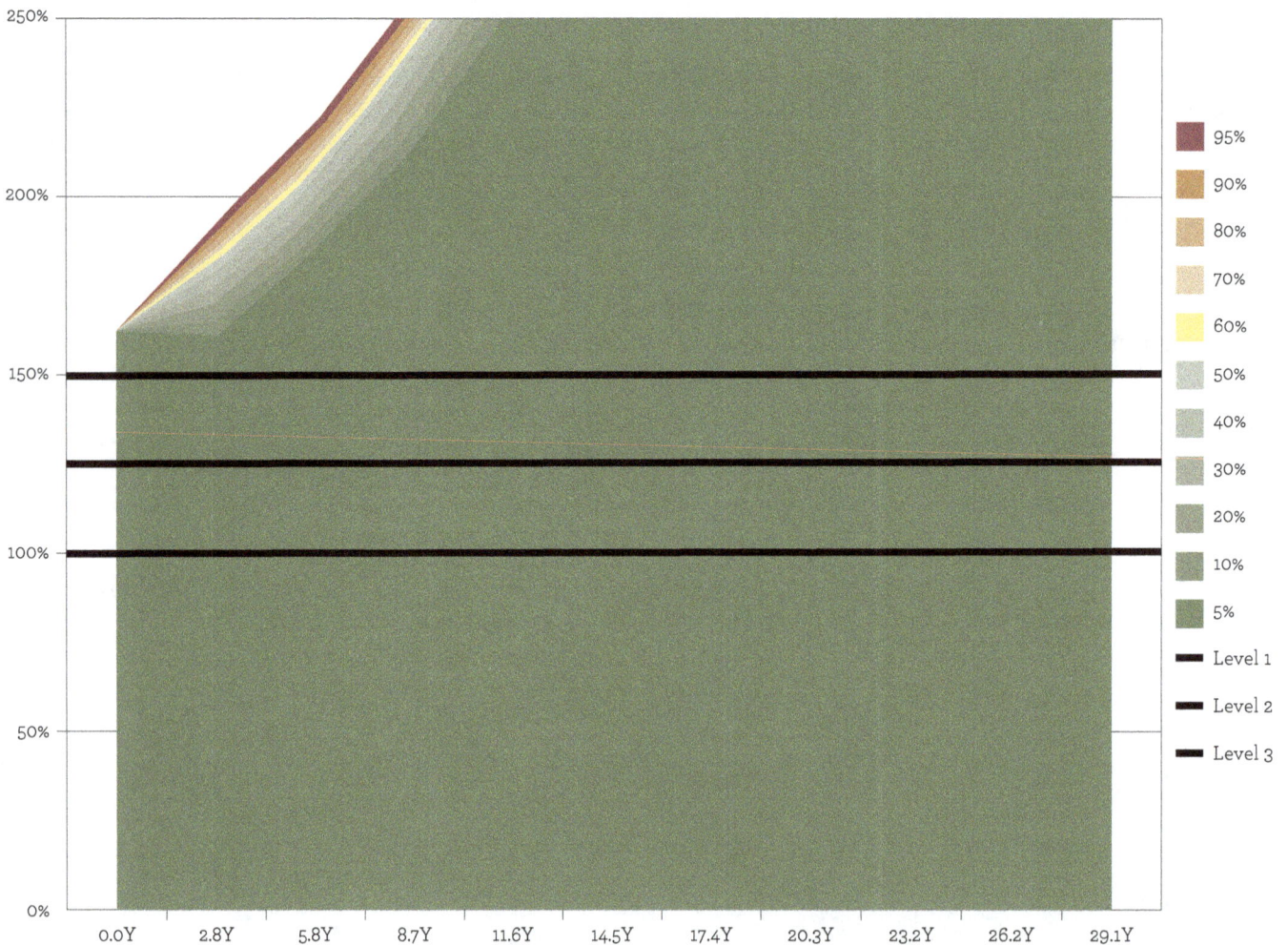

"How do these exhibits strike you?"

"Well," the investor slowly intones, "I don't see much of a danger zone, but ... what's the trick?"

The advisor acknowledges the acumen of the investor's remark and notes the ACR value starts at a healthy-looking 163 percent and, with few exceptions, continues upward from there. Has risk disappeared? It certainly seems like this is the case. Indeed, the graph reinforces this impression because each ACR level (the horizontal lines at 100 percent, 125 percent, and 150 percent) remains solidly in the dark green throughout the planning horizon. What's going on?

"You're looking at wealth-to-consumption ratios, not at income levels. The ACR for an income strategy that is 'pure float' almost always will be in the green region because, when you're adjusting spending based on portfolio value, there is little danger that you will fully deplete your assets—as assets decline, spending declines, but the ratio values appear to remain relatively stable. Here's the catch: There is a danger that the level of your spending will decline below acceptable target levels. When you go into a store to buy something, you don't check your wallet for income ratios, you check it for money. The ratios are like the traffic light on the street outside of the store. The light serves a critically important purpose, but you can't take it into the store and buy anything with it."

The advisor offers a simplified version of the calculations underlying the two visuals. As the portfolio's value fluctuates over time, the yearly withdrawal amount also changes. A portfolio that increases in value will, over time, throw off higher income levels than a portfolio that decreases in value. But the ACR calculation takes future income levels—both higher and lower—and determines whether the new wealth-to-consumption ratio can be sustained throughout the remaining planning horizon or not. Like Alexander Pope, it assumes that "Whatever Is, Is Right." This means that when an investor asks the risk model: "Can I sustain an income strategy based on an income level equal to 4.8 percent of portfolio value?" the answer is yes because the calculation algorithm is singularly unconcerned about the dollar amount of income thrown off by this strategy. As the advisor remarks: "If you set up a floating income target and ask the risk model if it is sustainable, you always will receive a positive answer. You may not receive much actual money, but you always will receive your target percentage. Be careful what you ask for because you may get it (Collins and Stampfli 2001). There are certain perils hiding in this option, but you will see them only when we examine risk model outputs based on income levels."

OPTION THREE

The investor is curious about the ACR profiles for the remaining two spending strategies. The hybrid spending strategy calls for a fixed, inflation-adjusted monthly distribution of $10,000 per month combined with a floating distribution calibrated to 2.4 percent of the portfolio's annual value withdrawn monthly. Initially, this amounts to a $10,000 monthly withdrawal under the "budget certain" election, and an additional $10,000 monthly withdrawal under the "2.4 percent of corpus" election.

DATA TABLE FOR FIGURE 4.4: OPTION THREE—RANGE OF ACTUARIAL COVERAGE RATIOS FOR HYBRID STRATEGY ANNUAL WITHDRAWAL

	Years from Today										
	0.0Y	2.8Y	5.8Y	8.7Y	11.6Y	14.5Y	17.4Y	20.3Y	23.2Y	26.2Y	29.1Y
95%	150%	217%	253%	302%	371%	462%	581%	729%	908%	1156%	1348%
90%	150%	204%	237%	281%	344%	424%	532%	665%	832%	1031%	1280%
80%	150%	186%	216%	253%	307%	376%	467%	580%	717%	897%	1112%
70%	150%	174%	199%	232%	281%	341%	414%	505%	624%	758%	898%
60%	150%	163%	184%	214%	258%	307%	366%	445%	541%	635%	730%
50%	150%	152%	171%	197%	233%	275%	326%	384%	448%	503%	548%
40%	150%	141%	157%	179%	208%	243%	279%	317%	357%	365%	366%
30%	150%	129%	141%	159%	182%	207%	228%	240%	252%	222%	149%
20%	150%	114%	123%	135%	152%	160%	168%	163%	139%	82%	0%
10%	150%	94%	98%	104%	107%	104%	88%	39%	0%	0%	0%
5%	150%	73%	78%	78%	72%	61%	21%	0%	0%	0%	0%
Level 1	100%	100%	100%	100%	100%	100%	100%	100%	100%	100%	100%
Level 2	125%	125%	125%	125%	125%	125%	125%	125%	125%	125%	125%
Level 3	150%	150%	150%	150%	150%	150%	150%	150%	150%	150%	150%

The advisor reiterates that the data table for figure 4.4 shows conditional probabilities as they unfold through time. The sample population of 10,000 investors has a known ACR value of 150 percent currently. As time unfolds, ACR values change dynamically for the population of surviving investors. Unlike the spending strategy that provides budgetary certainty ($20,000 per month) and that first exhibits an initial zero-percent ACR value at year 14.5, a zero-percent ACR value initially appears at year 20.3—investor age 94—for the hybrid spending election. The hybrid policy reduces the conditional probability of portfolio depletion relative to the budget-certain policy, but it increases the conditional probability of portfolio depletion relative to the floating "4.8 percent of corpus" policy.

Figure 4.4 confirms this interpretation.

FIGURE 4.4: RANGE OF ACTUARIAL COVERAGE RATIOS, 2.4% + $10,000

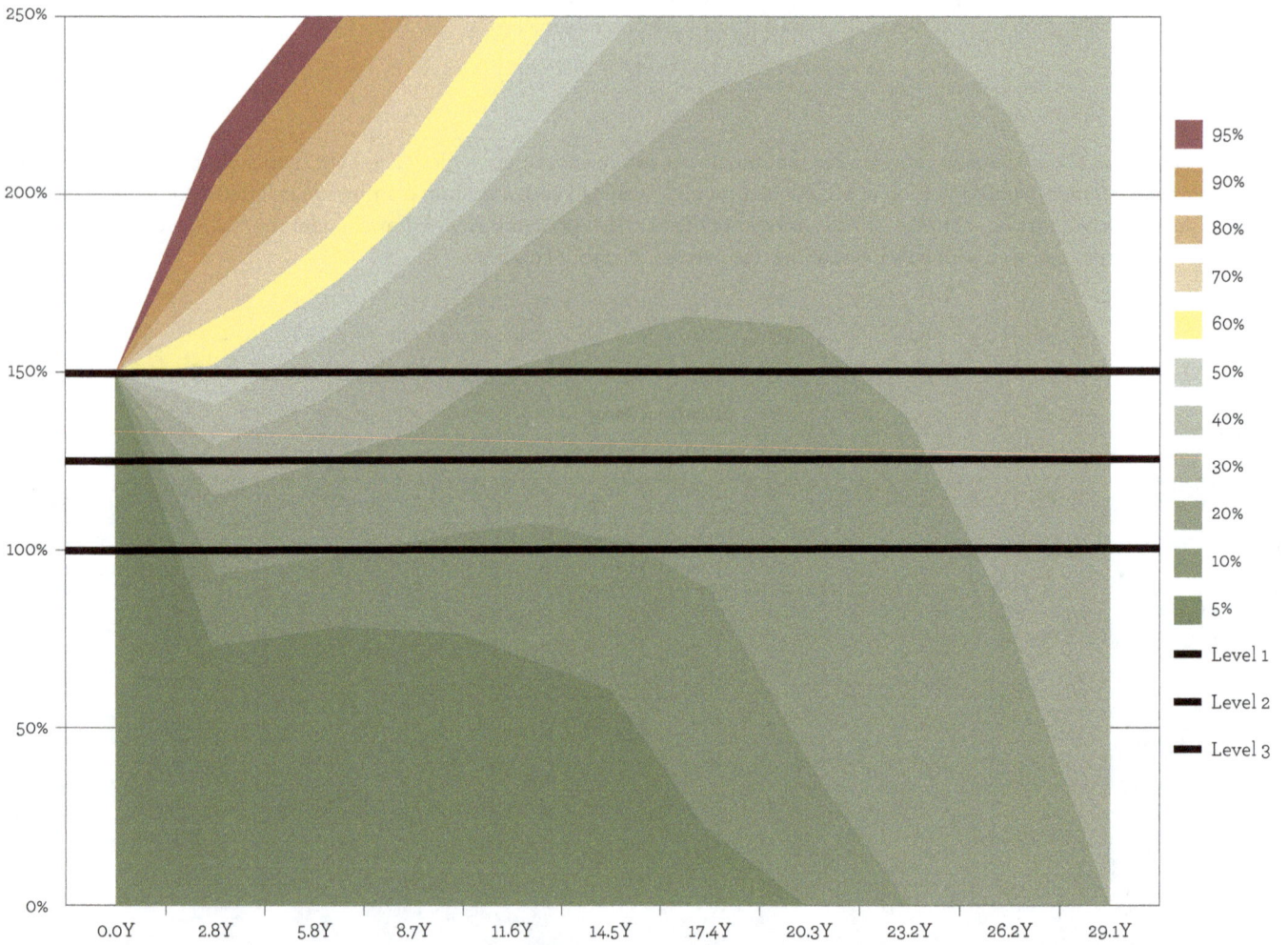

However, the advisor again cautions the investor that the ACR calculation algorithm is not testing for income levels. Rather, it is testing for feasibility—in this case, the feasibility of maintaining partially floating income levels throughout the remainder of the planning horizon. Feasibility, under certain spending elections, is not adequacy, i.e., income sufficiency.

OPTION FOUR

Finally, the data table for figure 4.5 evaluates the projected feasibility trajectory for the front-loaded spending policy providing an initial yearly withdrawal of $360,000, decreasing yearly by $12,000, until it levels off in year 15 to a fixed $180,000 (with all values adjusted for inflation).

DATA TABLE FOR FIGURE 4.5: OPTION FOUR—RANGE OF ACTUARIAL COVERAGE RATIOS FOR FRONT-LOADED SPENDING STRATEGY

	Years from Today										
	0.0Y	2.8Y	5.8Y	8.7Y	11.6Y	14.5Y	17.4Y	20.3Y	23.2Y	26.2Y	29.1Y
95%	126%	227%	304%	443%	712%	1231%	1152%	1638%	2189%	3068%	4164%
90%	126%	203%	267%	377%	591%	1018%	914%	1202%	1689%	2256%	3468%
80%	126%	176%	224%	312%	465%	779%	655%	818%	1063%	1383%	1798%
70%	126%	158%	198%	269%	386%	623%	485%	589%	704%	811%	909%
60%	126%	144%	177%	233%	324%	506%	363%	430%	481%	551%	619%
50%	126%	130%	158%	201%	270%	405%	274%	295%	304%	291%	369%
40%	126%	118%	139%	169%	216%	312%	196%	185%	154%	94%	27%
30%	126%	106%	120%	139%	168%	221%	117%	74%	9%	0%	0%
20%	126%	92%	98%	105%	113%	119%	33%	0%	0%	0%	0%
10%	126%	74%	70%	62%	43%	0%	0%	0%	0%	0%	0%
5%	126%	59%	52%	35%	0%	0%	0%	0%	0%	0%	0%
Level 1	100%	100%	100%	100%	100%	100%	100%	100%	100%	100%	100%
Level 2	125%	125%	125%	125%	125%	125%	125%	125%	125%	125%	125%
Level 3	150%	150%	150%	150%	150%	150%	150%	150%	150%	150%	150%

This option also passes the initial test for feasibility, albeit at a slightly lower ACR value. Likewise, it suggests that, although it would take some low probability shocks to push the ACR value to 0 percent, nevertheless a zero-percent value initially appears for the population of surviving investors in year 11.6 at the 5th percentile of outcomes.

Figure 4.5 confirms the prudence of electing the front-loaded retirement-income strategy:

FIGURE 4.5: RANGE OF ACTUARIAL COVERAGE RATIOS, $30,000, DECREASING TO $15,000

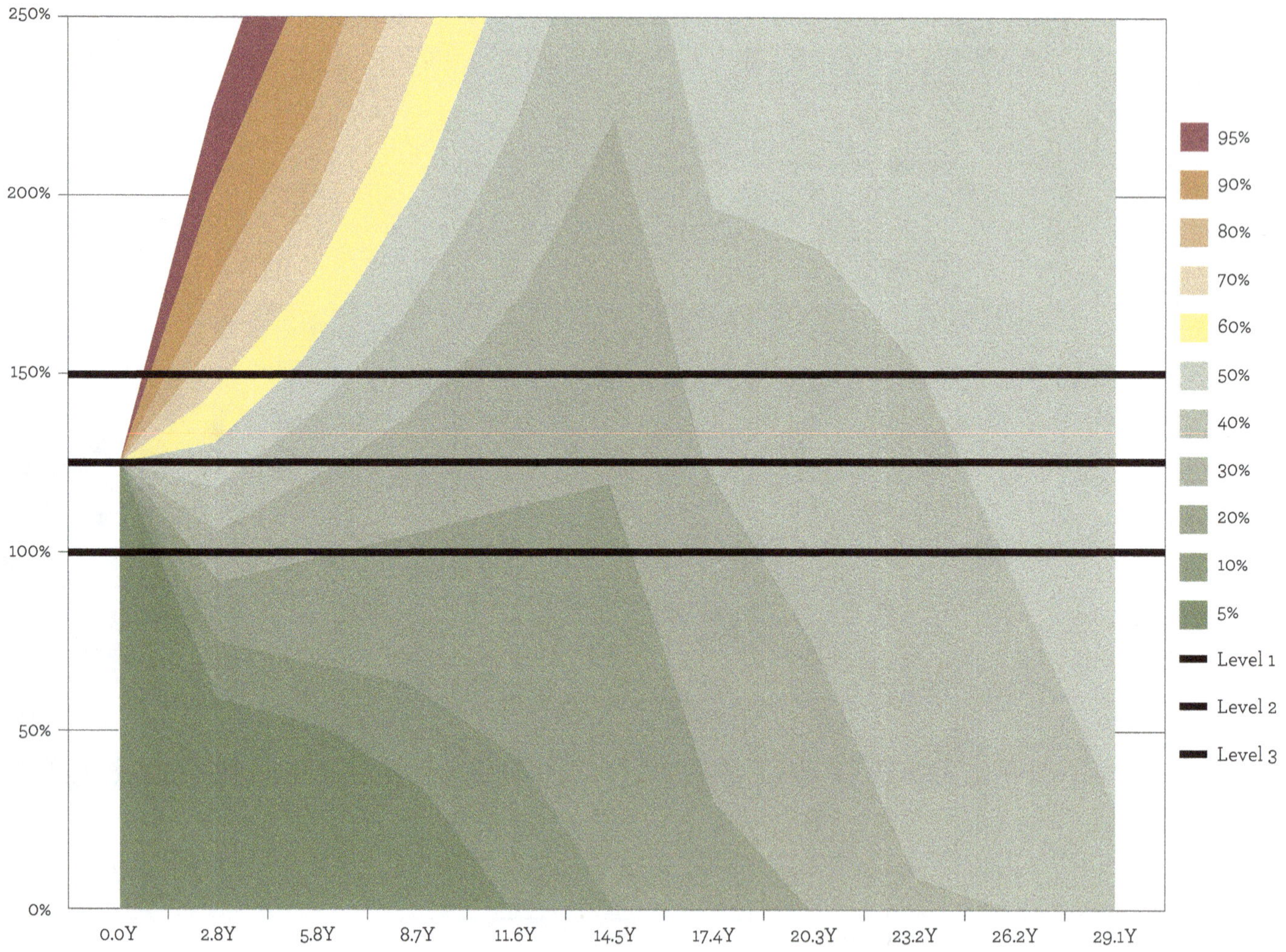

The investor is glad to have taken this brief tour of feasibility ratios because it assures her that:

■ Her retirement-income preferences are, at least for now, feasible

■ There is a mechanism for monitoring future developments to assess the continued prudence and suitability of her spending strategy

The advisor reminds her that the ACR projections provide only an initial glimpse into (1) what might happen to her financial resources (her investment portfolio), (2) what might happen to her liabilities (her spending demands), and (3) their relative valuation. If her spending is in equilibrium with her financial resources, she is solvent; if the value of her assets exceeds the cost of her spending, she exhibits a surplus; if her spending exceeds the value of available resources, she exhibits a deficit. The ACR analysis requires periodic monitoring on both sides of the balance sheet. ACR monitoring and evaluation is a technique for alerting investors that they may be trying to spend more than they have. It is the essence of an asset-liability management system.

The next topic focuses exclusively on income. How much can she spend? How likely is it that a spending target is sustainable? What is the interrelation between spending policy and bequest objectives? The ultimate question to be answered is which spending policy is most preferred by the investor. Will her spending policy jeopardize her bequest objectives? Which spending policy produces the most favorable reward-to-risk trade-offs, i.e., the greatest utility? Upon completing the planning session, the investor will have a multi-dimensional look at retirement as a risky project. She will then be able to tell the advisor what she would like to do.

PART FOUR: PROJECTING FUTURE INCOME

Once the retirement-income risk model indicates that a specific income path is currently feasible, what is the likelihood that it can be sustained? This is the focus of the next section for Case Study 2.

OPTION ONE: DISTRIBUTION OF OUTCOMES FOR $20,000 PER MONTH INFLATION-ADJUSTED LIFETIME INCOME

Assuming an asset allocation of 50-percent stocks/50-percent bonds, the advisor displays the data table for withdrawal option one, which shows projected income (all values in constant dollars). This income strategy is particularly appropriate for investors preferring budgetary certainty, perhaps because they lack spending flexibility or because they value knowing exactly how much income is coming in each month. Option One tracks three fixed spending levels:

- $240,000 annual income ($20,000 constant-dollar monthly spending)
- $222,000 annual income ($18,500 constant-dollar monthly spending)
- $180,000 annual income ($15,000 constant-dollar monthly spending)

The investor may have informally selected the monthly income targets or the income targets may be determined through a more rigorous and systematic analysis of personal spending goals. In Case Study 2, the $240,000 target represents the investor's "aspirational" goals, e.g., extensive travel, entertainment, gifting, etc., the $180,000 target represents the lower-bound or "threshold" monthly spending level required to fund an acceptable standard of living, and the $222,000 target splits the difference.

The retirement-income risk model offers the following information:

DATA TABLE FOR OPTION ONE

	Years from Today										
	0.0Y	2.8Y	5.8Y	8.7Y	11.6Y	14.5Y	17.4Y	20.3Y	23.2Y	26.2Y	29.1Y
95%	$240,000	$240,000	$240,000	$240,000	$240,000	$240,000	$240,000	$240,000	$240,000	$240,000	$240,000
90%	$240,000	$240,000	$240,000	$240,000	$240,000	$240,000	$240,000	$240,000	$240,000	$240,000	$240,000
80%	$240,000	$240,000	$240,000	$240,000	$240,000	$240,000	$240,000	$240,000	$240,000	$240,000	$240,000
70%	$240,000	$240,000	$240,000	$240,000	$240,000	$240,000	$240,000	$240,000	$240,000	$240,000	$240,000
60%	$240,000	$240,000	$240,000	$240,000	$240,000	$240,000	$240,000	$240,000	$240,000	$240,000	$240,000
50%	$240,000	$240,000	$240,000	$240,000	$240,000	$240,000	$240,000	$240,000	$240,000	$240,000	$240,000
40%	$240,000	$240,000	$240,000	$240,000	$240,000	$240,000	$240,000	$240,000	$240,000	$240,000	$240,000
30%	$240,000	$240,000	$240,000	$240,000	$240,000	$240,000	$240,000	$240,000	$240,000	$240,000	$240,000
20%	$240,000	$240,000	$240,000	$240,000	$240,000	$240,000	$240,000	$240,000	$240,000	$205,001	$189,250
10%	$240,000	$240,000	$240,000	$240,000	$240,000	$240,000	$195,541	$139,042	$102,308	$74,820	$56,725
5%	$240,000	$240,000	$240,000	$240,000	$240,000	$219,499	$101,892	$71,049	$57,486	$40,493	$23,173
Level 1	$240,000	$240,000	$240,000	$240,000	$240,000	$240,000	$240,000	$240,000	$240,000	$240,000	$240,000
Level 2	$222,000	$222,000	$222,000	$222,000	$222,000	$222,000	$222,000	$222,000	$222,000	$222,000	$222,000
Level 3	$180,000	$180,000	$180,000	$180,000	$180,000	$180,000	$180,000	$180,000	$180,000	$180,000	$180,000

The income objective is to generate, if possible, $240,000 constant-dollar lifetime annual income payable at the rate of $20,000 per month. Is this goal sustainable? How likely is it that the monthly income dips as low as $18,500, or $15,000? If such an event occurs, when might the income falloff first occur?

As the investor scans the data, answers to some questions present themselves. For the sample population of investors remaining alive in year 14.5 (age ≈ 89), only 5 percent will experience an income shortfall. The far-right column demonstrates the conditional probability of a monthly income below $20,000 at year 29.1 (age ≈ 103) for surviving investors. This occurs at the 40th percentile of the distribution of age 103 income. Indeed, the unconditional probability of complete portfolio depletion during the investor's life span is less than 5 percent as indicated by the positive amount of income in the bottom far-right column cell. From the perspective of an income-only analysis, the $20,000 constant-dollar monthly income spending strategy appears to be a relatively safe bet. Indeed, somewhat tongue-in-cheek, the advisor asserts that, by the law of inequalities, if $240,000 annual spending is a safe bet so, also, are $222,000 and $180,000.

Figure 4.6 confirms this assertion.

FIGURE 4.6: RANGE OF DISTRIBUTION SNAPSHOT, $20,000

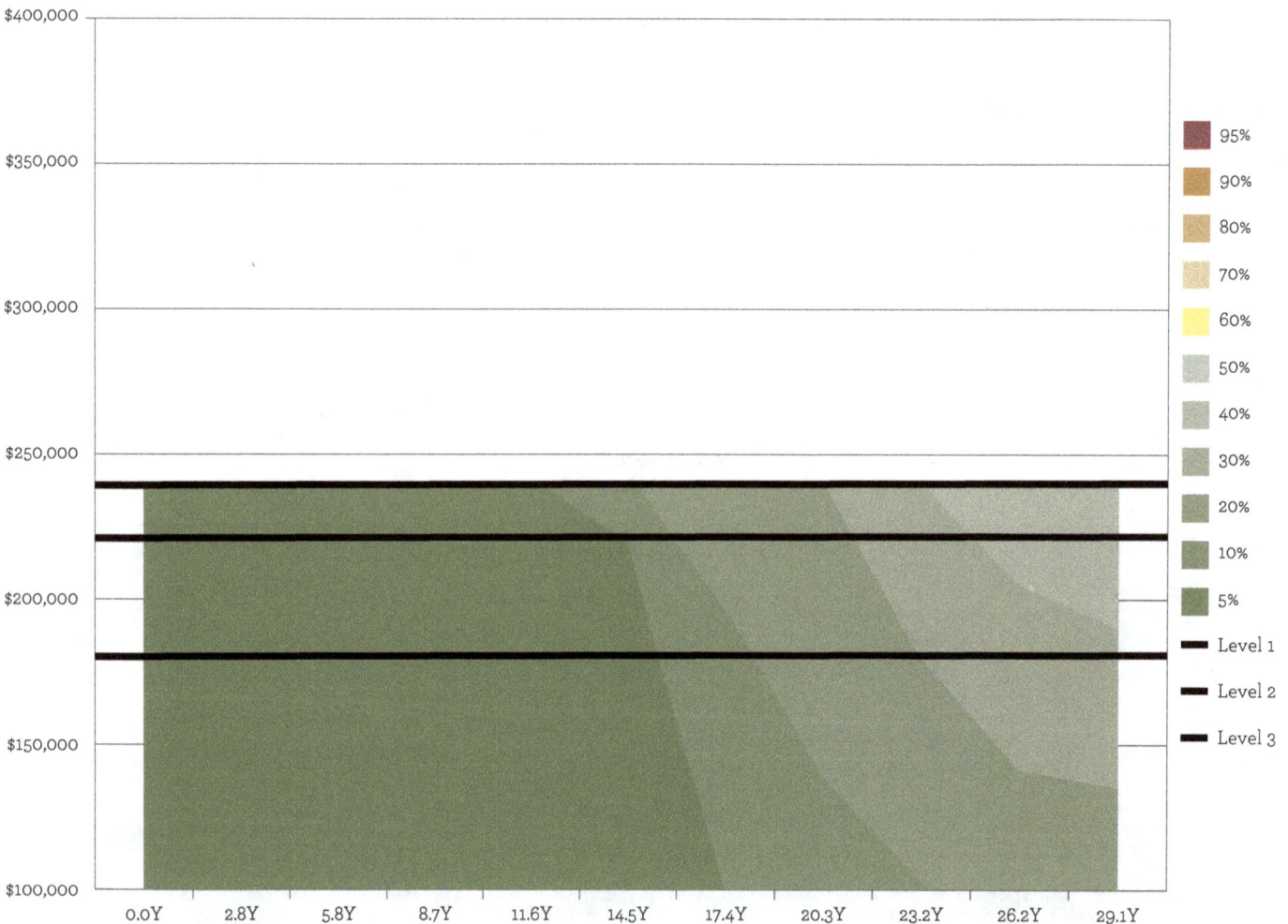

The investor, at first glance, is puzzled that figure 4.6 has no yellow, orange, or maroon components as does table 4.5. The advisor refers to the data table and notes that, in every column throughout the planning horizon, the $240,000 target amount is green (fully funded) at the 40th percentile of results and above. Figure 4.6, which tracks income levels across time, reflects this situation because it shows that the aspirational target succeeds at the 40th percentile of results even if the investor lives to age 103. The "worst case" color for the target corresponds to the 40th percentile color on the legend to the right. If the risk model was rerun to ascertain the success probabilities for generating higher amounts of income, the top horizontal line would move upward—more money is needed each month—with a corresponding decrease in the likelihood that the higher target income level could be sustained. Expressed differently, it would take a relatively low-probability event (< 40-percent likelihood conditional on living approximately thirty years) to knock the income objective off track. Bottom line: Green is good. The advisor explains that the investor can take some comfort because her target income levels remain in the green throughout the applicable planning horizon.

OPTION TWO: DISTRIBUTION OF OUTCOMES FOR A 4.8 PERCENT OF PORTFOLIO VALUE DISTRIBUTION POLICY

What if she opts for a floating rather than a fixed monthly income? The advisor presents the distribution of inflation-adjusted monthly income received by the investor under this election.

DATA TABLE FOR OPTION TWO

	\multicolumn{11}{c}{**Years from Today**}										
	0.0Y	2.8Y	5.8Y	8.7Y	11.6Y	14.5Y	17.4Y	20.3Y	23.2Y	26.2Y	29.1Y
95%	$240,000	$309,336	$361,128	$401,372	$434,352	$459,581	$483,159	$499,976	$520,991	$527,487	$555,217
90%	$240,000	$293,061	$331,579	$356,118	$376,864	$392,494	$407,836	$415,029	$432,080	$424,415	$446,428
80%	$240,000	$275,227	$299,148	$308,997	$317,953	$320,072	$323,937	$327,464	$333,695	$333,875	$323,030
70%	$240,000	$262,389	$275,920	$277,360	$276,631	$276,568	$275,490	$271,151	$265,550	$255,489	$247,640
60%	$240,000	$252,146	$255,764	$251,005	$245,326	$237,402	$232,424	$244,055	$211,558	$210,829	$207,806
50%	$240,000	$241,896	$238,271	$227,893	$217,288	$205,104	$198,760	$185,160	$177,462	$167,263	$170,537
40%	$240,000	$231,914	$220,347	$205,667	$190,181	$177,984	$169,507	$154,939	$146,787	$138,152	$138,869
30%	$240,000	$220,172	$199,839	$180,754	$164,847	$149,545	$138,993	$126,239	$118,230	$111,681	$119,624
20%	$240,000	$203,951	$174,084	$153,471	$136,484	$121,512	$109,764	$98,240	$90,754	$82,699	$84,087
10%	$240,000	$177,920	$142,425	$121,137	$102,340	$89,959	$78,183	$71,063	$64,495	$58,333	$48,291
5%	$240,000	$158,121	$121,780	$97,136	$81,255	$67,552	$59,650	$52,979	$50,315	$45,900	$35,921
Level 1	$240,000	$240,000	$240,000	$240,000	$240,000	$240,000	$240,000	$240,000	$240,000	$240,000	$240,000
Level 2	$222,000	$222,000	$222,000	$222,000	$222,000	$222,000	$222,000	$222,000	$222,000	$222,000	$222,000
Level 3	$180,000	$180,000	$180,000	$180,000	$180,000	$180,000	$180,000	$180,000	$180,000	$180,000	$180,000

After a brief examination, the investor remarks that the range of results is surprisingly broad. If the portfolio performs well in a low-inflation environment, the yearly distributions increase dramatically. The converse is also true. The range of distributable constant-dollar income extends from $309,000 to $158,000 at approximately year 3. Further examination shows, at the 50th percentile of the distribution, the $240,000 yearly aspirational target is not maintained and the percentage-of-portfolio-value distribution election pays out less than the minimum threshold target after year 20.

The advisor notes a trade-off between income sustainability and income sufficiency. Income, albeit at sometimes low levels, continues throughout the investor's life span; however, in some cases it falls well below the threshold target. Although she is attracted to the upside income potential, the investor admits that she is not comfortable with what she considers to be an unacceptable level of downside income risk. She does not, however, rule out this election and she asks to see the corresponding graph (see figure 4.7):

FIGURE 4.7: RANGE OF DISTRIBUTION SNAPSHOT, 4.8%

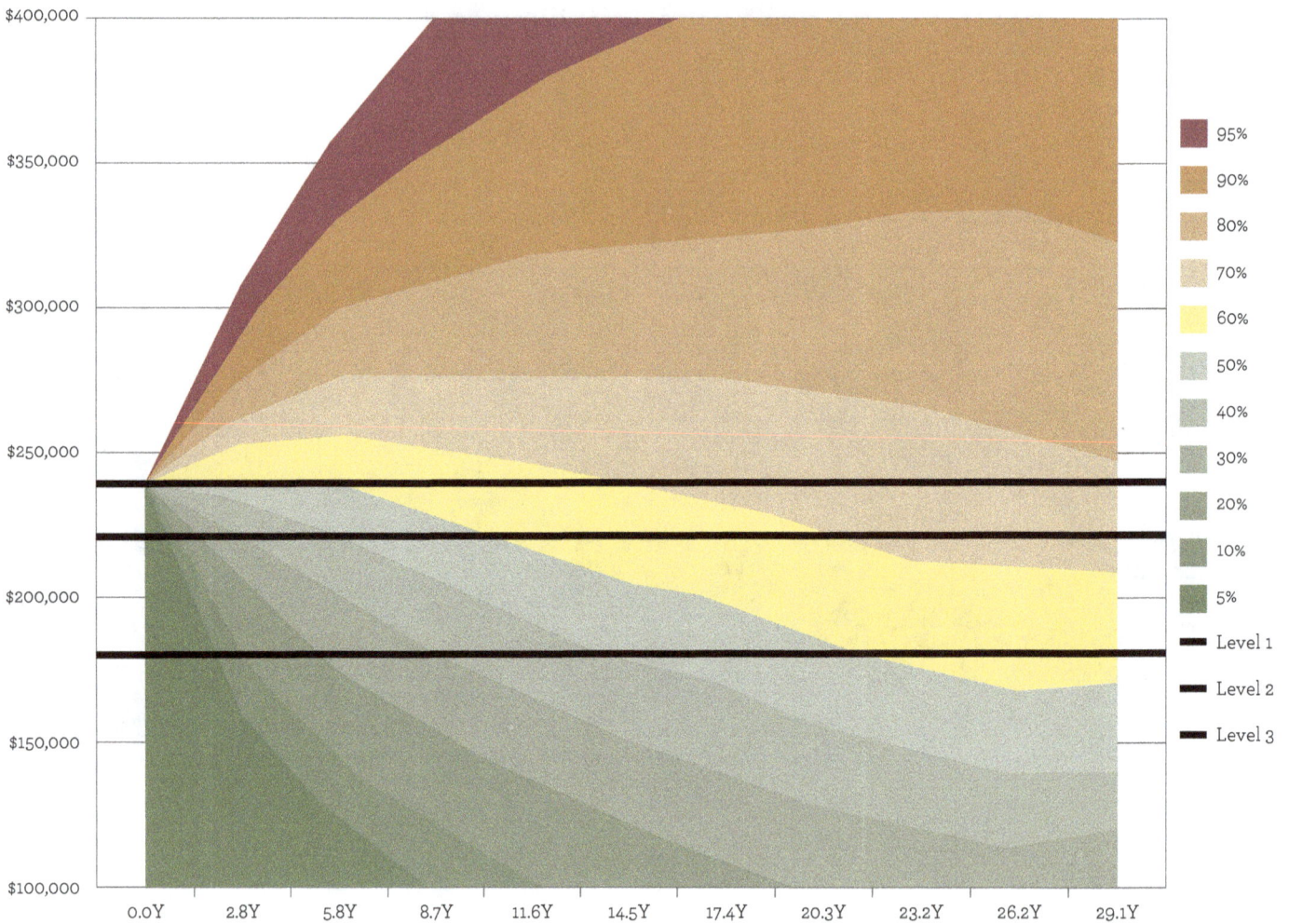

Unlike figure 4.6, which exhibited only green, figure 4.7 has a wider range of color. The higher the target income level, the more likely it is that, at some point in the planning horizon, it will pass through colors signifying a heightened need for awareness (yellow), caution (orange), or danger (maroon).

The advisor indicates that the best way to read figure 4.7 is to draw an imaginary vertical line through the time-period-of-interest. For example, a vertical line extending from the horizontal axis at the 2.8Y point, matches up exactly with the distribution depicted in the data table for option two. Approximately 10 percent of results are in the red, another 10 percent are in the orange, and another 10 percent are in the yellow with respect to the $240,000 annual income target. At a glance, the viewer notices that the ratio of green to other colors becomes less favorable as time progresses. If the investor enjoys a sufficiently long life span, the likelihood that this strategy will provide her target income diminishes. By time-point 23.2 (≈ age 97), the threshold income level enters the yellow. Matching this result against the color-guide on the figure 4.7 legend indicates that there is only an approximately 40-percent likelihood of economic success for the remaining population of long-lived investors.

OPTION THREE: DISTRIBUTION OF OUTCOMES FOR A $120,000 FIXED, INFLATION-ADJUSTED LIFETIME YEARLY INCOME COMBINED WITH A 2.4 PERCENT OF PORTFOLIO VALUE DISTRIBUTION POLICY

The investor is curious about the range of outcomes produced by the retirement-income risk model for a hybrid portfolio withdrawal policy consisting of $10,000 per month, constant-dollar income combined with a 2.4-percent floating percentage-of-portfolio-value withdrawal. The advisor calls her attention to the data table for figure 4.8:

DATA TABLE FOR OPTION THREE

	Years from Today										
	0.0Y	2.8Y	5.8Y	8.7Y	11.6Y	14.5Y	17.4Y	20.3Y	23.2Y	26.2Y	29.1Y
95%	$240,00	$274,765	$304,136	$327,812	$350,466	$373,715	$391,787	$417,983	$441,875	$494,456	$531,604
90%	$240,00	$266,910	$286,976	$302,310	$316,628	$330,873	$340,040	$356,085	$369,593	$389,302	$397,919
80%	$240,00	$257,674	$268,902	$276,464	$282,296	$286,480	$286,535	$290,220	$295,480	$300,577	$318,981
70%	$240,00	$251,266	$257,414	$259,784	$259,970	$257,647	$255,603	$254,904	$255,861	$252,928	$256,850
60%	$240,00	$245,786	$247,026	$245,263	$242,230	$237,601	$231,000	$226,190	$225,254	$216,755	$215,427
50%	$240,00	$240,543	$237,276	$232,823	$226,959	$220,481	$211,712	$204,993	$199,642	$192,308	$187,204
40%	$240,00	$235,297	$227,802	$220,137	$211,820	$203,822	$195,072	$187,910	$179,995	$169,198	$162,056
30%	$240,00	$228,940	$217,470	$206,821	$196,743	$187,436	$178,640	$169,008	$161,079	$150,118	$138,659
20%	$240,00	$220,958	$205,865	$192,507	$182,060	$170,991	$161,172	$152,045	$144,288	$135,262	$123,225
10%	$240,00	$208,012	$189,075	$175,424	$163,210	$151,902	$142,745	$134,288	$127,390	$104,328	$78,532
5%	$240,00	$198,603	$176,738	$162,687	$150,086	$140,376	$130,784	$122,951	$80,426	$49,856	$29,431
Level 1	$240,000	$240,000	$240,000	$240,000	$240,000	$240,000	$240,000	$240,000	$240,000	$240,000	$240,000
Level 2	$222,000	$222,000	$222,000	$222,000	$222,000	$222,000	$222,000	$222,000	$222,000	$222,000	$222,000
Level 3	$180,000	$180,000	$180,000	$180,000	$180,000	$180,000	$180,000	$180,000	$180,000	$180,000	$180,000

The hybrid spending election offers a less-favorable upside income level, but it provides a greater measure of downside protection. For example, the 4.8-percent floating withdrawal option provides a range of annual income in year 14.5 (age ≈ 89) extending from a high of $460,000 to a low of only $68,000. By contrast, the hybrid election is bounded between $374,000 at the 95th percentile and $140,000 at the 5th percentile. The investor opines that she finds this to be a more comfortable range of outcomes.

Figure 4.8 confirms the lower-bound protection for this election. The threshold target ($180,000 constant-dollar annual income) remains in the green throughout the planning horizon. The investor begins to create a tentative order of preference for available options.

FIGURE 4.8: RANGE OF DISTRIBUTION SNAPSHOT, 2.4% + $10,000

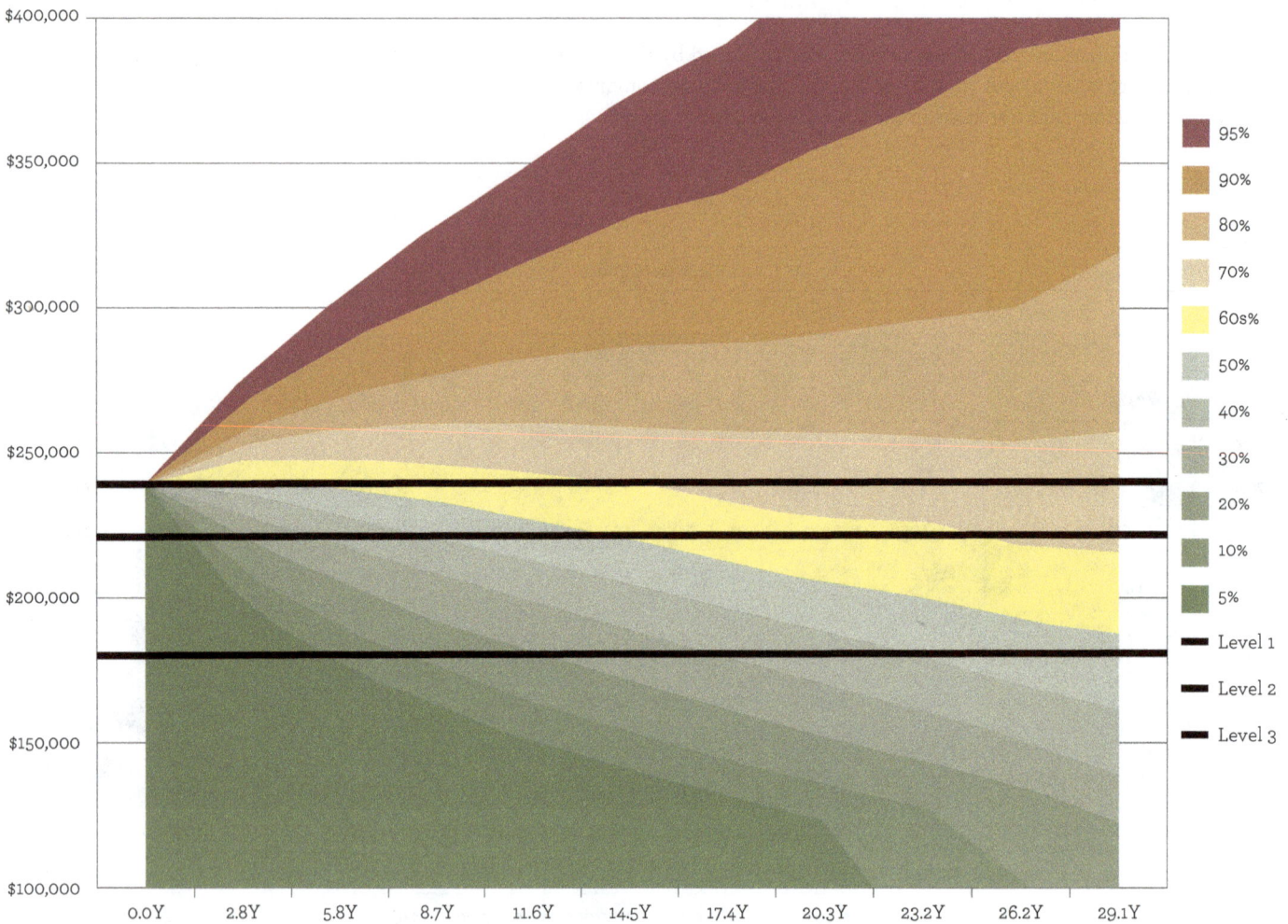

OPTION FOUR: DISTRIBUTION OF OUTCOMES FOR AN INITIAL $360,000, INFLATION-ADJUSTED YEARLY INCOME DECREASING BY $12,000 PER YEAR TO $180,000 INFLATION-ADJUSTED INCOME BY YEAR 15 AND THEREAFTER

The advisor explains that Option Four front loads retirement income so that she has more spending power for near-term consumption such as travel and entertainment. The trade-off is to accept a lower income target in future years when, of course, income is conditional on her survival. The advisor reminds her that the retirement-income model illustrates a starting annual income of $360,000 ($30,000 per month), tapering off gradually over a 15-year period to an annual constant-dollar lifetime income of $180,000 ($15,000 per month) beginning at age 89.[19]

Although success is tracked only in terms of the long-term $180,000 base income target, the data table for figure 4.9 illustrates the efficacy of the spending election throughout most of the planning horizon. Indeed, only at the 5th percentile of the distribution of results at time-point 14.5Y does the election initially fail to provide the targeted glide-path income.

---

19. Given the glide-path income strategy, the calculation algorithm for success in meeting the target income is unique. By design, the withdrawal election forces an income decrease during each of the first 15 years. If the long-term target income level is set to either $360,000 or $240,000, the awareness/caution/danger colors would "bloom" in abundance on the heat-map table and chart. It would appear that significant failures were occurring when, as a matter of fact, the withdrawal election operates as desired.

	Years from Today										
	0.0Y	2.8Y	5.8Y	8.7Y	11.6Y	14.5Y	17.4Y	20.3Y	23.2Y	26.2Y	29.1Y
95%	$360,000	$327,000	$292,000	$257,000	$222,000	$187,000	$180,000	$180,000	$180,000	$180,000	$180,000
90%	$360,000	$327,000	$292,000	$257,000	$222,000	$187,000	$180,000	$180,000	$180,000	$180,000	$180,000
80%	$360,000	$327,000	$292,000	$257,000	$222,000	$187,000	$180,000	$180,000	$180,000	$180,000	$180,000
70%	$360,000	$327,000	$292,000	$257,000	$222,000	$187,000	$180,000	$180,000	$180,000	$180,000	$180,000
60%	$360,000	$327,000	$292,000	$257,000	$222,000	$187,000	$180,000	$180,000	$180,000	$180,000	$180,000
50%	$360,000	$327,000	$292,000	$257,000	$222,000	$187,000	$180,000	$180,000	$180,000	$180,000	$180,000
40%	$360,000	$327,000	$292,000	$257,000	$222,000	$187,000	$180,000	$180,000	$180,000	$180,000	$180,000
30%	$360,000	$327,000	$292,000	$257,000	$222,000	$187,000	$180,000	$180,000	$180,000	$175,332	$163,682
20%	$360,000	$327,000	$292,000	$257,000	$222,000	$187,000	$180,000	$180,000	$148,358	$118,876	$108,945
10%	$360,000	$327,000	$292,000	$257,000	$222,000	$187,000	$135,579	$95,211	$73,870	$60,459	$46,460
5%	$360,000	$327,000	$292,000	$257,000	$222,000	$117,733	$74,328	$49,175	$37,553	$29,767	$18,838
Level 1	$180,000	$180,000	$180,000	$180,000	$180,000	$180,000	$180,000	$180,000	$180,000	$180,000	$180,000
Level 2	$0	$0	$0	$0	$0	$0	$0	$0	$0	$0	$0
Level 3	$0	$0	$0	$0	$0	$0	$0	$0	$0	$0	$0

The front-loaded spending election fails for only a handful of long-term surviving investors and, as will be demonstrated shortly, it pays off handsomely for short-lived investors.

Although figure 4.9 confirms the prudence and feasibility of this election, it nevertheless requires a bit of explanation. Figure 4.9 assumes that the investor withdraws the threshold target income level of $180,000 inflation-adjusted income in each year. At this level of income, figure 4.9 shows the target income level passing continuously through the green safety region. Furthermore, the chart indicates the additional front-loaded income distributions and the investor's preferred glide path. Close inspection confirms the prudence (feasibility) and sustainability of this income election.[20]

20. On a technical note, this spending election decreases monthly distributions over 15 years by $1,000 per month ($12,000 per year), but it increases distributions to keep pace with inflation. Implementation is not trivial because it requires a well-designed monitoring system. An investor, during the period of a step-down in spending, needs to decrease the previous month's withdrawal amount by (in this case) $1,000 (not adjusted for inflation), and then make an inflation adjustment.

A hypothetical client income-calculation system, using constant inflation realizations of 3.5 percent, is as follows:

$360,000	Nominal					Inflation		0.035	Inflation Adjustment				
Month	Dist		Year	Dist		Current Inflation	Inflation Index		Month	Dist		Year	Dist
1	$30,000					0.00292	1.00292		1	$30,000			
2	$29,917					0.00292	1.00583		2	$30,004			
3	$29,833					0.00292	1.00875		3	$30,007			
4	$29,750					0.00292	1.01167		4	$30,010			
5	$29,667					0.00292	1.01458		5	$30,013			
6	$29,583					0.00292	1.01750		6	$30,015			
7	$29,500					0.00292	1.02042		7	$30,016			
8	$29,417					0.00292	1.02333		8	$30,017			
9	$29,333					0.00292	1.02625		9	$30,018			
10	$29,250					0.00292	1.02917		10	$30,018			
11	$29,167					0.00292	1.03208		11	$30,017			
12	$29,083		1	$354,500		0.00292	1.03500		12	$30,016		1	$360,152
13	$29,000					0.00292	1.03792		13	$30,015			
14	$28,917					0.00292	1.04083		14	$30,013			
15	$28,833					0.00292	1.04375		15	$30,011			
16	$28,750					0.00292	1.04667		16	$30,008			
17	$28,667					0.00292	1.04958		17	$30,004			
18	$28,583					0.00292	1.05250		18	$30,001			
19	$28,500					0.00292	1.05542		19	$29,996			
20	$28,417					0.00292	1.05833		20	$29,991			
21	$28,333					0.00292	1.06125		21	$29,986			
22	$28,250					0.00292	1.06417		22	$29,980			
23	$28,167					0.00292	1.06708		23	$29,974			
24	$28,083		2	$342,500		0.00292	1.07000		24	$29,967		2	$359,947

Interestingly, starting with $360,000 and, assuming a constant future 3.5-percent inflation rate, actual dollar-value spending remains close to $360,000. The income-tracking system reports a need to send $359,947 to the client in year 2. Furthermore, the risk model assumes inflation is stochastic rather than constant. The hypothetical calculation of income further assumes that inflation is additive rather than multiplicative. This is a first glimpse into the intricacies of portfolio monitoring and evaluation requirements.

MONITORING A FRONT-LOADED INCOME DISTRIBUTION ELECTION

FIGURE 4.9: RANGE OF DISTRIBUTION SNAPSHOT—$30,000 DECREASES TO $15,000

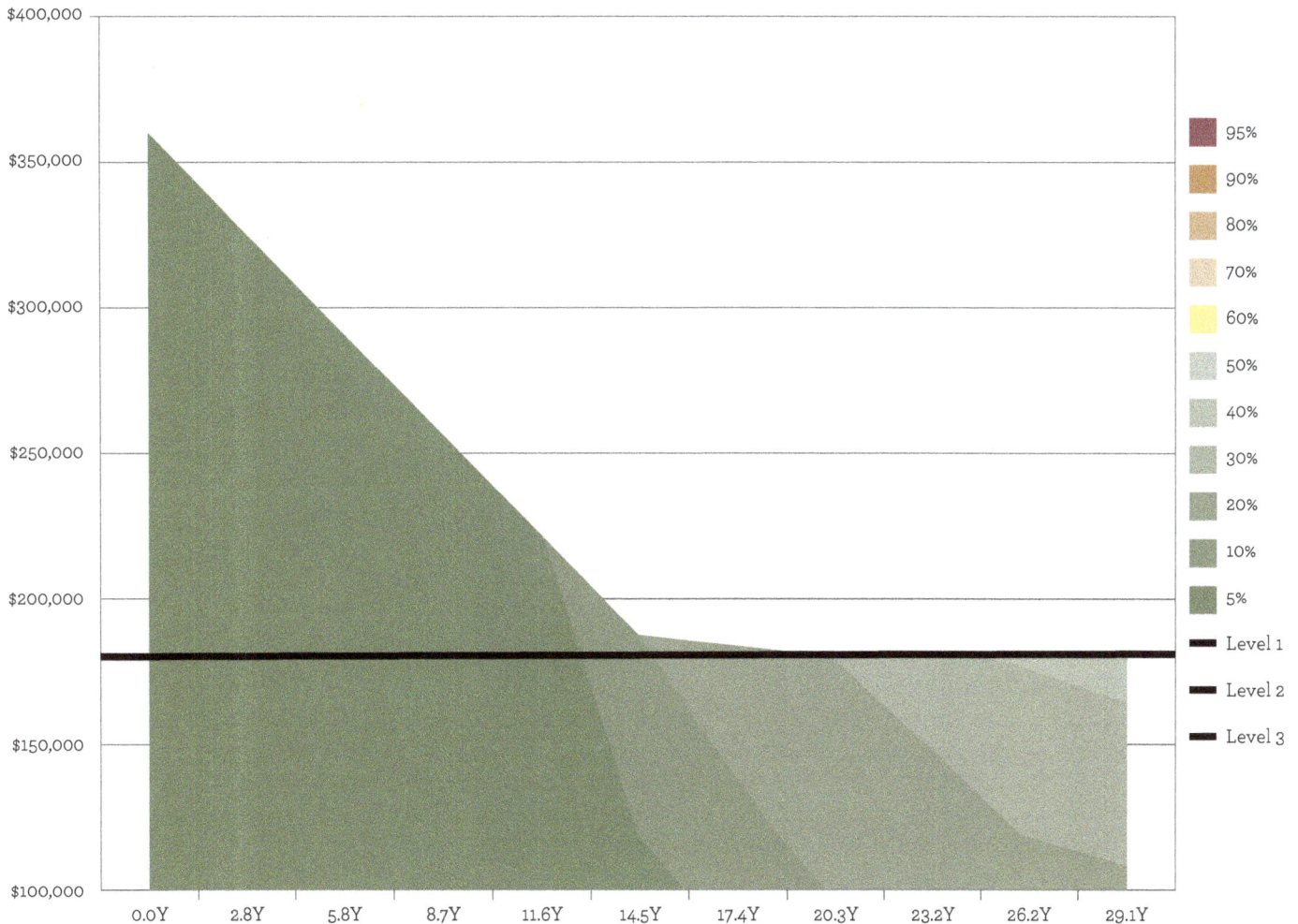

ADDITIONAL RISK METRICS

Before moving on to the investor's bequest-to-grandchildren goal, the advisor asks permission to present a table comparing "The Annualized Distributions over the Life of Simulation Trials." This output tracks, for each of the 10,000 trials: (1) how long a simulated investor survives, and (2) how much annual income, on average, each investor receives from 'time zero' through the 'end of the trial' (end of trial = end of investor's life span = month of investor death). It is an important measure of income stability as opposed to principal stability. For example, assuming an election to withdraw $240,000 per year in inflation-adjusted dollars, the remaining principal after, say, five years, will differ significantly across the range of portfolio values. However, it is less likely that the population of investors surviving for the full five-year period will experience significant income variation across the range of withdrawal values. Investors interested primarily in the amount and stability of lifetime income, as opposed to the amount and stability of principal, find this to be a helpful risk metric.

ANNUALIZED DISTRIBUTIONS OVER THE LIFE OF SIMULATION TRIALS

Once again, there is an opportunity to examine the range of possible results in both favorable and unfavorable environments. For investors surviving only a few years, odds are that their portfolios will fully support their lifetime income targets unless, of course, either income demands are wildly unreasonable or the portfolio is invested primarily in Enron stock. For investors enjoying a long life span, poor investment results or high inflation might undercut the portfolio's capacity for sustainable income at the target level. By contrast, good results show them merrily spending throughout retirement.

The advisor averages the annualized income over the range of distribution results bounded by the 80th percentile of annual income received over the "life of the trial" (best case) and the 10th percentile of annual income received over the investor's life span (worst case):

AVERAGE ANNUALIZED INCOME AT VARIOUS PERCENTILES OF SIMULATED OUTCOMES

Variable of Interest	Percentile	20K Fixed Spending	4.8% of Corpus	10K Fixed / 2.4% of Corpus	30K decrease to 15K over 15 years
Annualized Distributions: Life of Trial	80th percentile	$240,000	$283,698	$263,003	$312,500
Annualized Distributions: Life of Trial	50th percentile	$240,000	$233,649	$235,842	$275,500
Annualized Distributions: Life of Trial	30th percentile	$240,000	$200,161	$217,127	$255,412
Annualized Distributions: Life of Trial	20th percentile	$240,000	$177,654	$204,933	$247,310
Annualized Distributions: Life of Trial	10th percentile	$239,943	$149,705	$188,168	$238,384

There are several noteworthy observations:

1. At the median (50th percentile) of the $20,000 fixed-spending distribution, the investor can expect to receive $20,000 per month (annualized to $240,000 per year) constant-dollar income for life. It is not until the 10th percentile of results that the investment program fails to provide her aspirational income target. However, the drop-off from aspirational target is slight. This indicates: (1) Only a handful of investors will run out of funds having selected the "20K Fixed Spending" election and, (2) having kept it on auto-pilot from time zero, the condition of "run-out-of-money" occurs many years into the future. On average, even these few myopic souls will have realized an attractive income level for many years.

2. By contrast, the "4.8% Of Corpus" election allows yearly income to float as the portfolio fluctuates in value. This election tends to preserve bequest and gift-oriented goals at the expense of income stability. Above the 50th percentile of the distribution of income, the investor enjoys excess spendable income relative to her aspirational target, however, below the 50th percentile, her average annualized income diminishes. At the 20th percentile, the investor receives, on average, less than her designated threshold target.

3. The "10K Fixed / 2.4% of Corpus" election remedies the likelihood of generating average lifetime, below-target, spendable income. At the 80th percentile (good results) the investor benefits from excess income. At the 10th percentile (bad results) surviving investors receive, across their life spans, an annualized income above the threshold target level.

4. Finally, the "30K decreases to 15K over 15 Years" election provides interesting insights into the interrelation between mortality and income. At the 80th percentile, the investor receives a $312,500 annualized average lifetime income. Unlike the cross-section of investors at the 80th percentile of the distributional range for the "4.8% Of Corpus" election who receive large monthly checks because of long-term favorable investment results, the cross-section of investors at the 80th percentile of the distributional range for the "30K decreases to 15K over 15 Years" election had short life spans.[21] Brevity risk is precisely why some investors prefer to front load retirement income. Even at the less favorable percentiles of the income distribution range, the investor can expect to enjoy a favorable average lifetime income.

---

21. We think it unlikely that implementation of the front-loaded spending strategy caused this cross-section of simulated investors to experience an early demise. The average 80th-percentile income, $312,500, is greater than the $275,500 50th-percentile income because investors died before year 15, i.e., they "won" their front-loaded distribution bet.

RISK, UTILITY, AND INVESTOR OBJECTIVES

The advisor recognizes that the investor has two primary objectives:

1. Adequate lifetime income

2. Bequests for grandchildren

He restates the objectives and explains that there exists a tension between them. The greater the amount of lifetime income withdrawn from the portfolio, the less will be the bequest to grandchildren, all else being equal. Initially, the investor guesstimated that her utility function weights lifetime income at its full dollar value, but weights bequests at only 25 cents on the dollar. That is to say, a dollar of spendable income is worth four dollars of bequest according to her subjective preferences. Four-to-one is the balance point at which the investor's preferences are equally satisfied provided her threshold income requirements are fulfilled.

The advisor reminds her that, thus far, they have evaluated tests for both feasibility and sustainability of adequate lifetime income. He now plans to work through the economic consequences of various spending strategies in terms of her specific personal objectives. His goals are to provide her with an opportunity to confirm or modify her preferences and rank spending strategy options according to her personal preference criteria.

In a nutshell, he asks the investor to consider which election is the best fit for her.

He begins by showing her the following table:

LIFETIME CONSUMPTION AT SELECTED PERCENTILES

Investor Goal	Variable(s) of Interest	Percentile	20K Fixed Spending	4.8% of Corpus	10K Fixed / 2.4% of Corpus	30K decrease to 15K over 15 years
Lifetime Spending	Total Consumption	70th percentile	$4,360,000	$4,233,059	$4,317,801	$4,596,521
Lifetime Spending	Total Consumption	50th percentile	$3,484,197	$3,125,572	$3,381,956	$3,902,917
Lifetime Spending	Total Consumption	30th percentile	$2,540,000	$2,224,368	$2,455,962	$3,099,967

In this case, the variable of interest is "Total Consumption." Which spending strategy generates the greatest amount of spendable dollars throughout the investor's life span? To maintain manageable focus, the advisor illustrates results at the 70th, 50th (median), and 30th percentiles of the total consumption distribution.[22]

The investor calculates the following rank order [1 = best; 4 = worst] at each percentile:

1. The $30,000 per month decreasing spending election has rank 1 at each percentile.

2. The $20,000 per month fixed spending election has rank 2 at each percentile.

3. The $10,000 per month fixed spending combined with the floating 2.4 percent of portfolio value spending election has rank 3 at each percentile.

4. The floating 4.8 percent of portfolio value spending election has rank 4 at each percentile.

The investor remarks that she finds the above information to be interesting on its face, and helpful in establishing a "pecking order" for her decision-making.

The advisor next presents information about the range of possible bequests to grandchildren:

---

22. Technically, total or aggregate consumption reflects the interaction of several variables including inflation realizations, investment results, amounts available for withdrawal under the spending strategy algorithms, and longevity. The trial results from a well-performing retirement portfolio management strategy may end up in a low percentile simply because the investor suffered an early demise, i.e., did not live long enough to do much spending. Trial results from a less-efficient strategy may end up in a higher percentile simply because the investor was long lived. Investors seek the answer to the question: "Which spending strategy produces the most money?" Unfortunately, this requires the investor to answer simultaneously the question: "How long will I live?" All table values are in constant dollars.

BEQUEST AMOUNTS AT SELECTED PERCENTILES

Investor Goal	Variable of Interest	Percentile	20K Fixed Spending	4.8% of Corpus	10K Fixed / 2.4% of Corpus	30K decrease to 15K over 15 years
Bequest Objective	Portfolio Value	50th percentile	$4,278,031	$4,502,426	$4,334,421	$3,617,219
Bequest Objective	Portfolio Value	30th percentile	$2,426,530	$3,246,297	$2,885,251	$1,958,932
Bequest Objective	Portfolio Value	20th percentile	$1,308,599	$2,542,073	$2,034,468	$975,585
Bequest Objective	Portfolio Value	10th percentile	$—	$1,787,683	$1,028,117	$—

The analysis considers only the lower half of the distribution of bequest outcomes under each spending strategy. The advisor points out that the 50th percentile represents the median value and that the grandchildren will receive greater bequest amounts if the retirement portfolio management results exceed the median. What is of primary concern, however, is the risk to the investor's bequest objective should the portfolio achieve below-median results. In this case, the advisor depicts outcomes at the 50th, 30th, 20th, and 10th percentiles.[23]

After a few moments, the investor remarks that she now understands the implications of the advisor's statement that her goals may be conflicting. She notes that both the $20,000 fixed monthly option and the $30,000 monthly decreasing option leave no bequest value at the 10th percentile. She calculates the following rank order at each percentile:

1. The floating 4.8 percent of portfolio value spending election has rank 1 at each percentile.
2. The $10,000 per month fixed spending combined with the floating 2.4 percent of portfolio value spending election has rank 2 at each percentile.
3. The $20,000 per month fixed spending election has rank 3 at each percentile.
4. The $30,000 per month decreasing spending election has rank 4 at each percentile.

The "pecking order" is reversed. More lifetime spending means less money for the grandchildren.

Do the consumption or bequest outcomes prompt the investor to change her preference weightings? While discussing this question, the advisor reminds her that the outcomes assume that her initial spending strategy election continues without modification throughout her lifetime. An adequate monitoring and surveillance program, however, can alert her to unfavorable results before they reach a point of no return. Unlike a lemming who is condemned to walk over a cliff, she has the flexibility to modify her initial retirement-portfolio management elections. Ultimately, she decides that the original dollar weightings are a fair representation of her current preferences.

Having received this input, the advisor presents the table below. He explains that it combines her individual preferences over critical goals so that she can make an informed decision regarding her preferred strategy:

---

23. Portfolio value is the terminal value in the month prior to the investor's death.

TOTAL UTILITY—COMBINED CONSUMPTION AND BEQUEST PREFERENCES

Investor Goal	Variable(s) of Interest	Percentile	20K Fixed Spending	4.8% of Corpus	10K Fixed / 2.4% of Corpus	30K decrease to 15K over 15 years
Lifetime Spending	Total Consumption	70th percentile	$4,360,000	$4,233,059	$4,317,801	$4,596,521
Lifetime Spending	Total Consumption	50th percentile	$3,484,197	$3,125,572	$3,381,956	$3,902,917
Lifetime Spending	Total Consumption	30th percentile	$2,540,000	$2,224,368	$2,455,962	$3,099,967
Bequest	Bequest Adjusted Portfolio Value	70th percentile	$1,459,595	$1,420,970	$1,422,909	$1,290,570
Bequest	Bequest Adjusted Portfolio Value	50th percentile	$1,069,508	$1,125,606	$1,083,605	$904,305
Bequest	Bequest Adjusted Portfolio Value	30th percentile	$606,632	$811,574	$721,313	$489,733
Total Utility	Consumption + Bequest	70th percentile	$5,819,595	$5,654,029	$5,740,710	$5,887,091
Total Utility	Consumption + Bequest	50th percentile	$4,553,705	$4,251,178	$4,465,561	$4,807,222
Total Utility	Consumption + Bequest	30th percentile	$3,146,632	$3,035,942	$3,177,275	$3,589,700

The first three rows of data recap the information on total lifetime consumption. The middle three rows adjust the economic value of bequests according to her preference weights. The bottom three rows provide the total economic satisfaction (utility) derived from each strategy where satisfaction sums total consumption plus utility-adjusted bequest values.

The bottom three rows allow the investor to establish her order of preference for aggregated results:

TOTAL UTILITY OF WITHDRAWAL STRATEGIES

Investor Goal	Variable(s) of Interest	Percentile	20K Fixed Spending	4.8% of Corpus	10K Fixed / 2.4% of Corpus	30K decrease to 15K over 15 years
Total Utility	Consumption + Bequest	70th percentile	2	4	3	1
Total Utility	Consumption + Bequest	50th percentile	2	4	3	1
Total Utility	Consumption + Bequest	30th percentile	3	4	2	1

The investor observes that the rank order does not remain exactly uniform across all percentiles, but the $30,000-per-month decreasing election dominates the other choices. This said, the magnitude of its dominance is slight and the investor finds it somewhat remarkable that the utility-adjusted values of spending elections are so close to each other. She opines that she has a slight preference for the $30,000-per-month decreasing election based on the information she has seen thus far.

The advisor is pleased with the investor's progress up a rather steep learning curve. He now wishes to focus the discussion on some important risk metrics that will form the basis of an ongoing risk-monitoring and portfolio evaluation system unfolding over future years. Initial (time zero) risk metric values are as follows:

RISK METRICS

Risk Metric	20K Fixed Spending	4.8% of Corpus	10K Fixed / 2.4% of Corpus	30K decrease to 15K over 15 years
Likelihood Monthly Distribution ever falls below $15,000 (Inflation, Adjusted)	19.1%	48.2%	27.6%	20.9%
Likelihood Portfolio loses > 10% in first 12-months	14.7%	14.0%	14.0%	17.7%
Likelihood Portfolio loses > 20% in *any* 12-months	47.4%	45.6%	46.4%	50.9%
Likelihood Portfolio suffers > 40% peak to trough drawdown	33.7%	26.8%	30.2%	38.6%
% of investors surviving for 15 years and with $0 portfolio value	3.3%	0.0%	0.4%	5.2%
% of investors surviving for 20 years and with $0 portfolio value	4.6%	0.0%	1.1%	5.3%
% of investors with $0 portfolio value at end of life	10.6%	0.0%	3.1%	12.0%

The advisor tells the investor that the first four rows of data represent unconditional probability: Over all 10,000 trials and throughout every percentile of the distribution of outcomes, the cell values reflect the likelihood that the risk metric of interest ever manifests itself. Given the operation of each spending strategy, the least risky election expressed in terms of a failure to provide a $15,000 monthly income is the fixed spending policy. By contrast, the floating percentage spending election is most likely to produce monthly income that drifts below a $15,000 constant-dollar monthly income.

Each of the other "likelihood" measures can be interpreted similarly. Each election carries a risk of the portfolio declining by more than 10 percent (after taking withdrawals into account). The risk model estimates this downside probability to be between 14 percent and 18 percent during the initial 12 months of operation. More eye catching, however, are the risks that, in any 12-month time period, the portfolio can decline in value by more than 20 percent (after withdrawals). This risk metric is between 45 percent and 51 percent. Peak to trough (after withdrawals), the risk model estimates the likelihood of a decline greater than 40 percent is between 27 percent and 39 percent over the planning horizon. Irrespective of the spending election the investor chooses, given a 50-percent stock/50-percent bond allocation, she should expect volatility of investment principal.

The investor remains concerned about running out of money during her lifetime. One of the annual spending strategies—withdraw 4.8 percent of portfolio value—is designed, in part, to avoid this outcome. Likewise, the hybrid spending election—withdraw a fixed, inflation-adjusted $120,000 per year plus 2.4 percent of portfolio value—is designed, in part, to mitigate the probability of this outcome. At the 10th percentile of the distribution of final wealth, i.e., money available for bequests, both spending elections show terminal wealth amounts greater than $1 million adjusted for inflation. By contrast, spending strategies one (withdraw $20,000 per month in constant dollars) and four (withdraw a monthly amount starting at $30,000 and decreasing to $15,000 in constant dollars) exhibit zero bequest values at the 10th percentile of the distribution of final wealth. This means that, sometime before the investor's death, the withdrawal election, assuming it operates without modifications throughout the entire horizon, forced the portfolio's value to $0.

VARIABILITY OF MONTHLY INCOME: MARKET AGNOSTIC

Thus far, the advisor has focused primarily on lifetime consumption. By contrast, this section focuses on the variability of periodic income throughout the planning horizon. Specifically, the advisor presents a snapshot of the withdrawals of monthly income at 60, 120, 240, and 300 months. He explains that the graphic illustrations group each spending election into five columns. Each column represents the amount of money withdrawn from the portfolio with the "best case" (70th percentile of the distribution) in the far-left column, followed by withdrawals at the 50th, 30th, 10th, and 5th percentiles. He reminds the investor that the evolution of spending over time assumes that all initial portfolio elections remain on autopilot.

Figures 4.10, 4.11, 4.12, and 4.13 depict results from a market-agnostic perspective:

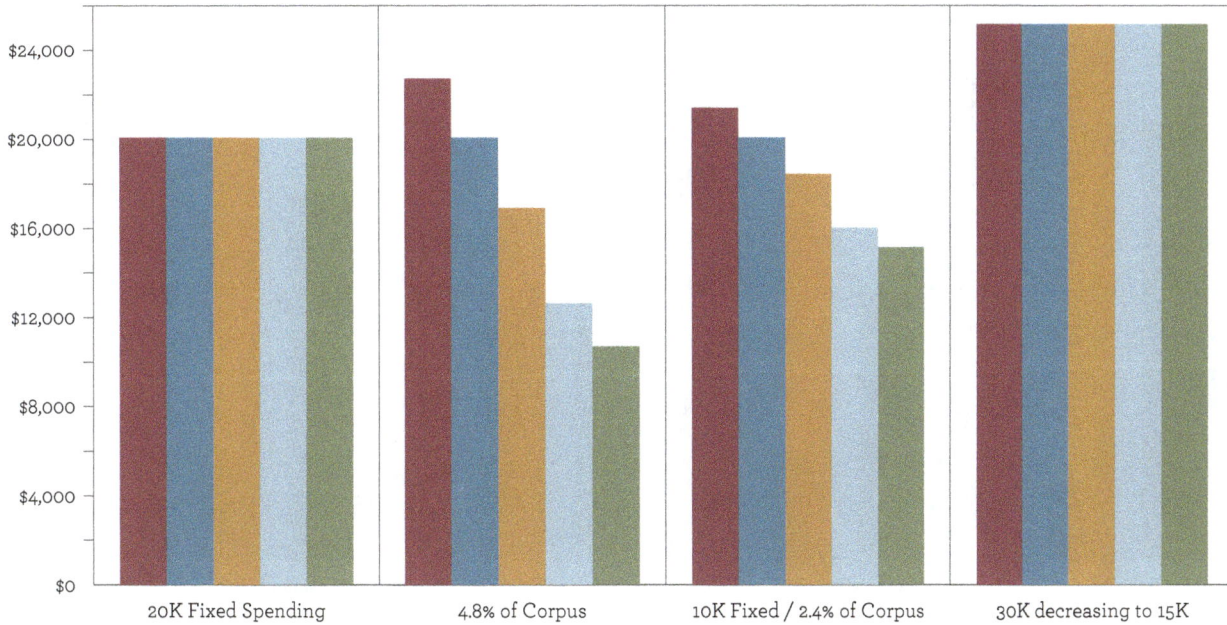

At month 60, the fixed spending and back-loaded spending elections provide the target income across the entire distribution of outcomes. The floating percentage elections provide a wider range of outcomes. By month 60, the 4.8 percent of corpus election provides income below the $15,000 per month threshold at both the 5th and the 10th percentiles.

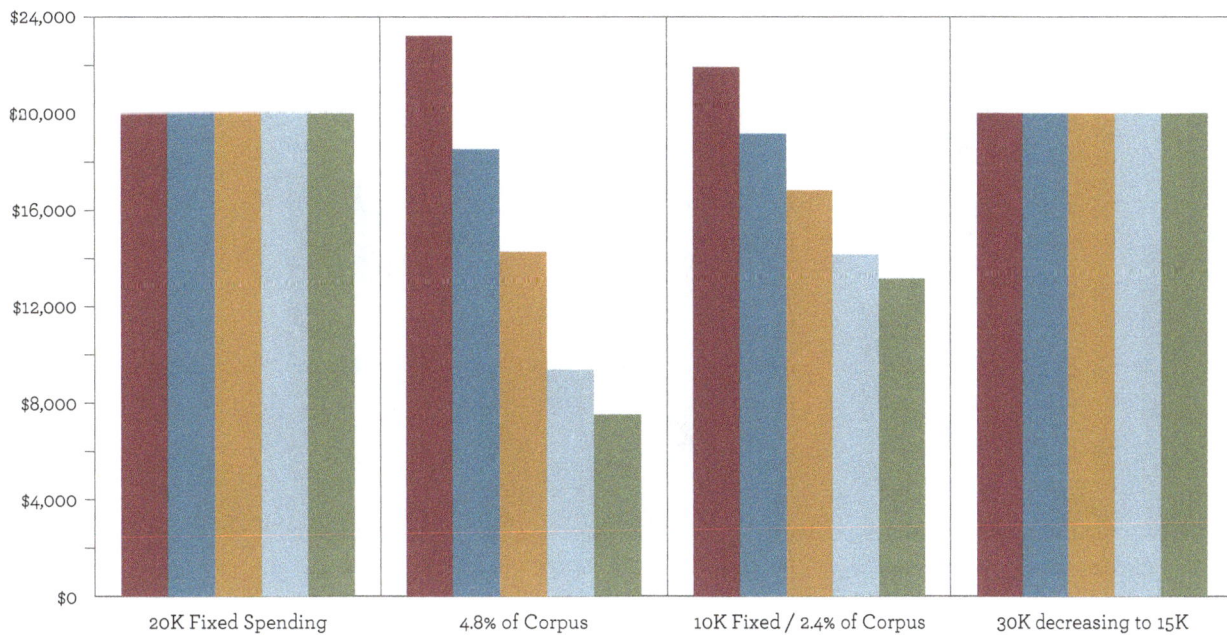

By month 120 the only significant change is the wider dispersion of results from the percentage-of-corpus spending elections. For example, although the 4.8-percent election now generates a projected $23,000 per month, the income fails to exceed the threshold target at 30th percentile of the distribution and below. At the 5th percentile, monthly income is approximately $7,500 per month for the 4.8 percent of corpus and $13,000 for the hybrid spending election.

FIGURE 4.12: INCOME VARIABILITY—240 MONTHS

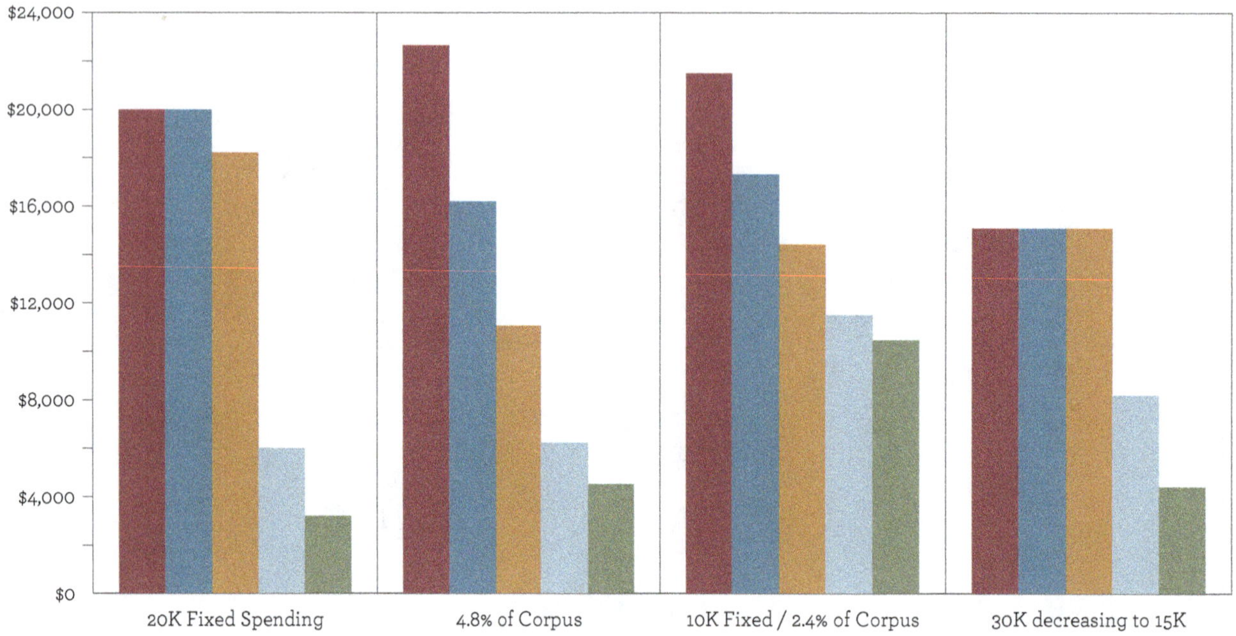

By the 240th month, the inflation-adjusted, fixed-budget spending elections are not providing target income at all percentiles. Interestingly, only the hybrid spending election produces a projected monthly income above $10,000 at the 5th percentile and above.

FIGURE 4.13: INCOME VARIABILITY—300 MONTHS (AGE 99)

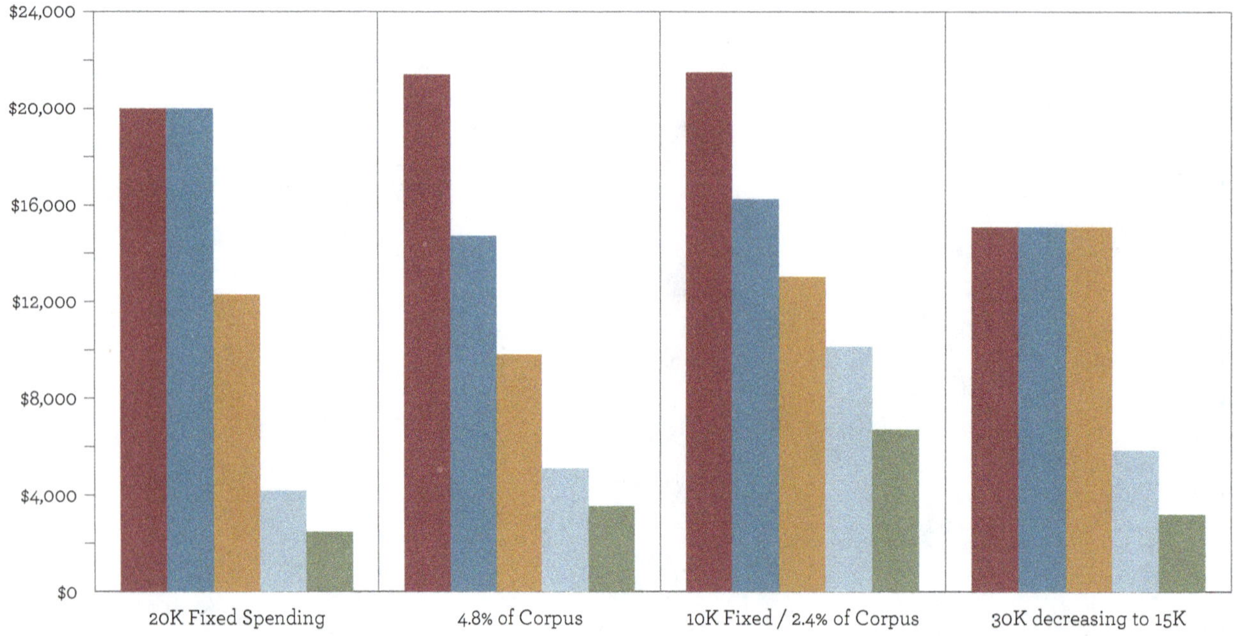

By age 99, absent any change in asset management elections, investment or inflation results below expectation may have a profound impact on spending. At the 50th percentile (median results) only the 4.8-percent spending election produces an amount less than the threshold $15,000 target ($14,638). Only the $30,000 decreasing election produces a projected monthly income of $15,000 above the 30th percentile.

The advisor now turns the investor's attention to projected outcomes that assume an immediate start to a bear market regime.

VARIABILITY OF INCOME: BEAR MARKET

FIGURE 4.14: INCOME VARIABILITY—BEAR MARKET START 60 MONTHS

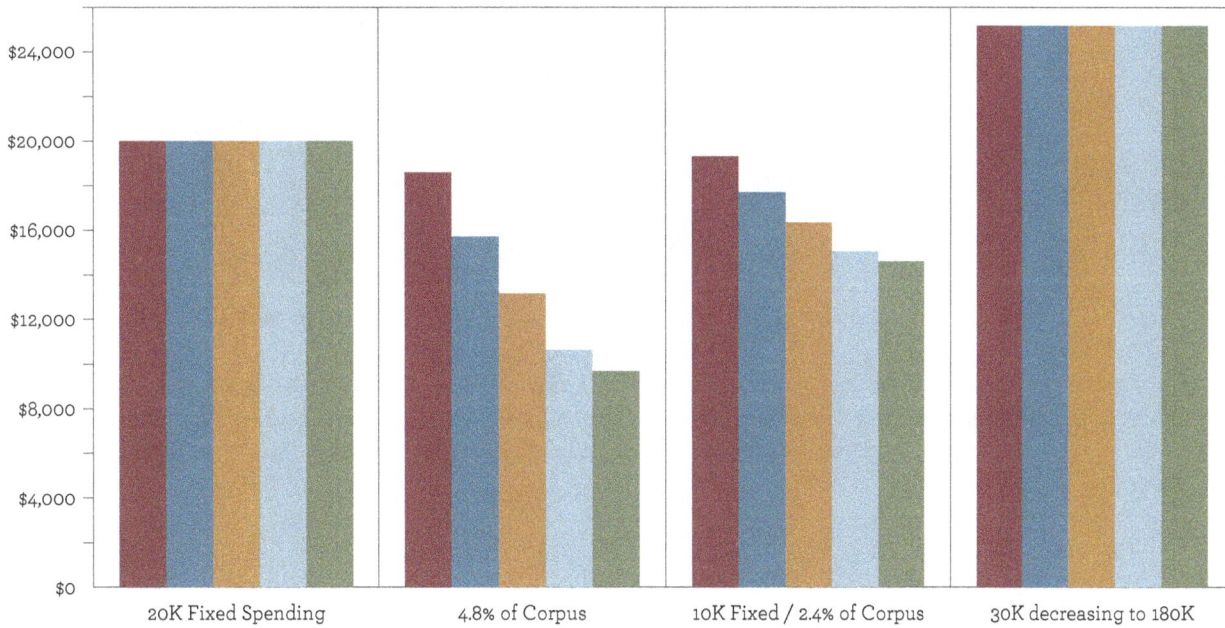

Examination of spending at month 60 indicates little effect of an initial bear market (see figure 4.14). The 5th percentile results for the 4.8 percent of corpus election indicates a decrease in monthly spending from $10,616 in the market-agnostic risk model to $9,648 in the start-bear risk model. For "best case" results, the 4.8-percent election produces an income of $22,618 at the market-agnostic 70th percentile compared with $18,566 at the start-bear 70th percentile.

FIGURE 4.15: INCOME VARIABILITY—BEAR MARKET START 120 MONTHS

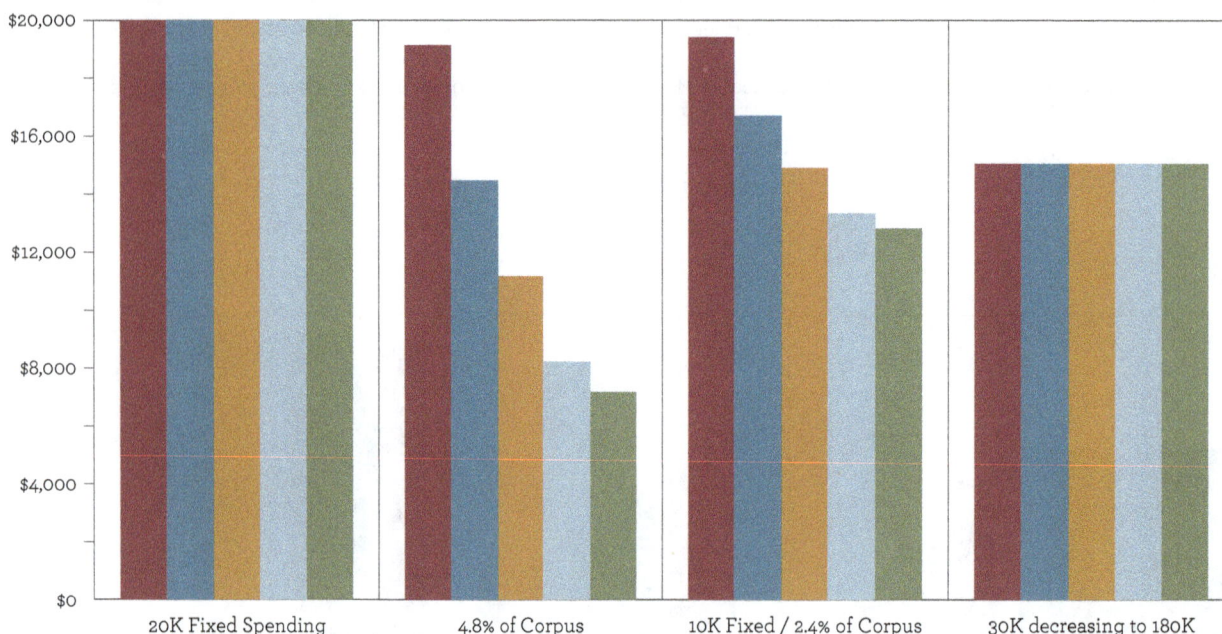

Likewise, the middle groupings of spending elections evidence a bit of a drop off at each percentile (see figure 4.15). For example, 50th-percentile income drops from market-agnostic risk modeling numbers of $18,519 and $19,110 for the floating and hybrid elections to $14,449 and $16,689 for the start-bear risk modeling numbers. Even at the 5th percentile, monthly income following an initial bear market is down less than $1,000 for both elections.

FIGURE 4.16: INCOME VARIABILITY—BEAR MARKET START 240 MONTHS

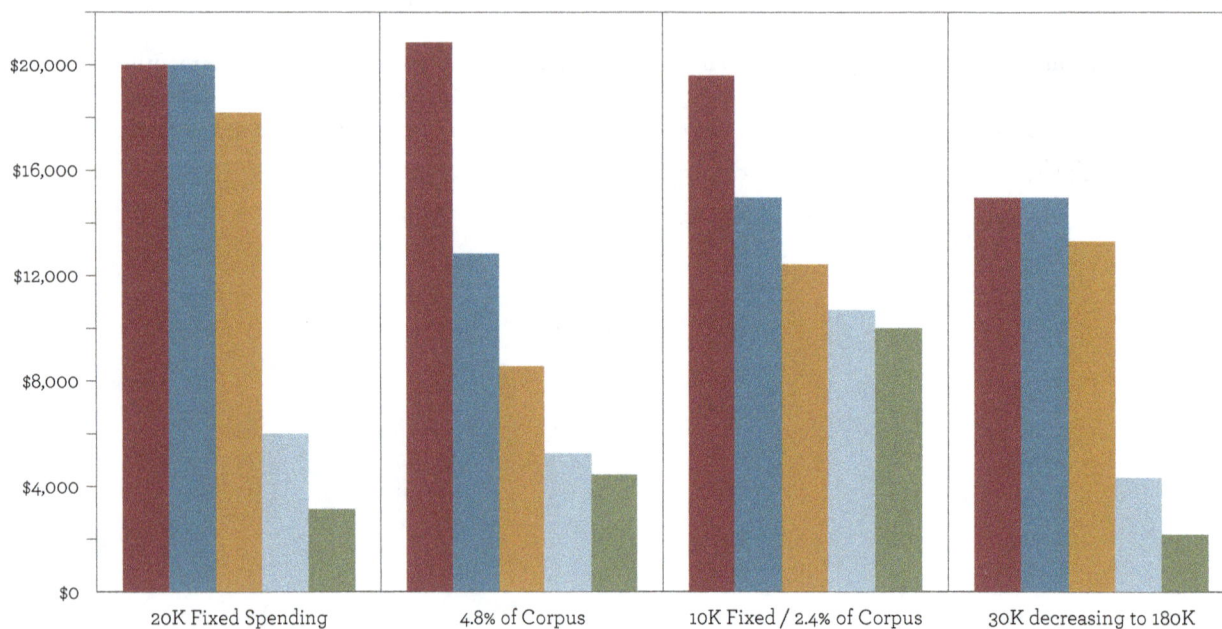

By the 240th month, the outer-two spending elections evidence an inability to support fixed, inflation-adjusted targets at the lower parts of the percentile of spending distributions (see figure 4.16). The floating percentile amounts exhibit relative convergence because, by the 20th year, much of the income variability impact of an initial bear market has subsided.

FIGURE 4.17: INCOME VARIABILITY—BEAR MARKET START 300 MONTHS (AGE 99)

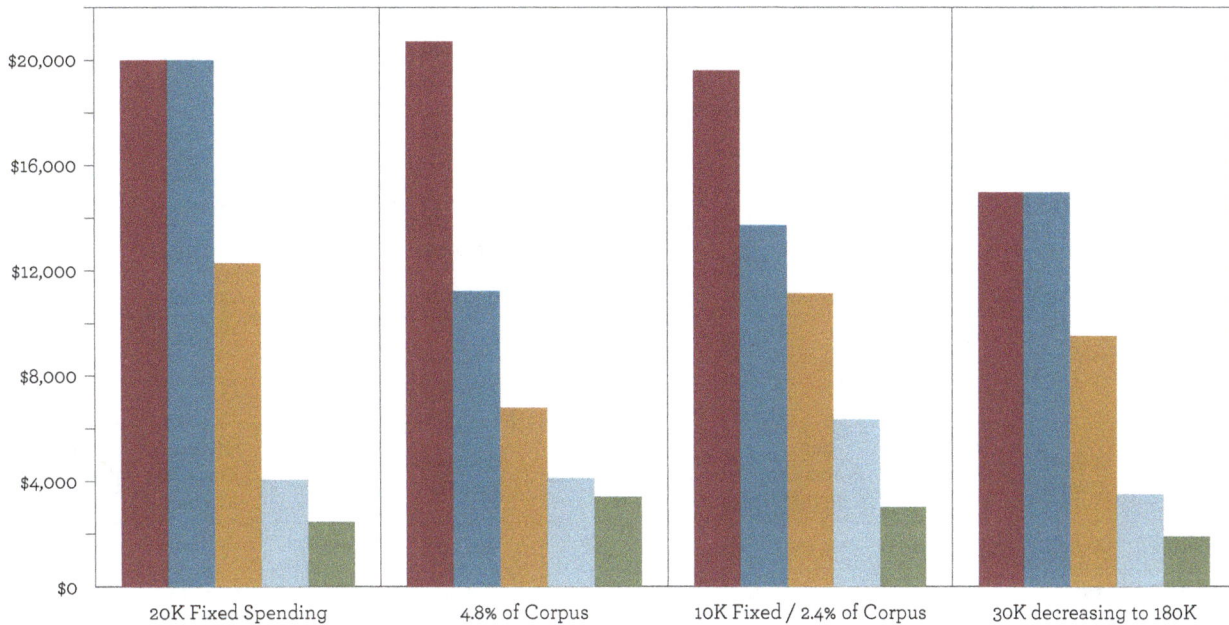

Finally, by age 99, the investor can expect to continue to receive target income (50th percentile) for both outer spending elections (see figure 4.17). However, results must be monitored carefully, lest lower-percentile outcomes push spending ability toward unacceptably low levels. The floating and hybrid elections both evidence slightly better worst-case results because of portfolio conservation of value for floating distribution elections.

The advisor summarizes results under both market-agnostic and bear market conditions:

SUMMARY OF INCOME SNAPSHOTS AT SELECTED PERCENTILES

CASE STUDY 2 / MARKET AGNOSTIC

CASE STUDY 2 / BEAR MARKET START

60 MONTHS INCOME VARIABILITY

Percentile	20K Fixed Spending	4.8% of Corpus	10K Fixed / 2.4% of Corpus	30K decreasing to 15K
70th	$20,000	$22,010	$21,305	$25,083
50th	$20,000	$19,823	$19,905	$25,083
30th	$20,000	$16,888	$18,414	$25,083
10th	$20,000	$12,536	$16,113	$25,083
5th	$20,000	$10,616	$15,057	$25,083

Percentile	20K Fixed Spending	4.8% of Corpus	10K Fixed / 2.4% of Corpus	30K decreasing to 180K
70th	$20,000	$18,566	$19,229	$25,083
50th	$20,000	$15,624	$17,664	$25,083
30th	$20,000	$13,151	$16,368	$25,083
10th	$20,000	$10,597	$15,012	$25,083
5th	$20,000	$9,648	$14,560	$25,083

120 MONTHS INCOME VARIABILITY

Percentile	20K Fixed Spending	4.8% of Corpus	10K Fixed / 2.4% of Corpus	30K decreasing to 15K
70th	$20,000	$23,159	$21,782	$20,083
50th	$20,000	$18,519	$19,110	$20,083
30th	$20,000	$14,250	$16,847	$20,083
10th	$20,000	$9,174	$14,067	$20,083
5th	$20,000	$7,450	$13,062	$20,083

Percentile	20K Fixed Spending	4.8% of Corpus	10K Fixed / 2.4% of Corpus	30K decreasing to 15K
70th	$20,000	$19,115	$19,368	$15,000
50th	$20,000	$14,449	$16,689	$15,000
30th	$20,000	$11,135	$14,893	$15,000
10th	$20,000	$8,125	$13,300	$15,000
5th	$20,000	$7,117	$12,728	$15,000

240 MONTHS INCOME VARIABILITY

Percentile	20K Fixed Spending	4.8% of Corpus	10K Fixed / 2.4% of Corpus	30K decreasing to 15K
70th	$20,000	$22,566	$21,520	$15,000
50th	$20,000	$16,160	$17,240	$15,000
30th	$18,192	$10,918	$14,381	$15,000
10th	$5,892	$6,116	$11,369	$8,114
5th	$3,119	$4,465	$10,413	$4,322

Percentile	20K Fixed Spending	4.8% of Corpus	10K Fixed / 2.4% of Corpus	30K decreasing to 15K
70th	$20,000	$20,785	$19,558	$15,000
50th	$20,000	$12,746	$14,876	$15,000
30th	$18,192	$8,423	$12,337	$13,262
10th	$5,892	$5,146	$10,640	$4,262
5th	$3,119	$4,352	$9,882	$2,131

300 MONTHS INCOME VARIABILITY

Percentile	20K Fixed Spending	4.8% of Corpus	10K Fixed / 2.4% of Corpus	30K decreasing to 15K
70th	$20,000	$21,368	$21,256	$15,000
50th	$20,000	$14,638	$16,157	$15,000
30th	$12,236	$9,784	$13,002	$15,000
10th	$4,048	$4,970	$10,140	$5,719
5th	$2,361	$3,439	$6,612	$3,085

Percentile	20K Fixed Spending	4.8% of Corpus	10K Fixed / 2.4% of Corpus	30K decreasing to 15K
70th	$20,000	$20,721	$19,582	$15,000
50th	$20,000	$11,193	$13,684	$15,000
30th	$12,236	$6,697	$11,070	$9,434
10th	$4,048	$4,053	$6,217	$3,445
5th	$2,361	$3,281	$2,920	$1,856

What is the investor's reaction to the distribution of periodic income under various spending elections? Sensitivity to income fluctuation reflects both economic and psychological factors. An impatience-to-consume factor generally motivates a front-loaded consumption path; attractive investment opportunities generally motivate a back-loaded consumption path. Impatience reflects investor psychology; investment rate of return reflects a rational assessment of future investment cash flows. Optimizing portfolio asset allocation or portfolio withdrawal policy based solely on a net-present-value criterion may miss the mark. It is difficult to derive closed-form representations of investor risk aversion to variation in consumption under conditions of uncertainty. Risk aversion itself is a probability distribution that changes with the ACR value.[24] In this case, risk aversion focuses on the investor's consumption level and the variability thereof.

---

24 . Risk questionnaires—as well as examination of previous personal choices, hobbies, and business decisions—are poorly suited tools for discovering an investor's risk aversion/risk tolerance.

Does secure flooring provide optimal income? Stylized economic models often assume complete markets, absolute certainty conditions, e.g., known life span, known future income stream, etc., and no consumption time-preferences ('impatience rate' equals 'risk-free rate'). The risk-free rate, in such models, is the premium demanded by investors to substitute future consumption for current consumption. In one sense, it measures the resistance to intertemporal substitution and, in many models, the optimal consumption path exhibits no variation. Given such assumptions, a commonly derived investment strategy is to form a portfolio of zero-coupon bonds where the maturity dates and amounts correspond to the investor's spending targets. This is an intellectual underpinning for portfolio flooring techniques. In such a case, absent any loads, a fixed annuity may place the retired investor on an optimal consumption path. However, even under conditions of certainty, whenever an investor's impatience factor is higher than the return offered on principal-guaranteed savings, there is a bias toward early consumption. By contrast, when the interest rate offered on savings is sufficiently high, there is a motivation to postpone spending in the expectation of increased future utility of consumption. Thus, the optimality of flooring, even under conditions of certainty, is questionable.

In this case, the advisor has acquainted the investor systematically with a broad range of economic consequences resulting from her selection of a preferred spending policy. Although a seemingly simple question—how much is it safe to spend?—turns out to be far more nuanced than the investor expected originally, the advisor is pleased with the investor's current level of comprehension. He is keen on knowing her preferred solution path.

CHAPTER FIVE

CASE STUDY 3—EMPHASIS ON SECURITY

- - -

SECURITY, UNCERTAINTY, AND PRECAUTIONARY SAVINGS MOTIVES

Multiperiod investing in "risk-free" assets can be very risky. Placing wealth in risk-free investments becomes a risky venture whenever growth and decline in the real economy alter the rates offered in savings accounts as well as the effective purchasing power of these accounts. However, investing in stocks further exacerbates the degree of uncertainty faced by retired investors. Multiperiod uncertainty (stochastic life spans, inflation rates, and investment returns) generates motives for maintaining liquid wealth. Liquid savings act as a buffer against future macroeconomic risks—not to mention shocks to personal or family well-being. Financial economists characterize the motivation to establish precautionary savings by the term "prudence."[1]

As Case Study 2 illustrates, each investor faces an individual tug of war: On the one hand, the uncertainty of future savings returns tends to weaken the precautionary savings motive (prudence); on the other, the investor's degree of risk aversion with respect to both the level and variability of consumption motivates increased prudence. Universal prescriptions both for and against flooring strategies are unlikely to find universal acceptance. Interestingly, a classic hallmark of imprudent behavior, i.e., decreasing liquid wealth in the face of uncertainty, is the purchase of contracts that provide actuarial guarantees when such guarantees are priced at levels greatly more than their actuarial fair value. High loads on insurance or annuity contracts transfer liquid wealth from the investor's balance sheet to the insurer's balance sheet. Full insurance is often optimal only in the absence of all loading factors.

Investors often face a similar tug of war with respect to security. Is security the same as stability of principal? If a stable principal provides an inadequate income, has a retired investor achieved security? On a preliminary basis, we define security as the investor's economic surplus—the amount by which the fair market value of current assets exceeds the stochastic present value of the liability to provide adequate periodic income. Assets, when narrowly defined, are the portfolio's investment securities. When more broadly defined, assets encompass entitlements such as Social Security, a home, or contingent assets such as an inheritance.[2] Liabilities, when narrowly defined, are the periodic income withdrawals from the portfolio. When more broadly defined, liabilities encompass contingent liabilities such as medical expenses, litigation costs, emergency repairs, and so forth.[3] Abstracting away from labor income—not usually a significant factor during retirement—the motivation for precautionary savings usually is decreasing with wealth or, more precisely, the motivation usually is decreasing with increases in the actuarial coverage ratio (ACR) value.

Security subsumes the notion of financial flexibility, and financial flexibility is an option with great value. Liabilities, even when predictable with respect to time, are stochastic with respect to discount rates. As economic and personal circumstances change over time, it is important to preserve flexibility. Maintaining financial flexibility is an essential aspect of risk management. Having sufficient current resources to meet contingencies means that the investor escapes the necessity to make immediate and unpleasant financial choices and also has the wherewithal to keep planning options in play until future uncertainties are resolved. This is the "real option value" of financial flexibility because decisions can be delayed until more information becomes available. Flexibility enhances an investor's ability to assume the risky retirement project. How much surplus is it prudent to consume, how much is it prudent to keep?

---

1. Prudence, in this context, is a mathematical term rather than a legal one. For a given investor utility function, risk aversion implies a negative second derivative, prudence implies a positive third derivative. A positive third derivative indicates that the investor is motivated to save money to offset adverse consequences of various future risks. A negative second derivative indicates that the investor is risk averse and will require increasingly large payoffs for units of additional risk. The literature on precautionary savings generally identifies two motives for accumulating liquid reserves: (1) rates on savings accounts are sufficiently attractive to induce investors to postpone consumption, and (2) protection against financial shocks especially when the investor is unable to borrow funds in the event of financial emergencies.

2. Assets, when broadly defined, indicate the investor's risk capacity. Risk capacity, however, is not the same as willingness to assume risk. An investor with a high ACR value may prefer a low-variance portfolio, and vice-versa.

3. A liability may be a positive event—for example, spending extra money to take advantage of a friend's offer to stay in his Paris apartment. Precautionary savings may be considered a liability because of an investor's decision to fund a low-return cash account and to maintain a minimum balance against future expenses. Reserve accounts, for example, are found on the liability section of an insurance company's balance sheet.

PART ONE: FACT PATTERN

In Case Study 3, the advisor meets married investors owning a portfolio that passes initial feasibility tests (ACR > 1) for their preferred spending strategy. He is age 69 and in good health; she is age 67 and also in good health. The portfolio's allocation is 60 percent to stocks and 40 percent to fixed income securities. The portfolio's current value is $5 million, and its periodic lifetime income target is $15,000 per month adjusted for inflation. The investors wish to investigate several questions:

What is the likelihood that:

- The portfolio can continue to provide the target income throughout their joint life span, i.e., until the date of the second death?
- The portfolio can continue to provide the target income throughout a single life span with a reduction to $10,000 per month for the life of the survivor (joint life target income equals 100 percent, single life target income equals 67 percent)?
- They will be able to make significant lifetime gifts to their daughter who is currently age 37?

The couple tells the advisor that their daughter, an only child, recently was divorced. The settlement did not leave her with sizable financial resources, her job as a teacher does not pay an ample salary, and she lives currently in a small apartment located near her job in a neighboring state with her eight-year-old son. She receives only a small monthly check from her ex-spouse who also is struggling to make ends meet on a teacher's salary. Two salaries financed an acceptable standard of living; a single salary makes things economically difficult.

The investors have offered some financial assistance to their daughter. This includes setting aside funds within a 529 college plan and gifting cash to cover some post-divorce expenses. Furthermore, they are considering revising their estate plan. The original will and trust provisions, although earmarking modest charitable bequests at the second death, allocate the bulk of the remaining estate for the benefit of their daughter and her, now, ex-husband contingent upon their marital status at the date of death. These provisions seemed reasonable because, when the estate plan was implemented originally, the daughter was still in her twenties and seemed relatively financially secure.

The advisor learns that the investors are concerned that, if the current estate plan remains their daughter's primary conduit for substantial resources, she may not enjoy financial benefits until close to her age 60, assuming a reasonable life span (early 90s) for one or both investors. Ideally, they would like to test the feasibility of the following financial options:

- Continue to withdraw $180,000 per year ($15,000 per month) on an inflation-adjusted basis from the portfolio which, when combined with Social Security benefits and a small pension check, is sufficient to fund a preferred standard of living.
- Continue to withdraw $180,000 per year on an inflation-adjusted basis while both investors are alive then withdraw $120,000 per year on an inflation-adjusted basis for the surviving investor's remaining life.
- Immediately withdraw a one-time amount of $300,000 to fund the purchase of a condominium. They would gift the condominium to their daughter who would then own it free and clear. This would eliminate the rental payments for her apartment, enhance her credit, and provide a sense of security and stability at a turbulent time in her life.
- Gift to their daughter an additional $1,000 per month starting immediately and continuing through grandson's age 21 (156 months) to cover property taxes, condominium fees, and ancillary expenses.

Although the investors have some disagreements regarding plan specifics, i.e., retaining condominium ownership in their names and forgiving monthly rental costs,[4] the advisor satisfies himself that the investors plan to review thoroughly these issues with their estate and trust attorney. The critical issue, on which they both wholeheartedly concur, is the impact of planning options on their future financial security. The nightmare scenario is running out of money while one or both remain alive. The prospect of everyone living in the condominium, however improbable, is unacceptable.

---

4. "Mom" favors gifting the condominium outright and is annoyed whenever "Dad" calls this the King Lear estate plan.

The advisor recognizes that circumstances are forcing the investors to rethink some long-term beliefs and financial objectives. Heretofore, the investors considered retirement security in terms of a financial strategy to provide adequate periodic lifetime income and relative stability of principal. Stability of principal, to the extent it could be achieved, served as a buffer against unexpected expenses or unplanned or unbudgeted repairs and maintenance costs. It also provided the expectation that family resources would benefit future generations. Although the investors never would employ the following vocabulary, the advisor suspects that they are beginning to realize that "family" is now the greatest potential threat to their financial security.[5] Unlike the focus in Case Studies 1 and 2, the investors must now deal with the issue: "How much is it safe to gift?" in addition to "How much is it safe to spend?"

PART TWO: ANALYSIS

The advisor, after taking time to analyze investor resources and objectives, prepares several exhibits that he feels will be useful in a forthcoming planning discussion. He meets with them the following week and outlines his preliminary findings. He explains that his analysis considers two retirement-income risk models: (1) projections assuming continuation of monthly $15,000 constant-dollar withdrawals throughout the investors' joint life, and (2) projections assuming monthly constant-dollar withdrawals of $15,000 during the period when both investors are living, with a reduction to a monthly $10,000 constant-dollar withdrawal for the survivor's remaining lifetime.

$15,000 JOINT-LIFE INCOME/100-PERCENT CONTINUATION TO SURVIVING SPOUSE

Following a recap of client goals and circumstances, the advisor explains that the forthcoming exhibits depict projections of the current portfolio's ability to successfully meet a sequence of increasingly challenging financial options:

1. A $15,000 inflation-adjusted monthly withdrawal throughout the investors' life span,

2. An immediate $300,000 gift for condominium purchase, plus a $15,000 inflation-adjusted monthly withdrawal throughout the investors' life span, and

3. An immediate $300,000 gift for condominium purchase, plus a $15,000 inflation-adjusted monthly withdrawal throughout the investors' life span, plus an additional $1,000 inflation-adjusted monthly withdrawal to provide family support through grandson's age 21 (156 months).

The applicable time horizon is the number of years over which at least one of the investors might remain alive. Given that they are both in their 60s and both in good health, a reasonable upper-bound time limit for the planning horizon is approximately 35 years. The advisor hastens to explain that there is only a small probability that one or both investors will experience a 35-year life span. The probability of such an occurrence is not zero, however, and therefore should be factored into the financial analysis. The questions under consideration are:

- How long is the portfolio likely to last under each of the above three planning options?

- Should portfolio depletion occur, what are the chances of experiencing lengthy periods in an alive-and-broke state?

Figure 5.1 offers a first look at these issues.

---

5.   The question "how much can I gift without undercutting my personal financial security?" is becoming more common as students, graduating with crushing student-loan debt levels, approach parents and grandparents for financial assistance. The question also extends to lifetime charitable gifting. At what dollar level does a gift become imprudent?

FIGURE 5.1: SURVIVAL AND PORTFOLIO DEPLETION RATES

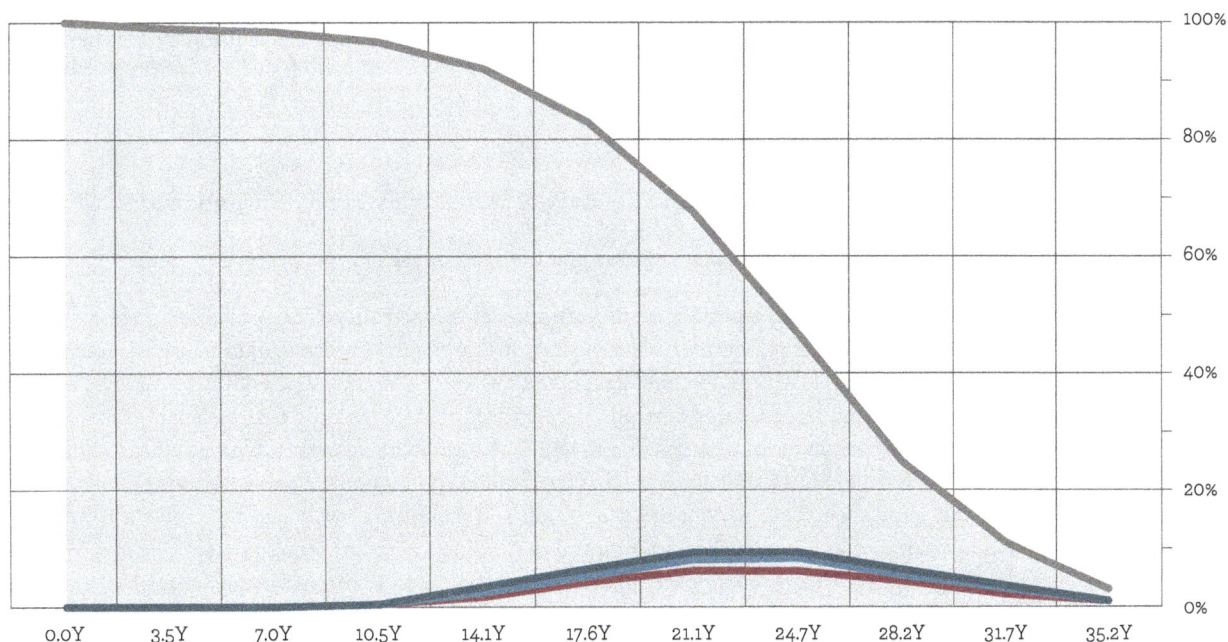

The shaded gray area depicts the likelihood of the survival of at least one spouse over time (bottom horizontal axis measures years). Drawing an imaginary line across the graph at the 50-percent height on the right-side vertical axis to intersect the shaded area indicates that there is an approximately 50-percent chance that one or both investors will enjoy a life span close to 25 years in length. It is unlikely, however, that one or both investors will experience a life span greater than 35 years.

The advisor turns the conversation to the three colored lines within the shaded gray area. He explains that each line reflects the probability of remaining alive-without-funds. The investors incur such a result by maintaining an initial portfolio withdrawal strategy without any mid-course corrections throughout the planning horizon:

- Red: $15,000 monthly withdrawal

- Turquoise: $300,000 initial real estate expense plus $15,000 monthly withdrawal

- Blue: $300,000 initial real estate expense plus $15,000 monthly withdrawal plus $1,000 monthly family support

In this instance, the economic result under consideration is the intersection of two events: at least one investor alive and a fully depleted portfolio. The shaded gray area addresses probability number one (likelihood of remaining alive); the colored lines indicate the probability of remaining alive without funds. The advisor points out that, for the very small population of sample investors remaining alive at year 35, approximately one-third of them will lack money. The red line exhibits the greatest amount of gray area above it. This is the strategy that avoids all gifting, and, therefore, the strategy that places the least stress on the portfolio. By contrast, the turquoise line (real estate purchase only) reduces the distance to the top of the gray area, and the blue line (real estate plus ongoing family support) places the greatest stress on the portfolio. It is the strategy most likely to bring the "depletion" line close to the "survival" line.

The investors express some discomfort with the graph's implications for their future financial security. The prospect of running out of money is not attractive. They opine that they probably should abandon their preferred lifestyle target income of $15,000 over their joint life span in favor of selecting either the option of reducing current joint income, or the option of reducing income at the first death to $10,000 per month. The advisor agrees that they may want to do this, but he suggests that such a decision is premature in a number of respects:

■ They have not yet had the opportunity to examine a reasonably complete information set.

■ They have not yet had an opportunity to quantify fully the timing and magnitude of failure should portfolio depletion occur.

A brief discussion of the distinction between "possible" and "probable" follows and the advisor asks for permission to continue.

He indicates that they are about to see a more comprehensive projection of portfolio values over time. The projection covers a range of possible results (which economists call a distribution of results), with the most probable results (which economists call statistically expected results) located at the middle of the range, and less-probable results located toward the extreme ends of the range. The middle of the range (median) is the 50th percentile; the risk model measures portfolio values through time over the entire distribution from the 1st through the 99th percentile. Again, a brief discussion follows, at the end of which the advisor is comfortable that they understand clearly that half of the projected outcomes are located above the median value (50th percentile) and half below. After apologizing for the jargon, the advisor reiterates that the range, i.e., distribution, contains both good and bad future outcomes, but a specific outcome cannot be known for certain today. He emphasizes that the investors' opinions about their investment strategy elections may change in future years as results unfold, as they acquire new data to evaluate, and as they assess the economic consequences of the new data. The challenge is to make a prudent and suitable decision today based on current information, to monitor the outcomes of that decision, and to reassess investment management elections periodically in terms of future goals and circumstances.[6]

Figure 5.2 illustrates the projected results.

FIGURE 5.2: PORTFOLIO VALUES OVER TIME, 50TH, 30TH, AND 20TH PERCENTILES

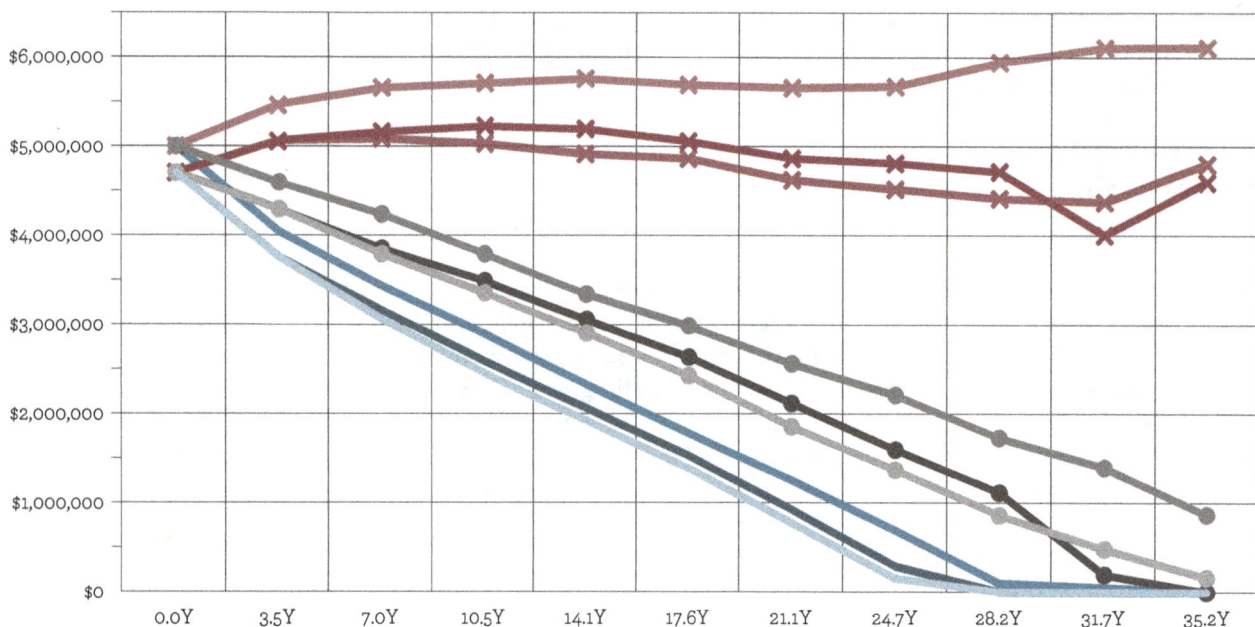

---

6. The advisor mentions that the possibility of their daughter's remarriage, for example, might profoundly influence their future spending or gifting preferences.

DATA TABLE FOR FIGURE 5.2: PORTFOLIO VALUES OVER TIME FOR THREE PLANNING OPTIONS

Portfolio	Percentile	0.0Y	3.5Y	7.0Y	10.5Y	14.1Y	17.6Y	21.1Y	24.7Y	28.2Y	31.7Y	35.2Y
$15K / Mo	50th	$5,000,000	$5,450,282	$5,658,395	$5,710,135	$5,756,941	$5,689,361	$5,655,271	$5,681,310	$5,945,054	$6,111,244	$6,099,314
$15K + Gift	50th	$4,700,000	$5,066,988	$5,144,332	$5,203,512	$5,173,321	$5,036,832	$4,844,335	$4,818,428	$4,711,455	$4,031,197	$4,611,301
$15K + Gift +$1K	50th	$4,700,000	$5,032,642	$5,098,839	$5,034,631	$4,915,781	$4,871,450	$4,635,866	$4,525,819	$4,414,664	$4,371,308	$4,790,262
$15K / Mo	30th	$5,000,000	$4,609,181	$4,250,080	$3,795,720	$3,333,105	$2,987,280	$2,538,832	$2,179,388	$1,705,884	$1,371,087	$834,307
$15K + Gift	30th	$4,700,000	$4,303,443	$3,874,915	$3,482,053	$3,051,667	$2,607,345	$2,101,484	$1,556,269	$1,088,865	$167,784	$—
$15K + Gift +$1K	30th	$4,700,000	$4,294,853	$3,816,396	$3,374,547	$2,909,519	$2,442,750	$1,867,076	$1,393,141	$849,903	$478,692	$146,147
$15K / Mo	20th	$5,000,000	$4,056,175	$3,427,781	$2,888,187	$2,307,158	$1,768,549	$1,237,853	$666,251	$66,814	$—	$—
$15K + Gift	20th	$4,700,000	$3,778,567	$3,162,191	$2,565,177	$2,041,293	$1,512,852	$899,853	$258,283	$—	$—	$—
$15K + Gift +$1K	20th	$4,700,000	$3,780,997	$3,070,582	$2,468,387	$1,904,516	$1,383,763	$751,716	$134,967	$—	$—	$—

"Let's walk through this jumble of data so that we can make sense of it. It projects future possible portfolio values at the 50th, 30th, and 20th percentiles of the distribution of investment/inflation outcomes."[7] The advisor is pleased that the investors quickly and correctly recognize that half of the projected portfolio values will be higher than those shown on the chart. "Yes, at this time we are looking only at the 'bottom half' of possible results."

Three groups of lines are traversing the planning horizon plane. The first set—marked with an "x"—projects the operation of the portfolio at the 50th percentile. The top line in this group begins with an initial value of $5 million and records the inflation-adjusted portfolio value trajectory for the status quo election, i.e., no gifting or ongoing family support. The middle line in the group projects the economic impact of the condominium purchase. Finally, the bottom line in the group projects the real estate purchase plus ongoing support through grandson's age 21. Each of the latter two portfolios starts at $4.7 million to reflect the estimated condo cost.

"Is there anything that strikes you as noteworthy about the 50th percentile results?"

Both investors quickly assert that they are pleasantly surprised to find that the risk model indicates that they may well be able to support their ambitious spending and family support objectives throughout their lifetime and have substantial terminal wealth to bequeath to their heirs. Indeed, this is the very outcome they hoped to see.

"OK. Let's look at the other two groupings. The middle grouping has three gray-shaded lines each of which is marked by a small circle. The initial values are $5 million for the status-quo spending election and $4.7 for the gifting/support elections. One way of interpreting the risk model's results is that your retirement-income portfolio generates outcomes that, 70 percent of the time, are equal to or better than the values recorded by the gray-colored trajectories." When asked, "Is there anything that strikes you as noteworthy about these results?" the investors remark that there appears to be sufficient wealth to produce the target income throughout the planning horizon; but for trajectories continuing to advanced ages, little or no money is available for a bequest. When the investors begin to refer to this part of the distribution graph as the "half-a-loaf" area—current wealth supports target lifetime income and an initial real estate purchase but eventually evaporates, the advisor cautions that the result occurs only for very long-lived retirees.

"OK, and what about the bottom group of lines without a marker?" They note that this group, at the 20th percentile of the distribution of projected future outcomes, crashes and burns around year 25 to 28 depending on the investors' initial level of generosity. If investors live beyond this time, there is a one-in-five chance of grave financial trouble. At this point in the analysis, the investors opine that none of the investment strategies under evaluation leaves them particularly vulnerable to early financial hardship. They begin to joke that by the time they go broke, their grandson may have moved out of the condo leaving them use of the spare bedroom. They inform the advisor that the new data makes them lean toward a strategy of an immediate real estate purchase (gift and titling issues to be ironed out in consultation

---

7. Outcomes are recorded for surviving investors only. Probabilistic assessments at the extreme end of the planning horizon are difficult because of the small remaining sample of active trials.

with their estate and trust attorney). After a brief discussion, they feel that they should communicate that an ongoing level of monthly family support is contingent upon future portfolio performance, and that they should make it very clear that planning to help is not the same as committing to help. The investors remark that the presentation has given them a higher level of confidence with respect to their gift and estate planning decision-making.

"Before we finish, I'd like to test your decision-making a bit further." The advisor explains that he would like to present two sets of additional information: (1) A close-up look at the economics of landing in the regime produced by the conditional probability of remaining alive without funds, and (2) an alternative measure of the investors' actual wherewithal for lifetime gifting.

The first information set simply provides an idea of the timing and magnitude of financial shortfalls should the investors outlive portfolio resources (see figure 5.3). "This information set is interesting in that, given outcomes expressed in constant-dollar terms, it indicates the amount of additional funds you might need today in order to avoid low-probability financial difficulties many years into the future." The advisor cautions the investors that the key word in the forthcoming analysis is "should." Should they fail to modify their initial spending or family support elections in the face of unfavorable investment results, and should one or both investors enjoy a sufficiently long life span, the risk model indicates the severity (time and magnitude) of possible future portfolio depletion.

FIGURE 5.3: YEARS ALIVE WITHOUT PORTFOLIO ASSETS

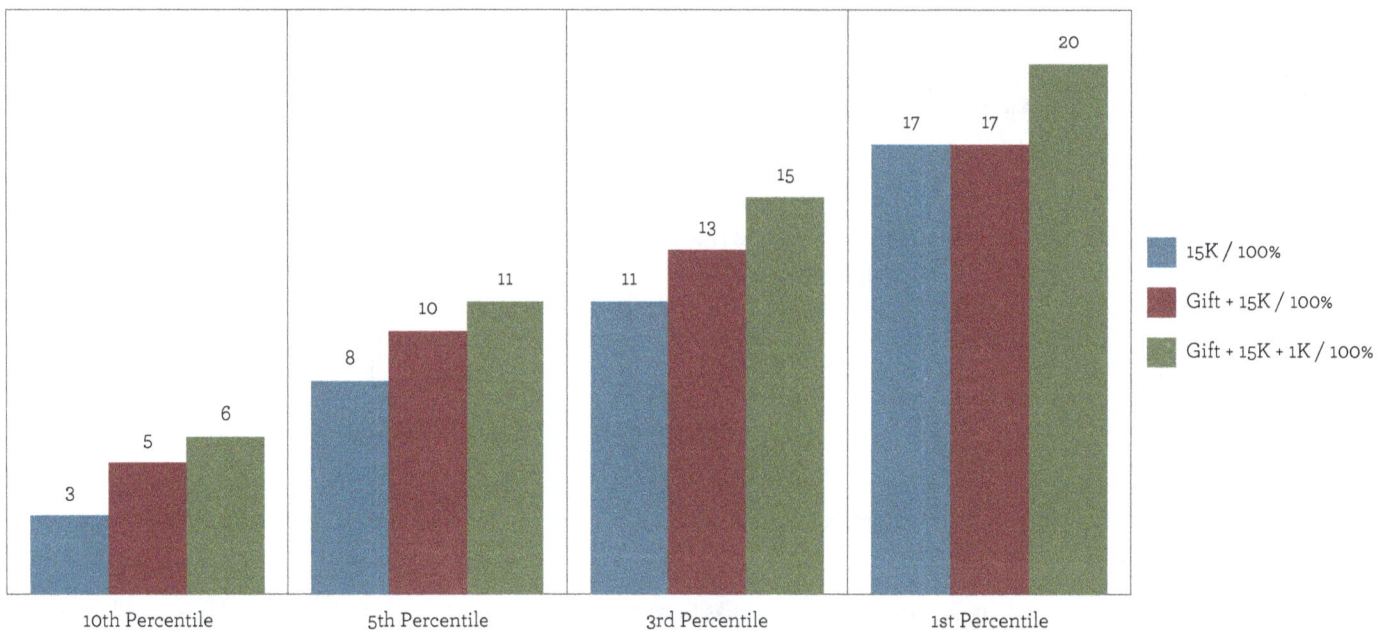

The advisor notes that figure 5.3 is a more detailed exploration of figure 5.1. "On the Survival and Depletion Rate chart, you noticed a gray-colored area for surviving investors with a hump-shaped area delineated by each colored line. But each colored line represents the likelihood that a portion of investors from the original sample of 10,000 would (1) remain alive[8] and (2) lack investment assets. Let's call the gray area above the lines, the "Region of Prosperity" and the gray area below the lines, the "Region of Depletion."[9] Figure 5.3 provides information about the Region of Depletion. Most investors (approximately 90 percent of the initial sample of 10,000) will never fall into the Region of Depletion.[10]

Figure 5.3 sorts the Region of Depletion (joint distribution of alive and broke) by its percentile ranking and asks what the magnitude of the income shortfall might look like. In English, figure 5.3 shows how long you may remain alive and broke if you run out of funds during the planning horizon. At the 10th percentile, the time alive without funds ranges from three to six years. At the 5th percentile, the time

8.   In this fact pattern, the line is hump-shaped because fewer and fewer investors remain alive with the passage of time. Although the portfolio depletion rate increases relative to the surviving population, the line slope eventually becomes negative as the absolute number of living investors shrinks toward zero.

9.   The Region of Depletion is not the same as the Region of Infeasibility. In the Region of Depletion, you are literally without funds; in the Region of Infeasibility, current funds, although potentially great, are not adequate, according to an actuarial measure, to support spending objectives.

10. To clarify, figure 5.2 and the companion data table record results for the population of surviving investors, not for the population of initial investors.

without money stretches from eight to eleven years depending on the initial spending election. And at the 1st percentile, investors find themselves having to fill an income gap lasting from 17 to 20 years. Although living many years usually is considered to be a good thing, these few myopic investors will experience poor investment/inflation realizations and live for many years without portfolio assets.

Whether membership in the alive-without-money group presents an insurmountable financial obstacle depends on the economic resources owned outside of the financial asset portfolio. But now, the advisor explains, you can quantify your financial vulnerability. In this case, vulnerability is measured by the likelihood and amount of a potential shortfall in financial assets, should such a shortfall occur. The data suggest the conditional probability of entering the Region of Depletion and the amount of additional assets that you would need to meet lifetime spending targets (personal income, gift, and family support goals). Additional income from sources such as a reverse mortgage or cash generated by moving to a smaller residence may more than cover conditional projected shortfalls.

"I'd now like to move to a second measure of financial vulnerability, an understanding of which should help better quantify your ability to achieve a financially secure retirement."

"Let's say that you tell a registered representative (stockbroker) that you have $5 million in cash to invest in a portfolio of financial assets. If you ask what a 60/40 mix of stocks and bonds might be able to provide for your retirement, he might show you something like the data at the 50th percentile of figure 5.2, but he'll caution you that the results are not guaranteed and actual outcomes may be better or worse. That said, you would note that the 50th-percentile outcome gets you pretty close to providing (1) your target lifetime income, (2) a real estate gift, (3) support for your grandson, and (4) a generous amount of terminal wealth for a bequest. This is great, except that you don't like the 'not guaranteed' language."

"Alternatively, let's say that you went to an actuary and remarked that you have $5 million in cash and that you want a guaranteed $15,000 inflation-adjusted monthly joint and survivor lifetime income. The actuary might remark that the cost of a guaranteed-income contract (single premium, inflation-adjusted, immediate annuity) is $4,436,557. However, if you wait a year—all else being equal—the contract will cost less because the passage of time (increase in joint age) decreases the length of the funding liability, i.e., the annuity cost. In fact, the actuary may present figure 5.4 depicting the relationship between your joint age and annuity cost:

FIGURE 5.4: COST OF ANNUITY SOLUTION

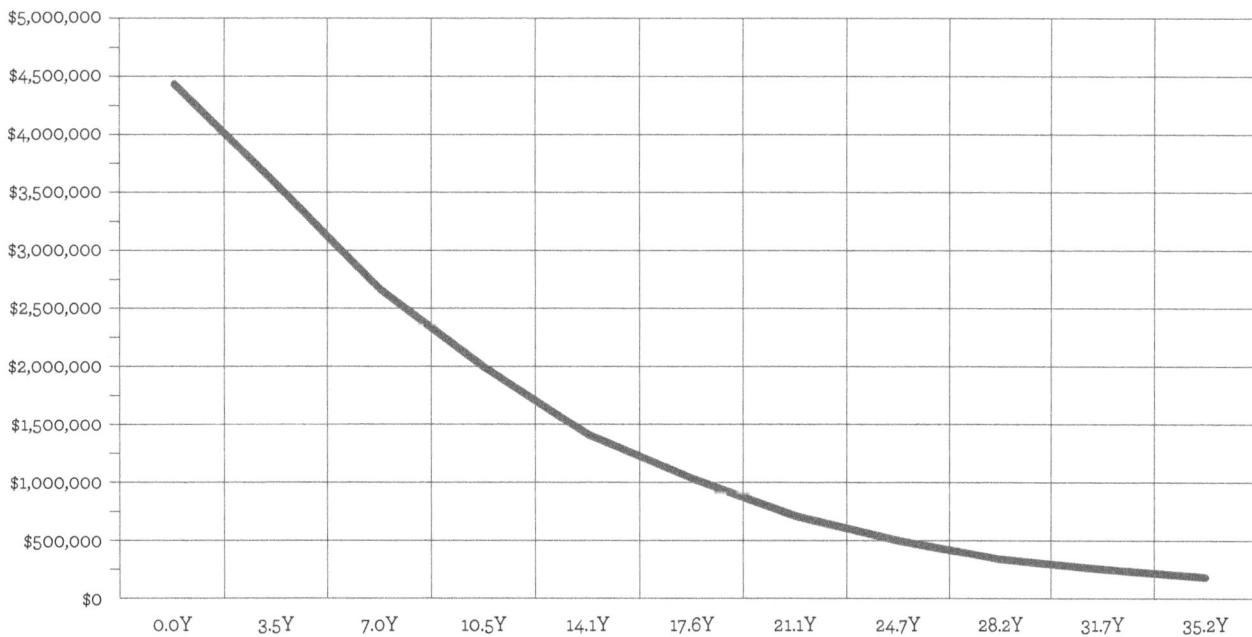

All else being equal,[11] annuity cost decreases with age simply because remaining expected life span becomes shorter."

"So, you're saying we should buy an annuity?"

---

11. For example, this assumes holding the level and shape of the yield curve steady, no change to population mortality risk, no change in insurance company taxation or regulation (reserving requirements), etc.

"Not exactly. You may want to do this someday—it's a lot cheaper if you wait—but if you do it today, you will soak up an enormous amount of your total nest egg with the result that little money will be left to meet expenses unrelated to producing periodic income."

"So, why are you calculating annuity prices?"

"If annuity prices represent the cost of a lifetime-income guarantee for your most critical financial objective—in this case, $15,000 inflation-adjusted income—then the difference between the current value of your portfolio ($5 million) and the cost of guaranteed funding ($4,436,557) measures your 'economic surplus.' All expenses, other than the cost of a guaranteed target income, are funded from surplus. In this case, you are contemplating asking a surplus account of approximately $563,000 to fund a $300,000 condominium purchase and a possible $1,000 inflation-adjusted support payment for 156 months (13 years), which we can round off to a present value of approximately $143,000 assuming an inflation-adjusted interest rate of 1.5 percent. This leaves a net economic surplus of $120,000. Of course, if you do not irrevocably commit to providing the additional monthly family support, your current economic surplus is $263,000. Just to be clear, after accounting for the actuarial cost of funding your preferred lifestyle and condominium purchase, current surplus amounts to $263,000.[12] The $263,000 is your current financial cushion. It is, however, only a virtual measure of surplus when measured actuarially.[13] Expressed otherwise, under this liability cost measure, you have current financial flexibility to the extent of $263,000 in the world of the actuary. In the investment world, surplus is a more probabilistic concept[14] and, in part, a function of the distributions of future investment and inflation realizations."

The advisor is uncertain whether the investors' silence reflects their astonishment as they contemplate the consequences of this risk measure, or their annoyance with him because of his stark presentation of their financial circumstances (or a bit of both).

"Well, we came in here thinking that we were in great shape because we owned a $5-million portfolio from which we are spending only 4 percent per year. Now, it seems as if we're only $250,000 away from becoming insolvent!"

"You're technically correct, but I think you may be surprised by what's coming next. Let's continue by putting all the pieces together to arrive at a comprehensive portrait of your financial position over time."

The advisor reminds them that the expected 50th percentile of portfolio value operating under each of their spending options is as follows:

Portfolio	0.0Y	3.5Y	7.0Y	10.5Y	14.1Y	17.6Y	21.1Y	24.7Y	28.2Y	31.7Y	35.2Y
$15K / Mo	$5,000,000	$5,450,282	$5,658,395	$5,710,135	$5,756,941	$5,689,361	$5,655,271	$5,681,310	$5,945,054	$6,111,244	$6,099,314
$15K + Gift	$4,700,000	$5,066,988	$5,144,332	$5,203,512	$5,173,321	$5,036,832	$4,844,335	$4,818,428	$4,711,455	$4,031,197	$4,611,301
$15K + Gift +$1K	$4,700,00	$5,032,642	$5,098,839	$5,034,631	$4,915,781	$4,871,450	$4,635,866	$4,525,819	$414,664	$4,371,308	$4,790,262

Projected annuity costs over time are:

Portfolio	0.0Y	3.5Y	7.0Y	10.5Y	14.1Y	17.6Y	21.1Y	24.7Y	28.2Y	31.7Y	35.2Y
$15K / Mo	$4,436,557	$3,564,679	$2,651,191	$2,013,579	$1,420,583	$1,046,655	$711,056	$511,557	$344,577	$257,443	$189,142
$15K + Gift	$4,436,557	$3,563,955	$2,653,360	$2,016,891	$1,424,652	$1,047,645	$717,738	$525,449	$360,352	$269,095	$189,688
$15K + Gift +$1K	$4,436,557	$3,565,777	$2,653,252	$2,013,299	$1,426,041	$1,054,356	$722,704	$524,651	$360,052	$263,558	$106,445

---

12. Simulation of the asset-liability management (ALM) approach to investment management often yields a more optimistic assessment of financial security as equity exposure increases up to the point where the benefits of positive expected equity risk premium and skew terms equal the detriment of positive portfolio variance and kurtosis terms. Beyond this point, additional allocation to stocks may be counterproductive. See Chapter 2, footnote 10 for a discussion about the benefit of using multiple models for decision-making in the fact of uncertain or ambiguous information. This book focuses on actuarial models and investment simulation models.

13. It would become an actual surplus if the investors committed to an immediate annuity purchase. Care should be taken to avoid concluding that the couple is unable to achieve financial success if expenses temporarily exceed the virtual surplus account value.

14. How likely is it that my assets will outpace my liabilities?

Subtracting projected actuarial costs from available portfolio resources generates projected economic surplus:

Portfolio	0.0Y	3.5Y	7.0Y	10.5Y	14.1Y	17.6Y	21.1Y	24.7Y	28.2Y	31.7Y	35.2Y
$15K / Mo	$563,443	$1,885,603	$3,007,204	$3,696,556	$4,336,358	$4,642,706	$4,944,215	$5,169,753	$5,600,477	$5,853,801	$5,910,172
$15K + Gift	$263,443	$1,503,033	$2,490,972	$3,186,621	$3,748,669	$3,989,187	$4,126,597	$4,292,979	$4,351,103	$3,762,102	$4,421,613
$15K + Gift +$1K	$263,443	$1,466,865	$2,445,587	$3,021,332	$3,489,740	$3,817,094	$3,913,162	$4,001,168	$4,054,612	$4,107,750	$4,593,807

"The risk model suggests that, at the current time, you are financially vulnerable. However, if you recall the sharply decreasing annuity cost chart presented earlier (figure 5.4), you can see that time is a strong ally, provided that realized portfolio values are close to statistically expected results. A short period of small consumer surplus can rapidly morph into a long period of substantial surplus."

Figure 5.5 illustrates a consolidated view for the target income/condominium purchase/family support spending election.

FIGURE 5.5: EVOLUTION OF SURPLUS

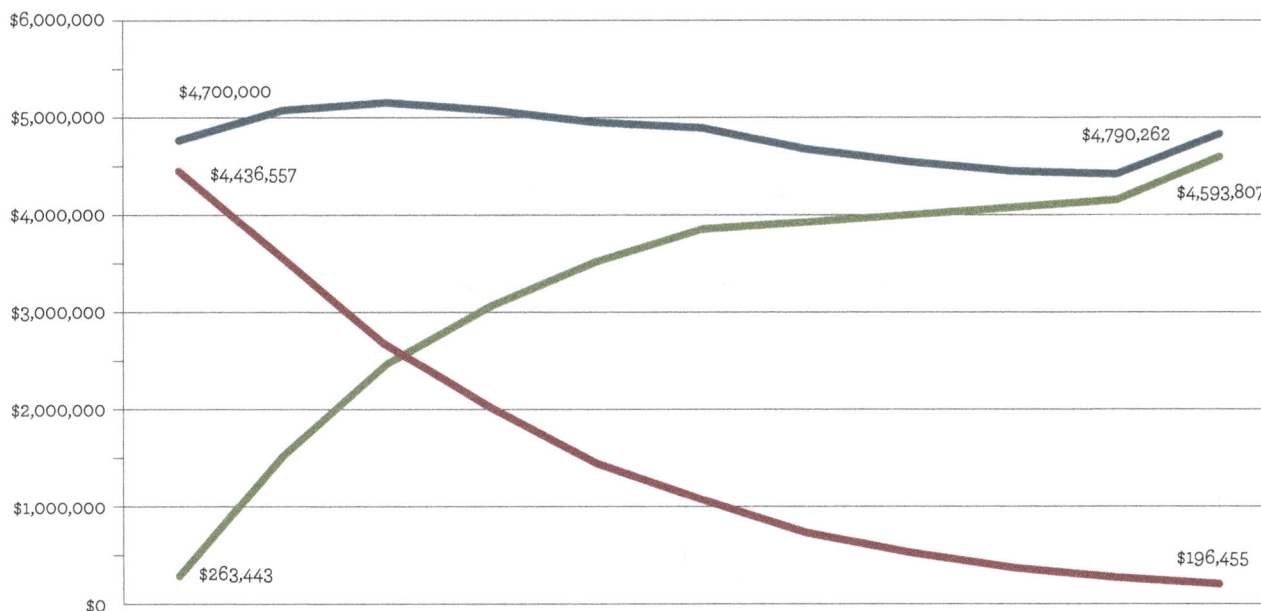

The red line shows the annuity cost, the blue line is the portfolio value projection, and the green line is the projected trajectory of economic surplus. The advisor notes that the investors' body language has changed to a more relaxed posture. He takes this opportunity to remind them that below-median results will change this picture. For example, at the 30th percentile, results are as shown in figure 5.6.

FIGURE 5.6: EVOLUTION OF SURPLUS—30TH PERCENTILE

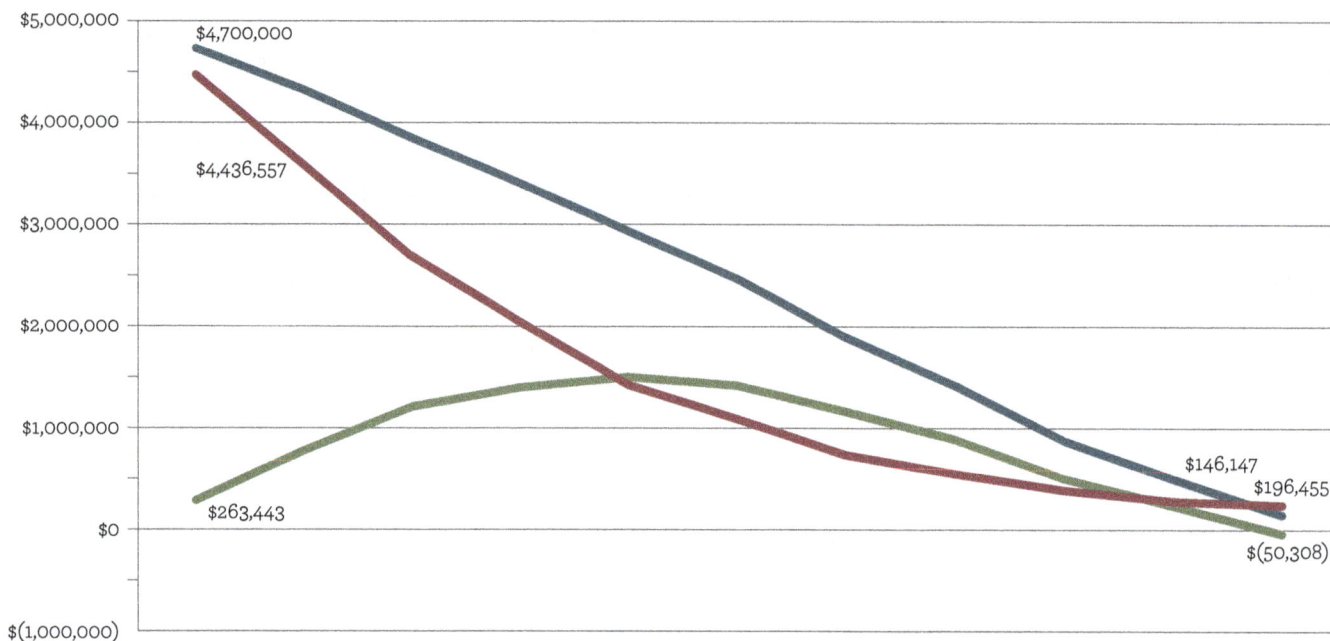

Although economic surplus is increasing initially (in this case, to a maximum of approximately $1.4 million), the trend does not continue. Surplus may not follow a linear path, its orbit may change direction and head toward negative future values. Surplus is a difference. In this case, it is a difference between projected resources and projected liabilities and, like many differential equations, surplus trajectory may be highly sensitive to initial values. Ongoing future financial security is not something that is necessarily detectable by extrapolating a trend line.[15] Retirement is a risky project.

$15,000 JOINT-LIFE INCOME/$10,000 CONTINUATION TO SURVIVING SPOUSE

The advisor, at this point, recommends a break so that everyone can recharge their attention span. When the meeting resumes, the advisor provides the following recap:

- The investors' current economic surplus [value of current assets minus actuarially calculated cost of spending liabilities] is $263,443 assuming immediate implementation of each and every spending objective, or $563,443 assuming only the lifetime income objective with 100 percent continuing to the survivor.

- The fact that the investors have a current surplus provides them with financial flexibility. For example, they have the luxury of waiting for investment and inflation results to unfold as they evaluate future planning options.

- The retirement-risk model projections suggest that a substantial surplus may emerge in the near future. This surplus, however, is not guaranteed. If the investors elect to implement all three elements of their spending strategy immediately, the proposed plan would not work throughout the entire potential planning horizon, i.e., the investors, if operating on autopilot, would be exposed to depletion risk below the 30th percentile of the distribution of financial outcomes. If outcomes track below this level, the investors will have a strong motivation to implement mid-course corrections.

---

15. On a technical note, as the ACR approaches a value of 1, the higher moments of the return distribution may become more consequential in terms of measuring an investor's retirement security. Distributions with equal return and variance expectations may not have equal utility for the investor. See Chapter 3, footnote 1 for a discussion of the impact of small changes in velocity and position on a spacecraft's orbit around a black hole.

There are several ways to view surplus. Surplus provides:

1. Flexibility in evaluation and selection of planning options

2. A buffer against unplanned or unforeseen financial shocks

3. Potential bequest benefits for the next generation(s)

4. Funds to cover contingent nursing home/end-of-life expenses

5. Extra lifetime consumption opportunities

At this point in time, the investors opine that they are beginning to see how they can use risk model outputs to make more informed decisions about security, flexibility, gifting, and spending opportunities. For example, they consider the possibility of making only limited supplemental cash gifts, over the next two to three years, so that their daughter can maintain an adequate standard of living. If economic surplus emerges as expected, they will be in better shape to implement substantial real estate and family support commitments.[16]

When the meeting first began, the advisor was under the impression that the investors were looking for a quick confirmation of the viability of their preferred spending strategy. Now, however, the advisor senses that the investors are beginning to see how intelligent planning is critical to their retirement security. At this point, he suggests that they should consider the investors' Plan B: reduce the income goal to a joint inflation-adjusted, monthly income of $15,000 with the survivor receiving a lifetime, inflation-adjusted, monthly income of $10,000. The investors agree and indicate that they are keenly interested in the trade-offs among surplus enhancement, reduction of consumption for the surviving spouse, and sustainability of the revised target income throughout retirement. This is the first time that they considered their retirement project as a series of trade-offs among competing objectives and opportunities. They volunteer that they are somewhat disconcerted to note that a $500,000 economic surplus could evaporate if the current portfolio experienced a 10-percent near-term, decline in value. Even though the risk model accounts for their planned withdrawal of 4 percent, they feel economically insecure because of the scant latitude for downside returns.[17]

The advisor indicates that they can focus on changes in their financial security resulting from voluntarily decreasing survivor income. A critical risk metric is the measurement of economic surplus. Figure 5.7 and its companion table indicate the security and financial flexibility enhancements achieved by modifying the income target:

DATA TABLE FOR FIGURE 5.7: EVOLUTION OF A FINANCIAL CUSHION

Financial Cushion—67%											
	0.0Y	3.5Y	7.0Y	10.5Y	14.1Y	17.6Y	21.1Y	24.7Y	28.2Y	31.7Y	35.2Y
$15K / Mo	$1,123,029	$2,001,727	$2,711,409	$3,106,617	$3,627,506	$4,029,872	$4,359,183	$4,746,089	$4,883,703	$4,640,597	$6,153,161
$15K + Gift	$823,029	$1,608,120	$2,287,701	$2,644,700	$3,162,575	$3,376,515	$3,685,820	$3,797,355	$3,952,955	$3,930,008	$3,350,573
$15K + Gift +$1K	$823,029	$1,596,027	$2,173,903	$2,479,037	$2,879,108	$3,110,332	$3,506,995	$3,614,671	$3,711,981	$3,594,390	$3,447,690
Financial Cushion—100%											
	0.0Y	3.5Y	7.0Y	10.5Y	14.1Y	17.6Y	21.1Y	24.7Y	28.2Y	31.7Y	35.2Y
$15K / Mo	$564,443	$1,885,603	$3,007,204	$3,696,556	$4,336,358	$4,642,706	$4,944,215	$5,169,753	$5,600,477	$5,853,801	$5,910,172
$15K + Gift	$263,443	$1,503,033	$2,490,972	$3,186,621	$3,748,669	$3,989,187	$4,126,597	$4,292,979	$4,351,103	$3,762,102	$4,421,613
$15K + Gift +$1K	$263,443	$1,466,865	$2,445,587	$3,021,332	$3,489,740	$3,817,094	$3,913,162	$4,001,168	$4,054,612	$4,107,750	$4,593,807

---

16. A comparable analysis may be undertaken profitably by those with lifetime charitable intent toward schools, churches, the arts, and so forth.

17. Waring and Siegel (2018) emphasize: "… risk is measured with respect to the certainty or lack of certainty of there being funds available to support whatever future spending the assets are being held to provide" (p. 6), and "… risk increases with a poorly designed spending plan…." (p. 14).

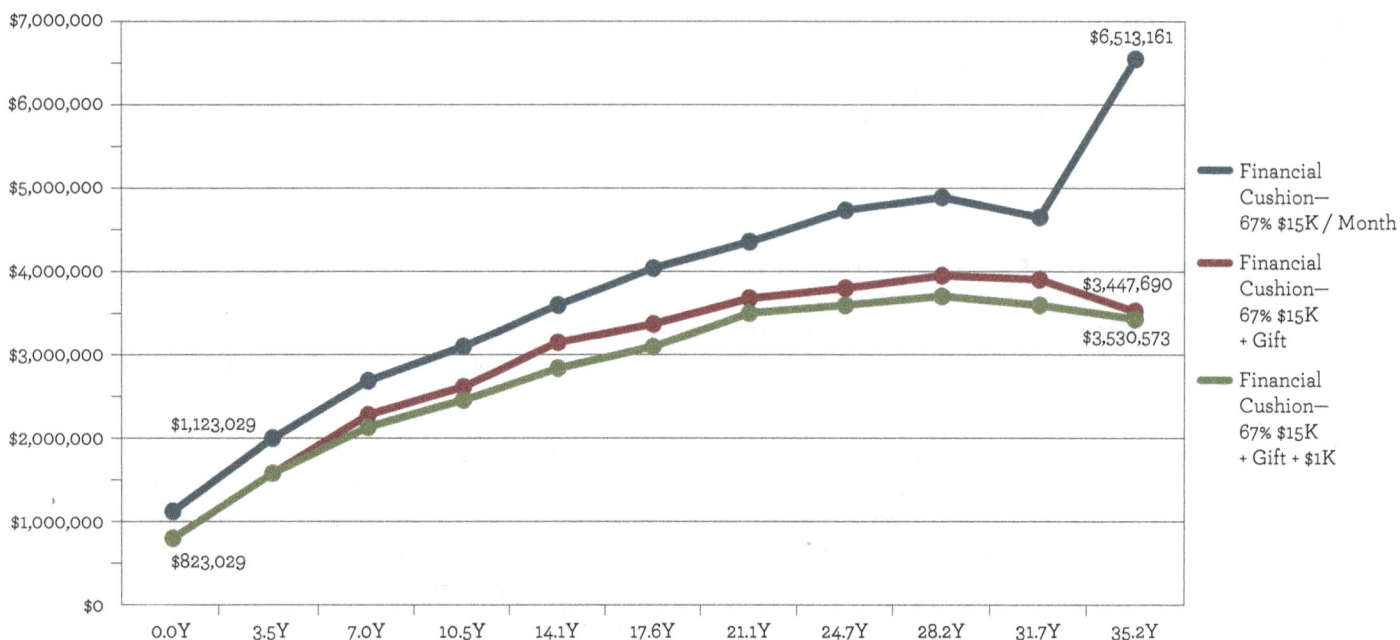

The risk model outputs suggest, not surprisingly, that a surviving spouse's willingness to reduce future income has a direct and noticeable effect on the investors' current economic surplus (an increase of $500,000+), and on their future financial wherewithal. Specifically, a reduction to a two-thirds income level indicates that the current portfolio can sustain an approximately 16-percent near-term decline in value assuming implementation of the real estate/support spending plans, or an approximately 22-percent near-term decline in value assuming a postponement of real estate and gifting strategies until new information regarding actual near-term portfolio performance becomes available.[18]

At this point in the discussion, the advisor is unsure if the investors will decide to adopt a staged-commitment retirement-spending policy or elect a more-aggressive policy to assist the next generation. However, he believes that the investors' awareness of the economics of the retirement project is expanding. Understanding their asset management elections—in this case, an election to modify future income, if economically prudent, at the death of a spouse, deliberately introduces variance in their spending pattern. This sounds like a bad thing. However, this perspective is instructive because it illustrates how variance can arise on either side of the accounting ledger—variance in spendable income produced by fluctuations in portfolio value versus variance in estimated retirement consumption needs and costs.[19] Financial flexibility is critical. Tracking variance in asset values and spending requirements within an integrated asset-liability management context exceeds, in large measure, the importance of optimizing portfolios in an asset-only context. The longer the retirement planning horizon and the greater the uncertainty of cash flows on both sides of the ledger, the greater the significance of the variance term and the greater the value of financial flexibility.

Waiting until next period's results are known prior to making investment decisions is a hallmark of adaptive and dynamic portfolio management. This differs from tactical asset management. Tactical strategies call for predictions about inflation and investment returns; adaptive strategies call for prudent responses to newly revealed information.[20] A dynamic investment strategy requires the investor to consider the economic consequences of gain or loss in the prior periods before deciding how best to proceed in the next period(s). However, financial flexibility is an essential element. Economic surplus creates conditions in which the investor is both willing and able to manage risk prudently.[21]

---

18. All curves evidence an increasing surplus on a concave-down trajectory. The upward spike at the far right of figure 5.7 for the $15,000-per-month election is an artifact of the small remaining sample of surviving investors.

19. Ignoring the variance term on the spending/cash needs side of the balance sheet may give asset allocation greater weighting than it deserves in the planning process.

20. Refer to the discussion on "Recourse Decisions" in Chapter Fourteen.

21. Risk management elections reflect an investor's risk aversion. Both rationalist and behavioralist commentators recognize that the risk-aversion function may change across the wealth domain. As the ACR approaches a value of 1, reactions and solutions vary. Advisors, subscribing to the belief that it is optimal for investors to employ constant relative risk aversion, may recommend a stay-the-course/trust-the-market response; advisors who assume that investors exhibit decreasing absolute risk aversion may suggest risk reduction in periods following substantial decline in portfolio value.

CHAPTER SIX

MONITORING AND EVALUATION—PAST

■ ■ ■

Most investment advisors are familiar with the investment policy statement (IPS).[1] This chapter, as well as the next four, focuses on how to fulfill IPS requirements regarding the monitoring and surveillance of investment strategy in terms of the investor's needs, purposes, and personal circumstances. A yearly comprehensive monitoring and evaluation report revisits the investor's resources, goals, and preferred asset management elections. It updates the client's understanding of his current economic circumstances (and how they have changed over time) by providing:

- Past performance evaluation
- Current feasibility evaluation (solvency criteria)
- Current measure of security (financial flexibility)
- Future sustainability evaluation (shortfall risk metrics)

This chapter discusses past performance measurement. The following chapters discuss how to evaluate and report on feasibility, sustainability, and security measures.

PAST PERFORMANCE

Measuring past performance is big business in the investment advice and consulting industry. Investors—both institutional and individual—like to feel that they have received their money's worth for the fees and expenses associated with their investment programs. Performance evaluation traditionally involves application of statistical methodologies, often derived from modern portfolio theory (MPT), either to measure performance relative to a benchmark, or to quantify the return-to-risk efficiency of portfolio investment strategies.[2]

A cynic might argue that performance evaluation presentations provide a chance for investment advisors to exhibit a veneer of sophistication by employing a dense, jargon-filled vocabulary to discuss arcane material in the field of financial economics. Ideally, however, presentations should provide insight into the investor's asset allocation and investment management decisions without inducing a strong soporific response.

That said, the advisory community, if it is to remain credible and trustworthy, must adhere to performance presentation standards such as those developed by the CFA Institute and enumerated in such documents as the *Standards of Practice Handbook*, the Asset Manager Code of Professional Conduct, and the Global Investment Performance Standards (GIPS).[3] Performance measurement and presentation is complex[4] and, when accounts managed by CFA® charterholders are discretionary, they are subject to fiduciary management and performance reporting standards. A primary challenge is to balance (1) quantitative-oriented assessments subject to industry-standard calculation methodologies and presentation formats, and (2) qualitative-oriented judgments regarding how well or poorly an investor is doing relative to personal financial goals. If the qualitative aspects of reporting are shortchanged, the investor may be confounded and stupefied. If the quantitative aspects are shortchanged, the investor may feel only a vague afterglow arising from a cleverly applied dose of

---

1. For an in-depth discussion of the nature and scope of the IPS, see Collins (2016).

2. Commonly used benchmarks include the S&P 500 stock index or the aggregate U.S. bond index, customized indexes representative of global asset-class weightings or portfolio risk-factor exposures, or a comparable investment manager peer group. Commonly used benchmark-relative evaluation measures include Jensen's differential alpha, the information ratio, and many others. Performance measures not directly related to a benchmark include the Sharpe ratio and the Modigliani squared ratio. Extensions of MPT performance ratios lead to holdings and style-based performance analysis, confidence interval tests for manager skill, trading and implementation shortfall measurement, and many other tests in areas of interest.

3. These documents are available on the CFA Institute website, https://www.cfainstitute.org.

4. The CFA Institute offers an academic program leading to the Certificate in Investment Performance Measurement. The CIPM program tests for competency in the areas of performance measurement, performance attribution, performance appraisal and manager selection, ethical standards, and performance presentation and GIPS standards. See https://www.cfainstitute.org/programs/cipm/courseofstudy/Pages/curriculum.aspx.

schmooze. Thus, it is manifestly obvious that just as a physician needs to assess quantitative information, e.g., the HDL/LDL cholesterol ratio, when evaluating patient health lest the doctor-patient consultation begin and end with "how do you feel?" so, also, the advisor needs to monitor and understand the implications of underlying quantitative data lest the discussion devolve into a mere storytelling session.

A variety of commercially available performance presentation software programs provide myriad quantitative performance measures based on statistics and probability, or derived from applications of these disciplines, i.e., econometrics, within the fields of finance and investments. Performance measurement software can focus at the individual security level, or on aggregate portfolio performance in either absolute terms, e.g., standard deviation, or relative to a benchmark, e.g., alpha values. Additionally, some investment advisory firms customize their presentation formats and provide information not readily available from commercial packages. The trend toward report customization also receives emphasis from practitioners in the behavioral finance (BF) school of thought who strive to provide a direct mapping from the performance of specific investment or sub-portfolio performance results to client goals. Although the appropriate level of granularity in investment communication is subject to debate, most clients appreciate discussion of investment results in terms of their personal objectives rather than in terms of Sharpe ratios or information on appraisal ratios.[5]

First things first, however. In this section, we consider one way to present past performance.

CASE STUDY 4: ANNUAL PORTFOLIO PERFORMANCE REVIEW

An advisor welcomes an investor to his office for an annual portfolio performance review meeting. The advisor has worked with the investor for several years and, beginning January 2006, they have met annually to review portfolio performance results. Presentations made in past-years' meetings covered the following topics:[6]

- Returns over the previous year and over selected additional time periods, e.g., two years, five years, since inception
- Returns in excess of inflation (real return)
- Portfolio risk as measured by its standard deviation
- Range of investment returns—highest monthly returns minus lowest monthly returns
- Distribution of returns—a histogram of monthly returns over the life of the portfolio
- The Sharpe ratio (return in excess of the risk-free rate ÷ standard deviation of returns)
- Current asset allocation versus target asset allocation (allocation drift)
- Investment position review—including notes on marketability, liquidity, tax-efficiency, and manager performance
- Discussions concerning continued prudence of maintaining existing investment positions
- Compliance with legal and regulatory requirements, e.g., no investments triggering unrelated taxable business income in tax-favored accounts

For today's meeting, the advisor prepares an exposition outlining important quantitative information about performance both during the past year as well as over the life of the portfolio. Previous meetings have gone well and the advisor is pleased generally with the investor's ascent up a learning curve since the initial 2006 portfolio review meeting. The investor knows, at least intuitively, the meaning of many important financial concepts. If she cannot precisely define the Sharpe ratio as a measure of the portfolio's efficiency in utilizing units of risk to generate units of reward, at least she recognizes it as a tool for assessing a reward-to-risk relationship.[7] The presentation depicts

---

5.   A more comprehensive discussion of this topic is found in Collins and Gadenne (2017). The robo-advice industry attempts to provide a "mass customization" solution.

6.   The reader will recognize the review items in terms of the key provisions in an IPS. Presentation formats and topics will differ across account types, e.g., taxable versus tax-deferred, and across advisory firms, e.g., financial planning-oriented versus investment-focused. We do not advocate for a one-size-fits-all presentation format or content.

7.   For a more technical discussion about how to apply MPT performance evaluation criteria in the context of prudent trust investing, see Collins (2011 a, b).

the year-by-year evolution of portfolio returns over time.[8] Each chart contains four geometric "characters." Taken in order, the sequence of snapshots is similar to an animated movie of the portfolio's behavior over time. The dramatis personae are the asset classes from which the portfolio is built, and, of course, the portfolio itself:

- Triangles—U.S. and foreign fixed income securities (bonds)
- Circles—U.S. stocks and U.S. securitized real estate
- Diamonds—foreign stocks including emerging markets equity
- Black Square—the investor's portfolio.

The advisor directs the investor's attention to figure 6.1. The portfolio's inception date is January 2005 and the initial snapshot is one year (period ending December 31, 2005). The advisor explains:

1. The vertical (Y) axis measures compound geometric return. The horizontal (X) axis measures risk as quantified by the standard deviation of monthly returns over the applicable period. Thus, the subject of the movie concerns (1) portfolio return, and (2) risk, over (3) time—the primary elements of investment performance evaluation.

2. The geometric "characters" occupy specific regions (sometimes overlapping) in the reward-to-risk plane. For example, in figure 6.1, triangles (fixed income investments) occupy lower-return/lower-risk land, foreign stocks (diamonds) occupy the "highlands," U.S. stocks (circles) occupy a middle region.

3. Individual asset classes, i.e., the building blocks of the square-shaped portfolio, are the indexes listed on the table located at the movie's end. It is like a table of ending movie credits. The bottom part of each frame snapshot contains the color-coded, asset class geometric key.

4. A straight line runs from the risk-free rate through the investor's portfolio square. This is the capital allocation line familiar to students of modern portfolio theory. The slope of the capital allocation line is the value of the portfolio's Sharpe ratio. The greater the positive slope, the more favorable the realized return-to-risk trade-off during the period under evaluation.

The advisor, wishing to engage the investor actively, asks what she notices in the picture of first-year portfolio performance. After some leading questions, she responds:

- The slope of the reward-to-risk trade-off is positive—this seems like a good thing (although she is mostly guessing at this point).
- There is a purple diamond far out on the risk line but very high on the reward line (she wishes she had put all her money in this investment). Looking at the key, she discovers that the investment is emerging market stocks.
- Bonds appear to be awful investments—short-term governments performed far better than either intermediate or foreign bonds (why did the advisor recommend these investments?).
- When the advisor points out that the green circle is the S&P 500, she notes that her portfolio earned more return with less risk during this period (this also seems like a good thing).
- Finally, she observes that foreign stock investments occupy a dominant position in the reward-risk plane.

The advisor also calls her attention to the fact that investment results are spread out widely across the plane. There does not appear to be a reliable relationship between risk and return—unlike emerging market stocks, some high-risk investments (U.S. small-cap and microcap stocks) exhibit high risk and anemic returns. This seems puzzling because the investor is familiar with charts that plot investment returns along a line of positive slope with low-risk/low-return investments located on the lower left with high-risk/high-return investments on the upper right. During this period, however, things did not work out as expected. Finally, the advisor points out that investors prefer to see the capital allocation line move in a counter-clockwise direction—more return per unit of risk.

8.　Returns are time-weighted monthly returns. The economic effects of withdrawal or contribution amounts and timing are not considered in order to focus on the performance of the strategic asset allocation codified in the IPS. The impact of timing and magnitude of cash flows is the subject of the next chapter. Appendix C provides details on asset allocation weights and data sources.

FIGURE 6.1: PORTFOLIO PERFORMANCE REVIEW, JANUARY 2005–DECEMBER 2005

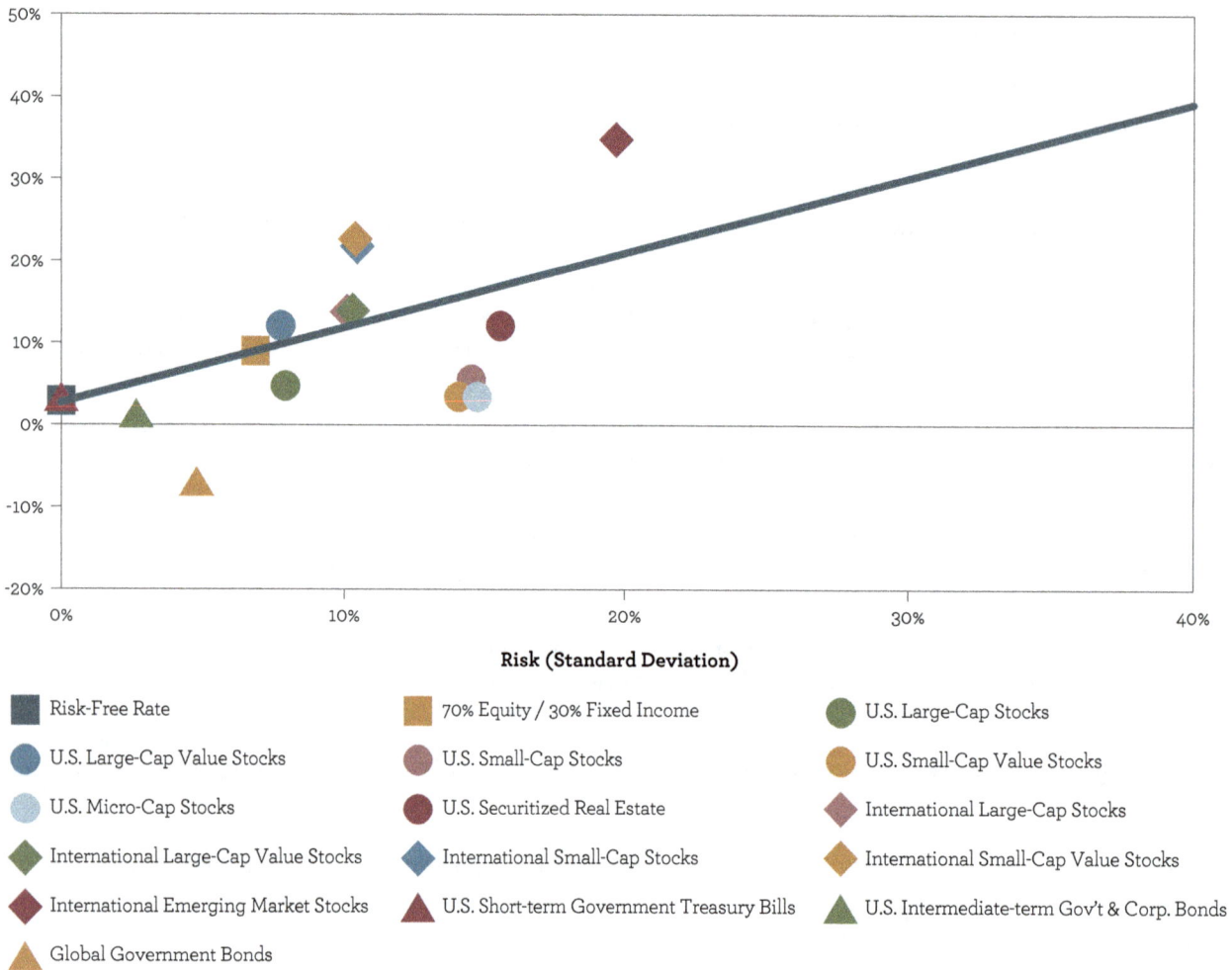

Returns (GM)

Risk (Standard Deviation)

Legend:
- Risk-Free Rate
- 70% Equity / 30% Fixed Income
- U.S. Large-Cap Stocks
- U.S. Large-Cap Value Stocks
- U.S. Small-Cap Stocks
- U.S. Small-Cap Value Stocks
- U.S. Micro-Cap Stocks
- U.S. Securitized Real Estate
- International Large-Cap Stocks
- International Large-Cap Value Stocks
- International Small-Cap Stocks
- International Small-Cap Value Stocks
- International Emerging Market Stocks
- U.S. Short-term Government Treasury Bills
- U.S. Intermediate-term Gov't & Corp. Bonds
- Global Government Bonds

With this background in hand, the advisor advances to the next frame snapshot, which covers the two-year period beginning in 2005 through the end of 2006 (see figure 6.2). Comparing figure 6.1 with figure 6.2 yields interesting insights:

- The line moves in a counterclockwise direction, i.e., exhibits a steeper slope. This indicates a favorable investment environment.

- The asset classes that occupied positions significantly above the line in figure 6.1 now are closer to the line. No one asset class appears to have provided a significantly superior reward-to-risk outcome over the two-year period. Likewise, many of the assets lying significantly beneath the line in figure 6.1 have moved closer to the line in figure 6.2.

FIGURE 6.2: PORTFOLIO PERFORMANCE REVIEW, JANUARY 2005–DECEMBER 2006

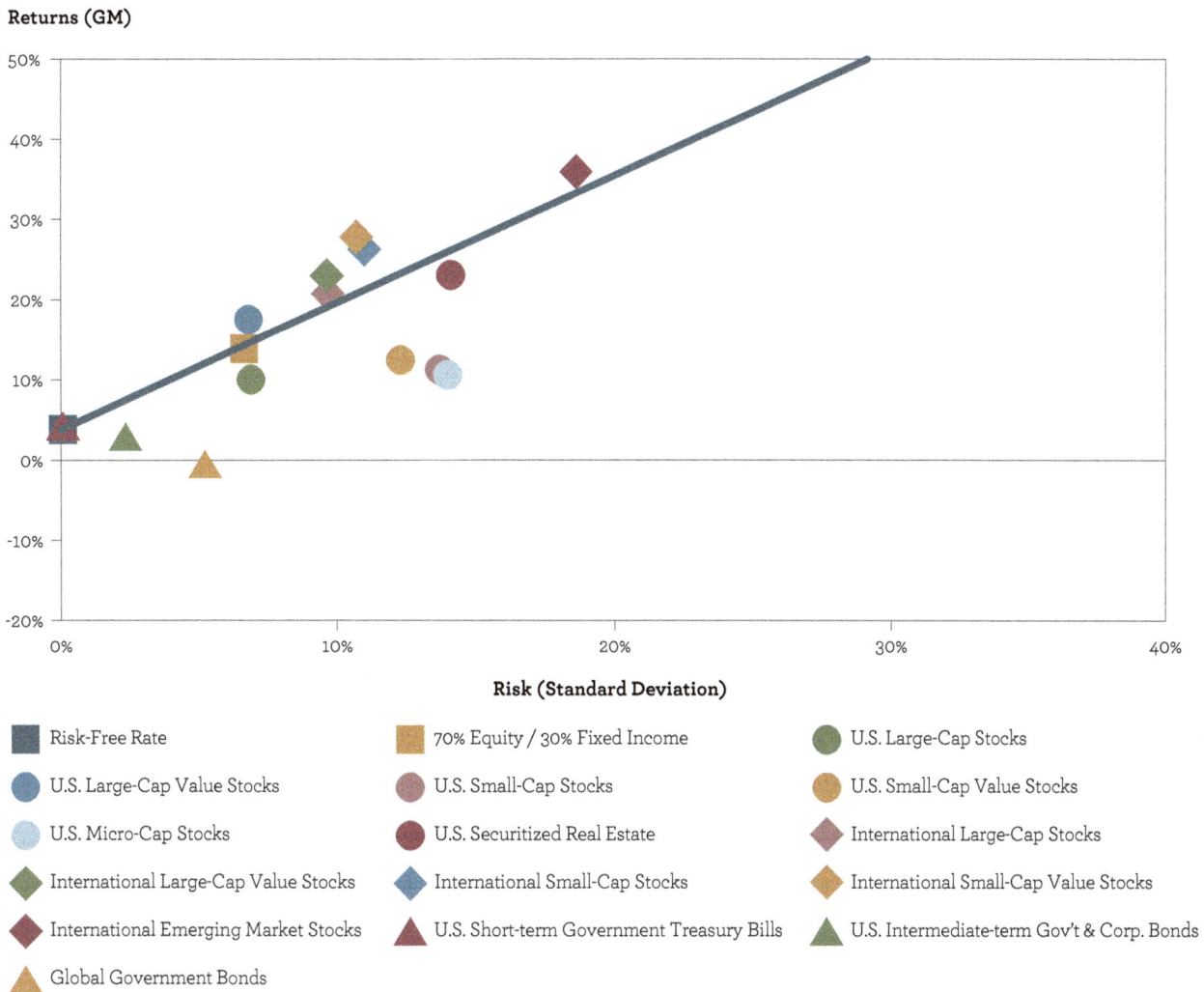

By figure 6.3, the investor notes that emerging markets again occupy a dominant position in the reward-to-risk plane. The advisor agrees but points out that the investment was not a free lunch—although the emerging markets asset class generated an outsized reward relative to other investment choices during this three-year period, its risk level exceeds that of other asset classes. Although the downside of emerging market stock risk has not materialized in this period, this does not mean that it is not embedded within the investment position. It remains as a kind of "iceberg" risk.

Additionally, the investor easily can see that the triangles continue to occupy both a low-risk and low-return region in the plane.

FIGURE 6.3: PORTFOLIO PERFORMANCE REVIEW, JANUARY 2005–DECEMBER 2007

Returns (GM)

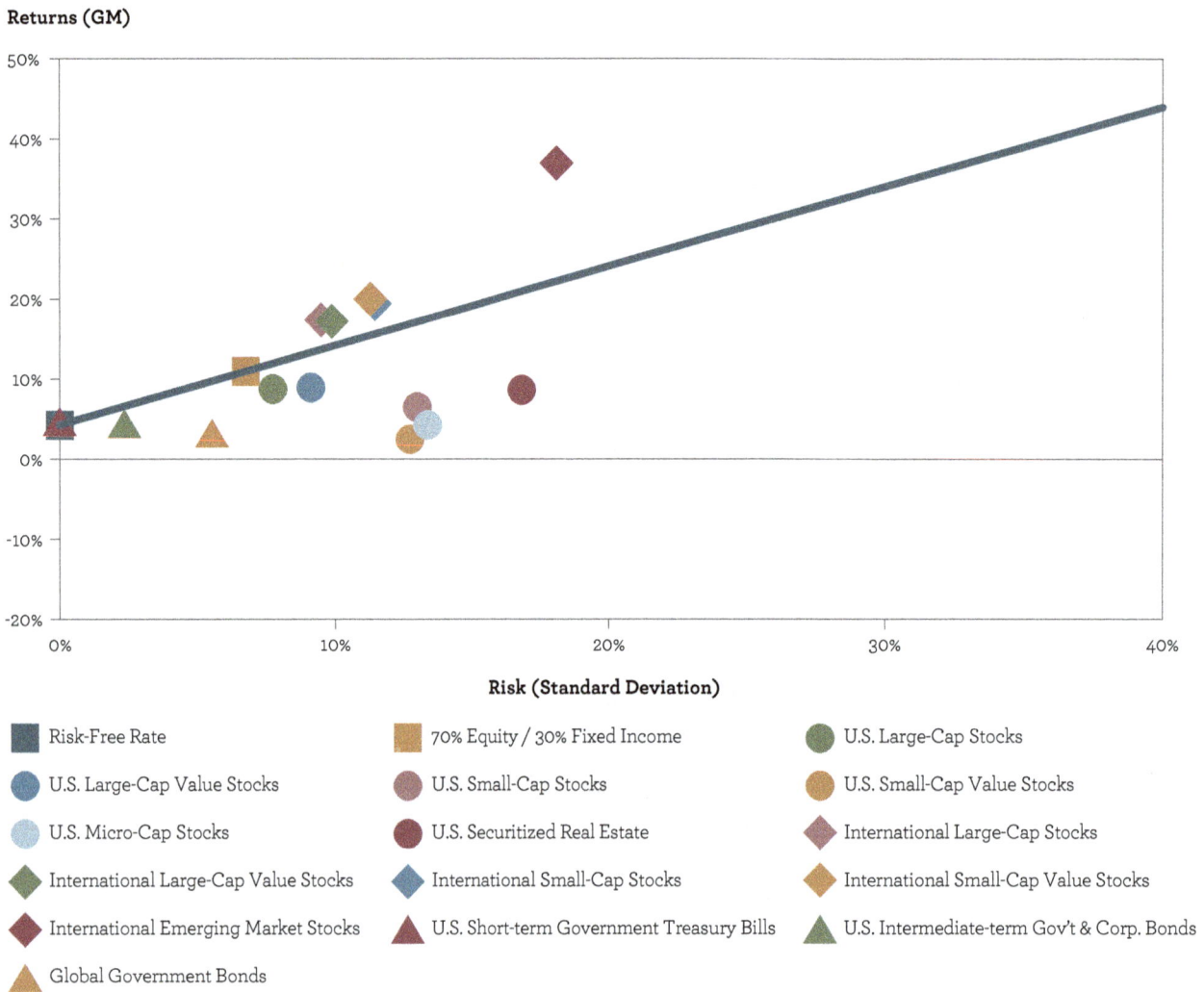

Before advancing to figure 6.4 (four-year period from 2005 through 2008), the advisor reminds the investor that her portfolio is about to endure the great global recession. The investor's curiosity is piqued—how did the portfolio behave? Did the bonds tank along with the stocks?

The investor is stunned by the picture in figure 6.4. The capital allocation line has moved clockwise and now exhibits a negative slope. Capital markets, rather than rewarding investors for assuming risk, have hammered them. Most asset class positions are sitting below zero percent on the Y-axis, i.e., they have negative returns for the four-year period. If most equity investments have declined significantly in value, the relative descent of emerging markets is breathtaking. In fact, it is clear that the helpful asset classes are the fixed income positions that formerly appeared to be a drag on portfolio performance.

The advisor also points out that most asset classes shift significantly to the right on the "X" risk axis. The recession robbed investors of cumulated profits, and placed them in a more unfavorable, i.e., higher risk, position on the investment plane.

FIGURE 6.4: PORTFOLIO PERFORMANCE REVIEW, JANUARY 2005–DECEMBER 2008

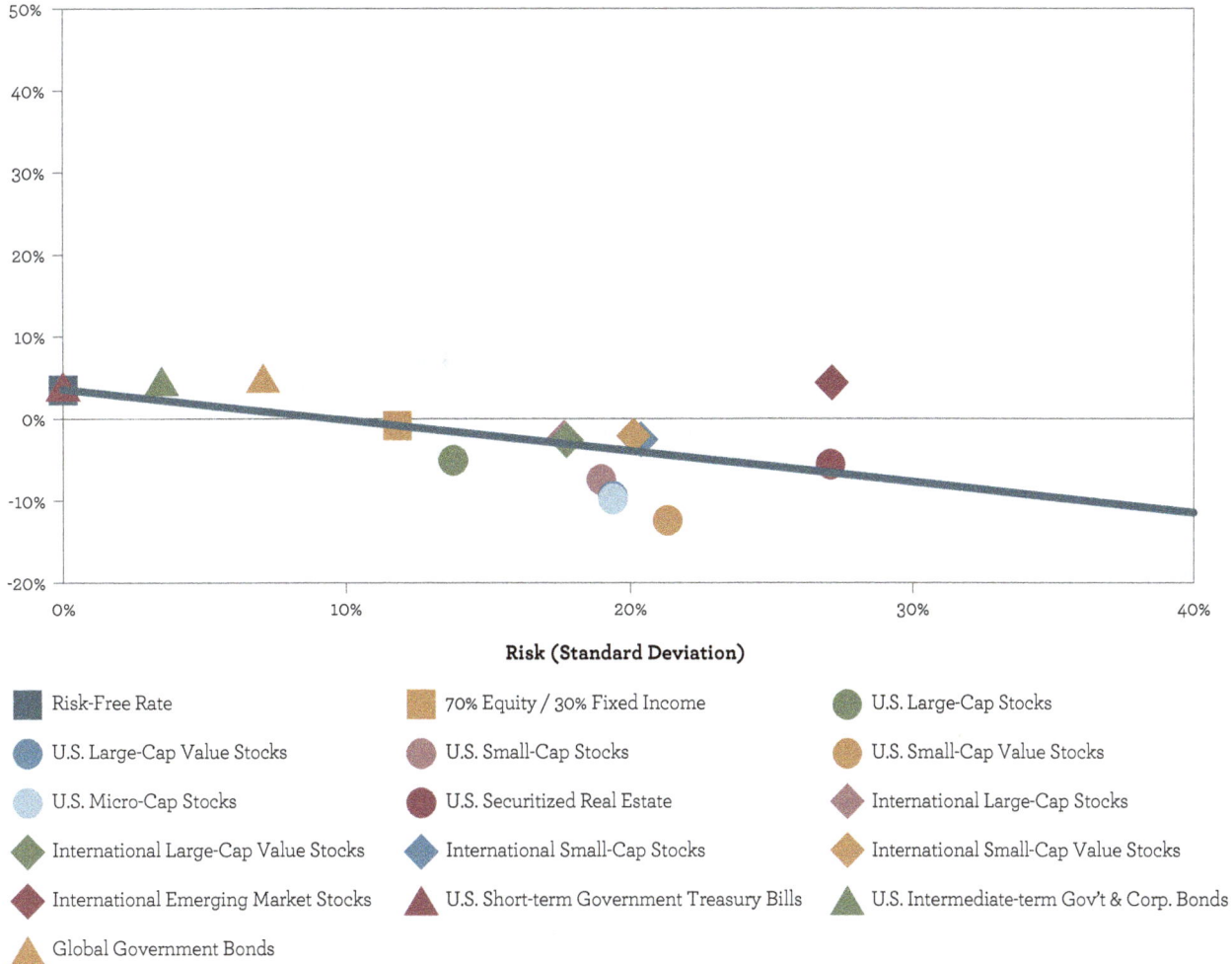

Moving forward one year, the investor sees a partial recovery for her portfolio. In figure 6.5, the slope of the line is now slightly greater than horizontal and securitized real estate has moved into the lead (far right) position on the risk axis. This is not surprising given that the roots of the recession lie in the subprime mortgage crisis. The three most-risky asset classes are now securitized real estate, U.S. small company value stocks, and emerging markets stocks. The S&P 500 (green circle) has produced approximately zero-percent compound annual return for the previous five years. It is cold comfort that the investor's portfolio has outperformed the S&P.

FIGURE 6.5: PORTFOLIO PERFORMANCE REVIEW, JANUARY 2005–DECEMBER 2009

Returns (GM)

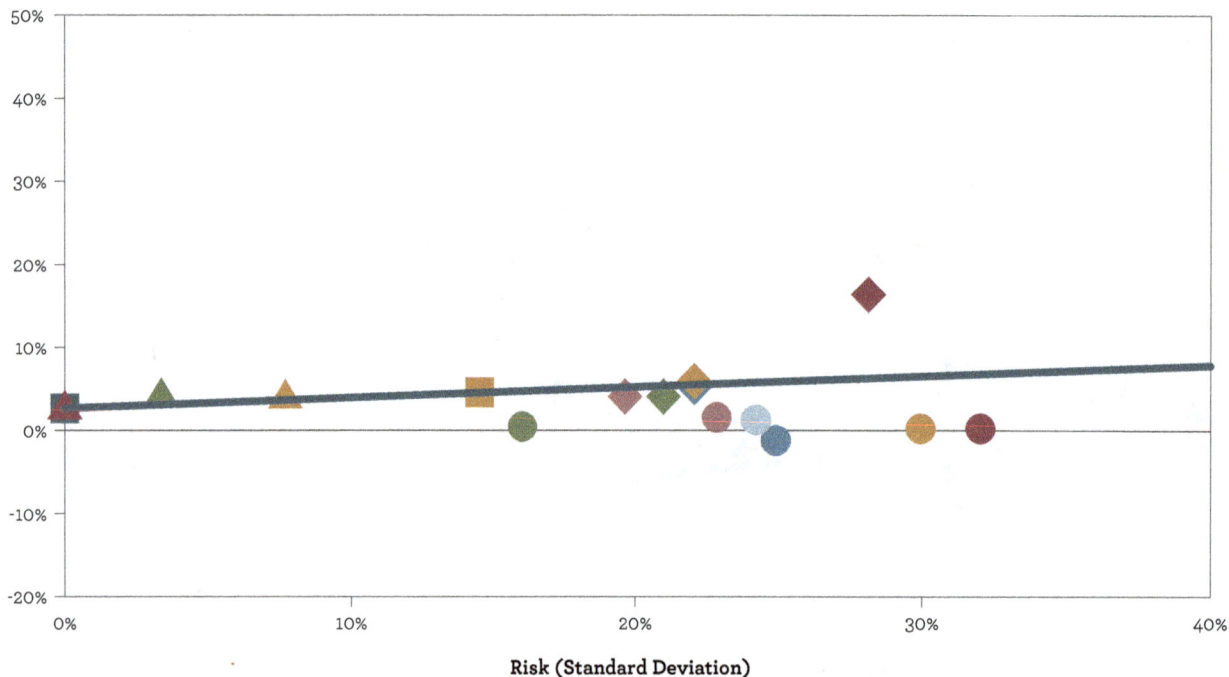

Risk (Standard Deviation)

■ Risk-Free Rate	■ 70% Equity / 30% Fixed Income	● U.S. Large-Cap Stocks
● U.S. Large-Cap Value Stocks	● U.S. Small-Cap Stocks	● U.S. Small-Cap Value Stocks
● U.S. Micro-Cap Stocks	● U.S. Securitized Real Estate	◆ International Large-Cap Stocks
◆ International Large-Cap Value Stocks	◆ International Small-Cap Stocks	◆ International Small-Cap Value Stocks
◆ International Emerging Market Stocks	▲ U.S. Short-term Government Treasury Bills	▲ U.S. Intermediate-term Gov't & Corp. Bonds
▲ Global Government Bonds		

Adding the next time period (through 2010) to the portfolio's reward-to-risk profile moves the capital allocation line in a favorable counterclockwise direction (see figure 6.6). (Are emerging markets a bullet proof long-term winner?) The investor notes that all asset classes now occupy spaces above the zero-percent compound return line. The advisor asks the investor to compare the dispersion of results in the reward-to-risk plane as of the end of 2010 with the one-year dispersion of results at the end of 2005 (figure 6.1). Looking at figure 6.1, the investor is struck by the extent to which time has decreased the range of outcomes expressed in rate-of-return terms.[9] It now seems as if empirical results are lining up in an approximately linear relationship between risk and reward.

---

9.   Rates tend to converge over time. Wealth levels do not converge because even small differences in rates, when compounded over many years, produce large differences in terminal wealth.

FIGURE 6.6: PORTFOLIO PERFORMANCE REVIEW, JANUARY 2005–DECEMBER 2010

Returns (GM)

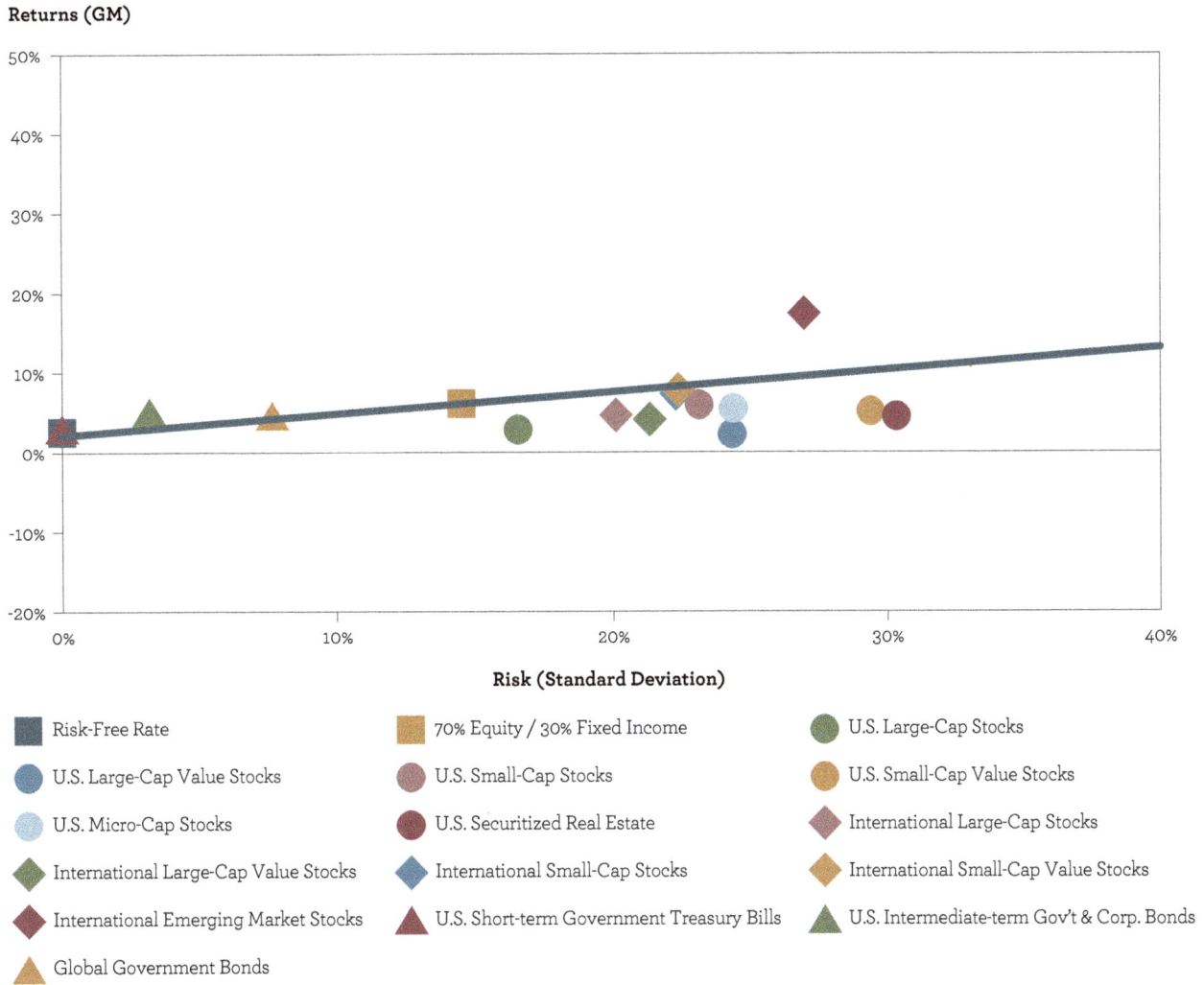

Risk (Standard Deviation)

■ Risk-Free Rate	■ 70% Equity / 30% Fixed Income	● U.S. Large-Cap Stocks
● U.S. Large-Cap Value Stocks	● U.S. Small-Cap Stocks	● U.S. Small-Cap Value Stocks
● U.S. Micro-Cap Stocks	● U.S. Securitized Real Estate	◆ International Large-Cap Stocks
◆ International Large-Cap Value Stocks	◆ International Small-Cap Stocks	◆ International Small-Cap Value Stocks
◆ International Emerging Market Stocks	▲ U.S. Short-term Government Treasury Bills	▲ U.S. Intermediate-term Gov't & Corp. Bonds
▲ Global Government Bonds		

The next two years produce one step forward and one step back (see figures 6.7 and 6.8). The risk-free rate of return intercept decreases toward the zero-percent mark on the Y axis. This, of course, reflects the U.S. Federal Reserve's attempt to maintain low interest rates post-recession. In many respects, the artificiality of this environment decreases and flattens the realized equity risk premium—higher-risk small- and micro-U.S. equities produce minimal return advantages over large, more liquid stocks. Figures 6.7 and 6.8 also indicate a modest shift leftward on the risk axis for most asset class positions.

FIGURE 6.7: PORTFOLIO PERFORMANCE REVIEW, JANUARY 2005–DECEMBER 2011

Returns (GM)

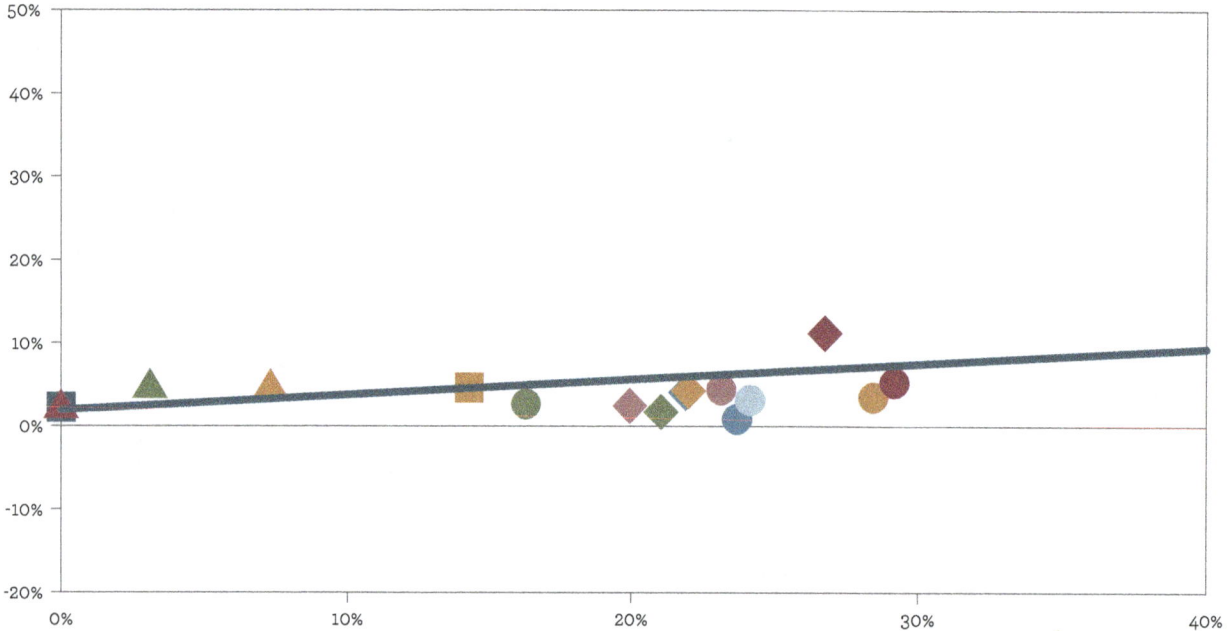

Risk (Standard Deviation)

■ Risk-Free Rate	■ 70% Equity / 30% Fixed Income	● U.S. Large-Cap Stocks
● U.S. Large-Cap Value Stocks	● U.S. Small-Cap Stocks	● U.S. Small-Cap Value Stocks
● U.S. Micro-Cap Stocks	● U.S. Securitized Real Estate	◆ International Large-Cap Stocks
◆ International Large-Cap Value Stocks	◆ International Small-Cap Stocks	◆ International Small-Cap Value Stocks
◆ International Emerging Market Stocks	▲ U.S. Short-term Government Treasury Bills	▲ U.S. Intermediate-term Gov't & Corp. Bonds
▲ Global Government Bonds		

FIGURE 6.8: PORTFOLIO PERFORMANCE REVIEW, JANUARY 2005–DECEMBER 2012

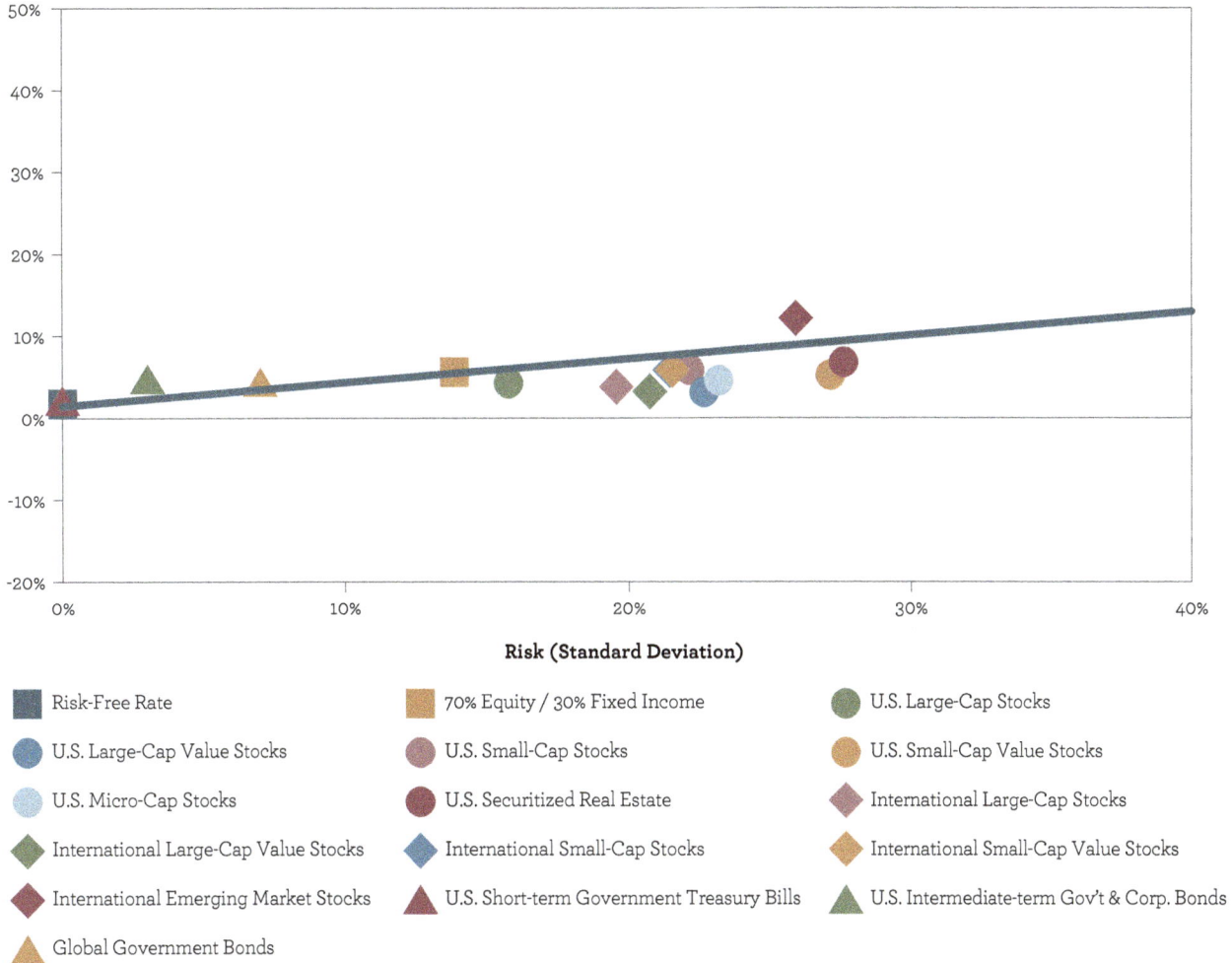

By the end of 2013, with the exception of the asset class of U.S. intermediate-term bonds, the compound returns of each investment considered in isolation lie below the capital allocation line (see figure 6.9). Despite the Great Recession, a diversified portfolio offered a better reward-to-risk outcome than most single-asset-class portfolios. Furthermore, over this period, the diversified portfolio produces approximately 6-percent greater yearly compound return than holding short-term U.S. treasuries. The cost of safety during this turbulent period is high.

The movement of individual asset class geometric shapes is more subdued as each yearly compound return is added incrementally to the time-weighted rate-of-return series originating in 2005. However, the investor, studying the periods ending in 2013, 2014, and 2015, remarks that the space occupied by foreign stock asset classes overlaps the positions of U.S. stock investments (see figures 6.9, 6.10, and 6.11). The advisor notes that this is, in part, a consequence of a strengthening U.S. dollar during this period.

FIGURE 6.9: PORTFOLIO PERFORMANCE REVIEW, JANUARY 2005–DECEMBER 2013

Returns (GM)

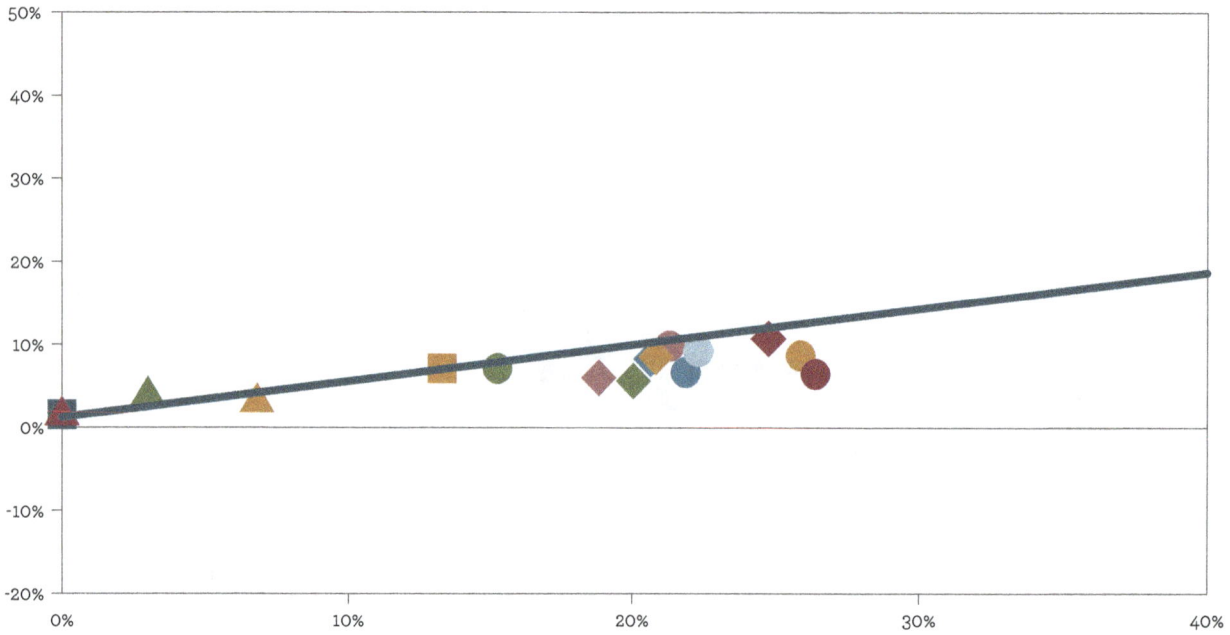

Risk (Standard Deviation)

■ Risk-Free Rate	■ 70% Equity / 30% Fixed Income	● U.S. Large-Cap Stocks
● U.S. Large-Cap Value Stocks	● U.S. Small-Cap Stocks	● U.S. Small-Cap Value Stocks
● U.S. Micro-Cap Stocks	● U.S. Securitized Real Estate	◆ International Large-Cap Stocks
◆ International Large-Cap Value Stocks	◆ International Small-Cap Stocks	◆ International Small-Cap Value Stocks
◆ International Emerging Market Stocks	▲ U.S. Short-term Government Treasury Bills	▲ U.S. Intermediate-term Gov't & Corp. Bonds
▲ Global Government Bonds		

FIGURE 6.10: PORTFOLIO PERFORMANCE REVIEW, JANUARY 2005–DECEMBER 2014

Returns (GM)

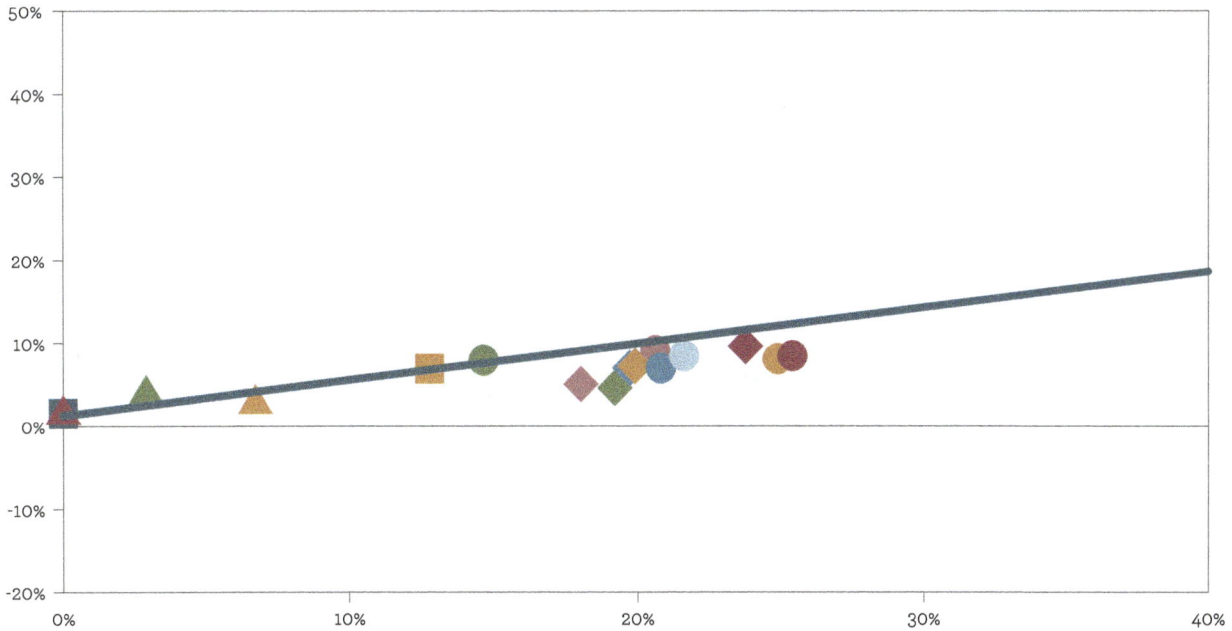

Risk (Standard Deviation)

■ Risk-Free Rate	■ 70% Equity / 30% Fixed Income	● U.S. Large-Cap Stocks
● U.S. Large-Cap Value Stocks	● U.S. Small-Cap Stocks	● U.S. Small-Cap Value Stocks
● U.S. Micro-Cap Stocks	● U.S. Securitized Real Estate	◆ International Large-Cap Stocks
◆ International Large-Cap Value Stocks	◆ International Small-Cap Stocks	◆ International Small-Cap Value Stocks
◆ International Emerging Market Stocks	▲ U.S. Short-term Government Treasury Bills	▲ U.S. Intermediate-term Gov't & Corp. Bonds
▲ Global Government Bonds		

FIGURE 6.11: PORTFOLIO PERFORMANCE REVIEW, JANUARY 2005–DECEMBER 2015

Returns (GM)

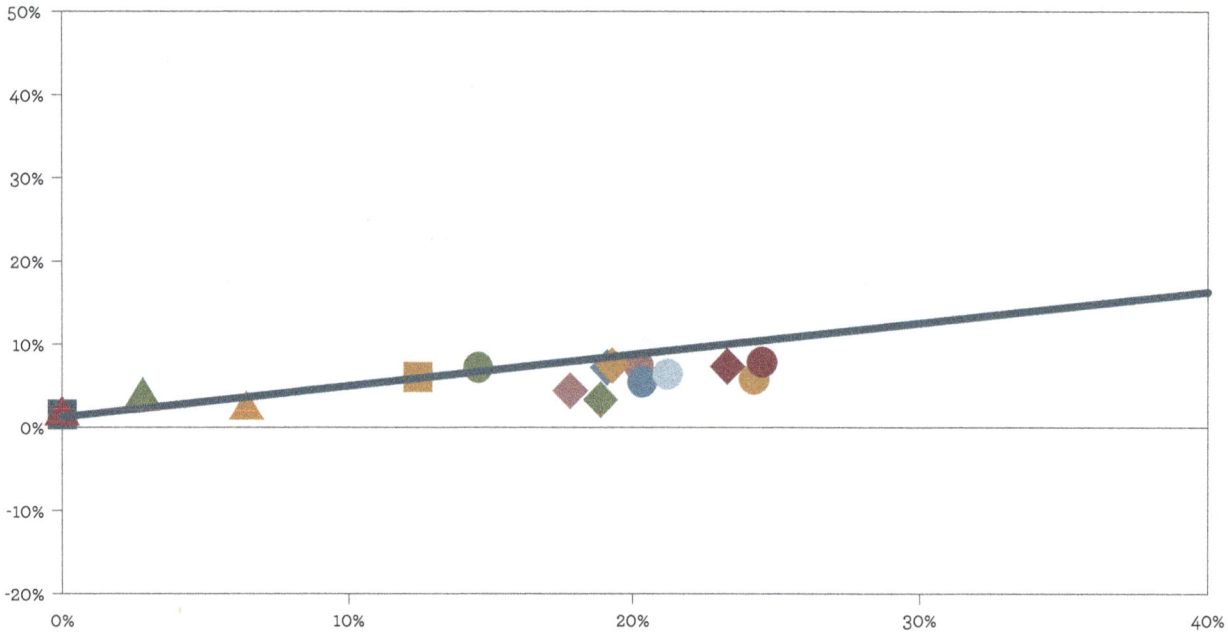

Risk (Standard Deviation)

- Risk-Free Rate
- 70% Equity / 30% Fixed Income
- U.S. Large-Cap Stocks
- U.S. Large-Cap Value Stocks
- U.S. Small-Cap Stocks
- U.S. Small-Cap Value Stocks
- U.S. Micro-Cap Stocks
- U.S. Securitized Real Estate
- International Large-Cap Stocks
- International Large-Cap Value Stocks
- International Small-Cap Stocks
- International Small-Cap Value Stocks
- International Emerging Market Stocks
- U.S. Short-term Government Treasury Bills
- U.S. Intermediate-term Gov't & Corp. Bonds
- Global Government Bonds

Over the 12-year time period, the portfolio earned an annual compound return approximately 5 percent greater than the risk-free rate (see figure 6.12). This was the (well-deserved) compensation for bearing risk during an extraordinarily volatile period. The investor could have earned roughly the same or higher returns by investing in many of the circle or diamond asset classes. The real investment accomplishment is not simply to earn a return above the risk-free rate, but to earn such a return at a suitable level of risk, i.e., a risk-controlled return.

Returns (GM)

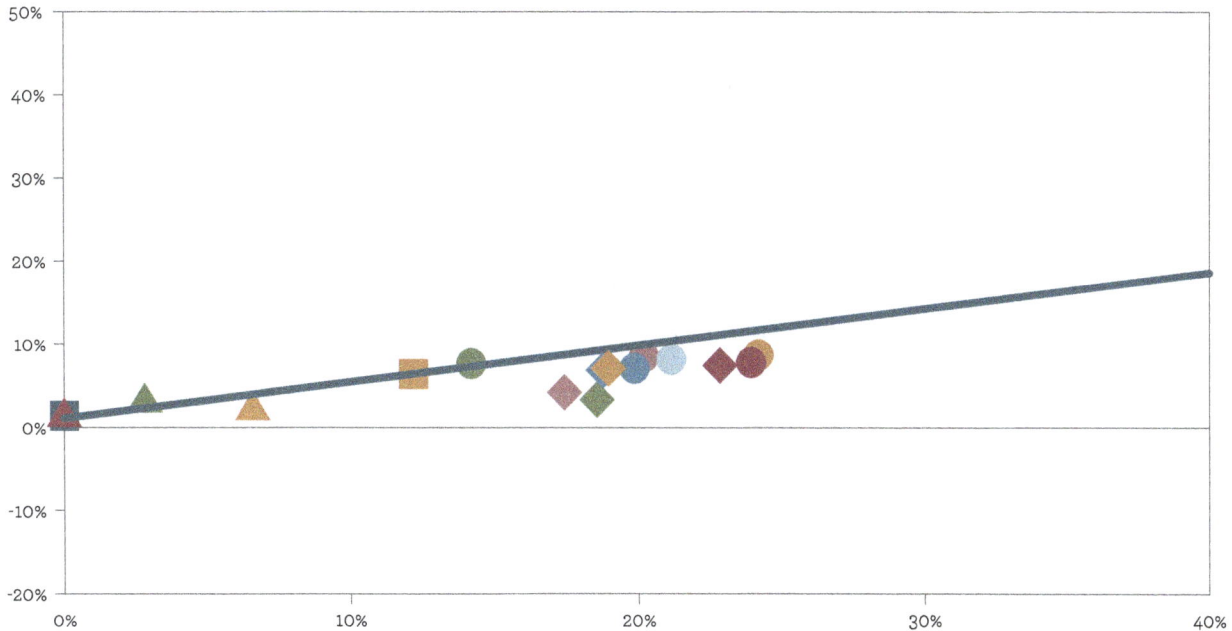

Risk (Standard Deviation)

■ Risk-Free Rate	■ 70% Equity / 30% Fixed Income	● U.S. Large-Cap Stocks
● U.S. Large-Cap Value Stocks	● U.S. Small-Cap Stocks	● U.S. Small-Cap Value Stocks
● U.S. Micro-Cap Stocks	● U.S. Securitized Real Estate	◆ International Large-Cap Stocks
◆ International Large-Cap Value Stocks	◆ International Small-Cap Stocks	◆ International Small-Cap Value Stocks
◆ International Emerging Market Stocks	▲ U.S. Short-term Government Treasury Bills	▲ U.S. Intermediate-term Gov't & Corp. Bonds
▲ Global Government Bonds		

As the investor considers figure 6.13, the advisor adds a second, rescaled view. Figure 6.13 depicts two lines: the capital allocation line and a line of best fit.

FIGURE 6.13: PORTFOLIO PERFORMANCE REVIEW, JANUARY 2005–DECEMBER 2016

Returns (GM)

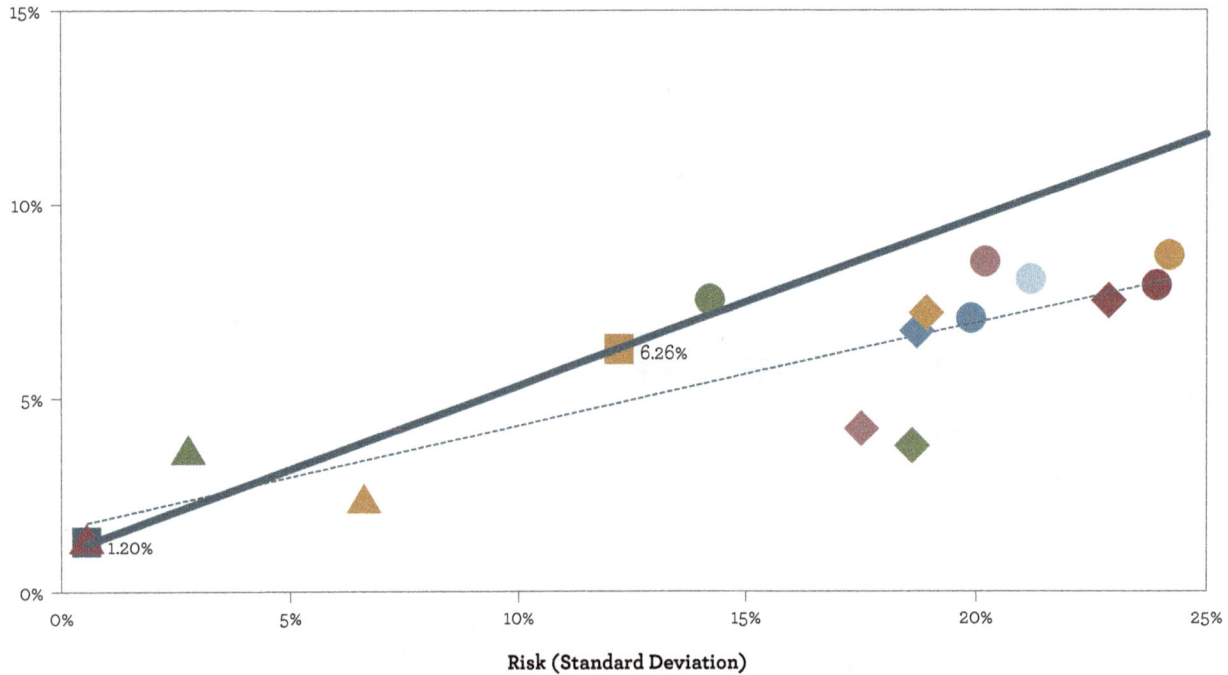

Risk (Standard Deviation)

■ Risk-Free Rate   ■ 70% Equity / 30% Fixed Income   ● U.S. Large-Cap Stocks

● U.S. Large-Cap Value Stocks   ● U.S. Small-Cap Stocks   ● U.S. Small-Cap Value Stocks

● U.S. Micro-Cap Stocks   ● U.S. Securitized Real Estate   ◆ International Large-Cap Stocks

◆ International Large-Cap Value Stocks   ◆ International Small-Cap Stocks   ◆ International Small-Cap Value Stocks

◆ International Emerging Market Stocks   ▲ U.S. Short-term Government Treasury Bills   ▲ U.S. Intermediate-term Gov't & Corp. Bonds

▲ Global Government Bonds   —— Capital Allocation Line   ----- Line of Best Fit

The solid line is the capital allocation line; the dashed line is the line of best fit. The advisor states that this is a statistical procedure that fits a line through the scatter plot of geometric shapes in such a way as to minimize the aggregate distance between the line and the geometric shapes.[10] He explains the new element's significance as follows: Although several asset classes earned higher compound returns during the period under consideration, the risk required to do so often was far greater than the portfolio's risk. Here is the key insight: The fact that the portfolio lies above the line of best fit demonstrates the benefits of the investor's asset allocation and investment management decisions. Only two asset classes—intermediate-term U.S. government bonds and the S&P 500 Index of U.S.

---

10.   The reader will recognize this as a least squares regression line. The portfolio "square" is not included in the best-fit calculation.

large-cap stocks—offered a more favorable compound return per unit of risk during this period. This said, hindsight is 20–20; there is no assurance that this will be the case over the forthcoming 12-year horizon.[11] After all, asset class positions shift constantly relative both to each other and to the capital allocation line in the return-risk plane. The investment results that unfold, over time, have many moving parts—hence the need for:

1. Understanding the dynamics of investment performance

2. Measuring and monitoring investment results

3. Assessing the probable consequences in terms of the feasibility, sustainability, and security of the investor's financial goals during retirement

These items form the main subjects of the following chapters.

---

11. The magnitude of the vertical distance between the line of best fit and the capital allocation line quantifies, in part, what some investment commentators refer to as "gamma"—the value of investment advice. (See, for example, Blanchett and Kaplan [2013]). Gamma is a somewhat nebulous concept, however, because it encompasses a variety of effects that are difficult to quantify with precision. The vertical distance between lines yields a more-precise measure of benefit in terms of compound return. At any point on the horizontal (risk) axis, an investor can see easily how much reward (units of return) is required to compensate for the risk to which wealth is exposed (units of risk). For example, in this period, although an investment in U.S. small-cap stocks earned a return higher than the portfolio's, the return is insufficient compensation for the risk of investing all wealth in small company stocks. Depending on portfolio construction principles and asset management strategies, the positive benefit may be due to some combination of (1) security selection or market timing, (2) diversification (benefit due to asset covariance less than unity), (3) asset weighting or factor loading decisions, (4) derivative usage, and (5) interactions among these elements. Tracking above the line of best fit is indicative of successful portfolio management, although care must be taken during recessionary periods, or when one asset class earns outsized returns over the period under evaluation.

CHAPTER SEVEN

MONITORING AND EVALUATION—PRESENT

■ ■ ■

This chapter discusses portfolio management through time. Prior to a portfolio's implementation, a written investment policy statement (IPS) codifies investment policy decision-making. Almost every IPS has boilerplate language outlining a protocol for periodic review of investments. Often, the investment review process evaluates the performance of investments in isolation, rather than within the portfolio context. Rather than determining an investment's suitability as a function of investor needs, goals, and circumstances, an IPS may mandate a comparison of each investment's risk and return characteristics to similar investments within the opportunity set. Undoubtedly, such a review can yield important insights, and can suggest opportunities to improve the portfolio, e.g., avoiding or replacing high-cost investment products). This chapter, however, is more about reviewing the aggregate portfolio than it is about finding five-star investment products that currently lead the investment return horse race.

Asset management encompasses monitoring and evaluating initial investment decisions. Monitoring incorporates assessments about past performance, current resources, and the likely future consequences of asset management decisions, i.e., stay-the-course or change strategy. Portfolio monitoring and evaluation is the basis for making prudent investment decisions.

THE PRESENT: FEASIBILITY AND THE ACTUARIAL COVERAGE RATIO

The previous chapter is primarily about the past—how the portfolio evolved. The current chapter is about what should be done today to secure a successful economic future. More technically, how does the investor assess probabilities and future outcomes given the current information set? Are these outcomes acceptable? What asset management elections should the investor consider now?

Generally, investors do not think in probabilistic terms. Rather, they ask: Are my goals achievable? Am I gaining or losing ground financially? These are the topics of interest, and the advisor's challenge is to translate quantitative insights into qualitative, i.e., understandable, vocabulary.

Technically, monitoring and evaluation is a process of forming "Posterior Probability Estimates" or "Conditional Probability Estimates." We borrow vocabulary from the ideas originally presented by Reverend Thomas Bayes.[1] Initial portfolio design and asset management decisions reflect return and risk preferences based on the investor's *a priori* probability distribution.[2] Once the investor understands how the portfolio arrived at its current state, the issue becomes how to update beliefs when faced with new evidence.[3] From the perspective of an advisor, the task is to help the client (1) understand events and learn from them as time unfolds, and (2) use the updated information to reassess preferences and, perhaps, modify behaviors. If new information is favorable, the investor may have an opportunity to increase consumption, gifting, or bequest levels; if new information is unfavorable, the investor may have the option to maintain or decrease consumption,[4] gifting, or bequest levels. Also included in the decision set is the option to changeinvestment-management strategy. For example, faced with changes in economic circumstances, is it prudent to initiate or delay an option to implement flooring? When is it appropriate to reset the stock-bond allocation for a buy-and-hold investing strategy? When is it prudent to acquire an annuity, a bond ladder, or other similar principal-protection strategies or products?

The initial challenge is to gauge the portfolio's current economic condition. Have the nature and scope of assets and liabilities changed over time, and has the portfolio maintained a surplus in the face of changes in asset and liability values? Operationally, this requires updating the actuarial coverage ratio (ACR) value based on current information. The question of interest is whether the investor's retirement-income objectives continue to remain feasible.

---

1.   Thomas Bayes (1701–1761) was an English statistician, philosopher, and Presbyterian minister who is known for formulating a specific case of the theorem that bears his name: Bayes' theorem

2.   Given what is known about the past, what is the investor's best guess about the future?

3.   Of course, the investor's risk aversion also may change with changes in wealth and liabilities. This means that the investor, over time, updates preferences as well as beliefs.

4.   Decreasing consumption may include keeping a withdrawal at the previous year's level by not adjusting upward for inflation increases.

Chapter Four (Case Study 2) devoted considerable time to decomposing the ACR into its component parts: available assets in the numerator and liability costs in the denominator, where we value retirement-income liabilities according to the annuity-pricing principle: [(cash flow needs multiplied by survival probability) ÷ (discount factors derived from the term structure of interest rates)]. Chapter Five (Case Study 3) added other liability components such as lifetime gifting or death time bequests. Chapter Three (Case Study 1) considered the economic effects of contingent assets (life insurance payoffs or inheritance expectations). Contingent liabilities can enter the retirement-income model either as a contingent reserve liability, a "negative inheritance" expectation, e.g., end-of-life expenses, or as a separately calculated stochastic cost that is zero in a good health regime and is a non-zero cost in a bad health regime.[5]

Case Study 1, our initial introduction to the ACR, demonstrates the variability of ACR values over time. The fact pattern generates an ACR with an initial value below 100 percent relative to the investor's aspirational income target. However, after a few years' time, the risk model projects a positive value (> 100 percent) "in expectation," i.e., 50th percentile.[6] Conversely, Case Study 1 also demonstrates how a positive ACR, over time, ultimately may turn negative (< 100 percent) "in expectation." The ACR is variable despite the static yield curve discount factor employed in this case study. Realistically, the yield curve changes constantly, and even small changes in the discount rate may generate large changes in ACR value over long-term planning horizons.

Feasibility evaluation, when using an actuarial benchmark, incorporates:

- Distribution and sequence of future investment returns
- Distribution and sequence of inflation realizations
- Distribution and sequence of retirement consumption (basic or aspirational standard of living goal)
- Distribution of future annuity costs—sequence of yield curve changes
- Health state differential (bad to worse, bad to good, etc.)
- Force and effect of mortality

Relationships among ACR factors are nonlinear, and the solvency test cannot be calculated on the back of an envelope. The advisor monitors and assesses variables within a high-dimensional context.

This is a "how should I plan" rather than a "what should I own" approach. The boilerplate investment review section of the IPS undergoes a metamorphosis and becomes a central element in the advisor's service set. It is the "monitoring and reporting in terms of client objectives" that is now the central level-of-service element in the ongoing client-advisor relationship. Portfolio monitoring is essential to prudent asset management.

Beyond this, however, the fact that a client knows what will be monitored, how it will be monitored, and how financial implications of unfolding events will be communicated has a profound effect on current actions. As time unfolds and new information arrives, investor preferences may change due to changes in economic circumstances (ability to accept risk) or in personal preferences (willingness to accept risk).[7] After meeting with the advisor, however, the investor knows that there exists a credible method for taking such developments into account, understanding their economic impacts, and formulating prudent and suitable responses. He cannot predict how personal preferences or circumstances may change, but adopting a retirement-as-a-risky-option perspective allows him to overcome decision paralysis: "This should be particularly important in a situation where the agent must decide today which options he wants to leave open in the future."[8]

---

5. Where the Markov transition model for health state is assumed uncorrelated with the economic state. In the presence of a state-dependent health modifier in a risk model, one cannot categorically assert that annuitization is optimal. Balls (2006) concludes that there "… are advantages to delaying annuitization, particularly when market returns available to the policyholder are superior to those available in the form of an annuity. However, the effect here is heterogeneous, depending also on the expected longevity of the policyholder." Balls' argument reinforces the necessity of monitoring and evaluating changes in investor-specific circumstances.

   See also, the discussion on the incorporation of liabilities in a retirement-income model given at the 2011 Society of Actuaries Conference, Yanikoski (2011), and Bajtelsmit et al. (2013) in which the risk model incorporates a variety of expenses for health-related risk factors.

6. This assumes a "market-agnostic" viewpoint instead of an "initial bear market" prediction.

7. The investor exhibits "temporal inconsistency" (Bordley and LiCalzi 2000).

8. Bordley and LiCalzi (2000, 63) point out that time horizon has an uncertain impact on option value. Increasing the time horizon often increases value; uncertainty regarding the amount of the target itself (a stochastic target) may decrease option value. We believe that future research into the merits of flooring strategies should incorporate these issues. What is the price of a put option held by an individual where the "payoff" is defined as a financially secure retirement, i.e., the amount required to restore an underperforming portfolio to the feasibility level? How should the option's value be calculated, e.g., the option's payoff is the ACR shortfall monetary calculation at a specified age? How does the option's price compare with the price of a single-premium immediate annuity contract, with a bond ladder, with a cash-flow-matching strategy?

The ACR provides an important component for reframing discussions about risks and rewards. A low ratio value suggests the need to consider corrective actions such as a spending reduction, a delay in lifetime gifting schedule, implementation of a reverse equity mortgage, or some combination of these and other planning options. A high ratio value suggests the need to revisit spending and gifting or bequest objectives to ensure optimal balance according to the investor's preference weighting (utility).

ACR, LONGEVITY RISK, AND PORTFOLIO VALUE

Retirement-income risk modeling, from the perspective of ACR analysis, yields interesting insights into longevity risk. Longevity risk may be a type of tail risk. Given the distribution of life spans, it is inevitable that some investors will survive well past their life expectancies. Some long-lived investors may incur the risk of portfolio depletion if they outlive their assets.[9] The traditional characterization of longevity risk is the joint conditional probability of (1) living beyond life expectancy, and (2) realizing investment returns insufficient to sustain the required lifetime target income. Consumer surveys suggest that retired investors worry about declines in portfolio value because they do not want to spend their final years unable to support an acceptable standard of living. They may express this concern in terms of not wanting to be an economic burden on family members, not wanting to apply for public or charitable assistance, and, ultimately, not wanting to sink into poverty.

The investor must be wary of longevity risk as age increases. Each year represents a greater proportion of remaining life expectancy, and, each year pushes life expectancy further into the future. The longer you live, the longer you're expected to live. As time in retirement passes, investors place greater and greater emphasis on their portfolio's dollar value if:

- The portfolio is on a downward dollar-value trajectory, and
- There is little flexibility in spending because current spending represents a greater proportion of portfolio value.[10]

Intuitively, many investors, lacking substantial wealth, realize that they are in a race between death and depletion. The stress meter can redline during periods of portfolio decline.

As the investor spends a greater and greater proportion of the remaining portfolio to sustain the target standard of living, will outcome volatility increase? How does the investor know if he or she is winning the race? What are the sources of outcome volatility for the late-in-life investor? An analysis should consider:

- Unfavorable inflation realizations
- Unfavorable investment returns
- Increases in liability values
- Changes in longevity risk

These are not uncorrelated variables. In an asset-liability management context, the deleterious effects of asset value declines due to higher interest rates may, in part, be offset by a correspondingly higher discount rate for valuation of liabilities.[11] Changes in longevity risk are especially interesting. Obviously, longevity risk may change with changes in health status. A cure for a disease, although having a beneficial impact on the general population, may have a detrimental economic impact on some retired investors if limited resources must be stretched further to accommodate longer expected life spans. However, there is another component to longevity risk. Actuarial data indicates, for example, that life expectancy for a white-collar, high-income, male retiree in current good health at age 65 is approximately age 88. However, life expectancy at age 88 for the population of surviving males is age 93. This means, absent any change in systematic population mortality risk, the population of age 65 male investors fortunate enough to live to age 88 will have a revised expectancy of surviving to age 93. Half of the age 88 population can expect to be alive beyond age 93. But no one is giving the portfolio an extra five year's life expectancy. If the initial age 65 investment planning contemplated the interactions of time, inflation, and investment returns to arrive at credible risk metrics and retirement-income projections, by age 88 the original numbers may be all wrong. Critical variables change merely with the passage of time. Was anyone monitoring the investor's situation?

---

9.   Longevity risk is also very real for any investor in danger of outliving limited resources irrespective of their age or actual longevity.

10. $40,000 withdrawn at age 70 from a $1-million portfolio is a far lower proportion than $40,000 withdrawn at age 85 from a $300,000 portfolio.

11.   Liabilities are here defined as the need to provide periodic income. Liabilities for late-in-life investors often increase because of health and disability issues.

SEQUENCE OF RETURNS RISK

As one ages, life expectancy increases. However, the number of years of expected remaining life decreases. At age 60, an investor may have a 30-year life expectancy (age 90); at age 89, the investor, if surviving, may have a four-year life expectancy (increase to age 93). The number of years of expected remaining life decreases from 30 years at 60 to four years at age 89.[12]

What is sequence of returns risk, and what does the above observation have to do with this risk? We first define and illustrate sequence of returns risk and then connect it to longevity risk to illustrate a complex, and not commonly understood, interrelationship.

SEQUENCE OF RETURNS RISK: DEFINITION AND ILLUSTRATION

Mathematically, sequence of returns risk usually is explained in terms of path dependency. Here is a simplified example:

We know (because multiplication is commutative) that $3 \times 2 \times 1 = 6$, and that $1 \times 2 \times 3 = 6$. The order of the numbers (returns) does not matter. This principle holds for any compound return series in which there are no cash flows. Consider, however, what happens when we introduce cash-flow requirements to the series. In this case, the investor withdraws one-half unit of value from the portfolio each period.

> Period One: $1 \times 3 = 3 - \frac{1}{2} = 2\frac{1}{2}$
>
> Period Two: $2\frac{1}{2} \times 2 = 5 - \frac{1}{2} = 4\frac{1}{2}$
>
> Period Three: $4\frac{1}{2} \times 1 = 4\frac{1}{2} - \frac{1}{2} = 4$ units of ending wealth

However,

> Period One: $1 \times 1 = 1 - \frac{1}{2} = \frac{1}{2}$
>
> Period Two: $\frac{1}{2} \times 2 = 1 - \frac{1}{2} = \frac{1}{2}$
>
> Period Three: $\frac{1}{2} \times 3 = 1\frac{1}{2} - \frac{1}{2} = 1$ unit of ending wealth

In the presence of withdrawals, the return order matters. An average return target is no longer a legitimate risk metric in the presence of portfolio distributions and return variance. Over time, when faced with the presence of cash flows, one can be exactly on track with respect to a portfolio's expected average return, but wildly off target with respect to the portfolio's actual dollar value. It is the dollar value, however, that must support financial objectives.

A common method for illustrating this risk uses the sequence of returns from the S&P 500 stock index during 1975–2009. If a portfolio, absent fees, taxes, trading costs, and other frictions, is completely and continuously invested in the S&P 500 Index, and if there are no contributions to or withdrawals from the portfolio during this period, the order of periodic returns has no effect on terminal wealth. Making an initial investment of $1,000 generates the same ending wealth if you reverse the historical return pattern, preserve the historical pattern, or scramble the returns. However, if you take $50 per year from the portfolio under the historically realized return pattern, your ending wealth is positive; if you reverse the return order,[13] you end up broke; and if you scramble the order, God knows what terminal wealth the return series generates. Final results are path dependent.

Many commentators advance the proposition that investor exposure to sequence of returns risk is greatest at the beginning of retirement. They correctly point out that when declines occur in the early retirement years, negative returns have an outsized effect. Early-in-retirement declines operate on substantial wealth, and the resulting loss of initial wealth compounds for many years. If late-in-life wealth diminishes, declines operate on smaller dollar-valued portfolios; therefore, some argue, the impact on the investor's financial security is less severe because the dollar wealth is less.[14]

---

12. See, also, the accompanying audience/participant discussion to Dempster and Medova (2011): "A male at 65 today has about a one-in-1000 chance of living to twice their life expectancy and life expectancy is, perhaps, 21 years. So at 65 are you going to live to 107? Probably not. But when you reach age 85, you have a one-in-ten chance of living to [twice] your life expectancy. In the same way that ... we need to take account of the variability of returns on investment assets so, I believe, we may need to look at the variability of longevity."

13. In this case, the initial annual return is the 2009 return, while the last return in the sequence is the 1975 return. The return order is the reverse of the realized historical return order.

14. "Sustainable withdrawal rates are disproportionately explained by what happens in the early part of retirement. Returns from later in retirement have minimal impact." Pfau (2017, 64).

Results obtained from our risk model suggest that sequence of returns risk is operative throughout retirement. Irrespective of a portfolio's dollar value, withdrawals at a dollar amount sufficient to sustain the investor's standard of living must continue. Withdrawals by some late-in-life investors may constitute a significant proportion of remaining wealth. Such investors are highly vulnerable to sequence of returns risk because they have limited risk capacity.

CASE STUDY 5: SEQUENCE OF RETURNS RISK FOR THE LATE-IN-LIFE INVESTOR

In Case Study 5, two things are going on simultaneously:

1. The investor withdraws larger and larger portions from a smaller and smaller portfolio each year
2. Each year of life pushes the applicable planning horizon further into the future

It is the joint interaction of these two factors that creates late-in-life vulnerability to sequence of returns risk.

A healthy 70-year-old woman wishes to withdraw $4,600 per month on an inflation-adjusted basis from a portfolio allocated to only two investment positions:

- 65 percent to the S&P 500 Index
- 35 percent to the U.S. Aggregate Bond Index

Other than the asset allocation design, the portfolio operates as specified in appendix A. The investor lacks gifting and bequest motives, but she seeks lifetime budgetary certainty. A risk model simulating returns by means of a Markov transition matrix, with the initial economic state selected randomly from either a bull market or a bear market suggests that her portfolio value, "in expectation" (50th percentile of results), should track her longevity closely with the result that, even if she lives to age 100, she will consistently achieve her target income goal (see figure 7.1).

FIGURE 7.1: AGE 70—SURVIVAL RATE AND EXPECTED PORTFOLIO VALUE

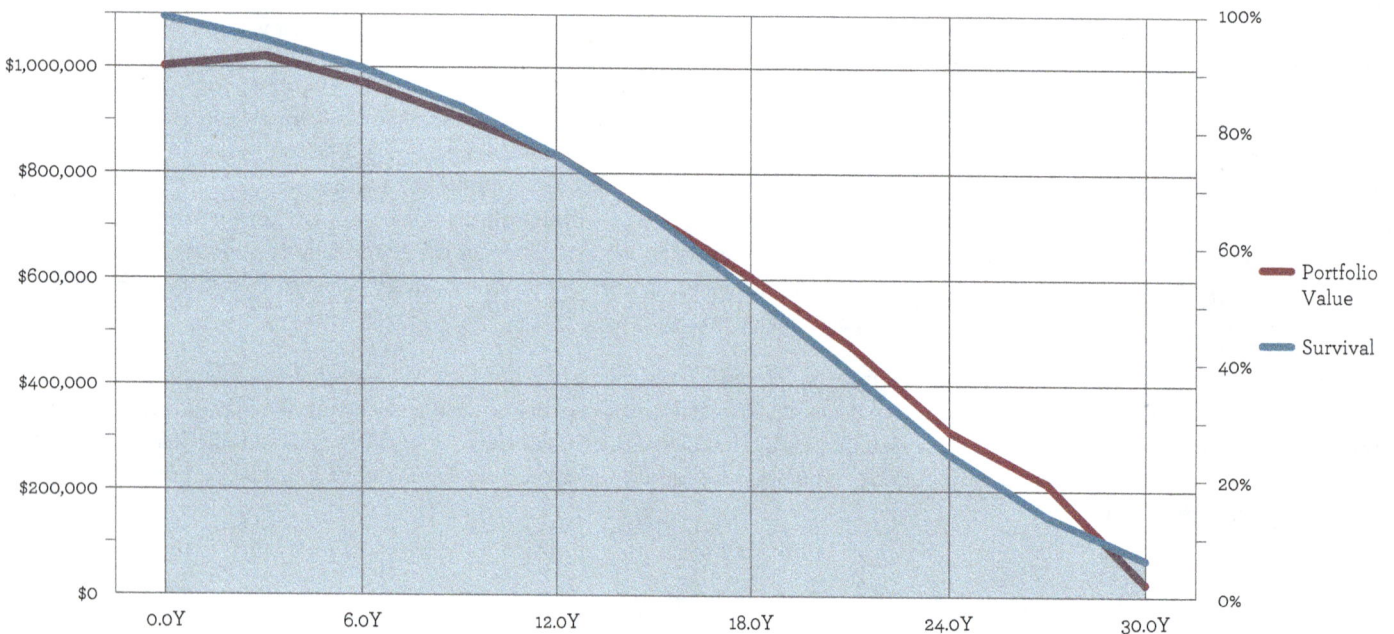

Fast-forward 15 years. The investor takes comfort from several fortunate outcomes:

1. Her health has remained good even though she is now age 85

2. Her portfolio has successfully weathered inflation and return vicissitudes, and it has generated the expected dollar value at the beginning of year 15, namely $693,500

Is she now less vulnerable to sequence of returns risk?

The answer may be yes if the survival expectation curve remains static. However, as the investor ages, the survival probability curve shifts further to the right.[15] As the investor grows older, in some ways she becomes more susceptible to sequence of returns risk because a bad investment return combined with a larger proportional share of wealth withdrawn for consumption can cause immediate problems. On the other hand, if her proportionate consumption is large relative to the returns then, in another sense, one may argue that her consumption of principal—not investment returns—is the dominating factor. However, as age increases in this case study, the impact of market declines becomes more pronounced as consumption, geared to deplete principal as the ACR value becomes less favorable, takes an even bigger bite.

Consider figure 7.2, which begins with the investor's financial position at age 85. At this time, the investor encounters a bear market. By year 12 (year 27 in terms of the age 70 analysis) she is out of money. However, she now has a longer survival expectation—approximately 20 percent of the initial population of 10,000 sample investors age 85 will survive to age 97. Here is the revised chart:

FIGURE 7.2: AGE 85—SURVIVAL RATE AND EXPECTED PORTFOLIO VALUE

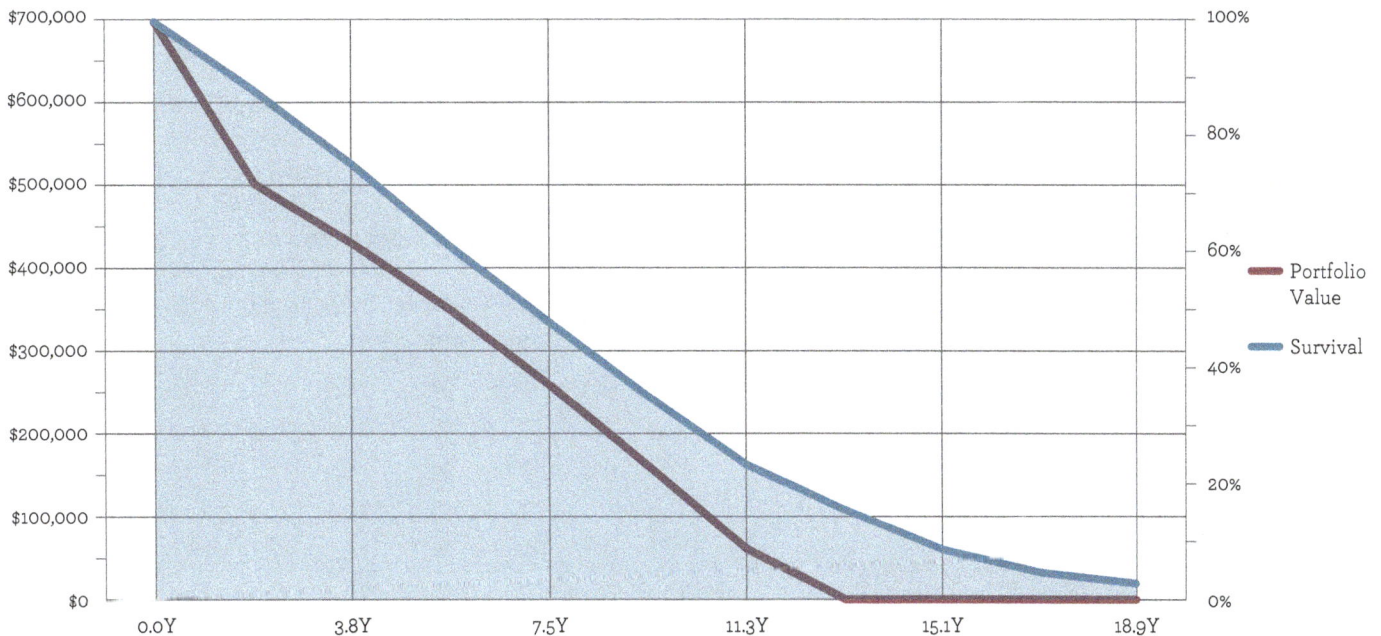

Whenever limited financial resources must sustain lifetime income, portfolio monitoring and evaluation is central to gauging investor retirement-income security. Given that the investor's expected longevity increases as she ages, all else being equal she remains vulnerable to downturns in portfolio value. But the extent of vulnerability is measured by the value of the ACR. An ACR slightly above 100 percent indicates financial vulnerability.[16] By contrast, if the older retiree's ACR exhibits a high value, the investor is less vulnerable to sequence of return risk.

---

15. Technically, the survival distribution's probability mass exhibits greater right-side skew.

16. Although beyond the scope of this book, ACR values for investors in poor health can be estimated by increasing the investor's age for risk modeling purposes. Age adjustment is common in the life insurance industry, and it is also found in "underwritten annuities" also known as "substandard annuity contracts," or "impaired life annuities." These financial instruments are common in personal injury litigation settlements. See Ainslie (2000) and Brown and Scahill (2010).

One implication is that, for retired investors of any age, the ACR is a key evaluation metric. An investor age 62 and beginning retirement with an ACR equal to 110 percent is exactly as vulnerable to sequence of returns risk as an investor age 92 with the same ACR value.[17] Advisors should redefine sequence of returns risk. It is a function of resources, longevity expectations, and consumption demands. Retirement, when faced with low ACR values, is a risky project at any age.

"Sequence" risk extends far beyond "sequence of returns" risk. It also encompasses risk factors listed at the chapter's beginning:

- Distribution and sequence of inflation realizations

- Distribution and sequence of retirement expenses

- Distribution of future annuity costs—sequence of yield curve changes

- Health state differential (bad to worse, bad to good, etc.)

- Force and effect of mortality

Sequence risk, in its most expansive definition, is a fundamental reason for improving the financial service profession's portfolio supervision and client communication skill sets.[18]

The bear-market case study depicts a race between principal depletion and the force of mortality. For modest-sized portfolios, older clients may experience more volatility in the "sufficiency space" because they consume more principal whenever return expectations are not met. Furthermore, tracking portfolio feasibility in terms of the ACR means that identical portfolios can have very different risk characteristics because the distance to the free boundary—a 1x coverage ratio value—differs greatly as a function of age. The annuity cost for a 75-year-old may be significantly less expensive than for a 65-year-old. Investment risk is age-related, as conventional wisdom suggests, but primarily as a function of the ACR value not as a byproduct of a rule of thumb, such as equity weighting should be approximately 100 minus current age.

Sequence of returns risk evaluation is a complicated topic, and it is difficult to identify the age range for which sequence order risk matters most. For example, a 40-year-old consuming a small fraction of the portfolio (or not consuming at all) has plenty of time to make up for a negative year. The low consumption won't take a big bite out of financial assets. Likewise, for an older investor, a bad upfront yearly return may not be a big deal because very few years are left, and consumption demands dominate capital gain/loss effects. However, at older ages mortality variability risk becomes very large,[19] and the investor may be potentially sensitive to a single bad investment year because both the consumption withdrawal and loss of principal put the portfolio on a catastrophic downward trajectory. The extent to which sequence of returns risk is operative is a facts-and-circumstances determination. Therefore, the value of the ACR is a monitoring benchmark. Sensitivity to this risk depends on the portfolio's distance from the feasibility boundary.[20]

---

17. This assumes comparable portfolios. In a bucketing approach to asset allocation, protecting against early downside risk by using low-volatility/low-return assets to fund initial consumption may generate a reverse glide path in which the portfolio's allocation to equity increases with investor age. An unintended result may arise if the older-age investor becomes more vulnerable to downside volatility as the planning horizon (remaining life expectancy) increases. A greater percentage of remaining wealth is exposed to equity risk as the planning horizon skews to the right.

18. Sequence of returns risk as traditionally defined provides additional intellectual underpinning for portfolio flooring or time bucketing asset-management strategies. A tilt toward fixed income early in retirement (the time during which the nest egg is, presumably, at its largest dollar value) undoubtedly has the effect of mitigating left-tail investment risk. At the start of retirement, selecting the asset allocation using this preferencing criterion allows the investor to achieve the optimal results with respect to the next time point (time 1). However, in the words of Rook (2014), such a portfolio selection criterion is flawed because "... it acts optimally on a local basis and ignores the long-term impact of each short-term decision." During the initial retirement periods "... it would place the retiree into a low volatility portfolio attempting to minimize P(Ruin) before the next withdrawal. The inflation/expense-adjusted returns with such a portfolio will struggle to outperform the ruin factor, causing it to increase over time. Eventually, the ruin factor may spike and the strategy would respond by shifting the retiree into stocks reflecting desperation." Rook emphasizes that "Minimizing P(Ruin) by using sequential optimization fails because the [allocation] at time t=0 has an impact on the probability of ruin at later time points." In mathematical terms: "... a collection of local optimums does not necessarily aggregate to a global optimum." Rook (2014) outlines the interrelation between decision-making that seems optimal in the short term and decision-making that produces the most favorable long-term outcome. "Selecting a low volatility portfolio ... early in retirement to avoid ruin at the next time point now comes with a price because that portfolio results in a higher value for the next ruin factor.... A larger ruin factor at the next time point increases the probability of ruin after the next time point...." He recommends a dynamic programming approach to identify a balance point between the competing risk factors. These observations reinforce the themes of "the cost of safety" and "investing as a prudent exchange of risk." Chapter Ten (Case Study 11) further develops these insights.

19. Ezra (2009) stresses this point. As retirees age, they must set aside a bigger proportion of remaining wealth every year because the standard deviation of life expectancy is a bigger proportion of life expectancy at older ages.

20. This is a variation on the theme of financial security explored in Case Study 3.

Consider, once again, the heat map presented in Case Study 2 for the fixed $20,000 monthly income election:

RANGE OF ACR VALUES THROUGH TIME

					Years from Today						
	0.0Y	2.8Y	5.8Y	8.7Y	11.6Y	14.5Y	17.4Y	20.3Y	23.2Y	26.2Y	29.1Y
95%	138%	261%	327%	415%	557%	746%	1001%	1386%	1914%	2814%	3790%
90%	138%	228%	279%	350%	453%	596%	782%	1051%	1342%	1981%	2684%
80%	138%	190%	227%	275%	339%	431%	550%	713%	857%	1215%	1575%
70%	138%	167%	194%	231%	277%	343%	422%	528%	603%	742%	973%
60%	138%	147%	170%	197%	231%	274%	322%	384%	395%	473%	687%
50%	138%	131%	147%	168%	192%	216%	244%	268%	250%	253%	250%
40%	138%	116%	126%	140%	155%	169%	171%	169%	112%	60%	15%
30%	138%	100%	107%	114%	123%	122%	109%	82%	2%	0%	0%
20%	138%	83%	86%	87%	85%	75%	45%	0%	0%	0%	0%
10%	138%	62%	61%	57%	45%	22%	0%	0%	0%	0%	0%
5%	138%	47%	44%	38%	20%	0%	0%	0%	0%	0%	0%
Level 1	100%	100%	100%	100%	100%	100%	100%	100%	100%	100%	100%
Level 2	125%	125%	125%	125%	125%	125%	125%	125%	125%	125%	125%
Level 3	150%	150%	150%	150%	150%	150%	150%	150%	150%	150%	150%

If you trace the yellow and orange caution zones throughout the planning horizon, there appears a pattern that we term "the danger smile." The warning and danger zone areas dip in the middle and rise at the beginning and end. In this case—it is difficult to generalize—there is clearly greater likelihood of a negative outcome at the beginning and the end of retirement. We think this pattern can be attributed to the outsized deleterious impacts of initial bad investment returns, the effect of which dissipates as multiple bad return periods become unlikely and the upward trend in expected return takes hold. However, at advanced ages, there is also greater sensitivity to sequence of returns risk because a few additional years of life make a big difference to ACR values at that time. If we were pressed to identify the ages for which the sequence of returns risk is greatest, we would surmise: (1) the very beginning of retirement for most investors with modest ACR values, and (2) the end of retirement for longer-lived investors.

It is difficult, and perhaps dangerous, to conclude that avoiding a sequence of negative returns at the start of retirement means that the investor is home free. Whenever there is a possibility of significant deterioration in the ACR, a bear market can prove financially devastating. Stated otherwise, sequence risk for modest-sized portfolios is often present throughout retirement—especially at the beginning and the end.

CHAPTER EIGHT

MONITORING AND EVALUATION—FUTURE

■ ■ ■

THE FUTURE: SUSTAINABILITY AND SECURITY

Monitoring is a precondition to prudent asset management. Asset-management options provide security (flexibility) because they enable the investor to modify, stage-by-stage, the risky retirement project. Initially, we considered portfolio monitoring as an activity within the set of free boundary problems. The boundary is "free" in the sense that (1) there is not a single, fixed dollar value lower bound for all investors,[1] and (2) the location of the boundary constantly changes due to complex interactions between investment returns, inflation, the nature and scope of liabilities, and the discount rate used to value liabilities.

When looking at retirement as a risky project from a free boundary perspective, it is the difference between assets (current financial wealth) and liabilities (investment costs and spending demands) that determines the boundary's location. This lower bound differs for each investor.[2] The boundary location also changes constantly as a function of investor aging, health changes, and other factors. In a bear market, the interaction of investment results with these factors tends to push portfolio value toward the boundary at either a slow velocity or, in the event of a perfect storm, at a rapid velocity. The free boundary, however, continues to be the point that determines the feasibility condition— the dollar value that separates the prospect of a successful financial outcome from the prospect of a painful standard-of-living adjustment or, worst case, portfolio failure and financial ruin. In terms of the actuarial coverage ratio (ACR) value, it is the financial condition where the ACR exactly equals 1. ACR values above 1 suggest future economic success in retirement, ACR values below 1 suggest the opposite.

Although penetrating the boundary is not an event that generates an explicit signal—many thousands of dollars may remain in the portfolio at the time the boundary is breached—it nevertheless is an event that the investor should not take lightly. In terms of portfolio management, it is perhaps the single most critical piece of information that the investor should know. The existence of the feasibility condition puts a premium on intelligent monitoring. It is crucial to know how likely it is that even a one standard deviation move to the downside of the statistically expected mean return could prove to be an economically nonsurvivable event. Investors need a monitoring system that lets them know whether they are in trouble, not whether their equity position has outperformed the S&P 500 or whether their portfolio is in the top quartile of balanced funds.

In terms of monitoring, we suggest that advisors and investors consider the following:

- Where is the free boundary (ACR > 1) or, equivalently, what is the current dollar value of the free boundary line?
- How far is the portfolio's current value from the line?
- Has investor risk tolerance changed with the change in portfolio dollar value; with the change in ACR?
- What is the probability that the portfolio will move into the region of economic infeasibility?
- If portfolio value continues to move toward the free boundary, is it prudent for the investor to continue a disciplined investment strategy, i.e., stay-the-course?
- If a portfolio drifts into the region of infeasibility, what is the probability that wealth will rebound and return, at a future date, to the region of feasibility?
- Is an asset-management strategy based on hope for such a rebound prudent, i.e., trust the market?

---

1. Unlike, for example, the fixed U.S. Department of Health and Human Services' poverty level for a family of four which, for 2021, is $26,500.

2. The assumption here is that the investor has specified the required minimum or lower-bound periodic withdrawal amount, irrespective of whether it is expressed in nominal or constant dollar terms. This is the amount that the portfolio must provide lest the investor experience a catastrophic economic result. Thus, the demands on the portfolio are net of any other sources of income such as Social Security or employer pension benefits.

Risk that is vague and ill-defined is not conducive to effective decision-making. A monitoring system that clearly illustrates ranges of probable outcomes along a decision path can greatly facilitate the selection and implementation of appropriate asset-management elections. Reference to the free boundary in terms of the ACR value may be the clearest way to depict the portfolio's current economic condition.

CARE, SKILL, AND CAUTION

This section continues the discussion about monitoring a retirement-income portfolio with requisite care, skill, and caution. Having selected a jointly determined asset allocation and withdrawal strategy, the investor is concerned that it remains prudent and suitable in light of current financial resources and objectives.

Thus far, the scope of inquiry includes examination of retirement risk in terms of solvency, sustainability, and security:

Retirement feasibility—assets greater than liabilities

Retirement-income sustainability—probability and magnitude of shortfall risk

Retirement security—level of dollar wealth meets or exceeds the level necessary for continued success in the face of changes in economic and personal circumstances

Translating this into the language of fiduciary standards suggests that a test for feasibility is an aspect of care, management strategies to enhance income sustainability are an aspect of skill, and monitoring retirement performance and financial flexibility is an aspect of caution. But, care, skill, and caution are the defining characteristics of prudent investment management: "A trustee shall invest and manage trust assets as a prudent investor would, by considering the purposes, terms, distribution requirements, and other circumstances of the trust. In satisfying this standard, the trustee shall exercise reasonable care, skill, and caution."[3]

CASE STUDY 6

Case Study 6 continues the theme of a portfolio-under-stress. It considers the behavior of a portfolio in financial trouble as opposed to analyzing what can be done with an emerging consumer surplus. For practitioners, working with investors facing the prospect of economic difficulties is challenging.

Case Study 6 considers a modest-sized portfolio that is losing value in a bear market. What is the likelihood that it will be unable to discharge its future financial objectives? The answer to this question quantifies portfolio depletion risk, namely, (1) the probability of portfolio depletion while the investor remains alive, and (2) the magnitude of the shortfall—the amount of time the investor spends without sufficient financial resources, or time alive-and-broke. This risk focuses on the likelihood of future portfolio depletion. Shortfall risk, a complementary risk metric, focuses on the likelihood that the investor will be unable to maintain threshold income or bequest targets. The portfolio continues to provide income, but the level is inadequate to support investor goals. The wealth and income targets might be expressed in aggregate dollar terms, i.e., a floor portfolio dollar value below which the investor does not desire to penetrate or, in periodic income terms, a minimum income that must be available each and every month during the applicable planning horizon. As shortfall risk increases, a monitoring system can anticipate problems and can help determine what corrective actions can be taken today lest the portfolio suffer failure in the future.

Stated otherwise, a credible retirement-income risk monitoring and evaluation system (1) gives the investor sufficient warning regarding the possibility of a potentially fatal blow to retirement aspirations, (2) provides an indication of the speed and magnitude of the problem should the portfolio realize lower than expected returns, and (3) provides sufficient time to rethink retirement-income portfolio strategies and consider alternative asset management elections.

---

3. Restatement Third of the Law Trusts. Family trust instruments often direct trustees to support the income needs of a current beneficiary—often a surviving spouse—while providing funds for remainder beneficiaries. The Uniform Prudent Investor Act [comments to §2 (a) through (d)] establishes a duty to monitor: "Managing embraces monitoring, that is, the trustee's continuing responsibility for oversight of the suitability of investments already made as well as the trustee's decisions respecting new investments." The authors of the CFA Level III course text (Arnott et al. 2007) echo this language: "Only by systematic monitoring can a fiduciary secure an informed view of the appropriateness and suitability of a portfolio for a client." Collins et al. (2014) provide a more complete discussion of this topic within the estate and trust context. For additional commentary, see Collins (2007, 2011a).

FACT PATTERN

In Case Study 6, the advisor reviews several years of portfolio results for an existing client. She retired at age 65 with a portfolio value of $2.3 million allocated 40 percent to stocks and 60 percent to fixed income.[4] Her current age is 68, she remains in good health, and her current monthly spending is $6,500. She anticipates adjusting this amount for future inflation. She has no gift or bequest goals. The portfolio is currently worth $1.7 million, i.e., it is down $600,000 over the previous three years. Several times during the review meeting she says, "At this rate, I'll be broke in eight years!"

ANALYSIS: CURRENT RESOURCES, THE ACR, AND THE RACE TO AVOID DEPLETION

Although spending ultimately depends on portfolio value, the advisor's challenge is to explain that, over long-term planning horizons, there is not a one-to-one correspondence between decreases in wealth and decreases in feasible spending. A wealth decline, in this case, of 26 percent may not necessitate an immediate 26-percent reduction in income. The issue is not the unfortunate loss of financial assets, but, rather, the ability of current assets to support income needs over the investor's remaining life given that she is now age 68.

The advisor decides to present figures 8.1–8.4:

FIGURE 8.1: PORTFOLIO SUFFICIENCY—50TH PERCENTILE

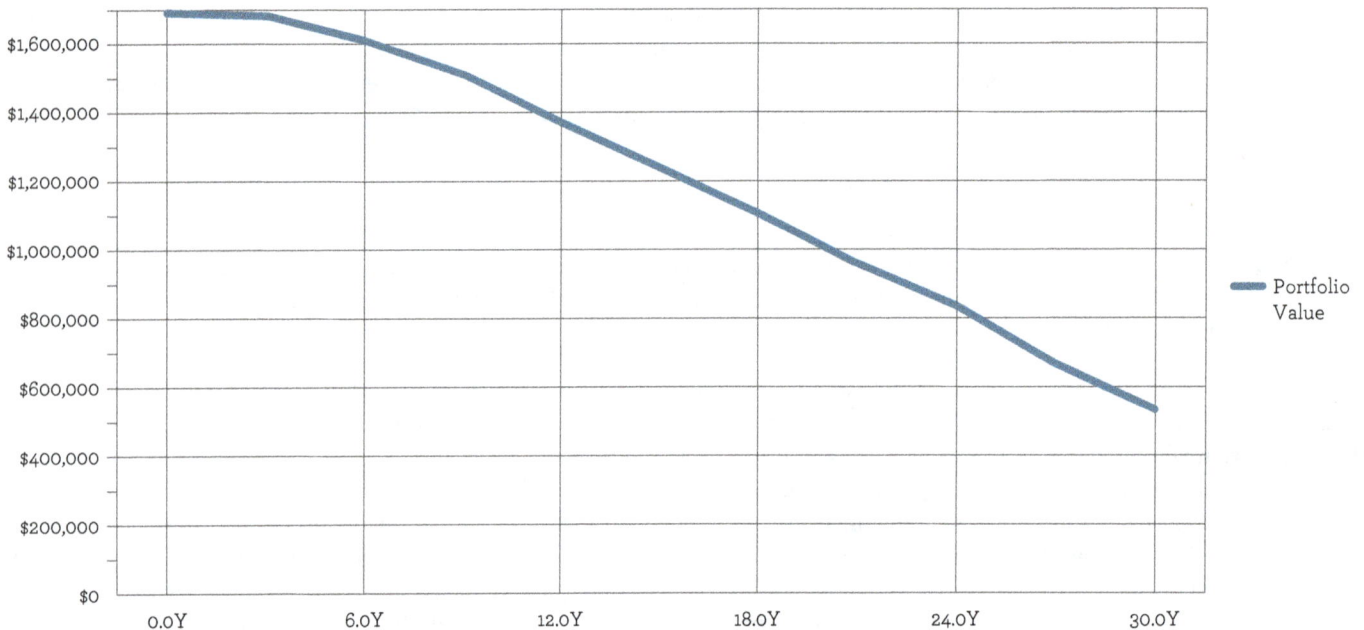

Figure 8.1 depicts the risk model's projection of her current $1.7-million investment wealth, over a 30-year period, at the 50th percentile of the distribution of outcomes. The expected outcome of withdrawing an inflation-adjusted monthly income of $6,500 results in projected terminal wealth slightly in excess of $525,000 after 30 years.

However, the advisor reminds her that expected results are not guaranteed results. Simplistically, he seeks to quantify the extent of bad luck so that the portfolio hits zero at the end of the planning horizon. The joke is that this is the bounce-the-check-to-the-undertaker investment strategy. Figure 8.2 suggests that she would have to experience results slightly above the 30th percentile of outcomes in order to hit a zero balance at the end of the planning horizon. Figure 8.2 indicates portfolio depletion at approximately year 28.

---

4.   The portfolio is diversified across the same investment positions as the portfolios previously presented (appendix A) in other case studies, and it has the same fee and cost structure. The risk model simulates 10,000 trials.

FIGURE 8.2: PORTFOLIO SUFFICIENCY—30TH PERCENTILE

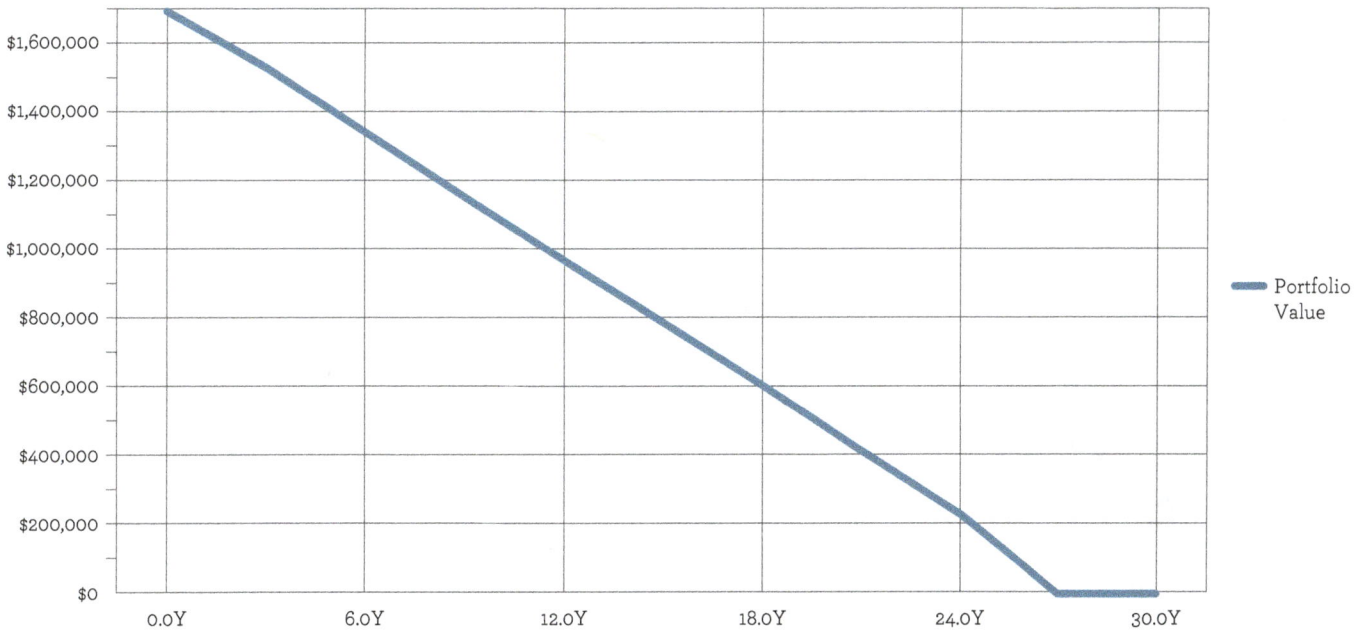

Joking aside, the advisor opines that, given the events of the previous three years, she will probably continue to be nervous about the outcome at either the 50th, 35th, or 30th percentiles because each percentile puts the portfolio on a decreasing value track. The client agrees and states that, rightly or wrongly, she is upset by portfolio value decreases.

ANALYSIS CONTINUED: IS FINANCIAL SECURITY INCREASING OR DECREASING OVER TIME?

If the goal is to achieve a lifetime income sufficient to sustain her standard of living, the primary concern is income sustainability as opposed to principal stability.[5] The advisor explains that he is going to add two additional elements to each figure: (1) survival rate and (2) ACR value. The investor acknowledges that each year she lives is one less year that requires her to fund an income from her portfolio. The advisor nods in agreement, but he recognizes that longevity is a more complicated subject because each year of survival also begets the expectation of additional life expectancy. Rather than pursuing difficult-to-grasp actuarial concepts, he decides to proceed with his planned presentation:

5.   Investing is a prudent exchange of risk, redux.

FIGURE 8.3: PORTFOLIO SUFFICIENCY—50TH PERCENTILE

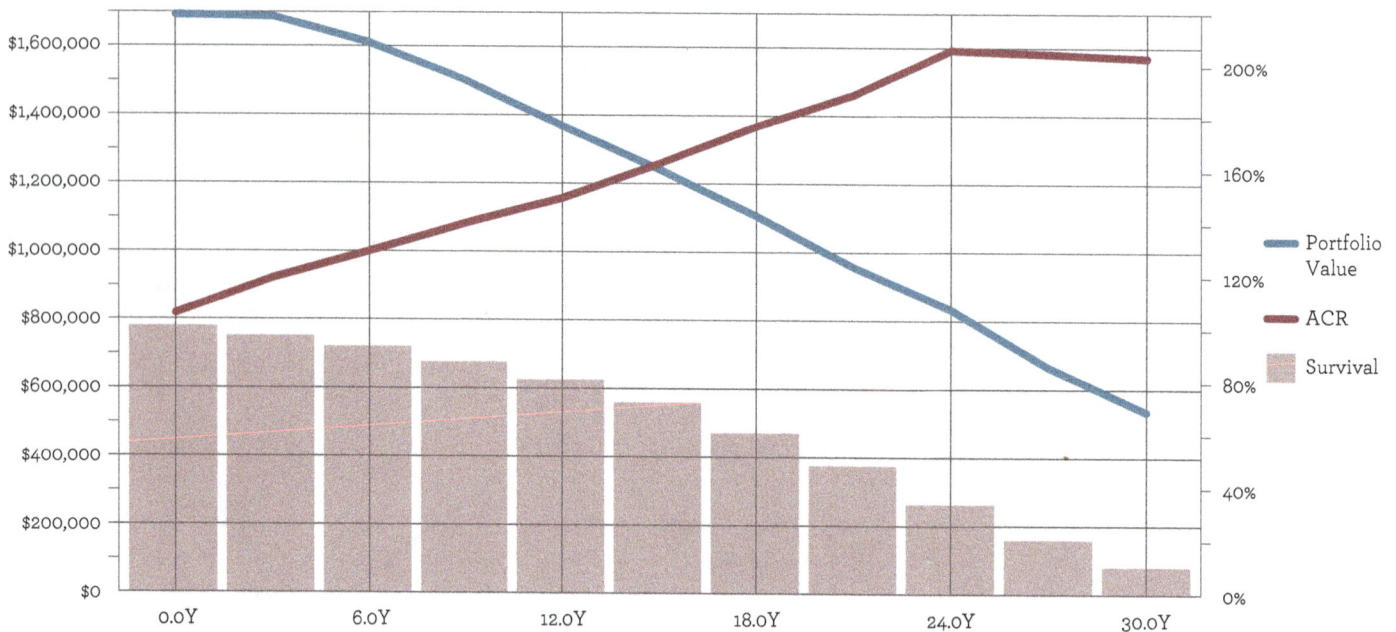

In figure 8.3, portfolio dollar value is measured on the left vertical axis; survival percentages and ACR value are measured on the right vertical axis. An ACR value greater than 100 percent indicates that the investor owns sufficient financial resources to finance lifetime income. At the 50th percentile of the distribution of outcomes, figure 8.3 suggests that, by year 30, the small percentage of investors surviving from the original 10,000 sample population will own a portfolio valued at approximately $525,000 in constant dollars. The great majority of investors will fail to attain a 30-year life span and, therefore, will have emphatically won their race to avoid portfolio depletion.

Although the investor intuitively recognizes that the process of aging has the somewhat perverse benefit of alleviating stress on her portfolio because it shortens the remaining planning horizon, she finds the strong upward slope of the ACR value line to be truly amazing. In terms of her most important personal objective, figure 8.3 suggests that, over time, her financial security is increasing despite the fact that her wealth is decreasing. The advisor remarks that, other than senior citizen discounts, she is looking at one of the few benefits associated with growing old.[6]

After further discussion, the advisor reminds her that downside dangers still remain. He presents figure 8.4:

---

6.   We have learned recently that shrinkage of nerves in gums makes certain dental procedures less onerous for older patients. It is important to take any-and-all the advantages of aging.

FIGURE 8.4: PORTFOLIO SUFFICIENCY—30TH PERCENTILE

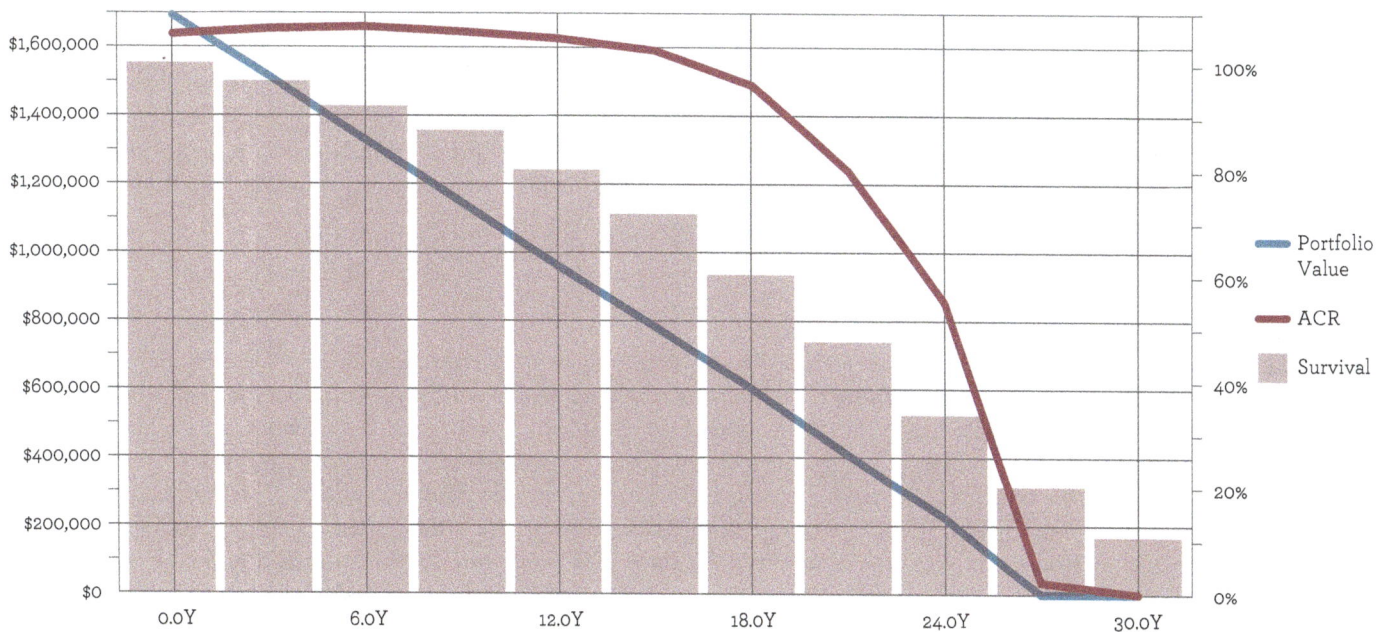

Figure 8.4 depicts results at the 30th percentile of outcomes. The survival probability measurement is the same, but the slope of portfolio decline is considerably steeper. Projected investment and inflation realizations are not favorable. A key risk metric is the projection of the ACR value. As long as the red line remains above 100 percent (on the right vertical axis), the investor has sufficient wealth to cover her income needs. The advisor points out that the ACR line does not dip below the 100-percent ACR value until approximately year 15. He asks the investor, "What do you think this means?" After a bit of thought, she guesses, "If things go badly and I get less than I expect, I should start to worry around year 12 when the ACR line starts to go down. But, I really should worry around year 14 when the amount by which it exceeds 100 percent is small."

Yes. The advisor tells her that she is in relatively good shape during the period when the ACR is more than 100 percent and its slope is increasing or stable. This does not mean that it should not be monitored because, at least in figure 8.4, it reaches a maximum between years 6 and 9 at the 30th percentile and turns downward thereafter. She is getting older, which is a good thing economically speaking, but she is continuing to take fixed amounts from a portfolio that is getting smaller and smaller in dollar value. This is the race—will the benefits of aging win or will the withdrawal stress on a shrinking portfolio win? At approximately the 35th percentile of outcomes, the race is a tie. Below the 35th percentile, she will encounter an economic environment in which she must consider cutting withdrawal amounts or, at least, consider refusing or postponing inflation adjustments. As a homeowner, she may want to investigate the merits of a reverse mortgage. If the market offers a late-in-life annuity, she may want to pull the trigger around year 12. But she doesn't have to make any of these decisions now.[7]

Some asset management elections, once implemented, are irrevocable. Things may either improve (the more likely result tracks above the 35th percentile of projected outcomes), or deteriorate (the less likely result tracks below the 35th percentile). If the former, the investor may regret early implementation of irrevocable management elections; if the latter, the time to change investment strategy may accelerate. Case Study 7 takes a closer look at this topic.

---

7. "In most instances however, investors will want to use their portfolios to finance consumption throughout their lifetimes. This has an important advantage, which is to allocate current risks of wealth into small risks on consumption over a long time horizon" (Eeckhoudt et al. 2005, 113).

CASE STUDY 7

This case study assumes a constant-dollar fixed amount withdrawal strategy. This is not to suggest that this strategy is the utility-maximizing strategy, the most sustainable strategy, the strategy that produces the greatest aggregate income, the strategy with the best reward (income) to variance (fluctuations in periodic income throughout the planning horizon) trade-off, or a strategy that dominates according to any of a large number of other preferencing criteria. Rather, we illustrate the strategy for three primary reasons: (1) it is simple to understand, (2) we assume that the withdrawal amount is the minimum required to support a threshold standard of living, i.e., the investor has little flexibility with respect to cash-flow amount and timing, and (3) it is a strategy that retirees interested in budgetary certainty for a threshold income often aspire to implement.

FACT PATTERN

In Case Study 7, the 68-year-old investor, following an initial simulation study by her advisor, sets an asset allocation of 70 percent to stocks and 30 percent to fixed income. Her spending policy seeks to provide a $5,000-per-month inflation-adjusted income ($60,000 constant-dollar annual withdrawal). The spending target represents the income level required to fund the investor's threshold standard of living needs. Two years later, at the investor's current age 70, and at a 1.5-percent-per-annum growth in the Consumer Price Index, the current annual income target is $61,800 ($5,150 per month). Current portfolio value is $1 million. The two-year performance outcome falls at the 20th percentile of the originally projected distribution of results. Given the changes in age, the realized withdrawal rate, and portfolio value, the investor is interested in knowing the amount of her current surplus, i.e., the distance between current portfolio value and the actuarially calculated value of her spending liability. Specifically, she wishes to know if her portfolio remains unambiguously in the region of feasibility.

ANALYSIS

The advisor estimates that $1 million can purchase a monthly income benefit of $5,676. This amount is the current cost of a single premium immediate annuity contract providing a 2-percent-per-year graded benefit to the age 70 female investor in good health. Given the monthly target income of $5,150, it appears that the investor is currently in the region of feasibility. Her economic surplus is approximately $100,000 [$5,150 ÷ $5,676 = 0.9073 × $1,000,000 = $907,300]. This is the dollar-valued distance above the feasibility boundary.

Although the distance to the free boundary is only 10 percent of the portfolio's current value, the annuity cost calculation occurs in an historically low interest-rate environment. Annuity payouts are sensitive to changes in interest rates and, given the mean-reversionary tendency of interest rates, there is a reasonable expectation that the ACR value may, all else being equal, improve. For example, the retirement-income risk model estimates that a 50-basis-point-upward parallel shift in the yield curve generates a 2-percent graded monthly benefit of $5,917, while a 100-basis-point upward parallel shift generates a 2-percent graded benefit of $6,162.[8] As interest rates revert toward their historical mean, the complex interactions between possible negative effects of rising rates on the financial asset portfolio and positive effects on the actuarial valuation of liability (spending) costs will either expand or shrink the distance from the free boundary, i.e., the ACR value.

Figure 8.5 illustrates the impact of differing interest-rate environments on a portfolio monitoring system during the high-stress period of a bear market. Projected outcomes continue at the 20th percentile of the range of outcomes and, as such, do not rely on a mere 'hope' for better times ahead. Given the pictorial depiction of the risk model of her financial circumstances, what will the investor decide to do? She could maintain her 70–30 stock-to-bond allocation; she could decide to reduce consumption temporarily by foregoing inflation adjustments in the withdrawal calculations; she could decide to tap into home equity, if available; or, with great difficulty, she could ratchet down her threshold standard of living. If things continue on a bad path, how soon must she face up to the new economic regime?

---

8.   For further insight into the sensitivity of annuity pricing to changes in interest rates, see Charupat et al. (2012).

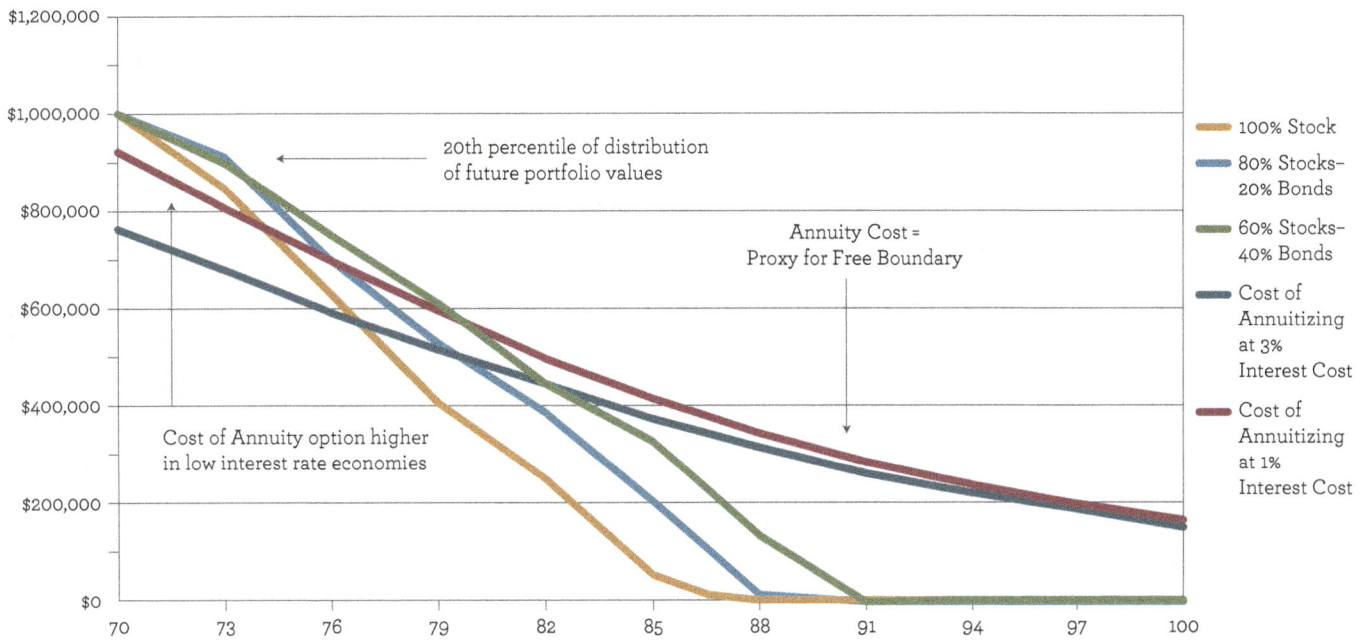

The advisor lists some asset-management elections available to her currently. She could, for example, elect to increase or decrease equity weighting in response to the recent declines in her portfolio's value. Figure 8.5 brackets her current allocation by changing equity exposure to 100 percent, 80 percent, or 60 percent. The advisor wishes to provide further insight into the following question: Given her portfolio's dollar value, how might continued investment in a risky-asset portfolio impact the short-term feasibility and long-term sustainability of her financial objectives?

Figure 8.5 portrays left-tail outcomes (the 20th percentile of results in a bull/bear regime switching model with the initial regime selected randomly). It depicts constant-dollar results for a 100-percent stock portfolio (orange line), an 80-percent stock portfolio (blue line), and a 60-percent stock portfolio (green line). If the investment climate continues to remain unfavorable, the x-axis time line indicates portfolio depletion for the 100-percent and 80-percent stock portfolios at approximately age 88 and depletion for the 60-percent stock exposure portfolio at approximately age 91. Additionally, the model suggests that trying to recapture lost portfolio value by increasing expected return through additional equity exposure is a risky-asset-management strategy in the face of a prolonged bear market.

Superimposed on the left-tail of the probability distribution are two free boundary lines. The red line is the cost of purchasing an annuity to provide an inflation-adjusted benefit of $61,800 per year assuming that current interest rates remain at 1 percent and that the level and shape of the pro-forma yield curve input into the retirement-income risk model does not change. The black line is the cost of purchasing an annuity to provide an inflation-adjusted benefit of $61,800 per year assuming that current interest rates rise to 3 percent and that there is a corresponding parallel shift in the yield curve. As the investor ages, the cost of purchasing an annuity sufficient to fund her lifetime threshold target decreases, all else being equal. Indeed, the annuity's price, at any interest rate, converges to the same amount as the investor approaches age 100. At this point in time, the effect of mortality dominates the effect of interest-rate exposure.

What does figure 8.5 indicate? Currently, the portfolio value is above the free boundary, i.e., in terms of the client's minimum income objectives, the portfolio fulfills the feasibility (solvency) condition. Although moving toward a riskier portfolio offers the expectation of higher future returns, a change in allocation requires close monitoring. There is an approximately 20-percent probability that increasing the equity weighting above 80 percent may accelerate the risk of violating the feasibility condition (falling below the free boundary) by age 75.[9] Indeed, if interest rates remain historically low, a 100-percent equity, swing-for-the-fences portfolio offers

9. Figure 8.5 assumes that the investor continues to withdraw the income required to maintain her threshold standard of living despite the risk of future portfolio depletion. Although investment results may force the investor to reassess her standard-of-living threshold, the purpose of figure 8.5 is to quantify the feasibility of her income target. The strength of bequest motives also may influence the investor's asset allocation decision.

a 20-percent chance of penetrating the free boundary by approximately age 74. If interest rates rise, however, the investor has more breathing room. The 20th-percentile results do not fall below the free boundary until the late seventies or early eighties. The investor has sufficient time to delay annuitization, and surplus wealth provides her with the luxury of waiting to see how the capital markets perform. Both the investor and the advisor expect better future results but neither can guarantee this result. Both agree, however, that economic surplus (flexibility) enhances retirement security.

BEHAVIORAL FINANCE IMPLICATIONS

Case Studies 6 and 7 illustrate the probabilistic nature of prudent decision-making. Decisions at each point in time depend on the outcomes of prior states. There is not a unique and immutable all-weather planning strategy. Rather, as time moves forward, decision-making becomes dynamic and adaptive. When it appears that a retirement-income strategy is creating negative surplus (ACR < 1), continued adherence to the strategy can destroy value, i.e., set the financial asset portfolio on a path toward depletion prior to the end of the investor's life span. In such a case, the strategy may become more protective. Conversely, if it appears that a sustainable surplus is emerging, strategy decisions may contemplate greater future spending or a more growth-oriented portfolio.[10]

The task of prudent asset management, however, requires a careful and ongoing assessment of client circumstances lest premature defensive measures, motivated primarily by fear rather than by intelligent evaluation, also destroy future value. It is not enough simply to observe gain or loss in the prior period before deciding the appropriate level of risk in future periods. Rather, a comprehensive monitoring system evaluates (1) the economic consequences of past results and (2) the future implications of changing investment policy.[11]

It is not only changes in economic circumstances that drive investment decision-making. Preferences are not absolute, and they can vary in intensity as time unfolds—for example, ill health may either increase or decrease the propensity to consume. Preference for near-term consumption may increase because life span shortens; preference for near-term consumption may decrease because the need to pay for substantial medical/end-of-life care costs may loom large. The effects of such changes on an investor's motivation for purchasing an annuity contract also are uncertain. Where in the pecking order of preferred strategic investment responses does an annuity purchase reside?

In one sense, Case Study 7's fact pattern suggests that if the next period's result lies around the 20th to 30th percentile of the projected distribution of outcomes during a period when interest rates are trending upward, the investor's financial position remains viable. Personal goals that are met at the 20th or 30th percentile may persuade the investor to follow a no-change-in-investment-policy strategy so long as results land in this percentile range, or better. However, if the next period's result lies around the 20th to 30th percentile of the projected distribution of outcomes, but the low-interest-rate environment remains steady, the investor's financial position becomes more perilous.[12] Interest-rate behavior is germane because the ACR calculates the cost of lifetime income according to the annuity-pricing principal. A main component of the calculation is the discount factor determined by the level and shape of the yield curve. In a trust/fiduciary law context, prudent decision-making is academically sound, administratively reasonable, and legally

---

10. The preferred asset-management elections reflect the investor's utility at a particular moment in time, in a particular economic or personal health regime, and at the given point in the wealth range. The point may be relative to a reference level of wealth such as distance from the feasibility bound or distance from the portfolio's highest dollar value. Investors exhibiting, for example, constant absolute/relative risk aversion will select strategies that differ from those selected by investors with decreasing/increasing, absolute/relative risk aversion. The use of the adjectives dynamic and adaptive are not prescriptions for investment market-timing strategies.

11. The iconographic representation of the Roman god Janus is worth keeping in mind. Janus, a two-faced god, simultaneously looks forward and backward. His depiction is emblematic of beginnings (January), time, transitions, and endings.

12. The analysis does not include precautionary reserves or resources other than the investment portfolio, e.g., family assistance. Risk modeling (not shown) in which reserves are used during bear markets and restored during bull markets suggests that investment reserves held in cash or near-cash do not have a significant effect on the economics of the retirement-income project. For example, a use-reserves-to-fund-withdrawals-when-returns-are-bad strategy does not materially change portfolio depletion times or depletion rates. Reserve accounts that pre-fund withdrawals through periods of six, 12, 18, and 24 months have a slight positive effect in models employing a start-in-bear-market-regime selection; a slight negative effect in models employing a random bull/bear-market-regime selection. Our findings support those advanced by Woerheide and Nanigian (2012). Our findings, however, are preliminary, and they in no way constitute an argument against establishment of precautionary savings to cushion the impact of future economic shocks.

Both the "buffer-stock" model developed by Carroll (1992) and the "prudence" model developed by Kimball (1990) offer important insights into motivations for savings. It is a puzzle why both the prudence model and the buffer-stock model are absent from the debate concerning the wisdom of creating a reserve to cushion retirement investment portfolio drawdowns during bear markets. For example, Carroll offers an "income statement" approach that may complement a comprehensive accounting-based retirement planning strategy. In this case, saving and consumption decisions depend on net worth and on permanent income so that the investor's goal is to achieve an optimal target ratio of net worth to permanent income.

defensible. Given the academic evidence of mean-reversion in the time series of interest rates, if the prevailing interest rate was in double digits, the defensibility of a stay-the-course decision for Case Study 7 may be more difficult to defend than a similar decision made in a low-rate environment.[13]

We must return to the topic of flooring. Investors with modest resources, who own portfolios generating poor results within the prevailing economy, value downside protection. A decline in portfolio value may be acceptable if it is likely that current resources, partitioned into reasonable periodic withdrawals over the planning horizon, will weather the ups and downs of portfolio volatility successfully. This was the lesson in Case Study 6. However, a decline in portfolio value may be of greater concern if the portfolio's ability to generate sustainable and adequate amounts of income is in serious doubt. Furthermore, lessons surrounding the cost-of-safety are, for investors lacking substantial wealth, often quickly forgotten in a turbulent economic environment. Although, objectively, the investor's planning horizon remains the same (income for life), subjectively, fear shrinks the horizon to today (further asset price declines are intolerable).[14] This is the province of behavioral finance.

Das et al. (2010), a seminal article co-authored by leading practitioners from both the rationalist and behavioralist finance schools, argues:

- Many private investors approach portfolio management in qualitative rather than quantitative terms
- They measure investment success primarily by progress toward personal financial goals
- Investors often compartmentalize goals, and mentally match investment resources to specific objectives (money for a trip, money to pay off a debt, money for emergencies, money to produce income, and so forth)
- It is difficult for investors to view their portfolios as a single, aggregated source of wealth arranged to integrate rather than segregate financial resources into a coherent strategy[15]

The suggested remedy is not to segregate assets into physically separate actual accounts but to allocate total wealth according to a prudent and suitable risk-reward posture, and then to segregate the integrated portfolio into virtual accounts. Although the investor benefits from coherent and coordinated asset management, the actual total portfolio is evaluated in terms of its ability to fund separate (virtual account) goals. This is central to Case Study 7 where critical goals are matched to the percentile of the distribution of wealth management outcomes. It is also central to Case Study 2's goal-oriented decomposition. Case Study 2 projects the aggregate portfolio's ability to fund distinct standard-of-living objectives: an aspirational standard and a threshold standard of living. Although we limited the Case Study 2 analysis to only two periodic consumption objectives, it is straightforward to include other specific spending and bequest goals. Once the concept of a virtual account enters the discussion, investor preference for strict matching between a specific goal and assets-earmarked-to-fund-the-goal may diminish. Focus turns toward the ability of total financial wealth to cover current and future goals and obligations. Investor demand for flooring, and its attendant cost-of-safety drawbacks, may recede if a monitoring and reporting system frames financial outcomes so that they become intelligible to the investor in contexts other than Maslowian pyramids.[16]

---

13. It is worth noting that the existence of an actuarial safety net—irrespective of whether an investor chooses to annuitize some or all wealth—influences the investment decision-making process. This point is stressed by Pang and Warshawsky (2009). Were annuities not available, households would reduce their exposure to equity substantially. Thus, the possibility of securing a floor income through an option to purchase an annuity contract makes a risk-averse household more comfortable with equity risk exposure irrespective of whether the option is ever exercised. Of course, the danger of not exercising the annuity option is that the portfolio's future value will be less than the future cost of securing the target-income annuity. For a technical discussion of the distribution of future annuity cost, see Li (2008) and Koijen et al. (2011).

14. Davies (2017) provides helpful background material.

15. In an asset-liability management context, this last point is particularly noteworthy. For example, a corporate-sponsored defined benefit pension plan has many stakeholders, each with differing interests and objectives—corporate executives with compensation tied to company profitability, retired workers interested in the security of forthcoming payments, active employees interested in increasing their projected future benefits, stockholders interested in the effect of pension decisions on share prices, etc. There is, however, only a single portfolio of underlying assets.

16. Many excellent insights of behavioral finance are, in our opinion, vitiated by its close, ongoing affiliation with the philosophy of the 1950s French psychologist Abraham Maslow, i.e., the "hierarchy of human needs" pyramid. Basing investment theory on questionable hypotheses—especially when subsequent empirical research within the psychology profession fails to confirm their validity—strikes us as problematic. Maslow's writings, it seems, offer a vocabulary that is tailor-made for the needs of 21st-century marketing departments. See the embedded links to a lengthy supplemental discussion on the history of behavioral finance research in Collins and Gadenne (2017).

The notion of virtual accounts can be expanded readily to include the concept of a virtual annuity. Building on the initial insights of Fullmer (2007),[17] Waring and Siegel (2015, 1) offer the most comprehensive development of this topic.[18] Although, in the authors' opinion, prudent spending can be defined in terms of an actuarial calculation, prudent asset management does not necessitate purchase of an actual annuity contract. The authors advocate a process of "periodic re-annuitization" that calls for annually recalculating the appropriate withdrawal rate by matching portfolio value to the income available through an annuity priced at an equivalent market value: "We call a portfolio managed according to this principle an *annually recalculated virtual annuity* (ARVA). ... the recomputed ARVA will vary each period as the current spending amount is adjusted to reflect gains or losses on the risky investment portfolio (as well as changes in the real interest and inflation rates used to price the virtual annuity)."[19] As the article's title suggests, the focus is on spending, and the authors' goal is to provide a fail-safe method for calculating a wealth-appropriate/age-appropriate spending level.[20] The control variables are asset allocation (an exercise primarily in risk control) and portfolio withdrawal amounts. A further insight is that investors can adapt the ARVA principle to a wide variety of spending strategies: "The ARVA need not provide for a constant real spending level but might have some other, perhaps front-loaded, *shape*. ...the shape of the cash flow payouts to a retiree can be engineered to be anything the retiree wants, so long as the various cash flow payouts have the same present value, on a risk-free real interest rate basis, as the available assets."[21]

At this point, we are ready to advance the argument that portfolio monitoring requires tracking virtual flooring. Flooring, as behavioralist commentators assert, is the safety net required to comfort investors lacking wealth significantly greater than required by their consumption, bequest, and gifting needs and aspirations. Willfully ignoring investor demands for flooring is foolhardy. However, implementation of actual flooring strategies, especially in low-interest-rate environments, creates a Gordian knot for investors wanting principal guarantees, income adequacy in the face of future inflation, and portfolio growth for enhanced security. One path out of this dilemma is to track a virtual floor while preserving options for cash matching, bond laddering, annuitization, or other flooring strategies. But tracking a virtual floor begs the question of asset management. It appears as if investment policy should be dynamic. A dynamic asset-management policy benefits from liquidity and surplus, and dynamic management has implications for investment policy. This subject is explored further in the next chapter.

---

17. Chapter 11 discusses Fullmer (2007) in greater depth.

18. "Our insight is that constructing a spending rule is itself an annuitization problem at heart but does not require purchasing an actual annuity ..."

19. Ibid, p. 2.

20. "It is thus easy to see that spending volatility is the risk—the only risk—you care about when setting your investment policy." Ibid, p. 7

21. Ibid, p. 10. Although the article points out the need to adjust spending levels, it does not fully address the issue of income adequacy. The authors, although advocating solutions, e.g., age-adjusted spending, similar to those developed by Pye (2012) seem unaware of Pye's work.

CHAPTER NINE

ISSUES IN RETIREMENT-INCOME PORTFOLIO MANAGEMENT

...

THE INVESTMENT POLICY STATEMENT

Some investors sidestep the issue of ongoing portfolio monitoring in favor of following pre-set, bright-line rules adopted at the time of portfolio implementation. In practice, such rules often are codified within a written investment policy statement (IPS). Under this static or architectural view of investment policy, sticking to pre-set asset management and withdrawal rules offers a high probability of achieving a safe and sustainable lifetime income. Practitioners, however, recently have started to implement more dynamic systems-engineering approaches to investment policy statements. We briefly discuss the investment policy recommendations promulgated by the CFA Institute regarding the importance of establishing a policy anticipating that a portfolio might confront an unsustainable future drawdown. This shift in emphasis, perhaps arising from severe equity-market downturns during the first decade of this century, augments the importance of an effective portfolio surveillance and monitoring policy. Paradoxically, some commentators recommend responding to investment turbulence by replacing a single bright-line rule such as the 4-percent-withdrawal-rate rule[1] with a veritable plethora of bright-line-rules-for-all-occasions. By contrast, we do not parse historical return paths searching for an elusive oxymoron—namely, a set of rules-to-follow-for-a-random-process. Reliance on a single historical path of realized returns to develop and codify rules for portfolio control variables such as asset allocation and distribution policy is, at the limit, an elaborate exercise in data mining.[2]

Monitoring becomes especially important during times of poor investment performance—either due to adverse market conditions or to an investor's unsuccessful asset-management elections. There are a number of responses to declining portfolio values. A common response is a sit-tight approach that advocates maintaining constant fixed-weight exposures to the portfolio's asset classes. The focus is on monitoring the current allocation's drift from the long-term strategic weights established in the IPS. This monitoring system is appropriate for investors manifesting constant relative risk aversion (CRRA), which assumes: (1) risk tolerance is invariant to changes in wealth, and (2) absent dramatic changes in investor health, longevity expectations, etc., the investor maintains a constant time preference rate for consumption.[3] Under this portfolio-management approach, a retiree suffering the effects of a bear market hopes for a market recovery sufficient to allow the portfolio to continue future target withdrawals. Many financial advisors caution clients to "trust the market," "stay the course," "maintain investment discipline," "avoid market timing," and so forth.

By contrast, dynamic asset management encompasses a variety of asset allocation and withdrawal strategies. Dynamic programming, for example, focuses on finding the optimal decision path given current resources, e.g., jointly considering asset allocation and consumption strategies by solving for formulae such as the Merton optimum in a continuous time finance model. Investment and consumption decisions are not separable.[4] Alternately, a portfolio-insurance strategy makes discrete time changes in asset weightings in response to changing portfolio values in order to replicate an option-like convex payoff structure. Finally, at the other end of the asset-management spectrum, some IPSs codify a variety of empirically based rules purporting to yield maximum portfolio sustainability. These rules may lack a firm

---

1. Each year, withdraw 4 percent of a portfolio's initial value with an adjustment for annual inflation. The result is a constant-dollar fixed retirement-income stream. Commentators sometimes use the term "synthetic annuity" to describe a self-managed fixed retirement-income stream, and to distinguish it from an annuity contract underwritten by an insurance company. The nomenclature can, at times, become confusing.

2. One type of data mining occurs when (1) a time-series analysis uncovers patterns or parameters that best fit the sample data, and (2) the same data is then used to develop and test the efficacy of asset management rules based on the patterns or parameters.

3. The investor's elasticity of intertemporal substitution is one divided by the risk aversion coefficient under a CRRA utility function. Some life-cycle models indicate that the optimal consumption path for individuals with CRRA preferences increases over time because future consumption is worth less than current consumption, i.e., to keep the utility of consumption constant, future consumption must increase. The rate of increase is a function of the force of mortality, and the level of consumption depends strongly on expectations for remaining life span. Other life-cycle models suggest that a high discount rate for future consumption leads to a preference for front-loaded retirement consumption. Investors with such a preference exhibit "Fisher utility," which leads to decreases in retirement spending over the planning horizon. In a model where the investor lacks any bequest motives, all remaining wealth is consumed in the period just prior to death. When the investor's time preference rate is exactly equal to the risk-free rate, optimal initial retirement spending can be strikingly low. Only a highly risk-averse investor would choose the extreme level of frugality in early retirement demanded by certain types of life-cycle models. An actuarial variation on such a spending trajectory is embedded in the U.S. tax code's minimum required distribution rules for individual retirement accounts.

4. For private investors, this is a hallmark of asset-liability management.

basis in economic theory, but they are recommended to investors because they would have produced successful results under previous bear market conditions. However, it may be dangerous to apply retirement withdrawal rules that lack mathematical necessity and investors may find it disconcerting to evaluate results when applying such rules to non-U.S. markets, e.g., to the Nikkei 225 stock index since its high-water mark at the end of 1989.

The need for effective portfolio monitoring increases during a bear market. If a portfolio suffers poor investment returns, it may be unable to fund an adequate and sustainable cash flow from a diminishing pool of capital. Although bear markets generally increase the desirability of capital-preservation strategies, winding down equity risk in a low-interest-rate environment may place the investor in a further bind. As stock values sink, a flight to quality often means acceptance of extraordinarily low yields on principal-guaranteed investments. Historically low yields on default-free investments often cannot protect against erosion of purchasing power. Even the distributional flexibility provided by percentage-of-corpus withdrawal formulae may not be able to solve the dilemma of too few resources and too much cash-flow demand.

Whenever a portfolio is in a pure accumulation stage—no cash flow from the portfolio—there is a presumption that, absent significant changes in investor circumstances, investment policy should remain largely static. An asset-only management perspective, however, may not be optimal for retirement-income portfolios. The CFA Institute, for example, acknowledges that "asset allocation policies are likely to change over time as characteristics of the investor change and as market circumstances vary" and that "... volatility as a descriptive measure of risk may be irrelevant beyond an absolute level of loss that would completely derail an investment portfolio" (CFA Institute 2010, §3c., 6). Reference to "... an absolute level of loss that would completely derail an investment portfolio ..." is a good expression for passing into the region of infeasibility.

In an asset-liability portfolio management context, the distance from the free boundary is a key measure of portfolio risk. The investor must closely monitor the dynamic interactions among asset price changes, the strategic asset allocation, and the value of the retirement cash-flow liability. Paradoxically, an asset-management plan that calls for periodic rebalancing to the strategic asset allocation target may not be the economic equivalent to a stay-the-course approach. For portfolios making periodic withdrawals in a decreasing market, portfolio risk emphatically does not stay the same. As current wealth declines, some investors put a premium on strategies to increase future expected return. The sooner a portfolio recovers investment losses, the happier all interested parties. However, strategies calling for higher-growth portfolios are more volatile. The higher expected growth may reverse investment losses, but the higher volatility also increases the probability that wealth will continue to decline.

There is a risk to increasing portfolio risk. At the limit, if the only response to losses is to seek investment gains by increasing risk, asset management becomes mere gambling. Return and variance move together, and any attempt to increase return also increases the probability of failure. Although increasing investment risk may be an appropriate and defensible response to investment loss, losses do not mandate increasing risk in order to recoup portfolio value. The IPS continues to retain its importance as a tool to prevent precipitous reactions to economic events. When committed to writing, investment policy protects the investment program from:

> ... ad hoc revisions of sound long-term policy. All too often, investment policy is both vague and implicit, left to be "resolved" only in haste, when unusually distressing market conditions are putting the pressure on and when it is all too easy to make the wrong decision at the wrong time for the wrong reasons (Ellis 1985, 53–54).

The strategies contemplated in an IPS assume that asset-management decisions are driven by personal circumstances, rather than transitory acute pessimism or optimism regarding capital markets. As monitoring and evaluation assume greater importance in the prudent management of retirement-income portfolios, 21st-century investment policy puts increased emphasis on a process that avoids ill-considered decisions. Policy incorporates the need to make informed judgments only after appropriate analysis. Decision-making criteria may become more adaptive; policy, however, will stipulate an analytical process that demands the investor looks before he leaps.

DIFFERENT PERSPECTIVES ON ACR AND INVESTMENT SURPLUS

It is easy to see that the current value of assets changes constantly as investment results are realized. In a single week, month, or quarter, the fair market value may rocket up or down depending on investment volatility. Likewise, changes in inflation and interest rates will change the discount rate for valuation of future cash payments, and life expectancy changes can increase or decrease the planning horizon. Indeed, the planning horizon—and thus the value of the aggregate liability—changes merely with the passage of time.

At any point in time:

Total Portfolio Wealth = the share to be withdrawn to fund a standard of living + the share to be gifted or bequeathed + taxes, fees, and other costs.

For an income-oriented investor, the gift or bequest amount is the economic equivalent of an investment surplus.[5] As long as the amount is positive, assets are sufficient to pay the projected income target. As the surplus shrinks, the risk that the portfolio will be unable to fund threshold needs increases. Retirement portfolio management becomes a contest between consumption and bequest goals. As the surplus shrinks, risk to the periodic income stream and to terminal wealth increases at an increasing rate.

Assume a $6-million portfolio with a $3-million estimate of the actuarial value of the spending liability. If we extend the concept of actuarial coverage ratio (ACR) to consider the wealth/surplus (W/S) ratio defined as: (wealth) ÷ (wealth – consumption), the current W/S ratio value is $6-million total assets ÷ $3-million surplus = 2.[6] At this wealth level, a 1-percent change in the value of assets translates to an approximately 2-percent change in the value of economic surplus, i.e., the portfolio's investment cushion. Assume, further, a 25-percent decrease in the value of assets to $4.5 million. The ratio is now 4.5 ÷ 1.5 = 3. This translates into a change in the value of the investment surplus of approximately 3 percent for each 1-percent change in the value of assets. Finally, assume a further decrease in portfolio value to $3.5 million. The ratio value is now 3.5 ÷ 0.5 = 7. This is a leverage factor of seven to one. As the investment surplus disappears, does the investor stay the course with respect to the asset allocation? For many investors risk tolerance is changing almost certainly as wealth decreases.

Equivalently, if wealth is the numerator and consumption is the denominator, the monitoring system tracks the ACR. If using a W/S ratio, the lower the ratio value, the better a portfolio can fund future liabilities. By contrast, a high ACR value suggests manageable demands against financial resources and a low ratio value suggests that adverse market conditions might stress the portfolio to the point where it no longer can be expected to generate the target income. The W/S ratio provides a complementary perspective on the role of tracking the ACR and indicates why such tracking is an important aspect of an appropriate portfolio monitoring program.

CASE STUDY 8: THE 'STEADY STATE' ACR

This section explores the sometimes-complex relationships between age, annuity costs, and the feasibility condition. The question of interest is this: What ACR is required assuming a two-fold goal of lifetime income plus preservation of principal on an inflation-adjusted basis? This issue is important for (1) investors assigning equal utility value for both lifetime income and terminal wealth, and (2) trustees tasked with the duty of impartiality between beneficiary classes. We consider two investors, a female age 50 and a female age 70, each with a starting ACR of around 1. Each could convert immediately to an annuity and leave no inheritance, or each could hold the investment portfolio and try to match her periodic consumption to the equivalent annuity payments. Assuming equal starting portfolio dollar values, the periodic annuity benefit payable to the 70-year-old investor is substantially higher than that payable to the 50-year-old investor. This is equivalent to saying that there is a greater mortality premium available at the older age.

---

5.   It may also be seen as a "buffer stock" in terms of Chapter Eight's discussion on precautionary savings. "Withdrawal surplus" is also a helpful term.

6.   The ratio is actually a ratio of two distributions rather than two numbers. The numerator reflects the probable range of short-term asset values, and the denominator represents wealth minus the probable range of short-term changes in the actuarially calculated value of liabilities. The current value of assets is a reasonable proxy for the numerator, and the mean of the liability distribution (50th percentile of aggregate distributions discounted for inflation) is a reasonable proxy for the denominator. The W/S ratio in this example does not consider fees and investment charges that would represent a further adjustment in the denominator's value.

Figure 9.1 depicts the evolution of wealth for the 50-year-old assuming an initial portfolio value of $1 million and a constant-dollar $5,000-per-month withdrawal. The coverage ratio (ratio of current portfolio value to the cost of an annuity) assumes that the equivalent annuity monthly payment ($5,000) grows by 3 percent per year. Although there is a basis discrepancy between portfolio withdrawals adjusted for actual inflation and the 3-percent graded annuity payout, we do not assert that the example presents a precise apples-to-apples comparison. Rather, we are interested in obtaining insight into the feasibility condition at various ages and for various financial objectives.

FIGURE 9.1: LIFE CYCLE WITH ANNUITY COMPARISON, 50-YEAR-OLD FEMALE INVESTOR

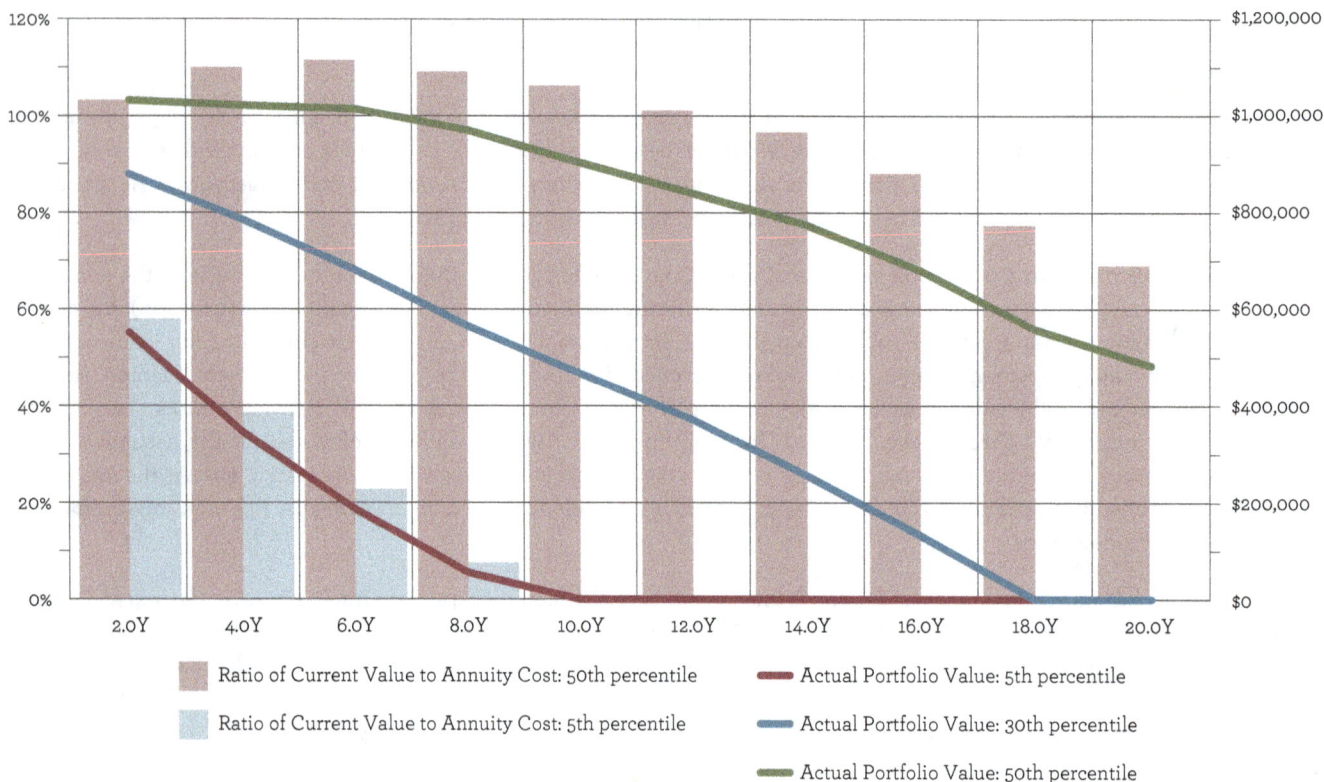

	Ratio of Current Value to Annuity Cost: 50th percentile		Actual Portfolio Value: 5th percentile
	Ratio of Current Value to Annuity Cost: 5th percentile		Actual Portfolio Value: 30th percentile
			Actual Portfolio Value: 50th percentile

The columns depict the ratio of portfolio value to the cost of an annuity at various percentiles of the distribution of constant-dollar portfolio value net after periodic withdrawals. The right-side axis measures net portfolio value evolutions which the graph illustrates with solid lines.

Figure 9.2 assumes a 70-year-old female who, from an initial portfolio valued at $1 million, withdraws an inflation-adjusted $6,500 per month increasing at a 3-percent annual rate.[7]

---

7.   The cost for $5,000 increasing yearly by a factor of 3 percent is $1 million for a 50-year-old female annuitant. A 70-year-old female annuitant can purchase $6,500 for the same premium amount.

FIGURE 9.2: LIFE CYCLE WITH ANNUITY COMPARISON, 70-YEAR-OLD FEMALE INVESTOR

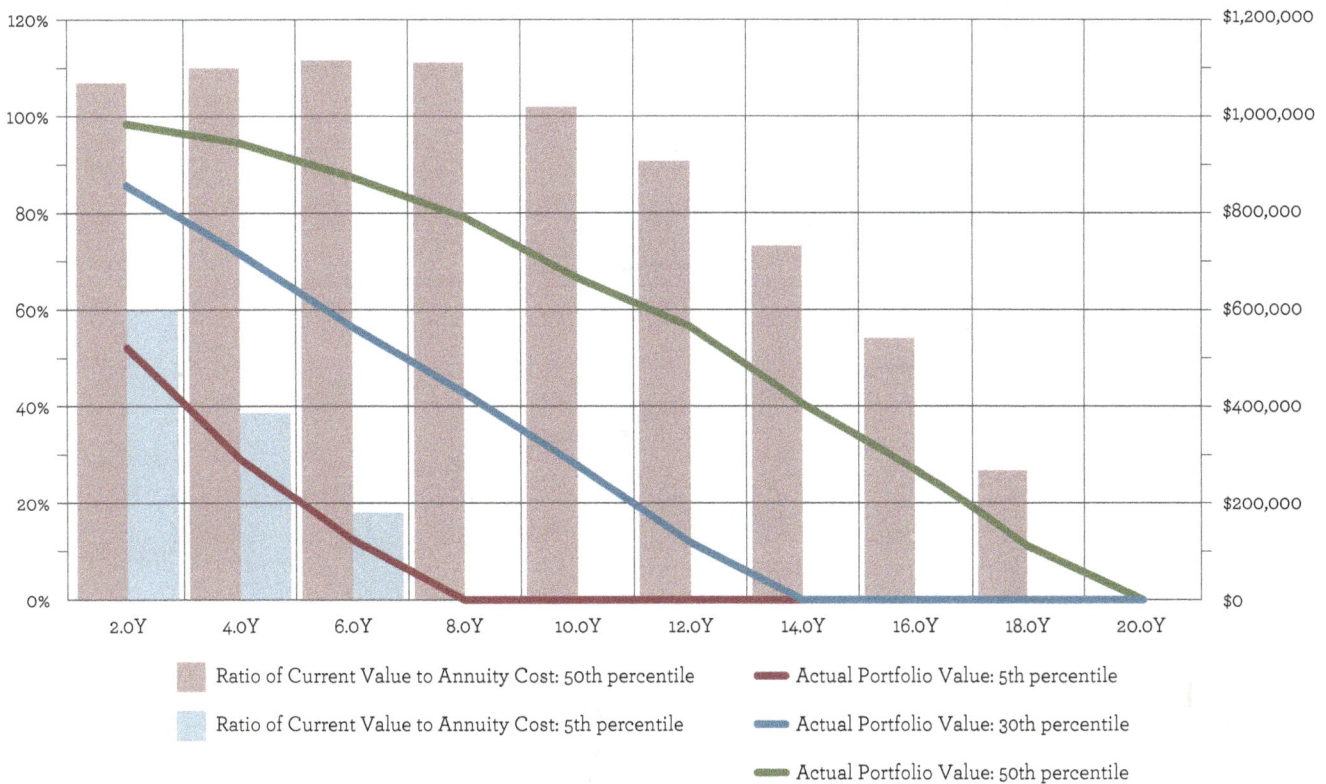

Both figures 9.1 and 9.2 illustrate the risk of trying to maintain a constant-dollar lifetime income and an inheritance. At the assumed withdrawal rates, neither investor can expect to match the annuity payout and protect the inflation-adjusted portfolio value for descendants. In other words, an investor incurs an expected cost for the option to provide a bequest. The older investor's wealth decays much faster—in the median case she depletes the portfolio at 20 years. This is not surprising because, when matching the annuity's periodic payout, the "bequest option" is cheaper for younger people.

But this raises a related issue: What is the "steady state" ACR for different ages, i.e., what ACR needs to be maintained, in the median case, to generate the expectation of both a lifetime income and an inheritance? This is a critical issue for trustees trying to produce income and, simultaneously, to preserve the value of the trust corpus. A trustee would benefit greatly from understanding the feasibility condition, i.e., what ACR is required lest the trustee attempt to satisfy the legitimate expectations of the settlor and the beneficiary classes when, financially, the trust is technically insolvent.[8] It turns out that the answer depends on age—the older the investor, the higher the required steady-state coverage ratio. Although a potential strategy for safe retirement income is to adjust consumption to always be equal to the age-dependent steady state ACR, this is an extremely conservative strategy because the goal is to sustain consumption rate in the median case forever.

---

8.   The trust's distribution to the current beneficiary may, for example, be the amount deemed necessary under an ascertainable standard provision (health, education, maintenance, and support).

To what degree must an investor or trustee adjust periodic income to lock in both a constant-dollar-income and a preserve-the-value-of-the-corpus expectation? Figures 9.3 and 9.4 approximate age-dependent, steady-state coverage rates (figure 9.3 for a 50-year-old and figure 9.4 for a 70-year-old) for a $1-million portfolio.

FIGURE 9.3: LIFE CYCLE WITH ANNUITY COMPARISON, 50-YEAR-OLD FEMALE INVESTOR

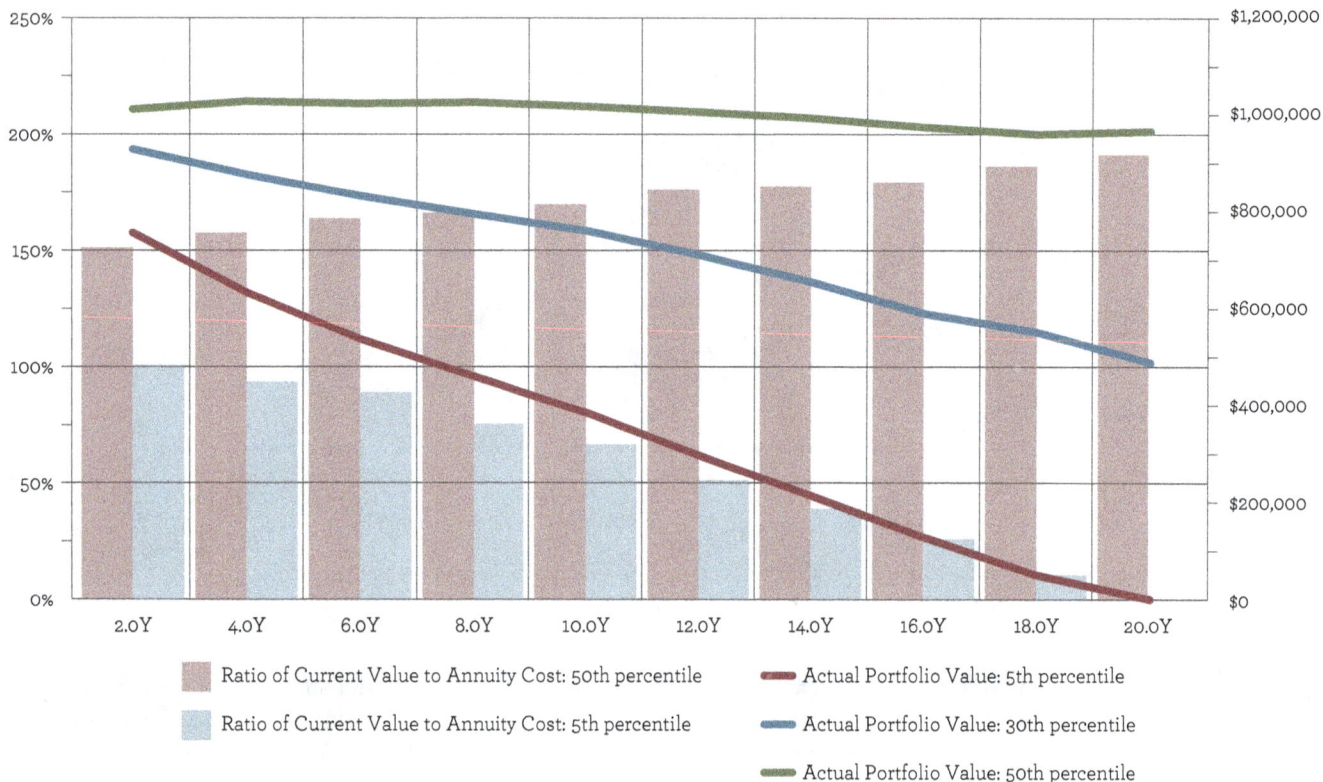

FIGURE 9.4: LIFE CYCLE WITH ANNUITY COMPARISON, 70-YEAR-OLD FEMALE INVESTOR

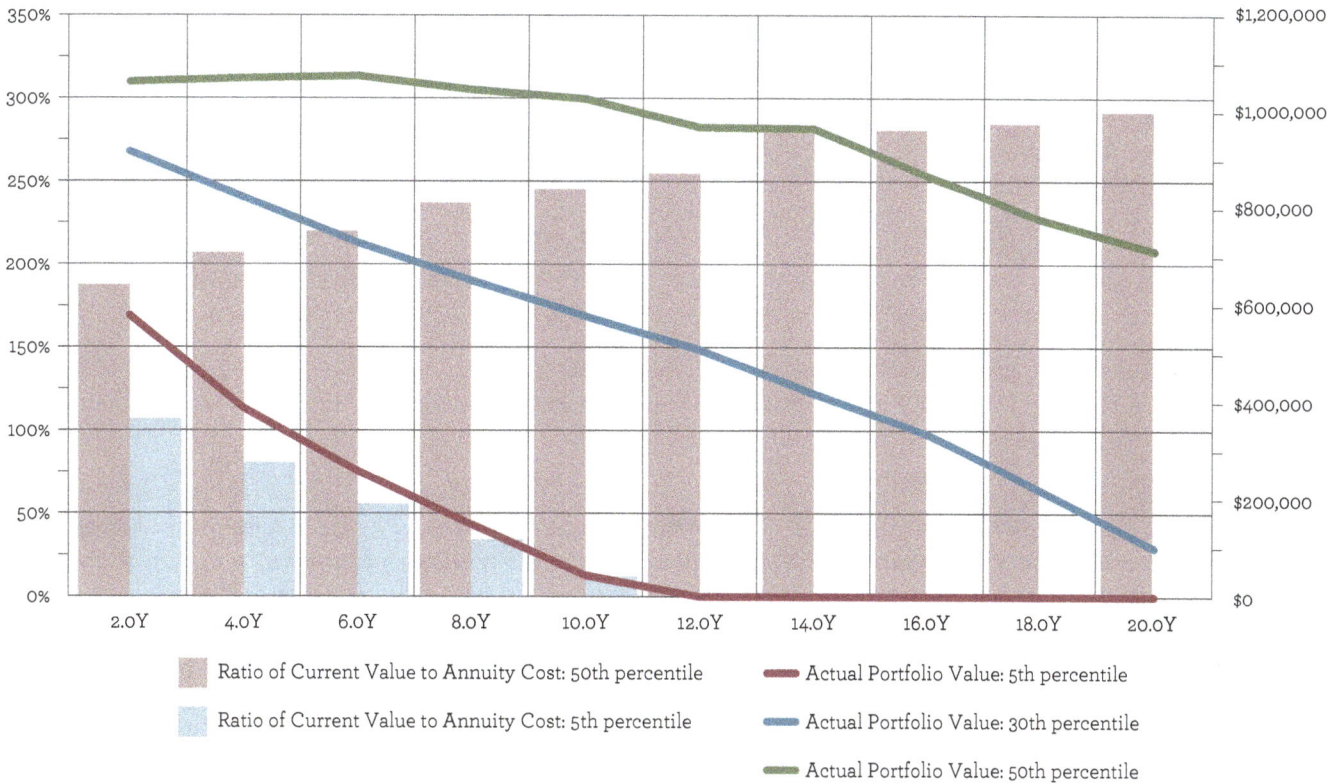

Legend:
- Ratio of Current Value to Annuity Cost: 50th percentile
- Ratio of Current Value to Annuity Cost: 5th percentile
- Actual Portfolio Value: 5th percentile
- Actual Portfolio Value: 30th percentile
- Actual Portfolio Value: 50th percentile

Given an initial $1-million portfolio value, the 50-year-old female investor requires an approximately 1.5x-coverage ratio to preserve the corpus. The revised ACR value requires her to reduce income to a $3,500 monthly withdrawal (graded upward by 3 percent per year). There is evidence of a modest decay in constant-dollar portfolio value over the 20-year planning horizon. The risk model indicates that the ACR increases slowly from approximately 1.5 to 2x coverage at the end of 20 years. Figure 9.3 suggests that given a withdrawal rate target of 4.2 percent adjusted for inflation ($3,500 × 12 = $42,000 per year), the hypothetical 50-year-old female investor can expect to maintain the inflation-adjusted value of the portfolio ($1 million) for 20 years.

Assume that she is now age 70 and has, in fact, maintained the constant-dollar equivalent of a $1-million portfolio. At age 70, a $4,000 monthly withdrawal rate with an approximately 2x coverage ratio works for the forthcoming 20-year period. Despite the higher monthly income, the ACR value is now between 1.5 and 2—largely due to increased mortality credits for older-age annuitants. The higher coverage ratio suggests that the 70-year-old is at a comfortable distance from the free boundary and, therefore, can finance more monthly consumption from her portfolio. But there's an important difference—the 70-year-old, despite starting the forthcoming 20-year planning horizon with a coverage ratio well above a value of one, can't maintain the upwardly revised 4.8-percent inflation-adjusted withdrawal rate ($4,000 × 12 = $48,000 per year) and, simultaneously, maintain the inflation-adjusted portfolio value. Bequest motives significantly change the location of the free boundary. Given portfolios of equivalent initial value, the initial steady-state coverage ratio per dollar of cash flow increases as age increases. At age 50 a 1.5x coverage ratio is enough, but by age 70 it should be closer to 2.5x, and age 80 may require a 3.5x or 4x coverage ratio. In other words, assuming the wish to maintain the portfolio's constant-dollar value, consumption needs to be even less than the current age steady-state ratio might suggest because the ratio must grow for the bequest to be sustained.

GOALS-BASED ASSET ALLOCATION VERSUS GOALS-BASED MONITORING AND SURVEILLANCE

Ideally, whenever an advisor reports quantitative performance results, the client also should understand progress toward or movement away from personal goals and objectives. For a retirement-planning engagement, this might necessitate tracking changes in feasibility of goals (solvency evaluation), sustainability (shortfall metrics), and financial security (flexibility in terms of a surplus over and above required funds).

A well-designed monitoring and surveillance program benefits investors by providing (1) timely alerts, and (2) insights into the scope of unfolding difficulties. It helps an investor distinguish between negative returns that are merely unpleasant and negative returns that are potentially catastrophic. Further, an effective monitoring system facilitates implementation of appropriate and timely adjustments. It enhances the ability to formulate prudent asset-management responses so that investor reactions are not byproducts of excessive fear or greed.

Goals-based asset allocation traditionally refers to the process of matching separate investment sub-portfolios to individual financial goals. The more critical goal fulfillment, the more capital is allocated to it. Consider, for example, the exposition of a goals-based asset allocation system provided in the Level III CFA course-of-study curriculum:

> *To illustrate, assume that a portfolio associated with a goal has an expected return of 7% with 10% expected volatility and the investor has indicated that the goal is to be met over the next five years with at least 90% confidence. Over the next five years that portfolio is expected to produce returns of 35% with a volatility of 22.4%. In short, this portfolio is expected to experience an average compound return of only 1.3% per year over five years with a probability of 90%; this result is quite a bit lower than the portfolio's average 7% expected return. Thus, rather than discounting expected cash outflows by 7% to compute the dollar amount needed to defease the goal over that five-year horizon, one must use a considerably lower discount rate and by implication reserve a higher level of capital to meet that goal* (Brunel et al. 2019, 291).

Given estimated values for the mean and standard deviation, the hypothetical goal described above requires initial funding in a goals-based approach so that the investor achieves "success" at the 90th-percentile probability level.[9] This is more than a plan-for-the-worst strategy; it is a fund-for-the-worst strategy. If an investor did not heretofore appreciate the "cost of safety," goals-based allocation guarantees such awareness. A goals-based asset allocation assumes a utility function rarely exhibited by retired investors. It induces a back-loaded spending policy,[10] when, more commonly, impatience, i.e., the subjective discount rate, motivates consumption paths that decrease over time.[11]

Goals-based asset allocation incorporates a probabilistic approach to portfolio design and, therefore, differs from strict asset-liability matching. Pfau (2017, 30) describes the asset-liability matching approach:

> *Asset-liability matching removes the probability-based concept of safe withdrawal rates from the analysis, since it rejects relying on a diversified portfolio for the entire lifestyle goal. The idea is to first build a floor of very low-risk guaranteed income sources to serve your basic spending needs in retirement …. such as building a ladder of TIPS or purchasing an income annuity…. With any remaining assets, you can invest and spend as you wish.*

> *Each approach shares, however, the burden of overcoming excessive implementation costs—especially in low-interest-rate economies. In a goals-based approach, the investor has the expectation of eventually releasing financial resources (liquidity for flexibility/security) if outcomes fall into more favorable percentile ranges. The asset-liability matching approach consumes financial resources, compromises liquidity, and has an uncertain effect on the investor's future security* (Vernon 2016, 25).

---

9. Refer to Brunel et al. (2019), Chapter 4, footnote 15, which discusses a random variable in terms of a possible outcome over a defined probability space. The CFA text places a somewhat greater emphasis on the nature of the probability space and its importance in portfolio design.

10. Ibid., p. 304. In an observation that is a model of understatement, the authors acknowledge: "... discounting needs based on probability-and-horizon-adjusted minimum expectations naturally means that these expectations will be exceeded under 'normal circumstances.' Thus, it is not unusual for the funding for a goal to seem excessive with the benefit of hindsight" pp. 292–293.

11. Table 1300 of the Consumer Expenditure Survey, U.S. Bureau of Labor Statistics (September 2018) supports the hypothesis that investors tend to front-load retirement consumption. Average 2017 spending decreased from $64,972 for ages 55–64, to $54,997 for ages 65–74, and finally to $41,849 for ages 75 and older. Theoretically, a high rate of return on deferred spending amounts induces back-loaded consumption paths. However, retired investors must balance this effect against "brevity risk" to arrive at optimal consumption/savings decisions.

Despite these drawbacks, some investors may implement a strict asset-liability matching approach for reasons other than its investment merit. Consider, for example, the following retirement-planning advice: "Select solutions that are easy to use and don't need continual monitoring and adjustment, or that protect retirees against fraud and mistakes due to cognitive decline." Just as there is a cost-of-safety, so also there is a cost-of-simplicity. These elements are part of the larger risk/return trade-off—investing is a prudent exchange of risk—that investors consider when making asset-management decisions.

By contrast, a goals-based monitoring and surveillance program tracks, among other critical metrics, a virtual floor (the free boundary as defined by ACR value) and preserves the option to implement flooring if it ever becomes appropriate to do so. To an adherent of the rational school of investing, the insights of behavioral finance seem more fitting within a risk-monitoring context than within a portfolio-design context.[12] Chapter Ten provides examples of goals-based monitoring systems and discusses how such systems facilitate asset management decisions.

---

12. See, for example, Mladina (2016): "Adaptive trade-offs can include goal reprioritization and modifications to goal thresholds, risk preference, time horizons, and expected returns."

REPORTING AND EVALUATING RESULTS

■ ■ ■

TRACKING INVESTOR SPENDING THROUGH TIME—A PROTEAN TASK

An investor says that he wishes to withdraw $50,000 per year from a $1-million financial asset portfolio. After reviewing a simulation analysis, he decides on an asset allocation, an asset management policy (constant mix, buy and hold, etc.), and a withdrawal policy (fixed periodic withdrawal, floating amount withdrawal, hybrid, etc.). The advisor records the decisions, makes sure the investment/spending policy passes the initial feasibility test (actuarial coverage ratio or ACR > 1), and memorializes important risk metrics, e.g., portfolio value never less than $x, monthly income never less than $y, probability of depletion never greater than z percent. At this point, the investor has used the information set presented to establish a prudent investment/spending program, and the advisor has set up metrics to follow how things are working out in terms of client goals and risk constraints.

- After three months, the investor needs $16,000 for a home remodel and repair project that can't wait.

- After eight months, the investor says that his grandson is looking to him to provide $15,000 to complete the final leg of an MBA program.

- After 20 months, the investor calls and says that his son-in-law has lost his job and needs temporary financial help to the tune of $20,000 (a grandson graduated but because of student loan debt has no extra money and needs to secure a car to commute to his new job).

- After 23 months, the investor calls and indicates that he has underestimated taxes because of qualified plan minimum required distribution rules. He needs $14,000.

At the end-of-year-two/beginning-of-year-three review meeting, the advisor's tracking record indicates that the investor has withdrawn the planned $50,000 × 2 = $100,000 periodic income (the investor did not implement an inflation increase in year two because of the unexpected expenses), plus $65,000 in one-off expenses. Total withdrawals over the first two years amount to $165,000.

At the review meeting, if markets have been good, little harm has been done. However, if returns have been poor, the investor may make changes in either allocation, rebalancing elections, inflation adjustments, or periodic spending. At this point a good record-keeping system becomes important. The advisor wants a continuous set of tracking metrics from the time of the investor's initial decision until the current date. This is the case even though the advisor no longer is tracking the same decision metric set. For example, the initial decision metric set was $50,000 from a $1-million portfolio; the new metric set might be something like $45,000 from a $780,000 portfolio at the investor's new age and health status.

Tracking in year three looks nothing like what the advisor started tracking in year one. But this is what dynamic asset management should look like—retrenchment if times are bad, additional reward if times are good. Although change is neither unexpected nor unwelcome, controlling volatility from the liability side of the balance sheet can be as important to meeting the retirement-income project successfully as controlling it from the asset side.

RECORD KEEPING

Given the heterogeneity of investor goals and circumstances, it should come as no surprise that there is no single best monitoring and evaluation system. Additionally, given the inevitable changes in investor preferences and circumstances, it would be a mistake to expect that all elements of today's monitoring system will remain unchanged into the future.[1]

---

1.   A basic property of decision-making is that people change their mind. One implication of this fact is that temporal discounting of reward may be hyperbolic rather than exponential. As time passes, the discounted value of rewards that seemed initially unattractive may, under a hyperbolic model, catch up to and surpass the discounted value of exponentially discounted rewards. Investor preferences change often with the passage of time. This observation has important consequences for optimal control approaches to decision-making when such approaches require a utility-based solution to the optimal decision-making strategy over time (Shadmehr and Mussa-Ivaldi 2012).

Recordkeeping is a prerequisite for an effective monitoring process. The following templates facilitate the accomplishment of this task. Template one tracks a threshold income level corresponding to the minimum income (threshold) level required to sustain an acceptable lifestyle for a single retiree. Template two tracks the income level sufficient to sustain a target standard of living for a single retiree.

We omit the straightforward extension for a template designed to record information for a retired investor plus spouse. The significance of the yellow-shaded column headings is discussed below.

TEMPLATE ONE: CLIENT RECORD-KEEPING SYSTEM

Year	Health-Adjusted Age	Inflation	Portfolio Value	Periodic Spending Threshold Target	Additional Anticipated Portfolio Withdrawals	Total Actual Withdrawals	ACR Target Value	Risk Metric One	Risk Metric Two	Risk Metric Three
1										
2										
3										
4										
5										
6										
7										

TEMPLATE TWO: CLIENT RECORD-KEEPING SYSTEM

Year	Health-Adjusted Age	Inflation	Portfolio Value	Periodic Spending Aspirational Target	Additional Anticipated Portfolio Withdrawals	Total Actual Withdrawals	ACR Target Value	Risk Metric One	Risk Metric Two	Risk Metric Three
1										
2										
3										
4										
5										
6										
7										

The advisor is, of course, free to add or delete elements to the templates. Likewise, additional template forms may be needed if the advisor tracks more than two target income levels (and their associated risk metrics).[2]

2.   For example, "threshold," "target," and "aspirational." Tracking multiple targets is the subject matter for Case Study 11.

The templates are primarily for the purpose of recordkeeping rather than for reporting and evaluation of actual results. The yellow-colored columns record variables, e.g., changes in portfolio value and client spending. Other columns record static parameter values. For example, a client's goals may include maintaining:

- An ACR of 1.1 for the threshold income level
- An ACR of 1.0 for the target standard-of-living income level
- A minimum portfolio (bequest) value of $x
- A risk of portfolio depletion less than z percent

The parameter values that record individual client goals may change; but, until such changes occur, template parameter values remain constant. In this respect, we distinguish the record-keeping templates from the retirement-income risk model. The risk model may change over time as the investor adjusts goals and preferences. For example, the retirement-income model's asset allocation in year seven may differ from the initial allocation weighting. The templates, however, assume that the advisor will, for the most part, use them to record information concerning the metrics that are tracked.

However, if a client prefers a retirement-income strategy calling for a floating percentage of corpus withdrawal policy as opposed to a fixed periodic income strategy, the risk metrics of interest may include:

- A minimum income of $y in any period
- An asset allocation that controls annual downside risk to portfolio value to less than z percent after planned withdrawals

The point is that the advisor—as well as the investor—should have a clear idea of what elements to measure, and how to track them. Irrespective of how the advisor chooses to modify the above templates to fit the demands of his or her practice, changes should be anticipated as time unfolds—although the specific nature and direction of some changes are currently unknown. Client tracking records are usually works in progress.

PRESENTING GOALS-BASED INVESTMENT OUTCOMES

Just as there is no one-size-fits-all record-keeping template, so also, there are many ways to present information about the results of client financial-management elections. The monitoring and evaluation of outcomes is an evolving field of practice management within the financial advisory profession. Selection of suitable presentation formats—including the information elements presented to clients—depends on the type of risk modeling applications available to the advisor as well as on individual client goals and preferences. Decisions about record-keeping templates and performance-reporting formats reflect advisor assumptions, based on the case fact patterns regarding how a dynamic monitoring system may unfold initially, and how it may change in future years. We move into the realm of the art of presenting quantitative information in a manner that is useful and readily understandable by the client. Often, this is facilitated by a tabular and graphic presentation.

CASE STUDY 9

In Case Study 9 the advisor begins to work in 2007 with a recently widowed investor. All debts are paid. In addition to portfolio income, she receives survivorship benefits from her husband's pension and from Social Security. A life insurance portfolio left her with a cash reserve that she divided between bank certificates of deposit and her checking account. Maintaining a threshold standard of living requires an annual inflation-adjusted withdrawal from the portfolio of $72,000. She wishes also to visit distant family and friends and estimates a yearly expenditure of $18,000 on trips, i.e., her target yearly withdrawal amount is $90,000 adjusted for inflation. Fortunately, the cash reserves are available to tide her over during the Great Recession of 2008 and 2009. In later years, she increases actual withdrawals to replenish, in part, her cash reserve accounts.

The investor and advisor meet each year to review portfolio performance information. Periodically, they find it useful to update the investor's retirement-income risk model. The advisor presents figure 10.1 and its companion data table (The large amounts of recorded "actual withdrawal" in years 2013 and 2016 are the cumulative withdrawals over the multi-year intervals).

DATA TABLE FOR FIGURE 10.1

Evaluation Date	SPENDING			Portfolio Value	Age	Approximate Life Expectancy (in Years)
	Standard of Living Target	Inflation-Adjusted Target	Actual Withdrawal			
2007	$72,000	$72,000	N/A	$1,800,000	66	22
2007	$90,000	$90,000	N/A	$1,800,000	66	22
2009	$72,000	$75,007	$14,000	$1,362,220	68	20
2009	$90,000	$93,759	$14,000	$1,362,220	68	20
2011	$72,000	$78,201	$35,000	$1,960,500	70	18
2011	$90,000	$97,751	$35,000	$1,960,500	70	18
2013	$72,000	$81,919	$170,000	$1,966,431	72	16
2013	$90,000	$102,400	$170,000	$1,966,431	72	16
2016	$72,000	$84,394	$330,000	$2,025,789	75	14
2016	$90,000	$105,493	$330,000	$2,025,789	75	14
2017	$72,000	$86,145	$98,000	$2,149,887	76	13
2017	$90,000	$107,681	$98,000	$2,149,887	76	13
2018	$72,000	$87,962	$220,000	$2,244,566	77	13
2018	$90,000	$109,952	$220,000	$2,244,566	77	13

FIGURE 10.1: PORTFOLIO SURPLUS (SECURITY) AND PORTFOLIO SUSTAINABILITY

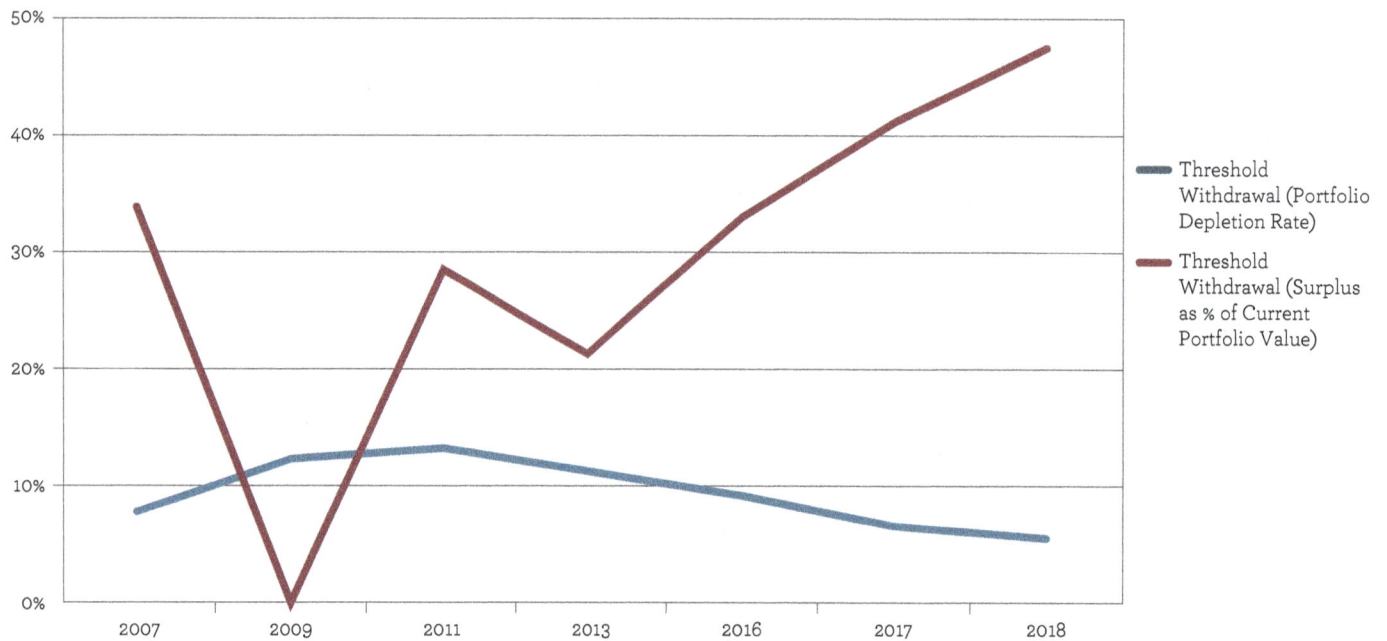

Legend:
- Threshold Withdrawal (Portfolio Depletion Rate)
- Threshold Withdrawal (Surplus as % of Current Portfolio Value)

BEQUEST			SUSTAINABILITY		FEASIBILITY	SECURITY	
50th Percentile Terminal Wealth	30th Percentile Terminal Wealth	10th Percentile Terminal Wealth	Portfolio Depletion Rate	Probability Assets Ever Below $500,000	Feasibility Boundary	Surplus	Surplus as % of Current Portfolio Value
$2,870,461	$1,602,084	$211,541	8%	14%	$1,191,895	$608,105	34%
$2,193,769	$997,958	$—	16%	23%	$1,489,869	$310,131	17%
$2,137,436	$1,109,933	$—	12%	20%	$1,355,581	$6,639	0%
$1,713,027	$634,851	$—	19%	28%	$1,694,481	$(332,261)	-24%
$1,996,108	$951,959	$—	13%	22%	$1,403,565	$556,935	28%
$1,610,960	$340,978	$—	24%	33%	$1,754,451	$206,049	11%
$2,187,640	$1,163,364	$—	11%	20%	$1,540,989	$425,442	22%
$1,817,389	$737,905	$—	18%	27%	$1,926,260	$40,171	2%
$2,096,630	$1,170,746	$94,667	9%	17%	$1,350,909	$674,880	33%
$1,808,752	$904,937	$—	14%	22%	$1,688,645	$337,144	17%
$2,337,782	$1,470,258	$317,900	7%	13%	$1,265,201	$884,686	41%
$2,054,718	$1,200,495	$—	11%	18%	$1,581,497	$568,390	26%
$2,464,114	$1,677,521	$428,103	5%	11%	$1,183,239	$1,061,327	47%
$2,271,635	$1,418,339	$58,369	9%	16%	$1,479,042	$765,524	34%

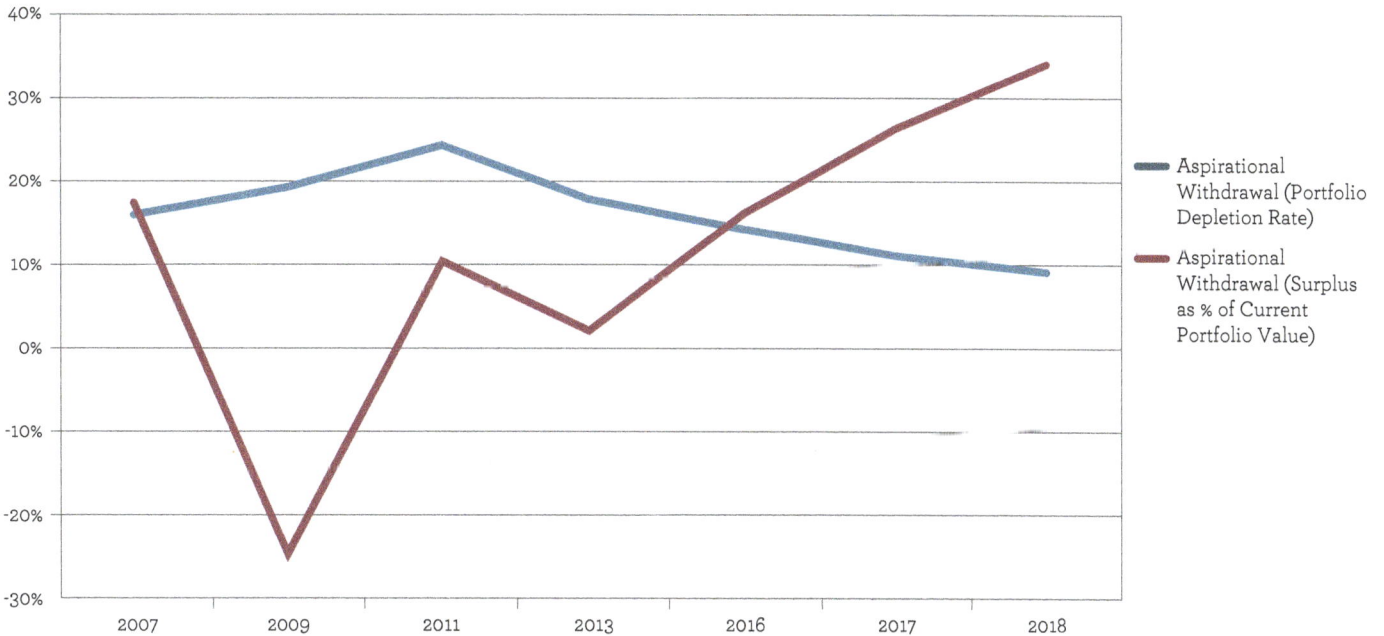

Several items are noteworthy:

- Portfolio withdrawals have been reactive to economic conditions; or, more simply, the investor exhibits lumpy spending.

- Although inflation over the period has been modest, nevertheless the threshold withdrawal amount has increased from $72,000 per year to $88,000; the target amount has increased from $90,000 to $110,000.

- Portfolio value has increased from $1.8 million to $2.24 million.

- Initially, at age 66, the investor's life expectancy is age 88. At her current age 77, her life expectancy is 90. The shift in life expectancy has profound implications with respect to sequence of returns risk for late-in-life investors.

- In all years of evaluation, the risk model indicates positive terminal wealth, i.e., amount available for bequest, at the 50th and 30th percentiles.

- Sustainability metrics focus on downside risk. During the period under evaluation, the unconditional probability of depletion at the threshold withdrawal target ranges from a low of 5 percent to a high of 13 percent, and, at the target withdrawal target, from a low of 9 percent to a high of 24 percent.

- The investor maintains feasible retirement-income objectives throughout the period with the single exception of the target income level in 2009.

The presentation provides a useful perspective about the investor's current financial position by mixing outputs from two distinct modeling approaches—investment simulation and actuarial estimation.[3] In this case, the investor has sufficient non-portfolio resources to keep withdrawals below target levels until the portfolio recovers. Thereafter, spending accelerates to reflect higher portfolio values plus the desire to replenish reserves.[4] The existence of a stock of buffer wealth provides sufficient financial flexibility for the investor to stay the course with respect to her 65-percent stock/35-percent fixed income asset allocation.

CASE STUDY 10

In Case Study 10, the analysis tracks three income levels for a retired married couple's joint life span. The husband is in his late sixties, his wife is in her early sixties. For each income level, the advisor tests the continued feasibility of a 100-percent joint and survivor income and a 100-percent joint with 80-percent survivor income. Additionally, for the 100-percent joint and survivor income election, the advisor presents sustainability (probability of eventual portfolio depletion), downside risk (probability of portfolio declines during its period of operation), and financial security (surplus) risk metrics. The assumed withdrawal inflation adjustment is 2.5 percent per year.

Initially, the portfolio has a value of $2,960,000. After one year, the portfolio value has increased to $3,050,000 after withdrawals and expenses. In table 10.1, the advisor presents a risk assessment based on the initial year's portfolio performance.

---

3.   "The decision maker's distrust of his model makes him want good decisions over a set of models …. Such decisions are said to be robust to misspecification of the approximating model" (Hansen and Sargent 2008, 27). Linear-quadratic dynamic programming approaches are appropriate when the decision-maker is confident that there is little or no model misspecification. Chapter 16 provides further insights into decision-making when an investor is uncertain about the true state of the world.

4.   See, the discussion on "precautionary reserves" In Chapter 8, footnote 12.

TABLE 10.1: RETIREMENT RISK METRIC SUMMARY—2018

Current Portfolio Value = $3,050,000

BULL/BEAR MARKET AGNOSTIC

Annual Net Distribution Target (adjusted for inflation)	$75,000
Feasibility Boundary 100% Joint	$2,020,000
Feasibility Boundary 100% / 80% Survivor	$1,810,000
Probability of Depletion	7%
Assets < $1 Million Inflation-adjusted	10%
Assets decline > 20% in a 12-month period	75%
Assets decline > 40% from peak to trough	46%
Financial Surplus 100% Joint (Cushion)	$1,030,000
Financial Surplus 100% Joint / 80% Survivor (Cushion)	$1,240,000

Annual Net Distribution Target (adjusted for inflation)	$87,500
Feasibility Boundary 100% Joint	$2,355,000
Feasibility Boundary 100% / 80% Survivor	$2,115,000
Probability of Depletion	8%
Assets < $1 Million Inflation-adjusted	11%
Assets decline > 20% in a 12-month period	75%
Assets decline > 40% from peak to trough	49%
Financial Surplus 100% Joint (Cushion)	$695,000
Financial Surplus 100% Joint / 80% Survivor (Cushion)	$935,000

Annual Net Distribution Target (adjusted for inflation)	$100,000
Feasibility Boundary 100% Joint	$2,690,000
Feasibility Boundary 100% / 80% Survivor	$2,415,000
Probability of Depletion	10%
Assets < $1 Million Inflation-adjusted	14%
Assets decline > 20% in a 12-month period	76%
Assets decline > 40% from peak to trough	49%
Financial Surplus 100% Joint (Cushion)	$360,000
Financial Surplus 100% Joint / 80% Survivor (Cushion)	$635,000

Planning Horizon: Joint Life Span

BEAR MARKET

Annual Net Distribution Target (adjusted for inflation)	$75,000
Feasibility Boundary 100% Joint	$2,020,000
Feasibility Boundary 100% / 80% Survivor	$1,810,000
Probability of Depletion	12%
Assets < $1 Million Inflation-adjusted	17%
Assets decline > 20% in a 12-month period	84%
Assets decline > 40% from peak to trough	59%
Financial Surplus 100% Joint (Cushion)	$1,030,000
Financial Surplus 100% Joint / 80% Survivor (Cushion)	$1,240,000

Annual Net Distribution Target (adjusted for inflation)	$87,500
Feasibility Boundary 100% Joint	$2,355,000
Feasibility Boundary 100% / 80% Survivor	$2,115,000
Probability of Depletion	16%
Assets < $1 Million Inflation-adjusted	21%
Assets decline > 20% in a 12-month period	85%
Assets decline > 40% from peak to trough	59%
Financial Surplus 100% Joint (Cushion)	$695,000
Financial Surplus 100% Joint / 80% Survivor (Cushion)	$935,000

Annual Net Distribution Target (adjusted for inflation)	$100,000
Feasibility Boundary 100% Joint	$2,690,000
Feasibility Boundary 100% / 80% Survivor	$2,415,000
Probability of Depletion	22%
Assets < $1 Million Inflation-adjusted	28%
Assets decline > 20% in a 12-month period	85%
Assets decline > 40% from peak to trough	62%
Financial Surplus 100% Joint (Cushion)	$360,000
Financial Surplus 100% Joint / 80% Survivor (Cushion)	$635,000

The advisor explains the various risk metrics. The bear market analysis is of great interest to the investors given that they are conservative in both their spending habits and portfolio allocation. They recognize that their greatest identifiable financial hurdle is to provide adequate lifetime income to a woman in good health currently in her early sixties. The applicable planning horizon may be 40 years or more. Given the initial year's data, they decide to forego increasing the annual distributions by an approximately 2-percent realized inflation factor.

A year has passed and the advisor has prepared the second annual review analysis. He prefaces his presentation with the following comments:

- Your portfolio is now valued at $50,000 less than last year
- Interest rates have decreased making the cost of lifetime income more expensive
- You are now each one-year older

Do you think your financial situation has improved, stayed the same, or deteriorated?

The investors' opinion splits with the husband opining that things have deteriorated and the wife suggesting the opposite. Table 10.2 shows the updated financial analysis.

TABLE 10.2: RETIREMENT RISK METRIC SUMMARY—2019

Current Portfolio Value = $3,00,000

BULL/BEAR MARKET AGNOSTIC

Annual Net Distribution Target (adjusted for inflation)	$75,000
Feasibility Boundary 100% Joint	$1,910,500
Feasibility Boundary 100% / 80% Survivor	$1,701,000
Probability of Depletion	7%
Assets < $1 Million Inflation-adjusted	10%
Assets decline > 20% in a 12-month period	73%
Assets decline > 40% from peak to trough	46%
Financial Surplus 100% Joint (Cushion)	$1,089,500
Financial Surplus 100% Joint / 80% Survivor (Cushion)	$1,299,000

Annual Net Distribution Target (adjusted for inflation)	$87,500
Feasibility Boundary 100% Joint	$2,229,000
Feasibility Boundary 100% / 80% Survivor	$1,984,500
Probability of Depletion	8%
Assets < $1 Million Inflation-adjusted	12%
Assets decline > 20% in a 12-month period	75%
Assets decline > 40% from peak to trough	49%
Financial Surplus 100% Joint (Cushion)	$771,000
Financial Surplus 100% Joint / 80% Survivor (Cushion)	$1,015,500

Planning Horizon: Joint Life Span

BEAR MARKET

Annual Net Distribution Target (adjusted for inflation)	$75,000
Feasibility Boundary 100% Joint	$1,910,500
Feasibility Boundary 100% / 80% Survivor	$1,701,000
Probability of Depletion	12%
Assets < $1 Million Inflation-adjusted	18%
Assets decline > 20% in a 12-month period	84%
Assets decline > 40% from peak to trough	58%
Financial Surplus 100% Joint (Cushion)	$1,089,500
Financial Surplus 100% Joint / 80% Survivor (Cushion)	$1,299,000

Annual Net Distribution Target (adjusted for inflation)	$87,500
Feasibility Boundary 100% Joint	$2,229,000
Feasibility Boundary 100% / 80% Survivor	$1,984,500
Probability of Depletion	18%
Assets < $1 Million Inflation-adjusted	23%
Assets decline > 20% in a 12-month period	85%
Assets decline > 40% from peak to trough	61%
Financial Surplus 100% Joint (Cushion)	$771,000
Financial Surplus 100% Joint / 80% Survivor (Cushion)	$1,015,500

Annual Net Distribution Target (adjusted for inflation)	$100,000
Feasibility Boundary 100% Joint	$2,547,000
Feasibility Boundary 100% / 80% Survivor	$2,268,000
Probability of Depletion	12%
Assets < $1 Million Inflation-adjusted	16%
Assets decline > 20% in a 12-month period	76%
Assets decline > 40% from peak to trough	52%
Financial Surplus 100% Joint (Cushion)	$453,000
Financial Surplus 100% Joint / 80% Survivor (Cushion)	$732,000

Annual Net Distribution Target (adjusted for inflation)	$100,000
Feasibility Boundary 100% Joint	$2,547,000
Feasibility Boundary 100% / 80% Survivor	$2,268,000
Probability of Depletion	23%
Assets < $1 Million Inflation-adjusted	29%
Assets decline > 20% in a 12-month period	85%
Assets decline > 40% from peak to trough	63%
Financial Surplus 100% Joint (Cushion)	$453,000
Financial Surplus 100% Joint / 80% Survivor (Cushion)	$732,000

The investors are now more familiar with the presentation format. They joke that each guess is correct—the husband notes a slight deterioration in the probability of depletion and other downside risk metrics; the wife notes an improvement in their financial security and income feasibility metrics.[5] She asks a penetrating question: "How can feasibility and security-related metrics improve while depletion and downside risk metrics head in the opposite direction?" For now, the advisor offers a simple explanation: "The risk metric summary draws from two distinct models: (1) an investment simulation model, and (2) an actuarial model for lifetime income. The analysis mixes the outputs so that you have the benefit of two perspectives on retirement-income risks." Although the investors are content with this explanation, we will pick up this issue at the beginning of the next chapter.

Case Study 10 presents portfolio monitoring as a tool for elucidating a spectrum of prudent asset management elections. In this case, the investors learn how they can control various risks by electing different forms of lifetime payouts ranging from 100-percent joint payout over both life spans to 100-percent/80-percent or even 100-percent/67-percent payouts.

Monitoring templates can be expanded or modified depending on the investor's asset management elections, circumstances, and goals. The template used in Case Study 10, for example, assumes a constant-mix asset allocation combined with a fixed, inflation-adjusted, yearly withdrawal target. If, however, the investors had selected a front-loaded withdrawal policy with an annually decreasing target, the reporting template may include the elements shown in table 10.3.

TABLE 10.3: RETIREMENT RISK METRIC SUMMARY—2019 (FRONT-LOADED WITHDRAWAL POLICY WITH AN ANNUALLY DECREASING TARGET)

Current Portfolio Value =

BULL/BEAR MARKET AGNOSTIC

Planning Horizon:

BEAR MARKET

Annual Net Distribution Target (adjusted for inflation) $Z to $Y (formula = yearly $△ or △%)	
Year of earliest projected depletion	
Average time w/o money conditional on depletion	
Standard Deviation of time without money	
Expected aggregate conditional shortfall amount	
Aggregate average (50th percentile) income	
Failure to achieve monthly income	
(= probability of portfolio depletion)	

Annual Net Distribution Target (adjusted for inflation) $Z to $Y (formula = yearly $△ or △%)	
Year of earliest projected depletion	
Average time w/o money conditional on depletion	
Standard Deviation of time without money	
Expected aggregate conditional shortfall amount	
Aggregate average (50th percentile) income	
Failure to achieve monthly income	
(= probability of portfolio depletion)	

---

5. Although not shown in the presentation, the financial cushion for a lifetime joint and 67-percent income stream with a 2.5-percent-per-year inflation adjustment increases to $913,000—a 30-percent surplus.

Alternately, if the advisor is tracking the financial status of a retirement-income portfolio operating only under a "floating"—percentage of corpus—withdrawal strategy, the reporting template may include the elements in table 10.4.

Current Portfolio Value = $3 million   **Planning Horizon: Joint Life Span**

BULL/BEAR MARKET AGNOSTIC   BEAR MARKET

Annual Net Distribution Target	% of Portfolio Value
Aggregate average (50th percentile) income	
Failure to achieve monthly income	
5th year snapshot spending	
10th year snapshot spending	
20th year snapshot spending	
Probability of failing to achieve monthly spending target	
Impact of spending election of expected terminal wealth	

Annual Net Distribution Target	% of Portfolio Value
Aggregate average (50th percentile) income	
Failure to achieve monthly income	
5th year snapshot spending	
10th year snapshot spending	
20th year snapshot spending	
Probability of failing to achieve monthly spending target	
Impact of spending election of expected terminal wealth	

Annual Net Distribution Target	% of Portfolio Value
Aggregate average (30th percentile) income	
Failure to achieve monthly income	
5th year snapshot spending	
10th year snapshot spending	
20th year snapshot spending	
Probability of failing to achieve monthly spending target	
Impact of spending election of expected terminal wealth	

Annual Net Distribution Target	% of Portfolio Value
Aggregate average (30th percentile) income	
Failure to achieve monthly income	
5th year snapshot spending	
10th year snapshot spending	
20th year snapshot spending	
Probability of failing to achieve monthly spending target	
Impact of spending election of expected terminal wealth	

Annual Net Distribution Target	% of Portfolio Value
Aggregate average (20th percentile) income	
Failure to achieve monthly income	
5th year snapshot spending	
10th year snapshot spending	
20th year snapshot spending	
Probability of failing to achieve monthly spending target	
Impact of spending election of expected terminal wealth	

Annual Net Distribution Target	% of Portfolio Value
Aggregate average (20th percentile) income	
Failure to achieve monthly income	
5th year snapshot spending	
10th year snapshot spending	
20th year snapshot spending	
Probability of failing to achieve monthly spending target	
Impact of spending election of expected terminal wealth	

In this template the variable of greatest interest is income realizations at the 50th, 30th, and 20th percentiles of the income distribution. The risk of portfolio depletion gives way to the risk of receiving wholly inadequate money to support the investor's standard of living goals.

Finally, if the advisor is tracking the financial status of a retirement-income portfolio operating under a hybrid (part fixed and part "floating"—percentage of corpus—withdrawal strategy), the reporting template may take yet another form as shown in table 10.5.

TABLE 10.5: RETIREMENT RISK METRIC SUMMARY—2019 (HYBRID WITHDRAWAL STRATEGY)

Current Portfolio Value =

Planning Horizon:

Allocation: 68% Stock / 32% Bond

BULL/BEAR MARKET AGNOSTIC

Annual Net Distribution Target (adjusted for inflation)	Fixed amount + % of Portfolio Value
Year of earliest projected depletion	
Average time w/o money conditional on depletion	
Standard Deviation of time without money	
Expected aggregate conditional shortfall amount	
Aggregate average (50th percentile) income	
Failure to achieve monthly income	
(= probability of portfolio depletion)	
5th year snapshot spending	
10th year snapshot spending	
20th year snapshot spending	
Probability of failing to achieve monthly spending target	
Impact of spending election on expected terminal wealth	

BEAR MARKET

Annual Net Distribution Target (adjusted for inflation)	Fixed amount + % of Portfolio Value
Year of earliest projected depletion	
Average time w/o money conditional on depletion	
Standard Deviation of time without money	
Expected aggregate conditional shortfall amount	
Aggregate average (50th percentile) income	
Failure to achieve monthly income	
(= probability of portfolio depletion)	
5th year snapshot spending	
10th year snapshot spending	
20th year snapshot spending	
Probability of failing to achieve monthly spending target	
Impact of spending election on expected terminal wealth	

Annual Net Distribution Target (adjusted for inflation)	Fixed amount + % of Portfolio Value
Year of earliest projected depletion	
Average time w/o money conditional on depletion	
Standard Deviation of time without money	
Expected aggregate conditional shortfall amount	
Aggregate average (30th percentile) income	
Failure to achieve monthly income	
(= probability of portfolio depletion)	
5th year snapshot spending	
10th year snapshot spending	
20th year snapshot spending	
Probability of failing to achieve monthly spending target	
Impact of spending election on expected terminal wealth	

Annual Net Distribution Target (adjusted for inflation)	Fixed amount + % of Portfolio Value
Year of earliest projected depletion	
Average time w/o money conditional on depletion	
Standard Deviation of time without money	
Expected aggregate conditional shortfall amount	
Aggregate average (30th percentile) income	
Failure to achieve monthly income	
(= probability of portfolio depletion)	
5th year snapshot spending	
10th year snapshot spending	
20th year snapshot spending	
Probability of failing to achieve monthly spending target	
Impact of spending election on expected terminal wealth	

Annual Net Distribution Target (adjusted for inflation)	Fixed amount + % of Portfolio Value
Year of earliest projected depletion	
Average time w/o money conditional on depletion	
Standard Deviation of time without money	
Expected aggregate conditional shortfall amount	
Aggregate average (20th percentile) income	
Failure to achieve monthly income	
(= probability of portfolio depletion)	
5th year snapshot spending	
10th year snapshot spending	
20th year snapshot spending	
Probability of failing to achieve monthly spending target	
Impact of spending election on expected terminal wealth	

Annual Net Distribution Target (adjusted for inflation)	Fixed amount + % of Portfolio Value
Year of earliest projected depletion	
Average time w/o money conditional on depletion	
Standard Deviation of time without money	
Expected aggregate conditional shortfall amount	
Aggregate average (20th percentile) income	
Failure to achieve monthly income	
(= probability of portfolio depletion)	
5th year snapshot spending	
10th year snapshot spending	
20th year snapshot spending	
Probability of failing to achieve monthly spending target	
Impact of spending election on expected terminal wealth	

The appropriate data set is larger because the hybrid withdrawal election contains risk elements common to both fixed and floating withdrawal elections.

The outputs provided by the advisor's modeling software application(s) determine the data elements within a portfolio monitoring template. One can monitor only what is measured. To date, commercial software programs focus, in the main, on outputs that facilitate portfolio design and implementation as opposed to ongoing monitoring and assessment. By contrast, this book tilts the discussion toward a consideration of outputs for the purpose of prudent retirement portfolio management. The ongoing asset management task requires the ability to assess the feasibility, sustainability, and security of client goals. But, because each client manifests different goals and preferences, it is difficult to envision a single, uniform tracking template. Goals-based monitoring and surveillance is a complex undertaking that presents unique challenges to financial advisors.

ASSET MANAGEMENT ELECTIONS AND MODEST-SIZED PORTFOLIOS

Developing prudent management responses requires clear and accurate information. A disclosure of the nature and magnitude of either hurdles or current opportunities, and an intelligent discussion of planning alternatives, can help investors decide how best to proceed. Responses can originate either from the asset side or from the liability side of the investor's balance sheet. Indeed, dynamic management from the liability side, e.g., periodic spending adjustments, is the flip side of asset management.

For example, a bear market may force owners of modest-sized portfolios to consider a variety of planning options, none of which is ideal:

1. The investor can stay-the-course and continue to invest according to the initial risk-reward guidelines established by investment policy. The danger in such a course is that, in the words of the CFA Institute, the investor may suffer "... an absolute level of loss that would completely derail an investment portfolio." If the dollar value of portfolio assets penetrates the free boundary, the investor can hope for a market recovery of sufficient magnitude to restore the portfolio's long-term viability, however, there is no guarantee of such a result.

2. The investor may conclude that a portfolio with a low ACR requires higher expected returns, even at the risk of speeding up the time to portfolio depletion. The investor will elect to increase exposure to growth-oriented assets in order to make up recent losses. This is especially helpful if the bear market terminates and there is a switch to a more-favorable investment climate. However, increasing expected future returns comes at the cost of increasing portfolio volatility. If the favorable conditions fail to materialize, shortfall probabilities may increase dramatically.

3. The portfolio owner can pursue a two-fund solution. This might take the form of moving the bulk of portfolio assets to cash in order to mitigate further investment losses. However, the opportunity cost of remaining in cash during low-yield environments may be so high that such an attempt to preserve principal merely exacerbates longevity risk.

4. If an effective monitoring and surveillance system is in place, the investor might elect to implement a dynamic asset allocation program where equity risk exposure is a function either of (a) a pre-set floor, or (b) the distance from the free boundary's location. As a bear market unfolds, a dynamic system typically moves the portfolio toward cash. Such a system—also commonly referred to as constant proportion portfolio insurance (CPPI)—is not commonly employed by investors with modest wealth.[6] It is more common for private investors to implement buy-and-hold or constant-asset-mix portfolio management approaches. Modest-sized portfolios may incur far greater expenses under a dynamic allocation approach, with the extra costs perhaps vitiating the risk control advantages.[7]

5. Another form of a two-fund solution is a division of the investment corpus into an annuity to provide secure lifetime income and a performance-oriented portfolio to provide growth opportunities. This is a buy-an-annuity/invest-the-difference approach, which parallels a buy-term-insurance/invest-the-difference approach to asset accumulation.[8]

6. The worst of all possible worlds is to discover that the free boundary has been breached, i.e., the current market value of assets is less than the stochastic present value of liabilities. In the case of insufficient funds, asset management becomes more of a gambling question, i.e., does the investor want to accept a certain but unhappy outcome or risk a worse disaster with a more-risky asset portfolio? The untenable nature of this situation highlights the importance of portfolio monitoring and surveillance policies.

Retiring investors, seeking to achieve retirement goals (liability funding) the value of which is close to the value of current financial assets, may be more motivated to seek professional guidance from a financial advisor than investors owning portfolios worth many times the cost of retirement aspirations. This subgroup of investors may face difficult choices as an uncertain future unfolds before them. Case Study 11 pursues this topic in depth.

---

6. There are important differences between a CPPI asset management approach and an approach based on a distance-from-boundary risk metric. CPPI focuses on asset levels only; a distance-from-boundary approach considers the dynamic interplay between asset and liability values. CPPI sets a floor to protect wealth; distance-from-boundary approach identifies a boundary to protect income.

7. See Collins and Stampfli (2009) for a more detailed discussion of dynamic asset allocation approaches for trust management. Scott and Watson (2013) suggest establishing a fixed income investment floor and investing excess wealth using a 3x leveraged equity exchange-traded fund.

8. Strong evidence suggests that, for many investors, an annuity option is not attractive despite its possible economic advantages. A 2012 study by Shu et al. (2016) found that of the 363 survey participants, 22 percent did not choose any annuity option even though all annuity options offered an expected payout with a net present value (NPV) of at least $160,000 and with some options offering an NPV over $200,000 for a $100,000 purchase. "This strong dislike of annuities with a high benefit relative to upfront costs (more than would ever be offered in the market, in fact) suggests some individuals are unwilling to consider annuities regardless of the benefit offered."

CHAPTER ELEVEN

CASE STUDY 11

■ ■ ■

Previous chapters moved sequentially through periodic assessments of investor portfolios in terms of feasibility, sustainability, and security. Such a process (1) reinforces investor awareness of critical risk metrics, and (2) updates portfolio values in terms of client targets. As Case Study 10 demonstrates, it is easy to spot trends that the advisor can highlight either in a tabular or graphic form. Although helpful, this approach is not sufficient for fully implementing a system of dynamic asset management. Further insights are necessary.

Case Study 11 spans the next three chapters. They differ from previous chapters in that:

1. The subject matter and exhibits become denser, and the reading speed necessarily slows.
2. Case Study 11 describes a chronological information tracking system set up by the advisor. The system is a prerequisite for dynamic asset management.

The exposition shifts from a how-to-present-information-to-the-client focus, toward a how-to-set-up-a-tracking-system focus. A primary interest is on a filing and organizational structure to fit the needs of the advisor rather than on facilitating client decision-making—although both elements remain intertwined because the task continues to be sequential decision-making under conditions of uncertainty. In Case Study 5 (the late-in-life investor),[1] we noted that an optimal strategy, when considered on a year-to-year basis, does not necessarily yield the optimal strategy over the entire planning horizon.[2]

PRELIMINARY TECHNICAL OBSERVATIONS

A brief detour through some technical observations is a necessary preface to adaptive, multiperiod-retirement-income planning.

1. Simulated portfolio values, over time, record a "population group" outcome distribution rather than a specific portfolio trajectory. For example, the 50th-percentile result in year three is almost certainly not from the same trial that occupied the 50th-percentile position in year one's outcome distribution.
2. Right-tail results suffer from a paucity of data (small sample bias). But it is the long-term surviving group of investors who make up the right-tail population. At advanced ages, the outcomes tend to split between dramatic successes and catastrophic failures. Outcome variance can explode. Confidence in model outputs decreases at longer planning horizons especially for a population of older-age investors.
3. A monitoring system may highlight both period-by-period portfolio value at the 50-percent percentile and actuarial coverage ratio (ACR) value at the 50-percent percentile. However, the ACR value output almost certainly does not correspond to the portfolio manifesting the 50th percentile portfolio value. Consider the following example that uses hypothetical numbers to describe a chronological progression of simulation outputs:

   ■ Age 73 ACR of 0.93 at year 0 at the 50-percent percentile of ACR output distribution: based on X thousands of initial population group members (trials).
   ■ Age 74 ACR of 1.02 at year 1: based on X thousands less decedents-to-date (fewer remaining trials).
   ■ Age 75 ACR of 1.09 at year 2: based on X thousands less decedents over two years (even fewer remaining trials).

---

1. See Chapter Seven.
2. Mathematically, this idea finds expression in the Bellman equation which is fundamental to optimal control policy. The Bellman equation is a central topic of Chapter Sixteen.

- Age 80 ACR of 1.03 based on X thousands less a substantial number of decedents. However, most decedents during the age 73 to age 80 period died with a positive value portfolio. There is, as yet, little indication of depletion failure or looming ACR trouble.

- Age 86 ACR of 0.40 based on X thousands less cumulative deaths, i.e., fewer investors remaining in the population group sample. The age 86 output distribution contains a hefty number of longer-lived investors who have, or are about to, run out of money. The 50th-percentile trial number for the age 86 sample is drawn from a very different, i.e., reduced sample, distribution from the original and, as stated above, the progression of 50th- percentile results, over time, does not represent a specific trajectory or orbit that follows any particular trial.

4. Some investors are booked as "successful" simply because of early mortality, i.e., a death before the portfolio ran out of money. The distribution over the surviving investor population is beginning to divide into subgroups of the haves and the have nots. Eventually, results can seem anomalous with the median portfolio value recorded as zero and the median ACR value as positive (or the opposite).

5. Investors worried about longevity risk need to consider how to cure an ACR < 1 even though the next 50th percentile ACR value shows a value > 1. By taking corrective actions now, pressure on the portfolios of long-lived investors is relieved. However, this is truly a facts-and-circumstances decision. As we shall see later in Case Study 11, several asset management options cure the ACR deficit by moving money from the future into the present. These include a reduction in a surviving spouse's income in order to maintain full consumption during a joint life span, and amortizing future projected surpluses in order to relieve pressure on the current portfolio.[3]

6. The advisor needs to run the simulation analysis periodically (1) in order to spot and address negative ACRs, and (2) because the shape of the survivorship distribution itself changes yearly (the longer you live, the longer you are expected to live is one way to characterize sequence of returns risk in the face of longevity). Furthermore, the older the investor, the greater is the outcome variability because of the variance around life expectancy. If life expectancy at age 90 is four years, living two years beyond this to age 96 represents a 50-percent increase in the portfolio's required funding period. There are multiple sources of outcome variance at older ages.

7. One way to mitigate small-sample bias arising from long-lived investors is to rerun the simulation analysis by moving forward year-by-year with updated inputs (new age, health and marital status, portfolio value, realized inflation, and so forth). The user resets the simulation's population group to its initial size, e.g., each year the new simulation starts with a 10,000-trial population group. The updated simulation replenishes the sample space each year.

8. Yearly updates are especially important if the advisor elects to include a shortfall or surplus analysis. For example, the investor may ask, "What steps can I take today in order to bring my ACR metric back to target in five, seven, ten years?" This question implicitly assumes that the investor remains alive during that period. Therefore, the software application must engage a counting system that lacks a mortality component. Without going into great detail, effective retirement-income planning software requires multiple counting systems and requires intelligent bookkeeping to assure that data is assigned to the correct bin. In effect, the computer is being asked to correct shortfalls by amortizing ever-changing asset and liability ratios, an updated state-estimation task in a highly stochastic, multidimensional environment, e.g., tracking an ACR value calculated with a mortality component in order to report an amortization metric lacking this component. This is like hitting a distant target with a bow and arrow while bouncing up and down on a pogo stick in the middle of a dense fog. An advisor needs to recalibrate yearly.

9. Monitoring, assessment, and evaluation of asset management options for corrective actions require a substantial commitment of both time and resources by the advisor. The tasks, however, are critical because corrections today can avoid catastrophic corrections down the road.

---

3. In this case, the pressure comes from minimum consumption constraints that appear to be binding.

ASSET MANAGEMENT OPTIONS

Case Study 11 presents information about previously discussed available asset management elections and also incorporates additional options.[4]

CURRENT ADJUSTMENTS TO MEET A FUTURE ACR TARGET

An ACR's future value is an alternative way to quantify a shortfall (or a surplus) in funds available for current spending. We characterize this portfolio evaluation approach by the term "amortization" metric. Ideally, a model's output indicates a positive ACR surplus currently, and projects continuation of a positive surplus throughout the planning horizon. Such an output suggests retirement feasibility, sustainability, and security. However, given the complex interplay among age (annuity cost), interest-rate changes, inflation, and investment returns, a retirement-income model that exhibits a current ACR deficit (ACR < 1) may project a future ACR surplus. Conversely, a retirement-income model exhibiting a current surplus (ACR > 1) may project low ACR values in future years.[5] Changes in ACR values during retirement are most common in portfolios with high withdrawal demands relative to available financial resources. How does an investor evaluate a model's output that displays, over time, changes in ACR value from negative to positive, or from positive to negative?

The amortization-relative-to-an-ACR-target is a Janus-like calculation in that it looks both forward and backward in order to equilibrate the future with the present.[6] "How bad off am I now if there is a projected future surplus; how much does a current surplus allow me to relax if the model projects future deficits?" The amortization metric is one way to provide an investor an answer to the following question: "If I'm still alive in X years, what should I be thinking of doing today in order to be reasonably confident that my ACR value will be Y at that time?"[7] For example, a retirement-income model projects an ACR surplus (ACR >1) turning to a deficit (ACR < 1) in approximately 10 years. Thereafter, the ACR value deteriorates rapidly and the portfolio risks subsequent depletion during the investor's lifetime. What is the current dollar magnitude of adjustments required to bring the projected 10-year ACR value to 1.1 or, even better, 1.25?

In the next year, the deficit (or surplus) is better or worse depending either on changes in the investor's personal situation or on investment/inflation results. At this point, a new simulation study resets the withdrawal/contribution schedule, and a new X-year schedule begins. The new schedule's amortization period is geared to the approximate date at which a newly projected ACR value turns negative. The monitoring, evaluation, and adjustment process continues for years three and forward until the portfolio risk metrics are back on track.

Alternately, surplus or shortfall can be addressed by tracking a return-required-to-achieve-the-target metric. This requires an adjustment to the investor's asset-allocation strategy as opposed to the investor's portfolio-withdrawal strategy.[8]

One template (tracking) structure takes a tree form where you have branching due to initial outcome(s) and then a subsequent branching reflecting either stay-the-course or adjust-to-converge-back-to-target strategies. For example, in terms of a spending adjustment, the advisor informs the investor about the adjustments required to return to a target ACR value given a sequence of possibly positive and negative outcomes after the initial year.[9]

ADJUST WITHDRAWAL POLICY

The investor may elect to change portfolio withdrawal policy from, for example, a fixed periodic withdrawal to a floating (percent of portfolio value) or to a hybrid (fixed + floating) withdrawal strategy. During bear-market declines, a floating withdrawal strategy may result in fewer dollars withdrawn.

---

4. Although Case Study 11 does not consider all these elections, the retirement-income model used in this book can accommodate most of them.

5. Surplus or deficits also can emerge because of a change in health status, numbers of dependents, marital status, exogenous economic shocks, and so forth. Retirement is a risky project.

6. See Case Study 7.

7. Currently, the model allows the user to input five, seven, or 15 for "X," and 1.0, 1.1, or 1.25 for "Y."

8. Or, perhaps, indicates an adjustment to both.

9. On a technical note, we observe that the "what if I'm still alive" question requires that the model ignore the force of mortality over the specified period. However, the model projects future ACR values over the distribution of surviving investors. The advisor must periodically re-run the model with updated values lest the quantification of surplus or deficit becomes stale. The modeling process constantly catches up with reality.

A variation on withdrawal-policy change is a decision to forego, for a temporary period, inflation adjustments to designated income levels. We encounter a further variation in Case Study 11 as yearly recalibrated future surplus, when calibrated to future ACR targets, creates constantly changing annual consumption.

ADJUST WITHDRAWALS TO A FEASIBILITY METRIC

The idea is to assess, on a periodic basis, the ongoing feasibility of the investor's originally stated objectives. If there are no major changes in metric values, this suggests a stay-the-course asset management; if the values improve, this suggests discussing how best to utilize the surplus; if they deteriorate, this suggests discussing other planning options including spending reductions or other asset management elections.

The process, as time unfolds, looks at a sequence of portfolio snapshots regarding the (money-left-to-spend-gift-or-bequeath) ÷ (cost of providing periodic income) ratio value. This is the ever-changing free boundary separating the regions of feasibility and infeasibility. One can extend the definition of liability beyond an income/gift/bequest liability to include sequences of unexpected shocks such as medical expenses and end-of-life-care costs. Likewise, one can extend the definition of assets to include contingent assets such as an expected inheritance or life insurance proceeds.[10]

ADJUST SURVIVOR BENEFIT INCOME PERCENTAGE

Thus far, the base-case retirement-income model generally assumes that a specified level or percentage-of-portfolio income continues to a surviving beneficiary/spouse. The income continues for the survivor's remaining lifetime. In Case Study 3 (Chapter Five), however, we presented an election to reduce survivor income from 100 percent of target during the investors' joint lifetime, to 67 percent following the death of the first. The retirement-income model can accommodate any integer decrease (from 1 percent to 99 percent) in income following the first death. A prudent and suitable reduction should, of course, not be mere guesswork by the advisor. Rather, a careful analysis of investor circumstances (including the internal dynamics of a family's relationships) often reveals an acceptable level of income reduction. In contrast to the amortization decision to move a projected future surplus into the present, the survivor income adjustment moves a portion of the remaining spouse's cash flow into the present.

ASSET ALLOCATION CHANGES

An investor's asset allocation policy reflects risk-return preferences incorporating standard-of-living goals (consumption utility) and wealth preservation, bequest, and gifting objectives (utility over the wealth domain). In an asset-liability-management framework, a prudent and suitable asset allocation policy decision mirrors, in part, the expected interplay between, on the one hand, an investor's personal goals and circumstances, and, on the other, the investor's financial resources.

OTHER ASSET MANAGEMENT OPTIONS

A number of additional actions are available to some investors. These include:

- A reverse mortgage
- Retirement delay
- Part-time employment
- Pre-fund one or more years of portfolio withdrawals
- Establish a precautionary investment reserve to be used in a bear market and replenished in a bull market
- Forego a scheduled consumer price index income adjustment either temporarily or permanently

The above-listed asset management elections are not mutually exclusive. A combination of two or more elections often produces significant improvements for portfolios during times of stress.

---

10. See Case Study 9, which utilizes a sequence of periodic snapshots to assess the portfolio's ongoing viability.

Although some practitioners may be unfamiliar with the above-listed management options, as Case Study 11 operationalizes them, they should become clearer.

CASE STUDY 11: INITIAL (AGE 74) EVALUATION UNDER A MARKET AGNOSTIC MODEL

The next three chapters focus on two topics: dynamic asset management, and the challenge of recording portfolio information in a useable format as it emerges over time.

In Case Study 11, the advisor meets with a husband and wife who are both age 74. Previously, they had self-managed their retirement-income portfolio. However, the combination of a bear market and higher than expected spending has diminished their financial resources to an uncomfortably low level. Although they are currently in good physical health with excellent mental acuity, they wonder if a strict do-it-yourself approach to portfolio management remains prudent. At the least, they would welcome an independent assessment of their current circumstances.

Following an initial fact finding, the advisor works with them to establish an asset allocation with which they are reasonably comfortable (60-percent equity/40-percent fixed income). A conversation regarding spending needs focuses attention on the liability side of their balance sheet. The advisor and investors agree that their threshold standard of living requires a monthly budget of $7,500, their target lifestyle requires a monthly budget of $10,000, and their aspirational lifestyle requires $12,500 per month income.[11] Given family circumstances, they would like, if possible, to bequeath some assets to descendants. They own their home free and clear and have no current installment-debt obligations. They concur that production of lifetime income is the primary goal of the financial asset portfolio. Accordingly, they place an initial utility weighting of 1 on each dollar of income, and a weighting of 0.25 on each dollar of terminal wealth.

In previous years, portfolio withdrawals often have been a function of what-they-wanted rather than what-they-budgeted. Now however, they would like to adhere more closely to withdrawing a fixed dollar amount from their portfolio. The monthly withdrawal amounts have not caused a great deal of perturbation in the principal. Indeed, in several years, they saw the value of the nest egg increase despite some generous spending on leisure activities. However, after a bear market, their principal has diminished substantially, and they wonder if they have funds sufficient to continue withdrawing the monthly target income amount of $10,000. The current portfolio value is $2 million. After a brief discussion, they inform the advisor that they would like to maintain spending flexibility, but they recognize the need to plan around a known budget. They have never scrupulously adhered to a precise budget, but they always have considered their yearly spending to be within prudent guidelines. Ideally, they prefer to adjust future spending for realized inflation.

Although they do not have a clearly earmarked fund to buffer investment shortfalls (a precautionary investment reserve), they maintain a rainy-day fund for both anticipated and unanticipated expenses. They explain that, in previous years, they were fortunate to travel extensively, but they do not have foreign travel plans or other known large expenses waiting in the wings. The aspirational income level ($12,500 per month) could provide an opportunity to enhance their current lifestyle through dining out more frequently, family gifting, overnight and weekend excursions, and so forth. Their subjective belief is that the financial market's slide is more likely than not to reverse, but they recognize that this is merely a hunch rather than a professional opinion based on objective evidence. Although they state: "We just feel that we will come out of this OK," they are not willing to bet the farm on their beliefs—many of which derive from predictions made by successful friends who are in the business or from TV, print, and internet media.

At this point in time, the advisor is primarily interested in (1) modeling their preferred portfolio configuration and asset management elections, and (2) setting up a monitoring template structure to track progress toward or away from their income and bequest objectives in future years. The advisor proposes to track their newly revised portfolio for a year and, at that time, to reassess their financial position. Following the initial year's results, they can consider additional asset management elections depending on the improvement or deterioration of their situation.[12]

---

11.   These are pre-tax amounts exclusive of Social Security and other entitlements.

12.   Initial (age 74) output for Case Study 11 is based on a 10,000-trial simulation. Although, in actuality, the underlying data (asset class returns and inflation realizations) change as each year's results are added to the data set, the returns and covariance matrixes used in this case study remain static—i.e., Case Study 11 does not create imaginary future asset class returns. As a consequence, some metrics may exhibit less than expected variability over time. The goal is to present a monitoring and evaluation structure rather than to create a hypothetical history.

In general, the templates used to track case-study output data follow the following structure:

1. A summary description page of portfolio characteristics and asset management elections currently available to and selected by the investor.

2. Output pages devoted to income levels corresponding to standard-of-living objectives.

3. A summary description page with risk metrics, actuarial coverage ratios, and feasibility bounds.

4. Output pages devoted to investment wealth, i.e., portfolio value, corresponding to different periodic withdrawal levels.

The advisor supplements output from a market agnostic viewpoint with a set of four corresponding templates that assume continuation of the current bear market regime.[13] Template 11.1 sets forth information about the clients' current portfolio design and asset management choices.

TEMPLATE 11.1: INITIAL (AGE 74) CLIENT CIRCUMSTANCES

CASE STUDY 11 [INITIAL SIMULATION: MARKET AGNOSTIC] DATA BASED ON 10,000 TRIALS

Current Age Male	Health Status	Current Age Female	Health Status
74	Good (5)	74	Good (5)
Approximate Joint Life Expectancy			18.5 years
Current Portfolio Value			$2,000,000
Macro Asset Allocation Election			60% Stock / 40% Bond
Precautionary Investment Reserve Value			N/A
Asset Management Elections			
Portfolio Strategy			Constant Mix
Withdrawal Strategy			Fixed Amount Adjusted for Inflation
Survivorship Income Election			100%
Rebalance to Target?			Yes
Rebalance to % Allocation different than Target?			N/A
$\triangle$ Income (Withdrawal) Target?			N/A
Amortize ($\pm$) to ACR Target?			N/A
Forego Income Inflation Adjustment?			N/A
Interest Rate Data for ACR Calculation			
Freddie Mac 5 Year ARM			3.28%
Freddie Mac 15 Year Fixed			3.50%

The summary page lists information about investor age, heath, portfolio value, and asset allocation. There is also a space to record the value of any investment reserve account from which an investor may draw during recessionary times. The account is distinct from a rainy-day fund for replacing a leaky roof or a broken water heater. If such a fund exists, its value is not included in the portfolio value and asset allocation calculations.

---

13. The advisor can decide which output elements to present during the planning conversations. It is important, however, to memorialize a significant amount of data at the beginning of the tracking process. Over time, investors may change spending and asset management elections, and the advisor often must focus on a subset of new and more currently relevant output. However, generating a rich set of baseline information facilitates visual communication of how investor decisions (actions made over estimated state probability distributions) generate economic results (states) that, in turn, require periodic reassessment of the feasibility, sustainability, and security of retirement goals. We explore this topic in more detail in Chapter Sixteen, "Discrete Time Stochastic Process Models and Simulation."

The "Asset Management Elections" section provides a list of options that may be in force currently or available in future implementation. These include the investors':

▪ Preferred portfolio management strategy (constant mix, buy-and-hold, etc.)

▪ Periodic withdrawal strategy (fixed, floating, hybrid, front-loaded, etc.)

▪ Survivorship benefit

▪ Rebalancing protocol

▪ Election to change asset allocation weighting percentages (not relevant to the initial year's template)

▪ Election to change the periodic withdrawal amounts (not relevant to the initial year's template)

▪ Amortization election to adjust current withdrawals to a projected future deficit or surplus (not relevant to the initial year's template)

▪ Election to forego a scheduled Consumer Price Index (CPI)-adjustment to the withdrawal amount(s)

Finally, the initial year's summary-page template records the current interest rates used to determine the applicable discount factor for future annuity payouts. The overall effect of the summary page is to (1) record initial information and client preferences, and (2) set up a menu of asset management options that may be useful in future years.

Template 11.2 records snapshots of projected, constant-dollar income at intervals of five, 10, 15 years and "projected income in final year of simulation." End of simulation is the month following the death of the surviving spouse. The output records projected income at threshold ($7,500), target ($10,000), and aspirational ($12,500) monthly standard of living levels. Finally, the model generates the feasibility boundary for each income level under evaluation.[14]

TEMPLATE 11.2: PORTFOLIO WITHDRAWAL (INCOME) SIMULATION—MARKET AGNOSTIC

Income	Utility Weighting Factor		1			
	Initial Income (Year Zero)	Percentile of Distribution of Withdrawal Amounts	Projected Snapshot Income in 5 Years	Projected Snapshot Income in 10 Years	Projected Snapshot Income in 15 Years	Projected Income in Final Year of Simulation
Threshold Monthly Income	$90,000	50th	$7,500	$7,500	$7,500	$7,500
$7,500	Plus 1+ Inflation	40th	$7,500	$7,500	$7,500	$7,500
Adjusted for Inflation		30th	$7,500	$7,500	$7,500	$7,500
		10th	$7,500	$7,500	$7,500	$5,780
		5th	$7,500	$7,500	$5,316	$3,071
Projected Aggregate Income to Snapshot Date		50th	$450,000	$900,000	$1,350,000	$1,575,000
		40th	$450,000	$900,000	$1,350,000	$1,447,500
		30th	$450,000	$900,000	$1,350,000	$1,305,000
		10th	$450,000	$900,000	$1,350,000	$922,500
		5th	$450,000	$900,000	$1,235,933	$735,000
Probability Monthly Income ever less than $7,500		13.00%				
Adjusted for Inflation						

Target Monthly Income	$120,000	50th	$10,000	$10,000	$10,000	$10,000
$10,000	Plus 1+ Inflation	40th	$10,000	$10,000	$10,000	$10,000
Adjusted for Inflation		30th	$10,000	$10,000	$10,000	$3,809
		10th	$10,000	$10,000	$5,955	$3,809
		5th	$10,000	$10,000	$2,893	$1,895
Projected Aggregate Income to Snapshot Date		50th	$600,000	$1,200,000	$1,800,000	$1,974,572
		40th	$600,000	$1,200,000	$1,800,000	$1,800,000
		30th	$600,000	$1,200,000	$1,800,000	$1,610,000
		10th	$600,000	$1,200,000	$1,525,711	$1,151,546
		5th	$600,000	$1,200,000	$1,289,278	$940,000
Probability Monthly Income ever less than $7,500		26.30%				
Adjusted for Inflation						
Aspirational Monthly Income	$150,000	50th	$12,500	$12,500	$12,500	$12,500
$12,500	Plus 1+ Inflation	40th	$12,500	$12,500	$12,500	$12,048
Adjusted for Inflation		30th	$12,500	$12,500	$12,500	$9,074
		10th	$12,500	$12,500	$3,990	$2,972
		5th	$12,500	$7,440	$2,097	$1,556
Projected Aggregate Income to Snapshot Date		50th	$750,000	$1,500,000	$2,250,000	$2,256,239
		40th	$750,000	$1,500,000	$2,250,000	$2,050,000
		30th	$750,000	$1,500,000	$2,237,500	$1,827,287
		10th	$750,000	$1,500,000	$1,565,594	$1,302,059
		5th	$750,000	$1,328,789	$1,328,747	$1,087,525
Probability Monthly Income ever less than $7,500		41.50%				
Adjusted for Inflation						
Total Distribution Annuity Cost [Actuarial Feasbility Boundary]	Threshold Income	$1,934,026				
	Target Income	$2,570,733				
	Aspirational Income	$3,212,729				

Upon studying the output, the advisor notes that the current portfolio appears able to support the threshold $7,500-monthly income assuming that the portfolio operates above the 10th percentile of the distribution of outcomes. The target $10,000-monthly income requires the portfolio to operate at or above the 30th percentile; the aspirational $12,500-monthly income requires outcomes to achieve 40th percentile or better results. The corresponding likelihood for the sustainability of income targets tracks these results. If the investors drop monthly withdrawals to the threshold, the likelihood of the portfolio failing to generate $7,500 income at a future date is 13.4 percent. If, however, the investors continue to withdraw the target income level of $10,000, there is a 26.8-percent chance that they will see future income drop below the minimum $7,500 goal. Finally, a $12,500-withdrawal strategy runs a 41.9-percent risk of depleting resources to the point where remaining portfolio value cannot support the $7,500 target in the future.

The output indicates an interesting trade-off in that the aspirational income produces the highest aggregate lifetime income, but it also generates the greatest risk of failing to produce the minimum monthly required income at a future point in time.[15] From one perspective, the aspirational-income withdrawal strategy produces the highest lifetime utility; from another, it produces the lowest. It is difficult to pick a single utility measure (function) for selecting an optimal asset management strategy for retirement-income objectives.

Finally, given the investors' current circumstances, the output indicates that only the $7,500-income target is feasible under the ACR metric. Although the portfolio withdrawal levels seem to be sustainable over most of the outcome distribution percentile ranges, there is a strong possibility of future trouble. ACR feasibility at their standard-of-living target shows a current-value shortfall in excess of $500,000. The advisor recognizes that this situation requires clear communication and diligent monitoring.

Template 11.3 tracks outputs oriented toward client wealth assuming a market agnostic point of view. Risk metrics focus on the $10,000-monthly-standard-of-living-target withdrawal.

TEMPLATE 11.3: INITIAL (AGE 74) PORTFOLIO RISK METRICS—MARKET AGNOSTIC

CASE STUDY 11 [INITIAL SIMULATION: MARKET AGNOSTIC] DATA BASED ON 10,000 TRIALS

Current Portfolio Value	$2,000,000
Risk Metrics	**Target Income: $10,000**
Likelihood Portfolio < $500,000 Adjusted for Inflation	37.00%
Likelihood Portfolio < 15% in first 12-months	11.10%
Likelihood Portfolio < 20% in any 12-months	69.60%
Likelihood Portfolio < 40% Peak to Trough	54.90%
Actuarial Feasibility Boundary	
Threshold Income	$1,934,026
Target Income	$2,570,733
Aspirational Income	$3,212,729
Surplus (Retirement Security—50th Percentile)	
Threshold Income	$65,974
Target Income	(-$570,733)
Aspirational Income	(-$1,212,729)

The summary page reports current values for selected risk metrics and the current surplus (retirement security) at each income level. The advisor immediately notices that only the threshold income level has a positive surplus, the remaining income levels evidence serious underfunding under an ACR metric.

The advisor uses wealth-oriented templates 11.4 through 11.8 to track projected portfolio values, a years-alive-and-broke analysis, changes (improvement or deterioration) in key risk metrics over time, the evolution of portfolio surplus (positive or negative), and aggregated income and wealth utility values. The investor-assigned utility of wealth value is 0.25. This implies that $1 of lifetime income is worth approximately $4 in bequests.

The tracking system requires several pages of detailed information.

---

15. Investing is a prudent exchange of risks.

TEMPLATE 11.4: PORTFOLIO VALUE (WEALTH) SIMULATION—MARKET AGNOSTIC

Wealth		Bequest Weighting Factor		0.25	
	Percentile Distribution of Portfolio Value	Projected Portfolio Value in 5 Years	Projected Portfolio Value in 10 Years	Projected Portfolio Value in 15 Years	Projected Portfolio Value in Final Year of Simulation
Projected Portfolio Value	50th	$2,108,395	$2,062,990	$1,959,134	$1,861,023
$7,500	40th	$1,908,093	$1,718,150	$1,479,708	$1,365,421
	30th	$1,692,313	$1,372,089	$1,044,361	$881,854
	10th	$1,090,973	$597,440	$165,759	$0
	5th	$841,913	$333,114	$0	$0
Projected Portfolio Value	50th	$1,934,818	$1,671,179	$1,303,785	$1,112,766
$10,000	40th	$1,743,130	$1,367,973	$909,227	$648,759
	30th	$1,528,881	$1,037,778	$517,994	$168,621
	10th	$942,574	$322,070	$0	$0
	5th	$716,292	$91,913	$0	$0
Projected Portfolio Value	50th	$1,774,492	$1,302,615	$715,899	$401,631
$12,500	40th	$1,589,439	$991,667	$335,965	$0
	30th	$1,388,838	$713,761	$142	$0
	10th	$820,165	$57,099	$0	$0
	5th	$590,670	$0	$0	$0

Template 11.4 is a straightforward projection of portfolio values at five-, 10-, and 15-year intervals, and at the end of the simulation (the month following the date of the surviving spouse's death). A quick scan indicates that the current portfolio is capable of supporting threshold and aspirational income levels throughout the projected joint-life span at the 30th percentile of the distribution of portfolio results. However, the aspirational income level requires the portfolio to generate results at or above the 50th percentile. From an investment-simulation perspective, there seems to be some future money with which to work; from a more conservative actuarial outlook, only the threshold income level appears feasible. This mixed-signal portfolio profile is not uncommon and indicates the need for close future monitoring and evaluation.

What if the portfolio runs out of money during the investors' lifetime? Template 11.5 projects the magnitude of the potential life-after-depletion problem.

TEMPLATE 11.5: SIMULATION OF YEARS OF LIFE FOLLOWING PORTFOLIO DEPLETION—MARKET AGNOSTIC

Life Remaining at Deplection $7,500	50th	5
Percentage of Portfolios Depleted	40th	6
13.40%	30th	8
	10th	12
	5th	14
Life Remaining at Depletion $10,000	50th	5
Percentage of Portfolios Depleted	40th	7
26.60%	30th	9
	10th	13
	5th	15
Life Remaining at Depletion $12,500	50th	6
Percentage of Portfolios Depleted	40th	8
41.90%	30th	9
	10th	14
	5th	16

Template 11.5 records the percentage of times the portfolio runs out of funds under each designated withdrawal level (13.4 percent, 26.6 percent, and 41.9 percent, respectively); and, should depletion occur, the distribution of time throughout which an investor is alive-and-broke.

Template 11.6 records risk metrics of interest at five-, 10-, and 15-year intervals and at the end of the simulation.

TEMPLATE 11.6: SIMULATION OF RISK METRICS—MARKET AGNOSTIC

Likelihood of Assets < $500,000 Adjusted for Inflation					
$7,500 per Month		0.80%	7.70%	15.60%	22.70%
$10,000 per Month		1.70%	14.10%	26.60%	37.00%
$12,500 per Month		3.30%	21.60%	40.30%	52.20%
Likelihood Portfolio < 15% in first 12-months					
$7,500 per Month		9.40%	9.40%	9.40%	9.40%
$10,000 per Month		11.10%	11.10%	11.10%	11.10%
$12,500 per Month		12.40%	12.40%	12.40%	12.40%
Likelihood Portfolio < 20% in any 12-months					
$7,500 per Month		27.40%	45.40%	56.30%	64.30%
$10,000 per Month		30.40%	50.60%	62.30%	69.60%
$12,500 per Month		33.10%	54.80%	68.30%	76.10%
Likelihood Portfolio < 40% Peak to Trough					
$7,500 per Month		11.80%	26.10%	35.50%	43.60%
$10,000 per Month		15.20%	33.50%	45.20%	54.90%
$12,500 per Month		19.20%	41.60%	56.70%	65.50%

Additional insight into the more conservative actuarial perspective is recorded via projected ACR values at five-, 10-, and 15-year intervals and at the end of the simulation (see template 11.7).

$7,500 Projected Surplus (+ / −)	50th	$656,583	$1,071,980	$1,329,889	$1,858,369
[Projected Portfolio Value –	40th	$445,183	$719,517	$848,007	$1,365,031
Total Distribution Annuity Cost]	30th	$202,409	$380,488	$416,995	$878,556
	10th	(-$421,187)	(-$418,737)	(-$477,709)	(-$430,372)
	5th	(-$679,174)	(-$691,698)	(-$750,581)	(-$685,231)
$10,000 Projected Surplus (+ / −)	50th	(-$3,975)	$372,858	$480,167	$1,111,025
[Projected Portfolio Value –	40th	(-$215,320)	$27,502	$76,697	$647,401
Total Distribution Annuity Cost]	30th	(-$439,448)	(-$291,099)	(-$340,837)	$164,624
	10th	(-$1,076,917)	(-$1,026,492)	(-$1,082,534)	(-$1,013,446)
	5th	(-$1,332,473)	(-$1,308,408)	(-$1,382,208)	(-$1,310,256)
$12,500 Projected Surplus (+ / −)	50th	(-$644,958)	(-$347,564)	(-$337,882)	$400,525
[Projected Portfolio Value –	40th	(-$868,210)	(-$648,244)	(-$710,242)	(-$517,798)
Total Distribution Annuity Cost]	30th	(-$1,103,750)	(-$951,668)	(-$1,035,362)	(-$921,178)
	10th	(-$1,732,182)	(-$1,669,866)	(-$1,727,718)	(-$1,653,337)
	5th	(-$2,009,873)	(-$1,962,013)	(-$2,006,730)	(-$1,948,584)

The distribution of red-colored values indicates the precarious situation when viewed from a feasibility metric. Only the threshold withdrawal level evidences a current positive value. However, the advisor notes, at the target income level ($10,000 constant-dollar monthly withdrawal) a current ACR deficit turns positive by year 10—at least at the 50th- and 40th-percentile outcomes. Indeed, at the end of the simulation, even the aspirational-level surplus turns positive at the distribution's 50th percentile. In subsequent chapters, we will explore the possibilities of using future surplus to enhance feasibility, sustainability, and security.

Finally, template 11.8 aggregates the utility-adjusted value of income with the utility-adjusted value of wealth to produce an indicator of which combination produces the greatest overall utility during the applicable planning horizon. At each interval, given the four-to-one utility weighting, the higher withdrawal levels dominate the lower withdrawal levels. The trade-off is now between a high consumption reward and the risk of running out of funds. This issue is explored in greater depth below.

TEMPLATE 11.8: UTILITY-ADJUSTED AGGREGATE WEALTH & INCOME—MARKET AGNOSTIC

Utility-Adjusted Aggregate Spending + Bequest	50th	$977,099	$1,415,748	$1,839,784	$2,040,256
$7,500 per Month	40th	$977,099	$1,415,748	$1,839,784	$1,912,756
Formula: (Aggregate Withdrawals x Income Utility Factor) + (Terminal Wealth x Bequest Utility Factor)	30th	$927,023	$1,329,538	$1,719,927	$1,646,355
	10th	$873,078	$1,243,022	$1,611,090	$1,142,964
		$722,743	$1,049,360	$1,277,373	$735,000
	5th	$210,478	$83,279	$0	$0
Utility-Adjusted Aggregate Spending + Bequest	50th	$1,083,705	$1,617,795	$2,125,946	$2,252,764
$10,000 per Month	40th	$1,035,783	$1,541,993	$2,027,307	$1,962,145
Formula: (Aggregate Withdrawals x Income Utility Factor) + (Terminal Wealth x Bequest Utility Factor)	30th	$982,220	$1,459,445	$1,929,499	$1,652,155
	10th	$835,644	$1,280,518	$1,525,711	$1,151,546
	5th	$779,073	$1,222,978	$1,289,278	$940,000
Utility-Adjusted Aggregate Spending + Bequest	50th	$1,193,623	$1,825,654	$2,428,975	$2,356,647
$12,500 per Month	40th	$1,147,360	$1,747,917	$2,333,991	$2,050,000
Formula: (Aggregate Withdrawals x Income Utility Factor) + (Terminal Wealth x Bequest Utility Factor)	30th	$1,097,210	$1,678,440	$2,237,536	$1,827,287
	10th	$955,041	$1,514,275	$1,565,594	$1,302,059
	5th	$897,668	$1,328,789	$1,328,747	$1,087,525

The advisor, upon reviewing the outputs, concludes that the portfolio may be unable to support client objectives at the more ambitious withdrawal levels at its current value. A brief review of the risk metrics and ACR values indicate that there is a significant chance that the investors, absent a recovery in the capital markets, may outlive their financial assets if they remain in good health. Only the threshold income of $7,500-monthly distribution strategy exhibits an ACR greater than 1 (Surplus = $65,974). Both target- and aspirational income levels show a negative surplus currently. However, the projected surplus (financial security) turns positive in a few years for the target income level ($10,000) assuming the portfolio performs at or close to the 40th-percentile level. The output metrics for an assumed bear market (see templates 11.9–11.13) reinforce the conclusion that the investors' financial situation is vulnerable. If the investors can weather the next year or so, however, they might be in better shape.

The portfolio will not run out of money any time soon. The life-remaining-at-depletion metric suggests that the portfolio, at the target standard-of-living withdrawal level, will fail to outlive the investors at the 10th percentile of the output distribution. If the investors are conservative during the forthcoming year(s), they may be able to weather the storm. If the bear market continues, they are in trouble. The bear market templates for both income and wealth appear below.

INITIAL (AGE 74) EVALUATION BEAR MARKET CONDITIONS

TEMPLATE 11.9: INITIAL (AGE 74) CLIENT CIRCUMSTANCES

CASE STUDY 11 [INITIAL SIMULATION: START BEAR] DATA BASED ON 10,000 TRIALS

Current Age Male	Health Status	Current Age Female	Health Status
74	Good (5)	74	Good (5)
Approximate Joint Life Expectancy			18.5 years
Current Portfolio Value			$2,000,000
Macro Asset Allocation Election			60% Stock / 40% Bond
Precautionary Investment Reserve Value			N/A
Asset Management Elections			
Portfolio Strategy			Constant Mix
Withdrawal Strategy			Fixed Amount Adjusted for Inflation
Survivorship Income Election			100%
Rebalance to Target?			Yes
Rebalance to % Allocation different than Target?			N/A
△ Income (Withdrawal) Target?			N/A
Amortize (±) to ACR Target?			N/A
Forego Income Inflation Adjustment?			N/A
Interest Rate Data for ACR Calculation			
Freddie Mac 5 Year ARM			3.28%
Freddie Mac 15 Year Fixed			3.50%

The initial summary page in template 11.9 is identical to the market-agnostic simulation model. Income and wealth values are, however, considerably less favorable.

TEMPLATE 11.10: PORTFOLIO WITHDRAWAL (INCOME) SIMULATION—IMMEDIATE BEAR MARKET

Income	Utility Weighting Factor		1	Start Bear		
	Initial Income (Year Zero)	Percentile of Distribution of Withdrawal Amounts	Projected Snapshot Income in 5 Years	Projected Snapshot Income in 10 Years	Projected Snapshot Income in 15 Years	Projected Income in Final Year of Simulation
Threshold Monthly Income	$90,000	50th	$7,500	$7,500	$7,500	$7,500
$7,500	Plus 1+ Inflation	40th	$7,500	$7,500	$7,500	$7,500
Adjusted for Inflation		30th	$7,500	$7,500	$7,500	$7,500
		10th	$7,500	$7,500	$4,456	$2,861
		5th	$7,500	$7,500	$2,240	$1,404
Projected Aggregate Income to Snapshot Date		50th	$450,000	$900,000	$1,350,000	$1,471,883
		40th	$450,000	$900,000	$1,350,000	$1,342,500
		30th	$450,000	$900,000	$1,350,000	$1,207,500
		10th	$450,000	$900,000	$1,142,289	$870,000
		5th	$450,000	$900,000	$969,209	$720,000
Probability Monthly Income ever less than $7,500		26.30%				
Adjusted for Inflation						
Target Monthly Income	$120,000	50th	$10,000	$10,000	$10,000	$10,000
$10,000	Plus 1+ Inflation	40th	$10,000	$10,000	$10,000	$9,057
Adjusted for Inflation		30th	$10,000	$10,000	$8,820	$6,763
		10th	$10,000	$9,330	$2,964	$2,323
		5th	$10,000	$4,672	$1,479	$1,157
Projected Aggregate Income to Snapshot Date		50th	$600,000	$1,200,000	$1,800,000	$1,750,000
		40th	$600,000	$1,200,000	$1,800,000	$1,581,241
		30th	$600,000	$1,200,000	$1,695,967	$1,404,117
		10th	$600,000	$1,178,844	$1,182,124	$1,018,888
		5th	$600,000	$1,023,787	$1,022,409	$876,854
Probability Monthly Income ever less than $7,500		44.50%				
Adjusted for Inflation						
Aspirational Monthly Income	$150,000	50th	$12,500	$12,500	$11,339	$10,165
$12,500	Plus 1+ Inflation	40th	$12,500	$12,500	$9,182	$8,204
Adjusted for Inflation		30th	$12,500	$12,500	$6,901	$6,071
		10th	$12,500	$5,381	$2,267	$2,016
		5th	$12,500	$2,585	$1,092	$997

Projected Aggregate Income to Snapshot Date		50th	$750,000	$1,500,000	$2,096,414	$1,850,000
		40th	$750,000	$1,500,000	$1,840,951	$1,665,546
		30th	$750,000	$1,500,000	$1,625,549	$1,492,775
		10th	$750,000	$1,200,759	$1,204,026	$1,112,500
		5th	$750,000	$1,077,467	$1,081,155	$986,007
Probability Monthly Income ever less than $7,500		61.90%				
Adjusted for Inflation						
Total Distribution Annuity Cost [Actuarial Feasibility Boundary]	Threshold Income	$1,934,026				
	Target Income	$2,570,733				
	Aspirational Income	$3,212,729				

Particularly striking to the advisor, template 11.10 illustrates the probability of future income levels failing to sustain their targets. This risk is considerably higher than in the market agnostic model.

The next section details model output for wealth-oriented information. It begins with a summary page in template 11.11 and continues with output data in template 11.12.

TEMPLATE 11.11: INITIAL (AGE 74) PORTFOLIO RISK METRICS—IMMEDIATE BEAR MARKET

CASE STUDY 11 [INITIAL SIMULATION: START BEAR] DATA BASED ON 10,000 TRIALS

Current Portfolio Value	$2,000,000
Risk Metrics	Target Income: $10,000
Likelihood Portfolio < $500,000 Adjusted for Inflation	57.20%
Likelihood Portfolio < 15% in first 12-months	49.90%
Likelihood Portfolio < 20% in any 12-months	83.50%
Likelihood Portfolio < 40% Peak to Trough	70.50%
Actuarial Feasibility Boundary	
Threshold Income	$1,934,026
Target Income	$2,570,733
Aspirational Income	$3,212,729
Surplus (Retirement Security—50th Percentile)	
Threshold Income	$65,974
Target Income	(-$570,733)
Aspirational Income	(-$1,212,729)

Wealth	Start Bear		Bequest Weighting Factor		0.25
	Percentile Distribution of Portfolio Value	Projected Portfolio Value in 5 Years	Projected Portfolio Value in 10 Years	Projected Portfolio Value in 15 Years	Projected Portfolio Value in Final Year of Simulation
Projected Portfolio Value	50th	$1,506,708	$1,293,336	$1,027,082	$894,156
$7,500	40th	$1,313,062	$1,026,877	$677,647	$486,363
	30th	$1,121,415	$767,972	$379,445	$126,077
	10th	$683,370	$232,297	$0	$0
	5th	$548,832	$67,864	$0	$0
Projected Portfolio Value	50th	$1,349,509	$941,216	$426,686	$209,456
$10,000	40th	$1,169,825	$697,873	$145,073	$0
	30th	$984,396	$472,835	$0	$0
	10th	$577,274	$0	$0	$0
	5th	$451,483	$0	$0	$0
Projected Portfolio Value	50th	$1,176,381	$576,716	$0	$0
$12,500	40th	$995,430	$336,825	$0	$0
	30th	$822,123	$120,854	$0	$0
	10th	$452,070	$0	$0	$0
	5th	$333,912	$0	$0	$0
Life Remaining at Depletion $7,500	50th	6			
Percentage of Portfolios Depleted	40th	7			
26.30%	30th	8			
	10th	13			
	5th	15			
Life Remaining at Depletion $10,000	50th	6			
Percentage of Portfolios Depleted	40th	8			
44.50%	30th	10			
	10th	14			
	5th	16			
Life Remaining at Depletion $12,500	50th	8			
Percentage of Portfolios Depleted	40th	9			
61.90%	30th	11			
	10th	15			
	5th	17			

Likelihood of Assets < $500,000 Adjusted for Inflation					
$7,500 per Month		3.60%	19.30%	31.40%	40.60%
$10,000 per Month		6.90%	30.50%	47.80%	57.20%
$12,500 per Month		12.30%	45.80%	63.70%	75.50%
Likelihood Portfolio < 15% in first 12-months					
$7,500 per Month		45.80%	45.80%	45.80%	45.80%
$10,000 per Month		49.90%	49.90%	49.90%	49.90
$12,500 per Month		54.60%	54.60%	54.60%	54.60%
Likelihood Portfolio < 20% in any 12-months					
$7,500 per Month		53.70%	65.50%	73.10%	77.90%
$10,000 per Month		58.50%	70.90%	78.90%	83.50%
$12,500 per Month		62.90%	75.90%	84.00%	88.10%
Likelihood Portfolio < 40% Peak to Trough					
$7,500 per Month		30.00%	43.00%	52.00%	59.00%
$10,000 per Month		36.20%	53.40%	63.90%	70.50%
$12,500 per Month		44.30%	64.50%	75.70%	81.60%
$7,500 Projected Surplus (+ / −)	50th	$57,187	$304,195	$390,961	$890,304
[Projected Portfolio Value –	40th	(-$146,381)	$26,119	$43,017	$484,341
Total Distribution Annuity Cost]	30th	(-$352,223)	(-$218,124)	(-$255,650)	$123,952
	10th	(-$823,244)	(-$785,775)	(-$824,872)	(-$776,280)
	5th	(-$1,007,334)	(-$977,657)	(-$1,020,094)	(-$978,604)
$10,000 Projected Surplus (+ / −)	50th	(-$575,960)	(-$342,495)	(-$404,583)	$208,399
[Projected Portfolio Value –	40th	(-$774,950)	(-$615,072)	(-$702,091)	(-$558,896)
Total Distribution Annuity Cost]	30th	(-$979,934)	(-$855,712)	(-$916,883)	(-$842,054)
	10th	(-$1,476,503)	(-$1,414,403)	(-$1,456,216)	(-$1,403,522)
	5th	(-$1,686,055)	(-$1,646,730)	(-$1,683,452)	(-$1,634,919)
$12,500 Projected Surplus (+ / −)	50th	(-$1,235,690)	(-$1,055,558)	(-$1,144,147)	(-$989,267)
[Projected Portfolio Value –	40th	(-$1,432,143)	(-$1,298,243)	(-$1,360,360)	(-$1,256,089)
Total Distribution Annuity Cost]	30th	(-$1,697,004)	(-$1,534,816)	(-$1,604,554)	(-$1,506,733)
	10th	(-$2,146,045)	(-$2,113,108)	(-$2,144,233)	(-$2,092,545)
	5th	(-$2,368,404)	(-$2,338,969)	(-$2,350,011)	(-$2,316,949)

A lot of zero or negative values appear in these templates. The future profile of the portfolio under bear market conditions is bleak. Only the threshold standard-of-living target appears to have long-term viability. The utility calculation section in template 11.13 also presents significantly lower values under a start-bear-market regime.

Utility-Adjusted Aggregate Spending + Bequest	50th	$826,677	$1,223,334	$1,606,771	$1,695,422
$7,500 per Month	40th	$778,266	$1,156,719	$1,519,412	$1,464,091
Formula (Aggregate Withdrawals x Income Utility Factor) + Terminal Wealth x Bequest Utility Factor	30th	$730,354	$1,091,993	$1,444,861	$1,239,019
	10th	$620,843	$958,074	$1,142,289	$870,000
	5th	$587,208	$916,966	$969,209	$720,000
Utility-Adjusted Aggregate Spending + Bequest	50th	$937,377	$1,435,304	$1,906,672	$1,802,364
$10,000 per Month	40th	$892,456	$1,374,468	$1,836,268	$1,581,241
Formula (Aggregate Withdrawals x Income Utility Factor) + Terminal Wealth x Bequest Utility Factor	30th	$846,099	$1,318,209	$1,695,967	$1,404,117
	10th	$744,319	$1,178,844	$1,182,124	$1,018,888
	5th	$712,871	$1,023,787	$1,022,409	$876,854
Utility-Adjusted Aggregate Spending + Bequest	50th	$1,044,095	$1,644,179	$2,096,414	$1,850,000
$12,500 per Month	40th	$998,858	$1,584,206	$1,840,951	$1,665,546
Formula (Aggregate Withdrawals x Income Utility Factor) + Terminal Wealth x Bequest Utility Factor	30th	$955,531	$1,530,214	$1,625,549	$1,492,775
	10th	$863,018	$1,200,759	$1,204,026	$1,112,500
	5th	$833,478	$1,077,467	$1,081,155	$986,007

The advisor decides that his initial presentation should focus on explaining the market-agnostic information. Only when the investors have a good grasp of the implications of model outputs, will the bear market results make their appearance. To this end, the advisor creates several graphs. The initial graph reflects portfolio values at both the 50th and 30th percentile for the monthly income distributions under consideration. The threshold distribution appears to have adequate current funding; the target income level appears to require the portfolio to operate at the 50th or higher percentile; and the aspirational income level appears to run a significant risk of depletion during the investors' joint-life span.

GRAPHICAL PRESENTATIONS

The advisor prepares the following graphs to focus client attention on feasibility, sustainability, and security metrics.

FEASIBILITY AGE 74: MARKET-AGNOSTIC/50TH AND 30TH PERCENTILES

FIGURE 11.1: AGE 74 PORTFOLIO VALUE—MARKET AGNOSTIC

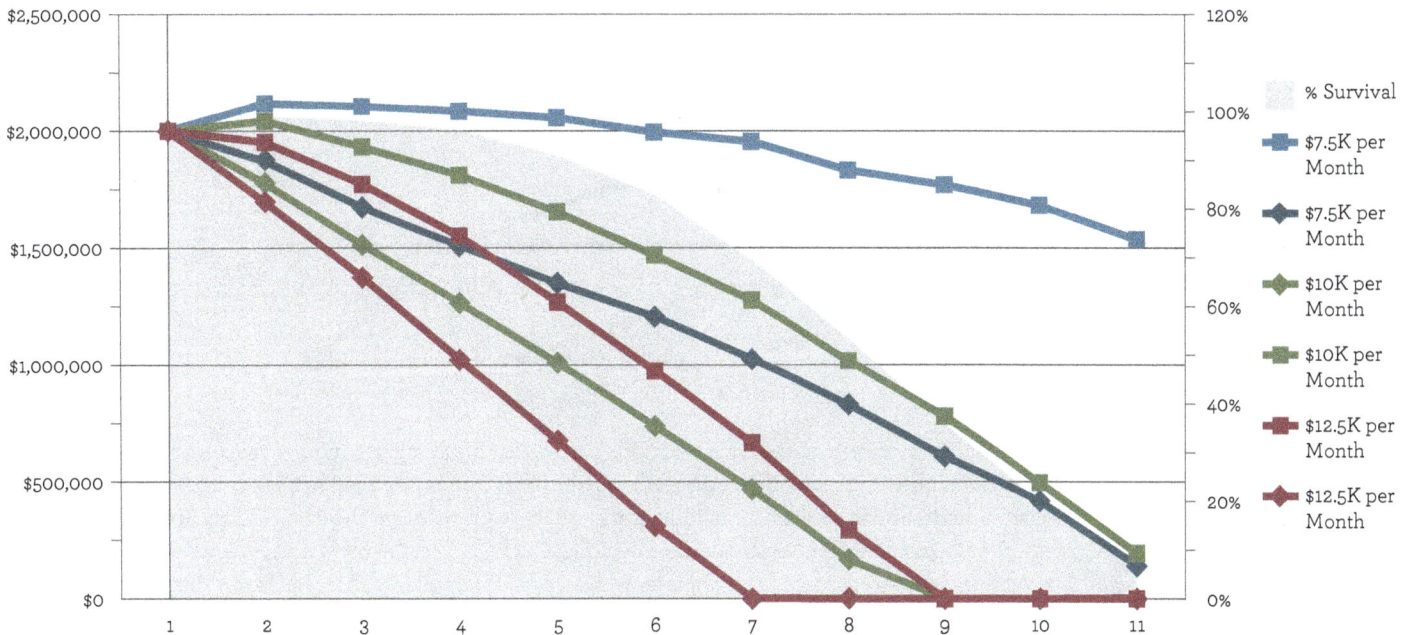

In figure 11.1, 50th-percentile outcomes appear with box markers; 30th-percentile outcomes appear with diamond markers. The shaded gray area depicts the survival probability curve. The greater the periodic withdrawal, the more likely the portfolio fails to avoid depletion during the life of the insureds. The advisor wishes to show that the current portfolio outraces the survival curve at the 50th percentile of outcomes for the $7,500 and $10,000 monthly withdrawal levels, and at the 30th percentile for the $7,500 withdrawal level—although the latter two races are very close.[16]

The advisor next prepares a chart depicting the evolution of ACR values for portfolio outcomes at the 50th and 30th percentiles of the distribution of outcomes at various withdrawal levels (see figure 11.2):

---

16. By "outrace," the advisor means preserves positive value throughout the planning horizon.

FIGURE 11.2: AGE 74 FEASIBILITY (ACR > 100%)

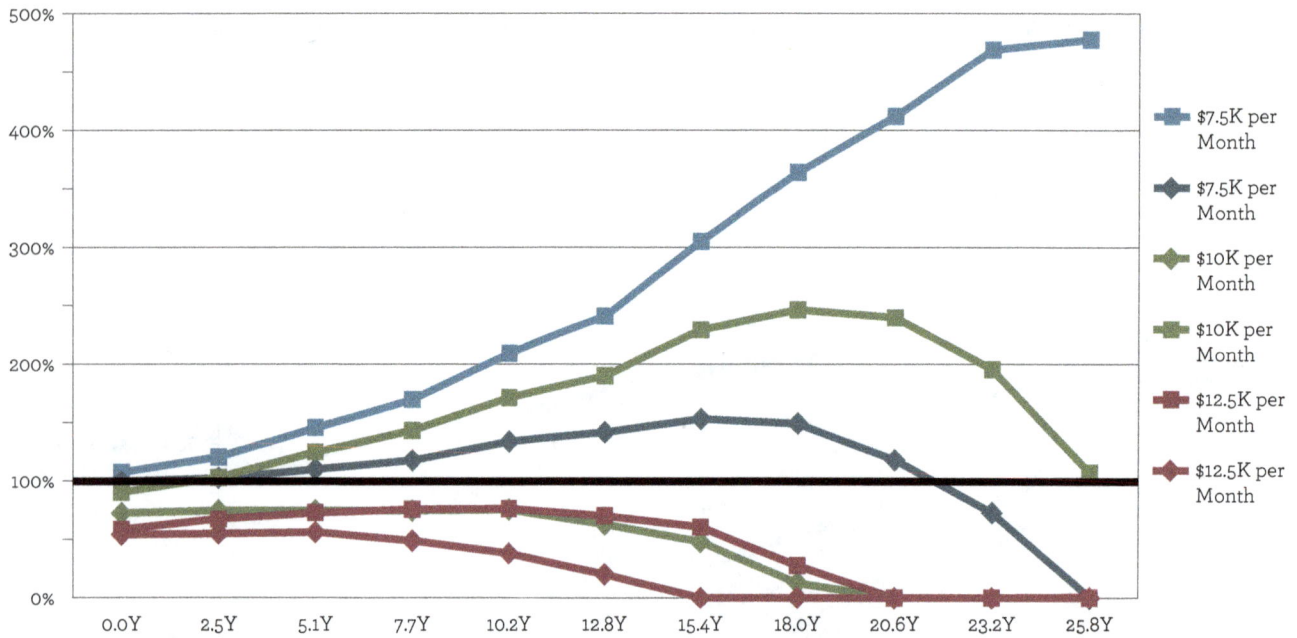

Figure 11.2 projects the evolution of the feasibility metric at the 50th and 30th percentiles of the distribution of results at each withdrawal level. The 50th-percentile outcomes are the lines with box markers; the 30th-percentile outcomes are the lines with diamond markers. The critical line for determination of actuarial feasibility is the horizontal line at the 100-percent point on the vertical axis. Initial feasibility is currently greater than one (100 percent) only for the threshold standard-of-living level. Over time, the projected ACR values rise above the feasibility (lower-bound) level for several withdrawal/percentile combinations. However, the higher withdrawal levels display a significant risk of eventual portfolio depletion (ACR value = 0).

SUSTAINABILITY AGE 74 $10,000 TARGET INCOME: MARKET-AGNOSTIC

The advisor next turns to a sustainability analysis. Figures 11.3 and 11.4 evaluate, at the 50th percentile of the distribution of outcomes, both the threshold- and target income levels according to several risk metrics.

FIGURE 11.3: PORTFOLIO VALUE AND SUSTAINABILITY RISK ($7,500/50TH PERCENTILE)

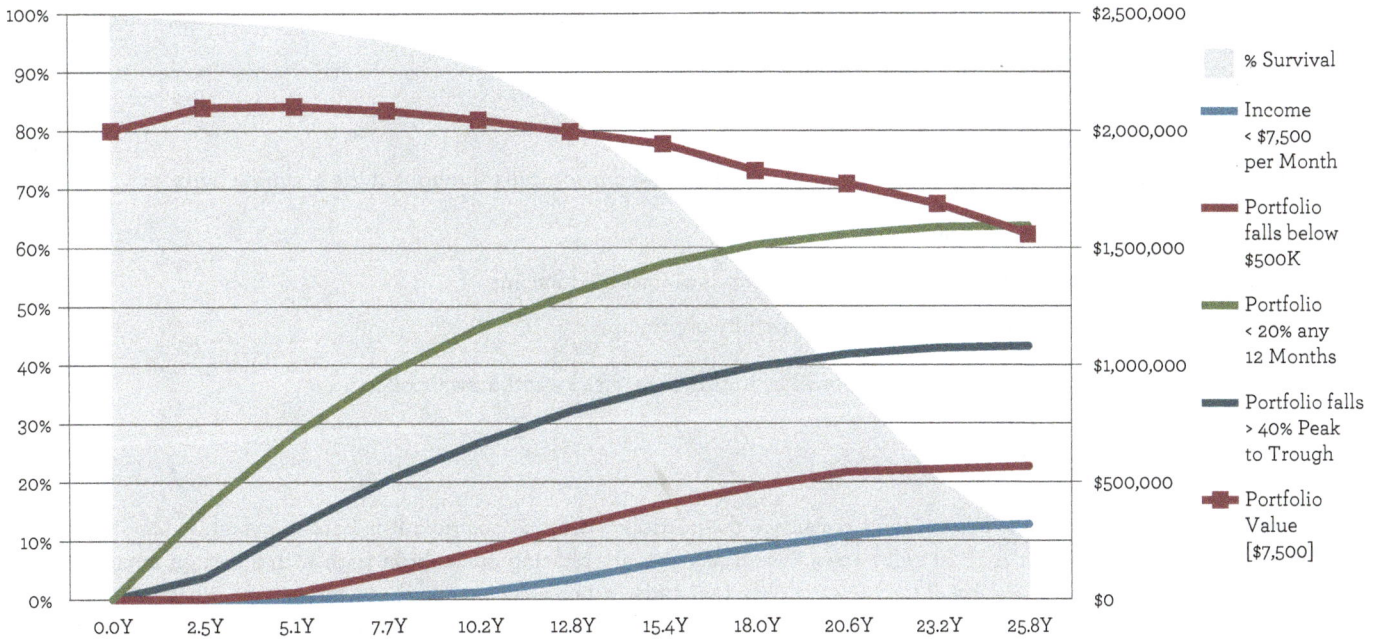

FIGURE 11.4: PORTFOLIO VALUE AND SUSTAINABILITY RISK ($10,500/50TH PERCENTILE)

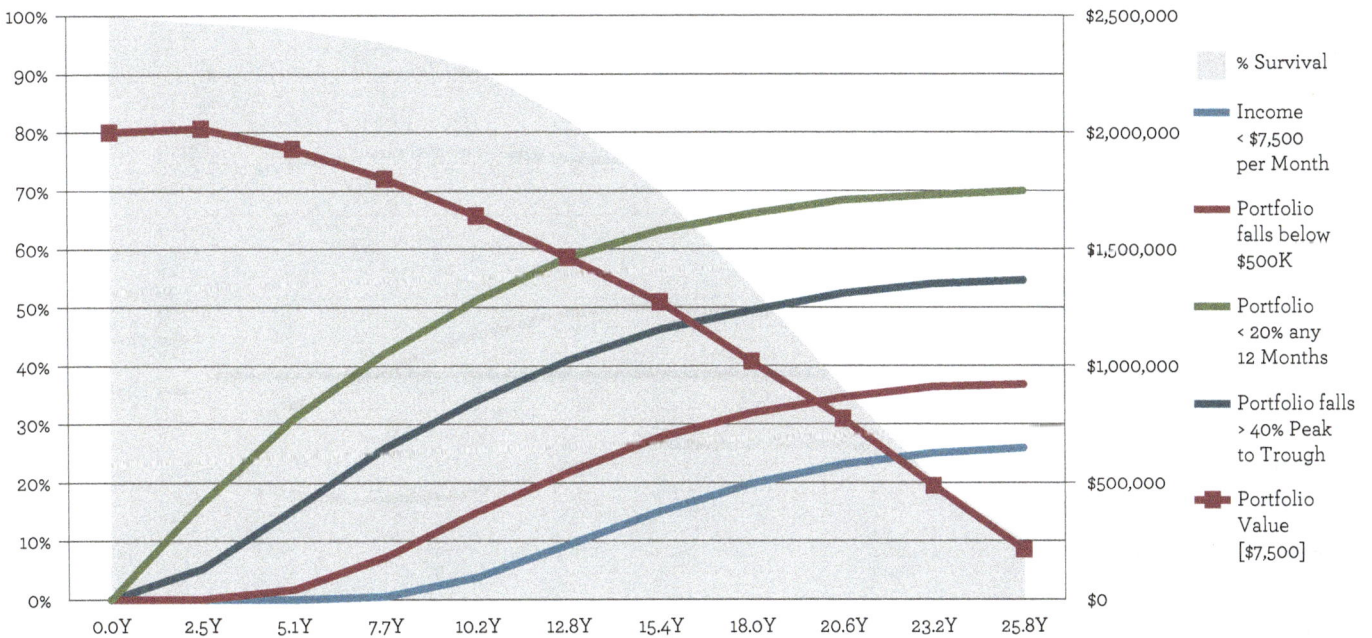

The companion table to figures 11.3 and 11.4 indicates the difference in risk metric values, at the 50th percentile, as a function of withdrawal policy:

COMPANION TABLE TO FIGURES 11.3 & 11.4—RISK METRICS AT 50TH PERCENTILE

	$7,500 Monthly Withdrawal	$10,000 Monthly Withdrawal
Portfolio Value End of Simulation (50th Percentile)	$1,551,657	$194,539
Income never drops below $7,500	13.00%	26.30%
Value ever less than $500,000	22.70%	37.00%
Portfolio ever down more than 20% in any 12-month	64.30%	69.60%
Portfolio ever falls > 40% Peak to Trough	43.60%	54.90%

The $10,000 per month target standard-of-living withdrawal level, if followed myopically throughout the planning horizon:

1. Fails to preserve the investors' bequest objective

2. Manifests an approximately one-in-four chance of failing to produce threshold income

3. Exhibits a high likelihood of subjecting the portfolio to volatility of principal

Budgetary certainty at the target standard-of-living level is, in this case, a risky withdrawal policy.

RETIREMENT SECURITY (SURPLUS) AGE 74: MARKET AGNOSTIC

The advisor also remains aware of model risk as he considers the portfolio's surplus position. It is hard to overstate the significance of a few extra years of longevity for ACR at older ages. Essentially you are plotting out a flight path with a certain amount of gas. Although being 50 miles off in the location of the runway doesn't matter so much when you have 500 miles to go, when you are setting up to drink that last drop of gas and discover the runway is 100 miles away instead of 50, you have a problem. Constant monitoring of surplus is critical.

FIGURE 11.5: EVOLUTION OF SURPLUS—50TH PERCENTILE

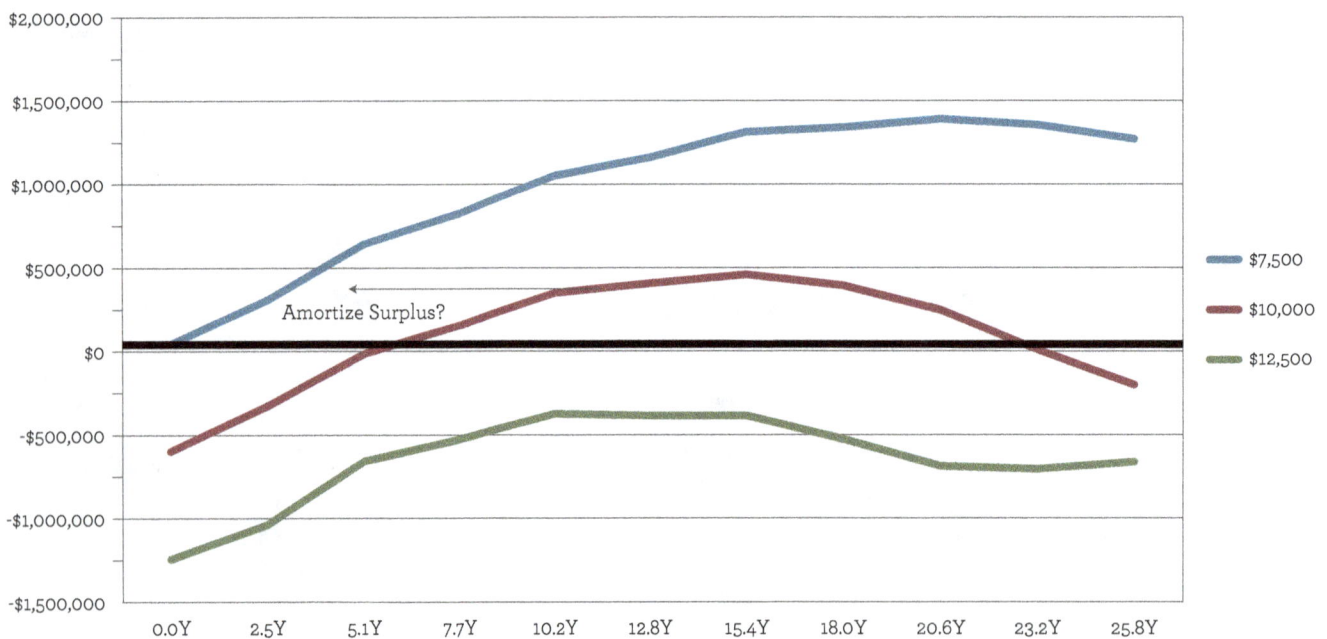

The surplus summary graph in figure 11.5 confirms the overall message of the advisor's age 74 risk model—the current portfolio exhibits an uncomfortable level of financial vulnerability. Regarding the risk metrics under evaluation, only the (blue) threshold income level passes tests for retirement feasibility, sustainability, and security. The (red) target income level, however, appears to exhibit positive surplus at and above the 50th percentile for approximately years six through 23. The hump-shaped curve starts in negative-surplus territory and rises into positive territory to reach a maximum at approximately year 15, when it again begins to decline toward negative values by the end of the horizon. For the advisor, the curve's humped shape as well as its location straddling the zero-surplus axis line is of great interest. Although the precarious state—relative to the investors' objectives—of the current portfolio precludes any borrowing from the future, the advisor recognizes that such an opportunity may present itself in a later year. Welcome to the topic of dynamic portfolio management which we explore in the next two chapters.[17]

Finally, figure 11.6 shows portfolio surplus at the 30th percentile of the distribution of outcomes.

FIGURE 11.6: EVOLUTION OF SURPLUS—30TH PERCENTILE

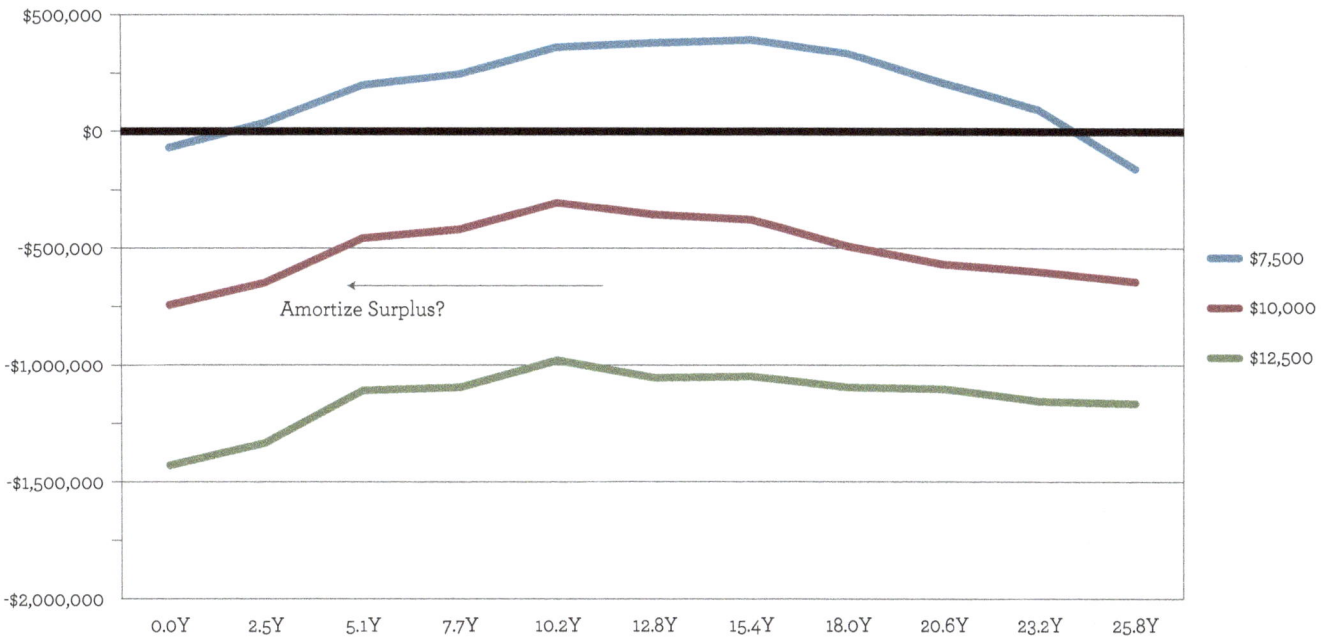

Although it is noteworthy that the threshold withdrawal target appears viable over most of the planning horizon, the target and aspirational surplus levels fail to achieve financial security at any time throughout retirement assuming 30th-percentile performance.

The investors feel that they now have credible information on which to base their asset management decisions. Both investors agree that frugality (as measured by the amount withdrawn from the portfolio) is desirable—at least over the forthcoming year. They plan to tap some savings to buffer any income shortfalls. They elect to adopt the 60-percent stock/40-percent fixed income allocation and to reassess their financial position next year.

---

17. We assume that the advisor will not raise this topic until a more appropriate time and under more favorable financial conditions.

CHAPTER TWELVE

CASE STUDY 11 CONTINUED—AGE 75

■ ■ ■

CASE STUDY 11: AGE 75 EVALUATION OF 'STAY-THE-COURSE'

The advisor closely monitored monthly portfolio values during the initial year of portfolio operation. Although a hoped-for spectacular recovery failed to materialize, the U.S. equity market did not experience further severe downward moves. Overall, most capital markets were up slightly. Inflation remained low [realized annual consumer price index (CPI) = 1.95 percent]; and, because the investors economized, the actual cash withdrawal from the portfolio was $87,500. At the end of the period, the portfolio value was $2.1 million. The advisor guessed that the slight increase in portfolio value, coupled with (1) an increase in age, and (2) a modest inflation rate were positive factors. However, the decrease in interest rates could offset any potential improvements to some risk metrics. As he runs the current numbers, the advisor is curious about where the investors stand.

In the next series of templates (age 75) the advisor first generates a 10,000-trial retirement-income model under the assumption that they continue to stay-the-course. The model updates inputs to reflect the current, i.e., age 75, values specified in the previous paragraph. The advisor's plan is to construct an updated profile under a market-agnostic viewpoint. In subsequent templates, the advisor extends the analysis by creating additional models incorporating new asset management options that the investors may wish to consider.

The updated, age 75, stay-the-course tracking template summarizes the model's output (template 12.1). As before, the income-oriented tracking template is followed by the wealth-oriented template.

TEMPLATE 12.1: AGE 75 CLIENT CIRCUMSTANCES

CASE STUDY 11 [INITIAL SIMULATION: MARKET AGNOSTIC] DATA BASED ON 10,000 TRIALS

Current Age Male	Health Status	Current Age Female	Health Status
75	Good (5)	75	Good (5)
Approximate Joint Life Expectancy			18.2 years
Current Portfolio Value			$2,100,000
Macro Asset Allocation Election			60% Stock / 40% Bond
Precautionary Investment Reserve Value			N/A
Asset Management Elections			
Portfolio Strategy			Constant Mix
Withdrawal Strategy			Fixed Amount Adjusted for Inflation
Survivorship Income Election			100%
Rebalance to Target?			Yes
Rebalance to % Allocation different than Target?			No
△ Income (Withdrawal) Target?			No
Amortize (±) to ACR Target?			No
Forego Income Inflation Adjustment?			No

Interest Rate Data for ACR Calculation	
Freddie Mac 5 Year ARM	2.81%
Freddie Mac 15 Year Fixed	3.20%
Realized Inflation	1.95%
Income Targets	
Threshold	$91,755
Target	$122,340
Aspriational	$152,925
Actual Spending Previous Year	$87,500

The age 75 income section now records additional information such as the previous year's withdrawal amount, realized inflation, and current interest rates. The income levels are increased by the inflation rate.

Income snapshots, adjusted for inflation, occur at five-, 10-, 15-year intervals and at the "end of simulation" date. Template 12.2 records outcomes ranging from the 5th through the 50th percentile of the distribution of cash-flow outcomes at each income level.

TEMPLATE 12.2: PORTFOLIO WITHDRAWAL (INCOME) SIMULATION

Income	Utility Weighting Factor		1			
	Initial Income (Year Zero)	Percentile of Distribution of Withdrawal Amounts	Projected Snapshot Income in 5 Years	Projected Snapshot Income in 10 Years	Projected Snapshot Income in 15 Years	Projected Income in Final Year of Simulation
Threshold Monthly Income	$90,000	50th	$7,646	$7,646	$7,646	$7,646
$7,500	Plus 1+ Inflation	40th	$7,646	$7,646	$7,646	$7,646
Adjusted for Inflation	$91,755	30th	$7,646	$7,646	$7,646	$7,646
$7,646		10th	$7,646	$7,646	$7,646	$7,190
		5th	$7,646	$7,646	$6,168	$3,539
Projected Aggregate Income to Snapshot Date		50th	$458,775	$917,550	$1,1376,325	$1,544,542
		40th	$458,775	$917,550	$1,1376,325	$1,414,556
		30th	$458,775	$917,550	$1,1376,325	$1,276,924
		10th	$458,775	$917,550	$1,1376,325	$886,965
		5th	$458,775	$917,550	$1,291,494	$695,809
Probability Monthly Income ever less than $7,500 + CPI		10.70%				
$7,646						

Target Monthly Income	$120,000	50th	$10,195	$10,195	$10,195	$10,195
$10,000	Plus 1+ Inflation	40th	$10,195	$10,195	$10,195	$10,195
Adjusted for Inflation		30th	$10,195	$10,195	$10,195	$10,195
$10,195		10th	$10,195	$10,195	$6,609	$4,800
		5th	$10,195	$10,195	$3,413	$2,338
Projected Aggregate Income to Snapshot Date		50th	$611,700	$1,223,400	$1,835,100	$1,947,245
		40th	$611,700	$1,223,400	$1,835,100	$1,784,125
		30th	$611,700	$1,223,400	$1,835,100	$1,603,058
		10th	$611,700	$1,223,400	$1,608,942	$1,131,645
		5th	$611,700	$1,223,400	$1,338,141	$911,683
Probability Monthly Income ever less than $7,500 + CPI		22.30%				
$7,646						
Aspirational Monthly Income	$150,000	50th	$12,744	$12,744	$12,744	$12,744
$12,500	Plus 1+ Inflation	40th	$12,744	$12,744	$12,744	$12,744
Adjusted for Inflation	$152,925	30th	$12,744	$12,744	$12,744	$10,675
$12,743		10th	$12,744	$12,744	$4,601	$3,443
		5th	$12,744	$8,722	$2,261	$1,715
Projected Aggregate Income to Snapshot Date		50th	$764,625	$1,529,250	$2,293,875	$2,255,644
		40th	$764,625	$1,529,250	$2,293,875	$2,039,000
		30th	$764,625	$1,529,250	$2,293,875	$1,825,898
		10th	$764,625	$1,529,250	$1,630,345	$1,307,490
		5th	$764,625	$1,398,074	$1,399,250	$1,083,219
Probability Monthly Income ever less than $7,500 + CPI		36.20%				
$7,646						
Total Distribution Annuity Cost [Actuarial Feasbility Boundary]	Threshold Income	$1,929,712				
	Target Income	$2,583,655				
	Aspirational Income	$3,228,860				

There is a slight improvement in risk metrics. If the withdrawal strategy is limited to threshold monthly income ($7,500), the probability of failing to achieve this level drops from 13.4 percent to 10.7 percent. Likewise, at the target ($10,000) level, the failure rate drops from 26.6 percent to 22.3 percent; and for the aspirational ($12,500) level, the failure rate declines from 41.9 percent to 36.2 percent. Although there is a slight improvement in the distance-to-the-feasibility-bound risk metrics at the threshold income level, the decrease in interest rates has pushed, by slight amounts, the target- and aspirational income levels further away from the feasibility bound. In other words, the benefit of reduced annuity cost from a one-year advance in joint age was almost exactly balanced by the decline in interest rates used to calculate the discount factor in the actuarial coverage ratio (ACR) denominator. This is not entirely bad news, however. The increase in portfolio value produces an improvement in the investors' surplus position (see table 12.1).

TABLE 12.1: CHANGE IN SURPLUS

Withdrawal Level	Age 74 Feasibility Bound	Age 74 Surplus	Age 75 Feasibility Bound	Age 75 Surplus
Threshold	$1,934,026	$65,974	$1,929,712	$170,288
Target	$2,570,733	(-$570.733)	$2,583,655	(-$483,655)
Aspirational	$3,212,729	(-$1,212,729)	$3,228,860	(-$1,128,860

The advisor records the model's output for the wealth-oriented section of the market-agnostic, age 75 simulation model in template 12.3:

TEMPLATE 12.3: AGE 75 PORTFOLIO RISK METRICS

Current Portfolio Value	$2,100,000
Risk Metrics	Target Income: $10,195
Likelihood Portfolio < $509,750 Adjusted for Inflation	33.00%
Likelihood Portfolio < 15% in first 12-months	10.80%
Likelihood Portfolio < 20% in any 12-months	67.30%
Likelihood Portfolio < 40% Peak to Trough	51.00%
Actuarial Feasibility Boundary	
Threshold Income	$1,929,712
Target Income	$2,583,655
Aspirational Income	$3,228,860
Surplus (Retirement Security—50th Percentile)	
Threshold Income	$170,288
Target Income	(-$483,655)
Aspirational Income	(-$1,128,860)

The advisor notes an improvement in the risk metric specifying the likelihood of bequeathing less than $500,000 (33 percent versus 37.0 percent). There are improvements in other failure-rate metrics geared to track results at the $10,000 monthly target withdrawal level. Specifically, the likelihood of suffering a decline of 15 percent or more in the next 12 months declines from 11.1 percent to 10.8 percent; the likelihood of a 20-percent or greater decline in any year declines from 69.6 percent to 67.3 percent; and the likelihood of a peak-to-trough decline greater than 40 percent decreases from 54.9 percent to 51 percent. A more detailed risk matrix for each income level that records simulation outputs oriented toward the evolution of investment wealth appears in template 12.4.

TEMPLATE 12.4: AGE 75 PORTFOLIO VALUE (WEALTH) SIMULATION

Wealth				Bequest Weighting Factor	0.25
	Percentile Distribution of Portfolio Value	Projected Portfolio Value in 5 Years	Projected Portfolio Value in 10 Years	Projected Portfolio Value in 15 Years	Projected Portfolio Value in Final Year of Simulation
Projected Portfolio Value	50th	$2,242,250	$2,196,279	$2,118,680	$2,058,746
$7,646	40th	$2,030,971	$1,844,155	$1,608,441	$1,541,865
	30th	$1,804,233	$1,480,127	$1,146,531	$1,022,090
	10th	$1,140,500	$650,949	$201,636	$0
	5th	$878,632	$387,055	$0	$0
Projected Portfolio Value	50th	$2,065,967	$1,801,589	$1,482,549	$1,332,999
$10,195	40th	$1,856,669	$1,468,107	$1,024,087	$855,900
	30th	$1,628,770	$1,137,220	$603,401	$381,862
	10th	$1,021,282	$386,884	$0	$0
	5th	$765,127	$127,482	$0	$0
Projected Portfolio Value	50th	$1,900,392	$1,413,306	$851,868	$654,453
$12,743	40th	$1,696,790	$1,089,864	$453,307	$180,120
	30th	$1,470,659	$793,037	$64,778	$0
	10th	$865,935	$92,539	$0	$0
	5th	$638,515	$0	$0	$0
Life Remaining at Depletion: $7,646	50th	5			
Percentage of Portfolios Depleted	40th	6			
10.70%	30th	7			
	10th	11			
	5th	14			
Life Remaining at Depletion: $10,195	50th	5			
Percentage of Portfolios Depleted	40th	6			
22.30%	30th	8			
	10th	12			
	5th	14			
Life Remaining at Depletion: $12,743	50th	6			
Percentage of Portfolios Depleted	40th	7			
36.20%	30th	9			
	10th	13			
	5th	15			

Projected portfolio values at all income levels show higher dollar amounts at age 75 than at age 74. This suggests an improvement in both sustainability and security metrics.

The next grouping of outputs (bottom half of template 12.4) focuses on the distribution of the "Life Remaining after Depletion" metric. If the investors outlive their portfolio, how long will at least one of them remain alive without portfolio income? There are two calculations:[1]

1. The likelihood of outliving portfolio resources, assuming a withdrawal policy of $10,000 per month adjusted for inflation, decreased from 26.6 percent at age 74 to 22.3 percent at age 75.

2. On average (50th percentile), the mean life span following portfolio depletion lasts five years in both age 74 and age 75 output. However, if the portfolio hits zero before the second death, there is a 5-percent (5th percentile) likelihood that the income shortfall may last for 15 years (age 74) or 14 years (age 75).

The calculation that one or both spouses remains alive without portfolio income is the first probability measure. The portfolio either fails or continues throughout the joint life span. If it fails, the second calculation quantifies the magnitude (duration in years) of the problem. The investors may better understand these statistical concepts in terms of a self-insurance liability. The advisor ponders the best way to explain: "There is roughly a one-in-four chance (22.3 percent) of depleting the portfolio if you withdraw $10,000 per month adjusted for inflation.[2] If this event occurs, you may have to find other resources to fund your target income. On average, conditional on a shortfall event, you must replace the lost income for five years. However, assuming depletion under worst-case conditions (an early depletion because of poor investment returns and an unfavorable inflation environment coupled with a long life span), there is a 5-percent risk that you may have to find alternative funding sources, i.e., self-insure, for as long as 14 years."

The next output (see template 12.5) quantifies other risk metrics of interest. For example, the age 74 output suggests that the investors, by deciding to withdraw the monthly target income, incur a 37-percent chance of leaving a bequest less than $500,000. At age 75, the metric improves to 33 percent. The advisor memorializes the results of several risk metrics so that they can be tracked and evaluated over time.

TEMPLATE 12.5: AGE 75 SIMULATED RISK METRICS AND PROJECTED SURPLUS

		5 Years	10 Years	15 Years	End of Simulation
Likelihood of Assets < $509,750 Adjusted for Inflation					
$7,646 per Month		0.80%	7.10%	14.00%	19.90%
$10,195 per Month		1.40%	12.70%	24.10%	33.00%
$12,743 per month		2.80%	20.50%	36.90%	47.10%
Likelihood Portfolio < 15% in first 12-months					
$7,646 per Month		9.60%	9.60%	9.60%	9.60%
$10,195 per Month		10.80%	10.80%	10.80%	10.80%
$12,743 per month		12.60%	12.60%	12.60%	12.60%
Likelihood Portfolio < 20% in any 12-months					
$7,646 per Month		26.80%	44.40%	55.00%	61.90%
$10,195 per Month		29.80%	49.00%	60.50%	67.30%
$12,743 per month		33.20%	54.30%	66.90%	73.50%
Likelihood Portfolio < 40% Peak to Trough					
$7,646 per Month		12.00%	25.40%	34.80%	41.60%
$10,195 per Month		14.70%	31.90%	43.50%	51.00%
$12,743 per month		18.60%	40.50%	54.40%	62.70%

1. We focus on the $10,000 (adjusted for inflation) target income level.

2. Will the investors be comfortable if a model predicts a 77.7-percent chance of retirement-income success?

$7,646 Projected Surplus (+ / −)	50th	$813,928	$1,244,962	$1,522,329	$2,058,609
[Projected Portfolio Value –	40th	$585,032	$891,085	$1,015,808	$1,541,865
Total Distribution Annuity Cost]	30th	$339,417	$518,485	$554,832	$1,021,432
	10th	(-$335,363)	(-$327,040)	(-$399,155)	(-$318,846)
	5th	(-$616,764)	(-$615,883)	(-$682,829)	(-$616,056)
$10,195 Projected Surplus (+ / −)	50th	$152,590	$546,837	$690,457	$1,332,348
[Projected Portfolio Value –	40th	(-$71,926)	$190,033	$266,318	$853,984
Total Distribution Annuity Cost]	30th	(-$313,116)	(-$143,194)	(-$195,367)	$380,431
	10th	(-$969,811)	(-$927,734)	(-$997,953)	(-$904,683)
	5th	(-$1,254,088)	(-$1,209,066)	(-$1,273,256)	(-$1,196,359)
$12,743 Projected Surplus (+ / −)	50th	(-$495,591)	(-$175,057)	(-$151,666)	$653,200
[Projected Portfolio Value –	40th	(-$719,385)	(-$490,315)	(-$560,306)	$179,255
Total Distribution Annuity Cost]	30th	(-$968,337)	(-$809,362)	(-$924,717)	(-$771,300)
	10th	(-$1,639,959)	(-$1,556,299)	(-$1,640,161)	(-$1,545,914)
	5th	(-$1,908,563)	(-$1,800,597)	(-$1,917,817)	(-$1,856,382)

The improvement in risk metrics over the course of one year places the portfolio on a firmer financial footing (see table 12.2).

TABLE 12.2: CHANGE IN RISK METRICS (AGE 74 TO AGE 75)

Age 74	$7,500 Monthly Withdrawal	$10,000 Monthly Withdrawal	Age 75	$7,500 Monthly Withdrawal	$10,000 Monthly Withdrawal
Portfolio Value End of Simulation (50th Percentile)	$1,551,657	$194,539	Portfolio Value End of Simulation (50th Percentile)	$2,058,746	$1,332,999
Income ever drops below $7,500	13.00%	26.30%	Income ever drops below $7,646	10.70%	22.30%
Portfolio Value ever less than $500,000	22.70%	37.00%	Portfolio Value ever less than $509,750	19.90%	33.00%
Portfolio ever down more than 20% in any 12-months	64.30%	69.60%	Portfolio ever down more than 20% in any 12-months	61.90%	67.30%
Portfolio ever falls > 40% Peak to Trough	43.60%	54.90%	Portfolio ever falls > 40% Peak to Trough	41.60%	51.00%

The portfolio even manifests positive value at the aspirational withdrawal level ($654,453—data not shown). The advisor notes the significant increase in portfolio value at the end-of-simulation date at both the threshold and target standard-of-living levels.

Finally, the age 75 template records the updated utility-adjusted aggregate values (see template 12.6).

TEMPLATE 12.6: AGE 75 UTILITY-ADJUSTED AGGREGATE WEALTH AND INCOME

		5 Years	10 Years	15 Years	End of Simulation
Utility-Adjusted Aggregate Spending + Bequest	50th	$1,019,338	$1,466,620	$1,905,995	$2,059,229
$7,646 per Month	40th	$966,518	$1,378,589	$1,778,435	$1,800,022
	30th	$909,833	$1,287,582	$1,662,958	$1,532,447
	10th	$743,900	$1,080,287	$1,426,734	$886,965
	5th	$678,433	$1,014,314	$1,291,494	$695,809
Utility-Adjusted Aggregate Spending + Bequest	50th	$1,128,192	$1,673,797	$2,205,737	$2,280,495
$10,195 per Month	40th	$1,075,867	$1,590,427	$2,091,122	$1,998,100
	30th	$1,018,893	$,1507,705	$1,985,950	$1,698,524
	10th	$867,021	$1,320,121	$1,608,942	$1,131,645
	5th	$802,982	$1,255,271	$1,338,141	$911,683
Utility-Adjusted Aggregate Spending + Bequest	50th	$1,239,723	$1,882,577	$2,506,842	$2,419,257
$12,743 per Month	40th	$1,188,823	$1,801,716	$2,407,202	$2,084,030
	30th	$1,132,290	$1,727,509	$2,310,070	$1,825,898
	10th	$981,109	$1,552,385	$1,630,345	$1,308,490
	5th	$924,254	$1,398,074	$1,399,250	$1,083,219

The advisor is especially interested in evaluating the "retirement security" metrics recorded at the target monthly withdrawal level [$10,000 Projected Surplus (+/-)]. Surplus, defined as the projected portfolio value minus the cost of an annuity designed to replicate the desired withdrawal pattern (100-percent lifetime joint-and-survivor income stream adjusted for inflation), represents a financial cushion available to absorb future economic shocks. A negative surplus indicates financial vulnerability. However, investors differ in how they interpret a positive surplus. An investor may place a favorable interpretation on a positive surplus because it suggests achievement, in whole or in part, of bequest or gifting objectives. On the other hand, an investor may see a positive late-in-life surplus as an opportunity cost because it suggests that higher lifetime consumption was not realized.

The possibility for mixed interpretations of end-of-life surplus does not exist for negative surplus values. A negative current surplus indicates that an investor lies below the feasibility bound as measured under an actuarial calculation. The investor may hope for a successful retirement but should not remain complacent about its attainment. The age 75 output for the $10,000-target income level indicates a current negative surplus (-$570,733), a negative surplus at the 5th year (-$3,975), and a positive surplus (at the 50th percentile of the distribution of portfolio results of +$1,111,025) in the final year of simulation. This compares to age 75 values of -$483,655, +$152,590, and +$1,332,348, respectively.

It is encouraging to see that the negative distance from retirement-income feasibility decreased by approximately $88,000. It is discouraging to see that the investors' portfolio remains approximately $480,000 short.[3] Furthermore, at levels below the 30th percentile of the distribution of portfolio value, the negative surplus persists. This is a troubling situation.[4] Figure 12.1 reflects the following model output.

---

3. The target withdrawal actuarial coverage ratio value at the 50th percentile is only 79.2 percent.

4. As stated, for some investors, a positive late-in-life surplus is a missed consumption opportunity. In this case, a dynamic portfolio management system may focus on adjusting current spending to maintain the likelihood of a positive surplus with an upper bound limit—for example, maintain an ACR of 1.25 at the 40th percentile of the distribution of results. Any funds above this limit are earmarked for consumption.

DATA TABLE FOR FIGURE 12.1

Name	Percentile	0.0Y	2.4Y	4.9Y	7.4Y	9.9Y	12.4Y	14.8Y	17.3Y	19.8Y	22.3Y	24.8Y
$7,646 Distribution	50th	108.80%	126.20%	147.30%	182.80%	215.10%	270.60%	319.90%	394.30%	443.90%	518.30%	543.80%
$7,646 Distribution	30th	102.20%	108.70%	115.80%	130.80%	141.60%	160.40%	171.00%	178.40%	155.50%	127.00%	60.10%
$10,195 Distribution	50th	79.20%	96.00%	114.70%	142.00%	166.30%	203.80%	234.70%	272.00%	277.70%	297.90%	238.70%
$10,195 Distribution	30th	76.70%	78.70%	79.10%	84.50%	82.00%	80.80%	67.50%	39.30%	0.00%	0.00%	0.00%
$12,743 Distribution	50th	65.00%	70.10%	74.70%	82.40%	82.20%	86.90%	76.60%	51.00%	4.00%	0.00%	0.00%
$12.5K Distribution	30th	61.30%	60.20%	57.40%	55.10%	45.60%	31.90%	5.40%	0.00%	0.00%	0.00%	0.00%
Survival %		100.00%	99.60%	98.20%	95.50%	90.20%	81.20%	68.70%	52.00%	35.10%	19.80%	9.20%

The lines with the box marker depict the 50th percentile of the distribution of actuarial coverage ratio (ACR) values; the lines marked with a diamond depict the 30th percentile.

FIGURE 12.1: AGE 75 FEASIBILITY (ACR > 100%)

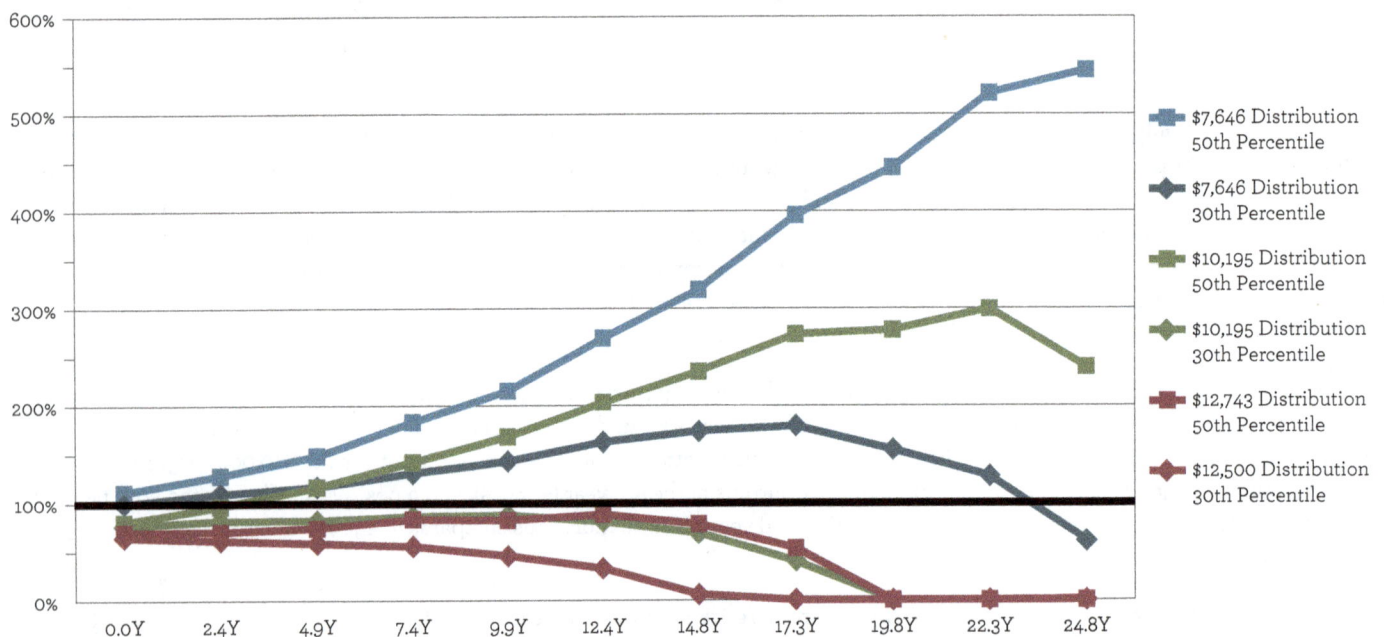

Initially, several ACR trajectories trend upward only to reverse direction in a future year. The temptation is to assume that an early upward slope indicates an emerging surplus (or emerging deficit reduction) that continues throughout all future periods. Small changes in initial values may have profound economic consequences that may not become apparent until many years have elapsed. For example, at the threshold standard-of-living income level, the portfolio's projected ACR value at the 30th percentile initially increases. However, at approximately year 17, it begins a lengthy slide downward over the remaining planning horizon.[5]

_____

5.   The ACR trend is unstable. The initially rising ACR value may mask the true magnitude of longevity risk.

As the percentile projections of portfolio wealth at the target standard-of-living withdrawal level illustrate (see table 12.3), should the portfolio's "expected values" fail to materialize over time, the downward path toward depletion can accelerate quickly.

TABLE 12.3: SIMULATED PORTFOLIO VALUE FOR $10,000 CONSTANT-DOLLAR MONTHLY TARGET WITHDRAWAL ($10,195)

		0.0Y	2.4Y	4.9Y	7.4Y	9.9Y	12.4Y	14.8Y	17.3Y	19.8Y	22.3Y	24.8Y
$10K Distribution: 50th Percentile	Portfolio Value	$2,100,000	$2,130,946	$2,068,232	$1,942,493	$1,805,723	$1,650,088	$1,489,595	$1,252,553	$1,004,976	$801,165	$505,902
$10K Distribution: 30th Percentile	Portfolio Value	$2,100,000	$1,883,983	$1,631,936	$1,388,969	$1,145,670	$887,806	$624,731	$314,256	$9,152	$-	$-

The instability of ACR values can increase dramatically at older ages because the variance in longevity has a potentially profound influence. A two-year addition or subtraction from life span for an investor in good health at age 65 only has a marginal influence on the sufficiency of financial resources; a two-year addition or subtraction from life span for a 90-year-old investor has a far greater potential impact on ultimate retirement success or failure. This is a rationale for careful and continual monitoring of retirement-income strategies, and an important reason not to wish-away deteriorating values.[6]

Deteriorating values, if left unattended, can jeopardize long-term income sustainability. In particular, the advisor notes that the $10,195-monthly-target income may deplete the portfolio to the point where it may not be able to support even the threshold $7,646 standard-of-living level (see table 12.4).

TABLE 12.4: RISK OF FAILING TO SUSTAIN THRESHOLD INCOME

		0.0Y	2.4Y	4.9Y	7.4Y	9.9Y	12.4Y	14.8Y	17.3Y	19.8Y	22.3Y	24.8Y
$10K per Month: 50th Percentile	Likelihood Monthly Income < $7,646 (Inflation Adjusted)	0.00%	0.00%	0.00%	0.20%	2.60%	7.00%	11.90%	16.30%	19.30%	21.10%	21.90%

Given the current portfolio profile, the advisor plans to suggest several asset management elections to improve the investors' chances for an economically successful retirement. These portfolio management options are the subject of the next section.

---

6. An analogous set of observations, made in the context of a defined benefit pension plan, appear in Leibowitz et al. (2017). For example, "Even with a high initial funding ratio (FR) and seemingly reasonable return assumptions, the funding ratio's 'orbit' may rise to a peak level, go into a 'stall, and then fall precipitously" (p. 8); or, "Orbits that rise at the outset but eventually peak and then fall are quite common" (p. 10). The Leibowitz et al. (2017) discussion does not consider the additional element of variance in life expectancy for individuals because its focus is on pooled investment accounts. They caution, however, "... the FR tends not to be stable over time, rising or falling depending on the assumed earnings rate and the prescribed liability payment schedule. Thus, it is necessary to move beyond a single-point estimate and focus on the FR orbit implied by the liability payment schedule, the initial funding status, and the return target" (p. 19). See, also, the discussion of orbital instability in the context of black holes in Case Study 1.

EVALUATION OF ASSET MANAGEMENT ELECTIONS

Evaluation of the age 75 stay-the-course output prompts the advisor to present four asset management elections for the investors' consideration:

1. Qualify for a reverse mortgage now to secure safety-net income if it is required in the future. The investors own their home free and clear; there is little doubt that they can complete a successful application.

2. Forego an inflation increase for the next five years. This election should not be too great a detriment to income because recent inflation has been modest. If the near-term inflation rate rises significantly, the investors can always elect to catch-up their withdrawal levels at a later time should portfolio results permit.

3. Revise survivor income levels from 100-percent continuation on the death of first spouse to 80-percent continuation. This adjustment requires less current frugality, and, if future portfolio performance permits, the investors can switch to an 85-, 90-, 95-, or 100-percent survivor income level.

4. Rebalance the portfolio to its long-term strategic asset allocation target (60-percent stock/40-percent fixed income).

The first election does not modify the portfolio or its operations. The revised template records the results of the other elections.

TEMPLATE 12.7: AGE 75 NEW ASSET MANAGEMENT ELECTIONS

CASE STUDY 11 [INITIAL SIMULATION: MARKET AGNOSTIC] DATA BASED ON 10,000 TRIALS

Current Age Male	Health Status	Current Age Female	Health Status
75	Good (5)	75	Good (5)
Approximate Joint Life Expectancy			18.2 years
Current Portfolio Value			$2,100,000
Macro Asset Allocation Election			60% Stock / 40% Bond
Precautionary Investment Reserve Value			N/A
Asset Management Elections			
Portfolio Strategy			Constant Mix
Withdrawal Strategy			Fixed Amount Adjusted for Inflation
Survivorship Income Election			80%
Rebalance to Target?			Yes
Rebalance to % Allocation different than Target?			No
△ Income (Withdrawal) Target?			No
Amortize (±) to ACR Target?			Yes
Forego Income Inflation Adjustment?			Yes
Interest Rate Data for ACR Calculation			
Freddie Mac 5 Year ARM			2.81%
Freddie Mac 15 Year Fixed			3.20%
Realized Inflation			1.95%
Income Targets			
Threshold			$91,755
Target			$122,340
Aspriational			$152,925
Actual Spending Previous Year			$87,500

The revised age 75 income-oriented summary page (template 12.7) now lists changes in the "asset management elections" section for survivor benefits, amortization of future surplus (the consequences of which will be considered separately), and suspension of CPI adjustments to income.

Template 12.8 records the economic consequences of changing survivor benefit and CPI adjustment elections. The initial five-, 10-, and 15-year, and end-of-simulation snapshots reflect the impact of reducing survivor income by 20 percent at each withdrawal level.

TEMPLATE 12.8: AGE 75 PORTFOLIO WITHDRAWAL (INCOME) ASSUMING CHANGES IN ASSET MANAGEMENT ELECTIONS

Income	Utility Weighting Factor	1			
	Initial Income (Year Zero)	Percentile of Distribution of Withdrawal Amounts	Projected Snapshot Income in 5 Years	Projected Snapshot Income in 10 Years	Projected Snapshot Income in 15 Years	Projected Income in Final Year of Simulation
Threshold Monthly Income	$90,000	50th	$7,646	$7,646	$6,117	$6,117
$7,500	Plus 1+ Inflation	40th	$7,646	$6,117	$6,117	$6,117
Adjusted for Inflation	$91,755	30th	$7,646	$6,117	$6,117	$6,117
$7,646		10th	$6,117	$6,117	$6,117	$6,117
		5th	$6,117	$6,117	$6,117	$3,755
Projected Aggregate Income to Snapshot Date		50th	$458,775	$917,550	$1,302,921	$1,422,202
		40th	$458,775	$891,553	$1,272,336	$1,302,921
		30th	$458,775	$860,968	$1,235,634	$1,175,993
		10th	$411,368	$784,505	$1,146,938	$810,502
		5th	$389,959	$760,037	$1,117,882	$631,580
Probability Monthly Income ever less than $7,500		8.10%				
Adjusted for Inflation						
Target Monthly Income	$120,000	50th	$10,195	$10,153	$8,156	$8,156
$10,000	Plus 1+ Inflation	40th	$10,195	$8,156	$8,156	$8,156
Adjusted for Inflation	$122,340	30th	$10,195	$8,156	$8,156	$8,156
$10,195		10th	$8,156	$8,156	$7,227	$4,822
		5th	$8,156	$8,156	$3,606	$2,456
Projected Aggregate Income to Snapshot Date		50th	$611,700	$1,223,025	$1,718,877	$1,809,235
		40th	$611,700	$1,184,659	$1,674,019	$1,665,863
		30th	$611,700	$1,141,840	$1,618,966	$1,496,626
		10th	$548,491	$1,039,890	$1,494,587	$1,051,281
		5th	$519,945	$1,007,266	$1,348,703	$838,029
Probability Monthly Income ever less than $7,500		13.50%				
Adjusted for Inflation						

Aspirational Monthly Income	$150,000	50th	$12,744	$10,195	$10,195	$10,195
$12,5000	Plus 1+ Inflation	40th	$12,744	$10,195	$10,195	$10,195
Adjusted for Inflation	$152,925	30th	$12,744	$10,195	$10,195	$10,195
$12,743		10th	$10,195	$10,195	$4,751	$3,676
		5th	$10,195	$9,256	$2,390	$1,782
Projected Aggregate Income to Snapshot Date		50th	$764,625	$1,513,958	$2,107,816	$2,131,528
		40th	$764,625	$1,468,080	$2,041,549	$1,947,245
		30th	$764,625	$1,412,008	$1,965,086	$1,740,292
		10th	$685,614	$1,282,764	$1,637,753	$1,228,498
		5th	$649,931	$1,241,241	$1,367,798	$1,011,854
Probability Monthly Income ever less than $7,500		30.50%				
Adjusted for Inflation						
Total Distribution Annuity Cost [Actuarial Feasibility Boundary]	Threshold Income	$1,710,823				
	Target Income	$2,337,960				
	Aspirational Income	$2,845,976				

Implementation of the survivor benefit and CPI adjustments greatly enhance the portfolio's ability to sustain the threshold income level throughout future economic environments (see figure 12.2).[7]

---

7. We refer the reader to the book-keeping discussion at the beginning of Chapter 11 ("Preliminary Technical Observations"). The failure rate numbers in figure 12.2 record a process over time; however, the five-, 10-, and 15-year, and end-of-simulation snapshot numbers record a distribution at a single moment in time. In later years, the snapshot is a record of only the subset of long-lived investors. However, many investors who died in early years were economically successful in that their portfolios remained solvent throughout their life span(s). Percentile ranks in the distribution of outcomes at a specific time are not comparable to failure rate frequencies throughout the entire planning horizon.

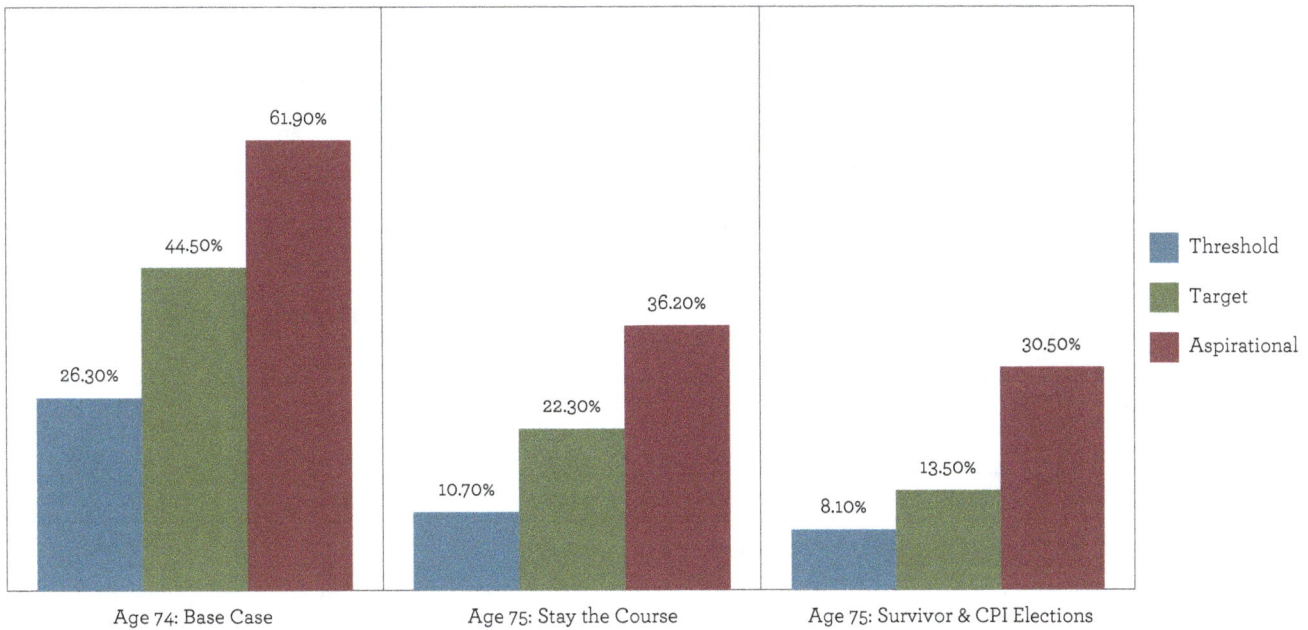

The advisor next examines the wealth-oriented template that records the impact of the new age 75 asset management elections. We present the entire wealth-oriented section without interspersing commentary (see templates 12.9 and 12.10). More detailed analysis follows.

TEMPLATE 12.9: AGE 75 RISK METRICS UNDER NEW ASSET MANAGEMENT ELECTIONS

CASE STUDY 11 [INITIAL SIMULATION: MARKET AGNOSTIC] DATA BASED ON 10,000 TRIALS

Current Portfolio Value	$2,100,000
Risk Metrics	**Target Income: $10,195**
Likelihood Portfolio < $509,750 Adjusted for Inflation	28.50%
Likelihood Portfolio < 15% in first 12-months	9.50%
Likelihood Portfolio < 20% in any 12-months	65.40%
Likelihood Portfolio < 40% Peak to Trough	47.40%
Actuarial Feasibility Boundary	
Threshold Income	$1,710,823
Target Income	$2,337,960
Aspirational Income	$2,845,976
Surplus (Retirement Security—50th Percentile)	
Threshold Income	$389,177
Target Income	(-$237,960)
Aspirational Income	(-$745,976)

TEMPLATE 12.10: AGE 75 SIMULATION OUTPUTS UNDER NEW ASSET MANAGEMENT ELECTIONS

Wealth	Percentile Distribution of Portfolio Value	Bequest Weighting Factor		0.25	
		Projected Portfolio Value in 5 Years	Projected Portfolio Value in 10 Years	Projected Portfolio Value in 15 Years	Projected Portfolio Value in Final Year of Simulation
Projected Portfolio Value	50th	$2,309,753	$2,356,307	$2,463,848	$2,411,394
$7,646	40th	$2,059,723	$1,907,327	$1,780,538	$1,755,009
	30th	$1,814,660	$1,516,573	$1,247,377	$1,210,796
	10th	$1,219,751	$763,067	$390,423	$182,073
	5th	$1,023,769	$560,662	$159,858	$0
Projected Portfolio Value	50th	$2,129,465	$1,917,858	$1,670,220	$1,653,119
$10,195	40th	$1,925,633	$1,577,806	$1,205,768	$1,130,043
	30th	$1,688,329	$1,247,139	$798,422	$661,074
	10th	$1,075,106	$483,572	$0	$0
	5th	$826,665	$217,411	$0	$0
Projected Portfolio Value	50th	$1,982,613	$1,634,658	$1,204,532	$1,173,000
$12,743	40th	$1,764,524	$1,256,377	$687,943	$597,866
	30th	$1,531,989	$892,368	$288,872	$96,397
	10th	$979,024	$279,962	$0	$0
	5th	$805,735	$80,433	$0	$0
Life Remaining at Depletion: $7,646	50th	4			
Percentage of Portfolios Depleted	40th	5			
7.00%	30th	6			
	10th	9			
	5th	11			
Life Remaining at Depletion: $10,195	50th	5			
Percentage of Portfolios Depleted	40th	6			
16.90%	30th	8			
	10th	12			
	5th	14			
Life Remaining at Depletion: $12,743	50th	6			
Percentage of Portfolios Depleted	40th	7			
27.90%	30th	8			
	10th	12			
	5th	14			

Likelihood of Assets < $509,750 Adjusted for Inflation					
$7,646 per Month		0.60%	6.20%	12.50%	17.70%
$10,195 per Month		1.40%	11.20%	21.20%	28.50%
$12,743 per Month		2.80%	18.20%	32.50%	41.80%
Likelihood Portfolio < 15% in first 12-months					
$7,646 per Month		9.50%	9.50%	9.50%	9.50%
$10,195 per Month		10.70%	10.70%	10.70%	10.70%
$12,743 per Month		12.30%	12.30%	12.30%	12.30%
Likelihood Portfolio < 20% in any 12-months					
$7,646 per Month		26.50%	43.70%	54.70%	61.50%
$10,195 per Month		28.90%	48.00%	58.80%	65.40%
$12,743 per Month		32.80%	52.70%	64.60%	71.00%
Likelihood Portfolio < 40% Peak to Trough					
$7,646 per Month		11.80%	25.10%	33.50%	40.10%
$10,195 per Month		14.80%	30.10%	40.40%	47.40%
$12,743 per Month		18.00%	38.50%	50.90%	58.20%
$7,646 Projected Surplus (+ / −)	50th	$1,038,006	$1,543,837	$1,970,714	$2,408,371
[Projected Portfolio Value –	40th	$804,165	$1,099,856	$1,303,444	$1,754,837
Total Distribution Annuity Cost]	30th	$549,964	$707,200	$758,057	$1,210,116
	10th	(-$91,206)	(-$56,357)	(-$132,547)	$181,935
	5th	(-$343,321)	(-$314,382)	(-$375,210)	(-$324,370)
$10,195 Projected Surplus (+ / −)	50th	$446,336	$852,526	$1,010,277	$1,653,119
[Projected Portfolio Value –	40th	$220,651	$480,646	$542,380	$1,130,043
Total Distribution Annuity Cost]	30th	(-$22,316)	$147,152	$136,627	$659,925
	10th	(-$690,011)	(-$644,514)	(-$721,028)	(-$607,450)
	5th	(-$965,769)	(-$937,456)	(-$1,059,963)	(-$937,259)
$12,743 Projected Surplus (+ / −)	50th	(-$106,725)	$324,092	$409,050	$1,172,538
[Projected Portfolio Value –	40th	(-$352,605)	(-$94,236)	(-$124,696)	$597,610
Total Distribution Annuity Cost]	30th	(-$600,399)	(-$449,042)	(-$539,749)	$96,338
	10th	(-$1,249,246)	(-$1,177,838)	(-$1,292,840)	(-$1,140,539)
	5th	(-$1,508,943)	(-$1,456,292)	(-$1,549,442)	(-$1,469,205)
Utility-Adjusted Aggregate Spending + Bequest	50th	$1,036,213	$1,506,627	$1,918,883	$2,025,051
$7,646 per Month	40th	$973,706	$1,368,385	$1,717,471	$1,741,673
	30th	$912,440	$1,240,111	$1,547,478	$1,478,692
	10th	$716,306	$975,272	$1,244,544	$856,020
	5th	$645,901	$900,203	$1,157,847	$631,580

Utility-Adjusted Aggregate Spending + Bequest	50th	$1,144,066	$1,702,490	$2,136,432	$2,222,515
$10,195 per Month	40th	$1,093,108	$1,579,111	$1,975,461	$1,948,374
	30th	$1,033,782	$1,453,625	$1,818,572	$1,661,895
	10th	$817,268	$1,160,783	$1,494,587	$1,051,281
	5th	$726,611	$1,061,619	$1,348,703	$838,029
Utility-Adjusted Aggregate Spending + Bequest	50th	$1,260,278	$1,922,623	$2,408,949	$2,424,778
$12,743 per Month	40th	$1,205,756	$1,782,174	$2,213,535	$2,096,712
	30th	$1,147,622	$1,635,100	$2,037,304	$1,764,391
	10th	$930,370	$1,352,755	$1,637,753	$1,228,498
	5th	$851,365	$1,261,349	$1,367,798	$1,011,854

'STAY-THE-COURSE' VERSUS IMPLEMENTATION OF OPTIONS

The impact of the newly proposed asset management elections is considerable. Focusing on the target standard-of-living income level ($10,195 per month), the advisor notes that the age 75 stay-the-course analysis indicates an initial surplus deficit of $483,606. Implementation of elections to (1) rebalance the portfolio to its strategic asset allocation target, (2) forego inflation adjustments for the forthcoming five years, and (3) reduce the anticipated monthly survivorship benefit by 20 percent, shrinks the surplus deficit to $237,936—an immediate improvement of $245,670.

Furthermore, at the 50th percentile of the distribution of portfolio results, the projected financial improvements restore the feasibility of the target income level within a reasonably short time. Particularly noteworthy is the fact that, with the exception of temporarily foregoing an inflation adjustment to monthly income, i.e., freezing income at $10,195 over the next five years, the substantial improvement in both current and projected surplus does not require current frugality. At this point in time, a painful downward adjustment to income is, by no means, either the sole or even the best control variable. Figure 12.3 and its accompanying data table depict the projected improvements of the asset management elections.

DATA TABLE FOR FIGURE 12.3

			0.0Y	2.4Y	4.9Y	7.4Y	9.9Y	12.4Y	14.8Y	17.3Y	19.8Y	22.3Y	24.8Y
Base Case	Surplus [+ or –]	$10K per month: No Elections [50th Percentile]	(-$483,606)	(-$210,739)	$40,359	$308,583	$454,763	$587,528	$636,286	$596,246	$448,571	$356,046	$100,731
All Elections	Surplus [+ or –]	$10K per month: All Elections [50th Percentile]	(-$237,936)	$38,699	$293,861	$590,466	$724,282	$881,250	$920,855	$882,834	$808,607	$698,045	$573,972
Surplus Improvement			$245,670	$249,438	$253,502	$281,883	$269,519	$293,722	$284,569	$286,588	$360,036	$341,999	$473,241

FIGURE 12.3: SURPLUS FROM ASSET MANAGEMENT ELECTIONS

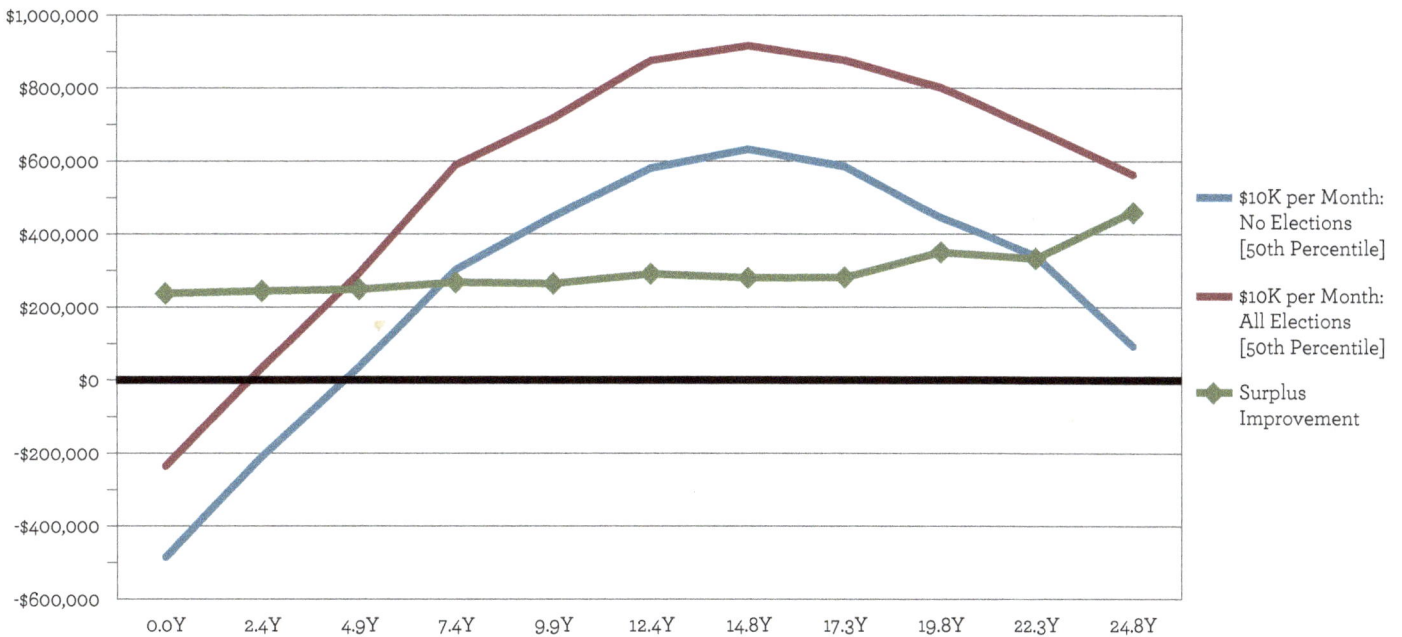

The blue line indicates the large current deficit ($483,606), i.e., the portfolio does not meet the feasibility test for the standard-of-living target. The red line indicates the current deficit after adoption of the asset management elections ($237,936). At the 50th percentile, the approximate time to erase the deficit is cut in half by implementing the proposed options. The green line quantifies the magnitude of dollar advantage—implementing the options generates an immediate gain of $245,670.

Further analysis (see table 12.5) indicates the relative benefits of asset management options both separately and in tandem:

- The election to forgo CPI adjustments over the forthcoming five-year period
- The election to reduce the survivorship benefit by 20 percent
- The election to implement both options

Lower numbers are better, i.e., the cost of providing long-term feasibility, sustainability, and security is cheaper.

TABLE 12.5: RELATIVE EFFECTS OF ASSET MANAGEMENT ELECTIONS

			0.0Y	2.4Y	4.9Y	7.4Y	9.9Y	12.4Y	14.8Y	17.3Y	19.8Y	22.3Y	24.8Y
Base Case	Lower Bound Actuarial Cost	$10K–50th Percentile	$2,583,655	$2,331,035	$2,047,482	$1,661,232	$1,375,965	$1,023,498	$850,295	$670,505	$577,259	$466,307	$407,222
No CPI 5 Years	Lower Bound Actuarial Cost	$10K No CPI	$2,523,540	$2,282,718	$2,043,260	$1,655,705	$1,370,025	$1,024,856	$853,874	$671,220	$575,266	$462,796	$401,518
80% Survivorship	Lower Bound Actuarial Cost	$10K 80% Survivor	$2,337,960	$2,101,859	$1,840,478	$1,483,483	$1,197,870	$818,738	$679,076	$532,701	$455,568	$367,137	$321,102
80% & No CPI	Lower Bound Actuarial Cost	$10K 80% No CPI	$2,286,516	$2,060,576	$1,836,526	$1,481,321	$1,189,750	$817,172	$676,476	$531,104	$454,230	$365,328	$319,461

As figure 12.4 suggests, the reduction in survivor benefit produces the largest improvement to the investors' current financial situation. The bottom purple line marks the base case, i.e., the stay-the-course option. The blue line follows the economic effects of changing to a nominal monthly income stream of $10,195 over the next five years. The red line shows the effects of reducing the benefit to the surviving spouse. Finally, the top green line highlights the combined impact of implementing both asset management options.

The advisor notes the change in slope direction (increasing to decreasing) at approximately year 16. The slope values that progress from negative (retirement infeasibility) to positive (retirement sustainability and security) do not remain stable.[8] Furthermore, at the 30th percentile, the projected surplus remains negative for approximately seven years, turns positive for approximately 10 years, and turns negative thereafter.[9] Trajectories often are unstable; trends may not persist; results often are dependent on initial conditions.

FIGURE 12.4: EVOLUTION OF SURPLUS—TARGET INCOME/50TH PERCENTILE

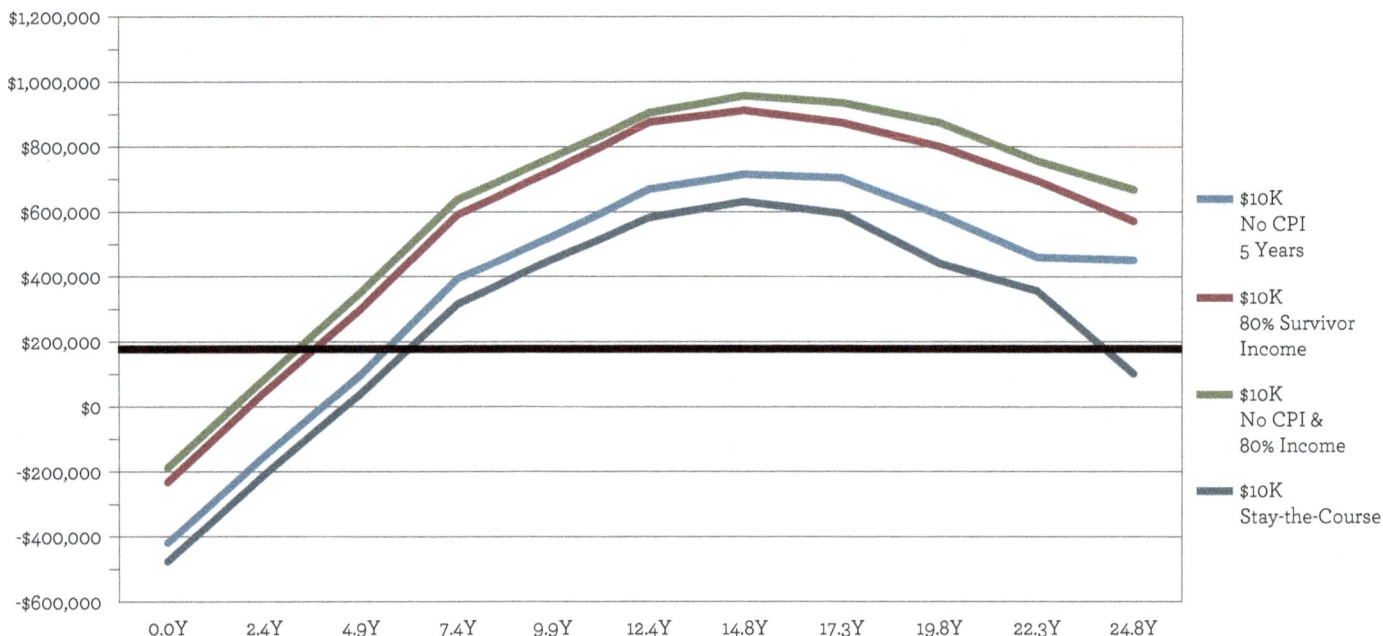

Upon reviewing the retirement-income model's output, the investors readily agree that implementation of the advisor's suggestions makes good sense. Their decision will set a new path for future portfolio monitoring and evaluation. They are gratified that their target standard-of-living funding goal is within their grasp. The goal is by no means secured; however, the slight market recovery that followed the severe bear market's jolt to their wealth has given them some breathing room. The advisor's asset management suggestions may, if things go well, restore the feasibility of their financial goals. If not, they are relieved to see that the threshold income level remains feasible, sustainable, and secure.

8.   The second derivative changes from positive to negative.

9.   Data not shown. Output for the $7,646-threshold income level shows an initial positive surplus. The dollar value of the surplus continues to grow throughout the planning horizon
      at both the 50th and 30th percentiles of portfolio results.

The investors are particularly pleased to hear that the CPI/survivor adjustments are reversible. If the portfolio evidences sufficient improvement over the next several years, they can restore the status quo ante in whole or in part.[10] In other words, unlike the options sold in financial markets, the asset management options under consideration are real options characterized by partial or complete reversibility. As such, they are powerful tools for dynamic portfolio management.[11]

REVISITING THE 'STEADY STATE' CONCEPT: A NEW SPENDING RULE?

Case Study 8 in Chapter Nine explores the challenges of withdrawing periodic income from a portfolio while maintaining a "steady state," i.e., preserving principal for a bequest objective. This section revisits the steady-state concept from the perspective of income objectives. One measure of income security is the ACR value. A current ACR value of at least 1 suggests that retirement-income objectives are feasible; an ACR value greater than 1 suggests that retirement income is sustainable; an ACR value trending upward over time suggests that there is sufficient financial flexibility to secure retirement income against unexpected shocks. Over time, a stable, or steady-state, ACR suggests an income stream that will remain feasible, sustainable, and secure. It is one method for answering a persistent question nagging many retired investors: "How much can I safely spend?"

The calculation of a steady-state ACR begins with the question: "If I'm still alive in 'x' years, how much current consumption can my portfolio support?"[12] The investor must:

1. Determine a financial target, e.g., for a designated income level, I would like my portfolio to exhibit an ACR value of 1.25 in 10 years at the 40th percentile of results.

2. Look backward over the planning horizon to determine the amount by which yearly portfolio withdrawals must be changed in order to meet the future financial target.[13]

3. Monitor all variables over time to implement the gradual yearly changes (increases or decreases to withdrawals) required to keep things on target.

The advisor recognizes that the actuarial cost of retirement income fluctuates primarily due to increases in investor age and interest rate (discount factor) changes. Likewise, the numerator of the ACR value changes primarily due to inflation and investment realizations. A constant ACR value sets a steady-state target at the cost of recommending yearly additions to or subtractions from the portfolio.[14] As new information unfolds each year, it is incorporated into the previous calculations (the Bayesian Prior) to generate a revised set of appropriate asset management elections (the Bayesian Posterior).

As is often the case in optimization problems, the best path to a goal is not the most direct. The advisor notes, at the 40th percentile of the distribution, there is a substantial current deficit ($247,119 shortfall) for the target income level even after postponing CPI adjustments and reducing the survivor benefit. The portfolio fails to pass the feasibility risk metric test. However, at the 40th percentile, the projected

---

10. Chapter Fourteen's section on "Recourse Decisions" explores this topic in greater detail.

11. The term "dynamic portfolio management" is sometimes used to describe "dynamic asset allocation." Although changing a portfolio's asset allocation is an asset management election, this book does not incorporate asset allocation changes into the case studies. Rather, we relegate asset allocation decisions to the portfolio design process rather than to the portfolio management process. Additionally, the large number of articles and books on asset allocation has, over time, resulted in definitional ambiguities. Is "dynamic asset allocation" market anticipating (market timing), market reactive (rebalancing an existing portfolio), or market updating (re-optimizing single or multi-period weightings to maximize criteria such as optimal growth, optimal utility, optimal mean-variance efficiency, etc.). Asset allocation for the purposes of surplus management (ALM) presents its own set of issues. We again cite Leibowitz et al. (2017), who argue that, of all the asset management elections available to investors, probably the least well understood is the economic consequences of changing strategic asset allocation weightings: "Funds that implement a glide-path strategy (shifting from equities to bonds as the FR improves) may face oscillating orbits that rise or fall with allocation shifts. If an FR increase leads to a reduced equity allocation and equity returns are insufficient to maintain asset growth, the result may be an FR decrease. This decrease may, in turn, require an increased equity allocation" (p. 10).

12. The "under-the-hood" calculations needed to approximate a credible answer to this straightforward question are formidable. The question itself assumes a zero-mortality state throughout the period under observation; and this, in turn, necessitates a change in underlying model assumptions. Retired investors may not wish to 'bet' on a mortality factor to assure the likelihood of success in securing lifetime income. However, model outputs recording projected future portfolio values, actuarial costs, economic surplus or deficits, and so forth, are based on distributions of results for surviving investors—one cannot simply state that current income must be reduced by a 10-year amortization factor because the model projects a negative surplus in 10 years. On the other hand, it is unrealistic (although, perhaps pleasant) to assume that every investor will live past age 100. Mortality cannot simply be ignored.

13. Although it would be convenient to adopt the methodology of backward induction to solve optimization problems using the Bellman equation, for technical reasons (discussed in Chapter Sixteen) a simulation approach is preferable. In analytic approaches, the dynamics of such a system often are specified by employing a variation of the Kalman filter. A simulation approach, by contrast, re-estimates the probability distributions(s) faced by investors as they consider updating asset management decisions each year.

14. Additions and subtractions most often are achieved by making changes to consumption (withdrawals). In an optimization context, the control variable becomes spending.

surplus turns positive at approximately year 3, reaches a maximum at approximately year 13, and shrinks thereafter until it becomes negative at approximately age 101, or year 25. Although the age 75 feasibility risk metric is flashing red, i.e., the investors should not take out the full amount of target income lest they exacerbate the actuarial funding deficit, is there another risk measure that they should consider? In the face of a projected future surplus, should they place a lesser weight on a feasibility risk metric that evidences a current deficit? How much weight should be given to data appearing in year 25 when there is only a remote probability that the joint life span will extend to age 101?

The advisor prepares an analysis under the following assumptions:

- The investors remain alive throughout the relevant planning horizon

- There is a specified ACR target (1.0, 1.1, or 1.25)

- The current surplus or deficit is "amortized" at the projected portfolio rate of return over the planning horizon

- The calculations reflect the current target income level ($10,195 per month)

TABLE 12.6: SPENDING ADJUSTMENTS REQUIRED TO ATTAIN FUTURE ACR VALUES AT 40TH PERCENTILE

40th Percentile	5 Years	7 Years	10 Years	15 Years
ACR 1	$38,552	$37,765	$33,395	$27,051
ACR 1.1	$10,790	$22,665	$26,517	$24,853
ACR 1.25	(-$29,973)	$535	$16,351	$21,647

If the investors wish to achieve a designated ACR value at a specific future year, they must adjust yearly portfolio withdrawals by the amounts shown in table 12.6. For example, if their objective is to attain an ACR of 1.25 in the next five years, the investors must decrease yearly spending by $29,973—from $10,195 per month to $7,698 for the forthcoming 60-month (five-year) period. However, if the ACR target is 1.1, the investors can increase annual spending by $10,790 (a monthly spending increase of $900 over the next 60 months). Reading down the columns, the amount of "extra" withdrawals monotonically decreases the more conservative the target ACR value.

The advisor explains to the investors that the calculations are forward-looking in that they project a future surplus or deficit. They amortize the surplus or deficit over the applicable time horizon and at the targeted ACR level. The investors remark that the presentation sounds a bit like a politician's declaration that a promised current tax cut will not balloon an already high deficit because his policies will create future growth sufficient to eliminate any and all revenue shortfalls. Are they not spending today future money that, in fact, may never materialize?

The advisor states that they are wise to remain skeptical:

- In some cases, it is better to eliminate an ACR shortfall as soon as possible either by reducing portfolio withdrawals or by changing asset management elections, e.g., no CPI adjustments, reduce the survivor benefit.

- The calculation inputs are specific trials representing a single percentile from the entire distribution of possible future results.

- The calculations are valid only at a specific moment in time. It is virtually impossible that the point estimate increase/decrease in yearly withdrawals will remain constant throughout the amortization-to-target-ACR period.

One way of mitigating the risk of overpromising and underachieving is to base asset management elections on calculations generated at the 30th percentile of the distribution of future outcomes. The advisor presents the revised table (see table 12.7) to illustrate the sensitivity of projected outcomes:

TABLE 12.7: SPENDING ADJUSTMENTS REQUIRED TO ATTAIN FUTURE ACR VALUES AT 30TH PERCENTILE

30th Percentile	5 Years	7 Years	10 Years	15 Years
ACR 1	(-$852)	$7,944	$13,663	$15,685
ACR 1.1	(-$29,216)	(-$8,377)	$6,428	$13,261
ACR 1.25	(-$72,495)	(-$32,387)	(-$4,598)	$9,656

The lower the percentile of investment/inflation realizations, and the higher the target ACR level, the more conservative the strategy. Indeed, the advisor suggests that most investors with reasonably long planning horizons, e.g., younger than age 90 and in good health, would not choose to calibrate current spending to an ACR level of 1 because of (1) the instability of future ACR trajectories, and (2) the high percentage variance in longevity at older ages. More succinctly, they may hit the target ACR = 1 level only to find a rapid deterioration in their post-target financial situation. In the 30th percentile presentation, the investors select a 15-year look-ahead period at the 1.25 ACR value. Granted, there is a 70-percent chance that the distribution of future results will be more favorable, but it is still a risky bet to maintain iron-clad confidence in long-term, point-estimate projections. Retirement is a risky project.

What, therefore, are the potential advantages revealed by the analysis? The advisor explains:

- It is a tool to calibrate withdrawal policy to investor utility. In this case, the investors assign a utility weight of 1 on income and 0.25 on wealth. Four dollars of lifetime income is equal to one dollar of bequest.[15]

- It is a tool to mitigate lost consumption opportunity costs. An ACR target analysis is a basis for a credible safe-spending rule because it takes into account both available financial assets and the cost of discharging the lifetime-income liability. All else equal, the change in future surplus is expected to have a positive slope (first derivative) given the decrease in annuity costs as an investor ages. Surplus is released merely with the passage of time, and surplus can be spent. Although not a perfect indicator, the ACR metric suggests how much of the projected future surplus improvement can be spent now.

- It is a tool to avoid immediate draconian reductions to income if there is a current ACR deficit (ACR < 1) because the investor can adjust (increase income or retrench) gradually.

The efficacy of the tool does not rest in its ability to provide a one-time, set-in-stone indicator of a prudent withdrawal amount. Rather, in a dynamic asset management context, the year-by-year recalculation of withdrawal amounts calibrated to a future ACR value synchronizes important elements of retirement-income portfolio management: portfolio sufficiency, income opportunities, retrenchment needs, and investor utility. By rolling forward the recalculated adjustments, and by yearly updating of portfolio withdrawal strategy, an investor achieves a steady-state ACR value; and, given that the ACR metric is important to determine feasibility, sustainability, and security, it provides a helpful perspective on retirement planning issues.[16]

UTILITY

The investors, after seeking additional information about some of the above-listed observations, request clarification of the word "utility." The advisor reminds them that, according to their stated preferences, a dollar of spendable lifetime income provides four times the satisfaction than does a dollar of terminal wealth (bequest). To the extent that heirs receive the portfolio's terminal wealth, an opportunity for additional lifetime spending has been missed. This is not to say that bequest dollars are unimportant; rather, that they have lesser importance in the investors' utility (satisfaction) pecking order. At this point in time, given current financial and personal circumstances, the investors are comfortable trading "final" dollars (principal) for "living" dollars (income) as long as the exchange rate is equal to or better than four to one. The utility value consolidates both principal and income satisfaction measures into a single, i.e., utility-adjusted, dollar value.

---

15. This weighting may change over time as investor financial preferences change with age and health status among other factors.

16. It is also worth noting that the amortization calculations provide important information to investors in the pre-retirement accumulation stage. The issue at hand is, "How much do I need to save for retirement given that I need to fund a target standard-of-living budget?" We assert that this method provides a superior calculation methodology when compared with the replace-a-percentage-of-income methods for determining retirement savings adequacy.

"But," the advisor opines, "there are some catches." The stated exchange rate may not hold across all wealth levels. In an asset-liability management context, whenever the ACR is less than one, many investors decrease the utility value of bequests. Lifetime income becomes a paramount concern. Conversely, whenever income is plentiful, the investor may increase the importance of bequest objectives.[17] "Perhaps an illustration might help explain." For each spending level (threshold, target, and aspirational) the advisor records the distribution of total utility of age 75 withdrawal levels assuming adoption of the CPI postponement and reduction of survivor benefit asset management elections (see table 12.8):

TABLE 12.8: SUMMARY OF AGGREGATE UTILITY FOR VARIOUS WITHDRAWAL TARGETS

Total Utility	Percentile	Life of Trial
Utility-Adjusted Aggregate Spending + Bequest	50th	$2,025,051
$7,646 per Month	40th	$1,741,673
	30th	$1,478,692
	10th	$856,020
	5th	$631,580
Utility-Adjusted Aggregate Spending + Bequest	50th	$2,222,515
$10,195 per Month	40th	$1,948,374
	30th	$1,661,895
	10th	$1,051,281
	5th	$838,029
Utility-Adjusted Aggregate Spending + Bequest	50th	$2,424,778
$12,743 per Month	40th	$2,096,712
	30th	$1,764,391
	10th	$1,228,498
	5th	$1,011,854

"It is not surprising, given your current income preference weighting, that the portfolio strategy that directs the maximum withdrawal amount produces the highest aggregate utility value. However, the maximum withdrawal strategy—aspirational monthly income—also produces the greatest likelihood of depleting your portfolio during your life span(s)." The advisor continues: "Although your current utility preference weighting indicates that you have a strong preference for an aspirational standard of living, are you willing to incur a non-trivial risk of running out of portfolio income while one or both of you remain alive?"

This question turns the discussion toward the topic of assets available to produce income in the absence of portfolio resources. To the extent that an investor owns assets outside of the portfolio sufficient to fund required income, the investor may be motivated to risk portfolio depletion by making high current periodic withdrawals. But this is a facts-and-circumstances issue. Does the investor own a second (vacation) home or a valuable coin or art collection? Is a reverse mortgage option available? Is there a substantial amount of pension entitlement income? Is there a strong inheritance expectation?

The investors state, "In the best of all possible worlds, we would like to withdraw the aspirational level of income if we will not be left 'high and dry'—no investment assets and no non-financial assets whatsoever. Although such a situation is the stuff of nightmares, we also know that an aspirational standard of living is the stuff of dreams."[18] The advisor apologizes for his cliché response ("if something can be done, it does not mean that it should be done"); and he offers to explore the economics of this strategy a bit further. Initially, he reminds them that the retirement-income model projects the distribution of number-of-years-alive-and-broke in the event of portfolio depletion.

---

17.   For some retired investors, the arrival of a grandchild often changes income/bequest trade-off preferences. These reactions comport with some tenets of behavioral finance.

18.   Investing is a prudent exchange of risks.

Specifically, the threshold income strategy indicates a 7-percent likelihood of depletion during the investors' lifetime, the target income strategy indicates a 16.9-percent likelihood of depletion, and the aspirational income strategy indicates a 27.9-percent likelihood of depletion. He reiterates that the failure odds assume that no corrective actions are taken in the face of investment underperformance or changes in investor circumstances. Of course, if future portfolio monitoring and evaluation reveal emerging difficulties, a dynamic asset management program may reduce the likelihood of eventual depletion.

"If portfolio depletion occurs, you are faced with a 'self-insurance liability.' If you spend your last dollar as the surviving spouse takes their final breath, the self-insurance liability is negligible. However, if the portfolio runs out of money early, you may need to use non-financial resources to fund monthly income. The question turns on the magnitude of the possible self-insurance liability and on your willingness to accept it. The model output indicates that:

- Given a 7-percent likelihood of depletion at the threshold income level, on average you will need nonfinancial resources sufficient to fund four years of income should depletion actually occur.

- Given a 16.9-percent likelihood of depletion at the target income level, on average you will need nonfinancial resources sufficient to fund five years of income.

- Given a 27.9-percent likelihood of depletion at the aspirational income level, on average you will need nonfinancial resources sufficient to fund six years of income.

The numbers record results at the 50th percentile of number of years-alive-and-broke outcomes.[19] If we look at the worst-case outcomes (outcomes below the median), here is the more complete range (in years) of the potential self-insurance liability (see table 12.9):

TABLE 12.9: RANGE OF DURATION OF SELF-INSURANCE LIABILITY

Life Remaining at Deplection $7,646	50th	4
Percentage of Portfolios Depleted	40th	5
7.00%	30th	6
	10th	9
	5th	11
Life Remaining at Depletion $10,195	50th	5
Percentage of Portfolios Depleted	40th	6
16.90%	30th	8
	10th	12
	5th	14
Life Remaining at Depletion $12,743	50th	6
Percentage of Portfolios Depleted	40th	7
27.90%	30th	8
	10th	12
	5th	14

19. If an investor does not possess substantial non-portfolio wealth, the analysis is not germane. However, a number of financial planning strategies pose interesting options for investors to consider. Among these are: (1) delay Social Security and use portfolio assets to fund early-retirement income, (2) fund early retirement income through a reverse mortgage when interest rates are low and hope that the portfolio will earn a higher rate of return, and (3) other elections such as the one discussed in this case study—take high early income and, if investment results are disappointing, use a safety net such as a reverse mortgage. We do not advocate for any strategy other than "look before you leap."

At the aspirational income level, the "expected" magnitude of the contingent liability is six years in length, however, the worst-case magnitude is 14 years or longer."[20]

Following a few moments deliberation, the investors announce their planning decision. Although they are relieved that the prospect of emerging future surplus mitigates some of the pressure of their current financial situation, they are reluctant to spend large amounts of current dollars based on uncertain future outcomes. They prefer to view anticipated future surplus as a kind of intertemporal safety net from which they will borrow only in the event of a current emergency or critical income shortfall. Their aspirational income target will, for now, remain just that—aspirational.

The in-depth exploration of the option to amortize a future surplus or deficit provides the advisor with insight into the investors' risk aversion. Usually, the topic of investor risk aversion focuses on investment selection ("stocks are too risky") or portfolio variance ("I can't afford to see my nest egg decrease in value because I'm not able to earn it back"). Much effort is put into documenting investor risk aversion in order to satisfy the "know your customer" standards promulgated by regulatory agencies. However, risk aversion in the current discussion focuses on retirement-income portfolio management rather than asset allocation and investment selection. Once the portfolio is set up, the risk-aversion discussion shifts from implementation to portfolio management. The process of presenting management options to the investor and recording the response to them serves to document the investor's risk-aversion profile. Acceptance or rejection of management options dynamically updates changes in risk aversion as (1) the investor ages, (2) experiences health changes, (3) receives inheritances or confronts financial difficulties, (4) takes into account inflation and investment realizations, (5) digests political, social, and economic news, (6) encounters changes in family circumstances, and so forth.[21] Insights offered by behavioral finance research may explain and predict changes in investor risk preferences.

---

20. Among the factors that contribute to bad outcomes (lengthy periods of funding from non-portfolio assets) are long life spans and lower than anticipated inflation-adjusted portfolio values.

21. Decision-making in a high-dimension context is the subject of Chapter Fourteen; Chapter Sixteen focuses on decision-making in an uncertain environment.

CHAPTER THIRTEEN

CASE STUDY 11 CONTINUED—AGE 76 AND BEYOND

■ ■ ■

AGE 76 TEMPLATE UPDATE

In the following year, the advisor updates the tracking templates to age 76 (see templates 13.1 and 13.2). Interest rates and inflation have increased slightly, actual withdrawals over the previous year amount to $103,400, and the portfolio's current value is $2,277,000. There have been no significant changes in the investor's health or family circumstances.

TEMPLATE 13.1: AGE 76 CLIENT CIRCUMSTANCES

CASE STUDY 11 [INITIAL SIMULATION: MARKET AGNOSTIC] DATA BASED ON 10,000 TRIALS

Current Age Male	Health Status	Current Age Female	Health Status
76	Good (5)	76	Good (5)
Approximate Joint Life Expectancy			17.3 years
Current Portfolio Value			$2,277,000
Macro Asset Allocation Election			60% Stock / 40% Bond
Precautionary Investment Reserve Value			N/A
Asset Management Elections			
Portfolio Strategy			Constant Mix
Withdrawal Strategy			Fixed Amount Adjusted for Inflation
Survivorship Income Election			80%
Rebalance to Target?			Yes
Rebalance to % Allocation different than Target?			No
△ Income (Withdrawal) Target?			No
Amortize (±) to ACR Target?			Yes
Forego Income Inflation Adjustment?			Yes (4 Years)

Interest Rate Data for ACR Calculation	
Freddie Mac 5 Year ARM	3.01%
Freddie Mac 15 Year Fixed	3.81%
Realized Inflation	2.19%
Income Targets (no CPI)	
Threshold	$91,755
Target	$122,340
Aspriational	$152,925
Income Targets (CPI)	
Threshold	$93,764
Target	$125,019
Aspriational	$156,274
Actual Spending Previous Year	$103,400

TEMPLATE 13.2: AGE 76 PORTFOLIO WITHDRAWAL (INCOME) SIMULATION

Income	Utility Weighting Factor		1			
	Initial Income (Year Zero)	Percentile of Distribution of Withdrawal Amounts	Projected Snapshot Income in 5 Years	Projected Snapshot Income in 10 Years	Projected Snapshot Income in 15 Years	Projected Income in Final Year of Simulation
Threshold Monthly Income	$90,000	50th	$7,646	$6,117	$6,117	$6,117
$7,500	Plus 1+ Inflation	40th	$7,646	$6,117	$6,117	$6,117
No Inflation Adjustment		30th	$7,646	$6,117	$6,117	$6,117
$7,646		10th	$6,117	$6,117	$6,117	$6,117
		5th	$6,117	$6,117	$6,117	$5,840
Projected Aggregate Income to Snapshot Date		50th	$432,536	$879,539	$1,277,443	$1,355,771
		40th	$428,397	$860,493	$1,248,560	$1,239,214
		30th	$422,875	$831,953	$1,214,237	$1,120,759
		10th	$387,505	$759,836	$1,134,963	$741,920
		5th	$368,672	$739,003	$1,110,991	$564,280
Probability Monthly Income ever less than $7,500		7.70%				
Adjusted for Inflation						

Target Monthly Income	$120,000	50th	$10,195	$8,156	$8,156	$8,156
$10,000	Plus 1+ Inflation	40th	$10,195	$8,156	$8,156	$8,156
No Inflation Adjustment		30th	$10,195	$8,156	$8,156	$8,156
$10,195		10th	$8,156	$8,156	$8,156	$6,948
		5th	$8,156	$8,156	$4,954	$3,691
Projected Aggregate Income to Snapshot Date		50th	$576,794	$1,171,583	$1,685,468	$1,734,778
		40th	$571,445	$1,145,935	$1,642,178	$1,585,321
		30th	$564,413	$1,105,671	$1,594,323	$1,424,246
		10th	$517,003	$1,011,335	$1,482,449	$975,964
		5th	$492,023	$983,730	$1,428,046	$746,229
Probability Monthly Income ever less than $7,500		11.50%				
Adjusted for Inflation						
Aspirationl Monthly Income	$150,000	50th	$12,744	$10,195	$10,195	$10,195
$12,5000	Plus 1+ Inflation	40th	$12,744	$10,195	$10,195	$10,195
Adjusted for Inflation		30th	$12,744	$10,195	$10,195	$10,195
$12,743		10th	$10,195	$10,195	$6,529	$5,062
		5th	$10,195	$10,195	$3,242	$2,682
Projected Aggregate Income to Snapshot Date		50th	$721,377	$1,462,250	$2,083,335	$2,073,171
		40th	$714,300	$1,424,419	$2,019,980	$1,894,311
		30th	$704,951	$1,373,007	$1,953,751	$1,696,613
		10th	$647,082	$1,255,347	$1,745,535	$1,181,085
		5th	$617,009	$1,219,717	$1,474,591	$929,322
Probability Monthly Income ever less than $7,500		22.10%				
Adjusted for Inflation						
Total Distribution Annuity Cost [Actuarial Feasibility Boundary]	Threshold Income	$1,561,599				
	Target Income	$2,084,899				
	Aspirational Income	$2,597,389				

The advisor notes that the current portfolio value ($2,327,000) exceeds the lower bound (feasibility risk metric) at both the threshold- and target-lifetime income levels. Indeed, the current value is closing in on the lower-bound for the aspirational level income ($2,597,389) as well. From the income perspective the financial health of the portfolio has improved.

The advisor next checks the portfolio from the wealth perspective (see templates 13.3 and 13.4):

TEMPLATE 13.3: AGE 76 PORTFOLIO RISK METRICS

CASE STUDY 11 [INITIAL SIMULATION: MARKET AGNOSTIC] DATA BASED ON 10,000 TRIALS

Current Portfolio Value	$2,277,000
Risk Metrics	**Target Income: $10,195**
Likelihood Portfolio < $509,750 Adjusted for Inflation	21.50%
Likelihood Portfolio < 15% in first 12-months	10.00%
Likelihood Portfolio < 20% in any 12-months	62.80%
Likelihood Portfolio < 40% Peak to Trough	43.10%
Actuarial Feasibility Boundary	
Threshold Income	$1,561,599
Target Income	$2,084,899
Aspirational Income	$2,597,389
Surplus (Retirement Security—50th Percentile)	
Threshold Income	$715,401
Target Income	$192,101
Aspirational Income	(-$320,389)

TEMPLATE 13.4: AGE 76 PORTFOLIO VALUE (WEALTH) SIMULATION

Wealth		Bequest Weighting Factor		0.25	
	Percentile Distribution of Portfolio Value	Projected Portfolio Value in 5 Years	Projected Portfolio Value in 10 Years	Projected Portfolio Value in 15 Years	Projected Portfolio Value in Final Year of Simulation
Projected Portfolio Value	50th	$2,498,529	$2,590,513	$2,650,655	$2,689,321
$7,646	40th	$2,252,819	$2,102,668	$1,968,713	$2,010,763
	30th	$1,983,583	$1,665,671	$1,411,266	$1,449,004
	10th	$1,329,953	$893,002	$511,146	$393,284
	5th	$1,124,124	$666,483	$272,474	$46,052
Projected Portfolio Value	50th	$2,318,518	$2,172,568	$1,993,980	$1,972,774
$10,195	40th	$2,109,095	$1,792,754	$1,489,414	$1,457,351
	30th	$1,867,146	$1,416,699	$1,018,577	$964,335
	10th	$1,187,969	$576,730	$45,628	$0
	5th	$911,370	$303,741	$0	$0

Projected Portfolio Value	50th	$2,172,519	$1,819,631	$1,416,653	$1,411,220
$12,743	40th	$1,955,795	$1,470,118	$924,402	$880,005
	30th	$1,720,021	$1,100,569	$516,523	$396,087
	10th	$1,046,834	$328,182	$0	$0
	5th	$800,115	$60,783	$0	$0
Life Remaining at Depletion: $7,646	50th	4			
Percentage of Portfolios Depleted	40th	4			
4.50%	30th	5			
	10th	9			
	5th	11			
Life Remaining at Depletion: $10,195	50th	5			
Percentage of Portfolios Depleted	40th	6			
12.20%	30th	7			
	10th	11			
	5th	14			
Life Remaining at Depletion: $12,743	50th	5			
Percentage of Portfolios Depleted	40th	6			
22.10%	30th	8			
	10th	12			
	5th	14			
Likelihood of Assets < $509,750 Adjusted for Inflation					
$7,646 per Month		0.00%	2.10%	7.70%	12.20%
$10,195 per Month		0.60%	8.20%	15.70%	21.50%
$12,743 per Month		1.20%	13.20%	25.10%	32.60%
Likelihood Portfolio < 15% in first 12-months					
$7,646 per Month		9.60%	9.60%	9.60%	9.60%
$10,195 per Month		10.90%	10.90%	10.90%	10.90%
$12,743 per Month		12.10%	12.10%	12.10%	12.10%
Likelihood Portfolio < 20% in any 12-months					
$7,646 per Month		26.60%	47.60%	60.80%	67.70%
$10,195 per Month		28.60%	46.50%	56.70%	62.80%
$12,743 per Month		30.90%	50.70%	61.60%	67.20%

Likelihood Portfolio < 40% Peak to Trough					
$7,646 per Month		9.10%	25.30%	36.60%	44.60%
$10,195 per Month		13.10%	28.00%	37.10%	43.10%
$12,743 per Month		16.10%	34.60%	45.30%	51.60%
$7,646 Projected Surplus (+ / −)	50th	$1,356,452	$1,853,730	$2,205,581	$2,687,275
[Projected Portfolio Value –	40th	$1,107,921	$1,385,056	$1,528,098	$2,009,677
Total Distribution Annuity Cost]	30th	$835,585	$939,234	$969,313	$1,448,863
	10th	$160,988	$139,334	$49,328	$391,151
	5th	(-$71,000)	(-$104,581)	(-$192,666)	$44,865
$10,195 Projected Surplus (+ / −)	50th	$792,733	$1,199,276	$1,392,688	$1,971,525
[Projected Portfolio Value –	40th	$566,236	$827,731	$905,361	$1,457,351
Total Distribution Annuity Cost]	30th	$315,170	$446,487	$405,293	$964,167
	10th	(-$387,929)	(-$412,364)	(-$537,776)	(-$416,795)
	5th	(-$678,962)	(-$742,579)	(-$874,500)	(-$725,618)
$12,743 Projected Surplus (+ / −)	50th	$282,967	$623,977	$673,668	$1,409,887
[Projected Portfolio Value –	40th	$36,955	$235,558	$189,312	$879,417
Total Distribution Annuity Cost]	30th	(-$225,024)	(-$120,355)	(-$227,668)	(-$396,087)
	10th	(-$936,044)	(-$955,932)	(-$1,086,976)	(-$918,729)
	5th	(-$1,235,176)	(-$1,291,712)	(-$1,418,114)	(-$1,288,287)
Utility-Adjusted Aggregate Spending + Bequest	50th	$1,057,168	$1,527,167	$1,940,107	$2,028,101
$7,646 per Month	40th	$991,602	$1,386,160	$1,740,738	$1,741,905
	30th	$918,771	$1,248,371	$1,567,054	$1,483,010
	10th	$719,993	$983,087	$1,262,750	$840,241
	5th	$649,703	$905,624	$1,179,110	$575,793
Utility-Adjusted Aggregate Spending + Bequest	50th	$1,156,424	$1,714,725	$2,183,963	$2,227,972
$10,195 per Month	40th	$1,098,719	$1,594,124	$2,014,532	$1,949,659
	30th	$1,031,200	$1,459,846	$1,848,967	$1,665,330
	10th	$813,995	$1,155,518	$1,493,856	$975,964
	5th	$719,866	$1,059,665	$1,428,046	$746,229
Utility-Adjusted Aggregate Spending + Bequest	50th	$1,264,507	$1,917,158	$2,437,498	$2,425,976
$12,743 per Month	40th	$1,203,249	$1,791,949	$2,251,081	$2,114,312
	30th	$1,134,956	$1,648,149	$2,082,882	$1,795,635
	10th	$908.791	$1,337,393	$1,745,535	$1,181,085
	5th	$817,038	$1,234,914	$1,474,591	$929,322

AGE 76 ANALYSIS, DISCUSSION, AND DECISIONS

Risk metrics have either improved or remained steady. For example, the likelihood of failing to achieve an inflation-adjusted bequest objective of $509,750 has decreased from 28.5 percent to 21.5 percent assuming the target standard-of-living withdrawal level. Most striking, however, is the improvement in the feasibility metric's lower bound. It has become "cheaper" to finance life-long income (see figure 13.1):

FIGURE 13.1: CHANGE IN FEASIBILITY BOUNDARY—AGE 75 TO AGE 76

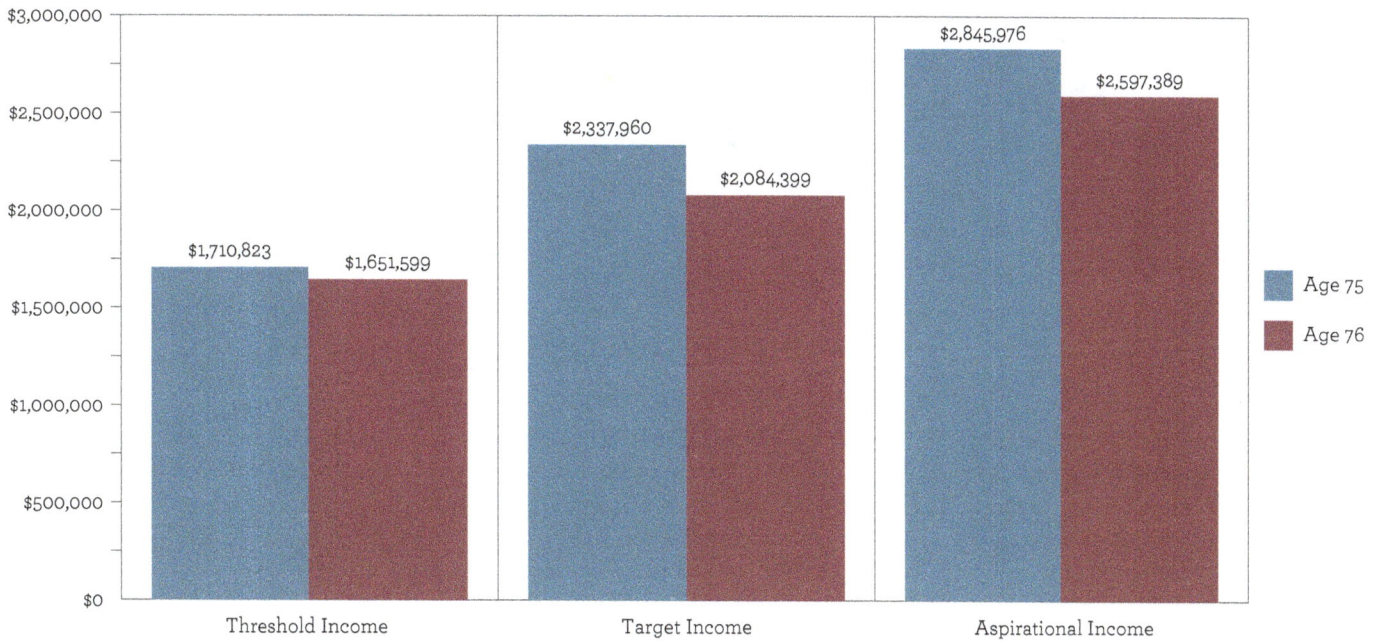

Over the past year, the interaction among mortality, inflation, investment returns, and interest rates has lowered the feasibility bounds. Both threshold and target income have current actuarial coverage ratio (ACR) values greater than one. In this type of high-dimensional context, the relevant metrics shift from "What was my investment return?" to "Given the interaction among variables of interest, am I likely to achieve my financial goals?" Figure 13.2 illustrates the improvement (from age 74 through 76) in the investors' retirement security (at the 50th percentile of the distribution of results):

FIGURE 13.2: SURPLUS (RETIREMENT SECURITY)

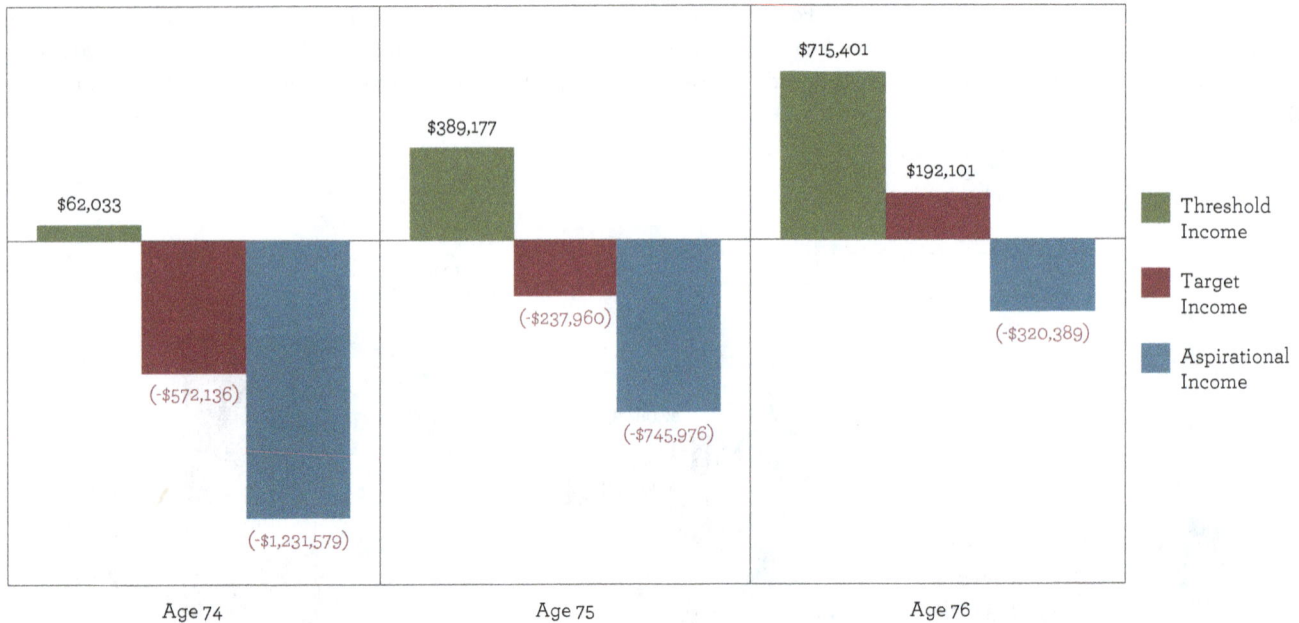

The question of interest is whether current output (no Consumer Price Index (CPI) adjustment for next four years/80-percent survivor benefit) indicates a stable upward trend for the ACR values.[1] At the 50th percentile, model output indicates both current feasibility and a steady upward ACR trajectory at the threshold and target standard-of-living income levels (see figure 13.3 and accompanying data table). However, the aspirational level continues to violate the feasibility condition and, not surprisingly, exhibits a downward slope at year 15. Ultimately, if the investors experience a long life span, the aspirational withdrawal level risks portfolio depletion.

DATA TABLE FOR FIGURE 13.3

Percentile	Income Level	0.0Y	2.3Y	4.8Y	7.1Y	9.5Y	11.9Y	14.2Y	16.7Y	19.0Y	21.4Y	23.8Y
50th	$7.5K 80% & No CPI	145.80%	171.80%	205.50%	265.10%	328.50%	404.80%	537.80%	644.50%	826.10%	966.10%	1099.10%
50th	$10K 80% & No CPI	109.20%	124.30%	142.70%	176.70%	207.30%	244.20%	302.80%	342.00%	395.50%	397.70%	397.10%
50th	$12.5K 80% & No CPI	(-87.70%)	(-97.00%)	107.80%	127.80%	141.50%	153.70%	178.60%	178.60%	162.80%	118.60%	(-39.40%)

---

1.   Each update of the dynamic asset management analysis produces a new set of initial conditions. Future ACR values are highly dependent on these initial conditions; therefore, ACR trajectories are inherently unstable—especially when surplus is close to the feasibility bound.

FIGURE 13.3: AGE 76 TRAJECTORY AT 50TH PERCENTILE

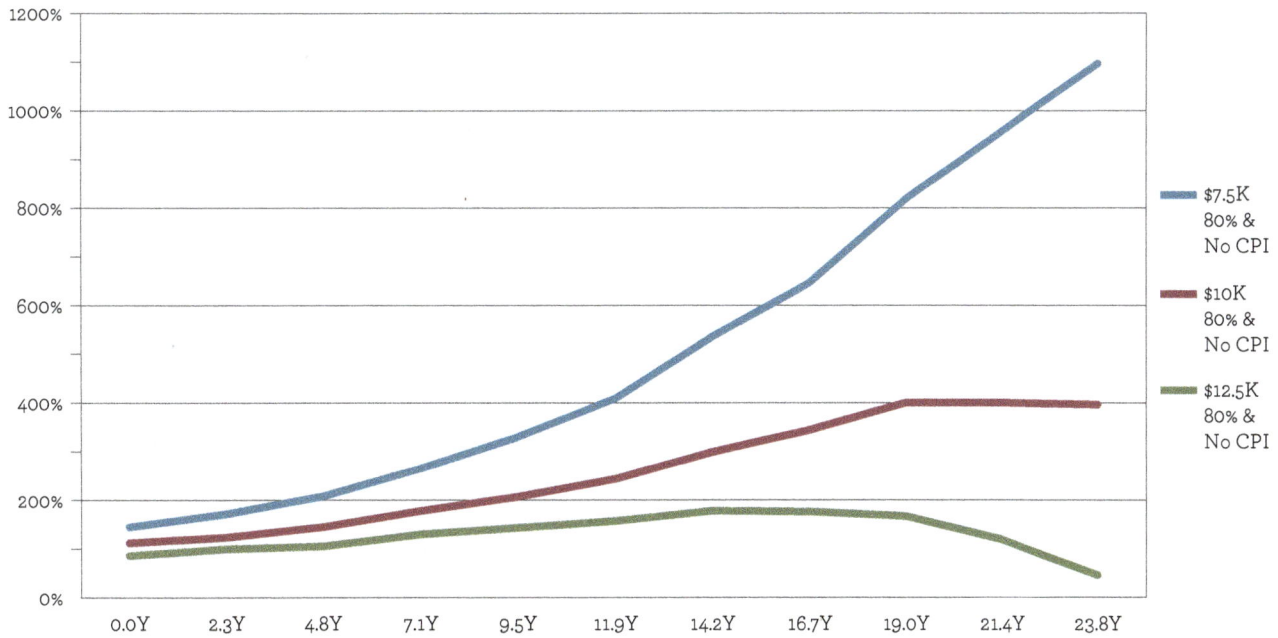

To test the sensitivity of the ACR values, the advisor reruns the analysis at the 40th percentile of the distribution of projected portfolio dollar values (see figure 13.4 and accompanying data table):

DATA TABLE FOR FIGURE 13.4

Percentile	Income Level	0.0Y	2.3Y	4.8Y	7.1Y	9.5Y	11.9Y	14.2Y	16.7Y	19.0Y	21.4Y	23.8Y
40th	$7.5K 80% & No CPI	142.10%	160.40%	182.80%	227.10%	267.30%	312.10%	396.60%	458.80%	541.90%	589.40%	608.90%
40th	$10K 80% & No CPI	106.50%	116.30%	132.00%	152.00%	171.90%	190.60%	228.70%	235.80%	248.60%	227.00%	165.70%
40th	$12.5K 80% & No CPI	(-85.40%)	(-90.30%)	(-96.20%)	108.10%	112.50%	113.00%	120.00%	(-95.90%)	(-59.50%)	(-0.00%)	(-0.00%)

FIGURE 13.4: AGE 76 TRAJECTORY AT 40TH PERCENTILE

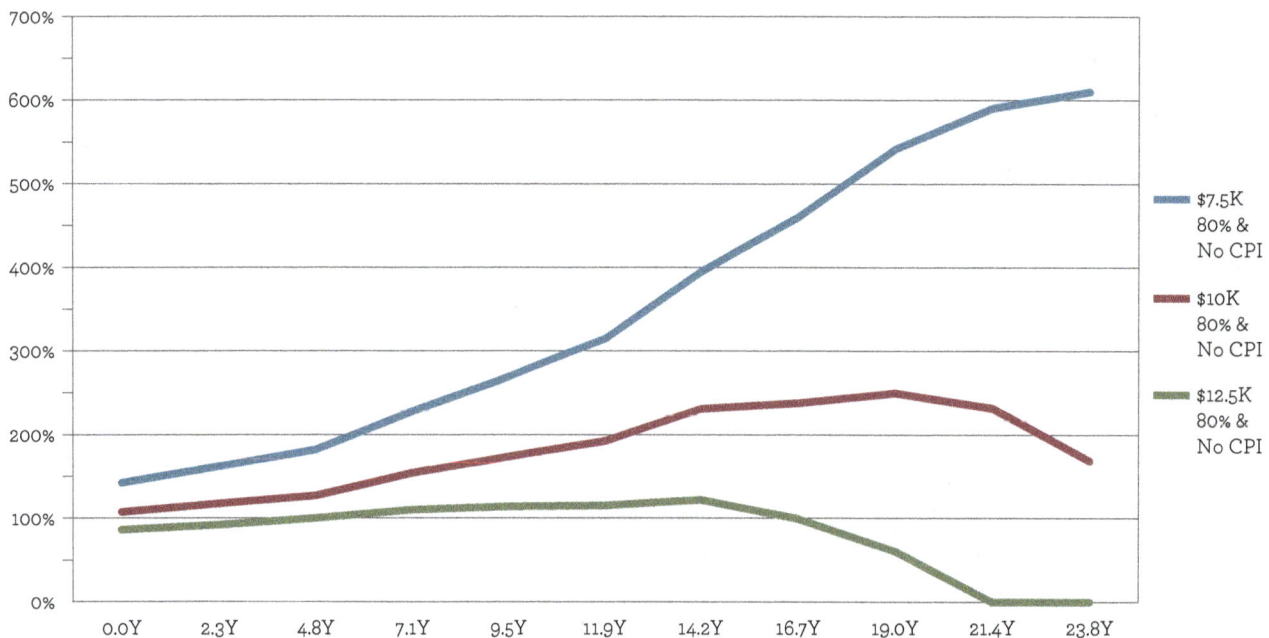

There are several messages here:

1. The aspirational level does not sustain itself for the long term.

2. Given current, i.e., initial, conditions, the threshold level maintains a steady upward trajectory throughout the planning horizon.

3. Although the target standard-of-living income level maintains an ACR above one, its slope changes from positive to negative at approximately year 19 and, therefore, may be subject to a rapid decline at a more advanced age.

At the 30th percentile of portfolio performance (data not shown), none of the income levels exhibits a long-term positive slope value, and both the target and aspirational withdrawal levels deplete the portfolio before the end of the planning horizon.

The investors are pleased with the improvements in the portfolio's profile. Although the advisor supplements the above analysis by illustrating the economic consequences of immediately restoring the elections to implement CPI adjustments and the survivor's percentage benefit level (data not shown), the investors decide to continue their present asset management track—at least for the near term.

SOME 'WHAT-IFS' AND A LOOK AHEAD

Space constraints (and reader attention span) prohibit replicating templates from every year throughout the investors' remaining life span. Rather, it is more productive (and interesting) to consider some hypothetical developments in future years.

A CHANGE IN HEALTH

Assume, at age 80, the wife receives a medical diagnosis that adversely affects the number of years she can expect to live. Heretofore, the model output assumed a force of mortality derived from the Society of Actuaries' table for high-income, white-collar retirees in good health. Following a discussion about the new, less-favorable medical status, the advisor changes model input by advancing the wife's age from 80 to 83. At this point in time, there is still considerable uncertainty about the medical prognosis, and, despite the undeniability of the bad news, there is still a hope-for-the-best attitude.

Although the five-year geometric sequence of inflation from age 75 through 79 produces an inflation factor of 13.89 percent for the period, the investors decided to forego inflation increases in their yearly income targets. However, from this point forward, they wish to restore the withdrawal policy election to incorporate inflation increases.[2] Current (age 80) portfolio value is $2,290,000. Inflation-adjusted withdrawal targets are $7,646, $10,195, and $12,743, respectively. The survivor benefit election receives careful consideration. The investors state that they would benefit from considering model output under both 80-percent and 100-percent benefit elections.

The advisor presents portfolio value projections at various income levels for both an 80-percent and 100-percent survivor benefit election. The first projection tracks model outcomes at the 50th percentile (figure 13.5 and accompanying data table).

DATA TABLE FOR FIGURE 13.5

	0.0Y	1.8Y	3.8Y	5.6Y	7.5Y	9.3Y	11.2Y	13.1Y	15.0Y	16.8Y	18.8Y
$7.5K 80% CPI	$2,090,000	$2,186,622	$2,228,531	$2,260,836	$2,267,134	$2,267,121	$2,332,392	$2,328,141	$2,436,072	$2,343,806	$2,502,830
$10K 80% CPI	$2,090,000	$2,122,762	$2,103,002	$2,061,055	$2,029,558	$1,945,472	$1,887,127	$1,772,821	$1,700,129	$1,515,253	$1,411,372
$12.5K 80% CPI	$2,090,000	$2,068,002	$1,992,002	$1,871,203	$1,745,313	$1,604,826	$1,452,255	$1,280,182	$1,064,881	$818,945	$581,330
$7.5K 100% CPI	$2,090,000	$2,170,084	$2,227,761	$2,213,032	$2,208,880	$2,181,284	$2,245,516	$2,222,453	$2,195,829	$2,051,101	$2,001,698
$10K 100% CPI	$2,090,000	$2,118,476	$2,093,742	$2,036,995	$1,965,472	$1,864,948	$1,789,900	$1,627,936	$1,502,357	$1,279,966	$1,012,002
$12.5K 100% CPI	$2,090,000	$2,058,611	$1,962,892	$1,829,517	$1,673,477	$1,479,525	$1,289,886	$1,041,120	$788,138	$468,283	$147,026
Survival %	100.00%	98.60%	94.70%	87.80%	76.20%	63.30%	48.40%	33.80%	22.00%	12.90%	6.50%

At each income level, the portfolio exhibits positive value throughout the planning horizon. The last row of the table indicates a 50-percent chance that one or both investors will remain alive until approximately 11.5 years, and a 22-percent chance that one or both investors will remain alive until approximately 15 years. The portfolio may have to generate adequate income over a long-term planning horizon, and it may be imprudent to reduce significantly the allocation to equity at this time.

---

2. They opt out of the election to catch up for some or all of previous years' inflation. One reason for their decision is that actual withdrawals in some years exceed the specified levels in the retirement-income model. This is one reason why it is important to track actual withdrawal history against model withdrawal assumptions.

FIGURE 13.5: PORTFOLIO VALUE 50TH PERCENTILE—80-PERCENT AND 100-PERCENT SURVIVOR BENEFIT

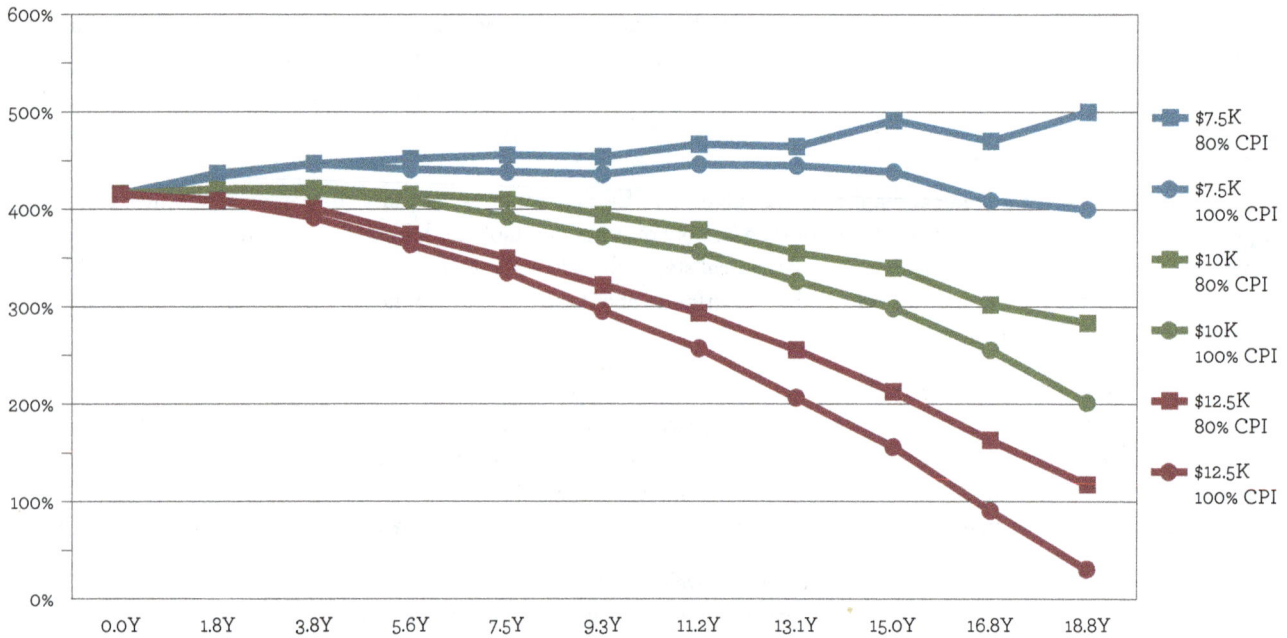

The downward trend in long-term portfolio value at the target- and aspirational income levels suggests that the investors' future financial security may be imperiled if inflation-adjusted portfolio values are too far below the model's median outcome. In order to gauge this sensitivity, the advisor checks results at the 40th percentile (see figure 13.6 and accompanying data table).

DATA TABLE FOR FIGURE 13.6

	0.0Y	1.8Y	3.8Y	5.6Y	7.5Y	9.3Y	11.2Y	13.1Y	15.0Y	16.8Y	18.8Y
$7.5K 80% CPI	$2,090,000	$2.084,592	$2,051,654	$2,006,962	$1,932,453	$1,865,290	$1,828,849	$1,790,412	$1,848,057	$1,643,811	$1,525,218
$10K 80% CPI	$2,090,000	$2,028,348	$1,937,538	$1,833,946	$1,736,742	$1,636,234	$1,494,264	$1,361,379	$1,258,633	$1,118,097	$961,413
$12.5K 80% CPI	$2,090,000	$1,974,594	$1,837,904	$1,652,978	$1,481,759	$1,292,617	$1,104,527	$882,033	$692,723	$423,022	$123,441
$7.5K 100% CPI	$2,090,000	$2,076,299	$2,040,544	$1,971,490	$1,882,942	$1,802,793	$1,752,797	$1,665,654	$1,564,999	$1,410,846	$1,290,117
$10K 100% CPI	$2,090,000	$2,021,812	$1,920,107	$1,786,295	$1,655,726	$1,511,157	$1,361,229	$1,179,389	$1,013,810	$753,634	$512,677
$12.5K 100% CPI	$2,090,000	$1,962,908	$1,791,343	$1,599,913	$1,368,005	$1,126,238	$903,362	$651,220	$375,773	$21,762	$0

FIGURE 13.6: PORTFOLIO VALUE 40TH PERCENTILE—80-PERCENT AND 100-PERCENT SURVIVOR BENEFIT

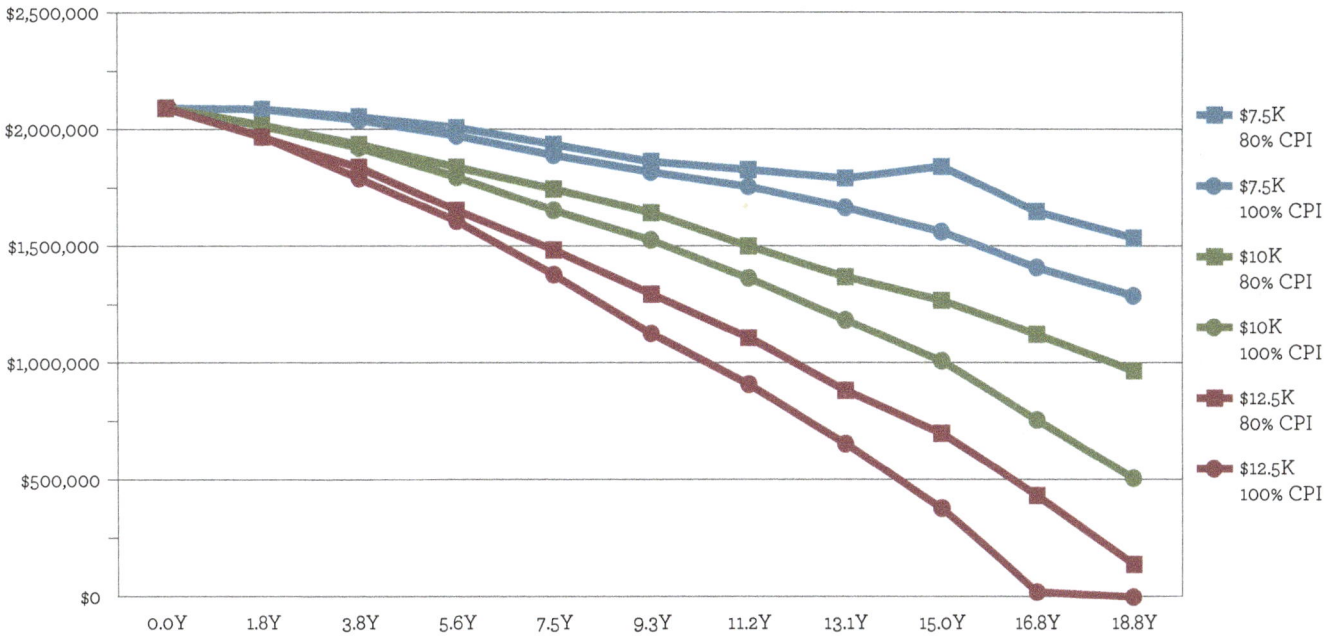

In this set of outcomes, the aspirational level at both 80-percent and 100-percent survivor income elections shows either depletion or perilously low value. If the investors choose to accelerate income to the aspirational level, the portfolio will continue to bear close monitoring.

Although, at some income levels, projected portfolio assets diminish substantially in later years, so, also, does the corresponding liability value, i.e., the amount required to fund lifetime income. The advisor checks the 40th-percentile portfolio value projections from the above table against the ACR values generated at the same percentile of outcomes (see table 13.1):

TABLE 13.1: PROJECTED ACR VALUES FOR ASSET MANAGEMENT ELECTIONS

	0.0Y	1.8Y	3.8Y	5.6Y	7.5Y	9.3Y	11.2Y	13.1Y	15.0Y	16.8Y	18.8Y
$7.5K 80% CPI	202.10%	222.10%	266.50%	318.10%	373.40%	433.50%	503.80%	562.60%	631.10%	615.10%	647.90%
$10K 80% CPI	151.70%	162.50%	188.40%	217.50%	250.90%	278.50%	303.50%	322.80%	328.80%	300.90%	275.20%
$12.5K 80% CPI	121.20%	126.10%	142.10%	156.70%	169.80%	177.00%	177.40%	165.10%	129.60%	71.50%	4.50%
$7.5K 100% CPI	180.10%	195.20%	229.00%	263.00%	301.60%	342.90%	386.70%	417.10%	431.50%	407.70%	415.80%
$10K 100% CPI	135.10%	142.60%	160.90%	179.70%	198.20%	212.70%	223.00%	217.90%	197.70%	150.10%	100.20%
$12.5K 100% CPI	108.10%	110.90%	119.90%	129.80%	131.70%	126.90%	115.90%	93.10%	52.10%	0.00%	0.00%

Not surprisingly, the aspirational-level income ACR values begin to exhibit negative slopes in approximately 10 to 12 years. The issue of late-in-life financial security remains—especially if current withdrawals place too much stress on the retirement-income portfolio. In order to quantify the likelihood and duration of this risk, the advisor generates the following data (see figure 13.7 and companion table).

DATA TABLE FOR FIGURE 13.7

	Percentile	$7.5K 80% CPI	$10K 80% CPI	$12.5K 80% CPI	$7.5K 100% CPI	$10K 100% CPI	$12.5K 100% CPI
Life Remaining at Depletion	50th	2	2	3	2	3	3
Life Remaining at Depletion	40th	3	3	4	3	4	4
Life Remaining at Depletion	30th	3	4	5	4	5	5
Life Remaining at Depletion	10th	6	7	8	6	8	8
Life Remaining at Depletion	5th	8	9	10	8	10	10
% Depleted		1.30%	5.60%	11.30%	2.70%	7.60%	15.20%

FIGURE 13.7: YEARS OF LIFE REMAINING AFTER DEPLETION

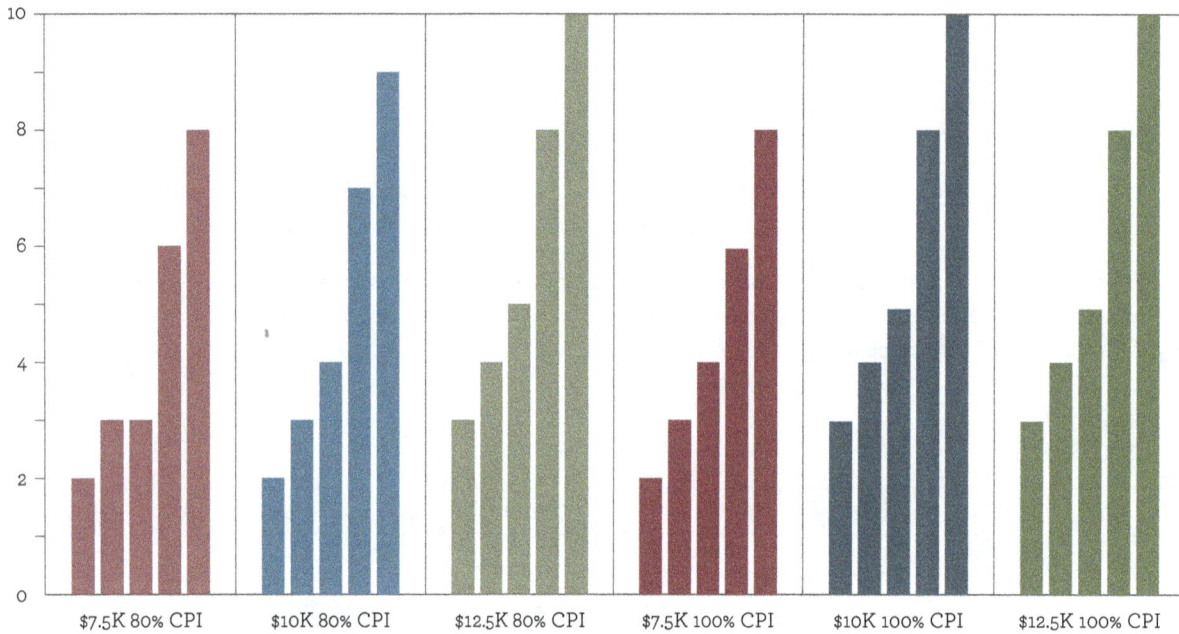

The target standard-of-living level has between a 5-percent and 8-percent likelihood of depletion (5.6 percent to 7.6 percent). Should depletion occur, the self-insurance liability funding period may last between two and 10 years.

NEW ASSET MANAGEMENT ELECTIONS

Following an in-depth discussion, the advisor realizes that the change in health status has increased the investors' propensity to consume—the utility of current income relative to future bequest amounts has increased.[3] This sets the stage for consideration of the following asset management elections:

1. Partial implementation of a reverse mortgage income stream, either currently or in the future, should the portfolio fail to produce the desired income.[4]

2. A decision to amortize projected future surplus in line with a prudent ACR target.

3. A change in withdrawal policy from a fixed, inflation-adjusted level amount to a front-loaded policy that grades down over time.

A model is not a financial plan. Rather, it provides guidance as to the feasibility, sustainability, and flexibility of the investors' forthcoming spending decisions.

The investors express interest in bringing some of the projected future surplus into the present. The advisor notes that projected surplus in seven and a half years at the 40th percentile of the distribution of portfolio value is $1,059,326 for the CPI-adjusted standard-of-living target income level with an 80-percent survivor benefit election, and $844,940 for the CPI-adjusted standard-of-living target income level with a 100-percent survivor benefit election.[5] If the investors implement a seven-year surplus amortization schedule to target a 1.25 ACR value, this releases an additional $7,918 monthly income throughout the seven-year period for the 80-percent survivor benefit election, and $5,846 for the 100-percent survivor benefit election.[6] If the investors implement a 10-year surplus amortization schedule, this releases an additional $5,202 monthly income throughout the 10-year period for the 80-percent survivor benefit election, and $3,664 for the 100-percent survivor benefit election. Given the potentially long planning horizon, targeting a five-year amortization schedule is probably too aggressive—the joint-expected-life span projection with the new mortality information is approximately 10 years.[7] The investors consider trade-offs between the higher extra seven-year-period money and the lower extra 10-year period money.

The advisor also models six front-loaded withdrawal strategies:

1. Initial monthly withdrawal of $13,000 grading down over five years to $8,000 per month at age 85 and thereafter. Withdrawals are adjusted for CPI with an 80-percent survivor benefit.

2. Initial monthly withdrawal of $13,000 grading down over five years to $8,000 per month at age 85 and thereafter. Withdrawals are adjusted for CPI with a 100-percent survivor benefit.

3. Initial monthly withdrawal of $14,000 grading down over five years to $9,000 per month at age 85 and thereafter. Withdrawals are adjusted for CPI with an 80-percent survivor benefit.

4. Initial monthly withdrawal of $14,000 grading down over five years to $9,000 per month at age 85 and thereafter. Withdrawals are adjusted for CPI with a 100-percent survivor benefit.

5. Initial monthly withdrawal of $16,000 grading down over five years to $11,000 per month at age 85 and thereafter. Withdrawals are adjusted for CPI with an 80-percent survivor benefit.

6. Initial monthly withdrawal of $16,000 grading down over five years to $11,000 per month at age 85 and thereafter. Withdrawals are adjusted for CPI with a 100-percent survivor benefit.

---

3. The advisor continues to track total utility, but, given the investors' revised preference for income, he changes the weighting factor for utility of wealth to 0.15. A change in health may decrease the demand for income if an investor's ability (or desire) for activities outside the home diminishes. Health changes make for a potentially fluid situation as time unfolds. If both spouses experience significant health changes, a low demand for current consumption can morph quickly into a high demand as home care and medical costs increase suddenly.

4. A reverse mortgage loan generally may take the form of a single disbursement, periodic income for a specified duration, or periodic lifetime income. Choice of loan timing, loan amounts, and loan type depend on age, interest rates (cost of the loan), investor circumstances, and a host of other factors. Reverse mortgage elections are outside the scope of the advisor's expertise and the client advisory engagement.

5. Data not shown.

6. If the portfolio results are below the 40th percentile, the withdrawal amounts will decrease, all else being equal, over time in order to maintain convergence to the 1.25 ACR target value; if results are above the 40th percentile, withdrawal amounts will increase. The amortization calculation indicates the initial withdrawal/contribution amount required to hit a future ACR target at a specified portfolio outcome percentile. This amount almost surely will change as the analysis is re-run periodically. As such, this withdrawal election is like a hybrid withdrawal policy where the inflation-adjusted base income remains fixed and the amortization of positive or negative surplus generates floating yearly income adjustments.

7. After 10 years, the actuarial cost of providing lifetime income (the denominator for the ACR calculation) drops quickly. Even if portfolio values decline, the denominator's actuarial costs decline at a rate that outdistances all but depression-economy investment results.

The trajectory of simulated future portfolio value at the 40th percentile of the distribution of outcomes is as follows (see table 13.2).

TABLE 13.2: PORTFOLIO VALUE, SPENDING, AND ASSET MANAGEMENT ELECTIONS

Withdrawal Policy Election	Portfolio Value	0.0Y	1.8Y	3.8Y	5.6Y	7.5Y	9.3Y	11.2Y	13.1Y	15.0Y	16.8Y	18.8Y
$13K to $8K 80% CPI	40th	$2,090,000	$1,948,045	$1,729,781	$1,513,442	$1,413,514	$1,326,722	$1,234,698	$1,121,125	$1,107,970	$950,299	$789,254
$13K to $8K 100% CPI	40th	$2,090,000	$1,942,321	$1,703,444	$1,466,726	$1,340,490	$1,221,275	$1,107,876	$957,642	$831,040	$647,396	$492,282
$14K to $9K 80% CPI	40th	$2,090,000	$1,928,594	$1,681,290	$1,457,340	$1,328,606	$1,204,907	$1,094,130	$946,951	$869,581	$616,041	$493,241
$14K to $9K 100% CPI	40th	$2,090,000	$1,913,669	$1,648,551	$1,381,098	$1,226,549	$1,091,530	$949,171	$748,769	$587,597	$382,286	$189,143
$16K to $11K 80% CPI	40th	$2,090,000	$1,877,865	$1,588,112	$1,308,239	$1,150,903	$979,014	$811,423	$604,147	$451,934	$208,172	$52,290
$16K to $11K 100% CPI	40th	$2,090,000	$1,867,345	$1,553,388	$1,231,023	$1,028,452	$820,430	$611,373	$385,549	$171,318	$0	$0

Each front-loaded withdrawal strategy sends the portfolio's value on a permanent downward trajectory. The investors ask the advisor to repost the survival projections so that they can better understand the risks of beginning a race between death and depletion. He presents the following survival information and withdrawal-strategy graph (see figure 13.8 and companion table).

FIGURE 13.8: AGE 80 FRONT-LOADED WITHDRAWALS—PORTFOLIO VALUE AT 40TH PERCENTILE

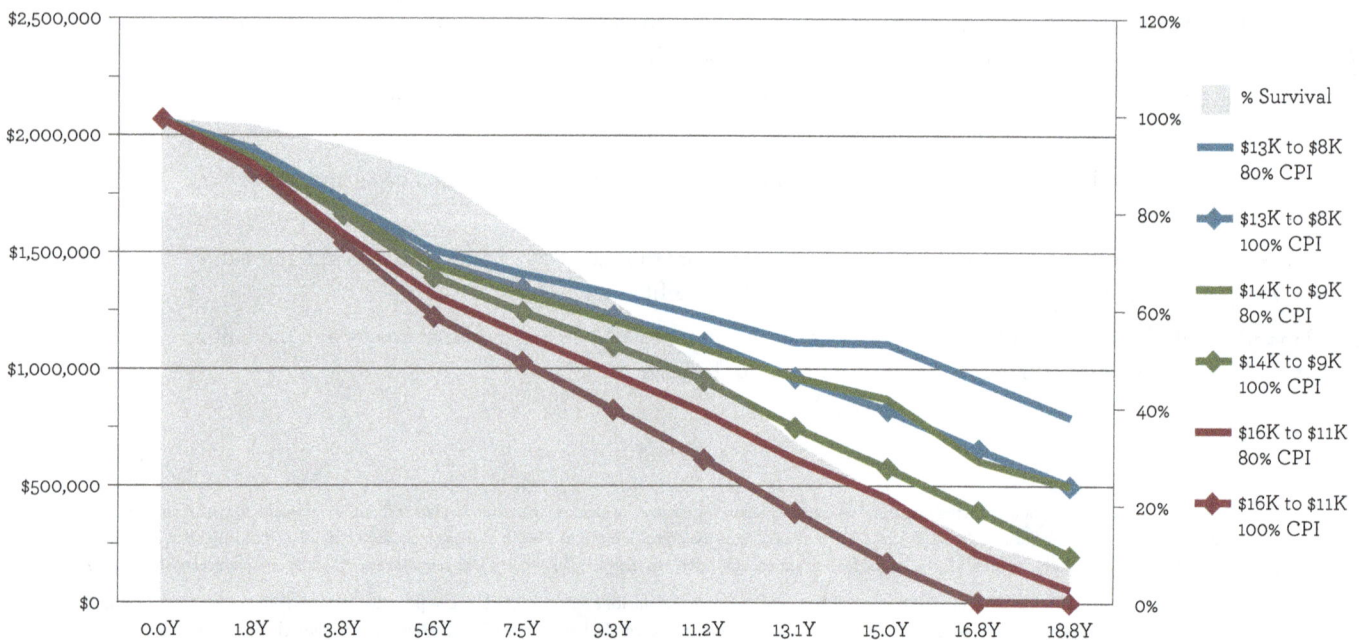

DATA TABLE FOR FIGURE 13.8

	0.0Y	1.8Y	3.8Y	5.6Y	7.5Y	9.3Y	11.2Y	13.1Y	15.0Y	16.8Y	18.8Y
% Survival	100.00%	98.60%	94.70%	87.80%	76.20%	63.30%	48.40%	33.80%	22.00%	12.90%	6.50%

The right-side axis records survival likelihood percentages; the left-side axis records constant-dollar portfolio values. Lines tracing the trajectory of portfolio value through time are marked with triangles for the 100-percent survivor benefit election. Lines without markers trace the trajectory of withdrawal amounts with an 80-percent survivor benefit election. The shaded area traces survival likelihood.

The investors readily see that the strategy calling for an initial $16,000-monthly withdrawal eventually fails to outrun mortality. The advisor reminds them that they are looking at the 40th percentile of the portfolio value outcome distribution, and with continued monitoring they can cut back on withdrawals in years two through five if it is prudent to do so. The strategy calling for an initial $13,000-monthly withdrawal projects a substantial cushion as age advances toward 100. The advisor reminds them that although this election is most likely to fulfill bequest objectives, the utility value of bequests is now quite low, and unspent wealth is a lost consumption opportunity. After a few minutes of additional Q&A, the investors tentatively conclude that they prefer a strategy calling for an initial $14,000 CPI-adjusted monthly withdrawal with an 80-percent survivor benefit. The advisor reinforces their conclusion by verifying the age 99 ACR values of the various withdrawal policy elections (see table 13.3).

TABLE 13.3: AGE 99 ACR PROJECTIONS AT THE 40TH PERCENTILE

Withdrawal Policy Election	ACR Value: 40th Percentile	18.8Y
$13K to $8K 80% CPI	Total Distribution Annuity Coverage	277.20%
$13K to $8K 100% CPI	Total Distribution Annuity Coverage	120.00%
$14K to $9K 80% CPI	Total Distribution Annuity Coverage	141.00%
$14K to $9K 100% CPI	Total Distribution Annuity Coverage	23.20%
$16K to $11K 80% CPI	Total Distribution Annuity Coverage	0.00%
$16K to $11K 100% CPI	Total Distribution Annuity Coverage	0.00%

At the 40th percentile, only the first $13,000 withdrawal election exhibits a higher long-term ACR value, and only two elections project an ACR value greater than 1.25. The advisor tests their preference by graphically depicting surplus in figure 13.9—positive or negative—generated by the various withdrawal elections at the end of the simulation (death of the surviving spouse).

FIGURE 13.9: PROJECTED SURPLUS AND SPENDING ELECTIONS

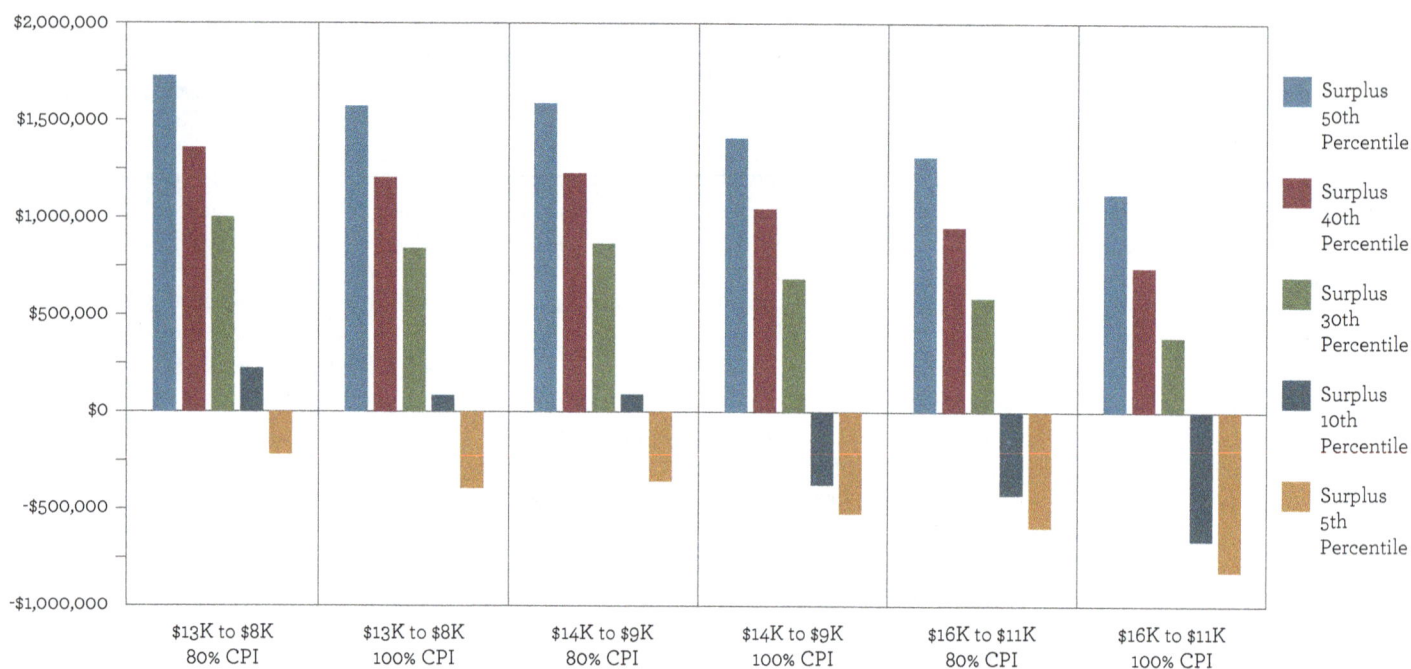

The investors are pleased to see that the initial $14,000 constant-dollar withdrawal strategy, combined with an 80-percent survivor benefit election, produces end-of-simulation surplus even at the 10th percentile of outcomes.

The question is whether the "amortization-of-projected-surplus" or the "front-loaded-withdrawal" option is the most appropriate portfolio management election. The investors weigh the 10-year/80-percent amortization program that releases an additional $5,202 monthly income throughout the period. This will provide, at the 40th percentile of portfolio value outcomes, an income of $15,397 ($10,195 + $5,202). This compares to their preferred front-loaded withdrawal strategy (also with an 80-percent survivor benefit) that provides an initial monthly income of $14,000 grading down over five years to $9,000. These are precisely the spending guidelines that the investors need. Even if they fail to adhere scrupulously to the specified withdrawal amounts, the projections provide upper-bound values beyond which spending would not be prudent given the current state of the portfolio.

A BEAR MARKET: AGE 80

Among the hypothetical events that may unfold in the investors' future, is the onset of another bear market. What might a dynamic portfolio monitoring, evaluation, and decision-making process look like under a bear market regime?[8] What asset management elections might be appropriate to consider?

Under a start-bear-market assumption, the retirement-income model generates outputs for withdrawal policies specifying threshold, target, and aspirational income levels. The templates set up a tracking structure for fixed, constant-dollar withdrawals under an 80-percent survivor benefit election. The investors' subjective expectation (fear?) of a forthcoming bear market diminishes the motivation for electing front-loaded withdrawal policies. The advisor changes the utility of wealth value from 0.25 to 0.15; current interest rates are unchanged (templates 13.5 and 13.6).

---

8.   Investment management decisions must be made under conditions of uncertainty brought about by interactions among "the investor's financial circumstances" and "the state of the economy." But there is also an important second-order element: "The investor's personal belief state about his or her financial circumstances and the state of the economy." Chapter Sixteen provides a further discussion of these topics.

TEMPLATE 13.5: AGE 80 CLIENT CIRCUMSTANCES—BEAR MARKET

Current Age Male	Health Status	Current Age Female	Health Status
80	Good (5)	80	Fair (2)
Approximate Joint Life Expectancy			10.8 years
Current Portfolio Value			$2,090,000
Macro Asset Allocation Election			60% Stock / 40% Bond
Precautionary Investment Reserve Value			N/A
Asset Management Elections			
Portfolio Strategy			Constant Mix
Withdrawal Strategy			Fixed Amount Adjusted for Inflation
Survivorship Income Election			80%
Rebalance to Target?			Yes
Rebalance to % Allocation different than Target?			No
△ Income (Withdrawal) Target?			No
Amortize (±) to ACR Target?			No
Forego Income Inflation Adjustment?			No
Interest Rate Data for ACR Calculation			
Freddie Mac 5 Year ARM			3.31%
Freddie Mac 15 Year Fixed			4.54%
Realized Inflation			2.89%
Income Targets (CPI)			
Threshold			$93,764
Target			$125,019
Aspirational			$156,274
Actual Spending Previous Year			$128,200

TEMPLATE 13.6: AGE 80 PORTFOLIO WITHDRAWAL (INCOME) SIMULATION—BEAR MARKET

Income	Utility Weighting Factor		1			
	Initial Income (Year Zero)	Percentile of Distribution of Withdrawal Amounts	Projected Snapshot Income in 5 Years	Projected Snapshot Income in 10 Years	Projected Snapshot Income in 15 Years	Projected Income in Final Year of Simulation
Threshold Monthly Income	$90,000	50th	$6,117	$6,117	$6,117	$6,117
$7,500	Plus 1+ Inflation	40th	$6,117	$6,117	$6,117	$6,117
No Inflation Adjustment		30th	$6,117	$6,117	$6,117	$6,117
$7,646		10th	$6,117	$6,117	$6,117	$6,117
		5th	$6,117	$6,117	$6,117	$6,117
Projected Aggregate Income to Snapshot Date		50th	$457,246	$841,088	$1,211,166	$896,140
		40th	$438,895	$821,207	$1,188,227	$792,152
		30th	$422,073	$801,327	$1,166,818	$680,516
		10th	$385,371	$756,979	$1,119,411	$402,193
		5th	$376,196	$744,745	$1,107,177	$290,558
Probability Monthly Income ever less than $7,500		8.00%				
Adjusted for Inflation						
Target Monthly Income	$120,000	50th	$8,156	$8,156	$8,156	$8,156
$10,000	Plus 1+ Inflation	40th	$8,156	$8,156	$8,156	$8,156
No Inflation Adjustment		30th	$8,156	$8,156	$8,156	$8,156
$10,195		10th	$8,156	$8,156	$3,598	$6,653
		5th	$8,156	$8,156	$2,023	$3,418
Projected Aggregate Income to Snapshot Date		50th	$609,661	$1,111,255	$1,578,186	$1,137,762
		40th	$585,193	$1,084,748	$1,543,523	$1,018,876
		30th	$562,764	$1,056,202	$1,504,782	$893,082
		10th	$513,828	$999,110	$1,197,526	$536,257
		5th	$501,594	$984,837	$1,025,124	$387,410
Probability Monthly Income ever less than $7,500		13,40%				
Adjusted for Inflation						

Aspiration Monthly Income	$150,000	50th	$10,195	$10,195	$10,195	$10,195
$12,5000	Plus 1+ Inflation	40th	$10,195	$10,195	$10,148	$10,195
Adjusted for Inflation		30th	$10,195	$10,195	$7,840	$10,195
$12,743		10th	$10,195	$6,875	$2,211	$4,404
		5th	$10,195	$3,070	$989	$2,133
Projected Aggregate Income to Snapshot Date		50th	$762,076	$1,371,228	$1,914,111	$1,349,561
		40th	$731,491	$1,335,545	$1,859,434	$1,210,656
		30th	$703,455	$1,299,862	$1,725,252	$1,076,759
		10th	$642,285	$1,224,495	$1,229,146	$670,321
		5th	$626,992	$1,109,189	$1,084,604	$484,262
Probability Monthly Income ever less than $7,500		23.70%				
Adjusted for Inflation						
Total Distribution Annuity Cost [Actuarial Feasibility Boundary]	Threshold Income	$1,023,125				
	Target Income	$1,365,106				
	Aspirational Income	$1,704,917				

The portfolio currently lies above the feasibility bound for each income level. This is good news and, as the model moves the capital markets into a bear-market state, the advisor is interested in how well it will fare in the forthcoming years. The model's reduction of yearly projected income to the 80-percent survivorship benefit level indicates that there is a better-than-even chance (> 50th percentile) that one of the investors will fail to survive over the next five-year period. This is an important piece of information because it suggests that a re-structured set of templates may be needed in the near future in order to track the evolution of a portfolio designed to support retirement income for a single investor (templates 13.7 and 13.8).[9]

9. This information is also a prelude to a potentially difficult discussion with the investors. This subject area often presents itself whenever there is a change in the number of dependents (current income beneficiaries), a change in health status or survival expectations, or a change in family status. For example, an investor who marries at an older age may suddenly find that former withdrawal levels are unlikely to be supportable throughout a joint life span.

CASE STUDY 11 [INITIAL SIMULATION: BEAR MARKET] DATA BASED ON 10,000 TRIALS

Current Portfolio Value	$2,090,000
Risk Metrics	**Target Income: $10,195**
Likelihood Portfolio < $509,750 Adjusted for Inflation	28.50%
Likelihood Portfolio < 15% in first 12-months	49.30%
Likelihood Portfolio < 20% in any 12-months	70.80%
Likelihood Portfolio < 40% Peak to Trough	50.40%
Actuarial Feasibility Boundary	
Threshold Income	$1,023,125
Target Income	$1,365,106
Aspirational Income	$1,704,917
Surplus (Retirement Security—50th Percentile)	
Threshold Income	$1,066,875
Target Income	$724,894
Aspirational Income	$385,083

The corresponding wealth-oriented output is as follows (see template 13.8):

TEMPLATE 13.8: AGE 80 SURVIVING INVESTOR PORTFOLIO VALUE (WEALTH) SIMULATION—BEAR MARKET

Wealth		Bequest Weighting Factor		0.15	
	Percentile Distribution of Portfolio Value	Projected Portfolio Value in 5 Years	Projected Portfolio Value in 10 Years	Projected Portfolio Value in 15 Years	Projected Portfolio Value in Final Year of Simulation
Projected Portfolio Value	50th	$1,578,806	$1,413,907	$1,250,404	$1,476,533
$7,646	40th	$1,396,541	$1,139,208	$902,408	$1,194,537
	30th	$1,219,196	$909,979	$607,382	$922,136
	10th	$884,579	$485,191	$120,078	$352,831
	5th	$776,456	$351,641	$0	$123,749
Projected Portfolio Value	50th	$1,447,426	$1,126,433	$740,806	$1,167,797
$10,195	40th	$1,258,477	$860,202	$416,614	$873,040
	30th	$1,061,677	$614,044	$134,284	$567,582
	10th	$619,793	$88,565	$0	$0
	5th	$492,583	$0	$0	$0

Projected Portfolio Value	50th	$1,298,141	$786,116	$215,260	$812,498
$12,743	40th	$1,101,726	$535,446	$0	$518,702
	30th	$919,982	$305,357	$0	$213,148
	10th	$508,389	$0	$0	$0
	5th	$388,436	$0	$0	$0
Life Remaining at Depletion: $7,646	50th	2			
Percentage of Portfolios Depleted	40th	3			
3.20%	30th	4			
	10th	6			
	5th	8			
Life Remaining at Depletion: $10,195	50th	3			
Percentage of Portfolios Depleted	40th	4			
13.40%	30th	5			
	10th	9			
	5th	10			
Life Remaining at Depletion: $12,743	50th	4			
Percentage of Portfolios Depleted	40th	5			
23.70%	30th	6			
	10th	9			
	5th	11			
Likelihood of Assets < $509,750 Adjusted for Inflation					
$7,646 per Month		0.10%	8.00%	13.80%	15.10%
$10,195 per Month		5.20%	20.40%	27.10%	28.50%
$12,743 per Month		8.90%	30.70%	38.50%	39.80%
Likelihood Portfolio < 15% in first 12-months					
$7,646 per Month		44.70%	44.70%	44.70%	44.70%
$10,195 per Month		49.30%	49.30%	49.30%	49.30%
$12,743 per Month		53.90%	53.90%	53.90%	53.90%
Likelihood Portfolio < 20% in any 12-months					
$7,646 per Month		49.60%	61.10%	65.80%	66.80%
$10,195 per Month		57.00%	66.00%	69.40%	70.20%
$12,743 per Month		60.90%	70.20%	73.70%	74.50%

Likelihood Portfolio < 40% Peak to Trough					
$7,646 per Month		22.40%	34.40%	39.50%	41.20%
$10,195 per Month		33.50%	44.70%	49.20%	50.40%
$12,743 per Month		40.60%	54.10%	58.80%	59.80%
$7,646 Projected Surplus (+ / −)	50th	$958,350	$1,041,858	$999,501	$1,476,533
[Projected Portfolio Value –	40th	$768,489	$758,457	$640,422	$1,194,537
Total Distribution Annuity Cost]	30th	$602,716	$528,312	$354,432	$922,136
	10th	$219,179	$98,720	(-$135,929)	$352,831
	5th	$79,415	(-$50,073)	(-$268,974)	$123,749
$10,195 Projected Surplus (+ / −)	50th	$620,655	$631,454	$401,718	$1,167,797
[Projected Portfolio Value –	40th	$408,797	$352,689	$83,472	$873,040
Total Distribution Annuity Cost]	30th	$213,209	$104,821	(-$201,791)	$567,582
	10th	(-$254,539)	(-$424,853)	(-$540,032)	(-$379,700)
	5th	(-$435,337)	(-$596,095)	(-$698,044)	(-$535,424)
$12,743 Projected Surplus (+ / −)	50th	$264,441	$164,611	(-$203,956)	$812,498
[Projected Portfolio Value –	40th	$56,680	(-$96,011)	(-$422,418)	$518,702
Total Distribution Annuity Cost]	30th	(-$138,491)	(-$330,282)	(-$543,235)	$213,148
	10th	(-$612,469)	(-$775,215)	(-$853,966)	(-$679,704)
	5th	(-$796,964)	(-$990,200)	(-$1,020,089)	(-$871,296)
Utility-Adjusted Aggregate Spending + Bequest	50th	$694,067	$1,053,174	$1,398,727	$1,117,620
$7,646 per Month	40th	$648,376	$992,088	$1,323,588	$971,333
	30th	$604,952	$937,824	$1,257,925	$818,836
	10th	$518,058	$829,758	$1,137,423	$455,118
	5th	$492,664	$797,491	$1,107,177	$309,120
Utility-Adjusted Aggregate Spending + Bequest	50th	$826,775	$1,280,220	$1,689,307	$1,312,932
$10,195 per Month	40th	$773,965	$1,213,778	$1,606,015	$1,149,832
	30th	$722,016	$1,148,309	$1,524,925	$978,219
	10th	$606,797	$1,012,395	$1,197,526	$536,257
	5th	$575,481	$984,837	$1,025,124	$387,410
Utility-Adjusted Aggregate Spending + Bequest	50th	$956,797	$1,489,145	$1,946,400	$1,471,436
$12,743 per Month	40th	$896,750	$1,415,862	$1,859,434	$1,288,461
	30th	$841,452	$1,345,666	$1,725,252	$1,108,731
	10th	$720,043	$1,224,495	$1,229,146	$670,321
	5th	$685,257	$1,109,189	$1,084,604	$484,262

Not surprisingly, the onset of a bear market creates several risk metrics with unfavorable values. A bear market reestablishes the grim race between death and capital market performance.[10] At the race's start time (age 80) however, the investors' financial state may not be too onerous:

- The feasibility criterion is met at all standard-of-living withdrawal levels
- For all withdrawal levels, model output indicates positive portfolio values at the end-of-simulation date at or above the 30th percentile of the distribution of portfolio results, i.e., portfolios evidence sustainability
- For all withdrawal levels, the current surplus (security) is positive, and remains positive through the end-of-simulation date for withdrawal levels through the 30th percentile of results

It appears that, in some cases, the investors may experience financial difficulty only for life spans in excess of age 95 given the immediate onset of bear-market conditions.

The decrease in the utility value of terminal wealth relative to current income reinforces the attraction of consuming at the aspirational income level. Despite the looming onset of a bear market, this might be prudent if the investment portfolio is monitored closely and if the investors are willing to exhibit flexibility in their future withdrawal amounts. Although the life remaining at depletion output indicates a rather low portfolio bankruptcy likelihood for the threshold and target income levels (3.20 percent and 13.40 percent, respectively), there is an approximately one-in-four chance (23.70 percent) of outliving the portfolio if the investors withdraw the inflation-adjusted aspirational income level on an auto-pilot basis. Should the portfolio fail to provide lifetime income, the model quantifies the bear market's distribution of time-alive-and-broke outcomes, i.e., the conditional self-funding liability.

In the face of longevity risk and a pessimistic market viewpoint, how much is it safe to spend given the investors' current circumstances and personal goals? If the investors wish to keep the pedal-to-the-metal for current income, the advisor wants to analyze the extent to which current and future surplus projections provide financial flexibility. Targeting a 10-year amortization of surplus schedule, the model indicates that maintaining a 1.25 target ACR value at the 40th percentile of portfolio results will initially release the following monthly amounts:

- $7,646 constant-dollar threshold with 80-percent survivor benefit: $3,808 over the projected 10-year period
- $10,195 constant-dollar threshold with 80-percent survivor benefit: $1,793 over the projected 10-year period
- $12,743 constant-dollar threshold with 80-percent survivor benefit: –$131 over the projected 10-year period

Thus, adjusting current spending for future portfolio surplus projections indicates a maximum feasible monthly current total withdrawal amount in the neighborhood of $12,000.[11] The amount derives from model inputs assuming immediate onset of a bear market, and appears to be a viable strategy through the 30th percentile of the distribution of investment results.

---

10. Further aspects of this race are discussed in Chapter Fourteen.

11. Average of monthly standard-of-living income levels plus extra monthly funds released or needed to amortize to a designated 1.25 ACR value (data not shown). To reiterate, the feasible monthly withdrawal amount changes each year as the advisor generates updated retirement-income-model output. Thus, the next year's discussion must consider the output for a 10-year amortization of portfolio surplus at the investors' joint age 81. The model sequentially projects the surplus value 10 years into the future and revises the withdrawal amount to maintain the percentile/ACR value targets on a rolling 10-year time frame. A 1.25 ACR target is consistently maintained throughout the planning horizon. At more advanced ages, the advisor will elect to use seven-year or five-year amortization horizons. As a further note, the retirement-income model accommodates use of a pre-funded investment reserve strategy. For example, an investor may elect to prefund two or three years of income in a money market account. Each year, depending on investment results, the annual designated income amount is withdrawn from the money market; and, concurrently, an appropriate/prudent amount is withdrawn from the investment portfolio to replenish the pre-funded reserve in whole, or in part. If it is a good investment year, the money market may be funded with more money than scheduled; if it is a bad year, the account may be funded with a lower amount (or zero). In an asset-liability management context, the investment reserve serves as a balancing item on the financial statements. This strategy is not discussed in Case Study 11 because the investors' financial condition did not permit a large set-aside of money to prefund future income needs. Precautionary reserves are discussed briefly in Case Study 7.

DYNAMIC ASSET MANAGEMENT

As time unfolds, the investors undoubtedly will encounter other changes that impact their financial condition and asset management preferences. Dynamic asset management—especially within an asset-liability management context—offers investment advisors a tool for (1) quantifying progress toward or away from investor goals, and (2) identifying useful management options to promote investor utility. A simulation approach facilitates communication of information vital for an understanding of the probabilistic nature of investing, and the range of outcomes that investor choices are likely to produce.[12]

Dynamic asset management is both a market-reactive and an event-reactive process. Its goal is to enhance the probability that investor resources can meet financial objectives successfully. Dynamic asset management can validate a stay-the-course investment decision or motivate actions to improve outcomes. Elections made under a dynamic asset management approach are often reversible, i.e., it may result in a return-to-course strategy in the future. As such, the elections are real options applied to a risky project. Although reactive, it is also a forward-looking management strategy that syncs present investment elections to projected risk and return preferences. Finally, dynamic asset management under an asset-liability management structure is labor intensive. It solicits an extensive and ongoing level of engagement between advisor and investor. No robo-advisors allowed.

---

12.   "… common sense does not replace computation. Models are most valuable when they predict something unexpected." (Blanchard et al. 2012, 293).

CHAPTER FOURTEEN

RETIREMENT—A HIGH DIMENSION PROJECT

■ ■ ■

COMPETING GOALS; MULTI-STAGE PLANNING HORIZONS

Retirement is a risky project. Limited financial resources often result in trade-offs among objectives. Commonly evaluated trade-offs are leisure time versus economic security and need for income versus preservation of wealth. The existence of competing goals often means that investors must pay a price to meet any single, specific objective. For instance, investors incur a cost of safety with bucketing strategies designed to secure retirement income. In exchange, a bucketing strategy may mitigate certain financial risks that the investor finds unacceptable. The advisor, when acting in a fiduciary capacity, does not advocate for or against investment preferences or strategies. Rather, the advisor helps the investor understand the nature and extent of trade-offs and quantifies the costs of prioritizing one goal over another. All anchor and no sail is not necessarily a good way to build a safe ship; all sail and no anchor invites disaster.

Trade-offs also are operative within a time dimension. Asset management strategies that seem appropriate in the short term may undercut a portfolio's chances of succeeding in the long term. An asset management approach that fails to consider and evaluate intelligently the claims of both the short and long term is difficult to defend. The race for some investors is between the opportunity cost of heavily weighting low-risk/low-return assets and the return requirements necessary to sustain an adequate long-term standard of living:

- Allocations tilted toward fixed income instruments may run an unacceptably high risk of depletion during the investor's life span because realized return falls below required return. Principal is safe, but cash flow is inadequate.
- Allocations tilted toward stocks may run an unacceptably high risk of depletion because realized downside volatility may create return patterns that exceed the portfolio's drawdown capacity.

Or:

- Allocations tilted toward fixed income securities may experience an unacceptable erosion of purchasing power.
- Allocations tilted toward stocks may necessitate substantial reductions in the investor's standard of living if the realized returns are unfavorable.

Time and financial objectives act together to shape the multi-stage investment planning horizon. Spending goals often dominate the discussion in early retirement. Some investors may show a strong preference for income prior to say, age 80, and a willingness to accept a lower periodic income at a later age. As investors age, wealth management goals may dominate the discussion. In the later retirement years, topics of interest may include: (1) the bequest and legacy issue; (2) the management control issue—especially in the context of cognitive impairments; and (3) end-of-life issues that extend into family dynamics, estate planning, medical security, use of home equity, and so forth.

It is unlikely that investor finances and preferences will remain constant throughout retirement. Although there is no hard-and-fast age for introducing a specific planning topic, it is wise to recognize that asset management decisions made tomorrow (based on future information and future preferences) are affected by decisions made today.

RECOURSE DECISIONS

"Recourse decisions" is a term from operations management. Generally, when forced to make a decision in the face of uncertainty, e.g., scheduling a picnic without certain knowledge of weather conditions, it is advantageous to have "recourse" (the ability to move the picnic table indoors). The recourse decision (stay outdoors or move indoors) is made only after the original ambiguity or uncertainty is resolved. The real options approach to retirement as a risky project draws upon some underlying concepts from operations research.

Recourse decisions permit flexibility in future decision-making. At this point, we extend the concept of flexibility beyond the notion of a financial cushion, to the ability to adapt, over time, to changes in risk preferences, return requirements, time horizon, and goal priorities. The previous chapter treated these elements in the context of dynamic asset management.

The next section considers the premium an investor is willing (or unwilling) to pay for early resolution of ambiguity in periodic income through purchase of an annuity.

ARGUMENTS FOR AND AGAINST IMPLEMENTATION OF ANNUITY-BASED FLOORING

Commentators are split on whether to:

- Annuitize as soon as possible lest a forthcoming bear market jeopardize the ability to secure threshold income; or,
- Delay annuitization for as long as possible to capture the expected investment risk premium and, potentially, enter into a lower-cost annuity contract issued at an older age.

The asset management option is to annuitize now to resolve ambiguities surrounding the sources and amount of future income or wait to annuitize for as long as a delay remains a prudent and suitable election.

As soon as you add liabilities to the decision problem, an annuity contract's illiquidity introduces risk because illiquidity reduces financial flexibility in the face of unexpected future expenses. The investor who elects an annuity solution resolves ambiguity only on the asset side of the balance sheet, not on the liability side. There are competing objectives, and it is important to know the costs of securing one objective at the expense of others.

The study by Babbel and Merrill (2007) presents an example of the "annuitize as soon as possible" flooring strategy. The authors suggest that a utility-maximizing investor will not pursue a strategy that leaves a positive probability of failing to support a threshold level of lifetime consumption. Their model directs the investor to allocate risk-free assets sufficient to support the minimum periodic income goal.

If the minimum consumption target requires periodic income greater than that available through government or corporate pension benefits, Babbel and Merrill advise the investor to annuitize immediately a portion of current wealth sufficient to fund the deficit. Excess wealth remains invested in a financial asset portfolio. In a multi-period context, the risk-free asset is an inflation-adjusted annuity. The authors argue for a bottom-up asset management approach, in that the investor, with little or no delay, converts financial assets into an annuity designed to provide threshold income. Only surplus wealth is allocated to a risky-asset portfolio—a buy-an-annuity-and-invest-the-difference strategy. If the proportion of wealth allocated to the annuity is large, however, the investor may not have remaining funds sufficient to implement the optimal allocation to the risky-asset portfolio.[1] Assuming that the risky-asset portfolio has a higher expected return than the annuity portfolio, the decrease in aggregate expected return (disutility) from investing only a small portion in stocks must be balanced against reduced uncertainty in future consumption (positive utility) by investing a large portion of wealth in annuities. The authors point out that the utility feedback loop plus the wealth constraint make an analytic solution impossible.

In contrast to Babbel and Merrill (2007), Fullmer (2007) espouses a top-down approach, where the option to annuitize is a last-resort asset management option. Fullmer asserts that the best strategy for managing retirement-income risk is to annuitize when necessary—but not before. The key to implementing a prudent portfolio management strategy is to evaluate continuously the option to annuitize financial assets. By exercising the option only when necessary to ensure a threshold standard of living, the investor takes full advantage of the option's time value.

---

1.   This is the fact pattern examined in Case Study 1.

Fullmer wrote: "The key for leveraging this optionality is setting the projected cost to annuitize the investor's desired lifetime income stream as a wealth goal in the objective function. Doing so effectively transforms longevity risk into investment risk, because now it is the portfolio's job to preserve the ability to annuitize the desired lifetime income stream. ... By monitoring the investor's wealth relative to the current cost of annuitization, the decision to invest or annuitize can be continually evaluated by a financial adviser."

This logic leads directly to a recommendation for "a dynamic allocation strategy." According to Fullmer, "When substantial cash flow risk is present, the objective function begins to take on more of the characteristics of a cash flow matching model."[2] The author terms this an "annuitization hurdle." Under this risk management approach, the investor monitors the cost of buying an annuity to fund threshold income and compares this cost with the market value of assets remaining in the portfolio. The decision becomes how much of the portfolio surplus to put at risk before exercising the option to annuitize. The argument is that there is time value in the option to delay annuitization (where annuitization may be thought of as a type of actuarial flooring) until future events resolve an investor's uncertainties.[3]

Additional studies investigating dynamic approaches to spending, allocation, and downside risk probabilities find a place in academic literature. A good example is found in Dus et al. (2005). Although, according to the authors, many investors choose to self-annuitize under a phased withdrawal approach, a fixed-amount withdrawal election carries the risk of outliving financial resources. By contrast, a fraction-of-remaining-wealth withdrawal strategy avoids this risk, but the periodic amount withdrawn may be substantially higher or lower than the fixed benefit amount.

The authors compare alternative retirement-income strategies. Traditionally, financial economists approach the problem by modeling a strategy to maximize discounted expected utility of uncertain future consumption and bequests. However, many utility-based models assume time-separable utility and constant-relative-risk aversion. These limiting assumptions may not adequately represent a retiree's risk preferences. Therefore, the authors present a risk-value model where reward is defined as expected return from any retirement-income strategy and risk is defined as the possibility of not reaching the desired level of consumption.[4] The authors stress that valid risk metrics must account for both the timing and the magnitude of losses. They anticipate an argument made in an article by Kitces (2012b).

Dus et al. (2005) demonstrates the benefit of "payout modeling" as opposed to "investment risk modeling"—income patterns are graphed over time instead of dollar wealth patterns. Income patterns, reflecting the investor's unique preferences, can manifest:

- "Back-loaded" retirement benefits;
- Stable benefits; or
- Benefits that decline over time.

Depending on the nature of the investor's utility of consumption function, one pattern may be preferred over another even though it produces a lower overall present value. Value is not simply monetary; it also encompasses a psychological dimension.[5] Risk, and the investor's response to it, becomes paramount. The retirement-income problem involves trade-offs between (1) budgetary certainty with an attendant risk of ruin, and (2) budgetary uncertainty with an attendant risk of insufficient periodic income. Investing is a prudent exchange of risks.

RECOURSE DECISIONS AND ADAPTIVE STRATEGIES

Several recent studies explore adaptive spending and asset allocation strategies. These are the recourse decisions discussed earlier. For example, Kitces (2012a) compares the use of equity-based strategies versus the use of flooring.

An annuity strategy provides a floor on income that cannot be outlived. However, in Kitces's opinion, the 4 percent withdrawal rule is also effectively a 'floor' strategy. Although it does not guarantee lifetime income, it has never failed in market history. Thus an annuity may be seen as an alternative way to achieve safe withdrawals but with a loss of liquidity and upside return potential. This is the 'cost-of-safety' dimension inherent in the bucketing (flooring) versus risky-asset portfolio strategy discussion.

---

2. The risk-management approach mirrors the hurdle race problem in that the "provision" must exceed the cost of securing the threshold living standard through annuitization (Vanduffel et al. 2003).

3. A more complete analysis of this topic is available in Collins et al. (2015b).

4. A "probability-of-consumption-shortfall" risk metric.

5. See Bernoulli (1954).

The safe 4-percent withdrawal rate is calculated based on a 30-year planning horizon whereas the annuity—which is backed by an insurance company guarantee, pays periodic income irrespective of the annuitant's actual life span. According to Kitces: "To truly fail, the couple needs to be unlucky enough to live through an investment environment worse than any found in history, i.e., no principal left at the end, and be the (approximately) one couple in six who are still alive at the thirty-year time horizon. When you combine low-probability investment disasters and low-probability longevity scenarios, you end up with some astonishingly low-probability scenarios, many of which could be further 'saved' by small midcourse corrections."

Furthermore, Kitces argues that "... extraordinary investment shocks that could destroy a thirty-year safe withdrawal rate could also threaten an insurance company ... the failure rate of a 4 percent withdrawal rate is about the same as the failure rate of an insurance company rated AA or better. ... Simply put, the tail risks are correlated."

He continues, "The bottom line is that choosing between immediate annuities and safe withdrawal rates is not a decision about *whether* to use a floor-with-upside approach; it's about choosing *which* floor is preferable in light of the trade-offs the decision entails." This implies that a 4 percent withdrawal strategy is almost as conservative a strategy for producing safe and sustainable income as is the purchase of an annuity. Both a 4 percent withdrawal rate strategy and an annuity offer "floor protection," but the annuity truncates upside potential. Annuitization strategies limit recourse decision making.[6]

'THE FOREVER WAR'

From a practitioner perspective, there is a "forever war" aspect to these debates. Decisions, however, should reflect investor preferences, needs, and circumstances, not investment dogma. An advisor's goal is to help investors reach prudent, defensible, and administratively practical decisions.

Is a simple investment solution indicative of a good solution? An annuity may be appropriate for investors who face dementia or other impairments, and who lack family and friends capable of running the household economy. But an annuity, like all financial products, cannot be acquired absent a cost. Product-based solutions are appropriate when their costs are judged reasonable in proportion to their expected benefits. Retirement investment planning is a function of resources, goals, time horizon, and a function of the investor's willingness and ability to plan. An investor unwilling to devote time and effort to retirement planning must default to product acquisition. The utility of a product-based approach derives, in part, from its simplicity, time savings, and freedom from the task of evaluating weighty economic decisions. Is defaulting to potentially high-cost products a good proxy for intelligent decision making? Is it an equitable trade? The answer has several dimensions, and depends on an investor's interests, preferences, and time constraints.

There is a difference between asking (1) what strategy is least risky, and (2) what strategy offers a prudent exchange of risk? The first question is single dimensional and fails to recognize that investment decisions involve trade-offs. The second is multi-dimensional, seeks to understand the applicable trade-offs, and attempts to carve out a reasonable solution path. If an investor purchases an annuity or implements another form of "flooring," "bucketing," or "risk-avoidance" strategy because he or she is asking the first question, the decision-making process may go off track.[7] Cost may not be measurable solely in terms of dollars spent on product loads. Additional costs may be forthcoming in terms of future budget constraints for both leisure activities and for meeting the costs of financial emergencies. If, however, the investor purchases an annuity because he or she is asking the second question, then the simple solution may indeed be the best.

Recourse decisions are valuable in high-dimensionality environments. As information unfolds, beliefs change, preferences evolve, and flexibility assumes heightened importance. Security and adaptability are two sides of the same coin.

---

6.   This is true whenever the investor exchanges all liquid financial wealth for an annuity contract at the time of retirement. It is less true for strategies considering sequential annuitization throughout retirement.

7.   An investor can be conservative right up to the time when he or she turns desperate because there has been only anemic portfolio returns.

CHAPTER FIFTEEN

SIMULATORS AND INVESTMENT ADVICE

Investors seek advice concerning a safe, sustainable, and secure retirement. However, retirement is a risky project because it requires multi-stage (intertemporal) decision-making for conflicting or competing objectives, under conditions of risk and uncertainty with incomplete or uncertain information regarding probabilities, asset management options, and the economic consequences of financial decisions.[1]

SIMULATORS: EFFICIENT EDUCATIONAL TOOLS

Allocating sufficient time to understand the risks and rewards of investment elections is often the single most-important planning step. In many respects, an economically efficient retirement depends on how well the advisor presents the merits and liabilities of planning options to the client. Certainly, it is an inefficient use of client time to expect that he or she become familiar with the derivation of risk-aversion coefficients used to design and implement portfolios constructed on the basis of the Merton optimum algorithm, the Black–Litterman algorithm, the Markowitz–Sharpe algorithm, or the many variations found within an asset-liability management context. Likewise, it is an inefficient use of client time to present mere pablum by bypassing complex but important financial topics. It is both an inefficient use of client time and a deviation from a fiduciary standard of practice when an advisor deliberately creates informational asymmetries to support a sales agenda.

There is no single, monolithic, rules-based, or optimal method for either portfolio design or asset management. Ultimately, an advisor must decide how best to address the client's needs, goals, spending requirements, and other circumstances.[2] We are partial to the use of simulation as a tool for helping clients explore and understand both the challenges and the opportunities that they face. We acknowledge that, like any tool, simulation models can be abused. When used to justify unwarranted investment positions, they can drive the client toward catastrophic financial failures. Practitioners adopt simulators specifically because they illustrate the range of results (including "tail risk") and allow the practitioner to construct reasonable approximations of risks and rewards for various asset management elections. Using a simulator, if its assumptions are credible and its structure sufficiently flexible, allows the client to scope out, in conjunction with the advisor, a good long-term strategy. If the strategy embraces the higher expected returns from equities and other risky assets, a simulator allows the user to recognize, as time passes, whether critical risk metrics are becoming more or less favorable and, therefore, allows them to adjust accordingly. Indeed, a central thesis of this book is that ongoing monitoring of retirement risk metrics in terms of client-specific goals is a critical prerequisite for dynamic and adaptive asset management. Risk means not having the amount of money you need at the time you need it. This is the heart of the matter—getting the client across the finish line successfully is of far greater importance than constructing a snazzy-looking asset allocation pie chart.

A second reason why we are partial to the use of simulation as an investment planning tool is because it gets the investor to "the other side of complexity."[3] If complexity is akin to John Bunyan's Slough of Despond, the advisor does not want to see a client become bogged down and fail to reach the Heavenly City.[4] Interactive simulators permit the client to grasp, sometimes with astonishing rapidity, the implications of complex economic decision making.

A third reason why we are partial to the use of simulation is that it allows the client to make the decisions. The investment plan is suitable because it is the client's plan—not the advisor's plan. Just as a flight simulator helps pilots determine which risks are acceptable and which to avoid; so, also, an investment simulator permits investors to test asset management elections prior to their implementation

---

1. For pre-retirement investors, uncertainty in the ability to meet savings objectives or spending limits is of equal importance.

2. A particularly difficult challenge is how best to address complex planning issues with time-constrained clients. In some respects, this is analogous to the problem of non-compliant patients in the medical profession. If the patient won't sit still long enough for a credible diagnosis or won't devote sufficient time to treatment programs, what is the practitioner's duty to the patient; and, what is the practitioner's liability for continued treatments and consultations? We elaborate on these issues later in this chapter.

3. This phrase is attributed to Oliver Wendell Holmes: "I would not give a fig for the simplicity this side of complexity, but I would give my life for the simplicity on the other side of complexity."

4. The "Slough of Despond" (or "swamp of despair") is a fictional, deep bog in John Bunyan's allegory *The Pilgrim's Progress*, into which the protagonist Christian sinks under the weight of his sins and his sense of guilt for them.

in the real world.[5] This process does much more than define the advisor as a life coach ("you can do it if you stick with my plan"), or as a financial therapist ("explore your money-life so that you empower yourself to act decisively and take responsibility for your financial future"). Simulation facilitates moving the client and the advisor into a planning partnership, but the advisor's role morphs into asking "do you really want to do this?" instead of "here's what I recommend." The dynamic is less about persuading the client to do something, and more about making sure the client knows what he or she is doing.

Simulators operate comfortably within a pictorial medium—they present a picture of what retirement reward and risk look like. Perhaps the closest analogy to the process of getting the client to "the other side of complexity" is found in the optometry profession. An optometrist is not a medical doctor but is skilled in the prescription of corrective lenses as well as in the diagnosis, treatment, and management of vision changes. As a skilled practitioner, the optometrist must earn a doctoral degree from a school of optometry and must pass requisite state licensing exams. The point is if you need eyeglasses, you don't want to hear long lectures about optics, cellular biology, eye abnormalities, and the effects of prescription medications. You do want assurances that the doctor knows about these things and that he can expertly bring a range of skill sets to bear on your vision needs. A rather straightforward set of diagnostic tools are available to solve a patient's needs efficiently and accurately. At the heart of the process, the basic exam for corrective lenses takes the form of an intelligently played game of trial and error: which is better, number one or number two? The patient, guided by the doctor's experience, education, background, and training, interactively makes decisions that best conform to his vision objectives (reading, driving, computer work, etc.). If selecting the "best" lens is analogous to evaluating the opportunity set, then experiencing firsthand, the range of corrective solutions is analogous to articulating a personal utility function. At the end of the day, the advisor, working interactively, arrives at the same place as the financial economist who develops mathematical expressions for risk tolerance or risk aversion. Simulators present information, and effective presentations are a prerequisite for clear articulation of personal preferences. Investors can't state their goals and preferences in a vacuum. They have to know their options so that they can make intelligent choices.[6]

SIMULATION MODELS AND THE REFERENCE CLASS PROBLEM

In 1983, I. J. Good, in a book entitled *Good Thinking* (no pun intended) wrote: "Every event in life is unique, and every real-life probability that we can estimate in practice is that of an event that has never occurred before."[7]

This is the "reference class" problem—to determine the outcome probability of any particular experiment it is necessary to place it in a reference class of similar experiments with known outcomes. From time-to-time, the reference class problem is the source of great confusion. For example, many investors considered that the laws of economics no longer were operable as we entered into the "new paradigm" economy at the end of the twentieth century. The new age of the information-technology economy was exceptional, unique, and unprecedented. Stock prices no longer were based on traditional valuation methods. Andy Grove, chairman of Intel, predicted "all companies will be internet companies, or they will be dead."[8] If the reference-class problem generated undue optimism regarding the "new paradigm" economy in the late 1990s, it had the opposite impact during the global recession of 2008 to 2009 during which the never-before-seen catastrophes in the banking system and housing markets bedeviled investor ability to assess the probable economic consequences of unfolding events. Nothing like this has happened in the past; no expert can foresee what will happen; what if the economy can never get back to normal? This is a difficult—almost intractable—problem. It is at the heart of much investor uncertainty.

A preliminary solution is to simulate thousands of possible outcomes—even outcomes that have never been realized historically. Why is this a solution? Because emergence of bad outcomes may be the result of war, nuclear accidents, natural disasters, political crises, economic depressions, medical or health crises, global terrorism, or some combination thereof. Indeed, simulated outcomes arise from causes not yet even imagined. However, simulation is unveiling not causes, but, rather, ranges of possible outcomes. But how trustworthy is simulation? Credible simulations should produce a range of results that are not bounded by a probability measure based on history. History cannot act as a probability measure because every minute is unique, i.e., never before seen.

---

5. The analogy to a flight simulator also occurs in Goldstein et al. (2008, 454). This article discusses the "Distribution Builder" application, developed by the authors to enable "… consumers to explore probability distributions of prospective outcomes …" (ibid., 440). They assert that interactive methods in which the investor actively participates in portfolio design and investment strategy decisions "… can be used to infer utility functions from distributions instead of from choices between simple two-alternative gambles, as was the dominant paradigm in the twentieth century" (ibid., 443).

6. "How people will act when they have choices is influenced by what people know" (Rappaport 2011).

7. Quoted in Russell and Norvig (2016, 491).

8. Quoted in Martinson and Elliott (2000).

A better solution is to blend several models: (1) investment-oriented models, e.g., bull and bear market regimes, and (2) actuarial-oriented models. The investment models focus on the growth and decline of assets; the actuarial models focus on the growth and decline of financial surplus. When presented with a once-in-a-century opportunity or a once-in-a-century catastrophe, a good decision-making process is paramount. Good decisions sometimes have bad outcomes (bad decisions sometimes have lucky outcomes—especially for the lotto-ticket winners), but a good decision-making process enhances the likelihood of good outcomes. Portfolio management is about choices, and the process used to make the decisions, e.g., prudence, greed, or fear. A decision may be informed, semi-informed, or flip a coin. During so-called unprecedented times, simulation is a tool to facilitate a careful review of asset management options—do nothing, go to cash, invest everything in tech stocks, establish a protective floor, utilize reserve accounts, maintain diversification—in terms of investor financial objectives.

INVESTMENT ADVICE AND CREDENCE GOODS: RECOMMENDING VERSUS SUGGESTING

If one definition of investing is "a prudent exchange of risk," what is a reasonable balance between risk-reward exposures? A "risk-is-bad" perspective leads to principal-guaranteed product solutions; a "risk-is-good" perspective leads to a view of risk as potential opportunity. Fear of risk leads to insurance-type solutions; acceptance of risk leads to an expectation (not a guarantee) of reward. Awareness of risk leads to good decision-making. Acceptance of risk is prudent as long as the investor is knowledgeable about the consequences of risk and is in an economic position to accept them. Investing is not wishful thinking, it is prudent judgment.

Retirement risk does not reside so much in the embedded accounting, investment, and statistical characteristics of the financial asset portfolio as in the decision to embark on retirement given inadequate resources (a low actuarial coverage ratio), or in the decision to adhere to retirement plan strategies in the face of a deteriorating actuarial coverage ratio (ACR) value. Risk is determined primarily by the wealth-consumption ratio—not the absolute level of wealth—and by the interrelationships, i.e., dependence structure, between changes in financial asset values and liability funding costs. These observations require advisors to (1) redefine retirement risk, and (2) rethink how to communicate it. The focus shifts to evaluating continually the feasibility of investor-specific goals, and to portfolio monitoring in terms of those goals.

Often, when critical information about the investor's financial position is made clear, appropriate solution paths suggest themselves. Who makes the decisions is as important as what decisions are made if the ongoing investor-advisor relationship is to remain productive. Advisors who relish the role of "recommender" often struggle through client meetings where time is wasted in defending past recommendations or in explaining why the advisor's recommendations will work in the future even though they have not yet panned out. By contrast, the advisor can shape a better relationship—a planning partnership rather than an exercise in promoting product-based solutions or in promulgating an investment theology.

The temptation to assume the role of recommender is great because it allows the advisor to maintain the trappings of intellectual prowess. There is, however, a subtle but important difference between these two notions: (1) If I say "X," I will appear to be an expert, and (2) if I'm an expert, I will know to say "X." Ideally, advisors should concentrate on becoming experts rather than on rehearsing techniques for projecting an aura of expertise. Most investors realize that an expert is a person who is not afraid to say, "I don't know."

Financial advice is a "credence good." Credence goods arise whenever the seller has a significant informational advantage over the buyer ("information asymmetry"). An extensive body of literature is built up around credence goods; indeed, a 1970 article by Nobel Memorial Prize-winner George Akerlof points out that cars, only a few months old, sell for drastically reduced prices because potential buyers are wary that the seller wants to get rid of a mechanically defective vehicle (Akerlof 1970). The buyer wants information that the seller may be reluctant to disclose; therefore, the buyer, fearing that he will be hornswoggled, refuses to offer the full or justified price even for cars in good shape. This, in turn, means that owners of truly road-worthy cars, who are reluctant to accept unfairly low prices, are reticent to bring their vehicles to market. Fewer high-quality cars are available for purchase—reinforcing the buyer's skepticism concerning all car sellers. Eventually, in extreme cases, the market may fail.

A good example of a credence good is medical care.[9] How do you find a good doctor or dentist? Medical services are next to impossible for a layperson to assess either before or after their delivery. Therefore, the value of trust and comfort: "My doctor listens and has a wonderful bedside manner." Without a deep knowledge of the profession, it is difficult to evaluate medical or dental procedures to determine the level of practitioner skill—as opposed to a comforting demeanor or social prominence. The same is true with financial advisors: "I have a wonderful advisor—she's on the board of several local charities and nonprofit organizations."

---

9.   We also include services provided by attorneys, accountants, electricians, mechanics, building contractors, and most of all, computer consultants.

Here's the key point: In the absence of an ability to judge the quality of a good, a buyer is inclined to go cheap. Quality disappears from the marketplace and public welfare decreases. Some might offer the opinion that the current market for financial advice is, in fact, a market for lemons, and some would argue that the rise of robo-advisors constitutes proof of this hypothesis. Although it may be difficult for investors to distinguish readily between advice and schmooze, most investors are sufficiently astute to know what they want when they see it. By redefining the nature and scope of retirement risk, and by presenting it in terms of feasibility, sustainability, and security (financial flexibility), advisors put investors in a position to self-recommend a prudent and appropriate retirement investment solution.

Technology is best used not to create the snazzy-looking asset allocation pie chart, but rather to help advisors frame investor risk-reward trade-offs appropriately. Why is this important?

1. It allows the investor to assess the opportunity set (distribution of outcomes) in terms of his or her personal risk-reward trade-off preferences given current goals and wealth; and

2. Investor utility is *revealed* as part of a prudent decision-making process rather than imposed prior to the process either by assumptions built into optimization software programs or by assumptions carried around in an advisor's head.

The intellectual challenge is to unify:

- Planning approaches grounded in the investor's personal financial circumstances rather than in a textbook,

- Advanced risk-modeling techniques,

- Monitoring metrics based on investor-specific goals, and

- Portfolio management based on investor-specific preferences (utility).

The advisor/practitioner challenge is to put the investor in a position where he or she can make informed decisions.

If "prudence" is an academically sound, legally defensible, administratively reasonable process to enhance the likelihood of a successful outcome, then the best answer to the investor's question: "As an investment advisor, what do you recommend?" is "use prudent judgment."

SIMULATION AND THE DECISION-MAKING PROCESS

At this point, it is appropriate to remark on the advisor's challenge when working with clients exhibiting various decision-making biases. Behavioral finance literature devotes considerable attention to identifying client types, or client psychometrics, so that advisor recommendations and presentations incorporate awareness of an investor's psychological predispositions.[10] If we are allowed a play on words, when the advisor recommends courses of action, the "advisor" becomes a "recommender." This dynamic has appeal for investors who exhibit "outcome-oriented bias." "Outcome-oriented thinking encourages a focus on the end state one wants to achieve." (Thompson et al. 2009, 1). In this dynamic, questions like "what should I own?" or "what do you think I should do?" are important; and doubtlessly, the advisor should have a good read on the client's comfort zone lest his recommendations fall on deaf ears.

The opposite of outcome-oriented bias is "process-oriented bias" that "involves elaboration on the step-by-step process that leads to a desired outcome" (Thompson et al. 2009). Although research indicates that process-oriented approaches to decision-making are more effective than outcome-based approaches, the process-oriented decision-maker often has greater difficulty in making a choice: "[W]e expect that individuals who engage in process thinking tend to form action-outcome links and weight more factors in their decisions than individuals who engage in outcome thinking, potentially making the choice task more difficult." Process-oriented decision makers "are less confident in their choices, and are less satisfied with the decision process than those who use outcome-oriented thinking."

---

10. "Once the adviser finds that the client has certain behavioral biases associated and consistent with a specific behavioral investor type, he or she will classify the client into the appropriate BIT [Behavioral Investor Type]." (Pompian et al. 2018, 113). The authors divide the investors into 'Passive Preservers,' 'Friendly Followers,' 'Independent Individualists,' and 'Active Accumulators.' "There is no doubt that an understanding of investor psychology will generate insights that benefit the advisory relationship." (ibid.,117).

For all but the wealthiest investors, retirement-income planning requires decision-making in a complex, high-dimension environment. It is possible to put both the outcome-oriented and the process-oriented investor on information overload.[11]

Time and attention become the new elements of the risk-return trade-off. We suspect that the disutility of time spent on planning is greater for outcome-oriented investors, perhaps because of their psychometric profile. Outcome investors are loss averse and want the advisor to produce a good outcome. Additionally, the outcome-oriented investor may wish to keep his or her time commitment to a minimum. Many 401(k)/defined contribution plan participants, either because of a lack of awareness about how to plan, or a general disinterest in acquiring at least a passing familiarity with investment concepts and investment jargon, irrevocably set their retirement elections on an unchanging and unmonitored course during the few moments set aside for plan enrollment. Undoubtedly, glide-path and target-date offerings are a godsend to many in this group.[12] Marketing campaigns are sometimes set up specifically to identify and appeal to outcome-oriented investors. Investors enhance welfare because they can dispatch the retirement-planning task with minimal effort; advisors enhance welfare because they can offer pre-packaged, simple to explain, intuitively appealing, and service-free products advertising downside protection as well as limited upside potential. Determination of the prudence or imprudence of this approach to retirement planning is a facts-and-circumstances issue. Were the extra fees and costs worth the savings in time and effort?

At the other end of the spectrum, advisors will recognize the process-mad client who seems to have an insatiable appetite for exploring the *nth* implication of every factor that could possibly affect retirement planning. The possibility of information overload does not exist for this client, and the client is often ill-prepared to arrive at an acceptable, not to mention, preferred solution. Such investors, if accepted as clients, often present an operational nightmare. A directory path through client file structure may take the form of Current Year / Allocation Strategy Six / Income Strategy Four / Contingent Assets / Bear Market only / etc., etc. Woe to the firm lacking an advisory agreement that calculates advisor compensation on an hourly fee basis, on a project basis not-to-exceed x hours, or on some similar provision. Whereas it is impossible to consider every alternative, it is worthwhile to offer these clients a short course in the benefits of "satisficing," i.e., picking a target and implementing the first course of action that meets target requirements.

---

11. This may be true for several of the case studies. Advisors may find that the time and attention demands exceed the limits of many clients. Fortunately, the learning curve does not have to be fully ascended at once.

12. "[T]arget-date funds offer a sole focus on an investment horizon without any protection of investors' minimum retirement needs. ... [They] do not adequately hedge the main risks related to retirement investing decisions, namely investment risk, interest rate risk, inflation risk and longevity risk." (Martellini et al. 2018, 3). Martellini et al. advocate a variation on a constant proportion portfolio insurance (CPPI) strategy. Traditionally, a CPPI strategy focuses on asset levels only. It sets a floor below which wealth is not allowed to penetrate; and it invests a multiple of excess wealth—i.e., the value of the portfolio above the floor. Martellini et al. recommend using this approach within an asset and liability management (ALM) context: "the allocation to equities does not stay constant and instead reacts to changes in the distance between current wealth and the floor, to protect the essential goal" (ibid.,8).

It is instructive to compare this approach to the Wilcox and Fabozzi (2009) "discretionary wealth" approach: "We define discretionary wealth in terms of an accounting balance sheet. ... On the left side are our investment assets, plus the time-discounted value of foreseen financial contributions to the portfolio. This present value is an implied asset. On the right side are our current debts, plus the present values of our foreseen financial commitments that must be satisfied by withdrawals. These latter make up an implied liability. The residual or surplus on the right side we term discretionary wealth. ... discretionary wealth in accounting terms is not an asset but rather more akin to book equity. It may be distinctly suboptimal to allocate an amount to risky investments precisely equal to our discretionary wealth." "... the ratio of the value of the investment portfolio to that of the surplus or discretionary wealth. ... We refer to this as implied leverage, or L, though no borrowing is involved, only a scaling of return." They continue: "[I]n addition, one can introduce reserves for unknown contingencies as an additional implied liability. This allows us to get the benefits of dynamic adjustment of risk aversion as we reach lower levels of discretionary wealth. The conventional practice of dedicating risk-free assets sufficient to cover all liabilities, as in some pension asset-liability management and insurance accounts, is demonstrably suboptimal unless transaction costs are very high."

The Martellini et al. (2007) strategy is concerned with investing a multiple (leveraged) amount above a floor value; the Wilcox and Fabozzi (2009) strategy is concerned with investing only discretionary wealth in a manner (the Kelly-system optimum) that retains a funding level sufficient to meet critical liabilities as they unfold over time. In neither case does leverage mean that the investor borrows funds.

We note: (1) Both approaches require, depending on the value of the "leverage" multiple, a relatively large portion of risky assets to be constantly bought and sold as portfolio values change, and (2) investors or advisors may find trading costs, administrative fees, and operational challenges to be extraordinarily high in such a system. However, both approaches employ the concept of an investment floor, comparable to the ACR, the value of which changes by virtue of returns on the asset portfolio relative to liability valuation change. Indeed, in many respects, our use of the ACR metric is akin to a "floor + multiplier" approach where the floor is a comprehensive ratio rather than a dollar value and the multiplier is set at a value of one. It is a straightforward extension to increase the multiplier to achieve a more growth-oriented strategy for "surplus." This book does not assert that a particular asset-liability matching (ALM) portfolio management system is inherently better or worse than well-thought-out alternatives. The investment advisory profession benefits as the number of thoughtfully designed studies focusing on retirement-income planning in an ALM context increases.

Simulators are ideal for bringing both outcome-oriented and process-oriented clients back toward the middle of the psychometric spectrum. They provide a rich information set, set up parameters for clear and efficient monitoring, and generate graphical presentations of client progress toward or away from financial objectives. The advisor can readily adapt simulation output into the classic two-page summary memo with supporting exhibits at the back. Simulators also provide important benefits to process-oriented investors. Haisley et al. (2013) indicates: "Confidence is significantly higher in the risk simulation compared to confidence in the description condition. This coupled with the finding that participants in the risk simulation condition feel more informed about their decision is a positive indicator that the risk simulation leads to positive subjective feelings regarding the allocation decision. … After receiving the outcome of their decisions from the financial market simulation, participants reported satisfaction with their returns. … Even for people whose return fell below the expected value of their allocation decision, satisfaction was not reduced for those in the risk simulation condition." (Haisley et al. 2013, 16). The authors argue that interactive simulation, as opposed to static communication of risk-return statistics, leads to more stable decisions and to increased investor confidence in the efficacy of the decision-making process. Investors become less reactive to market volatility, exhibit greater consistency in investment strategy over time, and are more likely to avoid significant changes in asset allocation. Simulation provides an opportunity for experiencing first-hand a wide range of possible outcomes, and "Decision making from experience can reduce or reverse decision-making biases" (ibid., 2).[13] Simulators are useful tools. But simulation outputs, statistically speaking, are noisy projections. It is the measuring, monitoring, and intelligent assessment of actual results, as they unfold over time, that help both investors and advisors manage an unstable present in order to obtain an economically secure future.

---

13. The Haisley et al. (2013) research is a seminal study on the use of simulations in investment decision-making. The more recent work by Bradbury et al. (2015, 2017) examines the effects of risk simulations of both final outputs and wealth paths over time. These studies confirm (1) "that risk simulations work as a 'substitute' for actual investment experiences" and (2) that allocations based on simulations remain stable over the multiperiod planning horizons.

CHAPTER SIXTEEN

DISCRETE-TIME STOCHASTIC PROCESS MODELS AND SIMULATION

■ ■ ■

STATES AND ACTIONS

Investors want to make good decisions even when they are faced with uncertainty. More precisely, investors make asset-management elections, e.g., retirement-income portfolio decisions, within an evolving system of random variables. The interactions of the random variables comprising the system generate changes in the investor's economic state. For example, a change in an investor's health can dramatically affect consumer surplus in an asset-liability management (ALM) modeling context. If the process is deterministic, it is possible to predict the direction, timing, and magnitude of surplus expansion or contraction; in a stochastic environment, we are uncertain how wealth surpluses or deficits will evolve. The random variables that determine the investor's state include:

- Security price changes
- Inflation realizations
- Health state transitions
- Mortality
- Change in marital status or number of dependents
- Changes in liability values (contractual or implicit liabilities)

Correctly assessing the true state is useful for determining optimal investment actions.[1] Investors have "state preferences," e.g., healthy, wealthy, and wise is better than sick, poor, and clueless, and they would like to know which actions are likely to enhance achievement and sustainability of economic goals. How can they get to and stay in a better state? However, in the context of retirement-income planning, states change merely with the passage of time, and correct identification of the true state is difficult.[2]

Preferred actions (asset-management elections) also may change as the investor ages. The actions (decisions) that affect the state transition process include:

- Spending
- Asset allocation
- Investment reserves
- Income, gifting, and bequest targets, i.e., goal setting
- Tax-strategy, insurance coverages, and so forth

This is a complicated picture of changing systems and time-sensitive actions. Simulation-based approaches to state evaluations and asset-management elections facilitate prudent decision-making. This chapter provides an intuitive understanding of (1) several types of random processes, (2) some "classical" mathematical approaches to modeling the processes, (3) decision-making challenges within specific process types, and (4) the role of numerical (simulation based) approaches for effective management of a retirement-income portfolio.

---

1. By "state" we mean the objective state of the individual rather than a more general and vague state-of-the-world idea. One objective measure is the investor's personal balance sheet. Other measures may include an investor's tax returns, medical charts, number of individuals living in the household, etc. Later, when we discuss the concept of a partially observable Markov decision process (POMDP), we will expand the notion of "state" to include the individual investor's subjective belief state.

2. At the start of 2008, for example, many economists believed that we were in an expansionary economy likely to continue throughout the year. In fact, the economic data published subsequently suggests that we may have entered into a recession during the fourth quarter of 2007.

The discussion focuses primarily on discrete-time processes. In a stochastic discrete-time process, the time variable takes on positive integer values. In a stochastic continuous-time process, the time variable takes on any positive real value. Whereas the simulation-based model used in this book models monthly stock and bond returns, inflation realizations, portfolio cash flows, etc., we limit attention to discrete-time processes.[3]

A RANDOM WALK

Most discussions of random (stochastic) processes begin with the "random walk." A simple random walk is best described by a series of flips of a fair coin where the player in the coin toss game wins $1 with heads, and loses $1 with tails. The game consists of a sequence of independent, i.e., past results do not influence the outcome of the next coin toss, and identically distributed, i.e., probability of gain = probability of loss = ½, or i.i.d. random variables.[4] After many tosses, by the central limit theorem, the probability distribution converges to a mean of zero.[5] If you start a "walk" at position zero on a number line, then a step to the right occurs with probability ½, and a step to the left occurs with probability ½. You may lurch several steps to the left or right during any time interval, but, as time increases, the distance from zero is unlikely to grow excessively large.

MARTINGALES

A random walk is a Martingale. A Martingale is a process where the expected value of a state at '$t + 1$' is exactly equal to its current value at 't': $E[(x_{t+1})]-(x_t)]=0$. Thus, in a Martingale process, the expected gain in the process for all future periods is 0: $E_{[t+1]} = X_t$.

Several Martingale properties (assuming i.i.d. increments with mean zero) are of interest. First, the process will randomly wander away from the initial starting value of zero. This is equivalent to flipping, by chance, a string of consecutive heads or tails. But the process cannot wander too far from expected value (it is unlikely that a player flips an infinite number of heads in a row). That is to say, the process is "bounded." Theoretically, it is bounded by ±t—the player flips at each time step 't' either heads or tails infinitely. In reality, it is unlikely that the accumulated gains or losses will be greater than ±$\sqrt{t}$.[6] In a Martingale process, the average displacement per move, i.e., position divided by move count, is mean reverting because position expected change is 0 and move count just increases with time. A player who spends a lot of time in either the winning column or the losing column will eventually wander from winner to loser. Furthermore, this happens infinitely often if the game never ends.[7]

Assuming a starting value of $0, a Martingale/random walk process continues to have an expected value of $0. A Submartingale, by contrast, is a random process that exhibits a positive trend (long-term slope of wealth change is positive); a Supermartingale process is a random process that exhibits a negative trend (long-term slope of wealth change is negative). Randomness around a horizontal, straight-line, zero-mean is often modelled as "white noise." Thus, a white-noise process is a Martingale. A Submartingale process exhibits noise around an upwardly sloped line; a Supermartingale process exhibits noise around a downwardly sloped line. A constant positive process without noise (variance of return) is analogous to a bank certificate of deposit (CD). In capital markets, the expected slope of the Submartingale line is steeper than the CD's slope. The difference in expected slope values is the result of the equity risk premium. You can't expect to get long-term growth benefits (higher expected slope value) without entering into a risky process (no risk/no reward).

---

3.   Time-series analysis and regression analysis are econometric approaches to discrete-time processes.

4.   The term "gambler's fallacy" refers to a failure to recognize that in a random walk process, the results realized over time interval one have no influence on expected results over time interval two. The probability distributions in each interval $0 \leq t \leq tn$ are exactly the same—i.e., the distribution is stationary in each time interval—the rules of probability do not change merely because you flipped a coin five consecutive heads. In roulette, a preponderance of black outcomes in the first 10 spins is not more likely to produce a preponderance of red outcomes in the next 10 spins. Results do not even out over adjacent periods.

5.   Convergence applies only to expected winning or losing percentages, not to expected gain or loss of dollars. After 100,000 coin flips, your winning percentage should approach 50 percent, but it is inconceivable that you will leave the game with break-even wealth. A 49.9-percent winning percentage means that you are $100 in the red if the betting amount is $1.00 on each toss. For one-million coin tosses, a winning percentage of 49.99 percent still leaves you down $100. The only way to come out even is to flip exactly 500,000 heads and exactly 500,000 tails. Good luck with that.

6.   Where 't' represents the number of flips in the interval of interest. The upper/lower bounds on the process are parabolic rather than linear.

7.   A random walk/Martingale differs, however, from a mean-reverting process such as the Ornstein-Uhlenbeck process used to model inflation (see appendix B).

Gambling games sponsored by casinos are Supermartingales (you're expected to lose money in the long run). Many capital markets, including the stock market, are Submartingales. Investing is not gambling. Simulation is a valuable tool to help investors calibrate the amount of required risk to the time remaining to achieve or sustain their goals given their current resources. An important task of effective investment education is to make the investor more aware of the type of process that he or she is about to undertake.

DYNAMIC PROGRAMMING

One approach to prudent decision-making under limited conditions of certainty is dynamic programming. The idea of solving a problem from back (the goal state) to front (the current state) lies at the heart of dynamic programming.

In discrete time, given initial state x_o, a dynamic program is the optimization

$$W(x_o): = \text{Maximize } R(a) := \sum_{t=0} r_t(x_t, a_t) + r_t(x_t)$$

Subject to:

- $x_t + 1 = f(x_t, a_t)$ over at $\in A_t$ where at is an individual action at time 't' selected from the set of feasible actions A;
- x_t is the state of the world at time 't' $[x \in X]$; and
- $R_T(X_T)$ is the dynamic programming objective, i.e., reward to be attained in the goal state 'T.'[8]

Given an initial state x_o, a dynamic program is the sequence of actions (a) taken at each time step (t) that maximizes a reward equation or, equivalently, minimizes a cost equation. The selected sequence of actions is termed the "policy" $[\pi]$. The best policy π^* maximizes the sum of rewards—where rewards can be thought of as consumption, gifting and bequests, investor satisfaction (utility), wealth, and so forth. The notation $W_t(x_t)$ = Maximum Reward $[R]$ given the best sequence of actions is commonly used.

The immediate action becomes a "constant" once the action is taken, i.e., it is fixed and irrevocable once implemented.[9] However, Max a_{t+1} is the best sequence of actions to take over future states. Given that an investor cannot control general economic forces reflected in inflation and security returns, it is this future sequence of asset-management elections that the investor seeks to optimize $[\pi^*]$. However, one must be cautious when using dynamic programing because the most commonly used form, linear programing, often gives extreme corner solutions, e.g., retain all wealth and consume nothing, i.e., postpone retirement, versus convert all wealth into a life-only, no-refund annuity, i.e., consume everything.

Two important extensions of dynamic programming are:

- Continuous-time dynamic programing, which is often used for deterministic processes; and,
- Optimal control for drift and diffusion processes (Markov chains), which is often used for certain processes exhibiting random behavior.[10]

A MARKOV CHAIN

A Markov chain process exhibits several properties. First, only the current state $[x_t]$ is important for a transition to the next state $[x_t + 1]$. All useful analytical information is contained in the current state and the history of previous state transitions can be ignored. An investor views history merely as a collection of randomly produced outcomes. Second, the current state transitions to a new state solely due to a randomness reflected by a probability distribution. No asset-management action $[a]$ or sequence of actions $[\varpi]$ is present during the state transition process.

---

8.   In the fields of finance and economics, the concept of "utility" is often substituted for "reward."

9.   It may prove helpful to view the initial action as the one that places the investor in a good position whatever future outcomes may arise. Thus, it is akin to the feasibility testing described in Case Study 1.

10.   These are processes for which the state transition probabilities are fully known.

Every period's state is independent of all past states; or, more technically, by the "separability principle," i.e., past states and future states are conditionally independent of the present state. Past events are not guides to future outcomes. The separability of states is a key to utilizing a dynamic-programming approach to asset management.[11]

A Markov chain consists of an initial state (x) and a probability distribution $[\lambda]$ over the state where λ is a vector of positive probabilities summing to 1. A 'Transition Matrix' $[P]$ governs the evolution from state x to state y: $\sum_{y \in x} P_{xy} = 1$. P is the probability that the current state at time 't' is 'x' and the next state at time '$t + 1$' is 'y.' However, when modeling the range of possible future paths for a retirement-income portfolio, the probability values within the bull-bear transition matrix do not remain stationary.

A MARKOV DECISION PROCESS (MDP)

When a set of actions is introduced to a Markov chain, the resulting process is a Markov decision process (MDP). An MDP is a discrete time, state-transition system. An MDP problem consists of four components:

1. A set of states that begin at the initial state (time zero) and transition to new states on a period-by-period basis.

2. A set of actions, e.g., asset-management elections

3. A set of transition probabilities that describe the dynamics of the system, e.g., bull-bear regimes

4. A measurable reward in each state, e.g., investor utility or ACR value

The transition to state $x_t + 1$ from state x_t is, in part, a consequence of the actions taken in state x_t.

An MDP problem often is solved through a dynamic-programming approach incorporating randomness, i.e., when a function is applied to a state, there is an element of randomness within the function; or, alternately, the function $[F]$ is, itself, a random variable. The investor determines the best se, i.e., sequence, of actions $[\pi^*]$ by summing, period-by-period, back through time (backward induction) from the rewards in the terminal goal state to the reward of being in the current state.[12] This summation occurs over all possible states given (weighted by) the fixed transition probabilities governing the system's evolution.

Most mathematical expressions for an MDP incorporate the concepts of (1) an instantaneous reward, (2) a discount factor $[\beta]$ to account for the fact that a current reward is more highly valued than a future reward of similar magnitude, and (3) a probability distribution over possible future states. Probability, in the form of 'Expectation' $[E]$, enters the picture:

$$R(x) = E_x\left[\sum \beta^t r(X_t)\right]$$

where the summation sign $[\Sigma]$ indicates an additive discrete time process. In a Markov chain, an investor either confronts a fully known initial state, e.g., recession, depression, stagflation, liquidity crisis, expansionary economy, etc., or an investor is uncertain about the initial state (perhaps the current state is the first stage of a bull market or a temporary upward perturbation in a bear market?).[13] Given a vector of probabilities for the initial state, the application of a 'Transition Matrix' governing state transition probabilities from state x to state y, yields a Markov chain. In terms of the simulation model used in this book, the matrix has the following form:

Bull Market to Bull Market	Bear Market to Bull Market
Bull Market to Bear Market	Bear Market to Bear Market

---

11.   The Principle of Separability rules out stock charting in a first-order Markov chain. In a second- or third-order Markov chain, only the previous two or three states $[x_t - 1 / x_t - 2]$ influence the transition process to $x_t + 1$. A first-order model assumes that current state variables contain all information required to characterize a probability distribution governing the transition to the next state, e.g., a random-walk transition process. A second- or third-order process looks back several time steps for relevant information on probabilities, e.g., weather prediction. A Markov chain on a state space assumes there are no strictly periodic cycles.

12.   In financial economics, it is common to consider the optimal policy as the one generating the highest investor utility value. The utility of a state is the expected sum of discounted $[\beta]$ utility from (1) occupying the current state [zero discount] and, (2) from executing the best policy $[\pi^*]$ to transition to future states. Mathematically, a policy is a mapping from states to actions.

13.   For expository convenience, we do not discuss health transition processes, household dynamics, liability changes, etc. In reality, a credible retirement-income model deals with multi-state, multi-attribute utility theory in an infinite (uncertain) planning horizon.

The future state is a random variable, but it is not completely opaque because the available information is in the form of probabilities. Furthermore, a transition to a "new state" (the transition can result in remaining in the current state), depends only on the current state—not on any stock/bond price history.[14] The highest sum of the indefinite-horizon discounted reward generated by the optimal policy is termed the 'Value' of the current state. The best policy gives the highest immediate reward plus the highest discounted reward by following the optimal policy [π^*] in each and every successor state. It assumes that the investor always will select the asset-management option that maximizes the 'Value' of the future.[15]

MDPs incorporate a sequence of decisions over evolving states through time. The investor decides what to do today [$a(t)$] given that he or she has the opportunity to decide again [$a(t+1)$] tomorrow. Immediately, however, potential obstacles present themselves. For example, the retired investor must know the number of periods prior to the final state 'T' (where T is the date of death), the transition probabilities along the possible future paths for each possible asset-management election ['a'] in each possible state until T, and so forth.[16]

THE BELLMAN EQUATION

It is only a short distance between an MDP and dynamic programming's workhorse equation: the Bellman equation. An alternate characterization of discrete-time dynamic-programming states that, given an MDP, the optimal reward [$W_t(x_t)$] is the best feasible action [a] such that 'a' maximizes current reward [$r_t(x_t,a_t)$] plus maximizes expected rewards for all future periods $E_{x_\tau a_\tau}[W_{\tau+1}(X_{\tau+1})]$:

$$W_t(x_t) = Sup\ a \in A\{(r_t(x_t,a_t) + E_{x_\tau a_\tau}[W_{\tau+1}(X_{\tau+1})\}$$

$W(x_0)$ is often termed the 'Value Function.' When the date of the terminal state 'T' is known, the Bellman equation provides an appropriate solution method. A classic example in finance is deciding the best time to exercise an American call option so that reward is maximized. If the investor decides not to exercise the option at x_t (where 'x' is the current price of the stock) the current reward [$r_t(x_t,a_t)$] is zero; the expected value of the reward under the best decision [a] is $E_{x_\tau a_\tau}[W_{\tau+1}(X_{\tau+1})]$ as in the above equation. In the case of the call option, if the investor is far away from 'T,' he or she should not exercise the option unless there has been a sharp increase in the stock's price. As time to 'T' grows short, the advisability of option exercise increases. The exact solution depends heavily on the standard deviation of the stock.[17]

OPTIMAL STOPPING TIME PROBLEMS

In the case of optimal time for option exercise, the number of days until expiration is known. If, however, the date of the terminal state 'T' is unknown, e.g., date of an investor's death, you are working to solve an 'Optimal Stopping Time' problem. Such a problem requires an adaptation of the MDP/Bellman equation:

$$Reward = E\left[\sum P^t x_t a_t\right]$$

---

14. Often, the transition matrix for a Markov chain leads to a "steady state" where the solution to a Markov chain problem eventually finds the static end-state of the dynamic system. However, for some transition matrixes, e.g., switching matrixes, there is no steady state because the underlying system (transition probabilities) changes at each time step. This is the case for the regime-switching matrix in our investment model. As new data become available, probabilities change for each table cell with the result that the expected fraction of time that the system remains in state 'x' is not fixed. The conditional probability table remains static only for a single year. See, for example, Strang (2019, 311–318).

15. In an MDP context, maximizing the value of the future is rarely achieved by implementing a "greedy algorithm" (GA) process. A GA always selects the action that yields the highest initial reward. Often, however, the highest long-term reward requires the investor to implement a policy generating low short-term rewards. The best action to take now is not necessarily the most comfortable action. A GA finds a series of local maximum; the investor is looking for the global maximum.

16. A somewhat technical problem encountered in standard dynamic-programming approaches to infinite/indefinite horizon problems is that the optimal policy is stationary (independent of time). Although the presence of a discount factor serves as a "trick" to avoid the problems of summing to infinity, in the real world, investors do not live forever. The discounted value over the time horizon is not reset at each state transition; rather, the force of mortality operates to set limits on life expectancy. Whereas time horizon for the dynamic-programming model does not change, the horizon for investors moves toward an upper limit. Therefore, the number of expected remaining time steps becomes an important factor in determining the optimal policy. Sid Browne comments on the consequences of a changing time horizon (albeit, in a continuous time process) as follows: "… the active probability-maximizing strategy gives results that are orders of magnitude better than the comparative results for the constant allocation (optimal-growth) strategy analyzed. The downside of course, is that under this strategy, the terminal value of the portfolio at time T has positive probability of being 0, as it is essentially an options strategy. … The major problem with probability maximization is that the payoff function is binary valued (1 at the investment goal and 0 elsewhere). Therefore, if there is a finite deadline, significant risk-taking occurs near the deadline if wealth is far from the investment goal" (Browne 1999).

17. The call option example assumes a non-dividend paying stock. The presence of a dividend-capture strategy complicates the analysis. This is not Black–Scholes mathematics (stochastic integration), which investors use to calculate the fair price of an option. Rather, once an investor has purchased the option, the Bellman equation is a tool to determine the optimal time to exercise it.

Infinite (indefinite) time MDP problems cannot be solved by backward induction because the time and/or value of the end state are unknown.[18] In this context, solving the Bellman equation still gives a solution to the MDP although the solution may be less exact than the one derived for finite time MDPs.[19] A standard form of the Bellman equation for maximizing reward in an infinite (indefinite) time context is:

$$R(x.\pi) = r(x,\pi_o) + \beta E_{x,\pi_0}) \left[R(X,\pi) \right]$$

Where:

- $r(x,\pi_o)$ is the instantaneous reward of the current state given the investor's policy action(s);

- β is an assumed constant discount factor[20];

- E_{x,π_0} is a probability distribution over possible state transitions following investor actions; and

- X-hat and π-hat are both random variables.

It can be shown that the mathematical expression for the optimal value function is the Bellman equation, and that a policy that satisfies the Bellman equation is the optimal policy [π^*] for generating the best outcome. A policy, i.e., choice of action, that depends only on the current state and not on prior history, i.e., time, or on a purely random selection of actions is a "stationary policy." Assuming a finite number of possible asset-management options, a stationary policy that satisfies the Bellman equation is the optimal policy.

However, when both the transition probabilities and the time horizon are unknown, closed-form solutions to MDPs are elusive. Even when transition probabilities are known, solving MDPs involves a two-step process: a search for the optimal policy candidate[21] followed by an evaluation of the candidate policy to validate that it is optimal, i.e., solves the Bellman equation. When transition probabilities are known, you are faced with an 'Optimal Control Problem;' otherwise, you are faced with a 'Reinforcement Learning Problem.'[22]

The difficulty in finding closed-form solutions through an analytical approach motivates the use of certain algorithms. In the case of indefinite-time, optimal control problems, the two most-commonly used algorithms are (1) the Value Iteration algorithm, and (2) the Policy Iteration algorithm. The Value Iteration problem assumes for every possible state of the world at t_o, the value of remaining in that state is zero. A systematic examination of actions taken to transition to the next state yields the action that generates the highest reward in the next state. That reward is then iteratively plugged into the Bellman equation to determine the best course of action, i.e., maximization of the reward function [W_{t+1}]. The new reward function value is plugged into the Bellman equation to identify the best action at the second time step, and so on. The algorithm calculates long-term values by summing every value over all states from $x_t + 1$ to x_T. As the assessment of 'Value' changes as the time steps progress, the algorithm:

1. Computes a whole new set of 'Value' (utility) outputs across an ever-growing number of paths—summing value from time T back to the current time; and,

2. Reassesses, iteration-by-iteration, its earlier policy recommendations.

---

18. An "infinite" horizon problem simply indicates that the time horizon is not fixed. It should not suggest that the relevant state transition process goes on forever.

19. The exact form of the Bellman equation may differ for reward-maximization problems as opposed to cost-minimization problems. Solving the Bellman equation for minimization of a cost function is less likely to produce an optimal solution.

20. For example, a discount factor [β] of 0.95 is approximately equivalent to a 5-percent interest rate [$(1/\beta) -1$]. The simulation model's output in this book uses, in most cases, a stochastic discount factor based on the change in the Consumer Price (Urban) Index.

21. A procedure known as "policy improvement."

22. Also termed "adaptive dynamic programming." See, for example, Gosavi (2015). In reinforcement learning problems, one often is uncertain regarding transition probabilities, time horizon, and the nature of the state [x] itself. This is a Yogi Berra world because, if you're not sure where you are, it's difficult to know where you're going (and what you need to do to get there).

With luck, the values converge to an identifiable maximum reward value that, by definition, is the reward generated by the best policy.[23] Tracing back from the highest-terminal-reward state to the current state reveals the best policy [π^*]. It is important to note that an action recommended at the initial step, even though it generates a transition to the highest-reward successor state, may be rejected ultimately because the algorithm operates over all possible paths.[24] The "quick riches" path is not always the best.[25]

Another commonly used algorithm is policy iteration. Policy iteration may be used when the form of the investor's utility function is uncertain. The Policy Iteration algorithm seeks the best policy, not the highest utility value. Whenever there is "stochastic dominance" (one set of actions produces, in every case, a better outcome than any other set), the policy's value is optimal for most every type of utility function. The search is conducted in terms of the best policy as opposed to the highest expected utility value:

1. Select and evaluate an initial policy by summing the utility values in all states that are generated by the policy, and

2. Select and evaluate a new policy to determine if there is an increase in expected value.

The algorithm operates until there is no marked increase in the value of the Bellman equation. A sampling algorithm is sometimes employed so that there is no need to update policy and utility values across all states at once.

There are several underlying assumptions when using the iteration algorithms for solving MDP problems:

- There are a finite number of states worth considering
- The investor knows the true nature of each state
- The investor knows the transition probabilities associated with each feasible action
- The investor has full knowledge of the "nature" (probability distribution over) of the successor state
- The investor's subjective assessment of the next state's value is accurate.

At this point it is easy to see that the infinite (indefinite) time MDP problem is potentially complex, and that the incorporation of numerical techniques may be necessary to arrive at a credible solution. This involves, however, something more than throwing a pre-packaged Monte Carlo simulation at the problem in the hopes of providing sufficient information for prudent asset-management decisions.

A PARTIALLY OBSERVABLE MARKOV DECISION PROCESS (POMDP)

Thus far, the discussion of solutions to optimal policies in state transition processes implicitly assumed that the investor fully and correctly understands the state of the world:

- In terms of the investor's personal situation (correct assessment of health state, financial profile, etc., and
- In terms of general macroeconomic conditions underlying security price change, inflation, etc.

It is extremely unlikely for an investor to fully see the big picture. The reliability of the observations of the parts about which the investor is aware is also questionable because observations are often "noisy." Uncertainty abounds about the state and the accuracy of observations thereon. The stochastic-process model must now account for partial observability.

The investor operates in a current state [x_t] (with an assumed probability distribution) over which he or she makes a set of observations. The selected asset management election [a] transitions to the next state [$x_t + 1$] in which the investor makes another observation and chooses another action. At each time step, the investor assesses the new information and observations to estimate the probability distribution in the new state. New information triggers a new assessment ("belief state") and, in turn, a new perspective on the state of the world.

---

23. Convergence to an exact solution is often not possible with a finite number of iterations.

24. This may occur because the initially recommended action is too risky in terms of reaching the ultimate goal state. Not surprisingly, in high-dimension problems, there are a variety of useful search algorithms including greedy best-first, breadth-first, depth-first, random-state sampling with Monte Carlo simulation, and so forth. See, for example, Russell and Norvig (2016).

25. The introduction of a discount factor, however, creates an interesting trade-off in the time dimension between speed and safety, e.g., early retirement versus secure retirement.

The "true condition" new current state remains partially hidden, and new actions represent the investor's best assessment of both state transition probabilities and the observation probabilities.[26] The partially observable Markov decision process (POMDP) solution path requires the investor to assess an asset-management election based on its state-of-the-world effects and based on its effects on the investor's belief state. The good news is that by incorporating the descriptive vocabulary of Bayesian updating— "priors" to "posteriors"— we set the POMDP framework into a modified Bayesian framework.[27] This framework is well understood and has been extensively studied. The bad news is that closed-form solutions are likely to become computationally intractable.

Simulating a POMDP process gives the advisor an opportunity to:

- Offer a probabilistic description of uncertainty,

- Reflect investor utility by presenting outputs in terms of goals, and

- Incorporate, systematically, new information (albeit partial), over time, in the retirement-income model.[28]

The investor's mental state is often identified as the "belief state" [b]. A belief state has a "sensor model" that incorporates a probability distribution—how much confidence can I place on my observations? Furthermore, given the evidence presented to me by noisy (uncertain) observations, what is the probability of observing this "evidence" [e] in state 'x' [$P(e|x)$]? That is to say, an investor selects an action, i.e., makes an asset-management decision, observes the transition from the current decision-making state to the next decision-making state, and, in a probabilistic manner, assesses the new "state space" to the best of his or her ability.

The investor's choice of action [a] depends on his or her current belief state [b] rather than the objective state-of-the-world [x] that is now partially hidden. Thus, a POMDP requires the investor to execute action [a_t] in the current belief state [b_t], observe evidence [e_t], and formulate a new belief state [b_{t+1}] based on evaluation of the evidence. What was the probability of observing evidence 'e' in state 'x_{t+1}' given action 'a_t' in state 'x_t'? For each subsequent action, the sensor model gives a probability distribution concerning the likelihood of observing 'e' that, in turn, leads to an updating of the investor's belief state. Mathematically, a belief state is a weighted combination of an investor's knowledge of the current economic state [x], observations evaluated according to a sensor model [e], and revisions to the previous belief state [a Bayesian prior].

For stochastic, partially observable problems, the policy becomes a conditional plan. The investor seeks to maximize utility by executing the best conditional plan given the best action in the initial belief state and the best conditional plan in future belief states. Given that there are infinitely many possible belief states, solving a POMDP usually involves focusing on both a subset of partially hidden states [x] and a subset of belief states [b].[29]

A commonly used mathematical tool for updating belief states, i.e., integrating our prior beliefs with current observations, is the Kalman filter. Students of statistics recognize the Kalman filter as a technique enabling a quick update of a time-series regression analysis based on new observations. Rather than re-computing the entire analysis from time zero, the most recent data is neatly appended onto the original matrix (which remains unchanged) through the addition of (1) a state update data matrix, (2) a measurement update matrix, and (3) a covariance matrix between (1) and (2). The original "regression matrix" is multiplied by the three additional matrixes derived from new data into a final "correction matrix" known as the Kalman gain matrix. In that respect, the Kalman filter comports nicely with the Markov chain property in that only the most current "state matrix" cell values are required for accurate estimation caused by new observational evidence. Although a detailed discussion of the Kalman filter is beyond the scope of this introductory exposition, we note that a variety of Kalman filter tools exist for use in updating belief states for deterministic processes as well as for stochastic processes.[30]

---

26. What do I think is the likelihood of observing outcome 'I' from taking action 'J,' if my assessment of the current state is correct? If I observe an unlikely outcome, is my probability distribution over my belief state incorrect—i.e., I should have expected to see outcome 'I;' or, is my state-of-the-world transition probability incorrect? There are many variations of the above. The current belief state transition to a successor belief state is, itself, an MDP process.

27. See discussion of Bayesian analysis in Chapter Seven.

28. All of which we operationalized in Case Study 11. The "prior," modified by new information, becomes the "posterior," which, in turn, becomes the new "prior," and so on.

29. Geometrically, the intersection of states creates a collection of hyperplanes.

30. A good introduction to the Kalman filter is found in Shadmehr and Muss-Ivaldi (2012). A variation of the Kalman filter known as the particle filter often is used to update priors in a stochastic process.

We are now moving into the field of reinforcement learning where approximate solutions are found by employing Bayesian nets, gradient descent algorithms, and other cutting-edge techniques beyond the scope of an introductory discussion. However, the tools and techniques of this approach call for making decisions based on forward projections of action sequences, evaluating a value function, and selecting the most favorable set of actions [π^*]. This process is akin to the simulation/evaluation/re-evaluation of an investor's retirement-income portfolio through time that we detailed in Case Study 11. The simulation process, however, presents ranges of outcomes rather than average, point-estimate, expected values.

EQUATIONS 'RE-SOLVE,' SIMULATIONS REVEAL

The extensive research into the nature of investor utility documents the difficulties of accurately defining and measuring an individual's utility function over both the wealth domain and the time domain. But optimization of expected utility over the relevant planning horizon requires a precise (and usually, constant) mathematical expression for investor utility, e.g., the gamma [γ] element in the Merton optimum discussed in Chapter Three.[31] In a non-deterministic world, however, we argue that it is preferable for an investor to exercise prudent judgment based on credible information rather than to seek an elusive "best" solution.[32] A good simulation model, in addition to revealing the consequences of choice within the available opportunity set, often reveals the answers to questions that were not originally asked of it. Wets (1996), for example, states:

> It is very unusual, at the outset of the modeling process, to have sufficient information about preferences to be able to construct an appraisal function. In fact, the building of a stochastic model is, or should be, used as a means of **discovering the shape of the appraisal function** [emphasis added].

Simulation of the individual investor's economic state [x] provides information on the ALM Markov chain environment in which decision-making occurs. Simulation of asset-management elections [π] provides information on the consequences of investor decisions [a] on future-state evolutions. The output is similar to interactive flight-simulation models created to provide pilots with the wherewithal to avoid a plane crash. Model output, in turn, assists the investor to discover information regarding the "shape" of their personal utility function and, as time unfolds, to revise their personal belief state [b] and state preferences. Ongoing monitoring in terms of the investor's personal economic goals measures the evolution of 'the value function' [V]. Ongoing monitoring, as illustrated in Case Study 11, involves a look-ahead/look-back dynamic-asset-management process. Although we contend that this is a better approach to investment advice than recommending "the 10 stocks to own now," we also stress that a simulation-based approach is compatible with, and deeply rooted in, the problem-structure of classical optimization of expected value defined by Harry Markowitz, Richard Bellman, and others.

---

31. The Merton optimum is derived from the form of the Bellman equation used to solve continuous-time stochastic processes. See, for example, Rogers (2013).

32. This is a variation on the "recommending" versus "suggesting" discussion in the previous chapter. The solution is suggested by the distribution over a space of wealth/consumption paths. It is the investor that adopts the solution according to the current distance from the goal(s) and the investor's view of risk and reward.

CHAPTER SEVENTEEN

CONCLUSION

■ ■ ■

THE OLD BECOMES THE NEW

Contemporary extensions of capital market theory incorporate multiperiod liabilities to create asset-liability management (ALM) models. Portfolio performance assessment tracks changes in assets, liabilities, health and marital status, longevity expectations, and other variables. Despite the challenges of assessment of investment opportunities and perils throughout retirement, recent research and technological developments show how both advisors and investors can benefit from dynamic ALM modeling. Advisors can translate investment performance jargon into a language based on specific client goals where goals appear as liabilities-to-be-funded on the client's balance sheet. Performance evaluation in an ALM context becomes, in the words of Wilcox (2003), an examination of the "time series of implied balance sheets." The financial economist and the corporate chief executive officer remain intensely interested in the "surplus efficient frontier;" the retired investor remains intensely interested in measuring progress toward or away from personal goals. Reporting quantitative performance results for individual investor clients means tracking changes in sustainability (shortfall metrics), feasibility of goals (solvency evaluation), and financial security (flexibility in terms of a cushion over and above funds required for lifetime income needs).

Something important has changed. Portfolio construction remains important, and optimization curves, indifference isoquants, and return-to-risk efficiency measures undoubtedly will remain in the advisor (or robo-advisor) toolbox. The "what to own" question remains important,[1] and information ratios, alphas, smart betas, and factor exposures undoubtedly will remain in play. However, the portfolio operates over a time span usually defined by investor longevity. These elements, initially memorialized in a written investment policy statement (IPS), often recede into the background as the IPS design and portfolio execution become more remote. Architects, although crucial for building design, rarely serve as property managers. The advisor's role changes, as well.

As time passes, the locus of action changes from the architectural activities required to create an IPS to the systems-engineering activities required to monitor results. This is the transition from retirement portfolio design to retirement investment management. As yet, there is scant discussion of how to go about the systems-engineering task in a meaningful way. Discussions about the nature and scope of the IPS often define ongoing portfolio monitoring as (1) a rebalancing protocol (how often and under what transactional algorithm), or (2) as investment manager monitoring (what are the investment criteria, and what are the IPS guidelines for replacing a poorly performing investment). As a general rule, commentators recommend that the client's economic and personal circumstances should be checked annually. If there are significant changes, the IPS should be updated to reflect the new circumstances. Although this advice is salutary, it does not provide suggestions about monitoring and evaluating critical developments, e.g., feasibility, sustainability, security, because they directly affect client goals and aspirations; nor does it provide guidelines about how best to quantify, present, and discuss appropriate asset-management elections to meet dynamically unfolding circumstances. How does the investor understand the economic consequences of new information? How does the investor adapt to it? How might the information to be revealed in the future create a need for an advisor who can assist in goal reprioritization and preference modification?

We argue that the best way to tackle these tasks is to develop a goals-based reporting system where the key element is a return to the centuries-old accounting identity: Assets = Liabilities + Net Worth.[2] In this case, retirement security is the current value of financial resources minus the actuarially calculated value of financial liabilities. For most retired investors, lifetime income is their largest balance sheet liability item. But the great virtue of double-entry accounting is its ability to give a clear, precise economic portrait within a structure allowing for intelligent assessment and informed analysis. It's an economic snapshot of the investor, not just the portfolio. The portfolio is of importance only in so far as it moves the investor closer to success, i.e., closer to personally defined objectives. It is difficult to see how portfolios that are not rationally constructed can benefit investors. It is just as difficult to see how investors can muster the attention span to review arcane portfolio-construction principles. The advisor, acting as a fiduciary within the scope of the engagement,

---

1. However, see Goldstein et al. (2008, 454): "The actual investment products in a portfolio should largely be irrelevant to the consumer. What matters is how investments combine to give an overall distribution of possible outcomes."

2. Luca Pacioli is credited with promulgating the rules for double-entry bookkeeping in a textbook published in Venice in 1494.

provides quantitative information and analysis; the advisor, acting in a counselor role, tells the client if he or she is on track. Rational and behavioral finance elements meet rather than compete, and monitoring and evaluation activity is the place where such a synthesis is both possible and desirable. Goals-based reporting is fundamentally an accounting activity.

THE VIRTUE OF DISCOMFORT

At the end of a working career, one of the biggest investment challenges is deciding that financial resources are sufficient to support lifetime income needs and standard-of-living goals. This is the feasibility question. It is the point in time where a more-money-is-better perspective is most likely to dominate, and, paradoxically, it is a point in time when fear of volatility motivates the investor to dial back investment risk. It is the point in time when simulators are most likely to be misused by advisors recommending high loadings to equity when such a strategy may not be in a client's best interest. It is a time when simulators are ignored by advisors pushing a go-conservative annuity or bond-ladder approach to avoid sequence-of-return risk. It is a time when the client seeks a comfortable resolution to critical issues and personal anxieties. It is a time when decision-making is difficult because the stakes are high. It is a time when an unbiased test for feasibility, based on current observables—as opposed to equity pipe dreams or annuity fears—is most needed. The actuarial benchmark exists in a context that is not shaped either by excessive greed or fear. This is the time for reality, not for investment dogma, and certainly not for sales agendas.

Contrary to virtually all conventional wisdom and practitioner-oriented literature, it is a time when an advisor wishes to make investors *uncomfortable* in at least two dimensions:

1. If an investor, owning a modest amount of financial resources, is predisposed to invest conservatively, the advisor should push back by highlighting the cost-of-safety penalty incurred by tilting investment strategy in a principal-guaranteed, low-variance direction. If a client is predisposed to invest in a growth-oriented portfolio, the advisor should push back by stressing downside risk to both wealth and income incurred by tilting investment strategy in a risky-asset, high-variance direction. Consumption (including gifts and bequests, when appropriate) is the key, i.e., how well can a principal-guarantee or risky-asset tilt support lifetime income and bequest objectives. Simulation can show when and if the safe approach is risky, or when and if the risky approach is safe. Neither the investor's beliefs nor the advisor's beliefs are actionable prior to looking at the numbers. When an investor, fully aware of available solution paths and the merits and liabilities of each, arrives at a final decision, both advisor and client can have high confidence that the best solution will be forthcoming. The investor reveals his or her utility function only when the advisor does not attempt to impose a point of view about the process.

2. When an investor is fully aware of available solution paths and the merits and liabilities of each, the investor will concurrently realize the importance of monitoring results through time in terms of how well or how poorly the portfolio meets his or her objectives. The investor has a heightened awareness that things can go wrong. Someone needs to look carefully at results unfolding over time lest, at some future date, the investor is surprised by a need for draconian change. An uncomfortable investor is keen on knowing if the ex-post investment decisions are moving his or her personal balance sheet in a favorable or unfavorable direction. Are risk metrics improving or deteriorating? Are economic goals moving closer or further away with respect to their ongoing feasibility? Is retirement security—as opposed to the portfolio's dollar value—on an upward or downward trajectory? An uncomfortable investor values objective assessment and intelligent evaluation of options (take a raise or dip into a reserve account); a comfortable investor may someday tire of hearing the advisor's rationale for why the recommended strategy will prove to be a winner soon.

Intelligent decision-making generates discomfort because the investor knows that things will go off track (in either a positive or negative direction). But the uncomfortable investor seeks to know how they are doing—not whether a manager exhibits an above-average record within a peer group. An uncomfortable investor wants a periodic audit and, if the financial situation is deteriorating, wants to discuss planning options. Monitoring and evaluation are prerequisites to asset management. If an advisor charges portfolio management and supervision fees, the time span over which the uncomfortable investor has a positive demand for such services extends for a lifetime.

A few words about a final paradox are in order. As the investor becomes more familiar with the monitoring and evaluation process and more aware that the advisor is acting in a fiduciary capacity where a fiduciary standard encompasses both a standard of conduct and a standard of competence, the investor becomes more comfortable. But this is the type of comfort that the investor and advisor want. When an anxious and skeptical investor meets a skilled advisor there is an initial, mutual level of discomfort. The advisor, as demonstrated in the case studies, is challenged to address adequately and intelligently the investor's concerns; the investor is challenged to decide, sooner rather than later, if he or she is being sold a bill of goods.

PRUDENT PORTFOLIO MANAGEMENT

There is a small library of books and articles on asset-allocation strategies and withdrawal formulae for retirement-income portfolios. These resources are largely devoted to retirement-planning analysis—what should I do? However, there is only a scant amount of advice about how to monitor wealth to assess whether goals continue to remain attainable. Credible methods for tracking and evaluating results relative to client goals answer the question: How are things panning out? One can argue, however, that this should be the primary focus of retirement-income portfolio management. If current portfolio value is less than retirement liabilities, the portfolio is technically insolvent. Investors can hope that things will work out satisfactorily, but they cannot expect them to do so.

This book advances the proposition that retirement-income portfolio monitoring can be greatly enhanced by basing decisions on current observables rather than on past results or future forecasts. If assets are greater than liabilities, economic objectives remain feasible because the investor has surplus wealth. Asset value is the current portfolio market value. The value of liabilities is the cost of providing a safe, sustainable, and sufficient income and, depending on the investor's goals, providing a target bequest. But this determination is an actuarial calculation as well as an investment projection. Therefore, the portfolio is best managed not to a rate-of-return bogey, but to an ALM objective subject to a constraint that surplus should not turn negative.

The most accurate and appropriate liability benchmark is the current cost of lifetime income as provided by an annuity contract. Annuity cost is a current market observable and does not depend on the accuracy of market forecasts, projections of the future expected equity and bond market risk premia, or the credibility of retirement-income risk models. There is no guesswork about the economic condition of the portfolio—if the portfolio violates the feasibility condition, both the retiree and heirs face a bleak economic prospect. In these circumstances, it is cold comfort to discover that the portfolio's rate of return beat a benchmark return series. We use the term "free boundary" to define the point at which the market value of wealth exactly equals the cost of funding liabilities. If an investor does not know the location of the free boundary, portfolio administration is based largely on hope rather than on a solid financial assessment.

We provide some case studies. Neither current asset values nor the investor's return forecasts are of primary importance in monitoring the economic viability of the retirement-income portfolio. Rather, the ratio of current wealth to annuity cost is the key risk metric. We term this risk metric the actuarial coverage ratio (ACR). The value of the ACR risk metric changes over time, and we illustrate a dynamic method for integrating solvency monitoring with retirement-income risk model outputs.

We conclude that prudent portfolio management benefits from knowing three sets of information:

1. The distance of current wealth from the free boundary that separates investor objectives into regions of feasibility and infeasibility—a solvency test,

2. The likely range of future wealth given periodic withdrawal demands—a sustainability test, and

3. The ongoing evolution of the ACR—a test for security and financial flexibility.

We conclude that a goals-based monitoring, evaluation, and reporting system is well-suited to communicating information regarding a client's financial state, and to assessing prudent and suitable asset-management elections. Although there is an extensive literature regarding goals-based asset allocation, much less has been written regarding goals-based portfolio performance reporting.

Retirement is a long-term, adaptive process—a risky project. Investment and spending decisions occur within a context of uncertainty. An asset-management election designed to provide short-term safety might have the unintended effect of undermining a portfolio's ability to provide long-term growth adequate to sustain a standard of living target.

PORTFOLIO COMPOSITION

■ ■ ■

The following table provides details about three asset allocations for the base-case $1.5 million portfolio described in Case Study 1:

Asset Class	50% stock / 50% bond	60% stock / 40% bond	70% stock / 30% bond
U.S. Large-Cap Stocks	$124,937	$150,000 (10%)	$175,063
U.S. Large-Cap Value Stocks	$124,937	$150,000 (10%)	$175,063
U.S. Small-Cap Stocks	$62,537	$75,000 (5%)	$87,463
U.S. Small-Cap Value Stocks	$62,537	$75,000 (5%)	$87,463
U.S. Securitized Real Estate	$62,537	$75,000 (5%)	$87,463
International Large-Cap Stocks	$124,938	$150,000 (10%)	$175,063
International Large-Cap Value Stocks	$62,537	$75,000 (5%)	$87,463
International Small-Cap Stocks	$62,537	$75,000 (5%)	$87,463
International Emerging Markets Stocks	$62,537	$75,000 (5%)	$87,463
U.S. Short-term Government Treasury Bills	$281,238	$225,000 (15%)	$168,762
U.S. Intermediate-term Government Bonds	$281,238	$225,000 (15%)	$168,762
Global Government Bonds	$187,488	$150,000 (10%)	$112,512

Extensions of the base-case model incorporate additional asset classes:

- U.S. Long-Term Government Bonds proxied by Bloomberg Barclays Long U.S. Treasury Index
- U.S. Treasury Inflation-Protected Securities proxied by Barclays Capital 1-10 Year U.S. TIPS Index

Given the controversies surrounding portfolio-optimization algorithms, the asset weights are only broadly suggestive of a well-diversified portfolio composition. Some commentators assert that portfolio optimizers are "error maximizers."

THE SIMULATION PROCESS AND RISK MODEL ASSUMPTIONS

■ ■ ■

Simulation is an approach to modeling that seeks to mimic a functioning system as it evolves. It is built on mathematical equations that express the assumed form of the system's operation. Simulation models assume a range of complexity from (1) a bootstrap of time-series data in which periodic returns are sampled with replacement to create a large number of reshuffled return sequences, to (2) a structural model such as a Monte Carlo simulation that draws random samples from a pre-specified distribution, to (3) more-complex simulation models that blend various types of distributions, or that switch among alternate distributions according to certain probability criteria. Whenever portfolios operate under conditions of cash flows (dollars going into or out of the portfolio), simulation analysis is an indispensable tool for evaluating the likelihood of economic success or failure.

The simulation model used in this book incorporates several elements:

The planning horizon. The applicable planning horizon can either be fixed or variable. When the planning horizon is measured by life span, the model simulates sample lifetimes using a Society of Actuaries 2014 annuity table based on "white collar" retirees from defined benefit pension plans. This table is conservative, i.e., exhibits a force of mortality lower than general population tables used by Social Security, and, therefore, suggests a higher likelihood of a long life. Unless otherwise indicated, the simulation reflects longevity expectations that assume good health.

The economy. The risk model divides economies into two regimes: A bear-market regime (defined as a 20 percent or greater peak-to-trough price decline for the Capital Appreciation S&P 500 stock index), and a bull-market regime. Using historical data from January 1973–2016, the historical lengths of bull and bear markets are determined. The simulation uses a Markov-switching regime model that offers the user a choice between a market-agnostic perspective (with a random selection for the initial economic regime) or a bear-market perspective (with an initial bear-market economic regime). The probability (p) that the initial economy is in a bull-market regime or a bear-market regime ($1 - p$) is based on historical frequencies. For all future periods, the simulation determines the probability of remaining in a bear market given that the last month was a bear, or of switching from a bear to a bull market given the total duration of the bear market to date. Similar calculations are made for the probability of remaining in or leaving a bull market regime.

Inflation. The risk model proxies inflation by the Consumer Price Index (CPI). The econometric model specifies the inflation-generating process as a serially correlated random variable with a "smoothed" reversionary factor. Specifically, the algorithm regresses the average value of the previous 12 month's inflation against the average value of the next 12 months. The value is calculated as:

Inflation_t = long-term inflation + Persistence Coefficient [Sum(inflation_{t-1} ... inflation_{t-12}) / 12 – long-term inflation] + error term

where the error term is an i.i.d., "white noise" process.

When the application has not yet produced 12 monthly simulated values, the application recursively calculates the average of the preceding 12 months by using the initial value to replace any missing terms. Therefore, the value for average prior 12-month inflation in the second month is 11/12 × the initial value + 1/12 × the value in the first month. The persistence coefficient determines the speed of CPI mean reversion. The coefficient's value is calculated via a regression of the rolling 12-month CPI against the rolling forward 12-month CPI. Thus, the model assumes that inflation is an Ornstein-Uhlenbeck process that includes a term for autocorrelation as well as for mean-reversion.

Investment returns. The simulation model generates investment returns utilizing common-matrix algebra techniques. Utilizing separate variance/covariance matrixes from historical bull- and bear-market regimes, the model executes, for each matrix, a Cholesky decomposition. It may also adjust dependence relationships by shrinking extreme off-diagonal elements to assure matrix invertibility. The Cholesky matrix algebra operation "divides" a variance/covariance matrix into upper and lower triangle matrixes that make them equivalent to the square root of a variance matrix. If there exists a lower triangle matrix C such that the historical matrix $V = CC^t$, then

C is a Cholesky matrix. The application simulates combinations of return series where each historical return series ($\vec{x}$) is transformed (by subtracting the mean and dividing by the standard deviation) into an independent standard normal variable ($\vec{z}$). The computer's random-number generation function simulates future evolutions for each independent return vector by drawing values for uncorrelated zero-mean variables. Pre-multiplying the vectors of simulated independent returns by $C\,C(\vec{z})$ restores their equivalency to each original return series ($\vec{x}$) = $C(\vec{z})$. The variance of the independent vectors is determined easily, and pre- and post-multiplication of the variance of ($\vec{z}$) by the appropriate lower triangle decomposition matrix C and its inverse restores the correlation structure by generating the required variance/covariance matrix $[V = CV(\vec{z})C']$.

Financial asset return series usually cannot be characterized as normal (bell-curve) distributions. Portfolio investment risk defined by the first two moments of multivariate symmetric distributions (Gaussian, Student's t, etc.) is often misleading. Monte Carlo simulations based on a normal distribution cannot realistically capture the frequency and magnitude of tail-risk events (leptokurtosis). To mitigate this deficiency, the application utilizes two normal distributions (bull and bear) with separately calculated means and variances for each regime. The distributions, according to the Markov transition probabilities described above, enable the model to capture the risk of outlier results that mirror real world frequencies.

Additionally, it is important to note that a regime-switching approach captures dynamic correlation and time-varying risk premia over different market conditions. Thus, instead of using average unconditional correlation values determined by the historical data, the risk model applies the historical correlation values conditioned on bull- and bear-market data. For example, over the entire sample period, an asset class may exhibit a mean of 10 percent and a standard deviation of 20 percent. However, during bull markets, the parameter values may be +18-percent mean and 15-percent standard deviation; while, during bear markets, the parameter values may be -23 percent and 25 percent, respectively. Thus, simply using the unconditional mean, standard deviation, and correlation values for the aggregate historical period does not capture realistic asset price behavior.

Fees, expenses, and transaction costs. Advisor fees are deducted at a rate of 1 percent across all portfolio values. Transaction costs assume each asset class incurs trading costs/custodial fees of 1 basis point per month. Asset classes are implemented by pooled investment products such as exchange-traded funds and mutual funds. Annual expense ratios are:

- 84 basis points for U.S. equity
- 112 basis points for foreign equity
- 36 basis points for fixed income

Finally, there is a factor for "implementation shortfall." Simplistically, implementation shortfall estimates the impact of bid-ask spreads incurred by trading in various capital markets. The risk model assumes a 40-basis-point shortfall for the U.S. large-cap equity market, a 60-basis-point shortfall for other U.S. equity markets, an 80-basis-point shortfall for international equity markets, and a 30-basis-point shortfall for fixed income capital markets.[1] Although the risk model can include the effects of taxes, in this book we do not consider tax implications either from realized gain or loss, or from receipt of ordinary income dividends and interest. Nor do we consider the tax implications of locating assets in taxable or tax-favored investment accounts.

Annuities. Annuity prices are an observable, market-based proxy for the cost of providing a lifetime income. The model benchmarks the cost of lifetime income by adding a 15-percent load factor to the estimated actuarial fair price of the specified lifetime income. Although the model assumes that annuities are single-premium, immediate contracts, it prices patterns of structured cash flows that commercially available contracts do not currently replicate. For example, Case Study 2 examines front-loaded and floating spending strategies. In these cases, the risk model uses the annuity-pricing principal to estimate the cost of customized lifetime portfolio withdrawal patterns. The model specifies either a nominal or inflation-adjusted payout to the annuitant. It assumes that the owner and beneficiary are the same and that contracts are owned by "natural persons" as defined in the U.S. Internal Revenue Code. Inflation-adjusted annuities increase benefits by a fixed 2.5-percent annual rate. Appendixes D and E provide additional information.

The simulation model inputs the above-listed elements to produce portfolio values over a wide range of possible future economies. Given the large number of simulation paths (10,000 trials), there is a rich set of future asset returns. It should be recognized, however, that any model is an imperfect representation of a more complex reality. In this case, (at least) two "model risks" should be considered:

1. Investors are interested in forecasts of a price-change process. However, the time series of asset prices is not statistically "stationary," i.e., exhibits the potential for infinite variance. It is only by "differentiating" the logarithm of prices on a period-by-period basis that the creation of a stationary series of returns is possible. It is only possible to model asset returns, but investors measure wealth based on asset prices—this is a subtle but important distinction. Returns are based on the single historical path of price changes, the realization of which is merely a manifestation of an unknown price-generating process. Simulation analysis greatly broadens our perspective about possible future outcomes, but any model of such a process must remain only a crude approximation of reality. Indeed, calculation of investment return is a function of the measurement interval (yearly, monthly, daily, intraday, continuous time) and, at the limit, may be meaningless in a statistical context.

2. The single historically realized return path for each asset class may be "representative" of the unknown price-generating process, or it may merely be an outlier result unlikely to persist. For example, an asset-allocation tilt toward small and value stocks is based on historical return data. If the premium for investing in small and value stocks reflects a reward for systematic risks, then investors have some confidence that they will continue to be rewarded for making these investments. If, however, the premium for such investments is merely an artifact of a chance historical price process, then investors may be increasing risk as they move their asset allocation deeper into the small/value gradient. Furthermore, investment volatility is measured by the variance statistic (the average squared difference between actual returns and average return). But if the historical return path is not representative, then the concept of average becomes meaningless and statistical measures are not illuminating.

Investors are rewarded for taking prudent and calculated risks. Investors may use the historical data to make inferences concerning the interrelationships between asset allocation, risk, and reward. However, in designing and implementing a portfolio, it is always wise to remain aware of parameter uncertainties. Past performance is not a guarantee of future results.

DATA SOURCES AND ALLOCATION WEIGHTS FOR SCATTER PLOT ANALYSIS

■ ■ ■

Label Name	Representative Index	Weighting
U.S. Large-Cap Stocks	S&P 500 Index	11%
U.S. Large-Cap Value Stocks	Fama-French Large Value	9%
U.S. Small-Cap Stocks	CRSP 6–10 Index	6%
U.S. Small-Cap Value Stocks	Fama-French Small Value	4%
U.S. Micro-Cap Stocks	CRSP 9–10 Index	4%
U.S. Securitized Real Estate	FTSE NAREIT Equity REITs	5%
International Large-Cap Stocks	MSCI EAFE	10%
International Large-Cap Value Stocks	MSCI EAFE Value	8%
International Small-Cap Stocks	S&P EPAC Small	4%
International Small-Cap Value Stocks	S&P EPAC Small Value	4%
International Emerging Markets Stocks	IFCI/S&P Emerging Composite	5%
U.S. Short-term Government Treasury Bills	U.S. 1-Year Constant Maturity	15%
U.S. Intermediate-term Government & Corporate Bonds	Barclays U.S. Intermediate Government/Credit	8%
Global Government Bonds	Citi World Government Bond Index	7%

THE ANNUITY BENCHMARK

■ ■ ■

Annuity cost benchmarks present several challenges for retirement-income risk modeling. A useful model is forward-looking in that it provides insight into both the expected values of critical variables and the extent to which actual results may differ from expectations. Just as there is a probability distribution of investment returns, inflation rates, and investor life span, so, also, is there a distribution of future annuity costs. Annuity prices are neither constant nor fully predictable from month-to-month and, therefore, the cost of discharging the liability to provide future income is also a random variable. Annuity prices are a function of several factors including the interest rate at the time of purchase, longevity expectations for the annuitant population, and the explicit and implicit costs of the annuity contract. The risk model must estimate current costs as well as project expected future costs. An expectation is a future-oriented value—it is a value that is more likely than not to be close to what is realized; a current cost estimate is a value that reflects the actual economic and demographic conditions of the day. In terms of the previous discussion of model risk in appendix B, the expected future annuity cost projection is a reasonable guideline for making long-term asset-management decisions; the actual price of an annuity is a measure of variance (risk) in the cost projection. *A priori*, we expect an increase in the magnitude of the difference between actual and expected during periods of abnormally low or high interest rates.

In one sense, finding the current price of an annuity is easy. Several websites allow the user to enter the requisite amount of monthly income as well as other contract features including graded payment increases in order to determine the contract's cost. Additionally, major custodians, e.g., Fidelity and TD Ameritrade, as well as mutual fund companies, e.g., Vanguard, provide prices for a select range of annuity contracts. The current annuity price determines the ratio of portfolio value to annuity cost—the actuarial coverage ratio (ACR). Thus, if an investor currently owns a $2-million portfolio and obtains a $1-million market price for an immediate annuity providing the lifetime target income, the ACR value is $2 \div 1 = 2$, or a 2x coverage ratio. Any ratio value below one signifies that current wealth is insufficient to fund the actuarial equivalent of the investor's target income stream. That is to say, the target income is not feasible given current resources, current interest rates, and other pricing factors including current age.

However, an effective portfolio-monitoring program needs to do more than simply present a single point-in-time annuity cost. The annuity cost is, itself, a stochastic variable. The monitoring and risk-evaluation program will want to estimate, over time, the ACR to provide insight into how the investor's preferred safety margin may unfold dynamically. For example, if the investor is committed to converting all or part of portfolio wealth to an annuity if the ACR drops below, say, 1.10, then examining the projected change in ratio value over time indicates the likelihood of a future conversion from financial assets to actuarial assets. Should annuitization not prove palatable, insight into the ratio value's trend provides useful information for determining if changes to asset allocation, investment strategies, tax and asset location elections, and so forth are prudent. The ACR is a solvency benchmark, it is not a recommendation to buy an annuity contract.

PRICING ANNUITIES IN THE RETIREMENT-INCOME RISK MODEL

■ ■ ■

Pricing annuities in a risk-modeling system presents significant challenges. The risk model described in this paper uses a pro-forma yield curve based on four parameters—the current level of inflation, the real short-term rate premium to inflation, the real long-term rate premium, and the curvature from short- to long-term rates. A fundamental assumption is that both of these premiums (short-term to inflation and long-term to short-term) remain constant over time. The pro-forma yield curve is not the current term structure of interest rates. Rather it produces an expectation—based on current inflation and historical risk premia—of what an investor might reasonably expect to pay, on average, for an annuity contract.

In the case of annuities, this assumption actually may be superior to assuming time-varying premiums reflecting forecasted changes in the yield curve's interest rates and shape. The purpose of the actuarial coverage ratio (ACR) calculation is to illustrate anticipated coverage ratios of portfolio assets to annuity costs. Introducing additional variance to the pro-forma yield curve model would allow for a range of possible premiums which, in turn, would create noise around the expected annuity cost, and therefore noise around the expected portfolio/ACR. The absence of variance is likely to provide a clearer answer to questions such as: "Will the investor be able to maintain a portfolio above the minimum asset level required to buy a replacement annuity" without biasing the answer either positively or negatively.

The rate model used to price annuities is independent from the returns calculated for fixed income instruments. Both equity and fixed income returns are modeled on one-month normally distributed (and appropriately correlated) returns within the appropriate economic regime—bull or bear. The annuities are priced on a pro forma, non-varying forward yield curve model. As a result, the change in the price of an annuity is based on changes to the annuity buyer's age and on the current rate of inflation. During periods of high inflation, annuities are relatively cheaper because future payments are discounted at a higher rate. During periods of low inflation the converse is true. Of course, a client-specific monitoring system should periodically input updates to age and interest rates to recalculate annuity costs and, by extension, current and anticipated coverage ratios.

Modeling the evolution of the wealth-to-annuity-cost ratio requires several steps. The first step is to determine the 'Starting Benefit Payment / Starting Price.' The 'Starting Benefit Payment' component equals the starting monthly benefit amount for a single premium immediate annuity purchased by the investor where the payment is measured in today's dollars. The starting periodic annuity payment may occur at month one (if the investor immediately opts to exchange financial wealth for annuity income) or, if the investor decides to defer the annuity purchase, the payment may start at any month thereafter. The 'Starting Price' component automatically rolls forward month-by-month to project the annuity's cost as the investor ages—keeping current health status constant. Despite the nascent market for purchasing annuity and structured settlement income streams by private investment groups, we deem a decision to purchase an annuity to be an irrevocable wealth transfer.

The second modeling step is to 'Adjust Starting Benefit Payment.'[1] If an annuity purchase decision is deferred, the investor is faced with the need to increase the future-date initial periodic payment to offset a decrease in purchasing power. We adjust the future-date initial payment by the realized path of inflation as calculated by the retirement-income risk model. For example, the hypothetical investor in appendix D with a $2-million current portfolio could elect to purchase the annuity today at a wealth/annuity income ratio of two; or the investor could wait and see how the inflation-adjusted wealth/adjusted annuity income coverage ratio plays out in the future—the coverage ratio is dynamic. An investor can estimate the likelihood that the ratio might either improve or deteriorate over time given the current asset allocation, target withdrawal amount, and projected mortality credits embedded within the annuity pricing structure. If the 'Adjust Starting Benefit Payment' input is zero, then the model assumes that the annuity benefit is nominal rather than inflation-adjusted. In a nutshell, the 'Adjust Starting Benefit Payment' calculation reflects the amount of the annuity payment to be purchased. This is a key input into calculating how much wealth must be exchanged—now or in the future—for lifetime income. It is the information that the investor needs to consider in order to decide if and when annuitization is appropriate.

1. This is the label of an input field in the retirement-income risk model.

The final modeling step is to specify values in an input field termed 'Growth after Start.' The 'Growth after Start' calculation reflects the amount the annuity income will change after the single premium immediate annuity contract's purchase date. Because the risk model treats future inflation as a stochastic variable, the model requires a reasonable input factor for increasing an annuity's future payouts once the annuity payout starts. If the input value is zero, the annuity payments, once started, do not increase. The risk model, in essence, asks the investor to elect an automatic yearly payout adjustment feature equal to 0 percent, 2 percent, 3 percent, 4 percent, or some other reasonable increase factor.[2] The larger the increase factor, the greater the cost of buying the annuity contract, all else equal. Although the specified rate of payment increase is unlikely to match precisely the realized inflation rate, it nevertheless mitigates adverse effects on future purchasing power.

Prior to periodic update reviews with clients, the risk model allows the advisor to input the actual current yield curve data, current investor age, annuity type (nominal or graded benefit), and other information in order to update the current cost of providing lifetime income via a commercial annuity contract. Thus, the application makes an important distinction between the pro-forma yield curve used for ACR projections and the actual yield curve data required for periodic portfolio monitoring and review.

In addition to setting reasonable expectations, a credible monitoring system also must estimate the variance around the expectation. In this case, we employ a model feature that calculates annuity costs given a parallel shift in the pro-forma yield curve. The user can specify the direction and magnitude of the shift. Thus, one component of the risk model builds a pro-forma annuity cost structure; the other checks to see how annuity prices may vary from expectations as interest rates change.

---

2. As stated, we assume a 2.5-percent 'growth after start' annual payment increase in all case studies.

REFERENCES

■ ■ ■

Abbas, Ali E., and James E. Matheson. 2005. Normative Target-Based Decision Making. *Managerial and Decision Economics* 26, no. 6 (September): 373–385.

Ahn, David, Syngjoo Choi, Douglas Gale, and Shachar Kariv. 2014. Estimating Ambiguity Aversion in a Portfolio Choice Experiment. *Quantitative Economics* 5, no. 2 (July): 195–223.

Ainslie, Ross. 2000. Annuity and Insurance Products for Impaired Lives (May). The Staple Inn Actuarial Society.

Akerlof, George. 1970. The Market for Lemons. *Quarterly Journal of Economics* 84, no. 3 (August): 488–500.

Albrecht, Peter. 1993. Normal and Lognormal Shortfall-Risk. Proceedings of the International Actuarial Association, Rome, Vol. 2: 417–430.

———. 1994. Shortfall Returns and Shortfall Risk. Actuarial Approach for Financial Risks, Proceedings of the 4th AFIR International Colloquium, Orlando 1994, Vol. 1, S: 87–110.

Ang, Andrew, Bingxu Chen, and Suresh Sundaresan. 2013. Liability Investment with Downside Risk. National Bureau of Economic Research Working Paper 19030 (May). http://www.nber.org/papers/w19030.

Arnott, Robert D., Terence E Burns, Lisa Plaxco, and Philip Moore. 2007. "Chapter 11: Monitoring and Rebalancing," in *Managing Investment Portfolios: A Dynamic Process* (3rd ed.), edited by John L. Maginn, Donald L. Tuttle, Jerold E. Pinto, and Dennis W. McLeavey. Hoboken, NJ: John Wiley & Sons, Inc.

Ashton, Michael. 2011. Maximizing Personal Surplus: Liability-Driven Investment for Individuals. *Retirement Security in the New Economy: Paradigm Shifts, New Approaches and Holistic Strategies*. Society of Actuaries 2011 Conference. https//www.soa.org/news-and-publications/publications.

Babbel, David F., and Craig B. Merrill. 2007. Rational Decumulation. *Wharton Financial Institutions Center Working Paper*. no. 06-14 (May).

Bajtelsmit, Vickie, Anna Rappaport, and LeAndra Foster. 2013. Measures of Retirement Benefit Adequacy: Which, Why, for Whom, and How Much? Society of Actuaries' Pension Section and Pension Section Research Committee. https://www.soa.org/globalassets/assets/Files/Research/Projects/research-2013-measures-retirement.pdf.

Balls, Kim. 2006. Immediate Annuity Pricing in the Presence of Unobserved Heterogeneity. *North American Actuarial Journal* 10, no. 4: 103–116.

Berkelaar, Arjan, and Roy Kouwenberg. 2010. A Liability-Relative Drawdown Approach to Pension Asset Liability Management. *Journal of Asset Management* 11, nos. 2/3: 194–217.

Bernoulli, Daniel. 1954. Exposition of a New Theory on the Measurement of Risk. *Econometrica* 22: 23–36.

Blanchard, Paul, Robert L. Devaney, and Glen R. Hall. 2012. *Differential Equations, 4th Edition*. Boston, Massachusetts: Brooks/Cole.

Blanchett, David, and Paul Kaplan. 2013. Alpha, Beta, and Now … Gamma. *Journal of Retirement* 1, no. 2 (fall): 29–45.

Bordley, Robert, and Marco LiCalzi. 2000. Decision Analysis Using Targets Instead of Utility Functions. *Decisions in Economics and Finance* 23, no. 1 (May): 53–74.

Bradbury, Meike A. S., Thorsten Hens, and Stefan Zeisberger. 2015. Improving Investment Decisions with Simulated Experience. *Review of Finance* 19, no. 3: 1,019–1,052.

———. 2017. Do Risk Simulations Lead to Persistently Better Investment Decisions? American Economic Association 2017 Annual Meeting. https://www.aeaweb.org/conference/2017/preliminary?sessionType%5Bsession%5D=1&organization_name=&search_terms=Bradbury&searchLimits%5Bauthor_last%5D=1&day=&time=.

Brockett, Patrick L., and Yehuda Kahane. 1992. Risk, Return, Skewness and Preference. *Management Science* 38, no. 6: 851–866.

Brown, Robert L., and Patricia L. Scahill. 2010. Issues in the Issuance of Enhanced Annuities. https://www.soa.org/globalassets/assets/library/journals/actuarial-practice-forum/2007/october/apf-2007-10-brown-scahill.pdf.

Browne, Sid. 1999. The Risk and Rewards of Minimizing Shortfall Probability. *Journal of Portfolio Management* 25, no. 4 (summer): 76–85.

Brunel, Jean L. P., Thomas M. Idzorek, and John M. Mulvey. 2019. Principles of Asset Allocation. CFA Program Curriculum, Level III, Vol. 3 (Wiley), p. 291.

Carroll, Christopher D. 1992. The Buffer-Stock Theory of Saving: Some Macroeconomic Evidence. *Brookings Papers on Economic Activity* 23, no. 2: 61–156.

CFA Institute. 2010. *Elements of an Investment Policy Statement for Individual Investors*. Charlottesville, Virginia: CFA Institute (2010), §3c., p. 6.

Charness, Gary, and Uri Gneezy. 2010. Portfolio Choice and Risk Attitudes: An Experiment. *Economic Inquiry* 48, no. 1 (January): 133–146.

Charupat, Narat, Mark J. Kamstra, and Moshe S. Milevsky. 2012. The Annuity Duration Puzzle (March 14). https://ssrn.com/abstract=2021579.

Collins, Patrick J. 2007. Prudence. *Banking Law Journal* 125, no. 1 (January): 3–70.

. 2011a. Trustee Asset Management Elections: Portfolio Performance Evaluation and Preferencing Criteria: Part One. *Banking Law Journal* 128, no. 2 (February). 130–179.

———. 2011b. Trustee Asset Management Elections: Portfolio Performance Evaluation and Preferencing Criteria: Part Two. *Banking Law Journal* 128, no. 3 (March): 237–284.

———. 2016a. Annuities and Retirement Income Planning, *Research Foundation Briefs* (February). Charlottesville, Virginia: CFA Institute Research Foundation: http://schultzcollins.com/static/uploads/2016/03/Annuities-and-Retirement-Income-Planning.pdf.

———. 2016b. *Portfolio Management: Theory & Practice*. https://www.amazon.com/dp/1541240324/ref=sr_1_8?ie=UTF8&qid=1482447399&sr=8-8&keywords=portfolio+management+theory+and+practice.

Collins, Patrick, and Francois Gadenne. 2017. The Shapes of Retirement Planning: Are You a Curve, a Triangle, or a Rectangle? *Investments & Wealth Monitor* 32, no. 4 (July/August): 52–60.

Collins, Patrick J., and Huy Lam. 2011. Asset Allocation, Human Capital, and the Demand to Hold Life Insurance in Retirement. *Financial Services Review* 20 (winter): 303–325.

Collins, Patrick J., and Josh Stampfli. 2001. Promises and Pitfalls of Total Return Trusts. *ACTEC Journal* (winter): 205–219.

———. 2009. Managing Private Wealth: Matching Investment Policy to Investor Risk Preferences. *Banking Law Journal* 126, no. 10 (November/December): 923–958.

Collins, Patrick, Huy Lam, and Josh Stampfli. 2015a. How Risky is Your Retirement Income Risk Model? *Financial Services Review* (fall): 193–216.

———. 2015b. Longevity Risk and Retirement Income Planning. Charlottesville, Virginia: CFA Institute Research Foundation.

Collins, Patrick J., Steven M. Fast, and Laura A Schuyler. 2014. Well-Performing Portfolios and Well-Disguised Insolvency. ALI-CLE Course of Study Materials: Representing Estate and Trust Beneficiaries and Fiduciaries (Chicago, 2014): 499–552.

Das, Sanjiv, Harry Markowitz, Jonathan Scheid, and Meir Statman. 2010. Portfolio Optimization with Mental Accounts. *Journal of Financial and Quantitative Analysis* 45, no. 2 (April): 311–334.

Davies, Greg B. 2017. New Vistas in Risk Profiling. Charlottesville, Virginia: CFA Institute Research Foundation.

Dempster, M. A. H., and E. A. Medova. 2011. Asset Liability Management for Individual Households. *British Actuarial Journal* 16, Part 2: 405–439.

DiBartolomeo, Dan. 2011. Asset/Liability Management for the Private Client. CFA Institute 28, no. 1 (March): 42–48. www.cfapubs.org.

Diecidue, Enrico, and Jeroen Van De Ven. 2008. Aspiration Level, Probability of Success and Failure, and Expected Utility. *International Economic Review* 49, no. 2 (May): 683–700.

Donnelly, Catherine, Montserrat Guillén, and Jens Perch Nielsen. 2014. Bringing Cost Transparency to the Life Annuity Market. *Insurance: Mathematics and Economics* 56 (May): 14–27.

Dus, Ivica, Raimond Maurer, and Olivia S. Mitchell. 2005. Betting on Death and Capital Markets in Retirement: A Shortfall Risk Analysis of Life Annuities Versus Phased Withdrawal Plans. *Financial Services Review* 14, no. 3 (fall): 169–196.

Edelen, Roger M., Richard Evans, and Gregory B. Kadlec. 2013. Shedding Light on 'Invisible' Costs: Trading Costs and Mutual Fund Performance, *Financial Analysts Journal* 69, no. 1 (January/February): 33–44.

Eeckhoudt, Louis, Christian Gollier, and Harris Schlesinger. 2005. *Economic and Financial Decisions under Risk*. Princeton, New Jersey: Princeton University Press.

Ellis, Charles D. 1985. *Investment Policy*. Homewood, Illinois: Business One Irwin.

Elton, Edwin J., and Martin J. Gruber. 1992. Optimal Investment Strategies with Investor Liabilities. *Journal of Banking and Finance* 16, no. 5 (September): 869–890.

Epstein, Larry G., and Stanley E. Zin. 1989. Substitution, Risk Aversion, and the Temporal Behavior of Consumption and Asset Returns: A Theoretical Framework. *Econometrica* 57, no. 4 (July): 937–969.

Ezra, Don. 1991. Asset Allocation by Surplus Optimization. *Financial Analysts Journal* 47, no. 1 (January/February): 51–57.

———. 2009. Who Should Buy a Lifetime Income Annuity? And When? CFA Institute Private Wealth Management (February). http://www.cfapubs.org/doi/full/10.2469/pwmn.v2009.n1.10.

Fan, Yuan-An, Steve Murray, and Sam Pittman. 2013. Optimizing Retirement Income: An Adaptive Approach Based on Assets and Liabilities. *Journal of Retirement* 1, no. 1 (summer): 124–135.

Fishburn, Peter C. 1977. Mean-Risk Analysis with Risk Associated with Below-Target Returns. *American Economic Review* 67, no. 2 (March): 116–126.

Friedman, Avner. 2000. Free Boundary Problems in Science and Technology. *Notices of the American Mathematical Society* 47, no. 8 (September): 854–861.

Fullmer, Richard K. 2007. Modern Portfolio Decumulation: A New Strategy for Managing Retirement Income." *Journal of Financial Planning* 20, no. 8 (August): 40–51.

Goldstein, Daniel G., Eric J. Johnson, and William F. Sharpe. 2008. Choosing Outcomes versus Choosing Products: Consumer-Focused Retirement Investment Advice. *Journal of Consumer Research* 35: 440–456.

Gosavi, Abhijit. 2015. Solving Markov Decision Processes via Simulation. *Handbook of Simulation Optimization*, Ed. Michael C. Fu (Springer, International Series in Operations Research and Management Science): 341–380.

Haisley, Emily, Christine Kaufmann, and Martin Weber. 2013. The Role of Experience Sampling and Graphical Displays on One's Investment Risk Appetite and Comprehension. *Management Science* 59, no. 2: 323–340.

Hansen, Lars Peter, and Thomas J. Sargent. 2008. *Robustness*. Princeton, New Jersey: Princeton University Press.

Ho, Kwok, Moshe Milevsky, and Chris Robinson. 1994. Asset Allocation, Life Expectancy and Shortfall. *Financial Services Review* 3, no. 2 (summer): 109–126.

Karagiannis, Evangelos. 2014. Stochastic Investment Horizons in the Asset Allocation Decision and Liability-Driven Investing. CFA Institute: 1–4. https://www.pacificincome.com/wp-content/uploads/2014/10/PIA_LDI-Whitepaper.pdf.

Kimball, Miles. 1990. Precautionary Saving in the Small and in the Large. *Econometrica* 58, no. 1: 53–73.

Kitces, Michael. 2012a. Annuities vs. Safe Withdrawal Rates: Comparing Income Floor-with-Upside Approaches (May 24). https://www.kitces.com/blog/income-floor-with-upside-comparison-annuities-versus-safe-withdrawal-rates-swr.

———. 2012b. Is The Retirement Plan with the Lowest 'Risk of Failure' Really the Best Choice (March 1). https://www.kitces.com/blog/is-the-retirement-plan-with-the-lowest-risk-of-failure-really-the-best-choice/.

Koijen, Ralph S. J., Theo E. Nijman, and Bas J. M. Werker. 2011. Optimal Annuity Risk Management. *Review of Finance* 15, no. 4 (October): 799–833.

Leibowitz, Martin L., and Roy D. Henriksson. 1989. Portfolio Optimization with Shortfall Constraints: A Confidence-Limit Approach to Managing Downside Risk. *Financial Analysts Journal* 45, no. 2 (March/April): 34–41.

Leibowitz, Martin L., Stanley Kogelman, and Anthony Bova. 2017. Funding Ratio Peaks and Stalls. *Financial Analysts Journal* 73, no. 3 (third quarter): 8–20.

Levy, Haim, and Moshe Levy. 2009. The Safety First Expected Utility Model: Experimental Evidence and Economic Implications. *Journal of Banking & Finance* 33, no. 8 (August): 1,494–1,506.

Li. Feng. 2008. Ruin Problem in Retirement Under Stochastic Return Rate and Mortality Rate and its Applications. MS Thesis, Department of Statistics and Actuarial Science, Simon Fraser University (spring). http://www.stat.sfu.ca/content/dam/sfu/stat/alumnitheses/MiscellaniousTheses/Li-2008.pdf.

Martellini, Lionel, Vincent Milhau, and John Mulvey. 2018. Applying Goal-Based Investing to the Retirement Problem. EDHEC Risk Institute. https://risk.edhec.edu/applying-goal-based-investing-principles-retirement.

Martinson, Jane, and Larry Elliott. 2000. The Year Dot.Com Turned into Dot.Bomb. *The Guardian* (December 29). 2000. https://www.theguardian.com/technology/2000/dec/30/internetnews.business.

Medova, E. A., J. K. Murphy, A. P. Owen, and K. Rehman. 2008. Individual Asset Liability Management. *Quantitative Finance* 8, no. 6 (September): 547–560.

Menezes, C., C. Geiss, and J. Tessier. 1980. Increasing Downside Risk. *American Economic Review* 70, no. 5 (December): 921–932.

Menoncin, Francesco, and Olivier Scaillet. 2003. Mortality Risk and Real Optimal Asset Allocation for Pension Funds. FAME Research Paper Series from International Center for Financial Asset Management and Engineering. https://archive-ouverte.unige.ch/unige:5785.

Merton, Robert C. 2014. The Crisis in Retirement Planning, *Harvard Business Review* (July/August).

Milevsky, Moshe. 1988. Optimal Asset Allocation Towards the End of the Life Cycle: To Annuitize or Not to Annuitize? *Journal of Risk and Insurance* 65, no. 3 (September): 401–426.

Mladina, Peter. 2016. Characteristics of a Sound Goals-Based Investing Method. *Investments & Wealth Monitor* 31, no. 3 (May/June): 22–23, 35.

Montesano, Aldo. 2009. De Finetti and the Arrow-Pratt Measure of Risk Aversion. Chapter 7 in *Bruno de Finetti Radical Probabilist* 8 (bepress): 115–127.

Munnell, Alicia H. 2008. The Role of Government in Life-Cycle Saving and Investing. In *The Future of Life-Cycle Saving and Investing* (2nd edition), Zvi Bodie, Dennis McLeavey, and Laurence B. Siegel (eds.). Charlottesville, Virginia: CFA Institute: 107–141.

Pang, Gaobo, and Mark Warshawsky. 2009. Optimizing the Equity-Bond-Annuity Portfolio in Retirement: The Impact of Uncertain Health Expenses. *Insurance Mathematics and Economics* 46, no. 1: 198–209.

———. 2010. Optimizing the Equity-Bond-Annuity Portfolio in Retirement: The Impact of Uncertain Health Expenses. *Insurance: Mathematics and Economics* 46, no. 1: 198–209.

Pfau, Wade. 2017. How Much Can I Spend in Retirement?: *A Guide to Investment-Based Retirement Income Strategies*. Retirement Researcher's Guide Series. McLean, Virginia: McLean Asset Management Corporation.

Pfleiderer, Paul. 2014. Chameleons: The Misuse of Theoretical Models in Finance and Economics. Stanford Business School Working Paper No. 3020 (August). https://www.gsb.stanford.edu/faculty-research/working-papers/chameleons-misuse-theoretical-models-finance-economic.

Pittman, Sam. 2013. Efficient Retirement Income Strategies and the Timing of Annuity Purchases. *Journal of Financial Planning* 26, no. 11 (November): 56–62.

Pittman, Sam, and Rod Greenshields. 2012. Adaptive Investing: A Responsive Approach to Managing Retirement Assets. *Russell Research* (March): 1–10.

Pompian, Michael M., Colin McLean, and Alistair Byrne. 2018. Behavioral Finance and Investment Processes. CFA Level III 2018 Program Curriculum, Vol. 2, Reading Seven.

Pye, Gordon. 2012. *The Retrenchment Rule: When It's Too Late to Save More for Retirement*. New York: GBP Press.

Rappaport, Anna M. 2011. Retirement Security in the New Economy: Developing New Paradigms for the Payout Period. *Retirement Security in the New Economy: Paradigm Shifts, New Approaches and Holistic Strategies*. SOA 2011 Conference.

Rogers, L. C. G. 2013. *Optimal Investment*. Springer Briefs in Quantitative Finance. Springer-Verlag, (Berlin, Heidelberg): 2–28.

Rook, Christopher. 2014. Minimizing the Probability of Ruin in Retirement (August 7). https://ssrn.com/abstract=2420747.

Rothschild, M., and J. Stiglitz. 1970. Increasing Risk: I. A Definition. *Journal of Economic Theory* 2, no. 3: 225–243.

———. 1971. Increasing Risk: II. Its Economic Consequences. *Journal of Economic Theory* 3, no. 1 (March): 66–84.

Roy, Arthur D. 1952. Safety First and the Holding of Assets. *Econometrica* 20, no. 3 (July): 431–450.

Russell, Stuart, and Peter Norvig. 2016. *Artificial Intelligence: A Modern Approach* (3rd ed.). Upper Saddle River, New Jersey: Pearson Education.

Savage, Sam L. 2012. *The Flaw of Averages*. Hoboken, New Jersey: John Wiley & Sons, Inc.

Scott, Jason S., and John G. Watson. 2013. The Floor-Leverage Rule for Retirement. *Financial Analysts Journal* 69, no. 5 (September/October): 45–60.

Shadmehr, Reza, and Sandro Mussa-Ivaldi. 2012. *Biological Learning and Control*. Cambridge, Massachusetts: The MIT Press: 308–316.

Sharpe, William F. 2017. Retirement Income Scenario Matrices. https://web.stanford.edu/~wfsharpe/RISMAT/.

Sharpe, William F., and Lawrence G. Tint. 1990. Liabilities—A New Approach. *Journal of Portfolio Management* 16, no. 2 (winter): 5–10.

Silver, Nate. 2012. *The Signal and the Noise*. New York: Penguin Press.

Shu, Suzanne, Robert Zeithammer, and John Payne. 2016. Consumer Preferences for Annuities: Beyond Net Present Value. *Journal of Marketing Research* 53, no. 2 (April): 240–262.

Strang, Gilbert. 2019. *Linear Algebra and Learning from Data*. Wellesley, Massachusetts: Wellesley-Cambridge Press: 311–318.

Thompson, Debora V., Rebecca W. Hamilton, and Petia Petrova. 2009. When Mental Simulation Hinders Behavior: The Effects of Process-Oriented Thinking on Decision Difficulty and Performance. *Journal of Consumer Research* 36, no. 4 (December): 562–574.

Vanduffel, Steven, J. Dhaene, Marc J. Goovaerts, and Rob Kaas. 2003. The Hurdle-Race Problem. *Insurance, Mathematics & Economics* 33, no. 2 (October): 405–413.

Vernon, Steve. 2016. A Portfolio Approach to Retirement Income Security. SOA Pension Section News (May): 24–27. https://www.soa.org/globalassets/assets/files/resources/essays-monographs/diverse-risk/2016-diverse-risks-essay-vernon.pdf.

Waring, M. Barton, and Laurence B. Siegel. 2015. The Only Spending Rule Article You Will Ever Need. *Financial Analysts Journal* 71, no. 1 (January/February): 91–107.

———. 2018. What Investment Risk Means to You, Illustrated: Strategic Asset Allocation, the Budget Constraint, and the Volatility of Spending during Retirement. *Journal of Retirement* 6, no. 2 (fall): 7–26.

Warshawsky, Mark J., and Gaobo Pang. 2012. Good Strategies for Wealth Management and Income Production in Retirement. Chapter 7 in *Retirement Income: Risks and Strategies*. Cambridge, Massachusetts: Massachusetts Institute of Technology: 163–178.

Wets, Roger J-B. 1996. Challenges in Stochastic Programming. *Mathematical Programming* 75: 20.

Wilcox, Jarrod. 2003. Harry Markowitz & the Discretionary Wealth Hypothesis. *Journal of Portfolio Management* 29, no. 3 (spring): 58–65.

———. 2014. Risk Management: Survival of the Fittest. *Journal of Asset Management* 5, no. 1 (June): 13–24.

Wilcox, Jarrod, and Frank J. Fabozzi. 2009. A Discretionary Wealth Approach for Investment Policy. *Journal of Portfolio Management* 36, no. 1 (fall): 46–59.

Woerheide, Walter, and David Nanigian. 2012. Sustainable Withdrawal Rates: The Historical Evidence on Buffer Zone Strategies. *Journal of Financial Planning* 25, no. 5 (May) 46–51.

Yaari, Menahem E. 1965. Uncertain Lifetime, Life Insurance, and the Theory of the Consumer. *Review of Economic Studies* 32, no. 2: 137–150.

Yanikoski, Chuck. 2011. Creating a Reality-Based Financial Decision-Making Model for Older Americans. Retirement Security in the New Economy: Paradigm Shifts, New Approaches and Holistic Strategies. 2011 Enterprise Risk Management Symposium, Society of Actuaries, March 14–16, 2011. https://www.soa.org/globalassets/assets/files/resources/essays-monographs/retire-security-new-economy/mono-2011-mrs12-yanikoski-paper.pdf.

Zhao, Yonggan, Ulrich Haussmann, and William T. Ziemba. 2003. A Dynamic Investment Model with Control on the Portfolio's Worst Case Outcome. *Mathematical Finance* 13, no. 4 (October): 481–501.

Ziemba, William T. 2003. The Stochastic Programming Approach to Asset, Liability and Wealth Management. The Research Foundation of AIMR.

www.ingramcontent.com/pod-product-compliance
Lightning Source LLC
Chambersburg PA
CBHW080524220326
41599CB00032B/6190